Bird of Time

*Dédié,
en profonde gratitude,
à Brigitte Hennessy*

Axel Klein

Bird of Time

The Music of Swan Hennessy

SCHOTT

Bibliografische Information der Deutschen Nationalbibliothek

Die Deutsche Nationalbibliothek verzeichnet diese Publikation in der Deutschen Nationalbibliografie; detaillierte bibliografische Daten sind im Internet über http://dnb.dn-b..de abrufbar.

978-3-95983-593-0 (Hardcover)
978-3-95983-594-7 (Paperback)

© 2019 Schott Music GmbH & Co. KG, Mainz

www.schott-buch.com

Alle Rechte vorbehalten.
Nachdruck in jeder Form sowie die Wiedergabe durch Fernsehen, Rundfunk, Film, Bild- und Tonträger, auch auszugsweise, nur mit Genehmigung des Verlags.

Contents

Acknowledgements 7

Introduction 11

Chapter 1
Cork to Chicago: The Origins (1830s to 1870s) 21

Chapter 2
Education in Europe (1878–1886) 29

Chapter 3
A Failed Anglo-Irish Family (1887–1903) 49

Chapter 4
In Search of Direction (1903–1907) 61

Chapter 5
An American Impressionist (1908–1913) 107

Chapter 6
Modernity and Celticity (1908–1914) 187

Chapter 7
Escape to Switzerland (1915–1919) 241

Chapter 8
An Engagement with Ireland (1920–1924) 249

Chapter 9
Swan's Way: Hennessy in Search of Lost Time (1925–1929) 333

Afterword
Six National Perspectives on Swan Hennessy 427

Appendix 1: List of Works 435

Appendix 2: List of Works in Opus Numbers 488

Appendix 3: Publishers' Plate Numbers 495

Appendix 4: Dedications and Dedicatees 500

Appendix 5: Sources 517
    A. Letters 517
    B. Reviews and Concert Programmes 521
    C. Music Manuscripts 522
    D. Mixed Items 548

Appendix 6: Bibliography 550

Appendix 7: Discography 555

Index 559

Acknowledgements

It must have been around 2007 when the Irish musicologist Barra Boydell asked me whether I had ever heard of the composer Swan Hennessy. Barra played the viola, with friends, in a string quartet, and they were just studying Hennessy's first quartet, published in Paris in 1913. It struck him that the first three movements sounded very French and the fourth movement overtly Irish. Despite my seeming expertise, I had *not* heard of him, but the name kept sticking in my head ever since. Obviously, 'Hennessy' was an Irish name, and a Cork name to be more exact, but the unusual first name no doubt contributed to remembering it for a good while.

In the course of my research of Franco-Irish careers in art music that I undertook since about the year 2011, the name propped up again from time to time, yet the person remained enigmatic. All existing information – from standard reference works to the internet – seemed extremely vague, not promising anything of sufficient quantity to even consider writing a biography. It seemed like he had written and published several works with a 'Celtic' flavour, among them piano works and some unusual chamber music settings, which kept my interest alive. In March 2014, a German photographer in Paris, Herbert Herterich, sent me a photograph of Hennessy's gravestone on the Montparnasse Cemetery, with three names on it: besides the composer there was his wife Claire, with an apparent Polish maiden name, who died in 1947 and Patrice (1910–1973), obviously their common son. The back of the stone seemed to feature a line from a French poem.

When I published my book on the O'Kelly family of Franco-Irish musicians[1] in May 2014, time had come to revisit Hennessy. I was helped immensely by the progress in the digitisation of library holdings and genealogical sources. But it was a rather unhappy coincidence that gave the decisive momentum to the project. In January 2016, Isadore Ryan, an Irish friend in Paris who had already supported my O'Kelly research, went again to the Cimetière Montparnasse to clarify for me the inscription on the back of the tombstone with the unidentified poem. He returned with the news that there was no inscription at the back side at all (obviously, the original photographer had mixed up two different stones in his e-mail to me), but that there was now a fourth name on the front side, besides Swan, Claire, and Patrice: Patrice's widow, who had died as late as December 2014. With this name I was able to identify current members of Swan Hennessy's family in France, all very much alive, including the composer's granddaughters Brigitte (*b.* 1939) and Aline (*b.* 1941).

Thus, this book owes its existence to coincidences initialised by Barra, Herbert, and Isadore. I am extremely grateful to all of you. You have given me some immensely pleasing and satisfying years, and I hope you are happy with the outcome.

Brigitte Hennessy is the family's main link to their obscure musical ancestor, of whom nobody in the family had ever heard a note played or recorded until very recently. For decades, the family had kept several large volumes of musical manuscripts,

---

[1] Axel Klein: *O'Kelly. An Irish Musical Family in Nineteenth-Century France* (Norderstedt: BoD, 2014).

carefully collected press reviews and concert programmes, and other material, dispersed over three locations in France: a treasure trove for a musicologist! And while there are, unfortunately, no letters or diaries in this collection, there still is enough material to undertake this research and rescue Swan Hennessy from his undeserved oblivion – or at least to provide the opportunity.

Further thanks are due to Janick Julienne in Paris who undertook research for me into Roman Catholic parishes in the Montparnasse quarter of Paris in order to establish the link between Swan Hennessy and Terence MacSwiney, the former Lord Mayor of Cork, who died on hunger strike in an English prison in 1920. This provided the basis for Brigitte Hennessy to ask for the baptismal record from the archives of the Archdiocese of Paris (unfortunately, this did not contain the information we were looking for). Many thanks to Nicolas Lods, great-grandson of Swan Hennessy, who was the first to investigate the composer's American roots, albeit years before documents could be found online, travelling to Rockford, Illinois, for this purpose. To his sister, Sophie Lods-Lenczner and her husband Lionel who provided their apartment in Paris for meetings and with whom my wife and I spent a lovely Saturday in southern Normandy among Hennessy's music manuscripts. To their son, Swan Lenczner, who initially established the contact between Brigitte Hennessy and me, and whose delightful first name prompted me to identify the right family. I cherish the generosity and trust with which you provided me with first-hand source material. Without all of you, this book would never have been written.

Some individuals at research libraries provided helpful and welcome support. Dr Nicole Bickhoff of the Landesarchiv Baden-Württemberg at Stuttgart provided me with information regarding the Stuttgart Conservatory where Hennessy studied. Birgit Renner of the Staatsbibliothek Berlin / Stiftung Preußischer Kulturbesitz very kindly arranged the reproduction of Hennessy's early scores from German music publishers and the ones published by Schott. Dr Sabine Kurth of the Music Division in the Bavarian State Library, Munich, unbureaucratically provided access and a scan of the only Hennessy music manuscript in a German collection (his Opus 14, part of the Schott Production Archive). Dr Jürgen Schaarwächter of the Max Reger Institute at Karlsruhe very kindly helped identify the link between Hennessy and Reger and provided the relevant document (a 1907 postcard). Esther Schönberger of the Thuringian State Music Archive ('Thüringisches Landesmusikarchiv') at Weimar, which houses the estate of the German music critic and folk music researcher Heinrich Möller, helped identify Möller's link to Hennessy, thereby unearthing many Hennessy publications with autograph dedications to Möller (Möller was based in Paris, *c.*1909–14). Brian McGee of the Cork City and County Archives has been most forthcoming enabling a visit despite severe constraints on personnel. Many thanks to David McMullin, music librarian at the New York Public Library, for trying to locate autograph material, even though the search was futile. Sonia Popoff at the Médiathèque Musicale Mahler in Paris was so kind as to scan for me the many articles and brief notices about Hennessy in *Le Guide du concert*. She also established the contact to Marika Green, copyright owner of the holdings in the Fonds Paul Le Flem in that institution, which contains three autograph dedications by Hennessy to Le Flem. To Marika Green, then, acknowledgement is due for the authorisation to have these works scanned for me. Roy Stanley, music librarian of Trinity College Dublin, very kindly reproduced manuscript dedications by Hennessy on printed music in their possession (see Chapter 8) and facilitated access to reviews in some issues of the *Monthly Musical Record* which were difficult to find in Germany, and which were then very kindly provided by Jonathan Frank of Westminster Music Library, London. In a more general way, Marie-Gabrielle Soret and Mathilde Belassène at the Bibliothèque Nationale de France in Paris were very forthcoming in responding to queries that arose in the course of my research.

My research has uncovered a number of autograph letters by Hennessy that had been hitherto unknown. Dr Roland Schmidt-Hensel of the Staatsbibliothek Berlin / Stiftung Preußischer Kulturbesitz very kindly identified (and made available to me) twelve autograph letters that Hennessy sent to the music publisher Schott, plus ten responses by the publisher, that have recently become part of the library's Schott Archive. Jacqueline Le Nail of the Bibliothèque de Rennes Métropole, Les Champs Libres, kindly provided the one autograph letter by Hennessy in their collection. Likewise, Mohamed Graine kindly sent me a scan from another single Hennessy letter at the Bibliothèque Municipale de Lyon. Dr Karen Moses of the Music Division at the Library of Congress, Washington D.C., discovered, after my tentative request, sixteen autograph letters in a Swan Hennessy file that forms part of the Irving Schwerke Collection at that institution, and facilitated their reproduction for me. In the latter regard, thanks to Kia Campbell for the friendly solution of bureaucratic hindrances and Chamisa Redmond for providing the material. Another (single) autograph letter in an American library was provided by Suzanne Lovejoy of the Irving S. Gilmore Music Library at Yale University. All these letters are documented in Appendix 4a. The German radio station SWR 2 in Stuttgart kindly provided me with their 2008 studio recording of Hennessy's *Quatre Pièces celtiques*, Op. 59, for cor anglais and string trio.

More people were supportive in many different ways, some of them musicians who brought Hennessy's scores to life for me (and partly for the public, too) or shared their interest. These include the members of the RTÉ ConTempo Quartet (Bogdan Sofei, Ingrid Nicola, Andreea Banciu, Adrian Mantu); Lesley Bishop, John O'Kane, Aidán Ó Dúbhgaill and, in particular, Eoin Brady at RTÉ (the Irish national broadcasting station) for the wonderful cooperation that led to the world premiere recordings of Hennessy's string quartets (published in April 2019); the producers of that recording, Laoise O'Brien and Ben Rawlins, who helped to bring out the essential elements of the music with great understanding and sympathy; the pianists Moritz Ernst in Badenweiler, Yukie Yamakata in Bad Nauheim, Thérèse Fahy, Niall Kinsella, and Úna Hunt in Dublin, the violinist Gillian Williams and the cellist Arun Rao, both in Dublin; Seóirse Ó Dochartaigh in Leckemy Co. Donegal; the Australian violist Valmai Coggins and her string trio Three Piece Suite for sharing with me their live recording of the *Petite trio celtique*, Op. 52; Ullrich Pühn and Cornelius Schmaderer of the Dejean Quartett in Germany for their interest in Hennessy and sending a rehearsal recording of the *Variations sur un thème de six notes*, Op. 58; likewise, Andreas Gosling and the Ensemble Più for our exchange regarding the *Quatre Pièces celtiques*, Op. 59;

Tina Darb and Tony Sheehan at the Triskel Arts Centre, Cork, for their interest and curiosity. All of this has been really encouraging.

Academics from whom I learned and who shared their expertise with me include Dr Paul-André Bempéchat of Harvard University; Prof. E. Douglas Bomberger of Elizabethtown College in Pennsylvania; Prof. emeritus Arbie Orenstein of the City University of New York; Prof. Howard Pollack of the University of Houston; Prof. Harry White MRIA and Dr Wolfgang Marx of University College Dublin; Dr Paul Everett, formerly of University College Cork; Dr Gareth Cox of Mary Immaculate College, University of Limerick; Prof. Lorraine Byrne Bodley, Dr Adrian Scahill, and Dr Laura Watson of Maynooth University; Dr Aidan Thompson of University College Galway; Dr John O'Flynn of Dublin City University; Dr Conor Caldwell of Queen's University Belfast; Dr Catherine Ferris, Dr Mark Fitzgerald, and Dr Maria McHale of the DIT Conservatory of Music and Drama in Dublin; Prof. Benjamin Dwyer of Middlesex University; Dr Yves Defrance, Associate Member of the Centre de Recherche Bretonne et Celtique (CRBC) at the Université Rennes II; Tim Schwabedissen of the Christian-Albrechts-Universität zu Kiel. Many thanks also to Dr Aaron C. Keebaugh of North Shore Community College, Danvers MA, for his continued interest in Hennessy and his warm encouragement, and also for providing me with his feedback on my first chapters.

I would also like to mention the positive feedback I received from music critics, and in this regard I would like to express my thanks to Michael Dervan of *The Irish Times*, Marjorie Brennan of the *Irish Examiner*, Christoph Schlüren of the *Neue Musikzeitung*, Oliver Fraenzke of *The New Listener*, and Jean Lacroix of the *Revue Générale* in Belgium, with hopefully more to come. The contact to Oliver Fraenzke enabled the wonderful reprint of some of Hennessy's chamber music in a better quality than ever before (with Musikproduktion Höflich, Munich).

Finally, antiquarian music dealers must be thanked for their sheer existence, but particularly kind and forthcoming were Bernd Katzbichler in Unterwössen, Bavaria, François Roulmann in Paris, Philippe Cabarat in Blois, Jacques Perroud in Carpentras, Austin Sherlaw-Johnson in Stonesfield, Oxfordshire, and the autograph dealers J. A. Stargardt in Berlin and Aguttes in Neuilly-sur-Seine.

I would also like to express my joy about this book appearing with Schott, a company that also published some of Hennessy's music. Many thanks to my editor, Sebastian Burkart who accepted my proposal without hesitation.

A number of my personal friends and colleagues beyond the area of music or musicology showed great interest in my subject of research, which I also perceived as a great encouragement. In this regard I would like to express my heartfelt thanks to Christof von Branconi, Benno Kahrens, Dr Benno van Dalen, and Dr Mingyi Yuan.

Last but not least, I thank my wife Michiko for her patience and understanding during the research and writing process. The project has presented us with travels to France, Switzerland and Ireland, numerous encounters and exchanges with amazing people, and a lot of pleasure but, no doubt, it has also meant restrictions on our leisure. Thank you from the bottom of my heart for going this route with me.

Introduction

*If I am to become known before I die I must make haste,
for the bird of time is on the wing.*

(Swan Hennessy to Irving Schwerke, Paris, 19 April 1929)[1]

Swan Hennessy (1866–1929) did not leave a diary, and although he must have been an active letter-writer, very little of his correspondence has survived. There are only few photographs, too, and most of those that exist are from his last ten to twelve years. And despite the fact that he was acquainted with many better-known composers of his time in France, his name does not appear in the biographies of any of his French contemporaries. It is difficult, under such circumstances, to write a proper biography of a standard that a 21st century reader can justifiably expect.

In addition, many of the facts about Hennessy's early life are unknown or obscure and will probably remain so. One reason is that his personal papers such as birth and educational certificates were destroyed, partly during the 'Great Chicago Fire' of 1871, partly during World War II in Germany. Because of the former, we have no birth or baptismal records, because of the latter, there are no documents of his musical education (at Stuttgart). Today, the internet gives access to emigration papers, census data and passport applications, but there remain large gaps and lacks of evidence in the chronicle, which probably can never be closed. It is for of these reasons that this book does not have a subtitle like 'The Life and Music of …' because the 'Life' part is so scarcely documented.

These also include some private details that Hennessy consciously hid from the public (Chapter 3). In fact, these may have been the reason why he did not keep a diary, because he would perhaps have entrusted to it thoughts that he may not have wanted others to see mixed up in the appreciation of his music. On the other hand, if he would have had no interest in being commemorated by later generations, he would not have kept such a careful catalogue of his own compositions in opus numbers and genres, he would not have taken the trouble to collect reviews and concert programmes in four volumes of press books that survived with the Hennessy family in France, and he would not have his manuscripts bound in volumes of marbled board and leather spines. He *did* want that somebody finds this material at some point. Yet, he could have made the biographer's work just slightly easier.

---

[1] This is the quote that I took as a basis for the title of this book. Half a year later, Hennessy had died. I considered it especially appropriate because of Hennessy's premonition of death and because of the image of Swan as a bird. Hennessy himself quotes an idea from the medieval Persian astronomer and poet Omar Khayyám's (1048–1131) collection *Rubáiyát* in Edward FitzGerald's English translation (1859). For the correspondence between Hennessy and the American music critic Irving Schwerke see Chapter 9.

Literature review

To say there is any state of research about Swan Hennessy would be an exaggeration. There is none, really, because he was almost never included, however briefly, in musical research in either France, Ireland, England, or the United States (nor, for his youth, in Germany). Therefore, for its biographical chronicle, this book relies almost entirely on early sources such as contemporary reviews, his occasional letters, and on family memory. Likewise, in terms of his music, the only sources available are the music itself (in print and in manuscript) and a large quantity of contemporary reviews of their publications and performances.

Hennessy has brief dictionary articles in Paul Frank's and Wilhelm Altmann's *Kurzgefasstes Tonkünstler-Lexikon* (Regensburg, 1936), in Carlo Schmidl's *Dizionario universale dei musicisti* (Milan, 1938), and in Wilibald Gurlitt's twelfth edition of the *Riemann Musik Lexikon* (Mainz, 1959), all focusing on superficial data and selected works (the *Riemann* has a wrong date and place of birth, making him Irish, born in Dublin!).[2] The French writer Guy Ferchault wrote the longest and most comprehensive article on Swan Hennessy in a reference work. It appeared, in German translation, in the first edition of the multi-volume encyclopaedia *Die Musik in Geschichte und Gegenwart* (MGG), vol. 6 (Kassel, 1957). For the biographical section, it is heavily indebted to a 1929 interview with Lucien Chevaillier in *Le Guide du concert* (see below). It has quite an extended list of works – the best so far in printed format – and an appreciation that emphasises the Irish aspect in Hennessy's music. Other brief dictionary entries can be found in Marc Honegger's *Dictionnaire de la musique* (Paris, 1970–76), Jozef Robijns' and Miep Zijlstra's *Algemene Muziek Encyclopedie* (Haarlem, 1979–84), Alberto Basso's *Dizionario Enciclopedico Universale della Musica e dei Musicisti* (Turin, 1986), and Nicolas Slonimsky's and Laura Diane Kuhn's ninth edition of *Baker's Biographical Dictionary of Musicians* (New York, 2001). Despite the various languages, these entries very much resemble each other. They draw their content from Chevaillier (1929) or Ferchault/*MGG* (1957) and do not present any new or individual research. So far, Hennessy has not made it into any of the editions of *Grove's Dictionaries*, and he has been dropped by the more recent editions of *MGG*, *Baker's*, and *Riemann*.

Some extended contemporary articles stand out and deserve special mention because of their length and because of some details that must derive from personal conversation of the author with the composer.[3] The first is an anonymous article simply headed 'Mr. Swan Hennessy' in a 1913 issue of *The London Musical Courier*.[4] This is the first portrait that reveals, among others, the name of Hennessy's teacher of composition in Stuttgart. The second article of note is by the well-known French music critic Henri Collet in his quite influential series of biographical sketches entitled 'La Musique chez soi' in *Comoedia* – a fine sympathetic portrait from a French perspective, reviewing

---

[2] Missing from the revised thirteenth edition published in 2012.
[3] For bibliographical details see Bibliography, section 2.
[4] (anon.), 'Mr. Swan Hennessy', in *The London Musical Courier*, 4 January 1913.

several of Hennessy's compositions and highlighting his Irish interests.⁵ An interesting portrait in an Irish newspaper is a lengthy article by Donnchadh Ua Braoin (a.k.a. Denis Breen) in a 1922 issue of the *Dublin Evening Telegraph*, with an updated 1923 version in *The Leader*.⁶ Written during turbulent political times, these accompany a brief period in the early 1920s when Hennessy enjoyed some performances in Ireland. The most significant and longest contribution is an interview that Lucien Chevaillier conducted with Hennessy for *Le Guide du concert* of 12 April 1929, entitled 'Un Entretien avec Swan Hennessy'.⁷ Most, however brief, articles that later appeared about the composer, who died six months later, refer to this source, and this extends both to what Hennessy disclosed and to what he chose to be silent about. Finally, a 1931 article about Franco-Irish relations in music includes several paragraphs about Hennessy.⁸ After that, Hennessy fell into oblivion.

It is hard to find Swan Hennessy even briefly mentioned in secondary sources or musicological studies. In a 1914 book on composition by Arthur Eaglefield Hull, Hennessy's *Étude* Op. 25 (published 1907) features as an example of polymetric composition.⁹

Some of the chamber music by Swan Hennessy is dealt with in *Cobbett's Cyclopedic Survey of Chamber Music* (London: Oxford University Press, 1929; ²1963) on just about one and a half pages written by Henry Woollett. These selectively list Opp. 14, 46, 49, 50, 52, 54, 58, 62, 63, and 65 only. The second issue of 1963 corrects his year of birth from 1886 to 1866 but still maintains that he was born in Ireland and omits his death in 1929.

Hennessy's name also occurs in René Dumesnil's *La Musique contemporaine en France* (Paris: Librairie Armand Colin, 1930; ²1949), vol. 1, p. 100, in a section on foreign influences in French music, here focusing on '*L'école anglaise*'. The phrase runs:

Bien que né en Amérique, Swan Hennessy fut avant tout un Celte et sa musique, quand elle n'exprime point un humour à la Satie, s'inspire de « âme gaélique ».

[Although born in America, Swan Hennessy was above all a Celt and his music, while it expresses a humour of Satie's kind, is inspired by the 'Gaelic soul'.]

---

⁵ Henri Collet: 'La Musique chez soi – XCVII. Œuvres de Swan Hennessy', in *Comoedia*, 5 December 1921, p. 4.
⁶ Donnchadh Ua Braoin: 'Swan Hennessy. An Irish Musician of To-day', in *Dublin Evening Telegraph*, 2 September 1922, p. 2; 'Craiftine': 'An Irish Musician of To-day', in *The Leader*, 7 April 1923, pp. 208–210.
⁷ Lucien Chevaillier: 'Un Entretien avec Swan Hennessy', in *Le Guide du concert*, 12 April 1929, pp. 791–793; online: http://lmhsbd.oicrm.org/media/ART-CHL-1929-10.pdf (accessed 16 March 2018).
⁸ Grace O'Brien: 'Synge at the Paris Opera – Franco-Irish Musical Associations', in *The Irish Press*, 10 November 1931, p. 5.
⁹ *Modern Harmony. Its Explanation and Application* (London & Boston, n. d. [1914]). Note also a review of this book in the *Harvard Musical Review* 3:5, February 1915, p. 8, pronouncing these as 'freak' examples'.

This is remarkable because it acknowledges that Hennessy had a humoristic *and* a 'Celtic' side. On the other hand, these two strands should be considered separate, as the composer never mixed them. Its placement in a section on foreign influences is, of course, incorrect. Firstly, Hennessy never exerted much influence on French composers, it was rather *vice versa*. Secondly, this section also deals (very briefly) with Eugene Goossens, Arthur Bliss, Ralph Vaughan Williams, Benjamin Britten, etc. – all 'real' foreigners, whereas Hennessy was based in Paris and was to a much greater extent integrated in French musical life than the other names. Perhaps, Dumesnil's assessment offers another explanation for Hennessy's neglect, namely that despite his French music and lifestyle, he was perceived as an outsider?

In 1936, Bruno Aulich and Ernst Heimeran published their very successful *Das stillvergnügte Streichquartett* (Munich: Ernst Heimeran Verlag), an entertaining volume aiming at popularising chamber music. The English edition as *The Well-Tempered String Quartet* (New York: H. W. Gray, 1938; with many later editions) contained numerous additions – composers and works from the Anglophone world – by the translator, David Millar Craig. Among these is Swan Hennessy.[10] His paragraphs runs:

> HENNESSY, SWAN (b. 1886) (T)
> The influence of Hennessy's native Irish folk-melody is at once the most noticeable and most attractive feature of his chamber music. He has written three string quartets. The first, a Suite, op. 46, makes some very attractive effects with folk-melodies simply harmonized. Like the Second Quartet, op. 49, it blends some devices of modern usage with classical style, and the form is of the simplest. Here, too, folk-melodies, or themes of similar-sounding character, are happily exploited, notably in the last movement, a series of Variations. The Serenade for String Quartet, op. 65, is somewhat more advanced in style but embodies many of the same attractive melodic features as the earlier quartets.

As is unfortunately typical with many sources on Hennessy, this paragraph combines quite a few mistakes and misunderstandings. Not only is the year of birth wrong and the year of death missing. Craig also boldly claims that Hennessy wrote three string quartets, namely the first (Op. 46), second (Op. 49), and a serenade, Op. 65, disregarding the third (Op. 61) and fourth (Op. 75). Obviously, Craig's source was *Cobbett's Cyclopedic Survey of Chamber Music*, which makes exactly the same omissions. For the quartet Op. 46 he should have mentioned that the 'folk-melodies' are used in the final movement (the 'Variations') only. Neither of Op. 49 or 65 uses any traditional melodies but rather those 'of similar-sounding character'. As a young man, Craig had participated in performances, as cellist, in Hennessy's early piano trio *Lieder an den Mond*, Op. 10 (1888),[11] but he had obviously lost touch with his music since.

Selected works by Hennessy, sometimes in combination with a brief biographical paragraph, can be found in handbooks on particular instruments. For example,

---

[10] Quoted from the 1951 edition, p. 99. The '(T)' in the headline to the paragraph means that this is an addition by the translator (not in the German version). D. M. Craig (1878–1965) was mainly known as an official (since 1924) and music editor (from 1926) at the BBC.

[11] In England in 1903 and 1905; see Appendix 1, section C.

Rudolph Maria Breithaupt in his *Die natürliche Klaviertechnik* (Leipzig, 1912) mentions eight piano works (all pre-dating 1910); Jean-Marie Londeix's *125 ans de musique pour saxophone* (Paris, 1971) lists Hennessy's works with alto saxophone; Cameron McGraw's *Piano Duet Repertoire* (Bloomington, ID, 1981) mention's Hennessy's *Petite suite irlandaise*; Maurice Hinson's and Wesley Roberts' *The Piano in Chamber Ensemble. An Annotated Guide* (Bloomington, ID, 2/2006) gives a short characterisation of Hennessy's *Sonatine celtique*, Op. 62 (ignoring all of his other chamber works with piano); likewise, the same authors' *Guide to the Pianist's Repertoire* (Bloomington, ID, 4/2013) refers to his *À la manière de …* volumes of piano pastiches (ignoring all of his original music for piano).

In saying, Hennessy 'almost never' occurred in modern research, there are three exceptions. The longest has been this author's own article in the *Journal of the Society for Musicology in Ireland* (JSMI), published in July 2018, which focuses on the Irish/Celtic aspect of Hennessy's career.[12] As for other authors, Irish musicologist Laura Watson mentioned Hennessy in an overview of Ireland as a theme for French or France-based composers that included observations of some works in the Celticist thread, maintaining that his music was rather conservative in a French context.[13] Also in 2015, the French researcher Yves Defrance included Hennessy in a discussion of Breton-Irish musical influences, putting forward the interesting argument that, in the days before universal travel, Breton musicians of the 1910s and 1920s gained their knowledge of Irish music from printed and performed works such as Hennessy's.[14] To the best of my knowledge, this is all there ever was before the present monograph.

For the contextualisation of Hennessy's music in Germany, England, Ireland, and (in particular) France, reference has been made in this study to selected pieces of research by Jane F. Fulcher, Barbara L. Kelly and other English-language experts on French music as well as Harry White and other experts on Irish music, all of whom are transparently cited and listed in the bibliography. However, Swan Hennessy's name does not appear in any of these studies.

Of some relevance for this book is the concept of regionalism in French music, in particular relating to the circle of Breton composers that Hennessy mixed with in Paris. However, much as French music is centralised on Paris, so is musicology, and there are not that many studies on regionalist aspects of music in France. So far, they do not play a role in the writings of the major contributors to French musical histo-

---

[12] Axel Klein: 'An Irish-American in Paris: Swan Hennessy (1866–1929)', in *Journal of the Society for Musicology in Ireland* 13 (2017–18), pp. 47–78; online at https://musicologyireland.com/jsmi/index.php/journal/article/view/176 (accessed 29 July 2018).

[13] Laura Watson: 'Ireland in the Musical Imagination of Third Republic France', in Una Hunt and Mary Pierse (eds.): *France and Ireland. Notes and Narratives* (Oxford etc.: Peter Lang, 2015), pp. 91–109.

[14] Yves Defrance: 'L'Irlande dans les musiques bretonnes actuelles', in Yann Bevant, Laurent Daniel (eds): *Bretagne/Irlande: quelles relations? / Brittany/Ireland: what relations?* (Brest: Centre de Recherche Bretonne et Celtique, Université de Bretagne Occidentale and Rennes: Université Rennes 2, 2015), pp. 159–196.

riography, be they American, English, French, or German, except for Kelly (ed., 2008), which features three essays in a section devoted to regionalism. This contains articles covering Dijon, Alsace and Lorraine.[15] Where this aspect comes more to the fore, such as in the writings of Musk (1999), Waters (2008) and Llano (2013),[16] the Breton side is also not covered. Only Bempéchat (2008)[17] has written specifically about the Association des Compositeurs Bretons (ACB), but both his essay and de Bellaing's *Dictionnaire des compositeurs de musique en Bretagne* (1992) will be found somewhat deficient. Bempéchat ignores that Hennessy was an early member of the ACB (and ignores other members as well; see Chapter 6), and de Bellaing is surprisingly short on the ACB while giving incomplete and partly inaccurate information on Hennessy.

There are two recent English-language biographies of French composers, contemporary to Hennessy, in which regionalism is an important aspect: Robert F. Waters' 2008 biography of Déodat de Séverac (1872–1921) and Paul-André Bempéchat's 2009 biography of Jean Cras (1879–1932).[18] While Waters' study focuses on the Languedoc resp. French part of Catalonia, Bempéchat's looks at Brittany.[19]

Any potential parallels have been taken into account, although it needs to be said that Hennessy's case is different insofar as he mixed with Breton composers but was not Breton himself. His music is Irish-influenced and as such he has no real parallel in France. Musical parallels would have to be sought in Ireland or England, but then his French residence makes him unique. The intersection uniting Hennessy with his Breton friends, at least in their own perception, was Celticism, which is not confined to a specific region and yet has many parallels with both musical nationalism and regionalism. Therefore, I do not wish to overemphasise the regionalist aspect for the simple fact that Hennessy *was not* a regionalist French composer. His inspiration is Irish (mostly).

Similarly, describing Hennessy as an Irish composer is difficult as well. His contemporaries in 1920s France did not hesitate to call him Irish, but Hennessy has never

---

[15] Barbara L. Kelly (ed.): *French Music, Culture, and National Identity, 1870–1939* (Rochester, New York: University of Rochester Press & Woodbridge: Boydell & Brewer, 2008); essays by Katharine Ellis, Detmar Klein, and Didier Francfort.

[16] Andrea N. Musk: *Aspects of Regionalism in French Music During the Third Republic: the Schola Cantorum, d'Indy, Séverac and Canteloube* (Oxford: Oxford University Press, 1999); Roger F. Waters: *Déodat de Séverac. Musical Identity in Fin-de-Siècle France* (Farnham, Surrey: Ashgate, 2008); Samuel Llano: *Whose Spain? Negotiating 'Spanish Music' in Paris, 1908–1929* (New York: Oxford University Press, 2013).

[17] Paul-André Bempéchat: *'Allons enfants de *quelle* patrie?' Breton Nationalism and the French Impressionist Aesthetic* (Cambridge, Mass.: Harvard University, Center for European Studies Working Paper Series No. 106, 2008).

[18] Roger F. Waters: *Déodat de Séverac. Musical Identity in Fin de Siècle France* (Farnham, Surrey: Ashgate, 2008); Paul-André Bempéchat: *Jean Cras. Polymath of Music and Letters* (Farnham, Surrey: Ashgate, 2009).

[19] Breton regionalist aspects are also covered in some French-language biographies, such as Mathieu Ferey & Benoît Menut: *Joseph-Guy Ropartz ou le pays inaccessible* (Troinex/Drize: Éditions Papillon, 2005).

had any sustained presence in Ireland, despite occasional performances. He did not mix with the Irish composers of his time. His Celticist repertory would ideally fit into an Irish context and would also compare well with a number of composers of the 'British Musical Renaissance' in the United Kingdom. Yet, the simple fact remains that Hennessy was not part of the Irish or British musical scene, although there are quite a few reviews of his published music in English journals, and although his first language was English. Hennessy chose to live in France and, by doing so, wanted to be perceived in a French context.

The concept of musical Celticism is another underrepresented area in musicology. In most cases, the discussion is applied to modern commercial variants of 'Celtic music' in the form of band arrangements of the traditional music of (formerly) Celtic regions in Europe, invariably ignoring that these post-1960s popular developments have a history and predecessors in art music. With the exception of Defrance (2015), there is no modern academic study of musical Celticism in the history (and present) of 'classical' music, apart from the research by Aidan Thompson on the music of Arnold Bax.[20]

Name variants of Swan Hennessy

Admittedly, the name of 'Swan Hennessy' is unusual – although there have been other composers who stylised their name in the form of two surnames, an example from Ireland would be Hamilton Harty. Since Hennessy never, neither in official documents nor in musical affairs, mentioned his proper first name Edward, many critics came to believe that Swan was his first name. Yet, particularly German critics did so unbelievingly, it seems, because there are numerous reviews of Hennessy's music in German journals and newspapers who suggested 'Svan' (perhaps as a variation of the Scandinavian name 'Sven') or as 'Iwan', suggesting a Russian provenance. To me, this does not look like the writers were not able to read the proper name, but like a stubborn unwillingness to accept a name they did not consider correct (an unfortunate German quality, perhaps). Thus, we find the name 'Svan Hennessy' in various issues of *Signale für die musikalische Welt, Die Musik, Allgemeine Musikzeitung,* or *Neue Zeitschrift für Musik* and in a 1913 concert review of the *Berliner Tageblatt*. Similarly, one also finds 'Iwan Hennessy' or 'Iwan Henessy' in *Signale für die musikalische Welt* and *Die Musik* as well as in a number of 1922 concert reviews in German newspapers. 'Swann' Hennessy also appears from time time, perhaps inspired by Marcel Proust, as do variants of his surname which may occur as 'Henessy', 'Henessey', 'Hennesy', or 'Hennessey'.

---

[20] Yves Defrance: 'Un Bretonisme musical (1860–1980)', in *Analyse musicale* no. 78, December 2015, pp. 104–113; Aidan J. Thompson: 'Bax and the 'Celtic North'', in *Journal of the Society for Musicology in Ireland* 8 (2012–3), p. 51–87. See also Martin Stokes, 'Celtic Music', in *The Encyclopaedia of Music in Ireland*, ed. Harry White and Barra Boydell (Dublin: UCD Press, 2013), p. 185–186; while this does mention the art music dimension, including Ireland and Brittany, its bibliography does not contain any item pertaining to this area.

I am pointing this out because the problem is that, when searching for information on Hennessy in newspaper databases, for instance, a researcher needs to consider an unusually broad range of keywords.

Supposed nationalities

Given the unusual name and (to many critics) unclear provenance, there was also considerable speculation as to Swan Hennessy's nationality. The earliest mention of any nationality is when *La Revue musicale* in May 1908 described him as *'Irlandais, ayant fait ses études musicales dans les conservatoires d'Allemagne et domicilié à Paris'*. Likewise, the *Allgemeine Musikzeitung* described him in March 1911 as *'geborenen Irländer'* ('native Irishman') and again in February 1912 as an *'Iren'* ('Irishman'). For the *Musical Standard* in April 1912 he was 'an Irishman', too.

The *Norddeutsche Allgemeine Zeitung* in Germany implied an English nationality when it wrote of Hennessy in 1911: *'Eine der merkwürdigsten Erscheinungen der modernen englischen Musikwelt dürfte unstreitig Swan Henessey sein'* ('one of the most noteworthy appearances in modern English music is, without doubt, Swan Henessey' [sic!]).

No room for doubt left the formulation of *'[die] Kunst des Schotten Hennessy'* ('the art of the Scotsman Hennessy') in another 1911 issue of *Allgemeine Musikzeitung*, perhaps because the author here reviewed *Annie*, subtitled 'chanson écossaise' (Op. 31 No. 1). He was Scottish also, for an issue of *Signale für die musikalische Welt* in February 1912.

Quite unique was the supposition of an *'anscheinend belgischen Komponisten'* ('apparently Belgian composer') in *Signale für die musikalische Welt* of May 1911.

From an Italian perspective, Hennessy was one of recent *'musicisti francesi'* ('French musicians'), according to an April 1912 issue of *Il Mondo del Arte*. Never tired of speculations, for *Signale für die musikalische Welt* of November 1913 he was a *'französischer[!] Komponist'* ('French composer'), too, after the same paper had previously asserted his Belgian and Scottish nationalities.

Taking 'Swan' for a version of the Scandinavian 'Sven', the Berlin daily newspaper *Die Zeit* claimed in 1922 he was *'der in Norwegen geborene, in Paris lebende Ire'* ('the Norway-born, Paris-resident, Irishman'), making the matter just a little more complicated.

Quite right then was the anonymous writer in the 1913 *London Musical Courier* who – evidently after having spoken to Hennessy – explains his birth in the United States and his father's Irish nationality. But the weirdest assumption can be found in the Irish newspaper *The Freeman's Journal* which wrote in January 1922: 'A feature of the occasion was the sonata in honour of Terence MacSwiney by a South American composer, Mr. Sean Hennessy, Mr. Arthur Darley conducted'. Not only would a sonata not need a conductor and his name was not Sean, 'South America' is a quite wild guess indeed.

A note on capitalisation and italicisation

There appears to be no clear-cut rule as to the capitalisation of titles in French – contrary to English where all major words (nouns, names, verbs, adjectives, organisations, etc.) begin with a capital letter or in German where all names and nouns are capitalised as in general language. Increasingly, in English-language publications about French topics the Chicago Manual of Style is used, and in music it has been adopted by the *New Grove* dictionaries, the *Oxford Dictionary of Opera*, and others. This does not use any capitalisation except for the very first word – often an article – or a place name. Examples would be *Le barbier de Séville* or *La vie parisienne*.

In France, one approach is to follow the usage of the Imprimerie Nationale, the government publishing house, as explained in its *Lexique des règles typographiques en usage à l'Imprimerie nationale*. According to this system, my examples above would read *Le Barbier de Séville* and *La Vie parisienne*. In Hennessy's case, sample titles would be *L'Américain qui a bien dîné* (Op. 47 No. 2) or *Le Chasseur noir* (Op. 73 No. 1).

Since alphabetical listings of works would never be sorted after articles like *Le* and *La*, and any such listing would never begin with a small letter (*barbier, vie*) my preferred use of capitalisation in this book is that of the Imprimerie Nationale and to abandon the increasingly standard but not very logical Chicago Manual of Style. I will extend that reading to titles that begin with a number or numeral, such as in *Quatre Pièces celtiques*, Op. 59, or *Deux Mélodies*, Op. 73. If any other spelling is used in this book, it is in quotes from an original source only.

In terms of italicisation, titles of musical works, of books and journals are italicised, but titles of articles in books or journals are put in simple commas. I also use italics in all quotations from a language other than English; this most frequently applies to French and German and will mostly be found in footnotes, as the originals to my own translations.

These rules are not simply my own fancy (which would be very presumptuous) but – in the absence of a general rule – they appear to me the most logical choice out of several established possibilities.

My approach to music analysis

In approaching the music of Swan Hennessy I do not follow any established school of musical analysis. In introducing an unknown composer such as him, it has been my aim to find a balance between the demands of fellow musicologists and musicians and the necessary brevity that is demanded by an overview of a lifetime's *oeuvre*. In each piece of music I try to identify the most characteristic, striking, or memorable elements that catches the essence of the work and that might make it worthy of attention for a musicologist or worthy of exploration for a musician. I am aware that one could write a lengthy article or book chapter about many of the individual compositions mentioned in this book, and I have no doubt that several of them would deserve such a treatment. I have also no doubt that other musicians and musicologists will see other or more things in this music than I do and may come to different conclusions.

A valid method of introducing an unknown composer may be to concentrate on pivotal works and omit (or only mention in passing) all the rest. While this approach has its advantages, I rather went for the 'overview approach', which gave me the opportunity to mention more or less all of Hennessy's works, with the length of treatment giving an indication of my assessment of importance. There is a realistic risk that it might take long until another musicologist would devote time to Hennessy's music – if, indeed, it ever happens. Therefore, I have had a vague feeling I should include as much as necessary and as many sources as I was able to find.

It is these sources, in fact, that I wanted to give space as well. Literature research in libraries, online resources and Hennessy's own press books reflect the views of contemporary critics, and I am documenting these alongside my own impressions of the music. Thus, my analyses/reviews/descriptions of the music will always conclude with the opinion of Hennessy's contemporaries. These bring further analytical insights into my own writing and complement the picture with additional perspectives.

It is hoped that this approach will be of interest and relevance. At the same time, I humbly accept more thoroughgoing analyses and look forward to them with keen interest, but from a relaxed distance. I have devoted a significant part of the past five years to the study of this man and his music, and my 'Life after Hennessy' begins in

August 2019
Axel Klein

Chapter 1
Cork to Chicago: The Origins (1830s to 1870s)

Hennessy is an Irish name that is traditionally to be found in and around the city of Cork in southern Ireland. The founder of the famous French cognac (brandy) company of Hennessy was from this area, too. Although there is no document of a direct relationship to the cognac family, it is striking that both families do not use the traditional Hennessy family crest – which shows a deer surrounded by three bundles of arrows – but the personal coat of arms of Richard Hennessy (1724–1800), the founder of the cognac dynasty, which shows an arm holding a hatchet. This refers to Richard Hennessy's twelve-year career in the French army which earned him French citizenship. This crest can not only be found on all cognac bottles of the firm today, but it was also on the letter-head that Swan Hennessy used in Paris, and it can be seen on the silver ring that Swan's father took with him when he emigrated from Ireland. It is still in family possession, now in France. From this, a distant relationship of the two families, reaching back to the 18th century, is not unlikely.

The name Hennessy was originally spelt in Gaelic as Ó hAonghusa, which means 'descendant of Angus'. The composer used this spelling at least once, on the title page of his *Petite suite irlandaise*, Op. 29 (1909).

The composer's father, Michael David Hennessy (1837–1919), was born in Cork (probably city, not county), 19 December 1837. The few musical reference works that include Swan Hennessy do not go into any details about his father. Guy Ferchault, the author of the Hennessy article in the first edition of *Die Musik in Geschichte und Gegenwart (MGG)*, wrote in 1957 that his father was an Irish lawyer; according to *Baker's Dictionary*, 'he was the son of an Irish-American settler'. Both is true and yet miles from the full story.

The names of Michael Hennessy's parents were David and Mary (née Hayes). This information is contained in Michael's death certificate and must therefore have come from Swan. However, neither the date of birth nor the names of Swan's paternal grandparents can be confirmed in the usual genealogical databases. In the absence of any surviving documents from the time we must rely on the information that Michael Hennessy has repeatedly given in official procedures such as passport applications.

The earliest passport-related document that has come to light is an 1897 exchange on passport matters contained in the *Papers Relating to the Foreign Relations of the United States, with the Annual Message of the President Transmitted to Congress December 6, 1897*.[1] Under 'Belgium', this contains the request of an official in the Legation of the United States in Brussels to the Department of State, dated 18 August 1897, requesting instruction on the issuance of a passport to Michael Hennessy under the unusual circumstance that all documents proving the identity and citizenship of the applicant were gone.

---

[1] https://history.state.gov/historicaldocuments/frus1897/pg_25 (accessed 15 June 2018).

It appears that Hennessy senior had originally received a passport on 11 January 1875 for himself, his wife, and his son. Both this passport and any further documents proving naturalization or citizenship had 'long ago been mislaid or lost'. Apparently, Michael claimed that he had been naturalized in Somerset, Perry County, Ohio and read law in Cincinnati. Various attempts to gain copies of those documents had failed because both the archives of Perry County and Cook County (for Chicago) were burnt, the latter during the 'Great Chicago Fire' of October 1871. The requested advice was obtained in September 1897 and the passport (headed 'Naturalized') was issued accordingly, dated 1 October 1897.

In this passport application, Michael Hennessy claims that he was born in Cork in 1837, emigrated in 1851, that he resided for 23 years (1851–74) in Chicago, and that he became a naturalized citizen of the United States at the Court of Somerset, Perry County, Ohio in 1858. Since January 1875 he had spent most of his time in the south of Europe for health reasons, occasionally returning to the USA on business, the last time in 1891.

Some years later, he got into similar trouble as is evidenced by a 1914 'Emergency Passport Application' (EPA), issued at the United States embassy in London.[2] This refers to the 1897 passport issued at the Brussels Legation. Because of the complicated case, the 1914 EPA contains long manuscript annotations by the embassy officials. Evidently, the information that was asked for in the form was not sufficient to explain the circumstances.

According to these annotations, Michael D. Hennessy emigrated to North America in 1853 (!) on board the 'Rory O'More', which travelled from Liverpool to an unnamed port in Canada, making a stop-over in Cork. Obviously, he cannot have remained in Canada for very long. He must soon have taken a land route to the mid-north of the USA. Again he says that in 1858 he became a naturalized citizen of the United States at [NB. the Court of Common Pleas in] Somerset, Perry County, Ohio and that the relevant document was lost due to a fire at the Court House.

Emigration from Ireland in the early 1850s was, of course, a mass movement. Around this time, hundreds of thousands of Irish men and women left their home to flee from the 'Great Famine' that had occurred following several years of a potato plight since the mid-1840s. Contrary to ships intended for US destinations, however, for Canadian ports at this period there usually don't exist passenger lists, so an important genealogical source such as this is unfortunately not available.

The 'Ireland Prison Registers, 1790–1924' database has an entry for a Michael Hennessy, aged 15 in 1852 (therefore born *c.*1837), who was imprisoned in Cork County Prison for 'stealing carrots'.[3] If this was indeed Swan's father (which is

---

[2] Available on request from https://sites.google.com/site/irishgleanings/home/1-0-extracts-from-passport-applications

[3] 'Irish Prison Registers, 1790–1924', database with images, *FamilySearch* (https://familysearch.org/ark:/61903/1:1:KMS4-DYS: accessed 12 October 2015), Michael Hennessy, 1852; from www.findmypast.com citing Cork County, Cork, Ireland, Cork County Prison, item 4, book 1/8/5.

impossible to ascertain), he probably had every reason to emigrate. In a country that exported food to England while its own population starved in hundreds of thousands and where one got imprisoned as a teenager for stealing carrots, there was little future.

An early document about Michael Hennessy's young family is a July 1865 census in the town of Rockford, Winnebago County, Illinois, 16 months before Swan's birth. This list is in form of a table, without giving addresses, in which Michael's household appears under 'M. D. Hennessy', and in the line for his name boxes are ticked that indicate one white female person 'over 10 and not over 20' years of age as well as one male and one female white person 'over 30 and not over 40'. In 1865, Michael was but 27 or 28 years old and not 'over 30', but perhaps he looked older and didn't have any document to prove that he was still in fact under 30. What we glean from this document is that by this time he was married (or at least lived together with a woman) and that there was a third (young) person in the house.

Another census document, now of 22 July 1870 in Chicago, Ward 20, is more detailed. Here, 'Hennessy M. D.', born in 'Ireland', is 36 years of age (wrong again, he was only 33), and following under the name of Hennessy are Sarah J., aged 37, born in 'N.Y.' (for New York state), then Lila, aged 18, born in 'Ohio', and Swan, aged 5 (he would only become four later in the year, in fact, but would then be in his fifth year), born in 'Ills' (for Illinois), and two domestic servants (see Fig. 1.1). Although the age indications are somewhat unreliable, this suggests that Lila was born before Michael's arrival in America. There are also two domestic servants from Holland, aged 36 and 27.

Fig. 1.1: Excerpt from 1870 Chicago census, showing the Hennessy household, Swan being in line 34 (Source: www.familysearch.com)

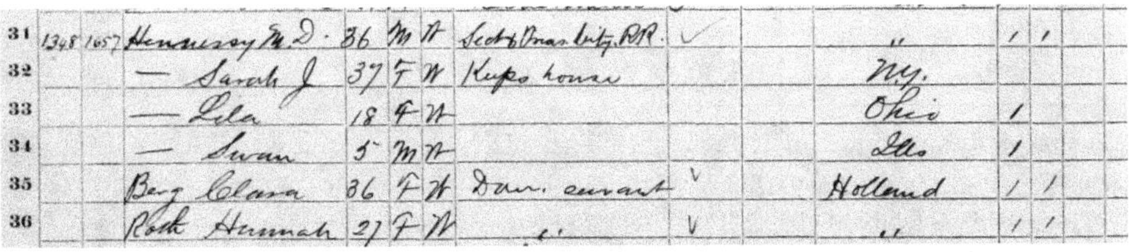

31	1348	1657	Hennessy M. D.	36	M	W	Sect & Man City RR	✓	"	/ /
32			— Sarah J	37	F	W	Keeps house		N.Y.	
33			— Lila	18	F	W			Ohio	/
34			— Swan	5	M	W			Ills	/
35			Berg Clara	36	F	W	Dom. servant	V	Holland	/ /
36			Roth Hannah	27	F	W	"	V	"	/ /

The maiden name of Sarah J. was Swan – which came to be the composer's putative first name. She had previously been married as McGiness and was probably widowed.[4] Thus, Lila was a step-daughter to Michael and a step-sister to Swan Hennessy.

No birth or baptismal record has been discovered for Sarah, but if she was 37 in 1870 she must have been born around 1832–3 and would have been just slightly older than Michael. She had an upper middle-class background; her father was Joseph Rockwell Swan (1802–1884), a prominent legal expert who came to some fame as a

[4] Information is included in Swan Hennessy's 1888 marriage certificate, see Chapter 3.

Supreme Court judge for Ohio (1855–9) and author of legal reference guides.[5] Joseph R. Swan was born in Westernville, New York State, and had moved to Columbus, Ohio, in 1824. It is not very likely, therefore, but not impossible, that Sarah was born in New York State, but Columbus is more likely. J. R. Swan was one of the founders of the Republican Party in the USA in 1854.[6]

* * *

Swan Hennessy was born on 24 November 1866 in Rockford, Winnebago County, Illinois. At this period, Winnebago County did not have a birth register yet, and no baptismal documents have come to light. His actual Christian name was Edward, but it never seems to have been used. Evidently, as the 1870 census records shows, he was called 'Swan' from early childhood. All through his life, Swan Hennessy gave 'Swan' as his first name, even at his marriage and when he applied for passports. Since no birth records existed, he never had to prove that this was not his first name. What's more, he was in fact known to his family and to himself as Swan from early on – with just one 1874 source suggesting an alternative (below).

He was apparently born at what was known for a long time as the 'old Holland House', or Holland House Hotel, situated at 200 South Main Street. When it was erected in 1855–6 it was named in honour of James A. Holland, an early citizen of Rockford who had died in 1855. It was long regarded as one of the best hotels in town before it burned down on Christmas Eve 1896.

How or why Swan Hennessy came to be born in a hotel remains unclear. Much later, his widow claimed that at this time his father practiced law in Rockford, but there is reason to be skeptical.[7] The family did live in Rockford at least for a few years (the Rockford census was in July 1865), and they would not have lived in a hotel during this time.

---

[5] In a passport application of 21 January 1921, in which he was required to disclose his American relations, he writes: 'My grandfather was Judge Swan of the Supreme Court of Ohio. I have cousins in Ohio.' Having consulted several genealogical websites, there is also the possibility that Hennessy indicated this relationship only to impress the American authorities, since a 'Sarah J.' Swan is not listed anywhere as a descendant of Joseph Rockwell Swan. However, an elder brother of his, James Swan (1796–1851) was married to a Sarah Brown (b. 1795), and they had a daughter named Sarah Jane Swan (no dates given). But with a year of birth around 1832–3 she would have been considerably younger than her three brothers (born between 1816 and 1821) and her mother would have been 37 or 38 years of age at her birth – not impossible but unlikely.

[6] Joseph P. Smith: *History of the Republican Party in Ohio* (Chicago: Lewis Publishing Co., 1898; online at archive.org); see also https://www.supremecourt.ohio.gov/SCO/formerjustices/bios/ swanJR.asp (accessed 22 March 2017).

[7] *Belvidere Daily Republican*, 17 September 1930, p. 5. The journalist may have misunderstood this point when he paraphrased from a much longer article in the *Rockford Daily Republic*, 15 September 1930, p. 1–2, which says '[…] the elder Mr. Hennessy, a lawyer, went to Chicago to practice.' In my understanding, Michael Hennessy only began to practice law from 1874.

Fig. 1.2: Holland House Hotel, Rockford (1871), where Swan Hennessy was born in 1866 (Courtesy: Rockford Public Library)

Not much later, Michael Hennessy was firmly settled in Chicago. In the 1870 Chicago census, his profession is given as 'Secr. Treas. City RR', 'RR' meaning railroad, and this is confirmed in another source. According to this, Michael Hennessy was Secretary and Treasurer of the Chicago City Railways between 13 January 1868 and 11 January 1872, and then President of the company until 8 Jan. 1874.[8] In the middle of this period, the 'Great Chicago Fire' of October 1871, one of the largest US disasters in the 19th century, destroyed two thirds of the city. In the handwritten note on the back of the 1914 EPA, there is a statement that

> Mr. Hennessy was 'President of the Chicago City Railways' & was instrumental in building up a good deal of Chicago. He practised 'law' in that city. He had large interests in the 'Chicago First Bank'.

While it is impossible to say how much the Hennessys may have suffered initially from the fire, in the long term they must have benefited enormously from 'building up a good deal of Chicago'. Michael's income must already have been above average before the fire, and if it is true that he was largely responsible for the re-building of the city, at least in terms of the traffic infrastructure, and held shares in a bank that

---

[8] Alfred Theodore Andreas: *History of Chicago*, vol. 3, *From the Fire of 1871 until 1885* (New York: Arno Press, 1975; reprint of an 1886 publication).

(most likely) also benefitted from giving out loans to fire victims, then this was the first step in his creation of wealth for the years to come. Following the period of his presidency of the Chicago urban railway company that ended in January 1874, he worked as a lawyer, presumably in his own practice. He became a very wealthy man – a remarkable career, especially if he really started out as a teen-age carrot thief.

There is conflicting information as to the duration of Michael Hennessy's residence in America. When he died in 1919 in Switzerland, he had already been living in Europe for a considerable time. But since when? This question is important, as he spent all (or most) of this time together with his son, accompanying him to various geographic locations and following (or supporting) his son's musical career. In fact, given the financial dependence of Swan on his father and the increasingly sensitive health-related dependence of Michael on Swan, it may have been the other way around, namely Swan accompanying his father.

Various sources provide the following information:

- In the 1897 passport application at the American Legation at Brussels, Belgium, he says that he lived in the United States uninterruptedly for 23 years, namely from 1851 to 1874, living in Chicago 'and other places', and that he last left the United States in 1891.

- In the 1914 EPA, he claims to have lived in Chicago for 44 years, expressly mentioning the years 1853 to 1897.

- In a December 1916 passport application by Michael Hennessy at the US consulate in Lausanne, Switzerland, repeated in a passport renewal in February 1918, he claims that he emigrated in 1854 and that 'I resided 35 years, uninterruptedly, in the United States from 1854 to 1889'. He also states that he last left the United States in 1903.

- In a January 1921 passport application by Swan Hennessy in Paris, he claims that his father emigrated to the United States in or about 1855, and 'that he resided 30 years uninterruptedly in the United States from 1855 to 1885 at Chicago, Ill.'. For the date of his father's naturalization, he indicates 'unknown'.

- In a 1930 interview for the *Rockford Daily Register*, Swan Hennessy's widow claimed that Michael Hennessy did not return to live in the United States after the tragic incident when he lost his wife Sarah in France in 1880 (see Chapter 2).

These sources include six possible years when Michael Hennessy may have left the United States: 1874, 1880, 1885, 1889, 1891, and 1897. Which is true? Since we cannot know for certain, an approach is needed that would reveal the most likely option. In attempting to do so, it is suggested that the direct documents from Michael should have priority over documents from his son and his daughter-in-law. Thus, the 1921 and 1930 sources should be dismissed in this respect. Claire Hennessy's version sounds all too romantic and does not match the opinion, transmitted in the family, that the marriage between Michael and Sarah was not a very happy one. Besides, in 1880, Swan was still a student in Stuttgart and therefore in a safe environment that did not necessarily need Michael's presence. Swan Hennessy's 1921 version is quite vague altogether and should be dismissed for that simple reason (and he was still a student in Stuttgart by 1885). Michael Hennessy's 1916 version is the most likely, not only because it comes from himself, but also because he repeats it exactly in 1918.

There are only two slightly irritating aspects about this theory. One is that he gives the year 1854 as the year of his emigration from Ireland and arrival in the United States. However, 1854 can perhaps be interpreted as the year he arrived in the US coming from Canada. The other is that the potential years in Ohio and Rockford, Illinois, are ignored. An explanation for the omission of Ohio is that perhaps he never lived there but only went there for the purpose of marrying Sarah (who then lived in Columbus, Ohio) and becoming a naturalized American citizen. Maybe his father-in-law, Joseph R. Swan, demanded this from Michael, wanting his daughter to marry an American rather than an Irishman. Rockford he may simply have subsumed under Chicago in order not to unnecessarily complicate the application form for his passport.

The year 1889 is also a likely year for his departure because Swan had married in December 1888 while living in London. Michael may have joined his son's young family, together, perhaps, with stepdaughter Lila. 1891 is another credible possibility because of Swan's early trouble in and with his young family.

Thus, for the purpose of this study, it is assumed that Michael D. Hennessy, following his period as President of the Chicago City Railway Company, worked as a successful lawyer in Chicago from February 1874 to 1889 or 1891. He eventually owned assets in the First Chicago Bank large enough to retire at age 61 or 62 and move to Europe.

A July 1874 source indicates that Swan Hennessy may have had another, a second, family nickname in his childhood – despite the fact that he appears as 'Swan' in the 1870 Chicago census. In that year, apparently, the Hennessy family spent the summer holidays in France. The Chicago-based newspaper *The Inter Ocean* reported, citing another journal: 'The American *Register* of June 20 contains the whereabouts of absent Chicago people as follows: Paris – [...] M. D. Hennessy and Miss Lila Hennessy, [...]'.[9] Similarly, the quoted paper itself, the London-based *The American Register*, featured a long table, covering the whole front page, under the headline 'Americans recently registered in London and Paris' (see excerpt in Table 1.1). Obviously, when intercontinental travel was still the pastime of a selected few, it was still possible (and of interest!) to name each of them. The family appears here under 'Paris' as:

---

[9] *The Inter Ocean*, 8 July 1874, p. 8.

Table 1.1: Members of the Hennessy family on European holidays (1874)[10]

Names	Where from	Residence
Hennessy, Mrs. M. D.	Chicago	73, Champs-Elysées
Hennessy, Miss Lila	Chicago	73, Champs-Elysées
Hennessy, Teddy	Chicago	73, Champs-Elysées

While it remains unclear whether Michael and Lila came in June and the rest of the family in July, the interesting item here is 'Teddy' for Swan Hennessy – Ted or Teddy being usual nicknames in the English-speaking world for someone called Edward. The address of 73 avenue des Champs-Elysées was the location of the Hotel Albe, which prided itself of their

> [...] meeting room, regular table, first-class restaurant à la carte, bathroom, English and French billiard room, special service at fixed prices including accommodation, service and meals; foreign languages spoken, hydraulic elevators …[11]

We see from this information that Swan Hennessy was accustomed to international travel and first-class hotels since childhood and evidently grew up in an environment where money was no scarce resource.

---

[10] *The American Register*, 4 July 1874, p. 1; https://newspaperarchive.com/london-american-register-jul-04-1874-p-1/ (accessed 25 March 2017).

[11] '… *salon de réunion, table d'hôte, restaurant de 1re classe, à la carte, salle de bain, salle de billard anglais et français, service spécial à prix fixe, comprenant logement, service et nourriture ; on parle les langues étrangères, ascenseurs hydrauliques …*'; *Annuaire-almanach du commerce et de l'industrie* (Paris: Didot Bottin, 1878), p. 1089.

Chapter 2
Education in Europe (1878–1886)

No information about Swan Hennessy's education in Chicago, musical or otherwise, has come to light yet. Various sources inform of studies in Oxford: *Baker's Dictionary* claims he 'studied general subjects at Oxford', without giving further details as to the exact subjects and period. Hennessy himself says his father wanted him to study something serious in Oxford but is also silent about the years and the exact place of his studies there.[1] Oxford University, on the other hand, has no records of him studying at any of its constituent colleges.[2] Ferchault in *MGG* says, 'After brief studies at Oxford, his enthusiasm for music drew him to Germany',[3] echoing Hennessy's statement 'I was there, but not for long. Music drew me away'.[4]

A 1921 passport application at the American embassy in Paris, which required him to outline the times he has lived in the United States, reveals that Hennessy left the US via New York City as a twelve-year-old, in 1878. This is supported by a portrait article of Hennessy in a 1922 issue of the *Dublin Evening Telegraph* that states that he 'came to Europe as a boy'.[5] Quite obviously, this is when he was sent to Oxford by his father, which therefore turns out not to have been university studies at all but a public-school education at one of the renowned institutions of that kind in the city. So far it has not been possible to identify this school.[6]

Since Swan Hennessy remained in Europe for the rest of his life, this makes him a rare case of an Irish-American who emigrated from America to Europe, and not the other way around as many thousands of others did at the same time. Although emigration figures from Ireland to North America for the 1870s had dropped by more than half compared to the 1850s when Michael Hennessy emigrated, these figures were still at over 40,000 annually. Swan Hennessy went the other way. One must only imagine the sight of hundreds of Irish people arriving by ship at New York City and young Hennessy entering it for the return journey to get an idea of the extraordinary experience this must have been for the teenager.

The next undetermined period are the seven years of study at Stuttgart. Unfortunately, the archive of the Konservatorium für Musik at Stuttgart was destroyed in the course of World War II, so no lists of past students exist anymore.[7] However, there is

---

[1] *'Mon père [...] désirait que je fisse des études sérieuses à Oxford.'*; Chevaillier, 'Entretien', p. 791.
[2] E-mail from Oxford University Archives to the author, 21 October 2015, summing up the research as 'It would appear, therefore, that he was not a member of the University'.
[3] *'Nach kurzem Studium in Oxford trieb ihn seine Musikbegeisterung nach Deutschland'*; Ferchault, 'Hennessy', p. 152.
[4] *'J'y fus et n'y restai point longtemps. La musique m'attirait.'*; Chevaillier, 'Entretien', p. 791.
[5] Donnchadh Ua Braoin: 'Swan Hennessy – An Irish Musician of To-day', in *Dublin Evening Telegraph*, 2 September 1922, p. 2.
[6] Denials were received from Dragon School, Magdalen School & College, and St. Edward's.
[7] Nicole Bickhoff & Elke Koch: 'Abgebrannt und umgezogen: Zur Überlieferung der Staatlichen Hochschule für Musik und Darstellende Kunst Stuttgart', in Joachim Kremer & Dörte

one exception: A *festschrift* published on the occasion of the 25th anniversary of the Conservatory in 1882 lists all current pupils as of the end of the semester in April 1882. This list contains 'Hennessy, Ed. Swan, Chicago (N.A.), Klavier'.[8] Apart from 'Teddy' for the seven-year-old boy in 1874 (see previous chapter), this is the first source that mentions Swan Hennessy's actual Christian name, Edward.

Fig. 2.1: The Conservatory of Music at Stuttgart as it looked when Hennessy studied there (Courtesy: Württembergische Landesbibliothek Stuttgart)

Seven years seems an unusually long period for musical studies. In establishing the exact period, a hint is given in Hennessy's first marriage, which took place in December 1888 at Edinburgh, more of which below. It means that the first half of 1888 (the academic year ended in mid-April) is the latest time by which he must have left

---

Schmidt (eds.): *Zwischen bürgerlicher Kultur und Akademie. Zur Professionalisierung der Musikausbildung in Stuttgart seit 1857* (Schliengen: Edition Argus, 2007), pp. 61–82. Also, e-mail from the secretariat of today's Staatliche Hochschule für Musik und Darstellende Kunst, Stuttgart, 21 January 2015.

[8] 'Zöglinge der Künstlerschule am Schluss des 50. Semesters, den 15. April 1882', in *Festschrift für das fünfundzwanzigjährige Jubiläum des Konservatoriums für Musik in Stuttgart* (Stuttgart: J. B. Metzler, n. d. [1882]), p. 12. I am indebted to Prof E. Douglas Bomberger of Elizabethtown College, Philadelphia, for pointing out this source to me. 'N.A.' stands for 'Nord-Amerika' (North America). Incidentally, Bomberger's Ph.D. thesis claims he arrived in Stuttgart in 1882, but this cannot be true because the 50th semester ending in April 1882 would have begun in September 1881. Hennessy must have arrived earlier; see Bomberger: *The German Musical Training of American Students, 1850 to 1900* (Ph.D. thesis, University of Maryland, 1991), p. 426 (full text accessible through the database *ProQuest Dissertations and Theses Global*).

Stuttgart. Counting seven years backwards, he may have started there in the autumn of 1881. This would mean three years for his Oxford schooldays (1878–81) – probably too long as, by all accounts, these were very short, probably not more than a year. The most likely period in Oxford would therefore be the academic year 1878–9, so the seven years at Stuttgart would be 1879 to 1886.

In late 1879 Hennessy would just have turned thirteen years of age, which would seem too young for conservatory studies. However, the Stuttgart Conservatory had a peculiarity among German music academies in that it had both a 'Künstlerschule' (artists' school), which provided for professional musicians, and a 'Dilettantenschule' for 'laymen' and younger people.[9] This is what Swan Hennessy must have attended in his first years there, before he proceeded to the 'Künstlerschule'. As we have seen above, for the academic year 1881–2 (or at least the second semester of it), Hennessy had already proceeded to the 'Künstlerschule', at age fifteen. This does speak for a considerable early talent.

Another clue for dating his years of study is given by Hennessy's first publications, which came out in Germany: Opus 1 was published with Breitkopf & Härtel in Leipzig in 1885, and Opp. 2, 3, 5, and 6 with the Stuttgart-based publisher G. A. Zumsteeg during 1886 and 1887. Zumsteeg appears to have been a second choice for Hennessy who would have preferred to see these works published with Schott in Mainz. The earliest preserved letter by Hennessy, written on 13 November 1885 (shortly before his 18th birthday, from a Swiss luxury hotel) offers *'einige kleine Klavierstücke'* to Schott, which they turned down (Fig. 2.2).

> Dear Sirs,
> I take the liberty of sending you the attached little piano pieces in the hope that you may find them useful. It should be a great honour for me if you would deem them worthy of your attention.
> In polite expectation of your benevolent response I sign
> in high esteem,
> Swan Hennessy.[10]

His next works (until Op. 10) appeared 1887–8 in London with Augener & Co., Op. 11 in Paris (1889). The German publications between 1885 and 1887 suggest his presence in the country at least until 1886. And he does seem to have been in London at least by 1887. One of the *Vier Lieder* Op. 3, published in Stuttgart in early 1886, is dedicated to "Fräulein Lucy Roper" – his future wife in England, an Anglo-Irish lady

---

[9] Nicole Bickhoff: *Im Takt der Zeit. 150 Jahre Musikhochschule Stuttgart* (Stuttgart: Landesarchiv Baden-Württemberg, 2007), p. 11.
[10] *'Sehr geehrte Herren! / Ich erlaube mir Ihnen gleichzeitig einige kleine Klavierstücke zu schicken, in der Hoffnung Sie möchten vielleicht für sie Verwendung haben. Es würde mir zur grossen Ehre gereichen sollten Sie sie ihrer Achtung würdig finden. / In höflicher Erwartung Ihrer gütigen Rückantwort zeichnet / in hoher Achtung ergeben, / Swan Hennessy. / Herren Schott Söhne / in Mainz.'*; Staatsbibliothek Berlin, Schott Archive, file no. 44614.

whose acquaintance he may have made in Stuttgart. There is no evidence yet, however, for any residence in Paris around 1889.

Fig. 2.2: Letter by Hennessy to Schott music publishers, 13 November 1885 (Courtesy: Staatsbibliothek Berlin / Stiftung Preußischer Kulturbesitz)

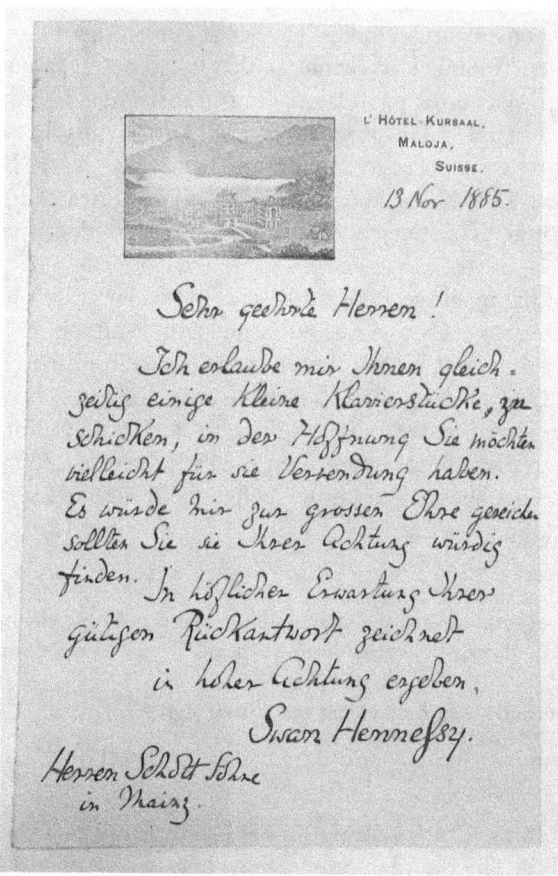

The letter to Schott is revealing with regard to Hennessy's excellent command of German (confirmed in a number of later letters) as well as to his financial situation. There would not have been that many students of music with the means at hand to reside in the latest luxury hotels in Switzerland (and in November, a period he would normally have to spend in the conservatory). No response to the letter has survived, but since no Hennessy work appeared with Schott in these years it cannot have been successful. The piano works he sent to Schott (and which therefore must have been completed by November 1885) are not mentioned and may not be exactly identical with the Opp. 2, 5, and 6 which were published with Zumsteeg. Schott had the laudable habit of giving reasons when they denied publication, and as a consequence Hennessy may have withdrawn works.

In the late nineteenth century, the Stuttgart Conservatory enjoyed an excellent reputation particularly among American and other English-speaking students. This reputation derived largely from its piano teaching. The Conservatory had been founded in 1857 by pianists,[11] the Mendelssohn pupil Immanuel Faisst (or 'Faißt', 1823–1894) and Sigmund Lebert (1821–1884), who enlisted the then prominent pianist and Liszt pupil Dionys Pruckner (1834–1896) as main teacher for piano from 1859.

Hennessy's own piano teacher was (Eduard Franz) Edmund Alwens. Very little is known about him. He was born around 1832 in Kaiserslautern and died on 25 September 1897 in Stuttgart. The only source that reveals his name in connection to Hennessy is the Paris-based American music critic Irving Schwerke, who was well acquainted with Hennessy during the late 1920s.[12]

In the 1882 list of current pupils, Hennessy's main subject is the piano, but he also studied composition, or at least the basics of it. His teacher in composition was the American Percy Goetschius (1853–1943) – Hennessy names him as his friend and teacher on the title page of his first published composition (Fig. 2.3).[13]

Goetschius was born in Paterson, New Jersey; he came to Stuttgart in 1873 to study music theory with Immanuel Faisst and the piano with Lebert and Pruckner, began to teach at the Conservatory from 1878, and in 1885 was made a *Königlich Württembergischer Professor* by king Karl Friedrich Alexander of Wurttemberg. After 17 years in Stuttgart, Goetschius returned to America in 1890 to teach at Syracuse University, and further in 1892 to the New England Conservatory, Boston, and the Institute of Musical Art at New York (1905–25), which became the Juilliard School in 1926.[14] In the United States, Goetschius enjoyed a reputation as one of the foremost, albeit conservative, teachers of composition. His American career is much better known than his years in Germany. His later pupils in the US included avant-gardists like Henry Cowell and Leo Ornstein as well as more conservative composers like Howard Hanson and Wallingford Riegger, among many others.[15]

In Stuttgart, Goetschius founded an English-speaking class at the Conservatory which Hennessy attended. His more prominent pupils included the American Edgar Stillman Kelley (1857–1944) and the Dublin-born Victor Herbert (1859–1924) (both also composition students of Max Seifriz, 1827–1885). Herbert was also a cellist in the Stuttgart court orchestra from 1881 to 1886. The Irish baritone Harry Plunket Greene

---

[11] Initially as 'Stuttgarter Musikschule'; it achieved conservatory status in 1865.
[12] Irving Schwerke: 'Funeral Services For Mr. Hennessy To Be Held Today', in *Chicago Tribune*, 30 October 1929. Schwerke had received this information from Hennessy in a brief autobiographical MS sketch of early 1929.
[13] 'Mr. Swan Hennessy', unsigned article in *The London Musical Courier*, 4 January 1913. Apart from the score of Hennessy's Op. 1, this article and the one by Schwerke (1929; see foregoing fn.) are the only bibliographic sources that mention Hennessy's teacher in composition.
[14] Caryn Hannan & Jennifer L. Herman (eds.): *New Jersey Biographical Dictionary*, 2008–9 Edition (Hamburg, Michigan: State History Publications, 2008), vol. 1, pp. 274–276.
[15] James Deaville & Nathan Broder: 'Goetschius, Percy', in *Die Musik in Geschichte und Gegenwart* (MGG), ed. Ludwig Finscher, biographical part, vol. 7 (Kassel: Bärenreiter, 2002), c. 1213.

(1865–1936) studied singing in Stuttgart at this time. Edward MacDowell (1860–1908) had also been attracted by the excellent reputation of the piano school at Stuttgart and studied there briefly for one and a half years during 1878 to 1880. However, Kelley, Herbert and MacDowell were all older than Hennessy, and any meeting of them would have been coincidental. A good friend of Hennessy's appears to have been the Canadian pianist Ernest Longley (1866–1889), a former child prodigy who died early of 'consumption' (tuberculosis). *'Seinem Freunde Herrn Ernest Longley'* Hennessy dedicated his *Carneval-Studien* Op. 6 (two volumes, Stuttgart 1886 and 1887).[16]

Fig. 2.3: Title page of Hennessy's first published composition (1885), dedicated to his teacher Percy Goetschius (Courtesy: Staatsbibliothek Berlin / Stiftung Preußischer Kulturbesitz)

Goetschius published an English-language harmony textbook in Stuttgart during Hennessy's time there, which is most certainly the method that Hennessy was taught. First published in 1882 under the title *The Material Used in Musical Composition*, it later

---

[16] Longley's death in Stuttgart on 5 December 1889 was reported in *Monatshefte für Musikgeschichte*, 1890, p. 96, and *The Dominion Illustrated*, 11 January 1890, p. 26.

went through numerous revised and expanded American editions. The original treatise was based on the harmony lessons of Faisst (to whom the book is, in fact, dedicated 'in token of the profound esteem and gratitude of its author'),[17] and Rainer Bayreuther suggested that it was in itself rather a harmony book than a method of composition.[18] According to Bayreuther, in the Conservatory statutes (versions of 1875, 1882, 1887, and 1895), there appears to have been no clear demarcation between the *'Dilettantenschule'* and the *'Künstlerschule'* with regard to the harmony classes. Only the third (of three) consecutive courses marked the transition from the techniques of composition to the composition of full pieces:[19] 'Only in the third course the composers of the *"Künstlerschule"* would have been among themselves.'[20]

Hannan & Herman (2008) gave the following characterisation of Goetschius' personality and approach to teaching:

> As a teacher Goetschius was a strict disciplinarian, and his 'bespectacled visage,' 'intellectual brow,' and 'closely cropped beard' gave an initial impression of austerity. He possessed, however, a delightful sense of humor, and his gracefully phrased lectures and agile piano demonstrations of musical structure and harmony made him a skilled pedagogue. He took a deep and sympathetic interest in the aesthetic problems of his student composers. His musical gods were Bach, Mendelssohn, and Brahms. Although his musical knowledge was encyclopedic, he had little interest in 'strict' counterpoint or the music of the seventeenth century. Nor did he approve of the direction taken by such composers as Ravel, Debussy, and Richard Strauss; and he described Wagner's harmonic technique as one of 'wandering harmonies' and warned his pupils against perverting it by extravagant or eccentric chords and tonal progressions.[21]

As we shall see, this description already includes some of the qualities that later characterises Hennessy's own music: the skilled, yet liberal approach to counterpoint, an admiration for the music of the baroque and of the German Romantics, and the scepticism towards certain modernists (although Hennessy applies this latter critique to different names of his own generation).

Naturally, for a harmony book of the early 1880s (and explicitly referring to the earlier model of Faisst), Goetschius' *The Material Used in Musical Composition* does not question but only explains the traditional tonal system. His view on dissonance, for instance, would soon sound utterly out of date, although it was still taught by him when he had returned to the United States:

---

[17] Percy Goetschius: *The Material Used in Musical Composition* (Stuttgart: G. A. Zumsteeg, 1882); here quoted from the 1903 New York sixth edition of 1903, online at http://hdl.handle.net/1802/21167 (last accessed, 7 May 2019).
[18] Rainer Bayreuther: 'Komponieren als akademische Disziplin. Von den Anfängen bis zur Gründung des Elektronikstudios', in Kremer & Schmidt (2007), pp. 301–302.
[19] *"Der ... Übergang von den Techniken des Komponierens zum Komponieren ganzer Stücke"*; Bayreuther, 'Komponieren', p. 302.
[20] *"Erst im dritten Cursus dürften die Tonsetzer der Künstlerschule unter sich gewesen sein."*; Bayreuther, 'Komponieren', p. 302.
[21] Hannan & Herman, *New Jersey Biographical Dictionary* (2008), p. 275.

> A Dissonance has, as the term indicates, a harsh sound which the ear will only accept on condition that it be reasonably brief, and that it be justified by the intervals which precede and (especially) follow it. By itself, a Dissonance is meaningless and unsatisfactory, and urgently demands a progression which will fulfil its tendencies and obligations.[22]

In a 'Concluding remark' to his book, Goetschius wrote:

> The chief and deplorably common error in modern Composition is the inclination to employ eccentric and complex harmonies, in endless succession, without relation or rest, and with studied evasion of vulgar 'Resolutions': The Composer who leads his auditor through a perfect labyrinth of harmonic by-ways, adding Suspensions (Irregular, of course) to every single succession, and fitting out the whole with an Organ-point, dare not wonder when his work is pronounced incomprehensible and unenjoyable. This truth cannot be too early and deeply impressed upon the scholar's mind; [...][23]

* * *

Michael Hennessy used to spend many of his holidays back in Europe. At one such occasion, a tragic accident happened that killed Swan's mother. All four members of the family (Michael, Sarah, Lila and Swan) spent time in Brittany, northern France, in September 1880. One day, Swan remained in the hotel while the others joined a boating cruise on a rather old sailboat called 'Grand Casimir', together with seven other people including the Viscount de Fleury, two of his servants, an English couple named Potter, and the coxswain. When an unexpected storm drew up, the boat was wrecked on the rocks of the coast of Roscoff and four people drowned including Sarah Hennessy, while Michael and Lila Hennessy were saved. Sarah had clung to the mast of the boat as long as it was possible. The dramatic scene was depicted in *Le Journal illustré* (Fig. 2.4) – the accompanying article repeats an earlier report in *Le Temps*.

The report in *Le Temps* blamed the coxswain for steering the boat through a passage between the rocks although he should have been aware of the currents there. Fresh breezes threw the boat on the rocks, and as it was so old it immediately broke apart and sank. One member of the party, described as a young and strong Russian, was a good swimmer and rescued several members of the group. When he thought to have brought them to relatively safe places on rocks (and the Viscount Fleury to the mast of the boat), he swam to the shore to call for help. But as he did so, the situation deteriorated:

> Meanwhile, the drama unfolded. Mrs. Hennessy, who had immediately plunged into the sea by the movement of the mast, covered incessantly by the waves, finally let go; she then clutched at the feet of one of her neighbours, who sank to the bottom of the sea; the unfortunate managed to disengage; the poor woman returned to the surface and tried to

---

[22] Goetschius, *The Material*, p. 72.
[23] Goetschius, *The Material*, p. 270; capitalisation as in the source.

seize him again but fortunately for him, she only took his hat, and she disappeared washed away by the waves.[24]

Fig. 2.4: The shipwreck in which Swan Hennessy's mother died (centre left, hanging on to the shoulders of another passenger), as depicted in *Le Journal illustré* of 19 September 1880 (Courtesy: Bibliothèque Nationale de France).

The drawing in *Le Journal illustré* probably shows Sarah Hennessy to the left of the mast hanging on to another passenger just before she lost touch. Lila Hennessy, Swan's step-sister, can be seen holding the rope of the mast to which the young Russian had brought her:

> ... the bowsprit of the ship only emerged, there he fastened a young American, telling her to wait patiently for relief he was seeking.[25]

---

[24] '*Pendant ce temps, le drame se déroulait. Mme Hennessy, qui à chaque instant plongeait dans la mer par le mouvement du mât, couvert incessamment par la vague, finit par lâcher prise; elle se cramponna alors aux pieds d'un de ses voisins, quelle entraîna au fond de l'eau; le malheureux parvint à se dégager; la pauvre femme revint à la surface et voulut le saisir de nouveau heureusement pour lui, elle ne prit que son chapeau, et elle disparut emportée par la vague.*'; *Le Temps*, 7 September 1880, p. 2; several reprints of the article in other newspapers including *Le Journal illustré*, 19 September 1880, p. 299, with the image on p. 301.

[25] '*... le bout-dehors du bateau émergeait seul il y a-t-attacha une jeune Américaine, en lui recommandant d'attendre patiemment les secours qu'il allait chercher.*'; *Le Temps*, as above.

The Viscount de Fleury who had a limp leg is seen holding on to the mast, shortly before he drowned. In the foreground, the young Russian swims to the shore to call help. The couple on the rock in the background are the Potters, also about to drown.

Meanwhile the young Russian returned from Roscoff with doctors, and the newspaper article describes the survivors:

> The young Russian barely ashore, although the body was horribly torn by the rocks, took a car and fetched relief from Roscoff for the survivors. The doctors departed with three sick shipwrecked: Miss Laïla Hennessy, the father who was saved with the help of two oars, and Justin, the servant of M. de Fleury, were soon driving back to Roscoff. [26]

This is the dramatic way Swan Hennessy's American mother died on the northern shore of France. Had the young musician, who was two months away from his fourteenth birthday, joined the family for the boat ride, he might not have survived. Even so, the incident must have weighed heavily on the boy's mind and may have influenced his decision, much later, to join a group of Breton composers and to associate with their aesthetic.

Swan's step-sister Lila seems to have remained in Europe for a short while before she may have returned to the United States. In a London census of the following year (1881),[27] she appears as a visitor to the household of Alexander and Isabella Ross, aged 65 and 62 years respectively, at 14 Longridge Road, Kensington. That this is indeed Swan's sister is suggested not only by her age, but also by another name in the said family, that of the daughter Isabella C. Ross, aged 35. An 'I. C. Ross' is the dedicatee of Hennessy's song *The Blackbird has a Golden Bill*, Op. 5 No. 1 (1886).

The name Lila Hennessy appears in a passenger list of the 'Gallia', a ship operated by the Cunard line, from Liverpool, arriving in New York on 26 April 1881. According to the list, she is 23 years old and a barrister. In 1881, she would have been 29, but we have already seen how cautious we have to have to be when it comes to age indications in censuses and other lists. If this was indeed Swan Hennessy's sister, she would have returned to the United States seven months after she lost her mother in that tragic incident. Yet, she may have died early: In the various passport extensions that survived from the WWI years, Swan Hennessy states that there are no close relatives anymore.[28]

* * *

---

[26] *Le jeune Russe à peine à terre, quoique le corps affreusement déchiré par les rochers, prit une voiture et vint chercher a Roscoff des secours pour les survivants. Les médecins partirent et les trois naufragés malades : Mlle Laïla Hennessy, le père qui s'était sauvé à l'aide de deux avirons et Justin, le domestique de M. de Fleury, rentraient bientôt en voiture à Roscoff.*; *Le Temps*, as above.

[27] 'England and Wales Census, 1881', database with images, *FamilySearch* (https://familysearch.org/ark:/61903/1:1:Q273-3SXQ: 18 August 2016), Lila Hennessy in household of Alexr Ross, Kensington, London, Middlesex, England; from '1881 England, Scotland and Wales census', database and images, *findmypast* (http://www.findmypast.com : n.d.); citing p. 13, Piece/Folio 50/57, The National Archives, Kew, Surrey; FHL microfilm 101,774,324.

[28] A potential year of her death is 1907, see Chapter 4.

Swan Hennessy's works of the 1880s are written in a late-Romantic musical language that has repeatedly been described as leaning on Schumann. This would not have been all too rare in 1880s Germany but is still not particularly advanced for a young composer in his early twenties. Apart from the last work of this period, the *Miniatures*, Op. 11 for piano, published in Paris by Durand et Schoenewerk (1889), all works were published in Germany or in London and have, with one exception, German and French titles.

While he was still living in Germany, six works were published, the piano works Opp. 1, 2, 4, and 6 and the songs Opp. 3 and 5. Op. 1 was published (without opus number) with Breitkopf & Härtel in Leipzig, the other five with G. A. Zumsteeg in Stuttgart.

Ländliche Skizzen, Op. 1 (1884) for piano

As explained earlier, the *Ländliche Skizzen*, Op. 1 was dedicated to his teacher Percy Goetschius (see Fig. 2.3). It was written in 1884 and published (without opus number) in the following year. The work consists of six separate pieces: *Am Bache, Waldvöglein, Ländler, Ringellied, Legende,* and *Die Sägemühle,* drawing their inspiration from nature and the built environment as well as German folk dances (*Ländler* and *Ringellied*). The *Musical Times* advertised them as *Rustic Sketches*; *Rural Sketches* would be a valid translation of the German title as well.

The first four works have the character of folksongs in a 'classical' arrangement, with undisturbed major tonalities devoid of modulations worthy to speak of. Numbers 5 and 6 (*Legende* and *Die Sägemühle*) are in minor tonalities with some more chromatic material. The opening *Am Bache*, for instance, in its straightforward melody in A major and its four phrases with interludes could easily be the tune of a song with piano accompaniment. The *Ländler* is a longer piece than most of the others, occupying three pages in the score compared to one each for four of the others (the longest is *Die Sägemühle*). Three of the four numbered parts of the 'ländler' stand in A flat major while no. 3 changes to D flat major, and there is a transitionary 'refrain' towards the end of parts 2 and 3. A 'ländler' is a popular dance form in 3/4 time common in the south of Germany, Austria and neighbouring regions in which a lot of hopping and stamping occurs. Hennessy's piece catches the spirit of the music – which he must have encountered frequently in Stuttgart – very well. The only slow piece, the *Legende*, is in 3/8 time and marked *adagio*. Notated in E minor, with frequent accidentals, its character reminds of a catholic church hymn. With a less memorable tune, *Waldvöglein* (E major) does not fully convince. *Ringellied* (D major) is simply too short and uncharacteristic to leave any lasting impression.

The most substantial piece in the collection is the last, *Die Sägemühle* ('the sawmill'). It is also the only one that seems to have received public performances by professional pianists in France, many years later (under the title of *Scierie dans la forêt*). It occupies six pages in print (but includes written-out repetitions). The piece (in mainly a G minor key) is dominated by melody-bearing chords on every beat in the right hand and, from bar 21, a subsidiary subject where G minor fourth chords dominate and present the only instance in the collection with slightly advanced harmony. The regular chordal beats most likely represent machinery in the saw mill, as perhaps do the modest harmonic dissonances, making the piece an early precursor of the programmatic pieces that Hennessy excelled with in the years preceding World War I.

Ex. 2.1: *Ländliche Skizzen*, Op. 1 No. 6 *'Die Sägemühle'*, bars 21–28

Technically, the six pieces of *Ländliche Skizzen* do not exceed the capabilities of the talented amateur. This was pointed out in the two reviews that exist of the piece, but it was not a negative judgement as can be seen in the following one (the earliest review ever of a Hennessy piece) in *Signale für die musikalische Welt*:

> Of course, these pieces are not merely 'sketches', i. e. unfinished drafts; they are light music that do not require much work at all, but there is nothing essential to add here. Some musicians would certainly begin to work now and nudge these innocent things with tormented middle parts, dissonances and highly embarrassing 'interesting melodies' until they become unrecognisable. That this went beyond the nature of the composer is pleasing about him; his so-called sketches fit, if not for musicians, then for all sorts of good people who would like to play or listen to a simple piece of music without any sophisticated art. This is also allowed.[29]

The *Monthly Musical Record*, which published brief reviews of all of Hennessy's works between Opp. 1 and 10, commented:

---

[29] *'Natürlich sind die Stücke nicht bloße "Skizzen", das heißt unausgearbeitete Entwürfe; sie sind zwar leichte Musik, die überhaupt nicht viel Arbeit macht, aber etwas Wesentliches hinzuzufügen giebt es hier nicht. Gewisse Musiker freilich würden nun erst recht zu "arbeiten" anfangen und diese unschuldigen Dinger mit gequälten Mittelstimmen, Dissonanzen und hochnothpeinlichen "interessanten Melodien" nudeln, bis sie unkenntlich würden. Daß dies über die Natur des Componisten ging, ist hübsch an ihm; seine sogenannten Skizzen passen, wenn auch nicht für Musiker, so doch für allerlei gute Leute, die gern einmal ein einfaches Musikstück ohne absonderliche Kunst spielen oder hören möchten. Auch das ist erlaubt.';* 'L. R.' in *Signale für die musikalische Welt* 43:73, 1885, p. 1154.

In these pianoforte pieces […] we make, no doubt, the acquaintance of a young composer and we will add at once that they seem to us a promise of future acceptable works from his hands. For the most part he writes melodiously and unaffectedly, although as yet not originally. Of the compositions before us the *Ländliche Skizzen* (Rural Sketches) are the most satisfactory, being indeed really pretty tone-pictures, simple but not commonplace.[30]

Ein Spinnerliedchen, Op. 2 (1885) for piano

With regard to Hennessy's Op. 2, the same author wrote: 'The *Ein Spinnerliedchen* (A Little Spinning Song), notwithstanding occasional harshnesses, must be pronounced pleasing.'[31] Rather than a collection, this opus number is a single piece only, perhaps one that the composer was especially pleased with at the time. The work, written in 1885 and published 1886, is in F major and 6/8 time throughout and is again quite programmatic. The right hand quite obviously represents the song of the spinner at work while the left hand resembles the regular and not always harmonious sound of the spinning wheel.

The 'occasional harshness' that the *MMR* reviewer perceived can be comprehended with a view to the continuously changing dissonances the two-part melody moves through in the course of its tune, especially in places where the left hand moves into the same space as the right hand (Ex. 2.2).

What may at first sight look harmonically advanced, is still within the scope of Goetschius' teaching. Hennessy's use of dissonances follows the rules set out in his teacher's textbook where he defined a dissonance as 'a harsh sound which the ear will only accept on condition that it be reasonably brief, and that it be justified by the intervals which precede and (especially) follow it'.[32]

Ex. 2.2: *Ein Spinnerliedchen*, Op. 2, bars 13–18

---

[30] *The Monthly Musical Record* 17:197, May 1887, p. 111.
[31] As above.
[32] As fn. 22.

Two Studies, Op. 4 (1886) for piano

The *Two Studies*, Op. 4 were written and published in early 1886 by Augener & Co. of London – the first of several of his compositions with that publisher. It almost looks like Hennessy had carefully prepared that move with making contact to Augener in advance while still living in Stuttgart. Opp. 5 and 6 were again published by Zumsteeg.

The at times somewhat patronising approach of the reviews in the *Monthly Musical Record* should be seen in this context, since the journal was also published by Augener & Co. and served as a medium to publicise their products. An outright negative review of an Augener publication can therefore be ruled out.

Number 1 of the *Two Studies* is entitled *Staccato* (D flat major), number 2 *Legato* (C minor). The *MMR* described them as 'good and effective', but was apparently more convinced by the *legato* study. Of the *Staccato*, the critic wrote it 'is a model of form, and as it is spiritedly written, is potentially attractive', a potentially polite formulation pointing to a perhaps more pedantic approach on the composer's part. He continues: 'In the legato the idea with which it is started is admirably carried out, and so both pieces are noteworthy enough to secure a welcome for other works of the same hand.'[33] Not only did this indeed materialise in the ensuing cooperation between composer and publisher, but Augener also published a second edition of Op. 4 four years later (1890, as no. 9 of a series called *Perles musicales*) and published the *legato* study as a supplement to the *MMR* in 1892.

This edition, *The Times* briefly considered as 'useful'.[34] The *Monthly Musical Record* applauded 'Swan Hennessy's anything but dry, in fact, strongly impassioned Study'.[35] In a second review, the critic found some remarkably fancy language to describe the work's character:

> SWAN HENNESSY'S Study (*Perles musicales*, 9), is one of those pieces in which the emotional and technical elements are almost evenly balanced. It is therefore a 'study' in the true sense of the word. The composer has most ingeniously maintained throughout the piece the figure which appears in the first bar, entrusting it to the left hand in the middle portion with the happiest effect. Were we asked to bestow a title on this piece, we should call it 'The Wail of the Wild West Wind.' If the composer meant something more human, he must forgive us. The 'wild wail' is there – whether of wind or human soul it is not in the province of music to tell.[36]

Carneval-Studien, Op. 6 (1886) for piano

Hennessy's last piano work of his Stuttgart years is the *Carneval-Studien*, Op. 6, composed in 1886 and published with Zumsteeg in two volumes, one in late 1886, the other in the first half of 1887 when Hennessy was (most likely) already living in

---

[33] All quotes in *The Monthly Musical Record* 16:184, April 1886, p. 88–89. The second volume was reviewed in issue 17:202, October 1887, p. 235.
[34] *The Times*, 26 December 1890, p. 2.
[35] *The Monthly Musical Record* 20:240, December 1890, p. 274.
[36] *The Monthly Musical Record* 22:253, January 1892, p. 9.

London. The work consists of thirteen pieces, eleven of which are numbered. Two unnumbered ones bring each volume to a close. These have independent titles but the preceding pieces do not end on final bars. The collection is dedicated to the Canadian pianist and fellow student at Stuttgart, Ernest Longley.

There are few works in which Hennessy resembles his early idol Robert Schumann more than in this particular composition. This was quickly pointed out in the *MMR* which warned

> The *Carnival Sketches* are a dangerous experiment. Unless a composer has the abundant *esprit* of a Schumann, he should not, like Schumann, indulge in the publication of such fragmentary thoughts, and, above all, should take care not to challenge comparison by similarity of title.[37]

The critic is alluding to Schumann's famous *Carnaval*, Op. 9 (first published 1837), very obviously the formal model for Hennessy here which he very consciously adopted. Both are collections of numerous character pieces, often brief, often containing allusions. Schumann's consists of 21 pieces, Hennessy's of 13 (in two volumes) (see Table 2.1). A number of formal parallels are striking such as *Papillons* (no. 9 with Schumann) and *Papillon* (no. 5 with Hennessy), the use of letters as titles as in *A.S.C.H. – S.C.H.A.* (no. 10 with Schumann) and *O.J.I.D.L.Y.S!* (unnumbered postlude to no. 6 with Hennessy), and the use of female forenames, *Chiarina* and *Estrella* (nos. 11 and 13 with Schumann) and *Alice* (no. 9 with Hennessy).

Table 2.1: Titles of Schumann's *Carnaval*, Op. 9 and Hennessy's *Carneval-Studien*, Op. 6

Schumann, *Carnaval*, Op. 9	Hennessy, *Carneval-Studien*, Op. 6
1. *Préambule. Quasi maestoso – Più moto – Animato (– Vivo) – Presto*	Vol. 1 ('*Erste Folge*')
	1. *Moderato, con espressione caricata*
2. *Pierrot. Moderato*	2. *Thema. Un poco più mosso*
3. *Arlequin. Vivo*	3. *Prestissimo*
4. *Valse noble. Un poco maestoso*	4. *Energico*
5. *Eusebius. Adagio*	5. *Papillon. Molto vivace*
6. *Florestan. Passionato*	6. *Prestissimo possibile – Agitato*
7. *Coquette. Vivo*	[n/n] *O.J.I.D.L.Y.S!. Leggiero*
8. *Réplique. L'istesso tempo*	Vol. 2 ('*Zweite Folge*')
9. *Papillons. Prestissimo*	7. *Velocissimo*
10. *A.S.C.H. – S.C.H.A. (Lettres dansantes). Presto*	8. *Thema. Andante molto*
11. *Chiarina. Passionato*	9. *Alice. Listesso tempo*
12. *Chopin. Agitato*	10. *Finale (alla 'G.'). Non troppo vivace*
13. *Estrella. Con affetto – Più presto*	[n/n] *G! Prestissimo, giocoso – Precipitandosi*
14. *Reconnaissance. Animato*	
15. *Pantalon et Colombine. Presto*	
16. *Valse allemande. Molto vivace*	

---

[37] *The Monthly Musical Record* 17:197, May 1887, p. 111.

17. *Paganini. Presto* 18. *Aveu. Passionato* 19. *Promenade. Con moto* 20. *Pause. Vivo* 21. *Marche des 'Davidsbündler' contre les Philist-* *ins. Non Allegro – Molto più vivo – Animato –* *Vivo – Animato molto – Più stretto*	

But on looking further into these parallels, not much remains of them but titles. Schumann's *Papillons* is in 2/4 time, B flat major and marked *prestissimo*; Hennessy's *Papillon* is in 3/4 time, C major and marked *molto vivace (quasi presto)*. The 'fluttering' of the butterfly's movements, expressed by Schumann in short, high-pitched chordal movements, is implemented by Hennessy in a curious shift of bars in the middle part of the piece, which begins in the left hand with a faked upbeat, so that the first beat with its *sforzando* chord falls on the second (suspended) beat of the right hand (Ex. 2.3).

Ex. 2.3: *Carneval-Studien*, Op. 6 No. 5 *'Papillon'*, bars 9–16 (middle section)

Schumann's lettered title *A.S.C.H. – S.C.H.A.* alludes to the Bohemian village of Asch, the home of his fiancée, and also constitutes the pitch basis of his composition (in English: A – E♭ – C – B). Hennessy's combination of letters *O.J.I.D.L.Y.S!* is impossible to implement in music. In fact, it is probably an abbreviation of something, perhaps the first letters of a full sentence (or exclamation), and perhaps one in English as there is a hardly a word in German that commences with Y. The rather enigmatic title probably remains a secret between Hennessy and his dedicatee. It is quite a striking piece without barlines, consisting of continuous triplets, beginning with a (repeated) part in piano, followed by a second part in a persistent crescendo from piano to forte. Musically, this procedure has no model in Schumann's work.

The other title with a letter, Hennessy's No. 10, *Finale (alla 'G.')*, followed by the postlude *G!*, may allude to Percy Goetschius. Neither the piece nor its postlude is in a G tonality. In fact, the two postludes *O.J.I.D.L.Y.S!* and *G!* are almost identical. The

Finale (alla 'G.') contains expressive markings like *quasi confuso* and *quasi ridendo*, that may allude to G's (whoever he is) character.

Hennessy's *Carneval-Studien* do not appear in his own list of works that he drew up towards the end of his life, suggesting that he has probably withdrawn them. In other words, one should perhaps not spend too much time on forming an opinion about this work. But in looking back on his early Stuttgart compositions it is worth pointing out that young Hennessy – he had not reached his twentieth birthday when he left Stuttgart – had an independent mind and a good deal of humour from early on in his career. Harmonically, he remains conservative – the chromaticism he applies is a German romantic one. But formally, he is quite innovative. In the *Carneval-Studien*, in particular, one comes across a number of unusual formal solutions – such as the disaligned bar lines in Ex. 2.3 and his dispensing with bar lines later – that make his sketches rather striking. In fact, it will be seen that these are early examples of a kind of non-conformism that is visible in many later works as well. On the one hand he does follow rules, but on the other, he allows himself a certain formal boldness or a cautiously experimental approach to distinguish himself.

Vier Lieder, Op. 3 (*c*1885–6) for voice and piano

A brief look at Hennessy's vocal compositions shall bring this chapter to a close. The first is a set of *Vier Lieder*, Op. 3 to words by Heinrich Heine. It is a small cycle of four songs, *Leise zieht durch mein Gemüth, Die blauen Frühlingsaugen, Mädchen mit dem rothen Mündchen*, and *Zum Schluss*. They were written around late 1885 or early 1886 and published in Stuttgart in 1886. No. 2 is dedicated to his later wife (*'Fräulein Lucy Roper gewidmet'*) from which we can assume that the couple met in Stuttgart, that Lucy Roper may have been a musician, too, and that she had blue eyes (or liked violets).

Heine's poetry has been a favourite with many composers of the nineteenth century (and beyond). All of the poems in Hennessy's small collection are well known and have frequently been set by a huge number of composers.[38] Of *Leise zieht durch mein Gemüth* (also known as '*Der Gruß*'), for instance, there exists a famous setting by Felix Mendelssohn-Bartholdy which Hennessy certainly knew. Hennessy's far-outreaching melody is a typical late Romantic specimen, a simple setting in 3/4 time and F major, accompanied by arpeggiated chords (rather in 6/8). *Die blauen Frühlingsaugen*, an *allegretto* in G major and 4/4 time, has folksong qualities, but remains rather pale. *Mädchen mit dem rothen Mündchen* was highlighted by the *MMR* reviewer as the best of the collection, but 'we have to point out that the words and the voice did not prompt the melody, as is evident, for instance, from the leap of a ninth which it takes at the beginning of the second phrase'.[39] One may disagree with this point of view, since the d at the beginning of the second phrase merely repeats the same beginning as in the first

---

[38] See Günter Metzner: *Heine in der Musik. Bibliographie der Heine-Vertonungen* (Tutzing: Hans Schneider, 12 volumes, 1989–94), lists 6,833 Heine settings, with a climax in the year 1884 when there were 1,093 settings by 538 composers. The Hennessy settings are in vol. 5, p. 304.

[39] *The Monthly Musical Record* 17:197, May 1887, p. 111.

phrase (which had ended on C). It is the only song in the collection with a change of tonality – from the initial (and final) B major to F minor for the middle stanza (in fact, Hennessy omits the actual third stanza of the Heine poem and ends on an abridged version of the first). It is indeed the change of mood expressed through the new tonality that is particularly fitting to the words. What Hennessy calls *Zum Schluss* ('in' or 'at the end') is a setting of *Sag, wo ist dein schönes Liebchen* which also happens to be Heine's last poem of the volume *Die Heimkehr* of the *Buch der Lieder* (1824). The cyclical character of the collection is emphasised by the last four bars in the piano which nearly resemble the accompaniment of the B major part of the previous song, an interesting little feature. It is also apparent in Hennessy's choice and sequence of poems which recall the beginning, the flowering, and the end of a couple's relationship.

Naturally, Hennessy's Heine songs are not representative of his later vocal music and stand in a firm German Romantic tradition. Except for the unusual ending of the collection, there is very little of his formal non-conformism alluded to above.

The Blackbird has a Golden Bill, Op. 5 (1886) for voice and piano

The same is true of the remaining vocal item from his Stuttgart years, the song *The Blackbird has a Golden Bill*, written (to his own words) and published in Stuttgart in 1886. The only extant print of this piece designates it as 'Op. 5 No. 1' and 'Second edition', suggesting there was an earlier version of Op. 5 with (perhaps) more pieces. Neither those potentially more pieces nor any earlier printed edition have come to light. In fact, when Hennessy drafted his list of compositions in 1929, this work appears as 'Op. 5' only.

Hennessy's poem is the following:

> The Blackbird has a golden bill,
> As emblem of its singing,
> And all the other birds are still,
> When thro' the woods with mellow trill,
> Its plaintive song is ringing.
>
> I know the blackbird's rival,
> No golden bill has she,
> But sweeter than the blackbird's far,
> But sweeter than the blackbird's far,
> Her singing seems to me.

The song is set in Schumann's favourite tonality, A minor, but ends on the major dominant, E major, a frequent feature in accompanying a melody in melodic minor (Schubert may have been another model here since he often used similar minor-major alternations). The piano accompaniment abounds with two-part writing in minor thirds with low octaves and fifths in the left hand, giving the piece a somewhat gloomy character despite the positive message of the poem.

Ex. 2.4: *The Blackbird has a Golden Bill* Op. 5 (ending)

Chapter 3
A Failed Anglo-Irish Family (1887–1903)

There are two gaps in Swan Hennessy's musical biography. One is the period of about 1889 to 1901, another occurs during World War I when he is unheard of between 1915 and 1919. These periods are characterised by a total lack of published compositions and of any reviews or other articles about him in journals and newspapers. In terms of his publications, the first gap is between his Opp. 11 (1889) and 13 (1901) (Op. 12 was published in London, 1902), the second between Opp. 50 (1915) and 49 (1920). Such 'gaps', of course, arouse curiosity, not least because they interrupted the composer's career and his public perception; they may even offer a (partial) explanation for his quick neglect by posterity.

The first of these periods is related to private circumstances that the composer quite obviously wished to hide, and only his close family knew about it. As explained in the previous chapter, Hennessy lived in London probably since the second half of 1886. On 7 December 1888 Hennessy married in Edinburgh. It is a carefully hidden aspect of his life mainly because the marriage was so short-lived and ended in trouble and divorce. It was celebrated at the 'Sheriff Court House George IV Bridge', Edinburgh, and reported in a newspaper as follows:

> December 7th, by special licence, SWAN HENNESSY, only son of M. D. Hennessy, Esq., Chicago, U.S.A., to LUCY HILDA ORMSBY, only daughter of the late ROBT. ORMSBY ROPER, of Hazelbrook, Co. Roscommon.[1]

A marriage by 'special licence' is a civil ceremony between (in this case) the Roman Catholic Hennessy and the Anglican (probably United Presbyterian) Lucy (Hilda Ormsby) Roper, warranted at the said 'Sheriff Court House'.

Why Edinburgh? Lucy Roper, two years younger than Swan, was (on her father's side) the descendant of an Anglo-Irish landowning family, which owned Hazelbrook House in Ballygalda, County Roscommon, a modest country mansion built in the 1790s by the Roper family (now in ruins for many years, see Fig. 3.1). Her father, Robert Ormsby Roper, was captain of the Roscommon Militia, an army unit first raised in Boyle, County Roscommon, in 1793, which became the 5th Battalion Connaught Rangers on 1 July 1881, following the sudden death of Robert Roper near Lucerne, Switzerland.[2] The leadership of the Roscommon Militia seems to have been dominated by members of the Roper family since its foundation – several sources referring to it reveal earlier members of the Roper family. Lucy's mother Elizabeth's (b. c1830) maiden name was Home, and the parents had married in 1858 in Berwick-upon-Tweed (Northumberland), Elizabeth's birthplace. Lucy Roper, Swan's wife, may have

---

[1] *The Scotsman*, 8 December 1888, p. 12.
[2] The *London Evening Standard*, 2 August 1881, reported in the classified ads section under 'Deaths': 'ROPER. – July 24, suddenly, at Morschach Lake, Lucerne, Robert Ormsby Roper, Esq. of Hazelbrook, county Roscommon'.

been born at Hazelbrook House in Ireland. But, following the death of her father, in 1883, the house had been sold to the Gilligan family.³ It is therefore rather unlikely that Swan Hennessy would have travelled to Ireland and seen the house.

Fig. 3.1: Hazelbrook House, County Roscommon, in 2014
(photograph: Colin Colleran, with permission)

Elizabeth Roper and her daughter Lucy had probably been living in Edinburgh since the death of her husband or the sale of the house in Ireland. Elizabeth's sister Mary, also a widow, lived at 23 Chalmers Street, in the centre of Edinburgh, close to the urban park area known as the 'Meadows'. Mary Home's (1827–1916) husband had been the well-known Presbyterian theologian John Eadie (1810–1876) of Glasgow. As the bride's birthplace in Ireland was no longer available, having been sold in 1883, the marriage between Lucy and Swan took place at the bride's mother's place of residence, Edinburgh. The address given in the marriage certificate is that of Lucy's aunt Mary (most likely also that of Elizabeth). Apparently, Swan's father did not come from Chicago for the marriage. His name is not listed among the witnesses, nor is his wife: the marriage certificate mentions the early death of Sarah J. Hennessy, née Swan. The only witnesses present on the occasion were Lucy's mother Elizabeth and aunt Mary.

Swan and Lucy lived in London and merely went to Edinburgh for the marriage. When the first child was born, the family lived at 93 Drummond Road in the Southwark area of London (part of St. James's Parish, Bermondsey). A daughter, Lucie (or

---

³ See http://www.svpal.org/~colleeng/connacht/tomKate.shtml (accessed 4 July 2016).

Lucy) Mabel Hennessy, was baptised here in the 'Established Church' on 29 June 1890,[4] but she must have been born in *c*1889.[5]

And this is because, interestingly, a second child was born six months later, on 6 December 1890, and the birthplace was Dublin, Ireland! It was a son named Martin Richard Furneaux Hennessy, the birth place being a large early Victorian house called 'Beachfield' in Sutton on the Howth peninsula (today the postal district Dublin 13) that is described as Hennessy's residence.[6] Situated at the end of a short driveway off Strand Road, the house offers a view on Bull Island and across Dublin Bay from the north. According to the notice in the General Register, the informant of the birth was Swan Hennessy's mother-in-law, Elizabeth Roper, 'present at birth', and it was registered on 15 January 1891, five weeks after the birth took place. Hennessy's profession is given as 'Gentleman'.

Although this document is no guarantee that Swan Hennessy has spent time in Dublin around 1890–1, it should be highly likely. It would be the first time we can be almost sure that he was in Ireland, and not only as a visitor. The Beachfield residence may not have been his own, though; more likely it belonged to the Roper family as their Dublin residence, and perhaps it was bought with the proceeds from the sale of the County Roscommon house.

* * *

Im Gebirg (In the Mountains), Op. 7 (1887) for piano and *Albumblätter (Album Leaves)*, Op. 8 (1887) for piano

Hennessy's compositions that originated in the late 1880s in London are a continuation of his early Stuttgart works. His opus numbers 7 to 10 were published by Augener & Co. – the first three being piano works and Op. 10 a piano trio. Augener also published the *Monthly Musical Record* so it is not surprising to find short reviews of his publications in this journal – probably by the same critic as before. The journal also published three of the four movements of *Im Gebirg*, Op. 7 (1887) as a music supplement, introducing him with the words: 'The name of Mr. Swan Hennessy will probably be new to most of our readers, but we have no doubt they will be pleased to make the acquaintance of these charming *morceaux* […]'.[7]

---

[4] London, England, Church of England Birth and Baptisms, 1813–1906, accessed via www.ancestry.co.uk, 13 May 2016.
[5] When she married on 5 December 1914, her age was 25.
[6] Registered in the first quarter of 1891 in registration district Dublin North, according to *Ireland, Civil Registration Indexes 1845–1958*, vol. 2, p. 453; accessed via www.familysearch.com, 14 May 2016. The exact date (15 January) and place was communicated to the author by the General Register Office of Ireland, Roscommon, 12 September 2017. The house was on the market for several years before the end of 2017, see http://www.independent.ie/life/home-garden/homes/lofty-splendour-at-victorian-beachfield-in-sutton-30369218.html (accessed 12 September 2017).
[7] In *The Monthly Musical Record* 17:200, August 1887, p. 178.

In a review of Opp. 7 and 8, the critic observed a development in comparison to his earlier compositions, but remained critical of what he perceived as 'fragmentariness, subtilisation, and Schumannism':

> These compositions give us an even better opinion of the composer than those we noticed on a former occasion. They are indeed more delicately felt and elaborated than anything of his we have as yet seen. There can be no doubt as to his possession of very considerable musical talent: he has a poetic temperament, refined taste, and artistic conscience. What he must guard against is overindulgence in fragmentariness, subtilisation, and Schumann-ism.[8]

He continued with a perspective on the briefness and sketchy nature of Hennessy's writing saying he should 'resist the tendency, very strongly developed in him, to stop short after slight suggestions and vague beginnings. If he fails to do so he runs the danger of raising curiosity and not satisfying it, [...]'. The critic here identifies a characteristic in Hennessy that he, in fact, never quite shook off in the years to come.

A critic in the *Musical World* offered a rather picturesque interpretation of *Im Gebirg*, but also implies that this is a youthful work:

> These pieces would seem to have been written during exceptionally fine weather, and as descriptive of mountains of very moderate elevation without a cloud to disturb the transparency of the atmosphere, and without a single trait of that grandeur and occasional storminess of mountain scenery properly so called. The idea of absolute serenity being thus reflected throughout the work, the element of a desirable contrast is absent. Nevertheless, these short sketches show a practised hand as well as refined taste and feeling, and they are especially welcome as an earnest [*sic!*] of more important things to come.[9]

Étude Fantaisie, Op. 9 (1888) for piano

With regard to the *Étude Fantaisie*, Op. 9 (1888), the *MMR* reviewer is more optimistic about the composer's development, although he begins his text in a curious fashion:

> We think a law ought to be passed forbidding young composers to write fantasias and suchlike compositions. To do this would be no less in the interest of the said composers than in that of the public. After this preliminary growl (not out of place, seeing that Mr. Hennessy manifests a particular fondness for that sort of thing) we have much pleasure in stating that the present Étude Fantaisie is by no means a bad specimen of its kind. It shows that the composer has learned something, and has something to say. It shows also that he can make the piano sound effectively, although there are passages that are written rather for the eye than for the ear. In short, it may be recommended to the attention and favour of pianists. We have no doubt that this is the best and most promising of his works as far as we are acquainted with them.[10]

---

[8] *The Monthly Musical Record* 17:199, July 1887, pp. 153–154 [153].
[9] *The Musical World* 65:39, 24 September 1887, p. 752.
[10] *The Monthly Musical Record* 18:208, April 1888, p. 89.

Lieder an den Mond, Op. 10 (1888) for violin, cello and piano

Hennessy's *Lieder an den Mond*, Op. 10 (1888), though termed 'Lieder', are his first piece of chamber music: a piano trio. Reviews seem to contradict each other, with the *Monthly Musical Record* calling them 'well-felt compositions, poetic and interesting, whose romanticism has its roots in Schumann';[11] similarly, the *Athenaeum* considered them 'three fanciful and pleasing little sketches, slightly suggestive of Schumann'.[12] But the *Musical Standard* described them as 'fantastically constructed, and bizarre rather than melodious'.[13]

The three short movements are called *Um Mitternacht* ('At Midnight'), to be played *largo*, *In der Frühe* ('Early in the Morning') in *allegretto*, and *Am Abend* ('In the Evening') in *andante con espressione*, suggesting different moods and situations of the moon's course, here beginning in the middle of the night. The title of the set is most certainly influenced by Schubert with his three different songs entitled *An den Mond*, but this is nothing more than a Romantic allusion, with no musical similarities.

For the opening *largo* movement, Hennessy starts with an eight-bar introduction in a relatively free form, in which two *sforzando* chords may have struck the writer in the *Musical Standard* as 'bizarre'. But what follows is an utterly Romantic passage with a gently sweeping melodic line in the violin that may well have sprung from the creative mind of any of the better-known German Romantics of the time (Ex. 3.1). The piano accompaniment is very simple (as are, in fact, the strings), sometimes supporting the violin line, only becoming richer towards the end when the regular quavers dissolve into widely spaced chords.

All three movements remain in F major, the second being a sprightly piece in 2/4 time and a delicate piano accompaniment that supports the interplay of the strings with a brief rhythmic idea that is then taken up by the strings and leads to the ending of the piece.

The third movement is the most attractive of the three insofar as it is less predictable. By using a number of repetitions, it is also the longest. It begins in 4/4 time and has a middle section in 3/4 with quiet *staccatos* before the opening *andante* is taken up again as a coda.

The pieces are certainly not difficult to play and may have been intended as 'Hausmusik' rather than for the stage.[14] They would probably still serve as an attractive short collection in a chamber music course for young musicians or perhaps as an *encore* in a concert programme. Even so, the *Musical Times* described it, after a performance in 1905 alongside the Brahms trio Op. 8 as 'most effective numbers'.[15]

---

[11] *The Monthly Musical Record* 18:209, May 1888, p. 106.
[12] *The Athenaeum* 2, 1890, p. 456.
[13] *The Musical Standard* 36:1277, 19 January 1889, p. 46.
[14] *The Morning Post*, 8 September 1888, p. 2, agrees, describing them as 'interesting contributions to the somewhat scanty store of trio music available for home performance'.
[15] *The Musical Times* 46:754, December 1905, p. 813.

Ex. 3.1: *Lieder an den Mond*, Op. 10 No. 1 *'Um Mitternacht'*, bars 9–18

Miniatures, Op. 11 (1889) for piano

Hennessy's Op. 11, a set of five *Miniatures* for piano, was published in 1889 with Durand et Schoenewerk in Paris. It is unclear how he made the connection to Paris. Did he go to visit the influential World Exhibition that took place in this year when the Eiffel Tower was unveiled? The scarcity of sources about this phase in Hennessy's life does not offer any explanation.

The first of the five pieces is dedicated to his wife Lucy, three others to what are probably personal friends (two English names and one Dutch or Flemish) and one to 'Gretchen Goetschius', apparently the daughter of his former teacher, Percy Goetschius. The work was characterised in the *Monthly Musical Record* (as earlier in this journal, with some fatherly advice) as

> VERY nice and very clever, but too finical, too *recherché*. Mr. Hennessy should endeavour to write in a more hearty and straightforward style; he should aim at greater vigour, fulness, and continuity of thought and expression. Unless he succeeds in this he is in danger of wasting, of frittering away, his *esprit*.[16]

Perhaps, Hennessy agreed with this assessment in retrospect, as he later withdrew this collection and reused one of the pieces (No. 1, *Vivace*), with absolutely no revision, under the title *Robert Schumann* in his first collection of pastiche compositions, *À la manière de …* (1926), mocking the style of the composer and admitting at the same time what a stylistic decal this early work represented.

* * *

Summing up Hennessy's first work-phase (Opp. 1 to 11), it appears as a period of learning and developing. The music is deeply rooted in German Romanticism with its melodiousness and richly modulating lyricism. These are also reflected in some of the works' dedications, such as his Op. 7 to Theodor Kirchner (1823–1903) and Op. 8 to Clara Schumann (1819–1896). There are early signs of his later, quite original stylistic elements such as a fair degree of playfulness and formal flexibility in works like the *Carneval-Studien* and the piano trio, although in harmonic terms they are quite conventional. This phase in his work is also notable for its total absence of the Irish or 'Celticist' elements that were to become such prominent features of his later music.

In the course of time, Hennessy himself dismissed these early works and seems to have withdrawn Opp. 6, 10, and 11. In the already mentioned 1929 interview with *Le Guide du concert*, he says that, at Stuttgart, 'I received an excellent education, very Romantic and Schumann-like, as you can imagine'.[17] Granting a certain pastiche character to these works and comparing them to a series of actual *intended* pastiches he became known for in the late 1920s, he goes on to explain that Clara Schumann had been quite

---

[16] *The Monthly Musical Record* 19:222, June 1889, p. 130.
[17] *'je reçus une excellente éducation, très romantique et schumannienne, comme vous pouvez penser'*; Chevaillier, 'Entretien', p. 791.

delighted about the dedication she received: 'I even dedicated one to Mme. Schumann who showed herself very happy about this dedication rendered to the memory of her husband'.[18] He says he needed to change his artistic environment in order to discover his true self, but that, what remained of this period, was a predilection for short pieces or movements, which, however, had nothing to do with the harmonic language:

> But it wasn't until I had left this somewhat cosy environment that I suddenly discovered myself. And henceforth nothing of Schumann remained in me except, perhaps, a taste for short pieces, for cut slices, for laying precise and sober traits about a person or a painting … but this has nothing to do with the style.[19]

* * *

Neither the 'somewhat cosy environment' of student life in Germany nor that of married life in England lasted long, as is evidenced by a Civil Divorce Record held in the UK National Archives.[20] It was based on a petition of his wife that was filed as early as 2 August 1892 in London and finally approved on 30 October 1893. When the petition arrived, Swan had already left the UK for Italy. The divorce file reveals that he did not even attend the proceedings; everything was managed between a London-based lawyer for the wife and one in Viareggio for Swan, and all communication passed through the British consulate at nearby Livorno (at the time known in English as 'Leghorn'); the court minutes also mention an affidavit that was read at the proceedings, written by one Arthur Wellesley Peckham Swan – judging from the name, probably an uncle or other relative from his mother's family's side. After Swan Hennessy had left his young family at Lucerne, he probably never saw them again.

In Victorian England, a divorce was difficult to obtain. Very few reasons were accepted as valid, and they were prescribed by the UK Matrimonial Causes Act of 1857:

> Adultery remained the sole ground for divorce, although wives could […] allege cruelty and desertion, in addition to the husband's adultery, in order to obtain a divorce.[21]

---

[18] *'J'en ai même dédié une à Mme Schumann qui se montra fort enchantée de cet hommage rendu à la mémoire de son mari.'*; Chevaillier, 'Entretien', p. 791.
[19] *'Mais ce n'est qu'après être sorti de cette ambiance un peu étouffante que tout à coup je me trouvai enfin moi-même. Et alors plus rien de Schumann ne resta en moi, sinon peut-être ce goût pour les morceaux courts, à l'emporte-pièce, situant en quelques traits précis et sobres un personnage, un tableau … mais cela n'a rien à voir avec le style.'*; Chevaillier, 'Entretien', pp. 791–792.
[20] The National Archives of the UK; Kew, Surrey, England; *Court for Divorce and Matrimonial Causes, later Supreme Court of Judicature: Divorce and Matrimonial Causes Files*; Class: J77; Piece: 497; Item: 15140; accessed via www.ancestry.co.uk, 14 May 2016.
[21] Quoted from https://www.parliament.uk/about/living-heritage/transformingsociety/private-lives/relationships/overview/divorce/ (accessed 20 July 2018).

And so it was done in Swan Hennessy's case. The divorce file gives as reasons 'adultery coupled with cruelty towards the petitioner'. We get a little better picture of what had happened from a newspaper article that appeared about the case under the headline of 'A Composer Divorced':

> The parties had at times lived abroad. While at Lucerne the respondent left the petitioner and told her he was going to England to look after a house to which she and the two children of the marriage could reside, but since that time she had seen nothing of him for the last two years. She received certain information as to the misconduct of her husband with a woman called Pauline in Vienna, and she then instituted the present suit.[22]

In other words, while Hennessy's eloping with Pauline from Vienna must have been cruel to Lucy and their common children, the cruelty should not be misunderstood as violent behaviour. It had to be described in such terms in order for the divorce to be granted. Hennessy clearly did not object to it and, to the dismay of his later family in France, regularly payed alimony to his former wife and children for many years. But the story clearly shows that Hennessy was a 'womaniser' (a characterisation confirmed in family memory) and also very immature at the time of his marriage. The burden of a family life with two young children, obviously a temporary phase in every family, seems to have overwhelmed him.

* * *

Further sources, also accessible via ancestry.co.uk, reveal that Hennessy's ex-wife married again in early 1903 (one Alexander Stuart) and that the life-dates of the two children were *c*1889–1964 (Lucie Mabel) and 1890–1941 (Martin).

When Lucie Mabel grew up, she married a wealthy English army officer, (Sir) Robert John Aldborough Henniker, on 5 December 1914, thus becoming 'Lady Henniker'. On registering her father's name, she gave 'Edward Swan Hennessy', profession: 'landowner' (Fig. 3.2).

This noble marriage made Lucie a member of the 'peerage', and as such she can still be found in a modern database,[23] which also mentions her father's first name as Edward, of 'Hazelbrook, County Roscommon, Ireland'. This marriage was reported in an English newspaper[24] as:

> A marriage has been arranged and will take place very quietly early this month, between Robert John Aldborough Henniker, Duke of Wellington's Regiment, son of the late John Granville Henniker, J. P., of Catcott Manor, Bridgwater, Somerset, and Lucy Mabel Hennessy, daughter of the late Edward Swan Hennessy and Mrs. Stuart of Hazelbrook, Co. Roscommon, Ireland.

---

[22] *Lloyd's Weekly London Newspaper*, 16 April 1893, p. 4.
[23] http://www.thepeerage.com/p43768.htm#i437671 (accessed 14 May 2016).
[24] *Daily Express*, 3 December 1914.

Fig. 3.2: The 1914 marriage register for Lucie Mabel Hennessy
(Source: www.ancestry.co.uk)

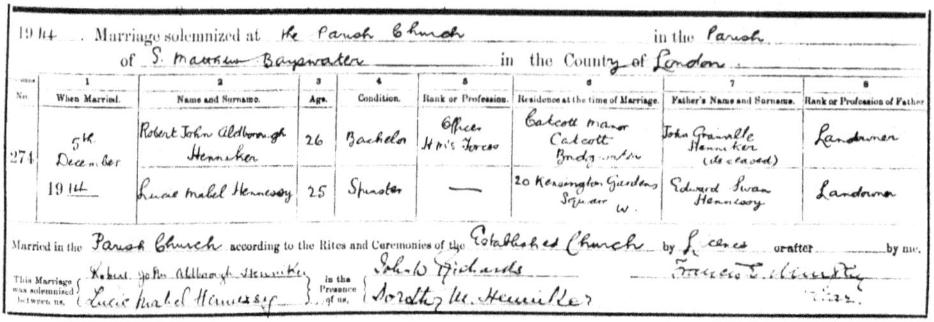
1914. Marriage solemnized at the Parish Church in the Parish of S. Matthew Bayswater in the County of London.

No.	When Married.	Name and Surname.	Age.	Condition.	Rank or Profession.	Residence at the time of Marriage.	Father's Name and Surname.	Rank or Profession of Father
274	5th December 1914	Robert John Aldborough Henniker	26	Bachelor	Officer H.M's Forces	Catcott Manor Catcott Bridgwater	John Granville Henniker (deceased)	Landowner
		Lucie Mabel Hennessy	25	Spinster	—	20 Kensington Gardens Square W.	Edward Swan Hennessy	Landowner

Married in the Parish Church according to the Rites and Ceremonies of the Established Church by licence or after by me,

This Marriage was solemnized between us, Robert John Aldborough Henniker, Lucie Mabel Hennessy; in the Presence of us, John W Richards, Dorothy M. Henniker

These two sources about the 1914 marriage of Lucie Mabel Hennessy confirm 'Edward' as Swan Hennessy's actual first name (which had first appeared as 'Ed.' in the 1882 list of pupils of the Stuttgart Conservatory). It remains somewhat strange, though, that the name Edward does not even appear in his 1888 marriage certificate. And when he became an artist, 'Swan' may have even been useful as an unusual name that attracted attention.

The fact that, in the newspaper announcement, Edward Swan Hennessy is described as 'the late' (i.e. deceased), should not surprise us. For one, during Lucie Mabel's childhood he had disappeared so thoroughly that he might as well have been dead. More importantly, however, in a public statement such as a newspaper notice of a marriage in the nobility, being the offspring of a failed marriage would have been considered awkward, socially, and may have given rise to unwanted questions, particularly as Lucie Mabel's mother's surname now was Stuart. As there was no risk that Swan would reappear, it was much safer to simply declare him dead for the newspapers. Otherwise, Lucie Mabel must have been well aware that Swan was still alive because of his alimony payments. Besides, she did not declare him deceased in the marriage register, whereas her father-in-law is (see Fig. 3.2).

Describing Swan Hennessy, in the marriage register, as a 'landowner' is another exaggeration. Although it cannot be fully excluded that he owned land somewhere in England or Scotland (bought from the money of his father), it is much more likely that this alludes to the time of Lucie Mabel's birth when the family of Hennessy's ex-wife may still have owned some land in Ireland, making Swan the temporary 'co-owner' by marriage. The description may also simply have been given because it looked more respectable than 'composer of music'.[25]

---

[25] Two photographs, dated 25 June 1926, of "Lucy Mabel (née Hennessy), Lady Henniker, Wife of Sir Robert John Aldbrough Henniker, 7th Bt; daughter of Edward Swan Hennessy", can be found on the website of the National Portrait Gallery, London, by the leading high society portrait photographer Bassano Ltd., see http://www.npg.org.uk/collections/search/person/mp64387/lucy-mabel-nee-hennessy-lady-henniker (accessed 13 May 2016).

Hennessy's Dublin-born son, Martin Richard Furneaux Hennessy Stuart, rose to some prominence as a civil engineer. He lived most of his life at Colchester, Essex, where he served his apprenticeship at a company called Davey, Paxman and Co. (1908–12), became an inspector of ordnance machinery during World War I in Belgium, France and Italy (from which he was decorated with a *Croce de Guerra* from the Italian king in 1919) and worked in several engineering companies, re-joining his original company at their London office from 1931. His last address was at 4 Standard Road, Colchester. He died, aged 51, on 14 May 1941 at St George's Hospital, Hyde Park Corner, London.[26]

It may be added that the English line of Swan Hennessy's family is no longer extant. Martin seems to have remained a bachelor. There was one offspring from Lucie Mabel's marriage, according to thepeerage.com, namely Ann Margaret Henniker (1915–1983) who married John Holroyd Bairstow (1909–1968) in 1946, and this couple remained childless.

* * *

Thus, from about 1892, Swan travelled around Europe, frequently returning to Italy, and probably in company of his father.

In his old age, Michael D. Hennessy suffered severely from stones in the bladder. He probably lived mainly in Europe at least from the time of his son's divorce, but probably earlier. In the 1914 Emergency Passport Application at the Brussels Legation (see Chapter 2), he relates that he had last left the USA in 1905 'in search of health', having spent the years since then in France, England, Italy, and Switzerland. He gives his (December 1914) address as Rue Chalgrin, Paris, and claims to desire the passport for the purpose of 'returning to residence in France, coming to England + returning to the U.S. America' [*sic*].

In the extended hand-written remarks on the back of the passport application form, he explains that since 1905 he had 'made several attempts to return to the U.S. but advanced years & failing health have prevented him'. The apparent minutes of the conversation between him and the embassy officer end with the statement: 'It is his intention to return to the U.S. to end his days, health permitting. Considers his case thoroughly meritorious. He has had during his residence abroad three capilar [*sic*] operations.' The document is signed by the 'applicant's son', Swan Hennessy.

In the 1929 interview for *Le Guide du concert*, Hennessy explained that after his brief stay at Oxford and his seven years of study in Stuttgart he travelled for ten years through Switzerland, France, Germany and Ireland, in between regularly returning to Italy. As there are no records of any musical activities during these years in the countries mentioned, this suggests that these travels were not primarily motivated by furthering his career, giving concerts, or by musical studies as has occasionally been

---

[26] Details from 1942 obituary in *Grace's Guide*, https://www.gracesguide.co.uk/Martin_Richard_Furneaux_Hennessy_Stuart (accessed 3 September 2017).

surmised.[27] Much more likely, given the knowledge about his failed Anglo-Irish family and reading Michael Hennessy's account of his travels above, is that he spent the first years in England, Ireland, Switzerland, and Italy, accompanying his father in his 'search for health'.

That England, too, was included in these travels, and that father and son travelled together, is documented in one of the few cases where their arrival at one of the prestigious hotels was recorded in the daily press. *The Observer*, of London, reported in January 1896 about the arrival of 'Mr. M. D. Hennessy, Mr. Swan Hennessy' at the Bristol Hotel.[28]

In terms of his compositional activity, this period represents the first of the two 'gaps'. The *Miniatures*, Op. 11 (1889) were his last composition for the time being. The next publication follows eleven years later (1900) – a sign of how deep the disruption was that was caused by the divorce.

Despite the eleven-year break in his published output, he does seem to have composed occasionally during this decade. This is suggested by a manuscript that had been catalogued in the 1950s in the New York Public Library that is now, unfortunately, lost. It was a song dedicated to David Bispham (1857–1921) when the famous American baritone was still in the early stages of his career, having just performed his first major role in opera as Beckmesser in Richard Wagner's *Die Meistersinger von Nürnberg* at the Royal Opera Covent Garden, London, in June 1892. The song, a Goethe setting in German, has been listed by Otto Edwin Albrecht in 1953 as *Nur wer die Sehnsucht kennt. Lied von Goethe in Musik gesetzt von Swan Hennessy*, Op. 14, apparently dated 1894.[29]

As his last published piece had been an Opus 11 of 1889, this manuscript suggests that he had written and discarded several compositions by the mid-1890s (Opus 14 has later been ascribed to a different piece, dated *c*1902–4). Albrecht describes it as '4 leaves 30 x 24 cm. Music on recto only. Song with piano accpt. Dedicated to David Bispham. New York Public Library.'[30]

---

[27] For instance, in the biographical note about Hennessy in Metzner, *Heine in der Musik*, p. 304, and in the booklet notes to the bremenradiohall CD recording of his *Trio*, Op. 54 (see Appendix 7).
[28] *The Observer*, 26 January 1896, p. 6.
[29] Otto Edwin Albrecht: *A Census of Autograph Music of European Composers in American Libraries* (Philadelphia: Univ. of Pennsylvania Press, 1953), p. 145.
[30] E-mail from NYPL to the author dated 24 March 2017 indicating that after much searching and consulting with curatorial staff, the piece could not be located.

Chapter 4
In Search of Direction (1903–1907)

Hennessy's activities, personal circumstances and whereabouts during the first few years of the twentieth century are difficult to pin down. Some of this time was still part of the ten years of traveling, if we presume that this lasted from the year of separation (1892) or divorce (1893) from his first wife until the Brussels recital in 1903 when he met Claire, his future second wife. He certainly resumed composing and having his music published around 1900. He may have lived in England again during some of these years, as some works of this time appear with Augener and the London branch of Schott. Paris is another option as a temporary residence, where he probably moved to around 1903. He may also have spent some time in Ireland, as among the earliest pieces of this period are the *Variations sur un thème original dans le style irlandais*, Op. 12 for piano and a *Sonate en fa (style irlandais)*, Op. 14 for violin and piano, both with first editions at Schott of London in 1902 and 1904 respectively. The manuscript of Op. 14, now in the Bavarian State Library in Munich, is the only proof of his residence in Paris from (at least) 1904: on the title page he gives his address as 4 rue Chalgrin in the 16th arrondissement of Paris – a small street within a stone's throw of the tree-lined Avenue Foch and the Arc de Triomphe.

Claire was of Polish birth; her maiden name was Przybyszewska. She was born in 1883 in Płużnica, a village in north-central Poland that was also known under its German name Plusnitz (the spelling she used to give in personal documents). Her mother, Rose Claire E. Przybyszewska, was a cousin of the well-known symbolist and revolutionary writer Stanisław Przybyszewski (1868–1927). Although of modest aristocratic background, her mother worked in the household of King Léopold II of Belgium from about 1885, so that Claire grew up at the Belgian court in Brussels. There is but speculative information about Claire's father, so that she retained her mother's surname. Claire's mother worked as a *'lectrice'* (reader or lector) to Queen Marie Henriette, and Claire succeeded her in this role. However, when the Queen died in September 1902, her future was in the open. As a result of this background, Claire was fluent in Polish, German, French and English.

There is no documentary evidence about the family-inherited knowledge that Swan Hennessy came to know Claire Przybyszewska in 1903 after a recital he gave at the Théâtre de la Monnaie, respectively a reception he attended afterwards at the royal castle. Given her uncertain position at the court, she was ready to follow Hennessy, and their destination was Paris. Why Paris, whether he had a residence there before 1903, whether Swan's father was living there as well – all this is unknown and unexplained. London was probably ruled out because of a too close proximity to his former family. Perhaps Paris seemed the most promising because of its musical life including publication and performance prospects. Certainly, a German musical centre may have been an option as well, given the fact that Swan Hennessy had studied there, and we will see later that Hennessy remained interested in publication and performance opportunities in Germany. Perhaps it was Michael Hennessy who had the last word in this decision.

Fig. 4.1: The earliest known photograph of Swan Hennessy, early to mid-1900s (Courtesy: Hennessy family)

Thus, from around 1903, Hennessy came to live permanently in Paris, the city he later described as 'the only place in the world where life is easy and agreeable',[1] probably sharing the apartment not only with Claire, but also with his father. Yet, there must have been something in London that now and again drew him there – a network of personal friends, perhaps his step-sister Lila – we will never know exactly what it

---

[1] *'le seul lieu du monde où la vie soit facile et agréable'*; Chevaillier, 'Entretien', p. 791.

was. For this book's storyline it does not seem essential, because if it was related to his musical career, there would surely be more traces that would extend beyond the February 1903 piano recital in London recounted below.

Berceuse, Op. 13 (1900) for violin and piano

Swan Hennessy's Op. 13 appeared in 1901 quite out of the blue – and it passed by without anyone taking notice. It was a *Berceuse* for violin and piano, written in 1900 and published in the following year with Enoch & Cie. in Paris. This publisher, founded in 1853 in Paris, had a strong connection to London, with 'Enoch & Sons' – founded by the brother of the Paris owner – being an independent company that also served as a distributor for their Paris publications. Yet, this does not fully explain the Paris connection. If Hennessy would have lived in London at the time he could have chosen the London house of Enoch. It was rather that he still travelled extensively, with home bases changing every now and then, between Italy and perhaps Paris and London. It should, however be kept in mind, that his Op. 11 (the last work of his first phase) had also been published in Paris (1889) – perhaps he had more trust in French publishers in terms of reputation. For his Op. 13, it is likely that Hennessy payed for the publication – the title page mentions it as being *'en dépôt chez'* Enoch, which is mostly a circumscription for a privately financed print.

The work is dedicated to Beatrice Langley (1872–1958), a quite prominent English violinist of the time. Yet, there are no traces of Langley having performed the work in public. In Hennessy's own list of works it appears as unperformed (he has not always been aware of performances, though). Also, there are no reviews of the work's publication.[2]

It seems highly likely, though, that Hennessy was in touch with Langley, having probably heard her playing in London, and it is also highly likely that he introduced this piece to her personally. Thus, around 1900, he must have considered it about time to resume his vocation. It is the earliest sign of the composer slowly returning from his European odyssey.

Choosing the route via a prominent artist is probably a good strategy, one that has been taken by numerous composers. In an ideal case, both sides – composer and dedicatee – benefit to equal measure: the composer's name is associated with the artist (so he must be respectable), and the artist is flattered by a composition specifically written for him/her – provided the composer has a name of repute or at least acknowledged promise. And this is where the problem may have occurred. Whereas Langley already had a good reputation, Hennessy had been hiding for ten years after a merely beginning career. Thus, he would have decorated himself with her name rather than *vice versa*.

---

[2] It is merely listed among pieces 'received for review' in *The Monthly Musical Record* (October 1903), p. 193. No review appeared after that. The work is freely available from the Gallica site of the Bibliothèque Nationale de France: http://gallica.bnf.fr/ark:/12148/bpt6k3185679 (accessed 14 January 2018).

The genre may have been another factor. A *berceuse* (lullaby) is by definition a rather calm piece of music and no showcase for the virtuosity of a performer. If anything, Hennessy's work would have functioned as an *encore* in a chamber music recital – and if in such a case the piece *was* actually performed, it might have escaped a critic's notice.

Hennessy's *Berceuse* is a brief piece in 2/4 time, to be played *allegretto con tenerezza*, the tonality of which moves mysteriously between C major and A minor, mainly tending towards C major, however. The first page (of three) of the score – 16 bars in the score with a reprise – contains the main theme in the character of a children's song, simple but rather beautiful and very catchy. After a piano interlude of 16 bars, the violin takes up again with a secondary theme in G major in which a persistent octaved B against a descending scale of G, F, E, D, C, A, and B makes an attractive effect. From an *'a tempo'* mark at the top of the third page the main theme then reappears in the piano, now 'accompanied' by the violin.

At two brief points only, the piece deviates from the dominating C major / A minor in somewhat unusual modulations that serve the purpose of ending a phrase. The first occurs at the close of the piano interlude, where a rather bold modulation from a D seventh chord via a B/F diminished, F minor and A flat sixth chord leads to the G major of the secondary theme. Then, in concluding the secondary theme, he moves from an E flat seventh chord (for two bars) via G major, C major, G major, and G major seventh back to C major. Here, the unusual element is the introduction of the E flat seventh chord.

* * *

Another contact with a female musician in London occurred just shortly afterwards, in 1902. It was the (then London-based) Irish pianist Carrie Townshend.[3] She appears in the contemporary press with many recitals in London and Dublin in the 1890s and the early 1900s, but she is now no more than a name in connection with the history of the Feis Ceoil, a notable music festival and competition in Ireland that was first held in 1897 and which still thrives. Here, Irish music students compete for a Townshend Cup. In later years she appeared as one of the few Munster members of the Feis Ceoil Association.[4] She was probably born in Cork, studied with Giuseppe Buonamici in Florence and was mainly active in England, at least during the period mentioned.

Townshend provided the fingering for a second edition (1902) of Hennessy's *Two Studies*, Op. 4 (originally of 1886). She also gave the first performance of Hennessy's Op. 12 in the Bechstein Hall, London, 2 February 1903.[5]

---

[3] Townshend (1870–1951) is an obscure figure in British and Irish music today. Larchet-Cuthbert lists her as 'Miss Caroline Townshend' and describes her as 'a very gifted musician both on the Piano and on the Irish Harp' with a strong Irish cultural consciousness. In advanced age she lived in Dublin and had a number of harp pupils; Sheila Larchet-Cuthbert: *The Irish Harp Book* (Cork: Mercier Press, 1975), p. 238.

[4] See, for example, the Feis Ceoil syllabus 1926, p. 41.

[5] Reviewed in *The Daily Telegraph* and *The Times*, 3 February 1903.

Variations sur un thème original dans le style irlandais, Op. 12 (*c*1902) for piano

As Hennessy's first 'Irish' composition, the *Variations sur un thème original dans le style irlandais*, Op. 12 is interesting to examine, as it is the earliest specimen of what was to become a key element of his personal style. Despite their French titles, both this piece and the *Sonate en fa (style irlandais)*, Op. 14 (1904) for violin and piano were published with Schott in London. The piano variations Op. 12 were originally published in 1902 with a revised edition as *Variations on an Original Theme in the Irish Style* in 1903. The work is dedicated to Carrie Townshend who showed her gratitude by giving the first performance.

Dating this piece is not easy as no manuscript appears to have survived. Hennessy's Op. 13 (the *Berceuse*) was evidently written in 1900 and has a publication date of 1901. His Op. 12 therefore should have been written between *c*1900 (if not before) and its first publication in 1902. However, as we have seen towards the end of Chapter 3, he had occasionally written music during his ten years of travel, even though he may have withdrawn most of it. Thus, there was an unacknowledged Op. 14 from as early as 1894. Therefore, at some point during the preceding decade, he must have rejected several compositions and renumbered his works. If the current Op. 12 is from the first series, it may even date from the early 1890s. I tend towards a later date because Hennessy explained in his 1929 interview with Lucien Chevaillier that he needed time to develop his own voice (in other words, his 'Celtic' identity). This piece may be regarded as a first result of that process and would therefore have to date from after his period of European travel. It probably even postdates the *Berceuse* Op. 13.

In any case, both Hennessy's Opp. 12 and 14 seem to have been written in England, which distinguishes them from the 'Celtic' music he produced during the 1910s and '20s. An important influence seems to have been the acquaintance with the Irish musician Carrie Townshend – and perhaps other Irish meetings and influences he encountered while living in London and, potentially, travelling in Ireland. The background to this piece would therefore have to be sought on the British Isles.

What Hennessy here calls *'style irlandais'* or 'Irish style' boils down to a melody that is modelled on the typical melodic and rhythmical contours of Irish traditional music, without quoting any existing folksong. This method turns out to be quite innovative. Most composers attempting to create an Irish style around 1900 would do so by quoting existing folk songs or dances and using them as thematic material in instrumental music. And the same is true for the Scottish style as practiced, for instance, by Alexander Mackenzie (1847–1935) or Hamish MacCunn (1868–1916). Quite wide-spread, of course, were arrangements of traditional music, or 'folk songs' and 'folk dances', as they were called at the time, for voice and piano – a practice going back 200 years and more.

But to consciously create an original Irish-style melody had not become an established practice yet. The case is different, interestingly, in vocal music. In the operatic field, the 1840s operettas of Samuel Lover are written in a humorous Irish style on original themes. Julius Benedict's *The Lily of Killarney* (1862) and Charles Villiers Stanford's *Shamus O'Brien* (1896) use original Irish-style tunes, as do some Irish-American musicals of the 1890s and early 1900s. Also, Stanford has written original song cycles in an Irish style (e.g., *An Irish Idyll*, Op. 77, 1901).⁶ But to find an original Irish-style theme in instrumental music can be quite challenging, especially if this is a theme with variations. Stanford is another case in point, with his Symphony No. 3, Op. 28, the 'Irish' (1887) where he mixes original material with pre-existing traditional tunes. Dibble described it thus:

> The scherzo, perhaps the most engaging movement of the four [...], with its modal flavour and compelling momentum, is a pseudo-Irish 'hop-jig' [...] Among the expansive thematic ideas inspired by the contours of the Irish ethnic repertoire is a fragment which Stanford claimed to be derived from a portion of an old Irish Lament, 'The Lament of the Sons of Usnacht' in Petrie's manuscripts.⁷

But Stanford – like Hennessy – continued to write music in an international, late-Romantic style. The Irish influence never wholly took over, and his use of Irish themes is in most cases limited to quotations of existing folk songs. As Harry White has noted:

> For Stanford, 'Irishness' was a remarkably simple (and commonplace) idea. It comprised the quotation of folksong. His own lyric impulse agreeably sustained this notion, with the result that many of the 'Irish' compositions have recourse to entire melodies which are arranged rather than recomposed into the musical fabric.⁸

Other composers using Irish material in one way or another were mostly younger than Stanford and Hennessy. So, for instance, Hamilton Harty's Piano Quintet dates from 1905 and was not heard in public before 1906 (in this case, according to Dibble, the piece contains '[...] synthetic pentatonicism to create an 'Irish' theme [...]'⁹). Percy Grainger (1882–1961) had not appeared before 1907. Relevant works by Granville Bantock (1868–1946) came later as well (his *Celtic Poem* for cello and orchestra, 1914), and so did a younger generation of composers who all contributed to musical Celticism in Britain like Rutland Boughton (1878–1960), Joseph Holbrooke (1878–1958), John Foulds (1880–1939), Hubert Bath (1883–1945), and Arnold Bax (1883–1953). And the same goes for Irish composers of the time – from Michele Esposito (1855–1929) and Robert O'Dwyer (1862–1949) via Carl G. Hardebeck (1869–1945) and Geoffrey M. Palmer (1882–1957) to John F. Larchet (1884–1967).¹⁰

---

⁶ So has, in Ireland, Thomas O'Brien Butler (1861–1915) with his *Seven Original Irish Melodies* (1903).
⁷ Jeremy Dibble: *Charles Villiers Stanford. Man and Musician* (Oxford: Oxford University Press, 2002), p. 184.
⁸ Harry White: *The Keeper's Recital. Music and Cultural History in Ireland, 1770–1970* (Cork: Cork University Press, 1998), p. 108.
⁹ Jeremy Dibble: *Hamilton Harty, Musical Polymath* (Woodbridge: The Boydell Press, 2013), p. 55.
¹⁰ For good current overviews of early 20th-century Irish composers, see *The Encyclopaedia of Music in Ireland*, ed. Harry White and Barra Boydell (Dublin: UCD Press, 2013), and *The Invisible Art. A Century of Music in Ireland, 1916–2016*, ed. Michael Dervan (Dublin: New Island, 2016).

Insofar, Hennessy's approach is quite unique indeed. With a view to Stanford, he may not have been the very first to write instrumental music in an Irish style, but even Stanford never went as far as creating an original theme in the Irish style and writing variations on it, as if it had been a traditional theme. We can safely assume that Hennessy was very aware of Stanford's music. He had been living in London, was an active concert-goer, and just slightly later exploited the Petrie Collection of Irish traditional music that Stanford edited, with the first two volumes appearing in 1902. Although Hennessy has never (publicly) acknowledged Stanford as an influence, it seems quite likely that he was among the early customers of Stanford's Petrie edition, which – besides the acquaintance with Carrie Townshend and his own travels – must have shaped his musical idea about Ireland.

Beyond Ireland, beyond Irish and British composers, the use of national musical characteristics is, of course, an important trend around the turn of the century that is, on the whole, well-researched. Critical attention has often focused on East European, specifically Czech, composers like Bedřich Smetana (1824–1884) and Antonín Dvořák (1841–1904), or on Scandinavia, with Edvard Grieg (1843–1907) and Jean Sibelius (1865–1957) writing music that is frequently associated with a national cultural identity expressed in music through recourse to traditional melody and rhythm. Expressing national identity through music certainly 'lay in the air'. In the present case, given the fact that Hennessy with his Opp. 12 and 14 had merely written two pieces of an Irish character – his next was to be Op. 28 four years later – it is too early yet to speak of national or cultural identity.

Notwithstanding the fact that there are not very many compositions with an original theme and variations in a folksong style, original themes with variations are nothing new in European classical and Romantic music. Franz Schubert published his eight *Variationen über ein Original-Thema*, Op. 35, in 1824; Hennessy's idol Robert Schumann wrote *Thema Es-dur mit Variationen*, better known as *Variations in E flat on an Original Theme*, WoO 24 (1854, the *'Geistervariationen'*). Likewise, Johannes Brahms' Op. 27 No. 1 (1857) is a similar work (a theme with eleven variations). Closer to Hennessy's time, Edward Elgar's *Enigma Variations* were originally called *Variations on an Original Theme*, Op. 36 (1899). There is no doubt that Hennessy was aware of these.

The theme of Hennessy's *Variations*, Op. 12 (see Ex. 4.1) is fully laid out in a four-part harmonic piano setting, eight bars long, with an upbeat, in A major. At first hearing, a non-expert in Irish traditional music would undoubtedly take the Irish inspiration for granted: the melodic downward movement at the beginning, the rough outline of the melodic line, the 'breathing space' in bar 4, the ending of phrases on repeated pitches, are typical elements of numerous pieces in the Irish traditional repertoire. The rather unusual length of the theme also reminds of variations on a folk song in which the theme is quoted once in its entirety.

On closer examination, however, this no longer quite holds true. Though rhythmically in form of a polka, a polka would be played considerably faster than the *Andante* marked here. The semiquaver leap C–E in the middle of bar 1 would rather move by step (C–D–E) in a traditional tune. And the allusions to a 'Scotch snap' in the second half of the theme (indicated by the bound-over notes towards the middle of bars 5, 6, and 7) rather remind of Scottish than of Irish music[11] – Hennessy's use of the 'Scotch snap' will be discussed in more detail in Chapter 8.

Ex. 4.1: *Variations sur un thème original dans le style irlandais*, Op. 12, bars 1–8 (theme) (from a 1929 reprint)

The theme is followed by eight short variations in quite different styles – the whole piece, including the theme, would not last more than about seven minutes. The variations in a medium tempo would not exceed 16 or 18 bars, only surpassed by the faster movements. The first variation is a *Maestoso* in A minor, played throughout in regular, full chords in quavers over a 2/4 bar structure. The second, again in 2/4, now with two-part crotchets in the bass and a light, dance-like movement in the right hand forming an attractive contrast to the B minor harmony (Ex. 4.2).

---

[11] For this brief analysis I gratefully acknowledge the advice of Irish traditional music expert Dr Adrian Scahill of Maynooth University.

Ex. 4.2: *Variations*, Op. 12, beginning of 2nd variation

Without a final chord, this leads directly into variation no. 3, a two-part canon in G major, in which the first part of the theme, mainly written in major thirds, is very well recognisable. No. 4 (*Vivacissimo*) interprets the theme in a lively C major; the 3/4 time structure is characterised by a chordal emphasis on the second beat. In no. 5 (*Vivace*, E major), the theme is rather alluded to, both rhythmically and melodically, compared to the more straightforward variations 3 and 4. No. 6 is very short (ten bars, no repetition), to be played *con tenerezza*. Notated in A major, the many naturals and flat signs that occur during bars 6 to 8 make the tonality overall quite ambiguous. Variation no. 7 (*Moderato*, A major) continues the strain of modulation, hiding the theme behind series of scales in quavers that have a baroque flavour.

This then prepares the way for the eighth and last variation, marked 'Fughetta' (*Allegro ma non troppo*), a two-part fugue, again in A major. The original theme is barely noticeable, and even the initial *fugato* increasingly dissolves into modulating intervals in the right hand accompanied by ascending scales in the left, ending in a broadly Romantic suspension sequence on the tonic (Ex. 4.3).

Ex. 4.3: *Variations*, Op. 12, ending of var. 8

The performance of the piece by Carrie Townshend at the recital in London's Bechstein Hall, in which she shared the platform for a few pieces with the prominent Italian violinist Achille Simonetti (1857–1928), was welcomed in *The Times* of the following day for her choice of pieces …

> […] that are fairly unfamiliar, such as a gigue in B flat major by Haessler, Raff's 'Rigaudon,' and Tausig's transcription of Strauss's 'Nachtfalter' waltz, in which last she obtained her greatest success. In two numbers of her programme the Irish pianist showed her patriotism, and if it cannot be said that her rather artless assemblage of Irish airs added much to the musical interest of the concert, the variations by Mr. Swan Hennessy 'in the Irish style' were decidedly successful; the theme and many of the variations are unmistakably Irish in character, whether the former be an actual traditional tune or not, and all are put together in a musicianly and effective way.[12]

The *Daily Telegraph* agreed with this assessment, describing Hennessy's variations as 'well-wrought and effective'.[13] Unfortunately, this remained the only documented performance of the piece until the mid-1930s, when it was heard twice in Paris.

Sonate en fa (style irlandais), Op. 14 (1902–04) for violin and piano

Contemporary British newspapers reveal a number of violin and piano recitals by Achille Simonetti and Carrie Townshend from the mid 1890s. The Turin-born musician had been living in London since 1891 and was best known as a chamber musician, especially as a member of the first London Trio (1901–12). After this period, he taught the violin at the Royal Irish Academy of Music, Dublin, from 1912 to 1919. Perhaps it is no exaggeration to say that a certain interest in Ireland was fuelled by musicians such as Carrie Townshend and Swan Hennessy.

This was the personal constellation that led to the composition of Hennessy's second work in an Irish style, the *Sonate en fa (style irlandais)*, Op. 14, for violin and piano. Again, the exact date of composition is not quite clear. The manuscript, preserved in the Bavarian State Library, Munich, is not dated, but the print is: it was originally published in London with Schott & Co. in 1904; and since it most certainly was written after his Op. 12, it is safe to say it was written 'between 1902 and 1904'. It may even be subsumed that Hennessy began work on it after the first performance of his Op. 12 in early 1903. In his own work-list, Hennessy clearly dates it to 1904, but some scepticism is appropriate with regard to this list. What the manuscript in Munich does reveal is that by now Hennessy lived in Paris: the cover page gives his address – which is why I tentatively date his move to Paris to 1903.

The exact title of the piece seemed to be undecided for a while. On the first page of the score, the work's title is '1re. Sonate' ('Sonata No. 1' in English) – the Irish-style connotation is on the cover page only.

---

[12] *The Times*, 3 February 1903.
[13] *The Daily Telegraph*, 3 February 1903.

The work was probably written with Achille Simonetti in mind; the dedication reads 'à son ami A. Simonetti', and they also gave its first performance together. Compared to the *Berceuse*, Op. 13 for the same instrumentation, the present work is a much more elaborate and ambitious piece. It is written in three movements, lasting about 17 minutes in performance.

As the title says, the work is written mainly in F major and stands in classical sonata form. The first movement (*Allegro, ma non troppo*) commences without introduction with the first theme of the exposition, the core of which is already contained in the first bar of the violin (Ex. 4.4).

Ex. 4.4: Violin Sonata Op. 14, 1st movt, bars 1–4

With twice accentuated piano chords, this quickly brings the violin to high registers (bars 15–17). A secondary theme (from bar 33) has a strong Irish flavour, deriving from intervals characteristic to Irish traditional music. This theme is the pivotal one in the whole work, occurring in various guises in all three movements. Here, it comes in an unusual tonality, D major, so to speak the parallel major to the (more normal) relative minor (although the seventh step, C sharp, is missing from the theme, occurring in the piano only) (Ex. 4.5). The theme itself begins an octave higher than the first theme and is almost an inversion of it.

Ex. 4.5: Violin Sonata Op. 14, 1st movt, bars 33–40

(contd)

There is a good deal of attractive thematic interaction between the two instruments without becoming all too difficult for the performers from a technical point of view.

The second movement (*Vivace capriccioso*) functions as a scherzo, beginning in A major and 3/8 time and the theme beginning in the piano. This movement contains a trio section in A minor (from bar 63, marked *Molto meno mosso*) in a much calmer mood where the violin rather cautiously imitates an Irish jig dance accompanied by single piano chords played on the first beat only. This jig theme (naturally) has a strong Irish connotation, including the typical ending of a phrase on repeated pitches, even though the first of those endings on G (bars 69/70) is not typical, the next one on A (bars 77–8), however, is (Ex. 4.6).

Ex. 4.6: Violin Sonata Op. 14, 2nd movt, bars 63–86

Overall, the violin has a more modest role in this movement, with less opportunities to shine in technical terms, its playing (except in the trio) being confined to thematic cells with short-sounding notes in contrast to legato playing and pauses.

The third movement is the most varied one of the sonata. It initially returns to F major and begins with a slow section featuring a lyrical violin melody accompanied by chords in quavers that modulate in a very Romantic manner betraying Hennessy's German education. From bar 36, this makes room for an extended *allegro*. Though notated in 2/4 time, this in fact resembles an Irish jig with the violin (or shall we interpret it as a fiddle?) playing in semiquaver triplets. The theme is based on the secondary theme of the first movement (Ex. 4.7). It is being taken up in the piano (bar 40ff.), and in the following it undergoes a number of small variants, with fragments thrown back and forth between violin and piano.

Ex. 4.7: Violin Sonata Op. 14, 3rd movt, bars 36–44

There follows a rhythmically accentuated intermezzo (marked *Sostenuto*), a reprise of the jig, a coda reminding of the original secondary theme of the first movement, and a brief *presto* finale.

All in all, it cannot be denied that in his Violin Sonata, Op. 14 Hennessy caught the spirit of Irish traditional music in the form of some characteristic melodic and rhythmic traits. He proves what has been denied by generations of Irish composers and musicologists, namely that Irish traditional music is very well suited for thematic treatment and development,[14] and in doing so his German educational background has certainly been beneficial. Formally and harmonically he is still deeply rooted in

---

[14] '… the essentially linear quality of traditional Irish music is not easily integrated into music that is essentially harmonic.'; Seóirse Bodley: 'Ireland, §I, 2: Art music', in: *The New Grove Dictionary of Music and Musicians* (London: Macmillan, 1980), vol. 9, p. 316; '[…] Stanford's music does exemplify a crucial miscalculation nevertheless, and that is the assumption that the traditional airs themselves (or edited versions thereof) could be absorbed into art music as the basis of an authentic *Irish* style.'; White, *Keeper's Recital*, p. 106 (White's emphasis).

German Romanticism; it is quite obvious that he has not yet come into any closer contact with music in Paris. The work may have been written in London and been influenced by music he has heard there.

The sonata was premiered by the dedicatee, Achille Simonetti, together with Swan Hennessy, at a semi-public soirée in Cannes at the Cote d'Azur on 14 January 1905. The Paris premiere took place at the Palais des Beaux Arts, 7 May 1907, by Auguste Delacroix and a pianist named de Bruyne. This performance was reviewed in *Le Monde musical*, the reviewer (abbreviated as 'M.') pointing out influences like Grieg for the first movement and Mendelssohn for the beginning of the third, calls the second movement 'very picturesque' and ends his review with the words 'The work is clear, not without quality, and the performance was good'.[15]

For a 1914 Paris performance,[16] Hennessy – whose style had changed considerably by then – called the sonata *'une œuvre de jeunesse'* – despite the fact that he had been 36 or 37 years of age when he wrote it. But by calling it a 'youthful work' in Paris in 1914, he did acknowledge that the style was now somewhat antiquated and (perhaps) that it might as well have originated in his early years.

When the name of Swan Hennessy had finally reached Ireland in the early 1920s, the piece was included in a Gaelic League concert at the Cork Opera House, performed by Liam O'Brady (violin) and Carl Hardebeck (piano). Before the concert, one of Hennessy's closest contacts in Cork, Denis Breen (also known as Donnchadh Ua Braoin), introduced the work to the readers of the *Cork Examiner*. Whereas the French music critic in 1907 found stylistic parallels in the 19th century, Breen in 1922 wrote:

> The Sonata in F to be played next Sunday is thoroughly modern music, and yet it differs characteristically from any modern music I am acquainted with.

It is likely that such a statement is *not* representative for the status of Irish music criticism, as much as one may be inclined to think. It rather speaks for the musical background of Breen (see Chapter 8 for more details). In fact, the following sentence in his article is so full of national prejudices and clichés that it does not speak favourably for him either:

> It has neither the violence of the German nor the over-affected restraint of the French school. Still less has it the melodramatic declamation of the Italian music of to-day.

Yet, as an Irishman, Breen's assessment of the Irishness of the piece is remarkable. He wrote:

---

[15] *'L'œuvre est nette, non sans qualité, et l'exécution fut bonne.'*; *Le Monde musical*, 30 May 1907, quoted from Hennessy's first volume of press books.

[16] At the Salle Gaveau, 21 March 1914, played by Alcibiade Anemoyanni (violin) and one Mme Lavello-Stiévenard (piano); *Le Guide du concert*, 21 March 1914, and *La Critique musicale*, 30 March 1914.

Many passages are so strongly reminiscent of Gaelic scales that the least musical cannot fail to perceive where they had their origin. The second movement (vivace capriccioso) is the most original and interesting. It consists of two portions, the first having a fairy-like passage whose rhythm, repeated again and again with subtle and charming changes of key and tune, gives a perfect unity to the whole movement. A minor theme, slower in time, but not less charming, thoroughly Gaelic in character and yet quite unlike any other music, links the two major portions. The final movement is preceded by an andante which is the most perfectly beautiful, and yet the most emotional passage in the whole work. This short passage, whose liquid beauty overpowers and fills the soul like the visions of a delightful dream, is in itself sufficient to give its composer a high rank. It introduces what is the most characteristically Gaelic in type, but yet the least satisfactory portion of the Sonata. A rapid jig-like theme, succeeded by a suave and charming duet between two passages, given alternately to the violin and the piano, leads again to the beautiful andante, this time shortened and modified in other ways. The jig theme again returns, it also modifies itself, and with some changes of time and some musical devices of augmentation and imitation concludes the Sonata with an effective and characteristic Gaelic cadence. The last movement is lacking in the feeling of unity and logical completeness of the other two; the themes do not seem to hang together so well, and the whole movement has neither the impressiveness of the earlier portions nor the sense of completeness of the Rondo of Mozart or Beethoven. But the Sonata is of value to us in Ireland not only for its great intrinsic beauty, but as an example of what use an Irish composer can make of the materials that exists in such quantity ready to his hand.[17]

It shall not be withheld that French critics did not only remark about the somewhat outdated style. There were, in fact, several positive critical statements. After the 1914 performance, *La Critique musical* called it (obviously having seen Hennessy's self-assessment in *Le Guide du concert*) 'a work of youth, of serious and studious youth, where one already finds many traits of an amiable and spirited imagination'.[18] After a 1930 performance in Paris, Tristan Klingsor described it as a 'simple and touching work, by a composer who does not fit into any formula',[19] and for Charles Dyke it was 'well written and not lacking in freshness or charm'.[20]

Aus dem Kinderleben. 6 kleine Tonbilder, Op. 19 (1904) for piano

The January 1905 event in Cannes when the Violin Sonata, Op. 14 received its first performance was a two-day event, and the preceding evening saw another first performance by Hennessy, of a piano work entitled *Aus dem Kinderleben*. Written in 1904, the work was published in 1905 with Breitkopf & Härtel in Leipzig, with French and

---

[17] All three quotes in the *Cork Examiner*, 22 April 1922.
[18] *'une œuvre de jeunesse, de jeunesse sérieuse et studieuse, où l'on trouve déjà maintes poussées vers une aimable et spirituelle fantaisie.'*; 'L. S.' in *La Critique musicale*, 30 March 1914. Hennessy had previously introduced the work briefly in *Le Guide du concert*, 21 March 1914.
[19] *'œuvre simple et touchante, d'un auteur qui ne s'embarrassait pas de formules'*; Tristan Klingsor in *La Semaine à Paris*, 14 March 1930.
[20] *'bien écrite, et qui ne manque ni de fraîcheur ni de charme'*; Charles Dyke in *Le Courrier musical*, 15 March 1930.

English subtitles to the work and its six constituting parts. The opus number suggests that probably other works with the opus numbers 15 to 18 were discarded or withdrawn, because these numbers came to be assigned to works that were evidently written later. Thus, *Aus dem Kinderleben* (or *Scènes d'enfances / Scenes from Child Life*) is the next surviving work after the Violin Sonata. Though the work has probably been written in Paris, it may be interpreted as an attempt to revive his musical connections to Germany. Other works from this period (see below) point in the same direction – despite his residence in France, he was aware of the importance of the German market in music, and his proficiency in the German language was an advantage in pursuing his interests.

The six pieces in the collection are
1. *Puppenwiegenlied / Berceuse de la poupée / The Doll's Cradle Song*
2. *Puppentanz / Danse de la poupée / The Doll's Dance*
3. *Im Wald / Dans les bois / In the Wood*
4. *Erster Walzer / Premier valse / The First Waltz*
5. *Schläfriges Kind / Envie de dormir / The Sleepy Child*
6. *Auf Wiedersehen! / Au revoir / Goodbye*

Without doubt, Hennessy was aware of German Romantic music with similar titles and intentions, most notably Schumann's *Kinderszenen*, Op. 15 (1838) and Mendelssohn's *Sechs Kinderstücke*, Op. 72 (1842). The circumstances of the Cannes performance reveal that it is indeed Mendelssohn's collection that served as model. The key is contained in a review of the event in the *New York Herald* of 14 January 1905. This begins as follows:

> Some exceptionally fine and well-interpreted music was heard last evening at Mrs. Benecke's reception at the Villa Florence, the hostess (a cousin of Mendelssohn) having gathered together a notable group of first-rate tone-artists.

Mendelssohn experts will recognise the name Benecke. One of Felix Mendelssohn's daughters, Marie (1839–1897), was married to a Victor Benecke and lived in London. On a visit to London in 1842, Mendelssohn composed his *Kinderstücke* inspired by the playing of the Benecke children. Of course, the Cannes hostess cannot have been a cousin of the composer; she would be far too old by 1905. More likely she was a niece or a cousin of a niece. One Benecke name that occurs around the time with a connection to Cannes is Amy M. Benecke who can be traced as author of the guidebook *Cannes and its Surroundings* (London: George Allen & Sons, 1908). What exactly her relationship to Mendelssohn was, is difficult to reconstruct – perhaps she was indeed one of the Benecke children for whom the *Kinderstücke* were written. Hennessy must have been aware of the family connection and may indeed have written the piece especially for the event and hostess in Cannes as a friendly nod to her famous forebear (the print does not contain a dedication, though, and the manuscript appears to be lost).

After a sentence about Achille Simonetti, it is Swan Hennessy who is highlighted as one of the 'first-rate tone-artists' (no doubt because both the composer and the journalist were Americans). The review also characterises Hennessy's composition and what its effect on the audience was like:

> Another was the pianist, Mr. Swan Hennessy, who is on his first visit to Cannes. He and Signor Simonetti together interpreted a sonata of César Franck's and subsequently alone he made the piano tell a series of exquisite stories about children that were picturesque to the last degree.
>
> They are of Mr. Swan-Hennessy's own composition and are together called 'Scènes d'Enfance,' the individual titles being: 'Berceuse de la Poupée,' 'Danse de la Poupée,' 'Dans les Bois,' 'Première Valse,' 'Envie de Dormir,' 'Au Revoir.'
>
> 'It was a marvellous production,' said one who was telling of the conception, composition and execution of the series. 'You could shut your eyes and yet see those kids doing exactly in accordance with the titles. I do not know when I have heard anything to compare with it.'[21]

Apart from Hennessy's own composition, this event is the first documented occasion of Hennessy appearing as a pianist in other composers' works, here the well-known Violin Sonata (1886) by César Franck.

Like the Mendelssohn model, Hennessy's *Aus dem Kinderleben*, Op. 19 consists of six short pieces. But this is the only formal parallel. The *Doll's Cradle Song* is an *allegretto* in A flat major (though with a closing F minor seventh chord), slightly fast, perhaps, for a cradle song, but the delightfully swinging melody suits nevertheless. The following *Doll's Dance* (*Andantino*) with the marked up- and downward movement of the *pizzicato* melody in F major fully lives up to its title, with the modulatory middle section fitting in just right. *In the Wood* (again in F major, *Vivace ma non troppo*) is certainly a happy outing in the woods that is not marred by some harmonic frictions in the middle *andante* section (Ex. 4.8).

Ex. 4.8: *Aus dem Kinderleben*, Op. 19 No. 3 'In the Woods', bars 17–28

---

[21] 'First-rate Music Heard at Cannes. / Notable Tone-Artists Play at Reception Given by Mrs. Benecke. / Mr. Swan Hennessy's Success'; *New York Herald*, 14 January 1905, quoted from Hennessy's press books, vol. 1.

No. 4, *The First Waltz* – the third in a row that stands in F major – , might be a beginner's piece on the piano were it not for the somewhat large intervals in the left hand. The fifth, *The Sleepy Child*, is a *largo* setting of a pleasant tune in C major with some forays into A minor and a penchant for introducing the pitch of D sharp as both a melodic element and, after slowing down step-by-step, a suspension just before the final tonic, no doubt resembling an increasingly dreamy state (Ex. 4.9).

Ex. 4.9: *Aus dem Kinderleben*, Op. 19 No. 5 'The Sleepy Child', bars 23–32

The final *Goodbye* returns thematically to the first piece in the set, despite its F major tonality. It is a calm piece marked *lento cantabile*, conveying a positive and peaceful message, hoping for happy returns.

Hennessy's little collection was favourably reviewed in a German piano teacher journal:

> These little piano pieces seem like delicate improvisations during twilight hours. There is a fine poetic touch on each of these miniature images. They are not, however, made for children's hands; the wide span in the piano part alone would be an obstacle. [...] it should therefore only be given to pupils with normally developed hands. They will rejoice in these things, and when they are technically equipped for the intermediate level, they will also easily be able to embrace these images of child life.[22]

The reviewer also pointed out the simple harmony of *The Doll's Cradle Song* as a pedagogically suited piece for the learner on the piano, the humorous expression of the *Doll's Dance* which would demand a somewhat crude emphasis, the rhythmical

---

[22] '*Wie zarte Improvisationen einer Dämmerstunde muten diese kleinen Klavierstücke an. Es liegt ein feiner poetischer Hauch über den einzelnen Miniaturbildchen. Für Kinderhände sind sie nicht geschaffen, der weitgriffige Klaviersatz würde schon allein ein Hindernis sein. [...] man gebe es also nur Schülern mit normal entwickelten Händen. Sie werden an den Sachen ihre Freude haben und, wenn sie technisch für die Mittelstufe gefördert sind, sich auch inhaltlich die Bilder aus dem Kinderleben unschwer zu eigen machen.*'; M. J. Rehbein in *Der Klavier-Lehrer* 29, 1906, p. 187.

subtleties of *The Sleepy Child*, and the 'tender harmonic colour' (*'zarte Klangfarbe'*) of *Goodbye*. Another positive comment in a German journal is contained in a review by Hugo Rasch of several recent Hennessy works that appeared in a 1911 issue of the *Allgemeine Musikzeitung*:

> Compositions such as the above-mentioned Op. 19 are so deeply felt in their modest simplicity that one is instinctively inclined to exclaim: how sweet, how heartfelt! These are indeed the most accurate words to describe his music.[23]

* * *

During 1905 and 1906 Hennessy was very productive. But he seems undecided whether he is more inclined towards contemporary German or French music, with some works leaning more in the first direction and others in the latter. His indecision seems sometimes to have had advantages in his perception by critics as it appears to have been a distinguishing element.

Deux Études (en ut mineur) pour la main gauche seul, Op. 15 (1905) for piano

A work combining two studies for the left hand, the *Deux Études (en ut mineur) pour la main gauche seul*, Op. 15 (written in 1905 and published by Hamelle in 1906) attracted the attention of Lucien Chevaillier, even though this was as late as 1911. Many years later (in 1929), Chevaillier was to conduct the major interview with Hennessy for *Le Guide du concert* that is such a pivotal resource about Hennessy, but here, writing for *La Revue musicale*, he seems to have come across his name for the first time.

In his review he covered, besides the Hennessy, the *Prélude d'un ballet* by Roger Ducasse, a cello concerto by Joseph Jongen, and *Ma mère l'oye* by Maurice Ravel. After heavy criticism of Ravel, the author continues:

> What joy, after this incursion into the unhealthy realm of the near-by, what a joy to find oneself on familiar, settled, and illuminated ground, first with the two deft studies for the left hand by Swan Hennessy, an Irish composer of whom we can only gain by making his acquaintance, and especially with Joseph Jongen's cello concerto, who I hope is no stranger to the Parisian public.[24]

Another review appeared also with a considerable delay after the work's publication, in an issue of the *Allgemeine Musikzeitung* of April 1913:

---

[23] '*Kompositionen wie das erwähnte op. 19 sind in ihrer schlichten Einfachheit so tief empfunden, daß man unwillkürlich ausrufen möchte: wie lieb, wie innig! Das sind in der Tat die treffendsten Merkworte für seine Musik.*'; *Allgemeine Musikzeitung* 28:13, 31 March 1911, p- 376.

[24] '*Quelle joie, après cette incursion dans le domaine malsain de l'à-peu-près, quelle joie de se retrouver dans un pays dénommé, situé, éclairé, d'abord avec les deux adroites études pour la main gauche de Swan Hennessy, un compositeur irlandais dont on ne peut que gagner à faire la connaissance, et surtout avec le concerto de violoncelle de Joseph Jongen, qui lui, je l'espère, n'est pas un inconnu auprès du public parisien.*'; *La Revue musicale* 11:1, 1 January 1911, p. 18.

These two works by Hennessy, which date further back in time, already show his desire to go his own way and also, incidentally, a highly respectable compositional technique and the absolute ability to write gratefully and effectively for the piano. *The two studies for the left hand are likely to be extremely useful as exercise material*, as well as being valuable music in their own right.[25]

It is not known whether there was a specific reason (or performer) why Hennessy wrote these interesting studies for the left hand. Often such works were written for pianists with temporary handicaps in the right hand, but in this case, they seem to have been written as technical studies (with very musical ambitions) to strengthen the often less developed left hand.

Petit album, Op. 18 (1905) for piano

The *Petit album*, Op. 18, also originated in 1905, but was published only in 1907 with Schott & Co. in London. As with *Aus dem Kinderleben*, the titles of the seven constituting pieces in this album have been given titles in German, French, and English, the English ones being 1. *On the Road*; 2. *The Inn*; 3. *Passing Children*; 4. *From Old Times* (a. *Fughetta*, b. *Menuet*); 5. *Balletgirl on the Stage*; 6. *Sonatina*; 7. *Scherzetto* – all very straightforward, fresh, and often humorous (in particular, *The Inn*) and descriptive pieces. Their collection seems rather eclectic, in particular with the inclusion of the more abstract *Sonatina* and *Scherzetto*, which are, in fact, the longest works in the album and might well have appeared separately.

Stylistically, the first pieces would fit into a late-Romantic German tradition, the most contemporary or 'French' piece would be the *Balletgirl on the Stage*. He even treads on neo-baroque grounds in the two parts of *From Old Times* as well as in the *Sonatina* and the *Scherzetto*, which reminded the German critic Karl Thiessen of Max Reger:

> There are two souls dwelling in the breast of this collection of medium difficulty that is well suited for the more mature student. For, while in pieces like 'On the Road' and the 'Passing Children' it reminds of the sensual Romanticism of our Jensen, makes a bow to the galant era in the somewhat artificial 'Fughetta', the delicate 'Menuet', and the rather modern touch of the 'Balletgirl on the Stage', it then completely moves over into the camp of the Regerians with the one-movement 'Sonatina' and 'Scherzetto' with their baroque melody and harmony.[26]

---

[25] '*Diese beiden, in ihrer Entstehungszeit weiter zurückliegenden Arbeiten Hennessys zeigen schon den Willen, eigene Pfade zu wandeln, und nebenbei eine höchst respektable Satztechnik und die absolute Fähigkeit, dankbar und klangwirksam für das Klavier zu schreiben. Die beiden Etüden für die linke Hand dürften sich als Übungsmaterial äußerst nützlich erweisen, ganz abgesehen davon, daß sie wertvolle Musik an sich darstellen.*'; *Allgemeine Musikzeitung* 40:17, 25 April 1913, p. 610, written by Hugo Rasch, with Rasch's emphasis.

[26] '*Der mittelschweren, für reifere Schüler gut verwendbaren Sammlung wohnen zwei Seelen in der Brust: während es nämlich in Stücken wie der hübschen 'Fussreise', der Wirtshausszene und in den 'vorüberziehenden Kindern' an die sinnige Romantik unseres Jensen gemahnt, dagegen in der etwas gekünstelten 'Fughette', dem zierlichen 'Menuett' und der schon ziemlich modern angehauchten 'Tänzerin auf der Bühne' dem galanten*

A 1911 review by Louis Vuillemin in *Comoedia* provides a sympathetic French perspective on the collection:

> Imagine an *Album* projected by Schumann and started by Mendelssohn! It seems obvious that, in principle, this album is intended for children. However, some of its pages are not entirely easy to perform. Others, on the contrary, remain accessible to the majority. In between there is a nice piece like *The Inn*, a kind of picturesque and animated scene that is very German; *Passing Children* and *From Old Times*, the latter in form of a three-part *Fughetta* and a pretty *Menuet*; *Balletgirl on the Stage*, a waltz of amusing distinction; a well-written Sonatina, and a Scherzetto, where both hands fraternise in a work that only good pianists should undertake – this is what the *Album* of Mr. Swan Hennessy is made of. He is a perfect musician, rich in at the same time seductive themes and an appreciable virtuosity in his writing.[27]

Praeludium & Fuga, Op. 16 (1906) for piano

In this piece, written in 1906, Hennessy is again inspired by German baroque music, and although a reviewer in the *Monthly Musical Record* suggested the model of Bach, it is rather the spirit of Reger that would have been at work here. The piece was published in the year of its composition by Hamelle in Paris, probably simultaneously with the left-hand *Deux Études*, Op. 15. The (unnamed) English critic had the following to say about the work:

> ANY composer following Bach's own particular lines is little more than an imitator. Klengel tried and failed; Beethoven, on the other hand, in his Op. 110 went his own way, and succeeded. In the *Præludium* and *Fuga* under notice we find traces of Bach influence; while the devices of augmentation, retrogressive movement, and one or two strettos, recall the past; yet the music, as a whole, is modern. We perceive that already in the *Prelude*. The form is free. The arpeggio chords soon give place to a short, expressive *Andantino*, and just before their return the theme of the *Fugue* is heralded. Apart, however, from form, the modulations themselves are up-to-date. The *Fugue* is clever and interesting, and the subject, being short, is easily retained in the memory. Moreover, in one or other shape it is never

---

Zeitalter eine Verbeugung macht, schwenkt es in der einsätzigen 'Sonatine' und dem 'Scherzetto' mit ihrer durchweg barocken Melodik und Harmonik vollständig in das Lager der Regerianer hinüber.'; Signale für die musikalische Welt 71:38, 17 Sep. 1913, p. 1364. 'Jensen' is Adolf Jensen (1837–1879).

[27] 'On dirait un Album *projeté par Schumann et commencé par Mendelssohn! Il apparaît comme évident qu'en principe, cet album est destiné à l'enfance. Cependant, certaines de ses pages ne sont pas exemptes de difficultés d'exécution. D'autres, au contraire, demeurent accessibles aux plus menues phalanges. En route, joli morceau,* L'Auberge, *sorte de scène pittoresquement animée et très allemande,* Les Enfants qui passent, Aux temps passés *— cette pièce en forme de* fuguette *a trois parties —* un gentil Menuet, Danseuse sur la scène, *valse d'une amusante distinction, une* Sonatine, *bien écrite,* Scherzetto, *où les deux mains fraternisent en un travail que seuls de bons pianistes pourront entreprendre, composent l'*Album *de M. Swan Hennessy. Il est d'un très parfait musicien, riche à la fois et de thèmes séduisants et d'une virtuosité de plume appréciable.'*; *Comoedia*, 20 July 1911, p. 2.

out of hearing. Much use is made of a little demisemiquaver figure derived from the countersubject, and this adds to the life of the music.[28]

Mazurka et Polonaise, Op. 17 (1906) for piano

The *Mazurka et Polonaise* were written as an expression of love for Hennessy's Polish partner (and later wife) Claire Przybyszewska to whom they are dedicated, two movements of Polish traditional dances with long-established counterparts in art music. The work was published at Hennessy's own expense with Augener & Co. of London in 1906. It does not seem to have been publicly performed, and no review appeared of its publication.

The *Mazurka* is a delightful, gentle piece in B major, rhythmically intricate; the *Polonaise* a technically considerably more demanding piece in E flat major.

Au bord de la forêt, Op. 21 (1906) for piano

Like the *Mazurka et Polonaise*, *Au bord de la forêt*, Op. 21 is dedicated to 'Mademoiselle Claire Przybyszewska'. Written in 1906, it was his first publication with Demets in Paris and appeared in 1907 in a large folio edition. It also shared the fate of the former work in that it does not seem to have been publicly performed and received no review.

Au bord de la forêt is a descriptive piece in one movement in free rhapsodic form with several distinct parts. According to a comment in his own list of works, it was written immediately after returning from a walk in the woods. It begins with a cornet motif, repeated in *pianissimo* (resembling a greater distance). Since Hennessy in later works used the same allusion with an explanatory note in the score we can safely interpret this as a cornet signal by a group of boy scouts spending their leisure at the edge of a forest. This motif forms the basis of a canon at the fifth in slow tempo for bars 5–26. The ending of the canon sounds more contemporary French compared to earlier works, with a descending bass line under the minor third interval of B♭–D which, though notated without a key signature, ends on a nice gloomy cadence of G minor sixth followed by D minor. A two-part cornet signal follows in quick tempo for a mere eight bars, before the canon reappears in a variation (bars 35–62). Another brief interlude with a *misterioso* movement in the lower registers of the keyboard ends on another cornet motif (Ex. 4.10).

---

[28] *The Monthly Musical Record*, 1 October 1910, p. 226.

Ex. 4.10: *Au bord de la forêt*, Op. 21, bars 63–70

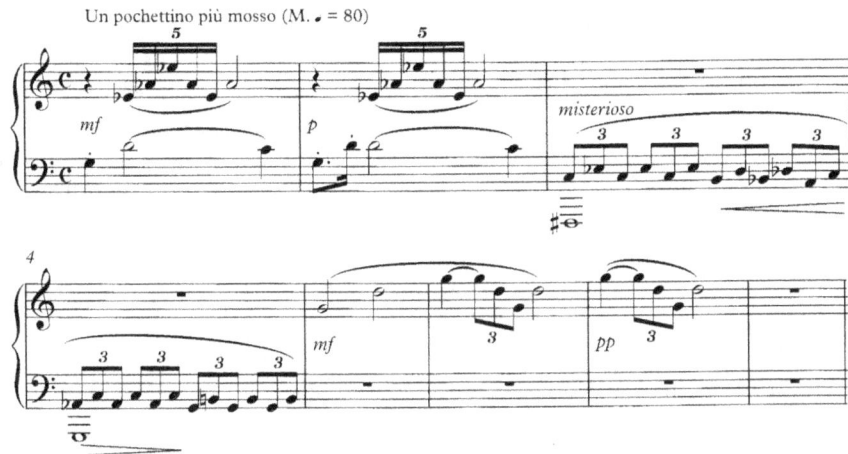

In a very pretty passage Hennessy then imitates the quick and interrupted movement of a squirrel (*'Petit écureuil'*), with quick up-and-down scales interrupted by rests (bars 71–86). For the rest of the piece the different elements reappear in various forms, ending on a high trill that is probably meant to resemble a bird call.

Hennessy uses numerous dissonances in scales and chords, but always 'with a purpose' that serves his programmatic ideas. In this, he is still close to the ideas of his teacher Percy Goetschius, although the latter would most certainly have complained about the virtual absence of traditional functional harmony. The effects are quite attractive, never overdone, never too long or outworn. As absolute music, it would be quite modern.

Eaux fortes, Op. 24 (1906) for piano

Eaux fortes is a collection of three pieces (1. *Sérénade espagnole*; 2. *Bergérie*; 3. *Petite mazurka*), written in 1906 and published with Demets in 1908. The title is the French term for 'etchings', and so the pieces may be interpreted as somewhat crude images of a Spanish musical evening scene and a peaceful sheepfold in the countryside, followed by the sketch of a mazurka.

There are no dedications in the published print, but the manuscript reveals dedications to (in this order) Gabrielle Pineau, Auguste Adam, and (again) Claire Przybyszewska. Although not printed, these were probably added just before publication in 1908. Gabrielle Pineau and Auguste Adam were probably personal friends of Hennessy. Pineau operated a private music school in Paris which occasionally organised public recitals of its pupils, and Adam may have been her husband. The performance records of Hennessy's works show several violin/piano recitals between 1908 and 1922 at which Hennessy accompanied a violinist called Ida Adam-Pineau who may have been a daughter of this couple (for instance, they performed the Violin Sonata, Op. 14, several times).

The *Sérénade espagnole* is Hennessy's first exercise in a Spanish idiom (with a few more to come), a sprightly *allegretto* in D major, syncopated rhythms and a 'Spanish' theme that ends on the parallel minor. *Bergérie*, an *andantino* in 2/4 time marked *'simple, enfantin'*, appears like a baroque minuet with a Romantic melody (like Schumann inspired by Bach) with some unusual modulations, particularly towards the end. The *Petite mazurka* (3/8 time, *moderato*) benefits from its rhythmic interest, with most of the motivic work in the right hand, that Hennessy enhances with triplets. The beginning and end is in C major while an extended and repeated part in the middle changes to the subdominant F major, although numerous sharps and flats throughout relativise this somewhat.

Eaux fortes received its two earliest performances by the English pianist and composer Herbert Fryer (1877–1957), then professor of piano at the Royal Academy of Music in London, the first on 5 March 1910 at the Aeolian Hall, London, the second a week later, 12 March, at the Salle Pleyel, Paris. There is no review of the Paris performance, but the London critics were not totally convinced. *The Times* called it 'merely mildly dull'[29] and for *The Morning Post* it was 'an incongruous grafting of unnatural modern harmonies upon the natural idiom of dance music'. Only the *Daily Telegraph* had a more constructive comment to offer:

> An unfamiliar name figured in the programme in that of Swan Hennessy, whose 'Eaux Fortes,' consisting of three pleasantly-written little pieces, betokened here and there the influence of Debussy.[30]

In France, a 1911 issue of *Comoedia* wrote about the published piece that these 'etchings' 'will delight the pianists as long as they are able to properly play this music, which is not at all preposterous, but rather seriously "written"'.[31]

Étude, Op. 25 (1906) for piano

It seems like, around 1906, Hennessy increasingly noticed that he cannot ignore the trends in contemporary music away from diatonic harmony and traditional forms. A number of the aforementioned examples went into this direction. And it actually fell on fruitful ground with Hennessy who has had a tendency to non-conformist and humorous expression from his earliest publications. Descriptive and programmatic music also gave him many opportunities to experiment with modern techniques as will be seen in many of his piano works in the future.

---

[29] *The Times*, 5 March 1910, p. 14.
[30] *Daily Telegraph*, 6 March 1910.
[31] *'Les* Eaux Fortes […] *feront la joie des pianistes à condition qu'ils soient en posture d'exécuter convenablement ces musiques, nullement abracadabrantes, mais très sérieusement "écrites".'*; *Comoedia*, 1 June 1911, p. 2.

The *Étude*, Op. 25, written in 1906 and published with Demets in 1908, is an experiment in form without any extra-musical programme. It is a polyrhythmic (or better: polymetric) composition that not only uses different metres within the piece (which would not be unusual) but between the left and right hand also so that bar lines are not at the same place. This becomes visible as soon as the right hand commences: on top of left-hand scale work in 5/8 the right hand begins in 2/4 time. The 'study' aspect of the work, therefore, is that of an exercise in counting and accentuation (Ex. 4.11).

Ex. 4.11: *Étude*, Op. 25, beginning

After 15 bars of 5/8 in the left hand, the hands change places and the theme moves down to the left hand, with the 'accompaniment' in the right hand moving two octaves (and a semitone) higher, now beginning on c sharp.

The work is (roughly) in sonata form, and a second subject (*andantino*) is introduced, notated in the dominant minor, G minor. Here, the right hand in 4/8 corresponds to a 3/8 time measure in the left (Ex. 4.12).

In a review of the work, which appeared in a 1910 issue of *La Revue musicale*, the fascinated critic described Hennessy as a 'very individual, curious, and inventive artist who is at the same time a solid technician'.[32] Apart from a formal description of the work's construction, the unnamed critic also pointed out motivic similarities between Hennessy's first right-hand theme and a '*pièce célèbre de Fr. Chopin*' and, towards the end, identifies Wagner's 'Tristan chord'. He also rightly remarks that such polymetric procedures have a model in some music of the Renaissance, notably Monteverdi, and that even Mozart applied it in the ball scene of *Don Juan*. The important thing should be whether polymetric applications make musical sense, apart from their function as a technical exercise, and in this assessment he has a clear opinion:

---

[32] '*Artiste très personnel, curieux, inventif, en même temps que technicien solide*, [...]'; *La Revue musicale*, 10:19, 1 October 1910, p. 428.

The essential thing is that we do not feel the effort, the research, and that the 'idea' – or rather the melodic 'thought' – does not suffer. It is necessary that the various kinds of superimposed rhythm appear as having presented themselves quite naturally to the composer's mind, as a spontaneous expression, perhaps even as the only possible way to express what he had to say. This is certainly the case with Mr. Swan Hennessy, whose connoisseurs will savour this original Study.[33]

Ex. 4.12: *Étude*, Op. 25, bottom of second page in the printed score

Similarly convinced was the German critic Hugo Leichtentritt in *Signale für die musikalische Welt*. Writing about a group of Hennessy scores he had received in 1910, he commented:

I cannot deny the rating 'ingenious' to all these pieces. They are always distinctive and inspiring. Some kind of very special finesse, be it in rhythm, harmony or piano writing, can be found everywhere. The Étude, for instance, lets both hands play in different bars, and is generally written in totally free, not bar-bound rhythms, in the manner of the old contrapuntists of the Lowlands; [...][34]

An English critic in the *Monthly Musical Record* also expressed a positive view, agreeing that

---

[33] 'L'essentiel, c'est qu'on ne sente pas l'effort, la recherche, et que "l'idée" – ou plutôt la "pensée" mélodique – n'en souffre pas. Il faut que les diverses modalités de rythme superposées semblent s'être présentées tout naturellement à l'esprit du compositeur, comme l'expression spontanée, et même le seul possible, de ce qu'il avait à dire. C'est certainement le cas de M. Swan Hennessy, dont tous les connaisseurs goûteront l'originale Étude.'; ibid., p. 429.

[34] 'Das Prädikat "geistreich" kann ich allen diesen Stücken nicht versagen. Sie sind immer apart und anregend. Irgend welche Finessen ganz besonderer Art, sei es in Rhythmik, Harmonik oder Klaviersatz sind überall zu finden. Die Etude z. B. lässt beide Hände in ganz verschiedenen Takten spielen, ist überhaupt in ganz freien, nicht taktmässigen Rhythmen geschrieben, nach Art der alten niederländischen Kontrapunktiker; [...]'; Signale für die musikalische Welt 86:47, 23 November 1910, p. 1787.

In the *Etude* before us, the constant changes of measure, and indeed mixtures of measure, are somewhat bewildering to the eye, but the effect is good. It is a clever piece.[35]

The work even made it into a contemporary textbook on modern compositional techniques, Arthur Eaglefield Hull's *Modern Harmony. Its Explanation and Application* (1914),[36] where it is mentioned, with a musical excerpt, as a prime example of 'modern rhythm', while also mentioning a more commonly notated example from Ravel's *Miroirs* (No. 3). The book, then, prompted an indignant response from the *Harvard Musical Review*, which called the Hennessy *Étude* a 'freak' example:

> There are several 'freak' examples given of strange tempi, which reach a climax of imbecility in a quotation from Swan Hennessy in which the right hand of the performer plays in two-four time against five-eight time in the left. This combination is spoken of as 'happy.' Let us hope that Mr. Hennessy's cult of beatitude dies an early death! But if these things occur in music, of course Mr. Hull must mention them.[37]

* * *

What unites all the aforementioned works of 1905–6 is that, unfortunately, they seem to have been hardly taken up by professional performers. Despite their favourable reviews (if any appeared at all), they do not seem to have aroused the interest of contemporary (French) pianists. A factor that contributed to this situation is that the publishers do not seem to have been very active in promoting the scores when they appeared. In some cases, it seems like Hennessy, after a few years, lost patience and sent some scores to music journals himself. As a result, reviews, for instance, of the *Deux Études*, Op 15 and the *Petit album*, Op. 18 only appeared as late as 1911 and 1913, the earliest of the *Étude*, Op. 25 in 1910.

It is no surprise, therefore, that Hennessy's reputation was slow to develop. From settling in Paris around 1903 it took about four years before his music was for the first time publicly performed (and reviewed) in Paris: in May 1907.[38] Before about 1911 he was perceived by critics only, in the form of reviews of his published music and not of his presence on recital programmes.

A similar fate befell a group of songs he wrote – all written in 1906 and for the most part published in 1908. These include *Lydia*, Op. 23, *Épiphanie*, Op. 26, the *Deux Mélodies*, Op. 30, and the *Trois Chansons écossaises*, Op. 31. They all received numerous performances in Hennessy's lifetime and beyond (see Appendix 1), but the earliest were in 1922 (!), increasing by the mid-1920s.

---

[35] *The Monthly Musical Record* (1 December 1910), p. 271.
[36] Arthur Eaglefield Hull: *Modern Harmony. Its Explanation and Application* (London: Augener Ltd. & Boston: Boston Music Co., n. d. [1914], pp. 177–178.
[37] *Harvard Musical Review* 3:5 (February 1915), p. 8.
[38] The *Sonate en style irlandais*, Op. 14, for violin and piano, performed at the Palais des Beaux Arts, 7 May 1907; see *Le Guide musical*, 19 May and 2 June, and *Le Monde musicale*, 30 May.

Table 4.1: Selected changes of opus numbers around 1906–7

Title	original opus no.	final opus no.
Épiphanie (1906)	25	26
Annie (1906)	26 / 1	31 / 1
Là-bas! (1906)	26 / 2	30 / 1
Le Revenant (*c.*1907)	[no op.]	30 / 2
La Fille aux cheveux de lin (*c.*1907)	[no op.]	31 / 2
Nell (*c.*1909)	[no op.]	31 / 3
Étude (for piano) (1906)	n/a	25

Hennessy's somewhat erratic use of opus numbers is visible here as well. The manuscripts of the songs reveal that the first of the *Deux Mélodies*, Op. 30, a setting of Joséphin Soulary's *Là-bas!*, was originally intended as Op. 26 No. 2 – as a companion piece to *Annie* (which became Op. 31 No. 1). The *Épiphanie* was originally Op. 25 (now occupied by the polymetric piano *Étude*). It may have been a publisher's decision and probably did not make much difference to Hennessy since they were all written in temporal proximity to each other.

Lydia, Op. 23 (1906) for high voice and piano

The only exception to the rule of late performances is *Lydia*, Op. 23, originally written for high voice and string quartet to a poem by Charles Leconte de Lisle (1818–1894). It is dedicated to the tenor, occasional composer and music critic Hugo Rasch who gave the first performance at the Sing-Akademie, Berlin, on 16 October 1906, accompanied by Karl Klingler and Joseph Rywkind (violins), Fritz Rückward (viola), and Arthur Williams (cello). It is not only the earliest documented performance of a Hennessy work in Berlin but also the earliest evidence of the association between the composer and Rasch – a few years later, both are involved in a common publication (Op. 38), and Rasch became a champion of Hennessy's works in the pages of the *Allgemeine Musikzeitung*.

Nowhere is Hennessy's search for stylistic orientation during these years – or rather, his indecision between a German and a French direction – more apparent than in his early French song settings, and *Lydia* is a prime example. It begins with an extended introduction of 18 bars, almost Mozartian in conception, in rich Romantic colours, but the quick chords in bars 14 and 15 and the trill in bar 18 are formal elements of an even earlier era (Ex. 4.13).[39]

---

[39] The string quartet original was not published, the manuscript is presumably lost. The piano score occasionally indicates particular cues for string instruments, such as the cello in Ex. 4.14.

Ex. 4.13: *Lydia,* Op. 23, bars 13–23

Of Leconte de Lisle's four stanzas, Hennessy uses nos. 1, 3, and 4, keeping arguably the most sensual of the author's love poetry. The first stanza is set to a melody in F major clearly deriving from the introduction. After this ended on a high F major chord and a bar's rest, Hennessy's second stanza where the poem speaks of 'numberless delights' emanating from 'divine fragrances' of Lydia's breast, the music begins in the parallel major (D major) and the harmony becomes considerably more chromatic and whole-tone-harmonic (bars 42–43 contain E♭, F, G, and A in the right hand of the piano) – and one might say 'more French'. The vocal line is an admirably faithful setting of the poet's words, here emphasising the words *'sein'* (skin) and *'délices'* (delights) on the highest pitch. The left-hand line indicates that this is to be played by a cello in the quartet version (Ex. 4.14).

'Lydia' has been set by a number of French composers, the earliest probably being Fauré's 1871 setting in his Op. 4 No. 2. Hennessy's song can stand the comparison very well. What's more, the German critic Heinrich Möller was of the opinion that these 1906 songs (expressly including *Lydia*) would also compare well with Hugo Wolf's songs:

> The present songs show Hennessy from his loveliest side: Youthful freshness in his invention and the sure-forming hand and mature serenity of the master; clear, imaginative and expressive melody and natural and seemingly simple, yet extremely characteristic and finely engraved texture. How many [composers] can still create such simple and warm melodies today without becoming banal or sentimental? Songs like 'Lydia', 'Epiphanie' and 'Le Revenant' are reminiscent of the most intimate songs by Hugo Wolf with which they need not fear the comparison.[40]

---

[40] *'Die vorliegenden Lieder [...] zeigen Hennessy von der liebenswürdigsten Seite: Jugendfrische in der Erfindung und die sicher formende Hand und reife Abgeklärtheit des Meisters; klare, phantasiereiche und*

Ex. 4.14: *Lydia*, Op. 23, bars 36–47[41]

Épiphanie, Op. 26 (1906) for high voice and piano

Épiphanie, Op. 26, originally published with Hamelle in 1907, is a setting of the poem of the same name by José-Maria de Héredia (1842–1905). It is a rather dark setting in *adagio* and G minor (although it ends, fittingly perhaps for the Christian message of the poem, on G major). Clearly, the poem stands in the foreground, and the piano supports it by chromatic two- and three-part writing, often in parallel quavers. The setting also includes two brief passages of recitative.

---

ausdrucksstarke Melodik und natürliche und einfach scheinende, aber doch äußerst charakteristische und fein ziselierte Faktur. Wie viele können heute noch so schlichte und warme Melodien bauen, ohne banal oder sentimental zu werden? Lieder wie "Lydia", "Épiphanie" und "Le revenant" erinnern an die intimsten Lieder von Hugo Wolf, mit denen sie den Vergleich nicht zu scheuen brauchen.'; Allgemeine Musikzeitung 38:38, 22 September 1911, p. 907.

[41] Interestingly, the manuscript deviates here from the print in that the intervals of the right hand of the pianist are set in dotted minims.

Deux Mélodies, Op. 30 (*c*.1906) for mezzo or baritone and piano

The *Deux Mélodies* consist of *Là-bas*, the setting of a poem by Joséphin Soulary (1815–1891), and *Le Revenant* by Charles Baudelaire (1821–1867). They were written in late 1906 or early 1907 and published by Demets, their first edition as separate pieces in 1907, followed by the Hamelle edition in 1908 of the *Quatre Mélodies* (see above).

Soulary's poetry in *Là-bas* is a melancholy memory of a love scene in the distant past of the protagonist, written from the vantage point of old age and a 'withered heart' (*'mon coeur indolent'*). Hennessy's setting captures the changing moods of the poetry perfectly, beginning with an *adagio* ($\quarternote$ = 48) centred around G major, with familiar late-Romantic modulations (a 'German' element?) and an ending of the first stanza on a very Ravelian chord progression (Ex. 4.15).

Ex. 4.15: *Deux Mélodies*, Op. 30 No. 1 *'Là-bas'*, bars 6–11

This is followed by five bars, representing a little more than half of the second stanza, marked *più animato* ($\quarternote$ = 63) that lead to the word *'deux'* (bar 17), signifying the end of loneliness for the protagonist and which briefly introduces a passage (until bar 24) with a move away from the slower 3/4 time to an agitated 4/4 time (*allegro*, $\quarternote$ = 104), a very clever and eminently suiting device. For the third stanza, the music returns to the initial tempo, ending on quick *staccatissimo* notes reaching into ever higher registers (Hennessy's third stanza is the original poem's fourth, as he dispenses with the third stanza of Soulary's poem).

Le Revenant is a setting from Baudelaire's *Flowers of Evil*.[42] In most English translations of the poem, the title is not 'the revenant' but 'the ghost', an interpretation of the rather eerie idea that the soul of a dead man returns to the night chamber of a woman giving her 'kisses cold as the moon' (*'des baisers froids comme la lune'*) and 'caresses of a snake' (*'des caresses de serpent'*). Again, Hennessy catches the mood of the poem perfectly in a setting in C minor with a number of chromatic scales, and with a few bars of chromatic triplets at the point with the caressing snake, which resembles the snake's lurching movement (Ex. 4.16).

When Opp. 23, 26 and 30 appeared as *Quatre Mélodies* in 1908, *La Revue musicale* summed them up as follows:

---

[42] This song is not contained in Helen Abbott: *Baudelaire in Song, 1880–1930* (New York: Oxford University Press, 2017), but it is in the accompanying database www.baudelairesong.org (accessed 31 March 2019).

Mr Swan Hennessy (Irishman, having studied music in conservatories in Germany and living in Paris) sends us four songs published by Hamelle: […] We recommend to all friends of the art of music these serious and personal works of a composer who has complete knowledge and respect for his art.[43]

Ex. 4.16: *Deux Mélodies*, Op. 30 No. 2 'Le Revenant', bars 14–19

Trois Chansons écossaises, Op. 31 (1906–9) for high voice and piano

The above-mentioned *Là-bas* from Op. 30 was originally (in the MS) coupled with *Annie* from the present collection, but the change was a prudent one, because Op. 30 now includes two songs for low voice reflecting on old age and death, whereas for the *Trois Chansons écossaises* Hennessy uses three poems by one writer, Charles Leconte de Lisle, all set for high voice. The title '*Chansons écossaises*' is borrowed from Leconte de Lisle; it was originally a section of six poems in his collection *Poèmes antiques* (1852), consisting of (in this order) *Jane, Nanny, Nell, La Fille aux cheveux de lin, Annie,* and *La Chanson du rouet*. For the Op. 31 album of songs, Hennessy uses poems no. 5, 4 and 3. The Scottish theme of the title therefore derives first of all from the poems.[44]

---

[43] '*M. Swan Hennessy (Irlandais, ayant fait ses études musicales dans les conservatoires d'Allemagne et domicilié à Paris) nous envoie 4 mélodies éditées chez Hamelle : […] Nous recommandons à tous les amis de l'art musical ces œuvres sérieuses et personnelles d'un compositeur qui a la connaissance complète et le respect de son art.*'; *La Revue Musicale* 8:10, 15 May 1908, p. 306.

[44] In later song cycles, Hennessy set two more of Leconte de Lisle's *Chansons écossaises*: *Jane* appears as Op. 66 No. 3 (*c*1921) and *La Chanson du rouet* as Op. 72 No. 1 (1926).

In his own list of works, Hennessy claims the collection was written in 1909, but the manuscripts disprove this. Clearly, the manuscript of *Annie* contains the date 1906, and *La Fille aux cheveux de lin* probably dates from 1907. Only for *Nell*, the year 1909 may be correct; in this case, the manuscript appears to be lost. There is no collective publication of this little cycle. *Annie* was published separately with Hamelle in 1907, *La Fille aux cheveux de lin* in 1920, and *Nell* in 1922, both with Demets – all three without their opus number.[45]

The poetry of the 'Chansons écossaises' has inspired many French composers from the nineteenth and the first half of the twentieth century, mostly for use as song settings, but Debussy's famous piano work *La Fille aux cheveux de lin* (no. 8 in the first volume of *Préludes*, 1910) speaks for their poetic inspiration that also found other ways of artistic expression (that also included paintings). But it is interesting that no other composer in France took up the meaning of the title and set the words to music that is actually inspired by Scottish traditional music – except Swan Hennessy. He really wrote 'Chansons écossaises' – Scottish songs (that the idiom did not differ fundamentally from Irish songs was certainly an advantage).

Structurally, the songs in this album are simple settings in a folk song manner. Hennessy avoids a strophic approach as, of course, he certainly did not intend to produce folk music. In all three songs he dispenses with some of the stanzas of the original poems, writing brief pieces of not more than one and a half or two minutes duration, each trying to catch the essence of the poem and the intended musical style.

Thus, *Annie*, set in D major and using stanzas 1, 2 and 4 of the original poem, features a melody that, with its typical interval leaps and the ending on repeated pitches, is characteristic of numerous Scottish (and Irish) traditional songs (Ex. 4.17). Likewise, if not quite so obvious, *La Fille aux cheveux de lin* is a similarly brief piece in C major that uses a Scottish/Irish melodic curve in places, such as in the poetic line set in bars 10 to 14 (Ex. 4.18). In *Nell*, a piece in G major that uses the first three of the four stanzas of the original poem, the 'Scottish lilt' appears predominantly in the initial four bars and its reprise later on.

Ex. 4.17: *Trois Chansons écossaises*, Op. 31 No. 1 '*Annie*', bars 8–12

---

[45] It cannot be completely ruled out that *La Fille* ... and *Nell* were not written before 1920–2, since the first performances did not occur before May 1922.

Ex. 4.18: *Trois Chansons écossaises*, Op. 31 No. 2 '*La Fille aux cheveux de lin*', bars 10–14

Yet, the idea did not convince the critic in the English journal *Musical Opinion* who failed to recognise the connection to Leconte de Lisle and whose judgement was:

> It is described as a 'chanson ecossaise,' but apart from the occasional introduction of the 'snap' there is nothing Scottish about it. And the concluding bars are unsatisfactory: the music is wrenched back to the opening key in a violent and unconvincing way. But there is some graceful melody in the song.[46]

This appears to have been the only, albeit late (1922) critical opinion of *La Fille aux cheveux de lin*. *Annie* received more favourable reviews, even though only one of them, from Germany, is more or less contemporaneous with its publication. Although the song receives no more than one sentence, the introduction by the critic Heinrich Möller is interesting:

> The highly individual art of the Scotsman Hennessy has already been appreciated in these pages, and one may hope, therefore, that some readers have taken the trouble of acquainting themselves with this lovely and original composer. Artists like him, who have the pride to do great things in the small forms, are a rare and doubly soothing phenomenon at a time of impotent bagginess and strong-arm tactics. [...] 'Annie' (Leconte de Lisle) is a delightfully graceful Scottish chanson of piquant appeal.[47]

And after a 1932 recital, the *Journal des débats* rightly noted the song's indebtedness to a German harmonic school, characterising it as 'pages of both Celtic turn and Schumannian spirit'.[48]

---

[46] *Musical Opinion*, February 1922.
[47] '*Die höchst persönliche Kunst des Schotten Hennessy ist in diesen Blättern schon gewürdigt worden; man darf also hoffen, daß einige der Leser sich die Mühe genommen haben, sich mit diesem sympathischen und originellen Tonsetzer bekannt zu machen. Künstler wie er, die den Stolz haben, in den kleinen Formen Großes zu leisten, sind eine seltene und in einer Zeit impotenter Aufgebauschtheit und Kraftmeierei doppelt wohltuende Erscheinung. [...] "Annie" (Leconte de Lisle) ist ein entzückend graziöses schottisches Chanson von pikantem Reiz.*'; Heinrich Möller in *Allgemeine Musikzeitung* 38:38, 22 September 1911, p. 907.
[48] '*Annie, page à la fois de tour celtique et d'esprit schumannien, qui fut "bissée"*'; *Journal des débats*, 1 March 1932, p. 4.

With the piano works *Au village*, Op. 22 and *Nouvelles feuilles d'album*, Op. 27 we are leaving this stylistically indecisive period of Hennessy's early years in Paris. Despite the gaps in their opus numbers, both were written, or at least completed, in 1907. It may be useful at this point to remember that despite publication dates that were close to the time of composition, most of the reviews cited above appeared considerably later, some after performances during the 1920s and '30s. As yet, there are no traces of Hennessy having appeared in Paris as a pianist in his own works. He may still have been unsure how much and what kind of effort was required to establish himself properly in the French capital.

In 1907 also, Hennessy visited the United States for the last time ever, returning to Paris permanently from October of that year. The year appears in passport applications of the 1920s, with no reason given. Perhaps, in late 1907, Hennessy made his final decision to remain in Paris for good. Another potential reason may have been the burial of his half-sister Lila who had died at some unknown date before WWI.

Au village. Petite suite caractéristique, Op. 22 (1907) for piano

Although *Au village* carries the opus number 22, it actually postdates *Eaux fortes*, Op. 24 and the *Étude*, Op. 25. In this case, this is probably not the result of a revision of opus numbers or the withdrawal of other compositions. It seems rather more likely that four of the five parts of the work were written around 1906–7, and the fifth most definitively in 1907. This can be deducted from the history of its dedication.

We have seen before Hennessy's stylistic indebtedness to the German late-Romantic Max Reger (1873–1916), and *Au village* is directly dedicated to him. Hennessy was interested in procuring Reger's consent, and it was arranged through a common acquaintance, the music critic, singer and occasional composer Hugo Rasch.

Reger had in March 1907 assumed a position as professor of composition at the Leipzig Conservatory. Apparently, Rasch had corresponded with him about his potential acceptance of a dedication by Hennessy, and his response to Rasch in a postcard dated 4 August 1907, probably to his holiday locality in Switzerland, has survived (Fig. 4.2).

> Dear Sir! Many thanks for your kind note. Of course, I should be very delighted if your friend Mr Hennessy would dedicate his latest 4 piano pieces to me. Up to now, with all my best efforts, I did not get the chance to write anything for voice and string quartet! So please, inform Mr H ! With best wishes, your devoted Max Reger[49]

---

[49] '*Sehr geehrter Herr! Besten Dank für Ihre freundl. Zeilen. Es wird mich selbstredend sehr freuen, wenn Ihr Freund Herr Hennessy mir seine neuesten 4 Klaviersachen widmet. Ich kam vor lauter Arbeit bis jetzt mit bestem Willen nicht dazu, etwas für Gesang u. Streichquartett zu schreiben! Bitte, verständigen Sie also Herrn H ! Mit besten Grüßen, Ihr ergebenster Max Reger*'. Postcard in the archive of the Max Reger Institut, Karlsruhe, Germany, with sincere thanks for the permission to reproduce it. The original request by Rasch to Reger has not survived.

Fig. 4.2a/b: Postcard from Max Reger to Hugo Rasch (1907) re Hennessy's dedication (Courtesy: Max Reger Institut)

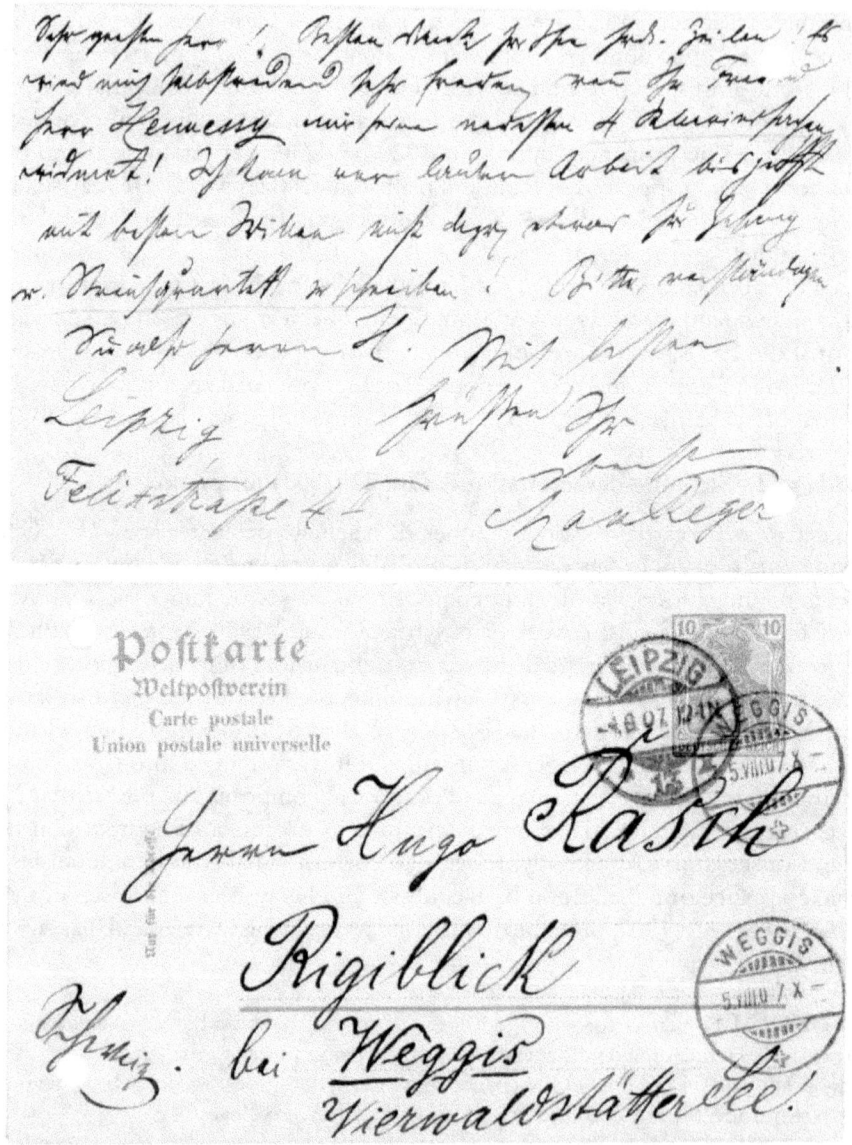

Rasch had previously sung Swan Hennessy's *Lydia*, Op. 23 to string quartet accompaniment in 1906 in Berlin. It seems like the format delighted the singer, especially since it had been originally written for quartet and not for piano, so much so that he had asked Reger to do the same – to no avail: he never wrote for this combination.

The postcard is enlightening in view of the fact that Reger writes of four pieces, whereas the work in question has five. The manuscript reveals a change in the handwriting in the fifth piece, *Au bord du ruisseau*, which is written more spaciously, with no more than four bars to a system, whereas the handwriting in the other pieces is considerably narrower. This is probably a piece that has been added after the dedication had been approved.

Au village ('In the Village') includes the five pieces *Noce campagnarde* ('Country Wedding'), *Fillettes* ('Girls'), *Basse cour* ('Barnyard'), *Sur l'herbe* ('On the Grass'), and *Au bord du ruisseau* ('At the Edge of the Stream') – titles suggesting that 'in the countryside' would have been an equally appropriate collective title for the set. We have seen in previous programmatic music by Hennessy that, although he evidently enjoyed urban Paris, he had a penchant for pastoral, rural scenes, a quality in which he did not differ from a large number of Parisian artists at the time, be they composers, painters or poets. It is, of course, his urban background (Chicago, Stuttgart, London, Paris) that informs Hennessy's love of the countryside in a technical and stylistic sense.

Ex. 4.19: *Au village*, Op. 22 No. 2 *'Fillettes'*, bars 1–12

As a brazen Romantic with neo-baroque leanings, Reger would have loved particularly the first and the last piece, with their rather clear diatonic language. *Noce campagnarde* is a short, straightforward piece in C major marked *vivace assai* that combines chordal play with, in between, a passage in neo-baroque sequences with a modest measure of modulation. *Fillettes*, notated in F major and marked *Andantino quasi allegret-*

to, is a first sign (and not the last, as we will see) of Hennessy's awareness of contemporary ragtime, both in rhythmic terms (albeit not so regular throughout) and in the applied harmony, inspired by his near-contemporary Scott Joplin (Ex. 4.19).

Basse cour, again notated in F major, is an image of a farmyard full of chicken, a very delightful work illustrating the business of the scene in quick *staccatissimo* chords and the excited cackling of the chicken in brief dissonant interjections in high registers (Ex. 4.20) while keeping in the jazz-tinged harmonic mood of the previous piece. It has a second, more calm part centred around C major (from bar 30) on which the piece ends.

Ex. 4.20: *Au village*, Op. 22 No. 3 'Basse cour', bars 13–16

Sur l'herbe is a slow movement that has twice been renamed before going to press (first *Le Soir*, then *Grillons*), as the manuscript shows. All three (potential) titles are illustrative of the composer's intentions: to depict an evening scene in meadows inhabited by crickets. It is a *lento* movement in C minor. The monotonous sound of the crickets is illustrated in repeated G pitches with an ascending *appoggiatura* on F♯.

The last piece, *Au bord du ruisseau*, is the longest in the set, occupying eight pages of the score compared to two or three in the preceding pieces. Beginning in C major marked *vivace ma non troppo*, it is characterised by semiquaver runs beginning in four bars of the left hand and continuing in two-part harmony of parallel fourths and fifths, it undoubtedly symbolises the rivulet of the title. After this idea went through some modulations, again with cautious neo-baroque allusions (as in the first piece) and a partial repetition, from bar 47 follows a passage with a *marcato* two-part theme reminding of hunting horns that will ultimately lead up to the end of the piece (and the set).

The critical reception of the work – now actually beginning in the year of publication by Demets in Paris – was mixed. While conceding that a series of works depicting village life may be, by definition, simple and old-style,[50] the critic Paul-Marie Masson

---

[50] *'Ils sont simples, alertes, et "le style en est vieux". Mais peut-il en être autrement au village?'*; Paul-Marie Masson in *La Revue musicale* 7:22, 15 November 1907, p. 253.

in *La Revue musicale* complained that several of Hennessy's creative ideas were not sufficiently developed and that 'true inspiration is often lacking'.[51]

'True inspiration' aside (about which opinions may differ), the question of the briefness of Hennessy's ideas ('ideas … not sufficiently developed'), props up frequently in the criticism of his music, again with some critics applauding the economic and concise construction and others wishing for more development. *Le Guide musical* briefly described *Au village* as 'simple, clear and, above all, easy'.[52] Louis Vuillemin in *Comoedia* attested Hennessy a 'charming virtuosity and exquisite sensibility'.[53]

Outside France, the *Monthly Musical Record* in England noticed the parallels between the first and the last piece in the set:

> 'CHARACTERISTIC' is a term which well suits this suite, and one of its characteristics is the strictly diatonic portions of certain parts. In the first section, entitled Noce Campagnarde, the bright opening theme with its piquant syncopated rhythm is of such kind, while in the closing section, Au Bord du Ruisseau, we find another simple and charming melody in the key of the dominant, the moving semiquavers being typical of the stream itself.[54]

In Germany, the *Allgemeine Musikzeitung* wrote after a performance of the work in Berlin in 1913:

> Recently, the focus of Hennessy's oeuvre lies, as far as I am concerned, in his piano compositions, above all in the short, aphoristic depictions of character and mood, which are in their own way real gems of pianistic small-scale art. The way he illustrates in just a few bars and in bold but artistically correct strokes a chicken farm … is exquisite.[55]

---

[51] *'En somme, pour finir par une banalité que bon voudrait pouvoir répéter un peu moins, il y a incontestablement dans ces œuvres, à des degrés divers, du savoir et du talent, mais l'inspiration véritable y fait trop souvent défaut. Aussi bien est-ce le fonds qui manque le plus.';* as fn. 47, p. 254.

[52] *'De son côté, M. Demets (2, rue de Louvois) donne satisfaction aux fractions diverses de sa clientèle de pianistes en publiant une petite suite de Hennessy,* Au village, *simple, claire et d'abord facile […]';* Henri de Curzon in *Le Guide musical*, 3 November 1907, p. 668.

[53] *'Au Village, suite caractéristique pour piano, nous entraîne loin de la capitale, sur le passage d'une* Noce campagnarde. *Les fillettes paysannes, la cacophonie de la basse-cour, une idyllique station sur l'herbe et au bord du ruisseau affirment chez M. Swan Hennessy une virtuosité de main charmante et une exquise sensibilité.';* Louis Vuillemin in *Comoedia*, 1 June 1911, p. 2.

[54] *The Monthly Musical Record*, 1 March 1911, p. 62 (no author mentioned).

[55] *'Der Schwerpunkt von Hennessys Schaffen liegt meines Bedünkens zurzeit in seinen Klavierkompositionen, vor allem in den kurzen, aphoristischen Charakter- und Stimmungsbildern, die in ihrer Art wirkliche Perlen klavieristischer Kleinkunst darstellen. Wie da in wenigen Takten der "Hühnerhof" […] mit kecken und dabei künstlerisch korrekten Strichen musikalisch illustriert [wird], das ist […] köstlich […].';* Paul Schwers in *Allgemeine Musikzeitung* 40:47, 21 November 1913, p. 1488.

Hennessy's opinion of Max Reger

From the dedication of Op. 22 to Max Reger and the various observable influences noted before, it seems like Reger had somewhat taken over the influential role that Schumann had played in Hennessy's youth. Yet, this is not unconditionally true. Hennessy had strong opinions on a number of his contemporaries, which he offered both privately and publicly. His own collection of published music of what he called the *'école moderne'*[56] contains a number of remarkable notices that he sometimes wrote in his unique, slow handwriting on the title pages of these pieces and sometimes as brief comments directly into the score.

For instance, Hennessy was extremely critical of Reger's piano series *Aus meinem Tagebuch*, Op. 82, in particular, vols 1 (1904), 2 (1906), and 3 (1910). Thus, he wrote on his copy of the first volume (see Fig. 4.3):[57]

Fig. 4.3: Hennessy's verdict of Reger's *Aus meinem Tagebuch*, Op. 82, vol. 1

Dass ein besoffener unverschämter Bauernlümmel solch ein Dreck schreibt ist wohl Heut zu Tage noch möglich – aber dass ein anständiger Verleger so was herausgiebt ist ganz unbegreiflich!
Swan Hennessy

Still not being content, he repeats his criticism in French on a second copy of the same piece:

Qu'une lourde brute alcoolique puisse accoucher de pareilles horreurs est de nos jours (hélas) encore possible – mais qu'un éditeur qui se respecte puisse les lancer dans la publicité est tout à fait incompréhensible !
Swan Hennessy

---

[56] The Hennessy Family Collection contains 15 hand-bound volumes of piano music, imprinted on the spine as *'École moderne – piano'*. In these, he mixes music of his contemporaries (French, German, Russian, Hungarian, Spanish) with his own, with numerous corrections in red ink where he discovered printing errors like missing or wrong accidentals and pauses. These include prints of works by Debussy, Ravel, Dukas, Ladmirault, d'Indy, Franck, Reger, R. Strauss, Shcherbachov, Rebikov, Moór, Turina, and others.

[57] 'That a drunken insolent lout writes such a mess is probably still possible today – but that a decent publisher is bringing it out is completely incomprehensible!'

The cover of vol. 3 features the comment *'Dieses dritte Heft ist womöglich noch lümmelhafter wie die beiden ersten'.*[58] On the copy of vol. 1 with the German text, there is an equally explicit response in the old-style German Kurrent handwriting, written in pencil and unsigned. In the original it reads:

> *Wenn Sie Reger's Werke genauer kennen würden, dann erlaubten Sie sich dies Urteil nicht. Dies zeigt die Enge Ihres Horizontes. Er ist in der Musikliteratur etwas mehr bekannt als Sie mit Ihren lächerlichen Kompositionsversuchen!*[59]

It is not sure whether Hennessy was not able to read Kurrent and whether that is the reason why he did not erase this rather insulting comment. More likely, he did not take it seriously as, with all the works gathered together in his collection, he was certainly not limited by a 'narrow horizon'. Unfortunately, we do not know the author of this response who must have been a private visitor to Hennessy's home. It is certainly not a friendly comment and cannot have come from one of Hennessy's German friends of the time like Heinrich Möller or Hugo Rasch.

Similarly, if not quite as polemic, Hennessy's opinion of Reger's *Variationen und Fuge über ein Thema von Joh. Seb. Bach*, Op. 81 was: *'Diese Komposition ist eine Lausbuberei! S. H.'* ('This composition is a rascallery!').

Verdicts such as these either show that Hennessy must have changed his mind about Reger at some point in time, or he was critical about some works while liking others.

Nouvelles feuilles d'album, Op. 27 (1907) for piano

With these 'new album leaves', Swan Hennessy makes another marked stylistic step towards his adopted home. What a difference to his first set of *Album Leaves*, Op. 8 of 1887! Once an involuntary copy of Schumann or Kirchner, he now merely takes the basic idea of brief characterisations that suits him so well (and that does derive from Schumann) and transports it to contemporary France.

The work was written in 1907, printed in 1908 by Demets, and consists of five short pieces of which the last two are designated as parts A and B of 'little Parisian scenes': the pieces are 1. *Madrigal*; 2. *Canon*; 3. *Style irlandais*; 4. *Petites scènes parisiennes*: a) *Montrouge le matin*; b) *Sortie de midinettes*. The work is dedicated to Hennessy's friend, the violinist and composer Auguste Delacroix (1871–1936), perhaps as a gesture of thanks for Delacroix performing Hennessy's Irish-style violin sonata (Op. 14) in May 1907.

The *Madrigal* is an unpretentious piece in the unusual key of G flat major that is written in three- or four-part harmony, much as a vocal madrigal would be. Hennessy's grasp of contemporary harmony is visible throughout and may perhaps be summed

---

[58] 'This third issue may be even more loutish than the first two.'
[59] 'If you knew more about Reger's works, then you would not allow yourself that judgment. This shows the narrowness of your horizon. He is a little better known in music literature than you are with your ridiculous attempts at composition!'

up in the highly chromatic final four bars that contain most of the work's characteristics (Ex. 4.21).

Ex. 4.21: *Nouvelles feuilles d'album*, Op. 27 No. 1 *'Madrigal'*, bars 47–50

The following two-part *Canon* has a very pleasant melody with a light and, in comparison, 'French' touch. It has a tonal centre in C major and is to be played in moderate tempo (the work is marked *Lento, con espressione*, but at 63 per crotchet it is not particularly slow). The piece has an A–B–A structure with a more chromatic middle part. It does not require sophisticated skills as a pianist, but the *'con espressione'* element should certainly be taken seriously to elaborate its qualities.

The third piece 'in the Irish style' (in F major marked *Andante*) would probably provoke dissent among performers of Irish traditional music, and most certainly so if they expect an Irish style based on the structure of traditional music. With a six-bar introduction and a repeated main section of sixteen bars divided into seven-plus-nine-bar phrases it would certainly not be similar to any existing folk song. Yet, in rhythmic terms it mostly resembles a harmonised ballad since it does not contain any dance rhythm. But the 'tune' does use recognisable Irish melodic patterns that we have encountered in previous works by Hennessy such as typical interval leaps and repeated pitches at the end of a phrase. Hennessy also makes extensive use of the 'Scotch snap' which he evidently regarded as a common feature of Irish traditional music – an issue that will be addressed in more detail later.

The most interesting parts of the *Nouvelles feuilles d'album* are the two Parisian scenes at the end of this volume, the first evoking a morning in the green Parisian suburb of Montrouge, the second entitled *Sortie de midinettes*, which one might translate as an outing of teenage girls. Thus, Hennessy created a contrast between the nature-dominated suburb and the more urban city centre with a group of teenage girls seeking their weekend diversions. The musical construction is curious since there is hardly a connection between the two parts, which are written in a different key, tempo and mode of expression, and separated merely by a *fermata*. What does unite them is the common idea of 'Parisian scenes' (perhaps underlining how diverse such scenes may be) and their very contemporary French style.

Montrouge le matin is a very tender little piece that derives its charm out of chains of chords including sixth and minor seventh chords that have lost their traditional harmonic function, often leading to abrupt and unexpected changes. In an Impressionist manner in the best sense of the word they serve to evoke this particular morning scene creating a mood of calmness, at the same time not becoming too idyllic, not hiding that they still depict an urban and not a rural scene (Ex. 4.22).

Ex. 4.22: *Nouvelles feuilles d'album*, Op. 27 No. 4A, 'Montrouge le matin', bars 1–7

Sortie de midinettes is livelier (*Vivace ma non troppo*, ♩ = 160), with a marked neoclassical melody, not unlike some works by Satie, that is first presented with single accompanying bass notes and then accompanied by chromatic chord shifts moving from the right to the left hand (Ex. 4.23).

Ex. 4.23: *Nouvelles feuilles d'album*, Op. 27 No. 4B 'Sortie de midinettes', bars 15–20

The *Nouvelles feuilles d'album*, and particularly the last part, established Swan Hennessy's reputation among some of the more important Parisian music critics – albeit in somewhat delayed reactions dating 1910 and 1911. He received almost enthusiastic reviews from *La Revue musicale* and *Comoedia*, also attracting a measure of attention in England and Germany. In both the French journals, the respective critics say they had observed Hennessy's development for a while and that he has now eventually convinced them of his talents. A critic abbreviated as 'S.' wrote in *La Revue musicale*:

> We have been following with great interest the development of the very real and personal talent of Mr Swan Hennessy. From the beginning, I had distinguished in him a very solid technique, an original turn of mind, a certain tendency (perhaps more intellectual than spontaneous) to rare forms, habits of a very conscientious style; – sometimes I would have liked a little more lightness of touch and some more liveliness. These recent pieces satisfy me fully. They are, as always, very neat (with some true four-part writing prevailing), but they are more natural, more out-going, and with a true sensitivity that is less academic. The Madrigal is charming, with phrases festooning in contours of exquisite elegance. The *Canon* may only live up to its title; but, what is more important, the page is worthy of a Schumann or C. Franck. Number 3 (*Style irlandais*) has great flavour. I was less taken with the impressionism (lacking sufficient melodic lines, a few bundles of notes) of *Montrouge le matin*. The last piece (*Sortie de midinettes*) is a composition full of spirit, of rare distinction, a true gem.[60]

The unnamed critic in *Comoedia* commented by pointing out Hennessy's gift of observing his (natural and urban) environment and using his experience as a source of inspiration.

> Mr Swan Hennessy's nature appears quite likeable. He does not write music for the pleasure of aligning one note behind the other. He does not care in any blunt way of simply writing a *méditation*, an *impromptu*, a *sonata*. No, Mr Hennessy looks around himself and having watched, he listens. Having listened, he writes. Isn't this the real *raison d'être* of an artist to express, day after day, the impressions that life suggests to him?
> In this way, Mr Hennessy undertakes translations, for instance in the *Nouvelles feuilles d'album* and its *Petites scènes parisiennes*. Here we find, sketched in a very funny way, the *Sortie de midinettes*. The 'meeting with the lover' takes place on a fallacious appassionato of a 'meno mosso assai'! The piece ends on an *Animandosi poco a poco* that soon becomes very cheerful. Are we to conclude that the girls unhesitatingly throw their cap over the mills?[61]

---

[60] 'Nous suivons avec grand intérêt le développement du talent très réel et personnel de M. Swan Hennessy. Dès le début, j'avais distingué en lui une technique très solide, un tour d'esprit original, une certaine tendance (peut-être plus intellectuelle que spontanée) aux formes rares, des habitudes de style très consciencieuses; – j'aurais désiré, parfois, un peu plus de légèreté de main et de vivacité. Ces dernières pièces me satisfont pleinement. Elles sont, comme toujours, très soignées (l'écriture à quatre parties réelles y prédomine), mais plus naturelles, plus allantes, et la sensibilité vraie y est moins entachée de recherche. Le Madrigal *est charmant; la phrase y festonne en contours d'une exquise élégance. Le* Canon *ne mérite qu'à moitié son titre; mais, ce qui est plus important, la page est digne de Schumann ou de C. Franck. Le numéro 3 (*Style irlandais*) a une grande saveur. J'aime moins l'impressionnisme (sans ligne mélodique suffisante, un peu en paquets de notes) de* Montrouge le matin. *La dernière poésie (*Sortie de midinettes*) est une composition pleine d'esprit, d'une rare distinction, un vrai bijou.*'; 'S.' in *La Revue musicale* 10:21, 1 November 1910, p. 479.

[61] '*La nature de M. Swan Hennessy apparaît comme essentiellement sympathique. M. Hennessy n'écrit point de la musique pour le vrai plaisir d'aligner des notes les unes derrière les autres. Il ne forme pas à brûle pourpoint le dessein de composer une* Méditation, *un* Impromptu, *une* Sonate. *Non, M. Hennessy regarde autour de lui, ayant regardé, il entend. Ayant entendu, il écrit. N'est-ce pas là la véritable raison d'être de l'artiste que d'exprimer, presque au jour le jour, les impressions que lui suggère la vie ? / M. Hennessy traduit donc tour à tour, en de* Nouvelles feuilles d'Album, *de* Petites scènes parisiennes, *par exemple. Nous y retrouvons, esquissée de façon fort amusante, la* Sortie des midinettes ! *La "rencontre avec l'amoureux" a lieu sur le fallacieux appassionato d'un "Meno mosso assai"! La pièce se termine sur un "Animandosi poco a poco" qui ne*

The *Monthly Musical Record* was also positive, again highlighting particularly the 'Parisian scenes'.

> IN the four *Album Leaves* which the composer presents to us, there is some very clever, piquant writing. No. 1, entitled *Madrigal*, is graceful and pleasing. No. 2, *Canon*, clever and expressive, has none of the stiffness which is so difficult to avoid in that particular form. No. 3, *Style Irlandais*, is very good. But it is in the No. 4, *Petites Scènes Parisiennes*, that the composer most displays his own individuality.[62]

The *Allgemeine Musikzeitung* was of the opinion that Hennessy in this work was at his most mature.

> [It] seems to me to be the by far most mature and substantive of all of Hennessy's works that I have seen so far. However, only the most advanced players should attempt them; they, then, will derive much pleasure and inspiration from the 'Madrigal', from 'Montrouge le matin' and especially the 'Sortie de midinettes'.[63]

It will be seen in the following chapters that Swan Hennessy never completely shook off the profound influence of the German Romantics on his musical development. But during these formative first years of his residence in Paris he convincingly demonstrates that he has listened to his French contemporaries and begun to absorb their harmonic language in order to amalgamate their style into his own world of ideas. There is a lot that he has always had in common with the Impressionists – the love of nature, at the same time the fascination with the technical and industrial novelties of contemporary urban life, the descriptive and programmatic motivation, the non-conformist approach to form. So far, Hennessy confines these qualities to the small forms of piano music and songs, and he will never go much further. But in any fair appreciation of Swan Hennessy's music there is no point in complaining about what he does or is *not*; he preferred the small form and was probably aware that this is where he is best.

---

tarde point à devenir fort gai. Faut-il en conclure que la Midinette n'hésite guère à jeter son bonnet pardessus les moulins?'; *Comoedia*, 1 June 1911, p. 2.

[62] *The Monthly Musical Record*, 1 January 1911, p. 17.

[63] '*Letzteres Album scheint mir von all den mir vorliegenden Werken Hennessy's das bei weitem reifste und inhaltlich bedeutendste zu sein. Es sollten sich aber auch nur fortgeschrittenere Spieler daran wagen; diese aber werden aus "Madrigal", "Montrouge le matin" und vor allem der "Sortie de midinettes" viel Genuß und Anregung schöpfen können.*'; Hugo Rasch in *Allgemeine Musikzeitung* 28:13, 31 March 1911, p. 376.

Fig. 4.4: Hennessy relaxing with a book in his apartment (before 1910) (Hennessy family)

Chapter 5
An American Impressionist (1908–1913)

In 1908, Swan Hennessy most likely visited Ireland (see Chapter 6), a journey that probably included London as well. For the London occasion, Hennessy had written a group of songs to words by Shakespeare. Written around 1908 or 1909, they were collectively called *Songs from 'As You Like It' (Shakespeare)*, with the opus no. 30, but later withdrawn: after cuts to his work-list, Op. 30 was later ascribed to the *Deux Mélodies*, which had been published in 1908 without an opus number; see Chapter 4).

The Shakespeare songs are preserved among the Hennessy manuscripts and include the three poems *Under the Greenwood Tree*; *Blow, Blow, thou Winter Wind*; and *It was a Lover and his Lass*. Hennessy provided German translations with the comment *'Deutscher Text frei nach Schlegel und Tieck'*, suggesting that they were essentially by Hennessy liberally using the nineteenth-century translations by Friedrich von Schlegel and Ludwig Tieck. The first is dedicated to the Paris-based German music critic Heinrich Möller, the second to the English soprano Marie Stark (already the dedicatee of the *Épiphanie*, Op. 26), and the third to another English singer, Annabel McDonald, who gave the first performance of the songs at London's Bechstein Hall on 7 May 1909 (with Madeleine Booth as accompanist). *The Morning Post* thought they 'proved to be eccentric rather than original'.[1] The first song was also given, in its German translation, in 1913 in Berlin by Marguerite Sonntag in a string quartet version played by the Marix Loevensohn Quartet, but the critics present on the occasion ignored it. Latest by that date, Hennessy must have decided to withdraw the songs.

There is no record of Hennessy having been present at the May 1909 London performance, but it is not unlikely given the composer's still frequent travels to England. Only two months later he chose London as the place to marry Claire Przybyszewska. It must remain a 'footnote' in this study, because nothing is known about the background, reasons or circumstances of this marriage far away from their Paris home. By this time, he had already dedicated five of his compositions to Claire, namely the *Mazurka et Polonaise*, Op. 17 (1906), the *Petit album*, Op. 18 (1905), *Au bord de la forêt*, Op. 21 (1907), the *Petite mazurka* (no. 3 of *Eaux fortes*, Op. 24, 1906), and the set of *Valses*, Op. 32 (1909). It must have been love, and he was heard, that's all we can say. And at age 42, he was certainly more mature than at his first (1888) marriage.

Valses, Op. 32 (1909) for piano

The last work devoted to 'mademoiselle' Claire Przybyszewska, the *Valses*, Op. 32 consists of four pieces, the second and third of which have descriptive titles, *Espagne* and *Suisse*. The first is marked *Allegro* and the fourth *Mesto*. Hennessy's 'arrival' among French music critics is manifested by a relatively long review in *La Revue musicale* (including three music examples), shorter ones in *S.I.M. Revue musicale mensuelle* and *Comoedia* as well as reviews from Germany and England. Despite the formal and stylistic

---

[1] *The Morning Post*, 8 May 1909.

diversity of the four movements, all reviews confirm that in their technical complexity and harmonic language they are on a par with those of his French contemporaries. The work was published by Demets and republished in an Eschig edition after Eschig had taken over Demets in 1923. The manuscript reveals that the work was composed in 1909 in Montrouge, one of Hennessy's favourite Paris suburbs that is very much part of the southern urban agglomeration of Paris. At this period, Montrouge was a rather green part of the city that was frequented by artists including Fernand Léger and, a little later, Pablo Picasso.

The critic in *La Revue musicale* (abbreviated as 'C.')[2] was a little irritated *('inquiétante')* by the beginning of the first waltz, yet seemed to like what he perceived as the *'morbidezza'* of the harmonic writing. In an F sharp major basic tonality, Hennessy's underlying rhythmic figure in the left hand starts off-beat and moves in unusual chromatic steps up and down while the right hand accentuates the first beat (Ex. 5.1).

Ex. 5.1: *Valses*, Op. 32 No. 1, bars, 1–10

He contrasts this bold writing by a subsidiary motif in plain major and with an almost ridiculously simple tune – as if to ironically say 'Look, if this was too modern for you, would you prefer this?' (Ex. 5.2).

If one follows Hennessy's type of humour, it is a very funny approach and a pleasure to play and to listen to. Both motivic ideas are developed to a limited extent that appears 'just right' without overstretching their essentially entertaining purpose.

---

[2] Possibly Jules Combarieu (1859–1916), the journal's editor; *La Revue musicale* 10:12, 15 June 1910, p. 303.

Ex. 5.2: *Valses*, Op. 32 No. 1, bars, 16–23

No. 2, subtitled *'Espagne'*, is Hennessy's first exercise in a Spanish idiom – several others are yet to follow. A ternary dance form in Spain, if not exactly a waltz, is the *jota* that Hennessy notates in 3/8 time. In this quite creative handling of the Spanish idiom, the composer is, naturally perhaps, at his 'most French' when he leaves the Spanish idiom behind, such as when, towards the end, he transforms the typical melodic phrases of a Spanish folkdance into a whole-tone variant (Ex. 5.3).

Ex. 5.3: *Valses*, Op. 32 No. 2 *'Espagne'*, bars, 97–102

Switzerland as the theme of the third waltz may have been close to Hennessy's heart as we shall see later that he spent quite a lot of his leisure time (or holidays) in this country, in fact since adolescence (see Fig. 2.2). The piece has a good measure of internal diversity, beginning in medium tempo *'con tenerezza'*, moving to an *animato* passage with more than twice the previous tempo marked *'Très rythmé, imitant la danse populaire de l'Oberland'* and further to a passage where he leaves the predominant F major for sixteen bars in A major marked *'brutal'* with a heavily accented rhythm that reminded this author of a *schuhplattler* (although this social dance form is not so typical for Switzerland) before returning to the initial tempo for the piece's conclusion. Harmonically it is comparable to the first waltz insofar as a contemporaneous French style at the beginning is contrasted with a very straightforward Swiss folkdance style extending from the *'Più mosso'* phrase in bar 17 right through the 'Oberland' and the ensuing 'brutal' phrase.

While the first three waltzes are technically quite demanding, the fourth is much easier. With a base in C minor, its melody changes from the left to the right hand, but while there is a certain degree of chromaticism in the harmonic language, it is, on the whole, less characteristic than the other movements.

The critical response to the *Valses* was quite positive. Despite the liberal formal structure of the first waltz, the critic 'C.' in *La Revue musicale* warned of a certain academic 'Conservatoire' approach that he perceived in this movement, continuing:

> I allow myself to translate this impression to Mr Hennesy: he has original, personal ideas; there are certain moments where it is no longer the idea that matters anymore but a quite visible care in the technical aspects of his writing. Moreover, this collection has serious artistic value: the author has a curious mind; he likes the diversity of modes and rhythms; he seeks and he finds picturesque effects.[3]

He further attested the second and third waltzes a *'très bon caractère'* and considered the fourth 'not unworthy of Chopin'.

The critic in *S.I.M. Revue musicale mensuelle* (a journal that was to merge with *La Revue musicale* after 1920) was particularly fond of the Spanish and the Swiss waltz:

> I especially like the 2nd called Espagne, where the rhythm is hammered by the clapping of the castanets and the 3rd, called Suisse, a mountain dance where we can hear the sound of heavy ironed shoes beating the ground.[4]

The critic and composer Louis Vuillemin – a little later to become good friends with Hennessy – recommended this particular work in the course of a review of several compositions by Hennessy that appeared in 1911 in the artistic weekly *Comoedia*:

> I cannot encourage too much our pianist colleagues […] to make their acquaintance with the compositions of Mr. Swan Hennessy. From the very first reading, they will appreciate the charm and will be seduced by their elegant and remarkably expert manufacture.[5]

In England, the *Monthly Musical Record*, which had accompanied Swan Hennessy's work from his earliest publications in the 1880s, resumed:

> THE composer of these Waltzes goes his own way, and in saying this we have in mind, not only the piece before us, but also previous compositions of his. At every moment there is something in the writing which comes as a surprise. Rhythm plays a large part in the music, but knowing how even fine music may suffer from lack of it, this is to be accounted to him as a virtue. Even the great Schubert used occasionally to persist in the same rhythm till it became monotonous. The four short Waltzes in question contain some of Mr. Hennessy's ripest thoughts and best workmanship.[6]

---

[3] *'Je me permets de traduire cette impression au sujet de M. Hennesy : il a des idées originales, personnelles ; à de certains moments, ce n'est plus l'idée qui apparaît, mais un soin d'écriture technique assez visible. Ce recueil a d'ailleurs une sérieuse valeur artistique : l'auteur a l'esprit curieux ; il aime la diversité des modes et des rythmes ; il cherche et il trouve l'effet pittoresque.'*; 'C.' in *La Revue musicale* 10:12, 15 June 1910, p. 303.
[4] *'Je goûte surtout la 2ᵉ intitulée Espagne, ou le rythme se martèle d'un claquement de castagnettes et la 3ᵉ, intitulée Suisse, danse montagnarde où l'on entend le bruit de gros souliers ferrés battant le sol.'*; *S.I.M. Revue musicale mensuelle*, 15 January 1911, p. 94.
[5] *'Je ne saurais trop inciter les "camarades pianists" comme dirait Robert Oudot, à prendre connaissance des compositions de M. Swan Hennessy. Dès la première lecture, ils en goûteront le charme et s'avoueront séduits par leur facture élégante et remarquablement experte.'*; Louis Vuillemin in *Comoedia*, 1 June 1911, p. 2.
[6] *The Monthly Musical Record*, 1 August 1911, p. 204.

Also reviewing a group of piano works dating from these years, Hugo Leichtentritt in the influential German-language journal *Signale für die musikalische Welt* summarised his opinion as:

> I cannot deny the predicate 'witty' to all these pieces. They are always distinctive and inspiring. Some finesse of a very special kind, be it in rhythm, harmony or piano writing, can be found everywhere. [...]
> The waltzes Op. 32 are most likely to correspond to the general taste in Central Europe. Although I prefer those of Strauss and Chopin, I also accept those of Hennessy, simply because they are very ingenious.[7]

Unfortunately, despite Louis Vuillemin's call on pianists 'to make their acquaintance with the compositions of Mr. Swan Hennessy', this was not heeded, at least not by professional pianists. There are no documented public performances of the *Valses* before 1922, and the only documented performance of the complete album was in July 1928.[8]

Introduction, XII Variations et fugue sur un thème obligé, Op. 38 (1909) for piano

This is a work with a somewhat advanced opus number, dating from 1909 and published with Demets in 1910. In his commented list of works, Hennessy introduces it as a collaborative idea among five friends after having enjoyed dinner together.[9] Apart from Hennessy, the other contributors are the German critic, singer and composer Hugo Rasch, the French composer-musicians Georges Loth and Auguste Delacroix, and the English pianist-composer Herbert Fryer. The initiative must have come from Hennessy who probably was the host at the dinner and who would have persuaded (or payed) Demets to publish it.

Some critics knew where the inspiration came from:[10] It was the first (and best-known) of several collaborative compositions led by Nikolai Rimsky-Korsakov,

---

[7] '*Das Prädikat "geistreich" kann ich allen diesen Stücken nicht versagen. Sie sind immer apart und anregend. Irgend welche Finessen ganz besonderer Art, sei es in Rhythmik, Harmonik oder Klaviersatz sind überall zu finden. [...] / Dem allgemeinen mitteleuropäischen Musikgeschmack entsprechen am ehesten die Walzer op. 32. Ich ziehe zwar diejenigen von Strauss und Chopin vor, lasse aber auch die von Hennessy gelten, dieweil sie eben geistvoll sind.*'; Hugo Leichtentritt in *Signale für die musikalische Welt*, 23 November 1910, p. 1787. The critic here also reviewed the *Étude*, Op. 25, the *Petite suite irlandaise*, Op. 29, and the *Kinder-Album*, Op. 35.

[8] See Appendix 1 for details.

[9] '*Après un dîner les cinq artistes suivants Swan Hennessy, Hugo Rasch, Georges Loth, Auguste Delacroix, Herbert Fryer ont prise l'engagegement d'écrire une oeuvre sur le thème fa sol fa sol, mi la mi la, ré si ré si, do do do do – [...].*'; typescript of Hennessy's work-list in the family's collection, p. 4–5.

[10] It is revealed by Hugo Rasch in *Allgemeine Musikzeitung* 28:13, 31 March 1911, p. 376 and Louis Vuillemin in *Comoedia*, 25 May 1911, p. 2. Rasch – also one of the contributors to this work – introduces it as 'If I am not mistaken ...', failing to mention that he was present at the very origin of the work.

originally entitled *Parafrazy*, better known perhaps as 'Chopsticks Paraphrases', first published in 1880, with a second extended edition of 1893. The French title is *Paraphrases sur le thème favori et obligé*. In Rimsky-Korsakov's case, it was he who led the project with twenty-four variations and a finale, followed by further variations in a wide range of forms by Alexander Borodin, César Cui, and Anatoly Lyadov. The present publication uses exactly the same theme (Fig. 5.1).

Fig. 5.1: Excerpt from the title page of Op. 38 including the theme

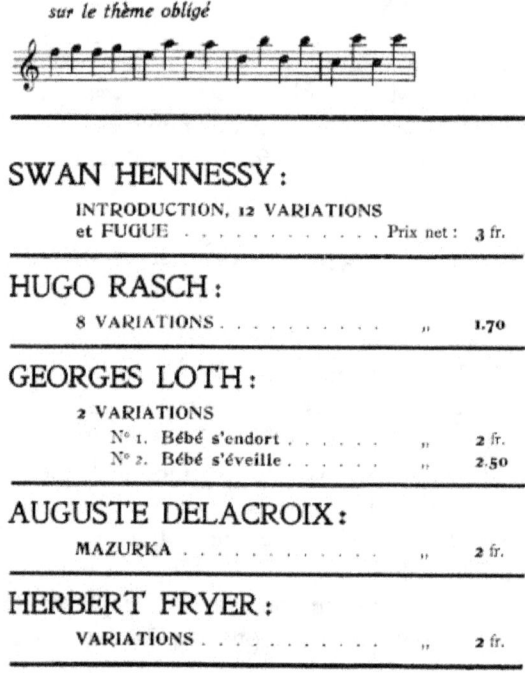

The work by Rimsky-Korsakov et al. is written for two pianos, with the first merely repeating the monophonic theme over and over again. This must have struck Hennessy and his friends at the convivial dinner table. Hennessy – like Rimsky-Korsakov leading the set, here with twelve variations and a fugue – confined the theme to the right hand (where it is also merely repeated, not varied) and adds music for the left hand only. There is a subtitle to his work reading *'pour la main gauche seule'* (for the left hand only), but this does not apply to the work as such, only to what Hennessy added to the theme.

Hennessy's lead role becomes apparent in the other pieces in this publication. The works of Rasch (*VIII Variations sur le thème obligé*, Op. 6), Delacroix (*Mazurka sur un thème obligé*) and Fryer (*Variations (sur un thème obligé)*) are dedicated to Hennessy, the only exception is Loth's two variations entitled *Bébé s'endort* and *Bébé s'éveille*, which are dedicated *'À ma petite Madeleine et à sa Maman'*. All works were published separately and in a collective album.

Hennessy's left-hand variations come in various tempi and moods and include dance forms such as a polka (var. VIII) and a rhythmically intricate waltz (var. X) with different bars in the left and right hand to accommodate a waltz to a theme in 2/4 (one bar in 2/4 corresponding to two bars in 3/8, effectively to be played as sextuplets), resulting in curious syncopations (Ex. 5.4). There is also a variation called *'Style irlandais'* (var. IX). The left hand of the piano does indeed perform variations on the theme, simultaneously with the repetitions of the theme in the right hand. The ensuing two-part fugue includes an expansion, inversion, and contrary motion of the theme.

Ex. 5.4: *Introduction, XII Variations et fugue*, Op. 38; var. X, first two (of five) systems

The whole project is a musical joke and must have been fun to conceive. That it is also best to be reviewed in a humorous manner was well understood by Louis Vuillemin in *Comoedia*:

> This is a lot of fun. Swan Hennessy, Hugo Rasch, Georges Loth, Auguste Delacroix, Herbert Fryer met. History does not tell us if it was evening, around the lamp. Their combined efforts, especially their lively imaginations, have resulted in a charming little collection. […] In truth, the work of the five 'accomplices' is full of spirit. It also shows great writing ability. Professionals will be as aware of this as they will be entertained. […] We should encourage our young musicians to play these innocent games. There is something for everyone. First the authors, who will have had a great time, then the readers, whose pleasure is certain. And, once again, this kind of paradoxical gymnastics is not incompatible with the music. The work by Swan Hennessy, Hugo Rasch – friend of Mr Hennessy – Georges

Loth – friend of Mr Hennessy – Auguste Delacroix – friend of Mr Hennessy – and Herbert Fryer – friend of Mr Hennessy – shows us this peremptorily.[11]

Other critics who did not recognise the Russian connection also found something to value. *La Revue musicale* considered the publication 'a little academic, but very original',[12] likewise, *The Monthly Musical Record* described it as 'in fact, a very original piece',[13] and *Signale* conceded '(t)here's enough spirit and wit in it.'.[14] A little more reservation demonstrated *La Revue musicale S.I.M.* which preferred the pieces by Loth and Rasch while expressing its opinion that '(o)ur authors often seemed to fight with [the theme] rather than to adapt to it.'[15]

Despite the interesting (and interested) reviews, there is no record of any public performance, whole or in part.

Kinder-Album. 24 kleine Präludien in verschiedenen Ton- und Taktarten, Op. 35 (1909) for piano

The *Kinder-Album*, Op. 35 was completed in 1909 and published with Schott in Germany in 1910. The choice of publisher shows that Hennessy tried to diversify his 'market'. By now he had given up publication in England (as he had done before with Augener & Co.), also preferring the Mainz headquarter of Schott to its London branch. To his advantage, he was still fluent in German and conversed easily in this language in his correspondence. Even the dedication is in German; it is to his father Michael Hennessy and reads *'Meinem lieben Vater gewidmet'* ('Dedicated to my dear father').

The present work is another specimen of Hennessy's particular humour, expressed in individual titles of the pieces, some unique playing directions and the music itself. Both the collective title and those of the twenty-four pieces in the collection are in German, and most have already been laid out like this in the manuscript. Some of the critics from France and England, however, provided translations of the more striking ones, and these have partly been used below.

---

[11] *'Ceci est très amusant. MM. Swan Hennessy, Hugo Rasch, Georges Loth, Auguste Delacroix, Herbert Fryer se son réunis. L'histoire ne nous dit point si ce fut le soir, autour de la lampe. De leurs efforts combinés, de leurs vives imaginations surtout, est résulté un charmant petit recueil. […] A la vérité, l'oeuvre des cinq "complices" est pleine d'esprit. Elle témoigne aussi d'une grande habileté d'écriture. Les professionnels en auront conscience autant qu'ils s'en divertiront. […] Il faut encourager nos jeunes musiciens à ces jeux innocents. Chacun y trouvera quelque attrait. Les auteurs d'abord, qui se seront énormément divertis, les lecteurs ensuite dont le plaisir est certain. Et puis, encore une fois, cette sorte de gymnastique paradoxale n'est point incompatible avec la musique. L'ouvrage de MM. Swan Hennessy, Hugo Rasch – ami de M. Hennessy – Georges Loth – ami de M. Hennessy – Auguste Delacroix – ami de M. Hennessy – et Herbert Fryer – ami de M. Hennessy – nous le démontre péremptoirement.'*; Louis Vuillemin in *Comoedia*, 25 May 1911, p. 2.
[12] *'un peu scolastique, mais fort original'*; *La Revue Musicale* 10:9, 1 May 1910, p. 237.
[13] *The Monthly Musical Record*, 1 August 1910, p. 178.
[14] *'Geist und Witz steckt genug darin.'*; *Signale für die musikalische Welt* 86:47, 23 November 1910, p. 1787.
[15] *'Bien souvent, nos auteurs ont eu plus l'air de se battre avec lui que de s'y adapter.'*; *La Revue musicale S.I.M.*, 15 January 1911, p. 94.

After *Aus dem Kinderleben*, Op. 19 (1904), this at first seems like a second essay in writing music for children, modelled after numerous historical prototypes. At second glance, however, this collection is perhaps rather targeted at adults with a childish sense of humour. Particularly when it comes to unusual time signatures like 3/16, 7/4, or 11/8 one begins to wonder if this is meant to be a counting exercise for children (and why not?) or an absurd expression of the theoretically endless choice of musical measures, taken literally and applied liberally.

A potential model for the conception of titles and the general spirit may have been the six pieces in Debussy's *Children's Corner* that had been published in the previous year, and which included a *Jumbo's Lullaby*, a *Serenade for the Doll* and the famous *Golliwog's Cake Walk*. Near-matches in Hennessy's work would be *Mietzi's Schlummerlied* ('Mietzi's Lullaby'), *Puppen-Menuet* ('Doll Minuet'), and *Begräbniss eines Bleisoldaten* ('The Lead Soldier's Funeral'). Further instructive titles with Hennessy are *Gesichterschneiden* ('Pulling Faces'), *Langweilige Geschichte* ('Boring Story'), *Der lustige Irländer* ('The Funny Irishman'), *Heute kommt der Lehrer nicht!* ('The Teacher Won't Be Here Today'), *Pfeifender Handwerksbursch* ('Whistling Handyman'), *Der Sandmann kommt!* ('The Sandman is Coming!'), etc. – conjuring up images enough to make children laugh and open-minded adults at least smirk.

Ex. 5.5: *Kinder-Album*, Op. 35 No. 7 '*Heute kommt der Lehrer nicht!*', bars 1–14

Of the twenty-four pieces, sixteen do not exceed one page in the score, the remaining six pieces have two pages each. Hennessy excels in brief characterisations of his themes, in generating creative and fanciful images of his ideas, while in this case being totally liberated from any burden to develop his themes at any length.

As some critics noted, a number of the more unusual time signatures do not seem necessary, such as 8/16 in *'Gesichterschneiden'* which might just as well have been notated as 4/8, or even 2/4. And even though the 2/8 metre for the Irish-style *'Der lustige Irländer'* will never be found in Irish traditional music, it seems perfectly indigenous, although a more common notation in 4/4 time with two groups of four quavers in a bar would have been possible (Hennessy notates four semiquavers in one bar in the right hand, accompanied by two quavers in the left). Some metres look weird, yet are nothing but sheer wit as his strange realisation of a 3/16 metre in *'Heute kommt der Lehrer nicht!'* (to be played 'jubilantly') (Ex. 5.5).

Other strange metres seem perfectly reasonable, such as the 7/4 in *'Aus der Heimat'* or the combination of 9/16 and 5/16 in *'Der Sandmann kommt'*, the latter to be played in a 'tired, sleepy' way (Ex. 5.6).

Ex. 5.6: *Kinder-Album*, Op. 35 No. 20 *'Der Sandmann kommt'*, bars 1–5

The collection received a fair measure of critical attention that, as can be expected, focused in equal measure on the humorous titles as much as on the unusual time signatures and, occasionally, tonalities. *The Monthly Musical Record* noted:

> The whole set of pieces is, in fact, clever and interesting. It is stated on the title-page that various keys and time-measures are employed. Among the former we find, for instance, the unusual one of E flat minor; and not only that, but enharmonic modulations necessitating many accidentals – a capital exercise in reading.[16]

In contrast, *The Musical Standard* enjoyed the amenable 'simplicity' in 'these days of overloaded music' and perceived a pedagogic aim in the rare rhythms:

---

[16] *The Monthly Musical Record*, 1 July 1910, p. 153.

His work is so clever, so melodious, so poetical, that it charms the hearer and delights the player. But he has a love of queer rhythms, as 7-4, 5-8, 11-8, which are, however, instructive for young learners.[17]

The Musical Times observed:

> The works are experimental miniatures, perhaps not intended to be taken seriously, and fit to be discussed as much as played. The workmanship is always careful, and there is more appeal to the mind of the musician than to that of the child.[18]

In Germany, Hugo Leichtentritt in *Signale für die musikalische Welt* acknowledged the collection's humour and originality while detecting influences of Debussy and Korngold. But he also expressed reservations towards some pieces in the collection in which he thought Hennessy went too far:

> Unfortunately, the interesting and ingenious alone is not enough to create a piece of art of significance. Ingenuity in music sometimes gets along very well with dryness, dullness, and I don't like this involuntary combination very much among the many interesting combinations of Hennessy.[19]

While also wondering about 'crazy' time signatures, Hennessy's critic-friend Hugo Rasch in *Allgemeine Musikzeitung* summarises:

> Those who have a sense of humour and love of children will get their money's worth playing through this little album. Pieces like: Gesichterschneiden, Heute kommt der Lehrer nicht, Begräbnis eines Bleisoldaten, and the delicious 'boring story' are gems of expressivity and sentiment.[20]

The most substantial review appeared in *La Revue musicale*, written by Jules Combarieu. He begins by pointing out that Hennessy's approach is not quite as unusual or new as it may seem, drawing a parallel to the …

---

[17] 'C. W.' in *The Musical Standard* 37:954, 13 April 1912, p. 234.
[18] *The Musical Times* 53:836, October 1912, p. 654.
[19] '*Leider genügt das Interessante und Geistvolle allein noch nicht, um ein Stück Kunst von Bedeutung zu schaffen. Geistvoll verträgt sich in der Musik bisweilen sehr gut mit trocken, poesielos, und diese unfreiwillige Kombination gefällt mir unter den vielerlei interessanten Kombinationen von Hennessy am wenigsten.*'; Hugo Leichtentritt in *Signale für die musikalische Welt* 86:47, 23 November 1910, p. 1787.
[20] '*Wer Sinn für Humor und Kinder lieb hat, kommt beim Durchspielen dieses kleinen Albums reichlich auf seine Kosten. Stückchen wie: Gesichterschneiden, Heute kommt der Lehrer nicht, Begräbnis eines Bleisoldaten und die köstliche "langweilige Geschichte" sind Perlen an Ausdruckfähigkeit und Gemüt.*'; Hugo Rasch in *Allgemeine Musikzeitung* 28:13, 31 March 1911, p. 376.

> [...] clavicinists of the 18th century ... Rameau and Couperin [who] abound in extraordinary titles, with malicious and caricatural tendencies, attesting to the musicians' habit to express, so to speak, all forms of life.[21]

Combarieu draws further comparisons to Schumann's idea of picking out single aspects of children's life that seem unimportant but always lead to a musical gem, to Stephen Heller who would be 'from the same school', to Mussorgsky for the realism of the expression, and even to operas by Gounod, Bizet or Wagner, that present series of musical genre paintings.

> The musician seems to tell us: 'These are the ideas suggested to me by this or that spectacle. Like all men, like all artists, I think after having observed, and what I write follows from what I have felt, but I express myself in a language of my own!' Moreover, the freedom of music is limitless, like that of the mind itself. And poetry is everywhere, both in the play of children and in the murmurs of the forest. Neither Mr Ravel nor Mr Koechlin will deny this.[22]

The critic continues with a more general assessment of Hennessy's music, based on having watched his development over some time:

> Mr Swan Hennesy's pieces are the fruit of a serious, original, solid and personal talent, which we have followed with interest since his beginnings. [...] I've enjoyed playing these little artistic fantasies, which, if played by skilful hands, will not fail to please. In a few, I regretted a little dryness, a lesser interest in melodic thinking, a certain laborious effort. In such short compositions, one has the right to be demanding.[23]

As with several compositions of this period, public performances came late – very late in this case – and Hennessy has not been able to witness them anymore, occurring in 1930 and 1931 (see Appendix 1).

---

[21] *'Les clavicinistes du XVIIIe siècle, pour ne pas remonter plus haut, Rameau et Couperin à leur tête, abondent en titres extraordinaires, à tendances malicieuses et caricaturales, attestant l'application du musicien à noter, pour ainsi dire, toutes les formes de la vie.'*, 'J. C.' [Jules Combarieu] in *La Revue musicale* 10:12, 15 June 1910, pp. 300–302 [301].
[22] *'Le musicien semble nous dire : "Voilà les idées qui m'ont été suggérées par tel ou tel spectacle. Comme tous les hommes, comme tous les artistes, je pense après avoir observé, et ce que j'écris vient à la suite de ce que j'ai ressenti; mais je m'exprime dans une langue qui n'appartient qu'à moi!" Au surplus, la liberté de la musique est sans limites, comme celle de l'esprit lui-même. Et la poésie est partout, aussi bien dans le jeu des enfants que dans les murmures de la forêt. Ce n'est ni M. Ravel ni M. Koechlin qui me démentiront.'*; ibid., p. 301.
[23] *'Les pièces de M. Swan Hennesy sont le fruit d'un talent sérieux, original, solide et personnel, que nous suivons avec intérêt depuis ses débuts. [...] J'ai éprouvé un vif plaisir à lire ces petites fantaisies artistiques qui, si elles sont jouées par des mains adroites, ne manqueront pas de plaire. Dans quelques-unes, j'ai regretté un peu de sécheresse, un moindre intérêt de la pensée mélodique, un certain effort laborieux. Dans des compositions aussi brèves, on a le droit d'être exigeant.'*; ibid, p. 301–302.

Croquis de femmes, Op. 33 (*c*1910/11) for piano

This work falls out of the order of opus numbers, being probably written in early 1911[24] and published in that year by Ch. Hayet, recent successor to F. Durdilly – Hennessy's only publication with this publisher.[25] That an opus 33 should have been written two years after Op. 32 and Op. 34 is curious and can only mean that Hennessy, for at least the second time, withdrew compositions and revised his work-list. Originally, opus 33 was assigned to the *Petite suite*, Op. 34 (1909, published 1911). Furthermore, among his music manuscripts, there is the unpublished score of '*2 Orientales*, Op. 37', separately entitled *Odalisque* and *Nubienne*, that have partly been used in the *Croquis*. The work is dedicated to Jules Combarieu (1859–1916), the editor of the first (i. e. pre-1920) *La Revue musicale*, a journal in which Swan Hennessy has often fared well (see, e. g., Op. 35 above).

In *Croquis de femmes* ('Women's Sketches'), Hennessy continues his humourist strain with an album in seven pieces intended to characterise different types of women. Their titles are *Au couvent* ('In the Convent'), *Bavardes* ('Chit-Chatters' or 'Gossipers'), *La Vieille tante* ('The Old Aunt'), *Mondaine* (a 'high-society' or 'worldly' woman), *Jeunes anglaises* ('Young English Girls'), *Dans les jardins du sérail* ('In the Gardens of the Seraglio'), and *Charmeuse de serpents* ('Charming Snakes'). Most certainly politically incorrect nowadays, the album was not perceived like that in Hennessy's time. On the contrary, critical reviews – written, of course, by males – were overwhelmingly positive. *The Monthly Musical Record* provided a merely descriptive review that may serve well as an introduction:

> IN these Sketches we have, as it were, musical pictures of various feminine types. In No. 1, *Au Couvent*, a chorale phrase depicts the religious atmosphere. The repeated opening figure may perhaps be intended to represent the uniform, calm life of the nuns. No. 2, *Bavardes*, with its ever busily moving semiquavers, express in a very realistic way chattering – of which the monopoly, by the way, is not confined to women. One other number, the bright *Jeunes Anglaises*, shows that the composer has met with some very pleasant English ladies. All, however, are light and tasteful specimens of programme music.[26]

Bavardes is a very good example of how Hennessy worked. The 'ever busily moving semiquavers' begin in bar 5 after very brief first 'exclamations'. The ensuing chatty 'conversation' illustrates agreement among the chatters as much as disagreement: the greater the disagreement (or the more excited the chat), the sharper the dissonances, with interjections representing, perhaps, a new speaker or an attempt at reconciliation

---

[24] It was evidently in print by early April 1911 when Hennessy presented a published copy to Ludwig Strecker, the director of Schott; see letter from Hennessy to Strecker, 4/5 April, with response from Strecker, 21 April; see below in the discussion of Op. 34.
[25] The score contains numerous printing errors (mainly missing bound notes and pauses in two-part writing), which must have angered Hennessy who was very strict in this regard.
[26] *The Monthly Musical Record*, 1 April 1911, p. 92.

(Ex. 5.7). Like most of the other pieces in the set, it is light-hearted music that clearly betrays his Parisian musical environment.

Ex. 5.7: *Croquis de femmes*, Op. 33 No. 2 'Bavardes', bars 9–16 (♪= 152)

Both *Dans les jardins du sérail* and *Charmeuse de serpents* play with an assortment of techniques associated with *fin-de-siècle* musical orientalism such as quintal harmony and chromatically ornamented melodic lines. The commonly alleged deceptiveness of snakes is depicted in the seventh piece by a rather sudden change from the predominant 5/4 metre to 7/4, and from C minor to C major, with some high-pitched rhythm in the right hand to a (less oriental) melody in the left (Ex. 5.8). This functions as a transition, after which follows a different type of melody more associated with Western instead of Eastern music, but following the rhythmic model from before the 7/4 passage. Speculating on his intentions, is this perhaps to suggest that after an orientally inspired seductive phase the relationship with this female character develops into something more common?

Ex. 5.8: *Croquis de femmes*, Op. 33 No. 7 'Charmeuse de serpents', bar 19 (♩ = 96)

The critical reception of *Croquis de femmes* was very positive, particularly in France and Germany, except perhaps that some critics regretted that the pieces were so short and wondered why that is the case. For instance, an unsigned review in *La Revue*

musicale – the journal of the work's dedicatee – expressed the opinion that '(t)his is, without doubt, only the temporary entertainment of a talented composer from whom we expect more considerable works',[27] and Hugo Rasch asked in *Allgemeine Musikzeitung*:

> The pieces are very short. Regretfully one asks again and again: Why doesn't this solid expert with his pronounced sense of part-writing write us something bigger? A string quartet or trio? Something good should come out of that.[28]

Apart from this mild critique (or expectation), the general tone of the reviews was encouraging. *La Revue musicale* wondered whether perhaps some of the effects would not work better in an orchestra or ensemble rather than on the piano, but stated

> They are pretty illustrations, genre paintings that are sometimes tiny, [but] well in the descriptive taste of contemporary music, where a composer of very serious technical knowledge enjoys following his fancy, and not without originality.[29]

Karl Thiessen in *Signale für die musikalische Welt* praised a composer in the footsteps of Debussy:

> [...] Swan Hennessy who every now and then finds delight in the innovative endeavours of the young French and their picturesque and uneven, as it were, Impressionist style of Debussy and his followers. The Croquis de femmes in particular, which indeed represent an interesting small gallery of women's heads depicted in tone-paintings, serve as strong evidence of this. It should be difficult to describe with so few strokes the most essential and important characteristics of a female character more aptly in music than has happened here in pieces such as 'La vieille tante' or 'Mondaine', for example.[30]

Louis Vuillemin wrote in *Comoedia*:

---

[27] '*Aussi bien n'est-ce là, sans doute, que le divertissement passager d'un compositeur de talent dont nous attendons des œuvres plus considérables.*'; *La Revue musicale* 11:8, 15 April 1911, p. 173.

[28] '*Die Stücke sind sehr kurz. Bedauernd fragt man immer wieder: Warum schreibt uns dieser gediegene Könner mit seinem ausgesprochenen Sinn für Stimmführung nicht mal was größres? Ein Streichquartett oder -Trio? Da müßte doch was gutes herauskommen.*'; Hugo Rasch in *Allgemeine Musikzeitung* 38:24, 16 June 1911, p. 672.

[29] '*Ce sont de jolies illustrations, des tableautins de genre parfois minuscules, bien dans le goût descriptif de la musique actuelle, où un compositeur de savoir technique très sérieux s'amuse à suivre sa fantaisie, non sans originalité.*'; as fn. 27.

[30] '[...] *Swan Hennessy, der hinwiederum mehr Geschmack findet an den Neuerungsbestrebungen der Jungfranzosen und an den malerischen, sozusagen abrupten Impressionsstil Debussy's und seiner Anhänger anknüpft. Dafür dienen namentlich die Croquis de femmes, die in der Tat eine interessante kleine Galerie tonmalerisch dargestellter Frauenköpfe repräsentieren, als sprechender Beweis. Es dürfte schwer sein, mit so wenig Strichen die wesentlichsten und wichtigsten Merkmale eines weiblichen Charakters noch treffender musikalisch zu schildern, als es hier z. B. in Stücken wie "La vieille tante" oder "Mondaine" geschehen ist.*'; Karl Thiessen in *Signale für die musikalische Welt* 69:21, 24 May 1911, p. 800.

One will love the chatter, the coquetry, the malice, even the soft irreverence of these different pieces written in a pianistic form that is quite seductive. Mr. Swan Hennessy certainly has excellent ears. His eyes aren't bad either![31]

Again, however, the uptake of these works on the concert stage was extremely delayed. There was never a complete performance of the full set, and even excerpts were not played in public before 1925. After a 1928 performance of excerpts in Brussels, a critic applauded them as 'small satires, fine, joyful, infinitely amusing';[32] after hearing a June 1929 performance in Paris, the *Journal des débats* praised works 'where the author's happy and fine musical sense proves itself',[33] *La Semaine à Paris* considered them 'extremely agreeable',[34] and in 1930 *Le Monde musical* thought they were 'delightful'.[35]

But all this proved that by 1911 Hennessy's reputation was still largely based on reviews of his publications. As yet, he had not found a way to open up the concert platform for himself.

Correspondence with Schott (part 1)

Beginning in 1905, Swan Hennessy published altogether six works with Schott, with the remaining two appearing in 1911.[36] These two works are the subject of the first part of the correspondence between Hennessy and the company's senior director, Ludwig Strecker, that has been preserved in the Schott Archive now housed at the Staatsbibliothek Berlin, Stiftung Preußischer Kulturbesitz.

Since we know so little about Hennessy's private life, his behaviour and character, this correspondence is a real treasure trove, giving a unique insight into Hennessy's life beyond the evaluation of music and reviews. Compared to later autograph letters by him (see Chapter 8), the Schott correspondence also contains copies of the responses by the publisher. These throw a spotlight on how he was perceived by this crucial intermediate between the composer and the public by revealing what the latter thought about the uniqueness and 'marketability' of his music. Finally, part 2 of the correspondence – following below after the discussion of Opp. 34 and 36 – reveals Hennessy's attitude to aspects like advertising and promoting one's work which eventually brought the business relationship between Hennessy and Schott to an end in 1912.

The main correspondent on Schott's part was the senior director and owner of the company, Ludwig Strecker (1853–1943), at the time one of the most successful

---

[31] 'On aimera le caquetage, la coquetterie, la malice, voire même la douce irrévérence de ces différentes pièces écrites dans une forme pianistique tout à fait séduisante. M. Swan Hennessy a certes d'excellentes oreilles. Ses yeux ne sont point mauves non plus!'; Louis Vuillemin in *Comoedia*, 25 May 1911, p. 2.
[32] 'petites satires, fines, joyeuses, infiniment amusantes', *L'Étoile Belge*, 29 April 1928.
[33] 'où s'avère le sens musical heureux et fin de l'auteur'; *Journal des débats*, 10 June 1929, p. 4.
[34] 'extrêmement agréables'; Tristan Klingsor in *La Semaine à Paris*, 14 June 1929.
[35] 'délicieux'; L. C. in *Le Monde musical*, 1 June 1930.
[36] See Appendix 3 for an overview of Hennessy's works with various publishers.

music managers in Europe who came to fame through, among other factors, his skill in dealing with Richard Wagner. Part 1 lasts from 4/5 April to 16 September 1911 and deals with the publication of Hennessy's Opp. 34 and 36. This thread, in fact, continues through 9 December 1911 when Strecker thanks Hennessy for the cheque, but is increasingly intermingled with letters explaining reasons for Schott's/Strecker's rejection of Opp. 39 and 40.

The exchange begins with a short letter by Hennessy that shows how he worked with publishers. Despite the distance from Paris, Hennessy had made an attempt to visit Strecker personally in Mainz, Germany, to play two works to him, but had apparently not announced his visit so that he stood before closed doors. He did not mention in any of the letters that Op. 34 already dated from (late?) 1909 and that Op. 36, too, was not one of his latest works. Thus, we also don't know whether he had made any earlier attempt to publish the works elsewhere. Because Op. 34 is dedicated to Eugène Demets (Schott's competitor), it is quite possible that he had offered it to him first, and it would be interesting to know why Demets did not take it. Unfortunately, despite the much longer relationship with Demets and Eschig, today's Eschig archive in Paris does not appear to have any correspondence.

Hennessy's letters are interesting for a number of revelations we might otherwise not have known, such as

- In the letter of 4/5 April 1911, he admits not to have a sufficient piano technique to play his own music well.
- On 23 April he says he is a very careful corrector of galley proofs.
- In the letters of June to September 1911, he communicates a number of different addresses of hotels in Switzerland to which proofs can be sent for correction. It seems like he spent that whole summer in various Swiss luxury hotels, returning to Paris every now and then – and this may not have been an unusual year.

Likewise, Strecker's letters to Hennessy reveal a number of interesting facts as well, such as:

- In the letter of 21 April 1911, we learn that he had a financial agreement with Hennessy (with details to follow later on) that extends to at least co-financing his own prints. It is not sure whether the sums in question relieved Schott of the full publisher's risk, but this is probably not the case (if it would, Strecker would not have needed to reject the later works Opp. 39, 40, and 41).
- In the same letter, he predicts to Hennessy 'We have the impression that your time is still to come', which – one hundred years later – may still be true.

The correspondence is documented in full below, with the German original and an English translation side by side.[37]

---

[37] The date line in the following documentation is represented here exactly as written in the respective letters (not translated). Likewise, the original German text in the letters themselves has not been edited (or corrected) but given exactly as in the autograph letters by Hennessy

Paris, 270 Boul^d Raspail
Paris, 4/5 April 1911

Sehr geehrter Herr,

Ich habe Sie vor einigen Tagen besucht in der Hoffnung Ihnen einige neue Klavier-Compositionen vorzuspielen. Leider waren Sie abwesend. Jetzt schicke ich Ihnen die Sachen und bitte Sie dieselben genau zu besehen. Ich glaube die Sonatine wird Sie interessieren. Sie dürfte wenigstens instruktiv sein. Mit den anderen beiden Stücken habe ich immer großen Erfolg bekommen, obwohl meine Klavier-Technik nicht ganz hinreichend ist. Ein guter Pianist sollte aber mit dem „Pariser Volksfest" ein grossen Effekt machen können.

Gerne hoffend recht bald von Ihnen eine günstige Antwort zu bekommen –

Mit vorzüglicher Hochachtung und bestem Gruss

   Swan Hennessy

Dear Sir,

I visited you a few days ago in the hope to be able to play to you a few new piano compositions. Unfortunately, you were not present. Now I am sending you these things and ask you to have a close look at them. I think that the Sonatina[38] should be of interest to you. At the least it should be instructive. With the other two pieces I have always had great success although my piano technique is not really sufficient. However, a good pianist should be able to make some great effect with the 'Parisian Fair'.

Hoping to receive a positive response from you soon –

With exquisite respect and best wishes

   Swan Hennessy

   Herrn Swan Hennessy
     Paris

Sehr geehrter Herr,

Die Durchsicht Ihrer uns freundlichst übersandten Kompositionen, sowohl gedruckte: Croquis de femmes, als Manuskripte: Fêtes, deux morceaux; und Sonatine op. 34 hat uns ausserordentlich interessiert, besonders die Croquis, die ebenso wie die kleinen Jugendstücke, die wir voriges Jahr gedruckt

   Mainz, 21. April 1911
   Mr Swan Hennessy
     Paris

Dear Sir,

The perusal of the compositions that you so kindly sent to us, the printed: Croquis de femmes as well as manuscripts: Fêtes, deux morceaux; and Sonatina, Op. 34, has interested us extraordinarily, especially the Croquis, which are, like those little children's pieces that we printed last year, really

---

and the machine-written responses by Strecker. I have applied occasional minor corrections in square brackets in Hennessy's German letters that may help understand his message for readers with limited German.

[38] As becomes clear later, this relates to the *Petite suite sur les notes mi do mi fa si mi* (originally called 'Sonatine' in the MS) Op. 34 (1909); the second piece is *Fêtes. Deux Morceaux descriptifs*, Op. 36 (1910); both were published in 1911 with Schott. The printed piece he sent with the same letter is *Croquis de femmes*, Op. 33.

haben wirklich ausserordentlich witzig und charakteristisch sind. Aber – wir befürchten, dass Sie mit dieser Musik immer noch Anstoss erregen werden, wenn auch einzelne Kritiker in letzter Zeit sich sehr anerkennend geäussert haben. – Es macht uns den Eindruck, als würde Ihre Zeit erst kommen, wenn man einmal musikalische Zeitungen hat, wie man jetzt gedruckte politische Zeitungen herausgiebt. Wir meinen, dass ein solcher Witz dann leichter genossen werden wird, als jetzt, wo er prätensiöser auftritt, indem er als Teil eines musikalischen Heftes zu einem verhältnismässig hohen Preis erworben werden muss.

Die Sonatine ist insofern ein kleiner Widerspruch, als man bis jetzt unter einem solchen Werk etwas ganz leicht ausführbares und einfaches, für den Unterricht gebräuchliches, verstanden hat. Diese Eigenschaft wird man vergeblich in Ihrer Sonatine suchen und wir möchten Ihnen anheim geben, einen anderen Titel zu wählen, vielleicht „petite suite" oder ähnliches. Auch die Widmung an die Katzen und die Hunde des Herrn Demets klingt nicht sehr pädagogisch. Immerhin sind wir bereit dieses Stück, sowie die beiden op. 36 herauszugeben unter den seitherigen Bedingungen und bitten Sie uns zu sagen, ob Sie damit einverstanden sind. –

Mit hochachtungsvollen Grüssen
[signature stamp] B. Schott's Söhne

P.S. Ich habe ausserordentlich bedauert, Ihren Besuch verfehlt zu haben, ebenso mein Sohn, der im Hause anwesend war, als Sie beim Hausmeister nach mir fragten. Ich bitte Sie jedenfalls in einem ähnlichen Falle nicht so rasch wegzulaufen und uns der Freude nicht

extraordinarily witty and characteristic. But – we fear that you will still offend with this kind of music, even though some critics have expressed their appreciation lately. – We have the impression that your time is still to come, when there are musical newspapers just like we currently have political newspapers. We are of the opinion that then people will more readily enjoy your humour than now as it appears more pretentious as part of a musical edition that has to be bought at a relatively high price.

The Sonatina is a little contradiction in that, until now, such a work has been understood to be something very easy to perform and that is usable in the classroom. This characteristic will not be found in your Sonatina, and we would like to advise you to choose another title, perhaps 'petite suite' or similar. Also, the dedication to the cats and dogs of Mr. Demets does not sound very pedagogical. However, we are willing to publish this piece as well as the two Op. 36 under the usual conditions and ask you to tell us whether you agree.

With respectful greetings,
[signature stamp] B. Schott's Söhne

PS.: I deeply regretted that I missed your visit, as did my son, who was present in the house when you asked the caretaker about me. In a similar case, I would ask you not to run away so quickly and not to rob us of the joy of speaking to you, even if it can only be for a short time.

Yours respectfully,
L. Strecker

zu berauben, Sie, wenn es auch nur kurz sein kann, zu sprechen.
    Hochachtungsvoll ergeben
      L. Strecker

                          270 Boul^d Raspail
                             Paris, 23, 4 11.

Sehr geehrter Herr,
Besten Dank für Ihren liebenswürdigen Brief. Es freut mich sehr dass Sie bereit sind meine Stücke (op. 34 und 36) herauszugeben und ich bin mit Ihren Bedingungen einverstanden. Betreffend den Titel von op. 34, scheint mir „Petite Suite sur le Thème [in staff notation, with syllables above] mi do mi fa si mi" am geeignetsten. Die Widmung kann ganz weg bleiben. Bitte sagen Sie mir die Summe die ich Ihnen zu schicken habe.

Ich habe mir sehr viele Mühe gegeben dass die Manuskripte ganz Fehler frei seien, aber zur Vorsicht und um Zeit und Mühe für Sie zu sparen möchte ich Sie bitten die ersten Proben revedieren zu lassen bevor Sie sie mir schicken. Ich weiss leider aus Erfahrung dass ich ein sehr bedürflicher Correcteur bin.

Gerne hoffend Sie auch in Paris zu sehen und einmal die Bekanntschaft Ihres Herrn Sohnes zu machen, mit besten Grüssen
    Hochachtungsvoll ergeben
      Swan Hennessy.

Dear Sir,
Thank you for your kind letter. I am very pleased that you are willing to publish my pieces (op. 34 and 36) and I agree to your conditions. Regarding the title of Op. 34, 'Petite Suite sur le Thème [in staff notation, with syllables above] mi do mi fa si mi' seems to me the most suitable. The dedication can be omitted completely. Please tell me the amount I have to send you.

I have tried very hard to ensure that the manuscripts are completely free of errors, but to be on the safe side and to save time and effort for you, I would like to ask you to revise the first samples before you send them to me. I know from experience that I am a very needy *correcteur*.

Very much hoping to see you in Paris some time and to make the acquaintance of your son I remain, with best wishes,
    Sincerely yours
      Swan Hennessy

                      270 Boul^d Raspail, Paris,
                               14, 6, 11.

Sehr geehrter Herr,
Da ich den ganzen Sommer von Paris abwesend sein werde, dürfte ich Sie bitten mir gefälligst zu sagen wann ich die Proben meiner Kompositionen „Petite Suite" und „Fêtes" bekommen

Dear Sir,
because I shall be away from Paris for the whole summer, I would like to ask you to please tell me when I will receive the proofs of my compositions

werde, damit ich Ihnen eine Adresse geben kann?
    Hochachtungsvoll ergeben
    Swan Hennessy.

'Petite Suite' and 'Fêtes', so that I can provide you with an address.
    Sincerely yours
    Swan Hennessy

    Herrn Swan Hennessy
    Paris
Sehr geehrter Herr,
    Entschuldigen Sie, dass ich Ihnen über die Stücke noch nichts geschrieben habe, es war aber noch nicht möglich den Stich zu beginnen, da wir sehr eilige andere Sachen zu erledigen hatten. Bis zur „rentrée" sollen sie aber fertig sein und ich bitte Sie, uns Ihre Sommeradresse zur Uebersendung der Korrekturen freundlichst angeben zu wollen.
    Mit hochachtungsvollen Grüssen ergebenst
    L. Strecker

    Mainz, den 16. Juni 1911
    Mr Swan Hennessy
    Paris
Dear Sir,
    Please accept my apologies for not having written anything yet about those pieces, but it was not yet possible to commence the engraving, because we had other urgent things to take care of. Before the 'rentrée', however, they should be finished and I would like to ask you to please send us your summer address for the corrections.
    With respectful greetings,
    Yours truly,
    L. Strecker

    Paris,
    17, 7, 11.

Sehr geehrte Herren,
    Wenn die Proben meiner op. 34 und 36 noch nicht nach Andermatt spediert worden sind, bitte ich Sie gefälligst dieselben nach
    Hotel zum Löwen
    Lungern (Obwalden)
    Schweiz
zu schicken.
    Hochachtungsvoll ergeben,
    Swan Hennessy

Gentlemen,
    In case the proofs of my Opp. 34 and 36 have not yet been sent to Andermatt, would you please be so kind and send them to
    Hotel zum Löwen
    Lungern (Obwalden)
    Switzerland

    Sincerely yours,
    Swan Hennessy

[letter head: Grand Hotel du Parc/Société Anonyme de l'Hotel Suisse/Vittel/130 Chambres/Ascenseur /Éclairage Électrique/Téléphone N°. 9]

16, 9, 11.

Sehr geehrter Herr!	Dear Sir!
Auf Seite 1 der „Petite Suite" sollte die Widmung: „à mon cher ami E. Demets" heissen statt „à mon cher ame"! (Letzteres wäre doch etwas zu zärtlich.) Auf dem Titelblatt derselben „Petite Suite" gehören zwischen „Vivace, ma non tanto" und „Moderato" ein Punkt und ein Strich. In der Musik finde ich nur einen Fehler, ebenfalls in der „Petite Suite" — Seite 12 sollte Tackt 11 wie folgt sein in der linken Hand (Bass): [one notated bar] also eine halbe statt eine ganze Note.	On page 1 of the 'Petite Suite', the dedication should read 'à mon cher ami E. Demets' instead of 'à mon cher ame'! (The latter would be just a little too tender.) On the title page of the same 'Petite Suite' there should a dot and a hyphen between 'Vivace, ma non tanto' and 'Moderato'. In the music I find but one mistake, again in the 'Petite Suite' — bar 11 on page 12 should be as follows, in the left hand (bass): [one bar in notation], therefore, a minim instead of a semibreve.
Mit besten Grüßen, Hochachtungsvoll ergeben Swan Hennessy	With best wishes, sincerely yours Swan Hennessy

At this point, Hennessy sends two further manuscripts with a letter dated 29 September 1911 that Schott rejects in a response of 3 October (discussed further below). Strecker adds in this response that Opp. 34 and 36 are now in print and should arrive shortly. However, on 5 October he sends another letter with corrections by Hugo Rasch[39] so that the printing was halted:

	Mainz, 5. Oktober 1911
Herrn Swan Hennessy Paris	Mr Swan Hennessy Paris
Sehr geehrte[r] Herr Hennessy,	Dear Mr Hennessy,
Soeben trifft der beifolgende Brief unseres gemeinschaftlichen Freundes Rasch ein, den ich Ihnen zur freundlichen Kenntnisnahme schicke, damit Sie die von ihm vorgeschlagenen und mir einleuchtenden Zusätze noch machen können.	The attached letter from our common friend Rasch has just arrived here that I forward to you for consideration so that you can incorporate the proposed additions that seem to make sense to me.
Es war mir möglich, den Druck, welcher gerade begonnen hatte, zu sistieren und es kann also Alles, was Sie	It has been possible for me to halt the printing process that had just begun so that everything that you deem necessary can be added.

---

[39] The letter by Rasch is not extant in the Schott Archive in Berlin. The corrections (or recommendations) have been additional tempo markings; see letter by Hennessy, 1/3 November.

für nötig halten, noch hinzugefügt werden.	With best recommendations,
Mit den besten Empfehlungen	Yours truly,
Ihr sehr ergebener	L. Strecker
L. Strecker	
	Attachment

1 Brief

In another letter of 1/3 November 1911 – documented below in part 2 – , Hennessy again asks when he would receive the prints of Opp. 34 and 36, claiming it was now seven months that Schott received the manuscripts and one month since the letter by Rasch, adding *'Die ganz kleine Ergänzung der Tempobezeichnungen könnte höchstens einen halben Tag brauchen.'* ('That little addition of tempo markings cannot have taken much longer than half a day.').

Strecker responds (3 November, also documented in part 2 below) with 20 copies each of the two works and adds that he agrees that those seven months sound like a long time but that this had been a 'dead time' during the summer when attention would have been low.

Table 5.1: Schott invoice to Hennessy re. Opp. 34 and 36

Preliminary calculation Hennessy	Opus 34	Opus 36 I	Opus 36 II
Tinplates	13,-	4,-	4,-
Zinc plates	5,-	1,25	1,25
Overprint	4,-	1,-	1,-
Retouch	1,60	-,40	-,40
Proof	1,60	-,40	-,40
Title-overprint etc.	6,-	6,-	6,-
Lithography	25,-	25,-	25,-
Rotation	5,-	2,-	2,-
do.	1,50	1,50	1,50
Cover paper	3,54	3,54	3,54
Music print	12,15	6,15	6,15
Hemming	-,75	-,75	-,75
	79,14	51,99	51,99
10% surcharge on expenses	7,91	5,21	5,21
	87,05	57,20	57,20
Extra costs on engraving	32,50	10,80	10,80
Plates: 13, 4, 4 à 1,-	21,-		
Correction of plates	20,-		
	160,55	68,-	68,-
	68,-		
	68,-		
	296,55		
25%	74,15		
	370,70		

Hennessy sends his thanks on 6/7 November, adding that he hopes these new pieces would find more acknowledgement than their predecessors.

On 6 December 1911, Schott (not Strecker personally) sent their invoice – a small sheet of paper in manuscript (Table 5.1). The overall sum is 370.70 marks. Hennessy responds on 7 December by sending a cheque of 347.50 francs, which he says corresponds to 277.70 marks – about 100 marks (or 25%) less than the sum on the invoice (no reading error). This appears to have been the arrangement between Hennessy and Schott.

* * *

Petite suite sur les notes Mi Do Mi Fa Si Mi, Op. 34 (1909) for piano

The *Petite Suite* was originally conceived as a sonatina on the theme mentioned and had been numbered opus 33. This partly explains why the current 'Op. 34' predates the *Croquis de femmes*, Op. 33. According to the manuscript, the work was written in Zweisimmen, Switzerland (a small municipality in the canton of Berne with a population of about 2,500 at the time), in August 1909, but the printed score says on the last page '*Septembre 1909*'.[40] Further delays to the publication with Schott in November 1911 are explained in the correspondence above.

The six-note theme, otherwise circumscribable as the pitches E – C – E – F – B – E, should be read in three pairs of Mi-Do, Mi-Fa, and Si-Mi and happen to be the names of the cat and two dogs of the music publisher Eugène Demets, to whom the piece is dedicated, the cat's name being Si-Mi. The manuscript carries a dedication, omitted in the print, reading '*À mon ami Eugène Demets, en souvenir de son chat et ses chiens: "Mi-Do", "Mi-Fa" et "Si-Mi"*'.[41] Of course, when Hennessy planned to write a piece of music on the names of the three pets, he could have chosen any combination of the three pairs, but this one appears to have appealed to him most. The title is another specimen of Hennessy's humour, inspired by a similar humour of his dedicatee.

As on previous occasions, it was Louis Vuillemin who instantly recognised the humoristic dimension (although he got the pets' names wrong) and who responded with an equally humorous analytical approach:

---

[40] The final manuscript ends on the words '*Zweisimmen, Août 1909*', an earlier version of the MS concretises this to '*Zweisimmen, 24, 8, 09.*'. The location is not mentioned in the print.

[41] Hennessy himself was fond of cats and dogs. Fig. 4.1 showed him with a fox terrier, and the 1929 Chevaillier interview mentions a Siamese cat living in Hennessy's apartment. More specifically, *Le Courrier musical* of 1 October 1927 features a photograph of Hennessy with the pianist Marthe Le Breton, with Hennessy holding on his arms the son of Si-Mi, '*le chat bien connu du regretté éditeur Demets*' ('the well-known cat of the late publisher Demets'); see Chapter 9. Strecker's letter of 21 April 1911 shows that it was he who suggested the dedication be changed with the effect that the explanation for the unusual title became suppressed.

Having opted for mi, do, mi, fa, si, mi – Here, Do! Will you stop it, Si! Bring it, Fa! – Mr. Swan Hennessy has grouped these notes at will, combining them in many different ways, separating them, amalgamating them, playing with them as with a ball of wool.[42]

Despite the apparent playfulness, Hennessy struggled with the exact wording of his title. In an early manuscript of the piece it is called '*Variations en forme de Sonatine*', changed to '*Sonatine & Prelude et fugue*'. This continues in a plural form of '... *sur les themes* ...', followed by the pitches as above and in a variant with C sharp instead of C and F sharp instead of F. In fact, both variants do occur in the work (not least because in the prevalent A major the pitches would be sharps anyway). In the final manuscript the piece is called '*Sonatine sur le thème* [pitches in the 'sharp' version]', and this, as we have seen in the correspondence above, was changed by Ludwig Strecker of Schott to *Petite suite sur le thème* ... . On the title page this is printed as pitches (Fig. 5.2) and at the head of the score in names of the pitches.

Fig. 5.2: Excerpt from the title page of Op. 34

But Hennessy struggled not only with his title, the musical construction is unusual as well and may point to structural difficulties he experienced in the process of writing the piece. Several critics pointed out that not only the theme itself is difficult to comprehend and not exactly attractive but that Hennessy's technique of linking the theme and its multiple variants (see below) as well as the unusual formal construction seemed at times awkward and their development far-fetched – the suite begins with an extended *allegretto* movement in A major, followed by a brief *Andantino semplice* in the character of an intermezzo in the same tonality, and concludes with an extended *Finale* beginning in C major, half of which is set off – without becoming an independent

---

[42] '*S'étant emparé de mi, do, mi, fa, si, mi — Ici, Do! Veux-tu finir, Si! Apporte, Fa! — M. Swan Hennessy a groupé ces notes à sa guise, les combinant de maintes façons différentes, les séparant, les amalgamant, jouant avec elles à la pelote.*'; Louis Vuillemin in *Comoedia*, 23 November 1911, p. 3.

movement – by a three-part fugue that returns to A major. In an otherwise positive review in *La Revue musicale*, a critic remarked:

> I would just like to make a very small observation. Mr. Hennessy is a very solid composer, admirably familiar with his trade, but, in some of these pages, I sense a little labour and effort – a pity! the fugue itself should be full of ease.[43]

Similarly, a writer in *Signale für die musikalische Welt* commented:

> [...] sometimes the pieces lack proper inspiration, one can see too well how they are calculated to have a really deep effect throughout. In the Petite Suite the formal structure is not fully successful, in the first and third movements one detail follows another, poorly linked by the relationship to the notes of the theme, but a form that seems satisfactory as a whole does not appear.[44]

The impression of 'effort' is supported by the two manuscripts of the work that survived in the family's collection. This is one of several pieces with extensive corrections not only in a first pencil draft (which has not survived but can be presupposed), but also in the first copy in ink and the clean copy he sent to Schott in which extended passages are pasted over, particularly in the first movement and the concluding fugue. While this offers another explanation for the long delay between 'completion' and publication, it may also point to either a technical difficulty or suggest an improvisatory approach in which there is a high degree of conscious arbitrariness. However, I would rather tend to an interpretation that suggests a discontentedness with initial solutions and a search for perfection that ultimately resulted, in this case, in a rather too visible effort to find perfection and that failed for this very reason.

Hennessy's usage of the theme may well be interpreted as a piece of musical humour itself. The theme, as notated on the cover page is by no means the only form that it takes in the work. It is transposed to several tonalities, reversed, mirrored, extended, varied rhythmically, to the extent that it is difficult to be recognised, not only aurally, but visually in the score as well. Very much aware of this, Hennessy chose to assist the performer (or the analyst?) by pointing out every occurrence of the theme as he interpreted it and let the reader partake in his unusual twists of thought and creative meanderings (Ex. 5.9, with four occurrences within nine bars).

---

[43] *'Je me borne à une toute petite observation. M. Hennessy est un très solide compositeur, connaissant admirablement son métier; mais, dans quelques-unes de ces pages, je sens un peu le travail et l'effort: c'est dommage! la fugue elle-même devrait être pleine d'aisance.'*; L. H. in *La Revue musicale* 11:22, 15 November 1911, p. 451.

[44] *'[...] es fehlt den Stücken doch zuweilen die rechte Inspiration, man sieht zu sehr, wie sie errechnet sind, als dass sie durchweg eine wirklich tiefe Wirkung ausüben könnten. In der Petite Suite ist der formale Aufbau nicht voll gelungen, im ersten und dritten Satz schliesst sich ein Detail an's andere, notdürftig verknüpft durch die Beziehung zu den Noten des Themas, aber eine als ganzes befriedigend wirkende Form kommt dabei nicht heraus.'*; W. H. in *Signale für die musikalische Welt* 70:9, 28 February 1912, p. 300.

Ex. 5.9: *Petite suite sur les notes Mi Do Mi Fa Si Mi*, Op. 34, 1st movt, bars 28–36

Notwithstanding those (potential) technical struggles – obviously not perceived as such by Ludwig Strecker of Schott – and relevant notices by critics cited above, the general critical reception of the work was very positive. Hugo Rasch – admittedly a friend of Hennessy's – emphasised in the *Allgemeine Musikzeitung* the originality of Hennessy's mind:

> As with most of the later compositions by Hennessy, the feeling that we are dealing with an absolutely peculiar and self-contained personality forces itself upon the reader again this time. And that's the great secret of art. [...][45]

Louis Vuillemin, after having described the various forms and tonalities in which the theme appears, found:

> The piece revels in a free musical approach and does not give the impression to be too arbitrarily put together. It is subject to certain fluctuations of movement, the effect of which is to avoid monotony.[46]

Apparently, he took particular pleasure in the *Finale*:

---

[45] 'Wie bei den meisten der späteren Kompositionen Hennessys, drängt sich einem auch diesmal wieder das Empfinden auf, daß man es mit einer absolut eigenartigen und in sich geschlossenen Persönlichkeit zu tun hat. Und das ist doch das große Geheimnis in der Kunst.'; Hugo Rasch in *Allgemeine Musikzeitung* 38:42, 20 October 1911, p. 1058.
[46] 'Le morceau demeure d'une libre musicalité et ne donne nullement l'impression d'être trop volontairement combiné. Il est soumis à certaines fluctuations de mouvement dont l'effet est d'éviter la monotonie.'; L. Vuillemin in *Comoedia*, as above.

The *Finale*, number three of the Suite – vivace ma non tanto – presents us with the domestic animals of Mr. Demets frolicking in an excellent spirit. They gallop, the dear beasts! Theme in F, in B minor, in all kinds of tones, really! It's quite some fun.[47]

An English review was equally impressed by the composer's skill:

THE Suite, based on five [sic!] notes, seems at first sight as if it were merely a *tour de force* to show what could be done with a theme which in itself is not particularly engaging. The music, however, should first be judged by the effect it produces, and only afterwards should it be analysed. Beginning with analysis, one is too much attracted by the composer's skill in presenting his theme with constant rhythmical alterations. There is poetry in the Allegretto, charme in the simple Andantino, while the Finale, a fugue, in modern style, is impressive.[48]

Unfortunately, it has again to be pointed out that despite the positive critical response in three European musical centres, there were hardly any public performances. According to Hennessy's records, the only performance of this work took place in Paris at the Salle des Agriculteurs, on 25 November 1922, played by Maurice Servais.[49]

Fêtes. Deux Morceaux descriptifs, Op. 36 (1910) for piano

The second piece that was accepted for publication by Schott in 1911 is *Fêtes*, Op. 36, which consists of two contrasting pieces depicting festivities in France at different periods: No. 1 is *Fête de village au XVIIIme siècle* ('Village Festival in the 18th Century') and No. 2 is called *Fête populaire dans la banlieue de Paris au XXme siècle* ('Popular Festival in a Suburb of Paris in the 20th Century') – the latter, of course, referring to the year 1910. It is consciously descriptive music, focusing on the change in the character of festivities not only over time but also between a rural village and urban Paris.

According to the manuscript, the score was completed in July 1910. The dedication in the print reads '*à Madame Betty Heffner, Hommage sympathique*'; in the manuscript this originally was '*Frau Professor Heffner gewidmet*'. Betty Heffner was the wife of Professor Carl Heffner, a German Impressionist painter and occasional composer who reappears in connection with the string quartet Op. 46.[50]

---

[47] '*Le Finale, numéro trois de la Suite – vivace ma non tanto – nous présente les animaux domestiques de M. Demets folâtrant avec un excellent entrain. Elles galopent, les chères bêtes ! Thème en fa, en si mineur, en toute espèce de tons, quoi! C'est très amusant.*'; L. Vuillemin in *Comoedia*, as above.

[48] *The Monthly Musical Record*, 1 December 1911, p. 323.

[49] The 1922 recital began with Beethoven's Sonata, Op. 28 *('Pastorale')*, followed by the Hennessy suite; thereafter followed the *Berceuse à Louisa* by Paul Dupin, *Musique pour deux petites filles* by Lucien Haudebert in a first performance of this work dedicated to Maurice Servais, and the final part consisted of *Thème et variations* by Gabriel Fauré and *Bourrée fantasque* by Emmanuel Chabrier (programme in Hennessy press book).

[50] The Heffners must have been private friends of Hennessy. Carl Heffner made artistic journeys to England, France (Paris) and Italy, and it is likely that Hennessy met them during one of those journeys (see Appendix 4).

The first piece is marked 'Mouvement de Rigaudon' and evokes the lively French dance of the name. Set in A major, the very melodious, sprightly neo-baroque piece in 2/4 duple metre contains a few mildly chromatic chord progressions that betray the work's composition in the early twentieth century while remaining very much in the mood of a baroque dance.

The *Fête populaire dans la banlieue de Paris au XXme siècle* is a very excited piece of programme music depicting a funfair in a Parisian suburb, with much of the musical excitement depicting the crowds in search of various pursuits and entertainments. That excitement derives from fast whole-tone scales and interspersed chord repetitions, counter movements between the left and right hand with semiquaver triplets, etc. One such downward run of semiquaver triplets leads to a noisy waltz, just four bars long, probably representing an orchestrion (Ex. 5.10). It is a hilarious piece, less than a minute in duration, but very funny, truly inspired and technically demanding.

Ex. 5.10 *Fêtes*, Op. 36 No. 2 'Fête populaire dans la banlieue de Paris au XXme siècle', bars 20–24

In the opinion of *La Revue musicale*, the two pieces 'indicate the refinement with which Mr. Hennessy treats the language of sound. He also finds, with a rare technique, very nice effects.'[51] The similarly titled *La Revue musicale S.I.M.* was considerably more critical, describing the first piece as a 'louisfifteenery without importance' and the second as a 'childish complication'.[52] The critic in the German *Signale* was more taken

---

[51] '[…] indiquent le raffinement avec lequel M. Hennessy traite le langage des sons. Il trouve d'ailleurs, avec une rare technique, de fort jolis effets.'; E. D. in *La Revue musicale* 12:1, January 1912, p. 5.

[52] '[…] d'une joie moins spontanée, la Fête dans la Banlieue de Paris de Swan Henessy : flonflons, refrains de bastringue, coups de grosse caisse, rien n'y manque : le tout est d'une complication enfantine. Du même auteur, une fête de village au XVIIIa siècle, louisquinzerie sans importance, […]'; *La Revue musicale S.I.M.*, 15 January 1912, p. 76.

with the neo-baroque first piece, while criticising the harmonic language of the second piece arguing that a programme seemed to allow for experiments that would not be justified in absolute music.[53]

As always, music criticism does not reflect objective views of any work's merits but is coloured by the individual taste and (sometimes) personal connections of the critic. As in reviews of previous works, the most positive and most extended criticism came from Hennessy's friend Hugo Rasch in *Allgemeine Musikzeitung* and from Louis Vuillemin in *Comoedia*. The friendly relationship to Rasch was established since at least 1906 while the one to Vuillemin was developing during these years (1910–12) through the critic's reviews of Hennessy's music. Not much later, Vuillemin – who was also a composer, a pupil of Fauré at the Conservatoire – and Hennessy would find themselves in the same circle of Breton composers (see below). Rasch wrote:

> If only the courageous artist could be found, who would publicly advocate this opus, which, by the way, has the additional advantage of concise brevity. The 'fête populaire du XXme siècle' is, as one can easily imagine, pianistically very difficult, but since one can never write enough notes into the fingers of today's virtuosos anyway, they also get their money's worth here. At the end of the second piece, in the composer's place, I would have made a repeat sign; because before you really know what's going on, this whole charming and incredibly 'real' sounding tone picture has already rushed past.[54]

Vuillemin focuses on the second, twentieth-century piece, and compares its character to the music of Gustave Charpentier (1860–1956), composer of the popular opera *Louise* (1900) and a conscious resident of Montmartre ('la Butte'):

> You would think the author has, as they say, given himself a heart's content! His lively, joyful, 'noisy' (as it should) music will amuse many. Fragments of popular waltzes – which the author recommends 'bringing out' as much as possible – come to colour this realistic composition, I was going to say: this 'sketch'.
>
> The virtuosos – and they alone – will have a great impact on their audience by performing Mr. Swan Hennessy's Fêtes. They will plunge into a perfect and delightful Gustave Charpentier, as sung from 'la Butte'.[55]

---

[53] '*Das in seiner Harmonik von Debussy beeinflusste Pariser Volksfest des XX. Jahrhunderts verfällt in den alten Fehler so vieler Programmstücke, alles was sich in der Musik als nicht rechtfertigen liesse, durch das Programm sanktionieren zu wollen.*'; W. H. in *Signale für die musikalische Welt* 70:9, 28 February 1912, p. 300.

[54] '*Fände sich doch der mutige Künstler, der gerade für dieses Opus öffentlich einträte, das übrigens noch den Vorzug prägnanter Kürze hat. Die "fête populaire du XXme siècle" ist, wie man sich leicht vorstellen kann, pianistisch reichlich schwer, aber da man den heutigen Virtuosen sowieso nie genug Noten in die Finger schreiben kann, kommen diese hier auch völlig auf ihre Kosten. An des Komponisten Stelle hätte ich am Schlusse des zweiten Stückes ruhig ein Wiederholungszeichen gemacht; denn ehe man sich recht besinnt, was eigentlich los ist, da ist dies ganze reizvolle und unglaublich "echt" klingende Tonbild schon vorübergerauscht […]*'; Hugo Rasch in *Allgemeine Musikzeitung* 38:42, 20 October 1911, p. 1058.

[55] '*Vous pensez que l'auteur s'en est, comme on dit, donné à cœur-joie! Sa musique vive, joyeuse, "bruyante" même comme il sied, amusera beaucoup. Des fragments de valses populaires – que l'auteur recommande de "faire*

Fêtes is the only Hennessy work of this period that received a performance relatively close to its publication – and by a virtuoso pianist, as demanded by Rasch and Vuillemin, albeit not in Paris. The prominent German pianist Ella Jonas-Stockhausen performed it under the curious title '*Impressions*' on 13 March 1913 at the Harmoniumsaal in Berlin in a programme designated as a 'Novitäten-Abend'. It consisted of the following items, with some works played in a duo with the cellist Marix Loevensohn:[56]

Albert Bertelin (1872–1951):
Sonata for Cello and Piano in D Minor (first Berlin performance)

Heinz Tiessen (1887–1971):
Sonata for Piano in C Minor, Op. 12 (in manuscript)

– Break –

Volkmar Andreae (1879–1962):
Frage, from Op. 20[57]

Théodore Dubois (1837–1927):
Les Bucherons / Die Holzhacker

Swan Hennessy:
Impressions. a) *Dorffest zur Zeit des Roccoco*; b) *Rummelplatz im heutigen Paris* (first performance)

Charles-Marie Widor (1844–1937):
Sonata for Cello and Piano in A major (first Berlin performance[58])

Several critics noticed the presence of Hennessy in the audience, taking a bow at the end of the performance – he was the only composer present apart from Heinz Tiessen.[59] The response by the Berlin critics to Hennessy's work was quite positive. The *Lokal-Anzeiger* noted 'two acclaimed "Impressions" by Swan Hennessy, charm-

---

ressortir" autant que possible – viennent colorer de lueurs faubouriennes cette composition réaliste, j'allais dire: cette "pochade". / Les virtuoses – et eux seuls – produiront grand effet sur leur auditoire en exécutant les Fêtes de M. Swan Hennessy. Elles plongeront dans un parfait ravissement Gustave Charpentier, chantré de la Butte.'; Louis Vuillemin in *Comoedia*, 25 January 1912, p. 3.
[56] Programme in Hennessy Press Books. Translations of titles and the composer dates by the author.
[57] No. 3 of *Sechs Klavierstücke*, Op. 20 (1910).
[58] Probably Op. 80 (1907).
[59] 'A. Sa.' in *Lokal-Anzeiger*, 16 March; Leopold Schmidt in *Berliner Tageblatt*, 19 March; and Paul Schwers, *Allgemeine Musikzeitung*, 21 March, p. 386.

ingly profiled small artefacts, more of an aesthetic than a strong intrinsic value'.[60] A review in *Signale* described the neo-baroque piece as *'belanglos'* ('insignifcant') but the more contemporary second piece as 'in its characterisation quite successful'.[61] Paul Schwers in *Allgemeine Musikzeitung* congratulated Ella Jonas-Stockhausen for her choice of works for the evening and commented on the Hennessy (focusing on the second piece):

> Especially the latter piece is a spicy bite for modern gourmets, a magnificent musical joke, only a little short. The composer who was present also received lively recognition for these spirited pieces.[62]

As we shall see below, this was not the only time that Hennessy promoted his music in Berlin. By early 1913 he had realised that he had to become more active and not wait until the fame of his works would have spread without any additional measures of his own. Part 2 of the Schott correspondence (below) reveals what his attitude to the marketing of his own music had been like up to now. It was going to change.

* * *

With the exception of Op. 36, each of the above treatments of Hennessy's Opp. 32, 38, 35, 33, and 34 ended – purposefully – on the astonishing fact that these works had to wait many years for their first public performance.

Correspondence with Schott (part 2)

Part 2 of the correspondence between Swan Hennessy and Ludwig Strecker, the director of the Schott publishing house in Mainz, Germany, overlaps somewhat with part 1 above. Before his Opp. 34 and 36 were printed and delivered, Hennessy already sent the next two pieces (Opp. 39 and 40), and a third one (Op. 41) a little later on. The following exchange of letters shows Strecker's scepticism towards certain aspects of Hennessy's music that would not be commercially viable and which lead to his decision not to publish these works. Hennessy for his part argues that a publisher needs to do more advertising to make such works more successful. After the rejection of Op. 41, Hennessy never offered anything to Schott again.

---

[60] '[…] *zwei beifällig aufgenommenen "Impressions" von Swan Hennessy, reizvoll profilierter Kleinkunst, mehr ästhetischen als starken Eigenwertes,* […]'; ibid.
[61] '*Abgesehen von einer belanglosen Gavotte "Dorffest zur Zeit des Rokoko" auch ein in der Charakterisierung recht gelungenes Stück: Rummelplatz im heutigen Paris.*'; Alfons Laugwitz in *Signale für die musikalische Welt* 71:12, 19 March 1913, p. 445.
[62] '*Namentlich das letztgenannte Stück ist ein pikanter Happen für moderne Feinschmecker, ein prächtiger musikalischer Witz, nur etwas kurz geraten. Dem anwesenden Komponisten brachten diese espritvollen Stücklein ebenfalls lebhafte Anerkennung ein.*'; Schwers, see fn. 59.

Sehr geehrter Herr!

Gestatten Sie dass ich Ihnen einige neue Klavierstücke zur Ansicht schicke.

„Incunabula", op. 39 (3 Stücke), und „4 Etudes d'après nature", op. 40.

Die drei ersten Nummern von op. 40 dürften, wenn entsprechend gespielt, ziemlich effektvoll wirken. N°. 4 ist sehr schwer. Das wird aber wohl nichts machen, denn es giebt eine ganze Menge Leute die sich nur für Musik interessieren die sie nicht spielen können.

Ich schicke Ihnen auch einige Kritiken aus verschiedenen musikalischen Zeitungen.

Es thut mir Leid dass ich Ihnen nicht selbst diese Stücke spielen kann – werde aber schwerlich diesen Winter nach Mainz kommen können.

In höflicher Erwartung Ihrer gütigen Rückantwort, mit besten Grüssen,

Hochachtungsvoll ergeben,

Swan Hennessy.

P.S. Ich mache Sie besonders auf Herrn Dr. Möller's Kritik aufmerksam. (Allgemeine Musik-Zeitung 22 Sept. 1911.)

Paris, 270 Boulevard Raspail,
29, 9, 11.

Dear Sir!

Please allow me to send you some new piano pieces for review.

"Incunabula", Op. 39 (3 pieces), and "4 Etudes d'après nature", Op. 40.

The first three numbers of Op. 40, if played accordingly, should be quite effective. No. 4 is very difficult. But that won't matter, because there are a lot of people who are only interested in music that they cannot play.

I am also sending some reviews from various musical journals.

I'm sorry I can't play these pieces to you myself – but I'll hardly be able to come to Mainz this winter.

In courteous expectation of your kind answer, with best regards,

Yours faithfully,

Swan Hennessy.

P.S. I would like to draw your special attention to Dr. Möller's review. (Allgemeine Musik-Zeitung Sept. 22, 1911.)

Herrn Swan Hennessy
Paris

Sehr geehrter Herr Hennessy,

Ihre freundliche Zuschrift vom 29. v.Mts. mit den Manuskripten Ihrer Op. 39 „Incunabula" und Op. 40 4 Etuden haben wir erhalten und danken Ihnen verbindlichst für das freundliche Anerbieten, uns diese Stücke zur Herausgabe überlassen zu wollen.

Sie werden uns in der Zeit unseres Verkehrs genügend kennen gelernt haben, um zu wissen, dass wir an Ihrer

Mainz, 3. Oktober 1911
Mr Swan Hennessy
Paris

Dear Mr Hennessy,

We have received your friendly letter of the 29th of the previous month with the manuscripts of your Op. 39 'Incunabula' and Op. 40 4 Etuden, and we thank you most sincerely for the kind proposal to offer these pieces to us for publication.

You will have come to know us well enough in the course of our relationship to know that we often take

Kunst oft eine wirkliche Freude haben, selbst wenn wir nicht in der Lage sind, Ihnen unsere Dienste zur Herausgabe zur Verfügung zu stellen.

Ein solcher Fall liegt nun mit diesen neuen Manuskripten vor. Wir verstehen ganz genau Ihre Absichten bei der Wiedergabe natürlicher Beobachtungen, mögen sie nun im ängstlichen Hin- und Herflattern von Schwalben, oder im Erklingen von Kuhglocken, oder von flimernden Mondlichtern bestehen, aber manchmal kommt uns Ihre Absicht doch als etwas vor, was sich mit den vorhandenen Mitteln, nämlich den Tönen eines Klaviers nicht erreichen lässt.

In den anbei zurückgehenden Kritiken rühmt man fast überall die gleichen Vorzüge, die wir eben erwähnten, was Ihnen beweisen mag, dass über diese Frage gar keine Meinungsverschiedenheit besteht. Was aber die Herren Kritiker weniger beobachten können wie der Verleger, das ist der Effekt, den diese Musik auf das musikliebende Publikum macht. Dieser Effekt ist leider negativ, denn man verlangt sie nicht und deshalb wagen wir zu behaupten, dass unser Ihnen schon verschiedentlich erteilter Rat, Sie möchten nicht Dinge auf dem Klavier darstellen wollen, die über seine Mittel hinausgehen, doch der richtige war und dass Sie über das Ziel hinausschiessen. Wir bedauern dies sehr, denn einzelne Stücke, bei welchen Sie nicht bis an die äusserste Grenze gehen, sind reizend und könnten eine allgemeine Verbreitung finden.

Nach dem Gesagten erlauben wir uns Ihnen die Manuskripte wieder zur Verfügung zu stellen, da wir als ehrliche Leute deren Herausgabe nicht übernehmen können, denn wir erachten die

real pleasure in your art, even if we are not able to provide you with our services for publication.

Such a case we now have in front of us with these new manuscripts. We understand your intentions in the reproduction of natural observations, whether they consist in the fearful fluttering back and forth of swallows, or in the sounding of cowbells, or of shimmering moonlight, but sometimes your intention seems to us nevertheless as something, which cannot be achieved with the available means, namely the sounds of a piano.

In the reviews that I am returning herewith, critics almost everywhere praise the same qualities that we have just mentioned, which may prove to you that there is no difference of opinion on this issue. But what the critics are not able to observe equally well as a publisher is the effect that this music has on the music-loving audience. Unfortunately, this effect is negative, because there is no demand for it, and that is why we dare say that the advice we have already given you on several occasions, that you should not present things on the piano that go beyond its means, was right and that you are overshooting the mark. We regret this very much, because individual pieces, with which you do not go to the outermost border, are charming and could find a general audience.

Having said as much we allow ourselves to return the manuscripts to you because as honest people we cannot undertake their publication because we consider the investment for it as lost.

Forgive us for speaking so frankly and openly. We would not have dared

dafür aufzuwendenden Kosten als verloren.

Verzeihen Sie, dass wir so unumwunden offen Ihnen unsere Meinung sagen. Wir würden es nicht gewagt haben, wenn wir nicht wüssten, wie aufgeklärt Sie über Alles, was Ihre Kunst betrifft, zu denken pflegen und dass Sie wohl zu unterscheiden wissen, ob eine Kritik aus guten Motiven entspringt oder nicht.

Die Stücke op. 34 und 36 sind im Druck und werden in ganz kurzer Zeit Ihnen zugehen.

Mit den besten Empfehlungen und wiederholtem Danke für Ihre freundliche Absicht zeichnen wir

Hochachtungsvoll ergeben
[signature stamp]
B. Schott's Söhne

Sehr geehrter Herr,
Es thut mir Leid dass Sie meine letzten Stücke, oder wenigstens die 4 Etuden, nicht behalten wollten.

Ich danke Ihnen herzlich für den liebenswürdigen Brief den Sie mir geschrieben haben.

Sie sagen meine Musik werde nicht verlangt. Haben Sie aber auch die nötige Thätigkeit dafür? Ich habe noch nie meine[n] Name unter Ihren Reklamen gesehen oder unter Ihre[n] Novitätensendungen meine Musik gefunden. Sie ist nicht einmal in Paris oder Berlin zu bekommen!

Das musikliebende Publikum kann nicht instinktiv wissen das[s] neue Klavierstücke von Hennessy vorliegen.

Ich kenne Leute die meine Musik gern hören und spielen, es wird wohl

if we did not know how enlightened you are about everything concerning your art and that you probably know how to distinguish whether a criticism arises from good motives or not.

The works Opp. 34 and 36 are in print and will reach you shortly.

With the best recommendations and renewed thanks for your kind intention we remain

Yours sincerely
[signature stamp]
B. Schott's Söhne

Paris, 270 Boulevard Raspail,
4, 10, 11.

Dear Sir!
I am sorry that you didn't want to keep my last pieces, or at least the 4 studies.

Thank you very much for the kind letter you wrote me.

You say there is no demand for my music. But are you really doing the necessary activity for it? I have never seen my name in any of your advertisements or found my music among your novelties. It is not even available in Paris or Berlin!

The music-loving audience cannot instinctively know that new piano pieces by Hennessy are available.

I know people who like to listen to and play my music, and there will be others, but they must be made aware of it.

andere geben, sie müssen aber darauf aufmerksam gemacht werden.

Da ich nicht konzertiere, und sehr zurückgezogen lebe, kann das nur durch den Verleger geschehen. Nicht die Güte der Musik macht es Heut zu Tage, sondern die Reklame. Es ist zweifellos der Reklame zuzuschreiben dass die willkürlichsten Unschönheiten womit ein gewisser moderne[r] Komponist die Verrücktheit einiger Hysteriker auszubeuten sucht, überall zu finden sind!

Sie sagen ich schieße über das Ziel hinaus. Ich ziele wenigstens in's Zentrum, und Sie werden zugeben dass es ein trauriger Künstler ist der gegen seine Ueberzeugung arbeitet.

Nehmen Sie es mir nicht übel dass ich so offen rede und genehmigen Sie die besten Grüssen von
Ihr hochachtungsvoll ergebener
Swan Hennessy.

Since I don't concertize and live in a very withdrawn way, this can only be done by the publisher. It's not the quality of the music that makes it successful nowadays, but the advertising. It is undoubtedly due to advertising that the most arbitrary uncomeliness with which a certain modern composer tries to exploit the madness of some hysterics can be found everywhere!

You say I am overshooting the mark. I am at least aiming for the centre, and you will admit that it would be a sad artist who works against his conviction.

I hope you don't mind that I speak so openly and please accept my best regards from
Your respectfully devoted
Swan Hennessy

Herrn Swan Hennessy
Paris
Sehr geehrte[r] Herr Hennessy,

Soeben trifft der beifolgende Brief unseres gemeinschaftlichen Freundes Rasch ein, den ich Ihnen zur freundlichen Kenntnisnahme schicke, damit Sie die von ihm vorgeschlagenen und mir einleuchtenden Zusätze noch machen können.

Es war mir möglich, den Druck, welcher gerade begonnen hatte, zu sistieren und es kann also Alles, was Sie für nötig halten, noch hinzugefügt werden.

Mit den besten Empfehlungen
Ihr sehr ergebener
L. Strecker

Mainz, 5. Oktober 1911
Mr Swan Hennessy
Paris
Dear Mr Hennessy,

The following letter from our common friend Rasch has just arrived and I am sending it to you for your kind information, so that you can make the additions he has suggested and which I can understand.

I was able to stop the printing that had just started, so anything you think is necessary can be added.

With the best recommendations
Your very devoted
L. Strecker

Sehr geehrter Herr Geheimrath,

Dürfte ich Sie höflichst bitten mir zu sagen, wan[n] ich meine op. 34 u. 36 kriegen werde? Es sind jetzt 7 Monate seit Sie die Manuscripte bekommen haben, und es wird bald ein Monat sein seit Herr Rasch Ihnen geschrieben hat. Die ganz kleine Ergänzung der Tempobezeichnungen könnte höchstens einen halben Tag brauchen.

Die Neugierde welche durch eine, für mich sehr günstige Besprechung in der „Allgemeinen Musikzeitung" erweckt wurde muss verloren gehen.

Ich kann es nur herzlich bedauern dass Sie für meine Kompositionen so wenig Interesse haben, umso mehr da es in der Regel bei kompetenten Musiker[n] nicht der Fall ist!

Genehmigen Sie, sehr geehrter Herr Geheimrath, die besten Grüssen Ihres sehr ergebenen
Swan Hennessy.

Herrn Swan Hennessy
Paris
Sehr geehrter Herr Hennessy,

Gleichzeitig mit diesen Zeilen gehen je 20 Exemplare Ihrer neuen Werke an Sie ab.

Sie haben unzweifelhaft recht, wenn Sie sich über die Dauer der Zeit seit Eintreffen Ihrer M.S.S. und der Ablieferung der fertigen Exemplare erstaunen; aber die Sache ist doch nicht ganz so schlimm, obgleich es so klingt, wenn man sagt, 7 Monate seien verstrichen. Diese 7 Monate waren die tote Zeit, in der nichts versandt hätte werden können und ausserdem sind durch Ihre verschiedenen Reisen die Korrekturen

Paris, 1/3 Nov. 1911.
Dear Privy Councillor,

May I politely ask you to tell me when I will receive my Opp. 34 and 36? It is now 7 months since you received the manuscripts, and it will soon be a month since Mr Rasch wrote you. The very small addition to the tempo markings would not take more than half a day.

The curiosity aroused by a review in the 'Allgemeine Musikzeitung', which was very favourable for me, must be lost.

I can only deeply regret that you have so little interest in my compositions, all the more so as it is usually not the case with competent musicians!

Please accept, dear Mr Privy Councillor, the best wishes of your very devoted
Swan Hennessy

Mainz, 3. November 1911
Mr Swan Hennessy
Paris
Dear Mr Hennessy,

With this same letter, 20 copies of each of your new works will be sent to you.

You are undoubtedly right to be surprised at the length of time since your manuscripts have arrived and the delivery of the printed copies; but the matter is not as bad as it sounds when you say that 7 months have passed. These 7 months were the dead time in which nothing could have been sent, and besides, due to your various trips, the corrections did not return here quite as regularly. After all, we will still

auch nicht ganz regelmässig wieder hierher zurückgelangt. Wir werden immerhin noch die beste Zeit des Winters zur Ausnutzung der Versendung an unsere Handlungen vor uns haben. Dass diese Versendung zur Ansicht an alle unsere tätigen Klienten das beste Propagandamittel ist, dürfen wir Sie versichern und glauben, dass Sie uns nicht ganz gerecht werden, wenn Sie meinen, wir hätten für Ihre Kompositionen wenig Interesse. Gerade das Gegenteil ist der Fall und es scheint nur, dass wir in letzter Zeit bei Ihnen in den Verdacht kommen, als kritisierten wir mit wenig Wohlwollen.

Wenn Sie unsere Briefe lesen, so müssten Sie eigentlich finden, dass es kaum einen ehrlicheren Bewunderer Ihrer Kunst gibt als uns, was ja nicht zu hindern braucht, dass wir gewisse Exzentricitäten im Interesse der Verbreitungsmöglichkeit bedauern. Es ist nämlich trotz aller guten Besprechungen, welche Sie in der Presse zu unserer Freude neuerdings erfahren, noch immer ein Widerstand gegenüber Ihrer Kunst vorhanden, den niemand besser beurteilen kann als wir. Denn uns schickt man die Exemplare, welche wir zur Ansicht hinausgehen liessen, zurück: Ein Beweis, dass sie keinen Liebhaber gefunden haben. Und gerade weil wir das bedauern, unterlassen wir es nicht, Sie darauf aufmerksam zu machen dass Sie sich gelegentlich etwas weiter als es Ihnen selbst dienlich wäre, von dem Pfad der als zulässig betrachteten Harmonien und Rythmen entfernen. Wer Ungewöhnliches will, darf die Geduld nicht verlieren, das ist eine Beobachtung, die noch jeder Neuerer hat machen müssen und die auch Ihnen nicht erspart bleibt.

have the best time of winter to take advantage of the shipment to our stores ahead of us. We can assure you that these inspection copies are the best means of propaganda for all our active clients and believe that you are not doing us justice if you think we have little interest in your compositions. Precisely the opposite is the case, but it seems that we have recently come under suspicion from your side, as if we were criticising with little goodwill.

If you read our letters, you should actually find that there is hardly a more honest admirer of your art than us, which should not prevent us from regretting certain eccentricities in the interest of dissemination. Despite all the good reviews that you recently, to our delight, received in the press, there is still a resistance to your art that nobody can judge better than us. Because the review copies we had sent out for inspection were returned to us: a proof that they had not found a lover. And it is precisely because we regret this, that we do not fail to draw your attention to the fact that you occasionally move a little further away from the path of harmonies and rhythms considered permissible than it would serve you well. Anyone who wants something unusual must not lose patience, this is an observation that every innovator has had to make and which you will not be spared either.

With respectful recommendations
most humbly
[signature stamp]
B. Schott's Söhne

Mit hochachtungsvollen Empfehlungen
   sehr ergebenst
   [signature stamp]
   B. Schott's Söhne

Sehr geehrter Herr Geheimrath,
   Besten Dank für die Sendung meiner op. 34 u. 36., und ganz besonders für Ihren liebenswürdigen Brief.
   Ich hoffe diese neuen Stücke werden mehr Anerkennung finden wie ihre Vorgänger.
   Mit besten Grüssen,
      Ihr sehr ergebener
         Swan Hennessy.

Paris, 6/7 Nov. 1911.
Dear Privy Councillor,
   Thank you for sending my Opp. 34 and 36, and especially for your kind letter.
   I hope these new pieces will gain more recognition than their predecessors.
   With kind regards,
      Your very devoted
         Swan Hennessy

Sehr geehrter Herr Geheimrath,
   Ich beehre mich Ihnen einen Cheque für 347 frs. 50 c. (277 M. 70 pf.) zu schicken – für die Publikation meiner op. 34 und 36.
   Sie haben die Umschläge meiner Compositionen benützt um für Ihre werthvollsten Novitäten Reclame zu machen. Ich bin selbstverständlich glücklich und stolz als Propaganda-Mittel für die feinen und höchst interessanten Werke von Oehme, Kronke, Nevin, Van Gael, und andere zu dienen, hoffe aber der Gerechtigkeit wegen dass diese Herren auch für <u>meine Reclame</u> zahlen.
   "Big fleas have little fleas upon their backs to bite'em,
   Little fleas have lesser fleas, and so "ad finitum"."
   Mit besten Grüssen,
      Ihr sehr ergebener
         Swan Hennessy

Paris, 7 Dez. 1911.[63]
Dear Privy Councillor,
   I have the honour of sending you a cheque for 347 frs. 50 c. (277 M. 70 pf.) – for the publication of my Opp. 34 and 36.
   You have used the covers of my compositions to advertise your most valuable novelties. I am of course happy and proud to serve as a propaganda tool for the fine and highly interesting works of Oehme, Kronke, Nevin, Van Gael, and others, but I hope that these gentlemen will also pay for <u>my advertising</u>.
   "Big fleas have little fleas upon their backs to bite'em,
   Little fleas have lesser fleas, and so "ad finitum"."
   With best wishes,
      Your very devoted
         Swan Hennessy
         (270 B^d Raspail.)

---

[63] As an exception, this letter was written on a printed letter head of '4, Rue Chalgrin / Avenue du Bois de Boulogne' – the address of Swan Hennessy's father.

(270 Bᵈ Raspail.)

Herrn Swan Hennessy
Paris

Sehr geehrter Herr Hennessy,

Wir bestätigen mit verbindlichstem Dank Ihren Check von Frs 347.50 – M 277,70, sowie den Ausdruck Ihres Missvergnügens über die auf den Umschlägen und leeren Seiten Ihrer letzten opus befindlichen Anzeigen von anderen Komponisten. Diese letzten sind infolge einer allgemeinen Anordnung in unserem Hause, dass keine Seite ohne Verlagsanzeige bleiben soll, gegen meinen Wunsch mit dieser Reklame bedruckt worden und ich bedaure dies sehr, denn ich hätte Ihnen lieber die Exemplare rein von Zutaten geliefert. Nur dürfen Sie nicht die Herren Kollegen, deren Namen Sie gelesen haben, dafür verantwortlich machen, denn die Schuld trifft ganz allein uns und ich werde dafür sorgen, dass etwas Aehnliches nicht mehr vorkommt.

Andererseits haben Sie aber vielleicht nichts dagegen, wenn auch Sie in andern Fällen auf Rückseiten erscheinen, denn jetzt haben wir von Ihnen doch schon so viele Werke herausgegeben, dass es nicht mehr komisch aussieht, wenn wir eine Liste derselben zusammenstellen und sie in der gleichen Weise verwerten, wie wir es neuerdings durchgängig tun.

Mit den besten Empfehlungen
Ihr sehr ergebener
L. Strecker

Mainz, 9. Dezember 1911
Mr Swan Hennessy
Paris

Dear Mr Hennessy,

We confirm with most obliging thanks your cheque of Frs 347.50 – M 277,70, as well as the expression of your displeasure at the advertisements of other composers on the envelopes and blank pages of your last opus. Due to a general order in our company that no page should remain without an advertisement from the publisher, these last ones were printed with this advertisement against my wish and I regret this very much, because I would have preferred to have delivered your copies free of any additions. But you must not blame the colleagues whose names you have read, because the blame lies entirely with us and I will ensure that something similar will not happen again.

On the other hand, you may not object if you also appear on the reverse side in other cases, because we have already published so many of your works that it would no longer look funny if we compiled a list of them and used them in the same way as we have recently done consistently.

With the best recommendations
Your very devoted
L. Strecker

In the next letter by Strecker dated 16 January 1912, he again rejects Hennessy's Opp. 39 and 40, with much the same arguments as before in his letter of 3 October 1911. It is not certain whether Hennessy had sent the scores again or if this is a(nother) late reaction to Hennessy's letter of 29 September. In the latter case, within three months Strecker seems to have forgotten that he had already seen and rejected these works before. There is no reaction by Hennessy, so Strecker's forgetfulness must be assumed here. Instead, Hennessy sends another work (2 February) that he describes as 'six unpretentious waltzes' without giving a title. Strecker names it in his response (7 February) as the *Valses caprices*, Op. 41, rejecting these, too. With that letter, the correspondence ends – and so did the business relationship between Swan Hennessy and Schott.

	Mainz 16. Januar 1912.
Herrn Swan Hennessy	Mr Swan Hennessy
Paris	Paris
Sehr geehrter Herr,	Dear Sir,
Empfangen Sie meinen besten Dank für die Sendung der Exemplare Ihrer interessanten Incunabula op. 39 und En passant op. 40, von denen mir besonders die letzteren gefallen. No. 1, 3 und 5 enthalten meisterhafte Wiedergabe[n] von Klängen, die jeder schon einmal gehört hat. Aber – Sie wissen zwar schon, was ich sagen will, ich muss es aber doch aussprechen – ich bedaure, dass Sie sich auf diese Art des Komponierens capriziren, denn so raffiniert Sie auch vorgehen: das Klavier hat nicht genug Varietät der Klänge, um nur annähernd zum Ausdruck zu bringen, was Sie sagen wollen. Sobald Sie Mögliches anstreben wie z.B. im langsamen Satz von op. 40 No. 5 ist alles gut und schön, sogar sehr schön, aber Rädergeräusche und Signalpfeifen sind keine Objekte für wirklich[e] Musik – wenigstens meiner Ansicht nach. Sie verhindern dadurch gewaltsam die Verbreitung Ihrer Arbeiten und das bedaure ich so sehr, weil ich sehe, wie ausserordentlich fein alles ist, was Sie veröffentlichen.	Please receive my best thanks for sending me copies of your interesting Incunabula, Op. 39 and En passant, Op. 40, of which I especially like the latter. No. 1, 3 and 5 contain masterful reproductions of sounds that everyone will have heard before. But – you know what I want to say, but I have to say it nevertheless – I regret that you seem to be so obsessed with this way of composing, because as clever as you proceed: the piano does not have enough variety of sounds to express only approximately what you want to say. As soon as you strive for the possible as for example in the slow movement of Op. 40 No. 5 everything is good and beautiful, even very beautiful, but wheel noises and signal whistles are not objects for real music – at least in my opinion. You are forcibly preventing the dissemination of your work and I regret that so much because I see how extraordinarily fine everything is that you write.
Mit hochachtungsvollen Grüssen	With respectful greetings
Ihr sehr ergebener	Your very devoted
L. Strecker	L. Strecker

Sehr geehrter Herr Geheimrath,
  Sie haben schon so viel von mir herausgegeben dass ich es doch noch einmal versuchen will.
  Ich schicke Ihnen diesmal keine Programmusik sondern 6 Klaviermäs[s]ige anspruchslose Walzer, die, obschon es keine Gassenhauer sind, vielleicht etwas für das allgemeine Publikum sein dürfte[n].
  In höflicher Erwartung Ihrer gütigen Rückantwort,
    mit besten Grussen,
    Hochachtungsvoll ergeben
    Swan Hennessy

Paris, 2 Feb., 1912.
Dear Privy Councillor,
  You have already published so much by me that I want to try it one more time.
  This time I am not sending you programme music, but 6 waltzes, unpretentious on the piano, which, even though they are no hit of the streets, may perhaps be something for a general audience.
  In courteous expectation of your kind answer,
    with best regards,
    Yours sincerely
    Swan Hennessy

  Herrn Swan Hennessy
    Paris
Sehr geehrter Herr Hennessy,
  Die freundlich übersandten 6 Valses caprices op. 41 erlaube ich mir mit bestem Dank gleichzeitig wieder an Sie zurückgehen zu lassen, da wir gegenwärtig so stark in Anspruch genommen sind, dass ich nicht die nötige Zeit zu finden weiss, um neue Kompositionen von Ihnen richtig zu lancieren. Ich habe sie mir natürlich angesehen und finde die Kompositionen wie alles von Ihnen höchst pikant, wenn auch nicht gerade für weitere Kreise geeignet.
  Mit besten Grüssen
  Ihr hochachtungsvoll ergebener
    L. Strecker

Mainz, 7. Februar 1912.
  Mr Swan Hennessy
    Paris
Dear Mr Hennessy,
  I would like to take the liberty of returning the attached 6 Valses caprices, Op. 41 to you with my best thanks, as we are currently so busy that I do not know how to find the necessary time to properly launch new compositions by yourself. I have, of course, looked at them and find the compositions, like everything of yours, highly piquant, albeit not exactly suitable for wider circles.
  With best wishes
  Your very devoted
    L. Strecker

Swan Hennessy's *Incunabula*, Op. 39, *En passant … (Études d'après nature)*, Op. 40, and *Valses caprices*, op. 41 were all published with E. Demets soon afterwards – as everything that Hennessy wrote until Eugène Demets died in early 1923. Hennessy must have entered an exclusive arrangement with Demets from early 1912 onwards. Whether this involved co-financing as with Schott, is not established. In any case, Demets does not seem to have had the problems that Strecker formulated when it came to the reproduction on the piano of sounds from nature, traffic and industry.

Descriptive programme music of this kind was not quite so unusual in France as it may have been in Germany, as works by Satie, Debussy, Koechlin, and many others prove. In fact, as Detlev Altenburg has pointed out, 'until the outbreak of the First World War, programme music was an important field of experimentation for innovation in the history of composition'[64] and so it was for Hennessy. Since he had made France his home, it was a good decision to have everything from now on published in the market that he primarily targeted – even though he kept an interest in making a name for himself in Germany as well, as will be seen.

At Demets, Hennessy certainly was in good company. The publisher was in the process of becoming one of the more prestigious music publishers in Paris, just slightly, perhaps, below the profile of Durand, Leduc and Sénart. He was the publisher of some works by Ravel – the *Pavane pour une infante défunte* (1900), the *Jeux d'eau* (1901), and *Miroirs* (1906) – and took on some of the humoristic works of Satie – the *Véritables préludes flasques (pour un chien)* (1912), *Descriptions automatiques*, and *Embryons desséchés* (both of 1913). During this extremely prolific phase of Hennessy's work – that also follows his settling down in a new family with his marriage (1909) and son (1910), the feeling of security and success that must have come with his many publications brought a creative stimulus to Hennessy's music that resulted in a prolific stream of new works during the years preceding the War. Of the thirty-one works published since his new orientation as a 'French' composer (Opp. 21 to 50, except Op. 49), twenty came out with Demets.

Part 2 of the Schott correspondence again throws a spotlight on Hennessy's character and on his reception in a way that could not be drawn from reviews of music. His humour comes to the fore when he writes about technically difficult piano music that it 'won't matter because there are a lot of people who are only interested in music that they cannot play' (29 September 1911) or when he complains about advertisements of works by others in publications that he co-financed: 'I am of course happy and proud to serve as a propaganda tool for the fine and highly interesting works of Oehme, Kronke, Nevin, Van Gael, and others' (7 December 1911). He is easily hurt when he gets the impression of being unfairly criticised, as when his Opp. 39 and 40 were rejected for their obvious programmes that Strecker did not consider appropriate on the piano, and he defends himself by pointing to his artistic integrity: 'You say I am overshooting the mark. I am at least aiming for the centre, and you will admit that it would be a sad artist who works against his conviction' (4 October 1911).

Most interestingly, we experience a key reason for why Hennessy's works did not appear in public recitals although they received such positive reviews, when he writes: 'Since I don't concertize and live in a very withdrawn way, this [the promoting] can only be done by the publisher. It's not the quality of the music that makes it successful nowadays, but the advertising' (4 October 1911). It is true that, up to this point, Hennessy had never appeared in public with his own music as did so many composer-

---

[64] '*Bis zum Beginn des Ersten Weltkriegs war die Programmusik [...] ein wichtiges Experimentierfeld für Innovationen in der Kompositionsgeschichte.*'; Detlev Altenburg: 'Programmusik', in *Die Musik in Geschichte und Gegenwart* (MGG), subject part vol. 7 (Kassel: Bärenreiter, 1997), c. 1842.

pianists, and he never paid musicians to perform his music, although he had the means to do so. His withdrawn lifestyle would also have contributed to his having relatively few contacts to musicians so that he really, rather naively perhaps, seems to have thought that having pieces published and reviewed would be enough. Again, we will see shortly that Hennessy was to change his strategy very soon: after the forced interruption caused by the First World War, all through the 1920s he did perform in his piano music and as an accompanist to his songs, and he did pay musicians to play his music. He certainly realised around 1912 that something had to change if he wanted to make a name for himself.

Strecker's opinion of the value of Hennessy's music is another highly interesting aspect of the correspondence – and one that should by no means be intermingled with their financial arrangement. As a 'neutral' person, as an intermediate to music critics and musicians, and as a business man, Strecker had to be absolutely honest about what he liked and disliked, and he expressed both very openly.

Strecker clearly says that 'we often take real pleasure in your art, even if we are not able to provide you with our services for publication' (3 October 1911) and 'there is hardly a more honest admirer of your art than us' (3 November 1911). But, on the other hand, Hennessy's 'certain eccentricities' and his occasional move 'away from the path of harmonies and rhythms considered permissible' would make sales difficult and contribute to a sense that 'there is still a resistance to your art'. And he closed that letter of 3 November 1911 with the noteworthy remark:

> Anyone who wants something unusual must not lose patience, this is an observation that every innovator has had to make and which you will not be spared either.

Hennessy insists on his integrity, but Strecker does seem to have lost patience, although he added, 'I regret that so much because I see how extraordinarily fine everything is that you write' (16 January 1912).

* * *

Following the new exclusive agreement with Demets – for which there is no document but the fact that all of his compositions were published with Demets from now on – continued his prolific stream of very 'French' piano music, including some of the best of his output.

Incunabula, Op. 39 (1911) for piano

Incunabula, rejected by Schott in October 1911, was published by Demets in 1912. The little album consists of three short pieces entitled 1. *Berceuse*, 2. *Bébé dort*, and 3. *Croquemitaine*. The first two are linked by their programme (a lullaby and a 'sleeping baby') and are to be played without a break. *Croque-mitaine* would translate as a bogey, bugbear, bugaboo, or spectre, therefore something like a counterimage to the idyllic scenes of the first two parts, though still remaining in the realm of a child's fancy – a fast piece in downward moving chromatic scales that requires considerably more pianistic skills than the other two pieces. Hennessy had a baby son at the time of composition, which may explain the origin of the idea to explore (again) he world of a young child's experience.

Incunabula was briefly reviewed in *The Monthly Musical Record*, *La Revue musicale S.I.M.* and *Die Musik*.[65] Ten years after its publication, a short review from a US journal shows a potential avenue of critical appreciation of Swan Hennessy in America, had he managed to secure a stronger foothold there. In the 1922 article, the critic perceived the influence of French Impressionists on Hennessy's music, describing it as the style 'we have come to recognize as the Debussy idiom' – generally speaking, a contemporary American response to Hennessy hardly existed, but this review demonstrates that there would have been opportunities.

> Here is a composer none too familiar to us in America, and it is sincerely to be hoped that we will become far better acquainted with his work, for a glance at the pages of this suite show that he has something very definite to say for himself. This particular set of pieces commences with a one page *Berceuse*, a delightful balm to a perhaps over-lullabied race of music-lovers. But there will always be a place for such cradle songs as this, a Berceuse which does not demand an advanced technique by any means. Like all of Mr. Hennessy's music, the piece is distinctly in what we have come to recognize as the Debussy idiom, but like his famous forerunner, M. Hennessy never forgets the formal structure he has in mind; he always has a definite mood or impression to convey to his audience. The composer never sacrifices sanity, or beauty, on the altar of novelty. [...][66]

Incunabula has never had a public performance. Swan Hennessy himself performed the two first pieces once in a radio broadcast in June 1929.

En passant ... (Études d'après nature), Op. 40 (1911) for piano

Opus 40 is the second of the two piano works that were rejected by Schott on the grounds that he was, in Schott's arguing, attempting sounds that could not be expressed on a piano. It will be seen that the sounds Hennessy produced were not at all that extraordinary, particularly from a twenty-first-century perspective, but even for French music of the time it was not atypical. But Schott (or its director Ludwig Strecker) evidently shied away from risking any experiments. Perhaps, in a German context, this kind of programme music was less usual than in France.

Mainly written in or before September 1911, *En passant ...* was published by Demets early in the following year. Originally (as the manuscript shows) the work consisted of four pieces (not five) and was entitled *Impressions de voyage* (the subtitle remained unchanged), a title that expresses just as well what the constituting pieces try to convey. The first four pieces are called 1. *Petit pâtre sur les hauts pâturages* ('Little Shepherd on High Pastures'); 2. *Champs de blé au clair de lune* ('Wheat Fields in Moonlight'); 3. *Dans une petite ville flamande le dimanche* ('In a Small Flemish Village on Sunday'); and

---

[65] See Appendix 1.
[66] *The Musician* 27:4, April 1922, p. 25.

4. *Cîmes neigeuses* ('Snowy Peaks'). A fifth piece was added in October, originally called *En Chemin de fer* ('On a Train'), which became *Sieste en chemin de fer* in the publication. As images of travels in the countryside, all five pieces most likely reflect on Hennessy's own experience as a frequent traveller.

The manuscript also shows that the shepherd in No. 1 was originally a mountain cowheard (*'vacher montagnard'*), but this is a minor difference for the sake of a better-sounding title (aiming at the similarity of *pâtre* and *pâturages*). He remains a shepherd of cows, though, it seems, because the score contains a passage imitating cow bells (Ex. 5.11). This is, in fact, the most 'modern' part of the piece, being framed by opening and closing passages in relatively clear F major, with a tune that evokes a happy person skipping across a green pasture in bright sunshine. The cowbell passage is an example for the formal and harmonic freedom that composers of descriptive programme music could allow themselves and which, without such a programme, would perhaps be regarded as an advanced formal experiment.

Ex. 5.11: *En passant …*, Op. 40 No. 1 *'Petit pâtre sur les hauts pâturages*, bars 15–21

Champs de blé au clair de lune is a beautiful albeit short exercise in harmonic shifts, with high-pitched chords to a comparatively low melodic line. Starting in an A major key with a D minor seventh chord, both the melody and the chordal accompaniment pass through a number of chromatic turns, including whole-tone scales. To remain in the image of the moonlit wheat field, the bright high-pitched chords would probably symbolise the monochrome light reflected in the field. The melody that is peeling forward from bar 3 onwards, may resemble shapes that slowly become visible once a visitor's eye got used to the nightlight.

No. 3, *Dans une petite ville flamande le Dimanche*, is characterised by its lively tempo and bright mood. Except for the last few bars, the right hand moves in constant semiquavers and frequently in alternating pitches while the left hand provides a harmonic footing in slower metres (between dotted minims and crotchets). Notated in an A major key, the piece revels in a positive airiness without ever developing a clear melody. The changing metrical pattern of the left hand give the piece some structure, as when the regular crotchets in major thirds dissolve into sevenths (Ex. 5.12). Towards the end, another bell motif reminds the listener that the piece depicts a Sunday in a village and, in a way, links back to the first piece which had already featured bells – and Hennessy sets the different yet related sounds (cow bell and church bell) extremely well on the piano.

Ex. 5.12: *En passant ...*, Op. 40 No. 3 '*Dans une petite ville flamande le Dimanche*', bars 5–12

In the fourth piece, *Cîmes neigeuses*, Hennessy depicts snowy mountain tops, moving the scene from the Belgian lowlands to the Swiss Alps that the composer already knew very well from his travels. Other than in an earlier essay in depicting an aspect of Switzerland (*Valses*, Op. 32 No. 3), he does not attempt to imitate or parody Swiss traditional music here. As may perhaps be guessed by now (after having becoming a little familiar with Hennessy's approach at programme music) he describes the 'snowy peaks' in high-pitched chords, spaced in fourths, with a melodic line in the left hand that also undertakes some unusually large interval leaps. The piece in F sharp minor ends on a widely spaced tonic seventh chord.

The most striking piece in the set is the fifth, the one that was originally not included in the proposal to Schott. *Sieste en chemin de fer* depicts a train ride, respectively the experience of a railway passenger who falls asleep in the course of the monotonous rattling of the wheels on the rail tracks only to be woken up suddenly as the train comes to a stop. Strictly speaking, it is not an '*étude d'après nature*' but, perhaps, the means to see these '*en passant*'.

The piece is not the first attempt to depict a train in music, an honour that goes to Charles-Valentin Alkan's early *Le Chemin de fer*, Op. 27 (1844). But it predates the well-known orchestral movement *Pacific 231* (1923) by Arthur Honegger by twelve years and, although the instrumental forces could not be more different, the beginnings of both works are so similar that one wonders whether it is a mere coincidence. Both works, for instance, begin with two sharp sounds of a signal whistle, followed by the slow setting in motion of the train and its gradual increasing of speed (Ex. 5.13).

Ex. 5.13: *En passant* …, Op. 40 No. 5 '*Sieste en chemin de fer*', bars 1–18

The piece – the longest of the five parts of *En chemin* … – consists of four clearly distinguishable parts that lead into one another in a well-crafted manner. The first covers the whole first page of the score, ending with bar 28. In this part 'the train' starts and picks up speed. Bars 29 to 44 transfers part of the 'movement' to the right hand (though remaining in the bass clef) with a variant of the rolling train motif with heavy accents in the left hand. The final bars 42 to 44 of this section slow down the dynamics somewhat ('*en ralentissant un peu*') and establish a motif with repeated pitches on the second and third beat of the bar. In a rich chromatic scoring, this forms part three of the piece (bars 45 to 60), the harmony of which reminds a little of the sound of the Parisian funfair that Hennessy depicted in the second piece of *Fêtes*, Op. 36. It may not be too speculative to interpret this scene as a dream of the piece's protagonist who is having his/her 'siesta' on the train, inspired by the sound of the train's wheels that reminds him/her of something else. Bars 61 to 72 form part four, which returns to the rhythmic model of part two but in slower tempo and with an additional melody that tends to clash with the underlying harmony. Clearly, the train passenger is still within his/her dream that becomes ever weirder. The rest of the piece (until bar 84) is mere concluding matter: the train slows down (evidently without the passenger noticing it) and, with another sharp signal from the locomotive and an abrupt step on the break, stops – the passenger is forced to wake up.

All this is technically extremely well made and harmonically fully up to date. Despite its brevity – the whole opus would not last longer than eight minutes – Hennessy achieves exactly what he aimed at: a work *'en passant'* – five brief observations that one makes 'in passing', while traveling. Yet, in an overall appreciation of Hennessy's piano music, this work should not be taken too lightly. It must surely rank as one of his best.

Fig 5.3: Decorative art nouveau image from the cover of Hennessy's *En passant … (Études d'après nature)*, Op. 40

In his review for *Comoedia*, Louis Vuillemin focuses on the idea of how an artist reacts to his natural or physical environment – and what he writes sounds like an Impressionist manifesto:

> Isn't it quite sympathetic, this inclination that a young artist affirms to constantly transport into the musical field things he has seen and always exactly felt? It seems to me that it should never be otherwise and that every composer has a duty to have an album in his pocket, adorned with the epigraph: 'What my ears have heard'. But alas, how many people know how to 'listen'? Many seek it, dangerously deviating from their true path and venturing into horizons where music must have difficulty to follow them. However, it would have been enough for them to have paused for a moment and to be attentive. Music is everywhere. Only the musician senses it, hears it. And it is up to him to reveal it to others. Because a musician, or painter, or poet – or all three together – the artist is only an intermediary between nature and … man. And it is precisely that which would not be expressible without him, that he has the mission to express. Nothing else.[67]

---

[67] *N'est-ce pas tout à fait sympathique, ce penchant qu'affirme un jeune artiste à transporter sans cesse dans le domaine musical des choses vues et toujours exactement ressenties? Il me semble qu'il n'en devrait jamais être autrement et que tout compositeur a le devoir de posséder en poche un album, orné de cette épigraphe: "Ce que*

Much more factual was a (anonymous) review in *The Monthly Musical Record*:

> The "En Passant" Etudes are a set of impressionistic pieces. No. 1 is of pastoral character. No. 2, "Cornfields by Moonlight" and "Snowy Heights," offer interesting studies in chromatic chords. "Sunday in a Flemish Town" is evidently not a dull day, while "A Doze in a Train" is a curious piece of programme music.[68]

In Germany, a review in *Die Musik* focused on *Sieste en chemin de fer*, which the critic called 'a little work of art in modern pianistic mood painting'.[69] The critic in the *Allgemeine Musikzeitung*, however, did not even mention it, preferring the pieces No. 1 and 3 and recommending Nos. 2 and 4 to the 'paradise of the waste paper basket':

> These two are typical for the fine mood painter that Hennessy is. Although he clearly avoids the Hanswurst shop of many of his Parisian colleagues, he remains fancy and original. All the more disappointing are pieces like 'Cîmes neigeuses' (how should such things be expressed in music?) or 'Champs de blé au clair de lune' (in the middle movement Schumann looks around the corner, suddenly and cheerfully, as in old times, as may be expected on such a moonlit night …). A solid musician like Hennessy could easily afford to hand over such unguessed children of his muse to purgatory if he didn't prefer the paradise of the waste paper basket.[70]

En passant …, Op. 40 is, unfortunately, no exception to the rule of late performances. The work was never publicly performed in its entirety. Hennessy himself played No. 3 (*Dans une petite ville flamande le Dimanche*) as *In einem vlämischen Städtchen am Sonntag* in November 1913 in Berlin, but all other parts of the work received performances by professional pianists only during the eleven years between 1922 and 1932. After a performance by Denyse Molié at the Salle Gaveau in June 1929 in a programme

---

mes oreilles ont entendu." Mais hélas combien savent "écouter"? Beaucoup cherchent, s'écartent dangereusement de leur voie véritable et s'aventurent vers des horizons où la musique ne saurait manquer d'avoir quelque peine à les suivre Or, il leur suffirait, s'étant un instant recueillis, d'être attentifs. La musique est partout. Seul, le musicien la devine, l'entend. Et le soin lui incombe de la révéler à autrui. Car musicien, ou peintre, ou poète — ou les trois ensemble — l'artiste n'est qu'un intermédiaire entre la nature et … l'homme. Et c'est ce qui sans lui ne serait pas exprimable, qu'il a précisément la mission d'exprimer. Rien autre chose.'; Louis Vuillemin in *Comoedia*, 25 January 1912, p. 3.

[68] *The Monthly Musical Record*, 1 February 1912, p. 45.

[69] *'"Sieste en chemin de fer" (aus dem ersten Heft) ist in der drollig-geistreichen Schilderung eines sich in Bewegung setzenden Eisenbahnzuges ein kleines Kunstwerk moderner pianistischer Stimmungsmalerei.';* Emil Thilo in *Die Musik* 11:17, first June issue, 1912, p. 308.

[70] *'Diese beiden sind typisch für den feinen Stimmungsmaler Hennessy. Trotzdem er den Hanswurstladen vieler seiner Pariser Kollegen in einem weiten Bogen ausweicht, bleibt es apart und originell. Um so enttäuschender wirken Stückchen wie "Cîmes neigeuses" (wie soll so was in Musik ausgedrückt werden?) oder "Champs de blé au clair de lune". (Im Mittelsatz guckt hier, wie bei solcher Mondnacht wohl verständlich, ganz plötzlich und fröhlich Schumann um die Ecke, wie in alter Zeit …) Ein gediegener Musiker wie Hennessy könnte es sich ruhig leisten, solche ungeratene Kinder seiner Muse dem Fegefeuer zu überantworten, sollte er nicht das Paradies des Papierkorbes vorziehen.';* Eugen Segnitz in *Allgemeine Musikzeitung* 39:43, 25 October 1912, p. 1104.

consisting of eighteenth-century music in a first part and works by Hennessy and Debussy in a second, Maurice Imbert wrote in the *Journal des débats* about her interpretation of the Hennessy works (which had included the *Sieste en chemin de fer* and some of his later Irish-coloured works):

> But it is by interpreting, if the term is acceptable, an important group of works of the 'French musician' that she [i. e. Molié] most forcefully affirmed her exceptionally sensitive nature. Listening to her then was a delight.[71]

Similarly, critic and composer Tristan Klingsor wrote of the same recital of the 'contemporary suite' by Hennessy, 'they are extremely pleasant and the last one, the *Sieste en chemin de fer*, is really full of spirit and rhythm'.[72] Little did Imbert and Klingsor know that they were writing about a work that by then was already eighteen years old.

Valses caprices, Op. 41 (1911) for piano

The *Valses caprices*, Op. 41 are another highlight among Hennessy's piano music of this period. Looking at the collective and the individual titles of the set, this work is most likely a humorous (or parodied) response to Maurice Ravel's *Valses nobles et sentimentales* (1911), which had received their first performance in May 1911, with its seven short waltzes followed by an *Epilogue*. This is reflected in Hennessy's work (written in October and November 1911) with its six short waltzes followed by a seventh '*Encore une valse*'. It may be regarded as the earliest of such ironic references, predating Satie's *Trois Valses distinguées du précieux dégoutée* (1914) by three years and by no means as insulting as Satie's.[73]

Hennessy's individual titles are 1. *Valse rustique* ('Rustic Waltz'), 2. *Valse canaille* ('Scoundrel Waltz'), 3. *Valse distraite* ('Distracted Waltz'), 4. *Valse boîteuse* ('Limping Waltz'), 5. *Valse érotique* ('Erotic Waltz'), 6. *À la Reger*, and 7. *Encore une valse* ('Another Waltz'). The work, rejected by Schott in February 1912 on the grounds of being 'highly piquant, albeit not exactly suitable for wider circles', was published by Demets in the same year (the earliest review appeared in November). Despite the one piece alluding to Reger and the descriptive titles (Ravel did not use such titles), the formal structure and the date most certainly point to his influence.

---

[71] '*Mais c'est interprétant, dans l'acception du terme, un groupe important de pages du "musicien français" qu'elle affirma avec le plus de force sa nature exceptionnellement sensible. L'écouter alors fut un délice.*'; Maurice Imbert in *Journal des débats*, 10 June 1929, p. 4.
[72] '[…] *une suite contemporaine de* […] *de Swan Hennessy; elles sont extrêmement agréables et la dernière, cette Berceuse en chemin de fer, est vraiment pleine d'esprit et de rythme.*'; Tristan Klingsor in *La Semaine à Paris*, 14 June 1929.
[73] Kelly explains that this work by Satie was intended as a musical attack on Ravel, which was not Hennessy's idea; see Barbara L. Kelly: *Music and Ultra-Modernism in France. A Fragile Consensus, 1913–1939* (Woodbridge: Boydell Press, 2013), p. 44–45.

A German critic compared Hennessy's work with Leopold Godowsky's *Walzermasken* (a work that includes 24 short waltzes in four volumes),[74] but this was only published in February 1912 and therefore cannot have influenced Hennessy. But the comparison is valid in terms of the satirical nature of the works, even though Hennessy's harmony is much more advanced than Godowsky's Romantic language. In terms of their character one may also regard them as a precursor to William Alwyn's *Fantasy Waltzes* (1956).

The manuscript, characterised by numerous corrections and pasted-over sections, reveals that the first four waltzes were composed in October 1911 and originally had no descriptive titles, merely being numbered I to IV. When the other three pieces were added in November, all were given descriptive titles. We have seen before that, in terms of his titles, Hennessy was open to suggestions by his publisher, so these subtitles may have been suggested by or in cooperation with Eugène Demets.

Another parallel to Ravel's work is that the single pieces follow each other without a break. Although Hennessy writes *'Enchaînez'* only between the first two pieces, this may be interpreted to be valid throughout, since he only uses simple double bar lines at the end of a piece, no proper ending on a bold stroke, except at the very end of the album. The brevity of the single pieces is another parallel, although Hennessy's are yet shorter than Ravel's, but it is a clear distinction to other, similarly titled works of which Hennessy was, no doubt, aware, such as the *Valses caprices* by Anton Rubinstein or Gabriel Fauré.

In Thomas Kabisch's opinion, Ravel's *Valses nobles et sentimentales* represent 'music about music' in the sense that he played with established forms like the Viennese or the slow waltz only to break away from them both rhythmically and in terms of their character.[75]

Following this idea (and the presupposition of a Ravel influence), Hennessy's waltzes are 'music about music about music'. His music is not meant to be dance but concert music and, much like the Ravel work, plays with established clichés about the popular image of a waltz. This becomes apparent from the beginning when in the *Valse rustique* a popular motif in thirds and sixths breaks out in double tempo from the syncopated nature of the previous material. This melodic cell (see bars 9–10 and 12–13 in Ex. 5.14) can be traced through most of the seven constituting pieces of the set, linking them by a simple motivic idea.

---

[74] Richard H. Stein in *Die Musik* 12:8, 2nd January issue 1913, p. 108.
[75] Thomas Kabisch: 'Ravel, Maurice', section 'Klaviermusik', in *Die Musik in Geschichte und Gegenwart* (MGG2), ed. by Ludwig Finscher, biographical part, vol. 13, cc. 1355–1356.

Ex. 5.14: *Valses caprices*, Op. 41 No. 1 *'Valse rustique'*, bars 1–15

This motivic idea is often hidden in formal variants that make it barely identifiable such as in the four bars (b. 23–26) interrupting two sequences of whole-tone scales in the *Valse canaille* (Ex. 5.15). But it also appears as a quite direct quote in F sharp major, mysteriously contrasted with a low E, in the *Valse érotique* that makes it sound like a distant memory (Ex. 5.16), and several times in different tonalities in waltzes nos. 6 and 7.

Ex. 5.15: *Valses caprices*, Op. 41 No. 2 *'Valse canaille'*, bars 16–28

Ex. 5.16: *Valses caprices*, Op. 41 No. 5 '*Valse érotique*', bars 13–24

The least dance-like waltz is the highly chromatic *Valse érotique*. And the syncopated *Valse boîteuse* (No. 4) poses yet other challenges resembling, perhaps, the stumbling of a dancer who has had a glass too many.

Critics were not united as to which of the seven waltzes they liked most. Louis Vuillemin seemed to have been taken by the *Valse canaille*, commenting:

> His sarcasm does not remind of bellowing. I even doubt that the places where we dance have ever heard such delicious harmonies. Yet, with each bar you can feel the intended, even childish, joking.[76]

He says nothing about the *Valse distraite* except '*Eh! oui*', but considers the *Valse boîteuse* one of the most curious pieces in the set because of the metric combination of 6/8 and 3/4 in the right hand with 2/4 in the left, about which he says:

> This is quite witty and skilfully realised. And don't worry: it is written as if it was the easiest thing on Earth.[77]

The Monthly Musical Record commented on the general form and harmonic language:

> [...] in the *Valses* there are some thoughts expressed, so to speak, in simple language; but at times the composer indulges in out-of-the-way harmonies and modulations. The music nevertheless is clever.[78]

---

[76] '*Sa canaillerie n'évoque aucunement le beuglant. Je doute même que les lieux où l'on danse aient jamais retenti d'aussi savoureuses harmonies. Pourtant, on sent à chaque mesure, l'intention plaisante, voire gamine.*', Louis Vuillemin in *Comoedia*, 21 November 1912, p. 3.

[77] '*C'est tout à fait comique et habilement réalisé. N'ayez aucune crainte: voilà qui s'exécute le plus facilement du monde.*'; ibid.

[78] *The Monthly Musical Record*, 1 January 1913, p. 19–20.

The same critic also considered the piece entitled *À la Reger* 'a curiosity', while German critics quite liked the Reger allusion. One wrote 'Strange, by the way, how easily Reger can be copied and how difficult it is to parody him',[79] another that it 'parodies a certain kind of Reger's occasional composing in a truly witty, unerringly accurate and yet not hurtful way'.[80]

The contemporary 'Impressionist' musical language of the work was well noted and remarked upon by several critics. Another German critic commented:

> 'Valse Canaille' and 'Encore une valse' are elegant and light in the revitalisation of their material, featuring harmonies of discreet and pleasant variation by mixing new colours.[81]

The composer and conductor Gabriel Grovlez remarked of Hennessy's *Valses caprices*, Op. 41 and the following *Gitaneries*, Op. 42 that the composer 'revels in good-natured Impressionism [and that] the numerous short pieces by this composer are not particularly difficult and should win everyone over with their charming musicality.'[82]

There was negative criticism, too, but it was of a somewhat snobbish kind, not untypical for contemporary music criticism in Paris, such as when *La Revue musicale S.I.M.* noted that the work was 'a small collection of characteristic dances, which will never make anyone dance'[83] or the opinion in *L'Echo musical* that they 'are made for the salons and cannot be of interest to a musician'.[84] Funny, on the other hand, is the comment in the London *Times* that 'the eroticism of the "Valse érotique" is undoubtedly platonic'.[85]

It was again the composer's German friend Hugo Rasch who wrote another passionate plea to pianists to explore the music of Swan Hennessy:

> Surely there is a lot to be found here, too – not surprising given the intimate genre of these compositions – which is best suited for the small circle. But how is this small circle supposed to know what delightful things Hennessy writes for it, if it is not a committed interpreter who draws their attention to them from a podium? Do the virtuosos always have

---

[79] '*Merkwürdig übrigens, wie leicht sich Reger kopieren, und wie schwer er sich parodieren läßt.*'; R. H. Stein, in *Die Musik*, op. cit.

[80] '[…] *parodiert in wahrhaft geistreicher, zielsicher treffender und doch nicht verletzender Weise eine gewisse Art von Regerscher Gelegenheitskomponiererei.*'; Hugo Rasch in *Allgemeine Musikzeitung* 40:10, 7 March 1913, p. 326.

[81] '"*Valse Canaille" und "Encore une valse" zeugen von Eleganz und Leichtigkeit in der Stoffbelebung und bringen in harmonischer Hinsicht diskrete und angenehme Abwechselung durch neue Farbenmischungen.*'; Fritz Crome in *Signale für die musikalische Welt* 71:23, 4 June 1913, p. 912.

[82] '*M. Swan Hennessy se complait dans un impressionnisme de bon aloi. D'une difficulté très abordable, les nombreuses petites pièces de cet auteur obtiendront tous les suffrages par leur charmante musicalité.*'; Gabriel Grovlez in *Musica*, June 1913.

[83] '[…] *petit recueil de danses de caractère, qui ne feront jamais danser personne.*', in *La Revue musicale S.I.M.*, 15 December 1912, p. 67.

[84] '[…] *sont faites pour les salons et ne peuvent point intéresser un musicien.*'; J. Peyrot in *L'Echo musical*, December 1912.

[85] *The Times*, 13 May 1913, p. 9.

to play things that require at least eighteen fingers to be executed? The musical delicacies presented here are so artistically refined that they can confidently adorn any serious concert programme if only the necessary master of heart and mind has them under his fingers. And shouldn't we be happy that in Hennessy we finally have a *humourist* of the first order? A superior, smiling connoisseur of life, who writes things in a deliciously unbiased and yet – I must use the word – aristocratic way, as life forces it into his pen.[86]

Alas, that 'committed interpreter' was not yet on the horizon. Surprising as it may seem in view of both the quality of the music and the positive critical response, the *Valses caprices* have never (as yet) been performed in public.

Fig. 5.3: Humorous Swan Hennessy, undated photograph probably early to mid-1920s (© Boris Lipnitzky / Roger-Viollet)

---

[86] '*Sicherlich ist auch hier wieder viel dabei – bei dem intimen Genre dieser Kompositionen nicht gerade verwunderlich – was sich am besten für den kleinen Kreis eignet. Aber wie soll dieser kleine Kreis wissen, was für entzückende Sachen Hennessy für ihn schreibt, wenn nicht ein berufener Interpret vom Podium herab auf sie aufmerksam macht? Müssen denn die Herren Virtuosi immer nur Sachen spielen, zu deren Execution mindestens achtzehn Finger vonnöten sind? Die hier vorliegenden musikalischen Leckerbissen sind von solch künstlerisch feiner Beschaffenheit, daß sie getrost jedes ernste Konzertprogramm zieren können, wenn nur der nötige Könner von Herz und Verstand sie unter den Fingern hat. Und sollen wir uns denn nicht freuen, daß wir in Hennessy endlich wieder einmal einen Humoristen feinster Crescenz haben? Einen überlegen lächelnden Kenner des Lebens, der mit köstlich unbefangener, und doch – ich muß das Wort gebrauchen – aristokratischer Art die Dinge zeichnet, wie sie ihm das Leben in die Feder drängt.*'; H. Rasch, op. cit.

Gitaneries, Op. 42 (1911) for piano

Another 1911 piano work may, perhaps, be dealt with quickly as it does not seem central to the narrative thread of this study. It shares the fate of the *Valses caprices* in that it never received a public performance. And if – as is the hope of this author – Hennessy's pre-War piano music and his post-War Celtic repertory should find new friends in the future, this particular work would probably not be part of it.

The *Gitaneries* show another interest of our composer, that in Spanish music, its modes and rhythms, an interest that is mainly informed by Hennessy's admiration for Georges Bizet's *Carmen* (and less in its more contemporary expressions such as in the music of Ravel, Laparra, de Falla or Turina). The Spanish idiom had for some one hundred years been a major vehicle for musical exoticism in France, even though the two countries were geographical neighbours. As Samuel Llano has shown, the French construction of Spanish music was an integral – and a very popular – part of the musical 'otherness' in French musical life – and this was strongly influenced by the immense success over several decades of Bizet's *Carmen*, originally premiered in 1875.[87]

Hennessy's *Gitaneries* are dedicated to the memory of Bizet. The titles of its four constituent pieces, 1. *Carmen*, 2. *Mercédès*, 3. *Jacinta*, and 4. *Manuelita*, all allude to more or less frequently occurring figures in the opera. The collective title *Gitaneries* is a clear indication that Hennessy more specifically sought to depict the female gypsy side of the characters in *Carmen*, which may originally have contributed to the modest success that the opera had in 1875–6. Llano had pointed out that

> the otherness surrounding perceptions of the Spanish female gypsy, reinforced by the display of deviant behaviors, most likely elicited a lukewarm critical reaction at the première[88]

Socially more acceptable revivals of the opera, leading eventually to the work's one thousandth performance by December 1904, had changed that perception, though, and the image of Spanish 'otherness' in opera had just very recently been superseded by Raoul Laparra's *La Habanera* (1908) and *La Jota* (1911). Llano emphasised that '*La jota* helped in regarding *Carmen* as an escape from the modernisms that some critics pointed out in Laparra's work'.[89]

It will therefore, at least briefly, have to be examined whether Hennessy's work must also be regarded as an 'escape from modernism' or whether he continued his modern harmonic language of the past few years into his interpretation of Bizetian figures. In this regard, it must be said that Hennessy rather followed Bizet's and not Laparra's lead. He does not quote from Bizet but – despite a few modulations in the first piece – he clearly prefers a late nineteenth-century harmonic language that largely remains within the confines of unaltered diatonic or modal scales. That is not to say that the *Gitaneries* are not interesting. For any pianist seeking a set of works in a Spanish

---

[87] Samuel Llano, *Whose Spain? Negotiating 'Spanish Music' in Paris, 1908–1929* (New York: Oxford University Press, 2013).
[88] Llano, *Whose Spain?*, p. 163.
[89] Llano, *Whose Spain?*, p. 166.

idiom that is entertaining and of great melodic and rhythmic refinement, these works should clearly be considered. In fact, it is quite amazing how, chameleon-like, Hennessy slips into the Spanish idiom as if it was his own.

It is this character that was applauded in the short reviews that are extant about this composition. *The Monthly Musical Record* thought they were written 'in a fresh, natural style'.[90] The critic in *Signale für die musikalische Welt* appears to have liked the set a lot, judging from his brief comment:

> From 'Gitaneries' Spain's sunshine and joy of dancing laugh towards us, and with a few strokes in 'Jacinta' and 'Manuelita' two flexible, piquant and black-eyed female figures are drawn.[91]

La Revue musicale S.I.M. was the only journal that wondered why Hennessy 'who must have been born far away from Spain, likes to divert his world by composing *Gitaneries*'[92] – an obvious and justified remark, but it did not offer any further comment.

Sonatine, Op. 43 (1911) for piano

Hennessy's Piano Sonatina is his first attempt at writing a more substantial work for the piano that would go beyond his clear preference for short and concise sketches. It is still comparatively short: with its three movements headed *Allegro appassionato*, *Tempo di menuetto*, and *Vivace ma non troppo* the duration is approximately nine minutes. It is this comparative briefness that must have led to the diminutive form of the term sonata, not its technical facility, since the work is quite ambitious.

Written in late 1911, it is probably another work that is, in its formal construction, influenced by a work by Maurice Ravel: his *Sonatine* of 1905. Both feature a three-movement structure with a minuet in the middle (Ravel calls it '*Mouvement de menuet*') and the neo-classical approach. For Hennessy's work so far, it is a rare example of an abstract piece of music without a concrete programme or any humorous aspects (but there were many more to come in the future).

Ravel's influence can not only be recognised in the formal arrangement of the movements but also in the character of the movements themselves. Both first movements of the two sonatinas feature a quick movement in Alberti figures in the left hand as the harmonic backdrop to a metrically diverse right-hand melody. Ravel places it in the higher middle register of the keyboard and Hennessy uses it as a 'classical' Alberti bass, yet the idea is the same (Ex. 5.17).[93]

---

[90] *The Monthly Musical Record*, 1 January 1913, p. 19.
[91] '*Aus "Gitaneries" lachen uns Spaniens Sonnenglut und Tanzfreudigkeit entgegen, und mit wenigen Strichen sind in "Jacinta" und "Manuelita" zwei biegsame, pikante und schwarzäugige Frauengestalten gezeichnet.*'; Fritz Crome in *Signale für die musikalische Welt* 71:23, 4 June 1913, p. 912.
[92] '[…] *M. Swan Henessy, qui a dû voir le jour fort loin de l'Espagne, se plaît à dérouter son monde en composant des* Gitaneries […]'; in *La Revue musicale S.I.M.*, 15 January 1912, p. 67.
[93] Ravel uses demisemiquavers and Hennessy semiquavers, but Ravel's tempo is '*Modéré*' and Hennessy's '*Allegro appassionato*', which almost equalises the respective tempi.

Ex. 5.17: *Sonatine*, Op. 43, 1st movt, bars 1–5

Both also use a contrasting second theme in the exposition that is considerably slower, in different rhythm and more lyrical. In fact, Hennessy's theme (from bar 23, see Ex. 5.18) is considerably more melodious than Ravel's, but of course Ravel did not aim at melodiousness whereas Hennessy most likely did. This is followed (in the Hennessy work) by a rather Romantic development section, before the 'classical' reprise of the themes.

Ex. 5.18: *Sonatine*, Op. 43, 1st movt, bars 23–30

In the middle minuet movement, both composers follow the regular ambitus of the eighteenth-century model. Ravel writes in 3/8 metre and Hennessy in 3/4, but again the thematic idea – contrasting bars of three regular beats per bar with other bars in up to six beats – is a parallel (Ex. 5.19).

Ex. 5.19: *Sonatine*, Op. 43, 2nd movt, bars 1–19

Even the conclusion of the movement, which breaks with the rhythmic regularity of the preceding music, introducing new material and stronger dynamics, is similar. Hennessy's, in contrast, is considerably simpler than Ravel's, as is the whole movement. Yet, the formal parallel is striking (Ex. 5.20).

Ex. 5.20: *Sonatine*, Op. 43, 2nd movt, bars 50–57

Also as in the Ravel *Sonatine*, Hennessy's third movement is a toccata in fast tempo, formally in an extension of baroque models with an inherent melodic line hidden in selected pitches of the rapid passages. If the pianist follows the *pianissimo* direction, it should be an effective movement that makes for a fine conclusion of the work.

With these strictly formal similarities, however, any sensible comparison with Ravel's work should end. Hennessy's *Sonatine* is a very attractive work in its own right, which, however, is considerably more conservative in stylistic terms. Although his score betrays his French environment here and there, its melodic and harmonic approach is clearly informed by late Romantic models. As always, Hennessy excels in clear and memorable melodies, which remain an essential ingredient of his music that he does not sacrifice for a modernist French style. Insofar, his first major abstract score in a while differs from his more programmatic scores in which he allows himself a more advanced harmonic and technical language.

The *Sonatine* is dedicated to the Paris correspondent of the *Allgemeine Musikzeitung*, the German critic Heinrich Möller, whom we already encountered in the withdrawn 1909 Shakespeare songs. Despite the connection, the review of this work in the German periodical was (again) written by Hugo Rasch who commented:

> Seriousness and passion speak from the Sonatine, op. 43, [...] which seems to me to be one of the most valuable of what Hennessy has written and which, due to the clarity of its structure and movement, is no less suitable for performance than it is for teaching purposes.[94]

Another German journal, *Die Musik*, wrote:

> The three-movement sonatina, if it is to sound well, will be too difficult for children, but will in any case be 'too easy' for adults. The middle movement, a charming minuet, deserves a special edition.[95]

In *Comoedia*, Louis Vuillemin focussed his attention on the second theme of the first movement (see Ex. 5.18 above), commenting on this theme's obvious indebtedness to the Romantic tradition:

> There are seductive inspirations in this *Sonatine*, and in particular, after the appassionato beginning of the first piece, a second theme is quite pretty. It looks like a Russian ballad that Chopin would have left behind in Poland and hummed while crossing Germany! See how Chopin, Rimsky and Schumann fraternise here for eight bars and rest in E minor, before separating.[96]

---

[94] '*Ernst und Leidenschaft aber spricht aus der Sonatine, op. 43, [...] die mir mit zu dem wertvollsten zu zählen scheint, was Hennessy geschrieben hat und durch die Klarheit des Aufbaus und des Satzes zum Vortrag nicht minder geeignet ist, wie zu Unterrichtszwecken.*'; Hugo Rasch in *Allgemeine Musikzeitung* 40:10, 7 March 1913, p. 326

[95] '*Die dreisätzige Sonatine wird, wenn sie gut klingen soll, Kindern zu schwer sein, von Erwachsenen aber in jedem Falle "zu leicht" befunden werden. Der mittlere Satz, ein reizvolles Menuett, verdient eine Sonderausgabe.*'; Richard H. Stein in *Die Musik* 12:8, 2nd January issue 1913, p. 108.

[96] '*Il y a de séduisantes inspirations dans cette Sonatine, et notamment, après le début appassionato du premier morceau, un second thème en ut tout à fait joli. On dirait d'une ballade russe qu'aurait retenue Chopin en*

The only documented public performance of the *Sonatine* was at the 12 November 1913 event in Berlin, when Swan Hennessy introduced several of his works to the German musical public (more about this event in Chapter 6).

Sentes et chemins (Nouvelles études d'après nature), Op. 44 (1912) for piano

The subtitle of *Sentes et chemins* alludes to *En passant* …, Op. 40 of the previous year, which was subtitled '*Études d'après nature*'. The present work is therefore intended as a continuation of the programmatic idea of setting in music scenes from nature as well as everyday human life – a strong trend among composers of this period, and particularly in France. It is indeed at the heart of the Impressionist idea of catching the essence of the moment. And Hennessy is again the keen observer of his environment that we have already come to recognise him by now.

As in his opus 40, there is again one exception to the idea of nature studies. In the previous work it was the 'doze on a train', now it is the very first piece, *Ouvriers allants à l'usine* ('Workers Going to the Factory'), which is followed by 2. *Promenade du philosophe* ('Philosopher's Walk'); 3. *À travers bois* ('Through the Woods'); 4. *Cornemuse en tête* ('Bagpipe [Sounding] in the Head'); 5. *Sur la route d'Amalfi* ('On the Road to Amalfi'); 6. *Sentier de Meudon au printemps* ('Meudon Trail in Spring'); and 7. *Par la pluie* ('Through the Rain'). The work was composed between June and September 1912.

The dedication '*à mon père*' is to his father, Michael David Hennessy, who celebrated his 75th birthday in Paris in 1912. The work is therefore most certainly a present in memory of the many travels that father and son undertook together since the 1890s.

Each of the seven short pieces (none exceeding two pages in the score) is preceded by a programmatic verbal introduction that prepares the player for the mood he is to convey in his performance and that helps interpret the various musical elements. The text for the first piece, for instance, is the following:

> Two workers go to the factory: one, an anarchist and dragging his leg, recriminates against the bosses, while the other shrugs his shoulders and whistles a joyful tune.[97]

While one may imagine how a dragging leg and a joyful whistling tune might be interpreted on the piano, the 'anarchist' is a little more difficult. Yet, it is probably this idea that helps interpret the rather 'un-ruly' harmonic treatment of the walking movement, which is indeed rather strange in its unusual and multifarious application of sharps and flats in the F minor score. The shoulder-shrugging fellow worker lurks through in between, for instance in bars 9 and 11 (Ex. 5.21).

Pologne et fredonnée en traversant l'Allemagne! Comprenez que Chopin, Rimsky et Schumann fraternisent ici durant huit mesures et se reposent en mi mineur, avant que de se séparer.'; Louis Vuillemin in *Comoedia*, 21 November 1912, p. 3.

[97] '*Deux ouvriers s'en vont à l'usine: l'un, anarchiste et trainant la jambe, récrimine contre les patrons, tandis que l'autre hausse les épaules et siffle un air joyeux.*'

An American Impressionist (1908–1913)

Ex. 5.21: *Sentes et chemins*, Op. 44 No. 1 *'Ouvriers allants à l'usine'*, bars 1–14

The *Promenade du philosophe* is headed 'The dream of a gentle and disillusioned old man' (*'Rêverie d'une vieillard doux et désabusé'*). It portrays the old man's walk in a repetitive 2/4 metric structure in the left hand and often rather sharp dissonances in the right hand. With a basic tonality in D minor and another dragging walking scene, the *Sentes et chemins* begin with two rather 'heavy' impressions of human 'nature'.

À travers bois is another calm piece, now in 6/8, in a tonality leaning on A major. The single-line left hand movement with its two tied tones per bar provides for a gently swinging movement that requires – as all seemingly simple scores – a sensitive interpretation. The introductory text speaks of the silence of a deep forest with a mysterious murmur that is the pulse of the heart of nature (*'les pulsations du cœur de la nature'*). A middle section of ten bars resembles a 'phantastic hunt' in the distance.

After three rather slow pieces, the mood in *Cornemuse en tête* is very different. In very straightforward F major and to be played very quickly with a clearly emphasised melody, it vaguely reminds of an unspecified traditional hornpipe in dotted rhythm. The accompanying text reads: 'Escorted by a group of kids, an old bagpiper crosses the village'[98] – most likely an experience the Hennessys had on one of their travels to Scotland (or, less likely, Ireland), and the tune remained in the head when the piper had gone. It is a rather unpretentious little piece.

The fifth piece, *Sur la route d'Amalfi*, alluding to the famous tourist town on the southwestern coast of Italy, is much like an Italian popular ballad, with a very singable tune worthy of a Paolo Tosti (Ex. 5.22). The introductory text sets the scene:

---

[98] *'Escorté d'une bande de gamins, un vieux cornemuseur traverse le village.'*

On the way to the market, a peasant perched on a small car dragged by a tiny donkey sings a popular chorus with his full throat, while a trattoria releases puffs of tarantella.[99]

The tarantella dance does indeed appear as a second thematic subject in bars 37–48. Otherwise, one may regard *Sur la route d'Amalfi* as a brilliant musical interpretation, in miniature format, of the charms of southern Italy, with a hint of satirical humour. Except in some chord progressions of the tarantella part, the piece does not contain major deviations from the dominant G major.

Ex. 5.22: *Sentes et chemins*, Op. 44 No. 5 '*Sur la route d'Amalfi*', bars 1–12

Sentier de Meudon au printemps is a strange and not very convincing piece. The introductory text describes birds singing in the sunshine, becoming quiet as the sky becomes cloudy, with only few timid chirps remaining. It is particularly the second part of the piece when the clouds suppress the birds' good mood that is a bit carelessly executed, with the same octave bass motif repeated over 24 bars and very little happening in the right hand, that is less than satisfactory.

Monotony is intended, on the other hand, in the last piece of the set, *Par la pluie*. The introductory note reads: 'The rain falls endlessly, monotonous and sad, on a grey landscape.'[100] But the musical realisation is excellent. In just 16 bars, Hennessy creates a wonderful miniature, in contemporary harmony and expression, of a rainy day that is not at all as depressing as the description may sound. There is a nostalgia expressed in the high-pitched D minor theme that a Minimalist composer of the closing twentieth century would extend to many more bars without finding an end, whereas Hennessy knows exactly the right moment when the musical material has exhausted itself. As in all of the other pieces of *Sentes et chemins*, there is a brief second subject – here a

---

[99] '*En route pour le marché un paysan juché sur une petite voiture traînée par un ane minuscule, chante à pleine gorge un refrain populaire, tandis que d'une trattoria s'échappent des bouffées de tarentelle.*'
[100] '*La pluie tombe sans fin, monotone et triste, sur un paysage en grisaille.*'

mere four bars long – before the repetitive rain drops occur again for the concluding few bars (Ex. 5.23) – a little masterwork in exactitude and conciseness.

Ex. 5.23: *Sentes et chemins*, Op. 44 No. 7 'Par la pluie', bars 9–16

All in all, *Sentes et chemins* is an uneven work, with highlights in Nos. 3 and 7, curious artistic solutions in Nos. 1 and 2, a harmless No. 4, a sunny No. 5, and less strength in No. 6. Hennessy, I think, was aware of the uneven quality. Judging from the performance history, which has certainly been influenced by Hennessy's personal choice and advice to performers, it is Nos. 1, 2, and 5 that received performances in Hennessy's lifetime and which may be interpreted as his own first choice.

It is noteworthy that in the 'nature studies' of opus 44 (in contrast to those of opus 40) music plays an important role as the object of portrayal. There is a singing worker in No. 1, strange tunes in the head of the old philosopher in No. 2, distant alienated hunting horns in No. 3, a bagpipe tune in No. 4, an Italian ballad in No. 5, singing birds in No. 6, and drumming rain drops in No. 7. Music as the object of descriptive programme music – there are not very many precedents!

The critical response was quite intense (because it included performance reviews), and opinions were strongly divided when it touched on matters of personal taste. On the positive side, Marc David wrote in *Le Guide du concert*: 'These piano pictures are treated with a very versatile feather.' And after having questioned the necessity of the introductory phrases, he continues:

> But let us not blame this way of doing things, provided that the music is always finely chiselled and follows, if not a plan, at least an existing line. This is the case with the work by Mr. Swan Hennessy, who finds the proper rhythm and nuance.[101]

---

[101] '*Ces tableautins pour piano sont traités par une plume très souple. […] Ne blâmons pas cette façon de faire, pourvu que la musique soit toujours finement ciselée et suive, sinon un plan, du moins une ligne existante. C'est le cas de celle qu'écrit M. Swan Hennessy, qui suit le Rythme et la Nuance.*'; Marc David in *Le Guide du concert*, 6 December 1913, p. 130.

An anonymous reviewer in *La Revue musicale S.I.M.* admits to have underestimated Hennessy on previous occasions and is now of the following opinion:

> He adds a series of Nature Sketches, taken from the lively everywhere with the same gift of surprising the popular soul. I have sometimes teased Swan Hennessy for his incoercible production; but I would like to take this opportunity to acknowledge the spontaneity of his music.[102]

In a 1922 review in the American journal *The Musician*, the critic looked at Hennessy's early *Au village*, Op. 22 and the present work:

> In these two sets of piano pieces the composer has written for more advanced players, but they are well worth the while of the concert player or the advanced pupil. *Au Village* is a group of rustic scenes, while the Nature Studies are highly useful etudes.[103]

After a 1931 performance in Paris of excerpts from *Sentes et chemins* by the pianist Janine Cools, the critic and composer Marcel Bernheim (1892–1963) wrote:

> Pleasantly descriptive, Swan Hennessy's music recommends itself by a sincerity of language that delights. Swan Hennessy does not seek to contradict the frank flow of his inspiration, he always expresses himself in a clear and limpid way.[104]

German critics seemed to have trouble with the music, mainly expressed in concert reviews of excerpts from Opp. 40, 44, and 47. In the Berlin daily *Die Post* a critic who was represented by a colleague wrote in 1913:

> All the more cruel, because overly realistic, were some mood paintings for piano, which the composer himself performed and which were to lead the audience to a 'small Flemish town', to a 'Parisian tailor's workshop' or to depict a troop of workers moving to the factory, etc. My colleague rightly asks whether such sketches in music are not generally a misguided direction. If such tone paintings, which are apparently to be set alongside Futurism and Cubism in painting, are to be characteristic – and this quality could not be denied – they would have to sound ugly, which they would also do abundantly.[105]

---

[102] '*Il y ajoute une série de Croquis d'après nature, pris sur le vif un peu partout avec le même don de surprendre l'âme populaire. J'ai parfois plaisanté Swan Hennessy sur son incoercible production; mais je tiens à saisir l'occasion de reconnaître la spontanéité de sa musique.*'; *La Revue musicale S.I.M.*, 1 February 1914, p. 68.
[103] *The Musician* 27:4, April 1922, p. 25.
[104] '*Agréablement descriptive, la musique de Swan Hennessy se recommande par une sincérité du langage qui plaît. Swan Hennessy ne cherche point à contrarier la franche coulée de son inspiration, il s'exprime toujours de façon clair et limpide.*'; Marcel Bernheim in *Le Courrier musical*, 1 Aug. 1931.
[105] '*Desto grausamer, weil übermäßig realistisch, muteten dagegen einige Stimmungsbilder für Klavier an, die der Komponist selbst vortrug, und die das Publikum in eine „kleine vlämische Stadt", in ein „Pariser Näherinnenatelier" führen oder einen Trupp zur Fabrik ziehender Arbeiter usw. darstellen sollten. Ob derlei Vorwürfe in Musik zu setzen nicht überhaupt eine verfehlte Richtung ist, fragt mein Vertreter mit Recht. Wenn solche Tonmalereien, die offenbar dem Futurismus und Kubismus in der Farbenmalerei zur Seite zu stellen*

Similarly sceptic, a critic in the fortnightly *Die Musik* wrote (on the basis of the printed scores of Opp. 44 and 47):

> Op. 44 and 47 show the likeable author on wrong paths. He would like to be young with the boys and paint a few quite naturalistic mood pictures with the most modern harmonic colours: Workers going to the factory; seamstresses in their 'atelier' and the like. That failed thoroughly; for what 'behaves absurdly' here is not a must. The music does not betray an exuberant temperament, but only shows a very bad way of doing things.[106]

A 1922 Berlin recital by the prominent pianist Bruno Eisner (1884–1978) still did not convince some critics:

> [...] spiritually entertaining small paintings of an emphatically harmless and cheerful outlook on life. A musical illustrator without the detailed intentions of the programme musician. They are also character pieces, but depths are avoided, even contrasts do not touch them [...] In the same cycle, even in short pieces old and new stylistic qualities are set in contrasts. 'Workers on the way to the factory', 'In a tailor's workshop' as Werfel-Mussorgsky expressions; 'In the forest', 'On the road to Amalfi' as expressions of Geibel-Weber. Already meaningless with Mussorgsky when he cites the source of his powerfully packed inspirations in introductory texts, Swan Hennessy is talkative and ambitious but unable to keep the promises of his signboards by compelling musical ideas. [...] – Bruno Eisner brought the piano pieces to best effect.[107]

It was Hugo Rasch who summed up much of the critical response, arguing that some of Hennessy's music would require time to be appreciated:

> It is really worthwhile to devote some attention to the work of this master of a highly distinctive small-scale art who creates [his music] in quiet seclusion. The fact that this kind

---

seien, charakteristisch sein sollen – und diese Eigenschaft könne man ihnen nicht absprechen – so müßten sie ja häßlich klingen, was sie auch reichlich täten.'; J. St–g. in *Die Post*, 17 November 1913.

[106] '*Op. 44 und 47 zeigen den sympathischen Autor auf Irrwegen. Er möchte gern mit den Jungen jung sein und ein paar recht naturalistische Stimmungsbilder mit den allermodernsten harmonischen Farben malen: Arbeiter, die zur Fabrik gehen; Näherinnen in ihrem "Atelier" und dergleichen. Das ist ihm gründlich mißlungen; denn was sich hier „absurd gebärdet", ist kein Most. Die Musik verrät nicht überschäumendes Temperament, sondern sie zeigt nur eine sehr üble Mache.*'; Otto Hollenberg in *Die Musik* 13:13, 1st April-issue 1914, p. 45.

[107] '[...] *geistvoll kurzweilige Kleinmalereien einer betont harmlos-fröhlichen Lebensanschauung. Ein musikalischer Illustrator ohne die ausführlichen Absichten des Programm-Musikers. Sinds auch Charakterstücke, so werden doch Tiefen gemieden, selbst Kontraste rühren nicht daran, [...] Im gleichen Zyklus, selbst im kurzen Stück alte und neue Stilqualitäten als Kontraste. "Arbeiter auf dem Wege zur Fabrik", "Im Schneiderinnen-Atelier" als Werfel-Mussorgsky-Expressionen; "Im Walde", "Auf der Strasse nach Amalfi" im Ausdruck Geibel-Webers. Bleibts bei Mussorgsky belanglos, wenn er die Quelle seiner kraftvoll gepackten Inspirationen in Ueberschriften angibt, so wirkts bei Swan Hennessy redselig ehrgeizig, wenn er die Versprechungen seiner Aushängeschilder nicht durch musikalisch zwingende Einfälle einzulösen vermag. [...] – Bruno Eisner brachte die Klavierstücke zu bester Auswirkung.*'; Otto Steinhagen in *Signale für die musikalische Welt* 80:47, 22 November 1922, p. 1350.

of music, which does not want to be revolutionary in any way, is not immediately accessible to everyone, certainly does not speak against it.[108]

Croquis parisiennes, Op. 47 (1912) for piano

The last piece in this small collection of three piano pieces has already been mentioned in some of the reviews of performances above. No. 3, *Dans un atelier de couturières* ('In a Tailor's Workshop'), was performed as *In einem pariser Näherinnen-Atelier* in Berlin in November 1913 (by the composer) and as *In einem Schneiderinnenatelier* in November 1922 (by Bruno Eisner). The other two works in the set are 1. *Promenade matinale au Jardin du Luxembourg* ('Morning Walk in the Jardin du Luxembourg') and 2. *L'Américain qui a bien dîné* ('The American Who Has Eaten Well').

The work was composed in Paris in 1912, published with Demets in 1913, and is dedicated to Louis Vuillemin (1879–1929), the Breton critic and composer. It will be remembered that Vuillemin was one of Hennessy's most faithful critics in the pages of *Comoedia* since he first encountered a work by Hennessy in May 1911. As Barbara Kelly has convincingly shown, the critic-composer relationship was highly influential in many composers' careers, notably with regard to Louis Laloy's and Émile Vuillermoz's response to Debussy, Roland-Manuel's to Satie, Henri Collet's and Paul Landormy's to *'Les Six'*, etc.[109] In Hennessy's case, at least for the years preceding World War I, it was Louis Vuillemin in Paris and Hugo Rasch in Berlin. At least since early 1912, Vuillemin and Hennessy knew each other well personally when they found themselves in the ranks of the Association des Compositeurs Bretons (see Chapter 6). The dedication is Hennessy's way to acknowledge this relationship.

The Breton aspect of this friendship has not influenced the music, though. The album is another set of programme music, this time not of the natural environment, but most likely of the life of the composer himself! It should be remembered that Hennessy was financially independent, and although several, albeit hidden, sources describe his withdrawn life-style, he was well able to live the life of a dandy in 1910's Paris. The individual titles of *Croquis parisiens* ('Parisian Sketches') may well describe the course of a day Hennessy enjoyed in the city, beginning with a morning stroll through a park in his vicinity (No. 1), enjoying his lunch in a restaurant (No. 2), and then visiting a tailor for a new suit (No. 3).

All pieces are furnished with appropriate onomatopoeia of the situations in the titles. Hennessy has set walking movements before, but never a 'normal' walk that would not limp or otherwise be syncopated. In the morning stroll in the park, he mainly uses regular crotchets in the left hand with dotted and tied quavers in the right that produce, in combination, an easy-going, well-tempered walking movement. And

---

[108] '*Es lohnt sich wirklich der Arbeit dieses in stiller Zurückgezogenheit schaffenden Meisters einer höchst aparten Kleinkunst etwas Aufmerksamkeit zu widmen. Daß sich diese Art Musik, die nicht revolutionär in irgend einer Art sein will, trotzdem nicht gleich jedem sofort erschließt, das spricht gewiß nicht gegen sie.*'; Hugo Rasch in *Allgemeine Musikzeitung* 40:10, 7 March 1913, p. 326.
[109] Kelly, *Music and Ultra-Modernism*, Chapter 3 'Polemics and Publicity: Composer-Critic Partnerships', pp. 67ff.

so, No. 1 begins, with a partial harmonic grounding in chromatic shifts of sixth chords (Ex. 5.24). This further develops in the course of the piece with more rhythmic variety, moving away from the regularity and returning to it towards the end.

Ex. 5.24: *Croquis parisiens*, Op. 47 No. 1 'Promenade matinale au Jardin du Luxembourg', bars 1–5

In No. 2, *L'Américain qui a bien dîné*, Hennessy most likely portrays himself, and it is from this movement that we can deduce that the whole opus is about himself. In theory, he may have had any American tourist in Paris in mind whom he merely watched in a restaurant. But given the fact that the Jardin du Luxembourg was in his Montparnasse neighbourhood and that he liked to dress well (visible in the photographs in later chapters), it is all too likely that in all three pieces he portrayed himself.

This piece has very little of the contemporary French musical elements that we had come to appreciate in Hennessy's piano music so far. There are no formal or technical experiments, and the harmonic language is a clear and unambiguous G major with a middle section in C major. There is also a very clear division into melody and accompaniment, and in the melody, Hennessy has created a very American tune that may have come from a popular Yankee songbook (Ex. 5.25). It is quite remarkable how easily Hennessy expresses the essentials of various national folk idioms, be it a Swiss waltz, a Spanish jota, an Irish song, or now an American one. The other aspect of the title, having 'eaten well', is probably expressed in the C major part where the syncopations of the accompaniment may represent the digestion of a (heavy) meal and the ensuing drowsiness in the slow four bars before the repetition of the initial theme.

On the other hand, if this was really meant as a self-portrayal, what does it tell us about the composer? Perhaps that deep within there is a musical soul rooted in the nineteenth century in unadorned diatonicism – it would not be totally far-fetched, perhaps.

Ex. 5.25: *Croquis parisiens*, Op. 47 No. 2 *'L'Américain qui a bien dîné'*, bars 1–9

The third piece is by far the most attractive (and the only one that had public performances, albeit not many). It is at the same time the technically most demanding. What makes orientation easier for the player is that it is set in C major, so the pianist does not have to pay much attention to the basic accidentals. The tempo is indicated as *Presto* (♩ = 144) and the main note value that is used almost throughout is *staccato* semiquavers. The piece is very much part of the contemporary trend to express the new soundworld of industry, technology, and traffic with musical means. Insofar it is comparable, perhaps, to his own *Sieste en chemin de fer*, Op. 40 No. 5. In the present case, this approach represents the rattling of sewing machines etc. – and we can be sure that this tailor's workshop had more than one.

Attention is also required in terms of rhythm. The piece in 2/4 time begins with eight bars of the *staccato* semiquavers. This is followed by a short thematic motif that is notated in 3/4 time for the right hand while the left hand continues in fast semiquavers in 2/4, which means two bars in the right hand correspond to three bars in the left.

There are three levels of complexity of this musical translation of sewing machines. The first is at the beginning where the semiquavers are kept in one hand (bars 1–14). Here, thirds and fourths alternate with a C as an anchor point. Then the motif moves into both hands (bars 15–22), now without *staccato*. After some different material (until bar 38) and an intermittent calmer phrase (until bar 54) follow another eight bars of the semiquaver motif, now in staccato and with an additional rising pitch leading to a climax (Ex. 5.26), after which the piece ends with a concluding phrase.

Ex. 5.26: *Croquis parisiens*, Op. 47 No. 3 'Dans un atelier de couturiers', bars 53–66

A critic writing in *The Musical Standard* compared this opus with earlier compositions by Hennessy and noticed the increasing use of dissonant intervals as an inconvenient sign of the times:

> Everybody acquainted with Mr. Hennessy's former works which are so pleasing to the ear must wonder what induced him in these sketches to employ, and that not once but frequently, such discords as a note against its augmented octave as he does in the first of these little pieces. But the like combinations are now met with so often, not only in Herr Schönberg's writings but everywhere, that we must expect in the next textbooks of harmony to be told that the concordant intervals are the second, the augmented octave, etc. The second number in this book, 'L'Americain qui a Bien Diné,' with its frequent syncopations is very pleasing. The remaining piece requires a particularly light touch and a quick alternation of the two hands.[110]

The critic in *Die Musik* who had been so sceptical towards Hennessy's Op. 44 at least acknowledges the realism of the first piece in Op. 47:

---

[110] *The Musical Standard*, 28 February 1914.

A single piano piece from Op. 47 is a pleasing exception: 'Promenade matinale au Jardin de Luxembourg'; despite its harsh dissonances, it does not appear to have been fabricated, but to have been experienced.[111]

French music critics seem to have ignored both this and the ensuing work, Op. 48. Perhaps, Louis Vuillemin thought it was improper to write about Hennessy now that they knew each other personally. It should also be remembered that Hennessy had still not appeared in public as a pianist in his own works (his first attempt was in Berlin in November 1913) and had not engaged French musicians to perform his music. Thus, hard to believe though it may seem, this delightful and well-made composition still awaits its first French performance.

Impressions humoristiques, Op. 48 (1913) for piano

Impressions humoristiques is an album of six (very) short pieces preceded by a prologue, written and published in 1913. The prologue comes in the form of a 'dedication to the friends of Russia', *Dédicace: Aux Amis de Russie* – no doubt this meant the friends of Russian composers, not of politics! The six following pieces are called 1. *Tupac-Polka*; 2. *"Das Fräulein stand am Meere / Und seufzte lang und bang" (Heine)*; 3. *Napolitains* ('Neapolitans'); 4. *En regardant une ronde de jeunes filles* ('Watching a Group of Young Girls'); 5. *Chanteuse de beuglant* ('Bawling ...' or 'Bellowing Singer'); 6. *Bébé prend sa medicine* ('Baby Takes Its Medicine').

Most of the pieces of this collection can be dealt with quickly. The *'Dédicace'* with its dark F minor tonality stands very much in the tradition of late nineteenth-century Russian music – another national idiom that Hennessy adapted without any problem. The *Tupac-Polka* may have originated from the visit to a funfair – it is strongly rooted in the vernacular of everyday life in the city. The title *Das Fräulein stand am Meere / Und seufzte lang und bang* are the first two lines of a Heine poem. Hennessy may have found pleasure in just the sound of these lines – there is little in it, though, that relates to the experiment in triplets that the piece basically consists of. *Napolitains* is another piece with 'popular' appeal, the idea of which Hennessy may have picked up anywhere in the streets of Paris. It is known from tales in his family that in the 1920s Hennessy was very fond of silent movies and frequented the first cinemas on Boulevard Montparnasse almost on a daily basis. A piece like *Napolitains* (or the *Tupac-Polka* also) sound like an anticipation of the music of a cinema pianist. The manuscript of *En regardant une ronde de jeunes filles* shows that it was originally entitled *Ronde d'ivrognes tristes* ('Group of Sad Drunkards'). How exchangeable are young girls and sad drunkards?! Set in D major, it is mainly written in 6/16 time which allows him to notate the rhythmically intricate middle section (bars 9–12) in a lucid way. Here, the happy melancholy of the main theme gives way to some organised chaos (or, perhaps, planned disintegration)

---

[111] *'Ein einziges Klavierstück aus op. 47 bildet eine erfreuliche Ausnahme: "Promenade matinale au Jardin de Luxembourg"; es wirkt trotz seiner schroffen Dissonanzen nicht gemacht, sondern als ob es erlebt sei.'*; Otto Hollenberg in *Die Musik* 13:13, 1st April issue 1914, p. 45.

that Hennessy ironically applies to young girls' (or sad drunkards') behaviour (Ex. 5.27).

Ex. 5.27: *Impressions humoristiques*, Op. 48 No. 4 *'En regardant une ronde de jeunes filles'*, bars 9–12

The *Chanteuse de beuglant* may well be regarded as a continuation of the funfair idea that already permeated the pieces Nos 1 and 3. This is the most dance-like of the three even though it sets out to imitate a bawling singer – it appears to depict a singer hopping from the left to the right foot while, perhaps, advertising a popular extravaganza.

Ex. 5.28: *Impressions humoristiques*, Op. 48 No. 6 *'Bébé prend sa medicine'*

The most striking piece in this album is the last, and with a length of only six bars Hennessy has exceeded by far even his standard preference for short pieces (Ex. 5.28). The title suggests that it depicts a baby taking its medicine, and it evidently helped, because the piece ends on a peaceful C major chord. But the preceding material can only be described as atonal. And the manuscript reveals that this was indeed intended, as it contains the following footnote: *'Malgré les apparences, l'enfant n'habite pas Vienne'* ('However it may seem, the child does not live in Vienna.').[112]

In other words, in the disguise of a sick baby in need of medical treatment, Hennessy depicts Arnold Schönberg! The note was apparently deleted by the publisher, because it does not appear in the print. It is at the same time a humorous as well as sarcastic and polemic critique of the twelve-tone composer – and neither the first nor the last attack that Hennessy launched on Schönberg, as we shall see. Coincidence or not, all twelve pitches of the Western scale do actually occur in the piece.

Swan Hennessy's critique of Arnold Schönberg (1)

The musical revolution that was Arnold Schönberg and the Second Viennese School was only just dawning when Hennessy identified it and perceived as a danger to the development of art music. From as early as 1912, Hennessy wrote letters to several music journals complaining about the impending decay of musical culture.

In the first of these, a letter to the editor of *The Musical Standard* in England, he argued that Arnold Schönberg was a charlatan merely trying to attract attention:

> SIR, – Referring to Mr. Heseltine's question whether Schönberg is a madman, the 'arch-humorist' of music, or a colossal genius (!) many years ahead of his time, may I venture to suggest an alternative? Is it not possible that he is merely desirous of attracting attention to himself at any cost? It is a sad fact that in these sensation-loving days, such absurdities such as Schönberg's 'Drei Klavierstücke.' Op. 11, are more likely to excite curiosity than a sincere work of art!
>
> PARIS, September 28, 1912 　　　　　　　　　　　Yours sincerely,
> 　　　　　　　　　　　　　　　　　　　　　　　SWAN HENNESSY.[113]

Three months after the first, another letter appeared:

> SIR, – May I venture to suggest that it is time papers devoted to the interests of musical art should cease devoting their valuable space on the absurdities of Arnold Schönberg? Surely the only really remarkable thing about such nonsense is the fact that people should be found who can take it seriously.
>
> December 1, 1912 　　　　　　　　　　　　　　Yours sincerely,
> 　　　　　　　　　　　　　　　　　　　　　　　SWAN HENNESSY.[114]

Hennessy's verdict of Schönberg's *Drei Klavierstücke*, a work first published and performed in 1910, is also unmistakingly clear in an autograph comment on his own copy of it (Fig. 5.4):

---

[112] In Manuscript Book III, no. 3.
[113] *The Musical Standard* 38:979, 5 October 1912, p. 218.
[114] *The Musical Standard* 38:988, 7 December 1912, p. 363.

An American Impressionist (1908–1913)

Fig. 5.4: Hennessy's opinion of Schönberg's *Drei Klavierstücke* (Courtesy: Hennessy family)

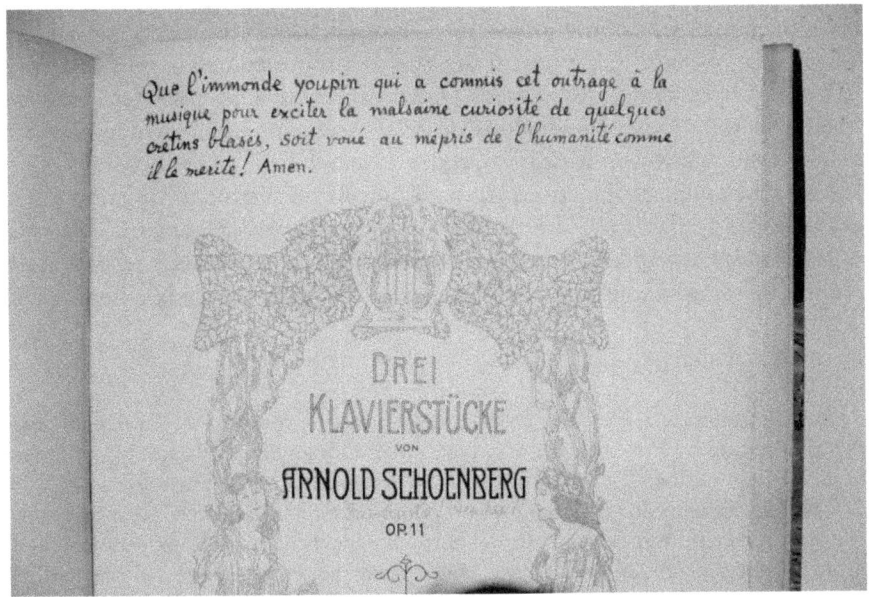

May the filthy kike who committed this outrage against music to arouse the sick curiosity of a few jaded morons be condemned to disdain for humanity as he deserves! Amen.[115]

And in pencil he adds to it, in German, *'Sauhund! Hep hep!!'* (see below under the composer's name).

It is interesting that the opinion Hennessy expressed in his two letters to *The Musical Standard* were echoed in very similar terms many years later by Vincent d'Indy. In 1928 he complained in a letter to *Comoedia* that for Schönberg and his disciples 'to earn money, to draw attention to themselves, they make noise, not music'.[116] Thus, Hennessy was one of the first and most outspoken opponents of what was to become known as the Second Viennese School. It is, however, important to note that Hennessy was concerned about the future development of music whereas the criticism of d'Indy and others was at least equally motivated by anti-Semitism. Even in later critical remarks about Schönberg (see Chapter 9), he is clearly worried about the direction that musical development would take and never mingles his view with anti-Jewish arguments and prejudices.

* * *

---

[115] *'Que l'immonde youpin qui a commis cet outrage à la musique pour exciter la malsaine curiosité de quelques crétins blasés, soit voué au mépris de l'humanité comme il le merite! Amen.'*
[116] *'Pour gagner de l'argent, pour attire l'attention sur eux, ils font du bruit, non de la musique.'*; quoted after Jane F. Fulcher: *The Composer as Intellectual. Music and Ideology in France, 1914–1940* (New York, Oxford University Press, 2005), p. 134.

Hennessy expressed his own alternative to a development that was increasingly influenced by the Second Viennese School, in a long letter, one might say article, in an October 1911 issue of *La Revue musicale*. It is headed '*Sommes-nous à la veille d'une plus complète expression musicale?*' ('Are we on the eve of a more complete musical expression?').[117] Apart from the lengthy 1929 interview in *Le Guide du concert* (see Introduction), this is the only source in which he describes elements of his own aesthetic approach – here at a time when his Irish/Celtic awakening had not yet occurred.

In this text he utilises the space given to him by the editor to describe the advantages and disadvantages of descriptive music, distinguishes between descriptive and imitative music, the ability of music to express the character and feelings of human beings, and the mutually supportive role of the voice and the accompaniment in vocal music.

He says, for instance:

> [...] Descriptive music is very often confused with imitative music. To be well understood, descriptive music requires the listener to have previous knowledge of the subject. Imitative music, on the other hand, will be understood by everyone without prior notice.
>
> These two genres are far from being modern products. Both were quite common in the eighteenth century and even before. There are wonderful examples of early descriptive music; but the imitative music of these periods was most often written in the spirit of a joke, a tour de force, and the imitation was generally quite inaccurate.[118]

He goes on to describe different ways to set bells in music, with examples from the 1900 opera *Le Juif polonais* by Camille Erlanger (1863–1919), the 1889 orchestral work *Impressions d'Italie* by Gustave Charpentier (1860–1956), and the piano work *Les Cloches de Casbeno* (1906) by Raoul Bardac (1881–1950).

The ability of intervals to express feelings is another topic, and he does not confine it to the difference between major and minor tonalities, arguing that the effect of intervals is also dependent on the tonal region. He gives an example of fifths in high registers and continues:

> These fifths will give everyone a feeling of coldness. If the minor third is added, the coldness decreases. The major third makes it disappear. Therefore, this impression only

---

[117] Swan Hennessy, '*Sommes-nous à la veille d'une plus complète expression musicale?*'; in *La Revue musicale* 11:20, 15 October 1911, p. 421–422. The following quotations can be found there. The editor introduces this text as follows: '*M. Swan Hennessy nous adresse une longue lettre d'où nous extrayons les lignes suivantes, le témoignage d'un compositeur sérieux étant toujours intéressant en pareille matière.*' ('Mr Swan Hennessy sent us a long letter from which we extract the following lines, the testimony of a serious composer who is always interesting in these matters.')

[118] '[...] *La musique descriptive est très souvent confondue avec la musique imitative. Pour être bien comprise, la musique descriptive exige de la part de l'auditeur une connaissance antérieure du sujet. La musique imitative, par contre, sera comprise de tout le monde sans avis préalable. / Ces deux genres sont loin d'être des produits modernes. L'un et l'autre étaient assez courants au dix-huitième siècle et même avant. Il y a de merveilleux exemples de musique descriptive ancienne; mais la musique imitative de ces époques était le plus souvent écrite dans l'esprit d'une plaisanterie, d'un tour de force, et l'imitation y était généralement assez peu exacte.*'

occurs in the upper position. In the bass the open fifths are of a completely different effect. Mr Claude Debussy gave us, in *Jardins sous la pluie*, the impression of being wet. [...]

Assuming that there can be no effect without a cause, it would be very interesting to look for the reason for these impressions, which are more than just a suggestion, since, as we already said, they are felt by everyone without prior knowledge.

It is true that whole-tone progression is a precious resource for imitative music, but it should not be forgotten that the same process cannot express one thing and the opposite of that thing. That is why some of our contemporary composers who try to express everything with the progression by [whole] tones end up not expressing anything at all. The same must apply to chromatic progressions.[119]

There are gaps in Hennessy's text because the journal did not print his full letter but excerpts only. Therefore, in some instances it would be advantageous to have more background or supporting ideas to his arguments. Yet, it becomes clear even so that Hennessy not only had a wide knowledge of recent and contemporary music but also studied the models of better-known composers, including Debussy, and formed his own opinion of the techniques they applied to achieve effects.

As to the role that the accompaniment takes in vocal music, Hennessy comes to a different model than most other theorists. For him, it is *not* the task of the accompaniment to express the words of a text:

Music can express emotions that cannot be expressed in words. The role of music begins where speech becomes insufficient. It is therefore not surprising that the greatest power of expression lies in the accompaniment, that it is rather the voice that accompanies with explanatory words the emotions expressed by the piano or orchestra.[120]

Hennessy concludes that the techniques available to the contemporary composer by far exceed the possibilities of earlier generations, which makes him wonder:

Would it be daring to say that we are on the eve of an even more complete musical expression?[121]

---

[119] '*Ces quintes donneront à tout le monde une impression de froid. Si l'on y ajoute la tierce mineure, le froid diminue. La tierce majeure le fait disparaître. Aussi n'est-ce que dans la position haute que cette impression se produit. Dans la basse les quintes ouvertes sont d'un tout autre effet. M. Claude Debussy nous a donné, dans* Jardins sous la pluie, *l'impression du mouillé.* [...] / *En partant du principe qu'il ne peut pas y avoir d'effet sans cause, il serait très intéressant de rechercher la raison de ces impressions qui sont plus que de la suggestion, puisque, comme nous l'avons déjà dit, elles sont ressenties par tout le monde sans avis préalable.* / *Il est certain que la progression par tons entiers est une précieuse ressource pour la musique imitative, mais il ne faut pas oublier que le même procédé ne saurait exprimer une chose et le contraire de cette chose. Voilà pourquoi certains de nos compositeurs contemporains qui essayent de tout exprimer avec la progression par tons finissent par ne rien exprimer de tout. Il doit en être de même des progressions chromatiques.*'

[120] '*La musique peut exprimer des émotions qu'on ne saurait exprimer en paroles. Le rôle de la musique commence là où la parole devient insuffisante. Ce n'est donc pas étonnant que la plus grande puissance d'expression se trouve dans l'accompagnement, que c'est plutôt la voix qui accompagne avec des paroles explicatives les émotions exprimées par le piano ou l'orchestre.*'

[121] '*Serait-il téméraire d'affirmer que nous sommes à la veille d'une expression musicale encore plus complète?*'

A year later, when he wrote his first letter to the editor of *The Musical Standard* he may have seen these achievements in danger. In a continuation of his argument, he began to fear that there was a development on the horizon that would remove the very reason why music should express anything beyond itself.

* * *

Swan Hennessy probably chose the title of his 1913 *Impressions humoristiques* carefully, combining in it two of the terms that dominated the contemporary musical debate for a long time: Impression(ism) and humorism. At the same time, the work marks the end of a period of about six or seven years during which he tried as best as he could to write in a contemporary French style and adapt it to his own ideas about descriptive programme music, humour, love of nature and his personal degree of (non-)conformism. The fact that he did not write in this style again until about 1922 is mainly due to the war years, but also to his beginning public success as a 'Celtic' composer (Chapter 6).

It is perhaps in this phase in Hennessy's artistic development in which he is, arguably, at his best in terms of quality, originality and his stylistic proximity to contemporary French music. One may intervene here and say, Hennessy has not created any major score for orchestra, the stage, even chamber music, and that even in the realm of piano music he has not written any extended score in which he would have further developed his ideas – all of which is true. The question whether he was not able or not willing to do this is a different matter and one that should not be judged upon prematurely, also keeping in mind that creating larger scores would not have been a financial incentive for him. In his chosen medium, that of piano miniatures, he has shown convincingly that he has learned from his French environment, but has not completely fallen for it. He evidently knows how to apply Impressionist colours, he is a keen observer of his natural and human environment, and he is able to translate this experience into original music of his own.

While the name of Debussy inevitably occurs in any discussion of French music of this period, a brief look at potential influences may not be out of place. In fact, as several reviews in this Chapter have shown, Debussy's influence was often detected, particularly by German and English critics, less so by the French. Also, when Hennessy's reputation had eventually reached Ireland in the 1920s, a 1922 portrait article in the *Dublin Evening Telegraph* found that

> Hennessy joins in a quaintly charming manner the old and the new. Without any doubt, he is a modern musician. Debussy has had no inconsiderable part in forming his style, though Hennessy himself thinks he has not come much under French influence [...][122]

---

[122] D. Ua. B. (= Donnchadh Ua Briain / Denis Breen), 'Swan Hennessy – An Irish Musician of To-day', *Dublin Evening Telegraph*, 2 September 1922, p. 2.

The last phrase would probably have been 'under Debussy's influence' in Hennessy's own words. When he was asked specifically about Debussy in the 1929 interview in *Le Guide du concert*, he toned down any specific influence of him while acknowledging that the composer has been influential for his whole generation, not only for himself:

> I understand that Debussy has revealed possibilities undreamt of by anyone else before him: this glory will not be taken away from him, and we all benefit more or less.[123]

I have argued in this chapter that perhaps Ravel was an even greater influence on Hennessy, at least in terms of titles, inspirations and forms, and at least for a while, with examples in Hennessy's *Valses caprices*, Op. 41, the *Sonatine*, Op. 43 – and later in Ravel's pastiche works in the style of other composers (*À la manière de Borodine* and [...] *Chabrier* of 1913) that were very successfully serialised by Hennessy in five volumes of *À la manière de ...* (published 1927–28, but begun around 1917).[124] It does, moreover, seem like Hennessy was personally acquainted with Maurice Ravel, but this would have occurred in the 1920s (see Chapter 9).

Swan Hennessy and Erik Satie

Another seemingly obvious influence is that of Erik Satie, given the humoristic approach to titles and the non-conformist attitudes that both composers maintained. They were of the same generation, having both been born in 1866. Given the fact that Hennessy has occasionally applied humorous titles to his works since at least 1909 and that his musical realisations are very different from Satie's, I regard this as a development independent of his contemporary, even though some of Satie's humoristic titles predate Hennessy's.

In fact, Hennessy had quite a strong opinion of Satie, which Lucien Chevaillier could only touch upon when he asked Hennessy about any influence in his 1929 interview. Hennessy declared himself a great friend of humoristic music and titles, but:

> [...] for apart from this superficial analogy, there is really nothing in common between Swan Hennessy and the composer of the pieces 'In the Form of a Pear', for which he did not seem to me to show any great liking ...'[125]

---

[123] *'Je comprends que Debussy a révélé des possibilités insoupçonnées jusqu'à lui : cette gloire ne lui sera pas enlevée et nous en profiterons tous plus ou moins.'* (Chevaillier, 'Entretien', p. 793).

[124] They also include pastiches of Borodin and Chabrier, besides Ravel, Debussy, and many others, 30 works in total. Contemporary critics responded overwhelmingly positive to these works.

[125] *'[...] car, en dehors de cette analogie superficielle, il n'y a vraiment rien de commun entre Swan Hennessy et l'auteur des morceaux En forme de poire, pour lequel il ne m'a pas semblé nourrir une sympathie exagérée ...'* (Chevaillier, 'Entretien', p. 791). NB.: Satie published his *Trois Morceaux en forme de poire* in 1903.

He had become more explicit in the fourth volume of his series of *À la manière de* ... (1926; published 1927) to which he added a '*Note de l'auteur*': 'This collection also contained Erik Satie, but I removed it, considering that my pastiche was more about literature than music. Here is the main passage:' (see Fig. 5.5)[126] He then adds a single bar with a fermata upon a pause and continues 'Do not use this empty bar to spit into the piano.'

Fig. 5.5: Hennessy's 'pastiche' of Erik Satie, from *À la manière de* ... vol. 4, p. 11

Ce recueil contenait aussi ERIK SATIE, mais je l'ai supprimé, estimant que mon pastiche relevait plutôt de la littérature que de la musique.

En voici le principal passage:

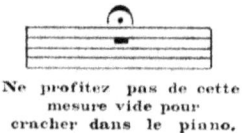

Ne profitez pas de cette
mesure vide pour
cracher dans le piano.

One can imagine the more or less hidden smile that must have crossed Swan Hennessy's face when he saw Erik Satie's 1913 publication of *Embryons desséchés* ('Desiccated Embryos') with Demets, which ends on a full-page advertisement of the '*Œuvres de Swan Hennessy*'.

* * *

Finally, although slightly premature, a comparison with *Les Six*, the group of young composers founded in 1920 as a reaction against the Impressionists – and who declared Satie their spiritual forefather –, may not be out of place. In summing up the legacy of this group, Barbara Kelly wrote

> Although Les Six stood for many things, many of which were serious, they are remembered for only a few of them, primarily for their call for music inspired by the everyday: low art music associated with Paris. [...] they welcomed the inspiration of the circus, the music hall and fair.[127]

If that is what most people considered the group's main achievement, then Swan Hennessy predated it in many of his works by at least ten years; see *Fêtes*, Op. 36, parts of *En chemin* ..., Op. 40, the *Valses caprices*, Op. 41, *Sentes et chemins*, Op. 44, three pieces from *Impressions humoristiques*, Op. 48 etc.

---

[126] Hennessy repeated this in a letter to Léon Vallas dated 25 June 1927 (Bibliothèque Municipale de Lyon, Ms Vallas 203, pièce 59).
[127] Kelly, *Music and Ultra-Modernism*, p. 69.

Chapter 6
Modernity and Celticity (1908–1914)

Just when, around 1908, Swan Hennessy was comfortably finding a stylistic place in French music, he also wrote two 'Irish' compositions – Opp. 28 and 29 –, which were probably inspired by a visit to Ireland. Briefly interrupting the chronological narrative with a recourse to these works seems to be sensible with a view to developments that followed in 1912.

Of course, writing an Irish folk music tinged piece has not required Hennessy in the past to undertake an actual journey to Ireland. Any such journey is almost impossible to prove since he never went to Ireland to concertize. This would have left some sort of trace like a printed programme or a review. But as we shall see below, the circumstances surrounding Op. 29 suggest a closer connection to Ireland, and Op. 28 may have been a side product of those circumstances.

Op. 28 is a set of variations on an Irish folksong for piano solo, Op. 29 a suite based on four Irish traditional tunes for piano duet. These two works are the first in which Hennessy uses existing Irish tunes rather than creating 'Irish-style' melodies himself. Both works derive from tunes in the Petrie Collection (in Stanford's edition of 1902–5).[1] The fact that Hennessy has not used actual traditional tunes before may mean that he had not come across the Petrie Collection before 1908. But again, this does not necessarily mean that Hennessy found it in Ireland, because he may also have done so on a journey to London. In fact, he may just as well have seen an advertisement and ordered the collection by mail to his address in Paris. It shows how unsafe the speculations may become when trying to ascertain any presence of Hennessy in Ireland.

In combination with the circumstances surrounding Op. 29, I would argue that Hennessy discovered the Petrie Collection on a journey to Ireland, either on the shelves of a music shop, by having the publication recommended to him by an Irish musician, or by hearing some of the music being performed in public spaces which may also have increased in the years following the publication of Stanford's edition.

With these two works, Hennessy aligns himself briefly with the 'mainstream' of folklorism on the British Isles, even though the heyday of variations on folk tunes was in the mid-nineteenth century. But the context here is, no doubt, the increasing trend to national elements in art music which resulted in a prolific body of folkloristic music in a wide range of forms and instrumentations. As already mentioned in the previous chapter, a number of composers used Irish traditional music in works of this kind, and these works were by no means by Irish composers alone. Simple arrangements

---

[1] George Petrie (1790–1866) was an Irish artist, musician, antiquarian and collector of Irish traditional music who published two volumes of his collection in 1855 and 1882. The London-based Irish composer Charles Villiers Stanford (1852–1924) edited and published them in three volumes of 1,582 tunes entitled *The Complete Collection of Irish Music as Noted by George Petrie* (London: Boosey & Co., vols 1 and 2: 1902, vol. 3: 1905); see also David Cooper (ed.): *The Petrie Collection of the Ancient Music of Ireland* (Cork: Cork University Press, 2002).

dominated the 'market' – Stanford, of course, comes to mind, both in some of his song collections and, on the piano, in his *Irish Dances*, Op. 89 (1903, but not published before 1907).

Yet, in terms of modern, i. e. early twentieth-century folklorism, Hennessy comes early. Stanford is most productive on these lines in the early 1920s, Herbert Hughes' well-known series of *Irish Country Songs* does not commence before 1909, and Hamilton Harty's relevant pieces are slightly later, too,[2] such as his chamber works *Irish Fantasy* (1912) and *In Ireland* (1915), his orchestral *Variations on a Dublin Air* (also known as *Variations on an Irish Air*) dating from 1912 as well. Thus, while being part of a trend, Hennessy's works are also unique insofar as there is no 'modern' variation work on an Irish tune before his Op. 28 and no 'Irish' work for piano duet before Hennessy's Op. 29.

Variations sur un air irlandais ancien, Op. 28 (1908) for piano

The 'Variations on an old Irish tune' were written in 1908 and published in the same year with the London branch of Schott. What is rather unique in comparison with other works of the variation type is that the theme is introduced as a single unaccompanied melody in the right hand. He does not harmonise the tune as so many of his contemporaries and predecessors but prefers to leave the tune intact, before commencing his set of twelve variations.

Hennessy did not name the tune he used and which is here presented in F major. But since he was evidently working with the Petrie Collection in this year, it had to be found there, and so it has. It is in the third volume, tune no. 1177, and is there described as from County Mayo, entitled (in Irish) '*Óch ón! A chuid an t-Saoíghil*'.

The theme is in AABA form which may pose a challenge for the arranger not to be over-repetitive on the A part. Hennessy solves the problem bravely by resorting to great rhythmic variety, both among the twelve variations as within each of them. While the tune is dominated by scales of quavers, it is the semiquaver leaps, illustrated in the 'A part' of the theme (Ex. 6.1), that provide the rhythmic variability.

Ex. 6.1: *Variations* Op. 28, bars 1–3

---

[2] Harty's *Irish Fancies* (*c*1904) for piano were not published and therefore unknown at the time. Likewise, it is highly unlikely that Hennessy would have been aware of Michele Esposito's works for violin and piano, such as the *Irish Rhapsodies* Opp. 51 and 54 and the similarly titled Opp. 56 and 57 (all 1901–3).

Variation no. 1 retains the beat of the theme, but considerably enriches it by dense, albeit conservative, harmony; no. 2, marked *'Gentiment'*, enlivens the ternary rhythm to a quicker 3/8 with a parallel movement in both hands; no. 3 is faster still, wholly focusing on the semiquaver element played in both hands, both simultaneously and in sequence; no. 4 is a slow waltz, miraculously moving the Irish tune to a Viennese funfair (Ex. 6.2); no. 5 is a two-part canon in slow tempo but with a strongly marked melody; no. 6 is headed *'Rustique'* and is characterised by quite forceful chords of the left hand in quartal and quintal harmony; in no. 7 the tune is contained in quick semiquaver *staccatos* accompanied by off-beat chords in the left hand; and so on. In two of the variations (nos. 1 and 11) the tune moves completely into the left hand, but in general it remains well recognisable throughout the work, even when it is disguised in a neo-baroque fugue as in the *Finale*.

Ex. 6.2: *Variations* Op. 28, var. 4, bars 1–10

While the rhythmic interest is the most memorable characteristic of this work, Hennessy becomes a contemporary harmonist in some parts, most notably in the 'Viennese' no. 4 and the mildly Impressionist no. 10. The latter is marked *'Simple'*, but this refers to the rhythm only with its straight quavers that bear the theme and the pseudo-minuet movement of the left hand. The chordal progression of minor and major thirds presents some harmonic clashes that may be interpreted as Hennessy's concession to modernity, and it works very well here (Ex. 6.3). Overall, however, Hennessy never once leaves the F major basic tonality.

Ex. 6.3: *Variations* Op. 28, var. 10, bars 1–8

The highly diverse nature of the *Variations* Op. 28 was very much noticed by the contemporary critics. *La Revue musicale* commented that the work contained 'much knowledge and technical interest', applauding the composer's 'very real and very earnest talent', not forgetting to mention his Irish roots (even though the critic confused Stuttgart with Leipzig).[3] The *Monthly Musical Record* wrote:

> In the work before us, although the composer afterwards deals freely with his theme, it can be clearly traced at the opening of each Variation, however modified, by rhythm, which, indeed, plays a large part in Mr. Hennessy's very ingenious music. One Variation is in the form of a Valse, another is marked 'Rustique,' while others are in canonic form.

German critics pointed to Hennessy's 'contrapuntal skill and rich fantasy'[4] respectively his 'individuality and personality'.[5]

In more recent times, Laura Watson has looked at the harmonic language of the work, writing:

> The variations mostly maintain the lyrical nature of the monophonic theme: forays into the more opaque impressionist sound-world are rare, with the exception of the tenth

---

[3] '*M. SWAN HENNESSY, dont nous avons déjà eu l'occasion de signaler le très réel et très sérieux talent de compositeur, et qui réunit en lui des esprits différents, c'est un Irlandais habitant Paris et ayant fait ses études de contrepoint au Conservatoire de Leipzig, publie, pour piano, des Variations sur un air irlandais ancien (op. 28) qui ont beaucoup de saveur et d'intérêt technique (chez Schott, Mayence et Londres).*'; *La Revue musicale* 8:22, 15 November 1908, p. 609.

[4] '*Auch hier zeigt sich Hennessy als Kontrapunktiker von Geschick und reicher Phantasie.*'; Hugo Rasch in *Allgemeine Musikzeitung* 28:13, 31 March 1911, p. 376.

[5] '*Mehr Eigenart und Persönlichkeit verraten die beiden wenn auch längst nicht so schwer gesetzten Klavierwerke op. 28. Variations sur un air irlandais ancien und op. 33. Croquis de femmes [...]*'; Karl Thiessen in *Signale für die musikalische Welt* 69:21, 24 May 1911, p. 800.

variation. Here, the juxtaposition of an Irish-tinged melody in the right hand and chromatic chordal sonorities of the modern French school in the left hand has the effect of musically linking the two countries.⁶

Bláithfhleasg bheag, d'fhonnaibh arsa Gaedhealacha as leabhar Petrie. / Petite suite irlandaise, d'après des airs anciens de la collection Petrie, Op. 29, (1908) for piano duet

Hennessy's *Petite suite irlandaise*, Op. 29 for two players on one piano was written in 1908 and published by Demets (without opus number) in 1909. This must be the earliest example of a composition published in Paris with a title in Irish – *Bláithfhleasg bheag, d'fhonnaibh arsa Gaedhealacha as leabhar Petrie* – executed in photostat handwriting on the cover. Even the composer's name appears in a Gaelic version (Suan Ó hAonghusa), and the title page features a Celtic ornament inspired by one of the medieval Irish manuscripts (Fig. 6.1).

Fig. 6.1: Title decoration on the front page of Hennessy's *Petite suite irlandaise*, Op. 29

Having seen Hennessy's handwriting, I am sure this is in his own hand, and this makes it an interesting item as it raises the question how he was able to write in Irish. It can be ruled out that he actually spoke Irish because that would have required a much longer physical presence in Ireland. Therefore, in this case somebody (an Irish person) must have shown him how his title and his name could be translated into Irish

---

⁶ Laura Watson, 'Ireland in the Musical Imagination of Third Republic France', in Una Hunt and Mary Pierse (eds): *France and Ireland. Notes and Narratives* (Oxford etc.: Peter Lang, 2015), pp. 91–109 [97].

– and it is not very likely that he would have found such a person in Paris in 1908. It may not be a fully convincing evidence, but this circumstance is the strongest indication so far that Hennessy was in Ireland at the time of writing the piece – perhaps for the second time after 1890 when the son from his first marriage had been born in Dublin (see Chapter 3).

In addition to the Petrie Collection, another inspiration may have come from France, respectively Brittany: the Breton composer (and later a friend of Hennessy's) Paul Ladmirault wrote two pieces of a similar manufacture, the *Rhapsodie gaélique* (1903) and the *Variations sur des airs de biniou trécorois* (1907), both for piano duet,[7] the latter published by Demets who also happened to be Hennessy's publisher. The scores of both pieces are indeed in what remains of Hennessy's collection of music in his family today. Like Hennessy, Ladmirault in the *Variations* also names the folksong collection that served as a source for the tunes, in this case it reads *'(tirés du Recueil de Quellien)'*.[8] If these works were indeed Hennessy's model, then he would have applied in an Irish style what he had heard (or seen) before in a Breton context.[9]

Rather than a through-composed suite, the work consists of four pieces, each one using a tune from the Petrie Collection of Irish music as arranged by C. V. Stanford.[10] The pieces correspond to the Petrie/Stanford numbers 983, 903, 1089/1247,[11] and 902, although Hennessy does not reference them. In his suite, they are called *Ancient Clan March*, *Cork Reel*, *Sagairt tar teorach*, and again *Cork Reel* – the latter better known as *Molly on the Shore*.

Hennessy's 'suite' is more or less a set of arrangements of these four folk tunes in an order and tonal sequence that would correspond to the movements of a classical suite. The introductory march is marked *allegro*, the first Cork reel *allegretto*, *Sagairt tar teorach* is a slow air in *adagio*, and the *finale*, the second Cork reel, in *vivacissimo*. To suit his purposes better, he transposes his arrangements to different tonalities than their originals (beginning and ending in C major, with F major and G minor for the middle movements) but otherwise leaves them mostly intact, with the exception of the initial march where he takes the tune apart after its first eight bars and distributes various fragments of it across the piece. For the other movements, he begins with a full statement of the folk tunes and processes and varies them in the course of the piece, albeit not in the form of a 'classical' set of theme and variations. The whole suite would not last longer than about eight minutes.

---

[7] Ladmirault also wrote a *Suite bretonne* (1908) for piano duet, which is an arrangement of excerpts from his opera *Myrdhin* (1903).
[8] Narcisse Quellien: *Chansons et danses des Bretons* (Paris: J. Maisonneuve & C. Leclerc, 1889).
[9] Interestingly, an English critic in 1922 found the same parallel, see *The Sackbut* 2:9, March 1922, p. 35.
[10] See fn. 1.
[11] One of many editorial mistakes that went unnoticed in this edition is that this particular piece appears twice. Besides, Hennessy also made a mistake in transcribing the Gaelic: in the third piece, the last word should read 'teóradh'.

The thematic focus of (some of) the movements of the *Petite suite irlandaise* on Cork may not only be interpreted as a nod towards his family, respectively his father who had been born in the city. It may also indicate that Cork was the place that Hennessy visited when he came to Ireland in 1908 – maybe to see for himself the place where his father was from, and perhaps even in his company. 1908 was an interesting year in the cultural life of the city as it saw the foundation of the Cork Dramatic Society by the well-known local writer and historian Daniel Corkery and the young dramatist Terence MacSwiney. MacSwiney was an increasingly politicised playwright who was to become a hero in the struggle for Irish independence when he was, briefly, Lord Mayor of Cork in 1920. In that role he went on hunger strike against the English occupation of Ireland and died in October1920[12] – which led to a dedication of Hennessy's second string quartet (Op. 49) to the memory of Terence MacSwiney in that year.

It has been the inherited knowledge in the Hennessy family that MacSwiney had been godfather to Swan Hennessy's son Patrice, who was born in Paris in July 1910. In the course of the research for this study, the baptismal record could be uncovered, but unfortunately it proves otherwise.[13] Would it have been possible to prove the connection with the help of this document, the speculation about Hennessy's presence in Cork in 1908 would not stand on such thin ice. However, the fact that the baptism took place on 29 September 1911, fifteen months after the birth, may yet speak for a long-cherished hope that MacSwiney would at some point be able to come to Paris to witness for the baptism. However, the reason may also have been much more profane: given the still high child mortality rates at this time, one may simply have wanted to be sure that the child would survive.

Yet, the facts remain that a) an Irish person must have shown Hennessy how to write his work title and name in Irish, and b) there is a (later) dedication to MacSwiney by Hennessy, the reason for which is not fully explained other than by sympathy. Together with the family story about the baptism in 1910/11, there is the possibility that Hennessy and MacSwiney knew each other personally, perhaps since 1908 and the foundation of the Cork Dramatic Society, and that it may indeed have been MacSwiney who was the person to teach Hennessy the writing in Irish. It is, alas, an unproven theory that would need further archival research [14] The Hennessy–MacSwiney connection does not appear so far in any MacSwiney biography or archival documentation, but neither does Hennessy's dedication of the string quartet in 1920. Obviously, there remain aspects of the MacSwiney story that are worth exploring.

---

[12] Dave Hannigan: *Terence MacSwiney. The Hunger Strike that Rocked an Empire* (Dublin: O'Brien Press, 2010).

[13] The baptism took place at the church of Saint Pierre de Montrouge, Montparnasse, Paris, 29 September 1911; godparents were Michael Hennessy and Ida (Adam-)Pineau.

[14] This author's enquiries at the MacSwiney collection in the UCD Archives in 2016 and a personal visit to the Cork City and County Archives in May 2018 did not yield any insights into the matter.

There is also the possibility that the Irish person who assisted Hennessy in the handwriting on his title page would have come from the wider circle of MacSwiney in Cork, for instance the musicians involved in the Cork Dramatic Society. This would primarily have been the company's music director, Denis Breen. However, as we shall see below, Breen does not appear to have known Hennessy before 1922.

The *Petite suite irlandaise* was received quite well, and it is one of the few of Hennessy's works with a response from Ireland. A writer in a 1909 issue of the newspaper *The Irish Nation* thought of it:

> The arrangements of these are without doubt some of the best that have hitherto been published. They are brilliant and clever and are entirely free from the extravagance of finger work, which is generally found in arrangements of the "fantasie" type, and both parts are evenly balanced. Mr. Hennessy has made a happy selection, and has displayed considerable skill in his arrangements. The "suite" should prove immensely popular.[15]

Many years later (1922), the aforementioned Denis Breen (a.k.a. Donnchadh Ua Braoin) in the *Dublin Evening Telegraph* wondered when he came across that 1909 article:

> Who could this Franco-Irish musician be that, in a foreign country, sent forth his music burdened with a title in a language almost unknown in its own land, and among its own people? The comment of the 'Irish Nation' of September, 1909 that 'this Suite should prove immensely popular,' has a more than ironic significance in view of the fact that the name of Swan Hennessy is yet unknown to more than a few dozen persons in Ireland.[16]

In France and Germany, both *S.I.M. Revue musicale mensuelle* and the *Allgemeine Musikzeitung* applauded the technically facile, yet attractive composition,[17] justifiably pointing out that – with the exception, perhaps, of the *vivacissimo* finale – the work is not difficult to play. *Comoedia* regarded it as a 'treat for gourmets'.[18] A review in the *Monthly Musical Record* was rather descriptive but pointed out 'clever devices' that made the suite attractive:

> VARIOUS pieces for pianoforte by M. Swan-Hennessy have been noticed in the columns of THE M. M. RECORD, and in them the composer displays considerable ingenuity – one might, indeed, say originality – in the treatment of his thematic material. In the Suite under notice, themes have been selected from the great Petrie collection of Irish folk music, of which, by the way, Sir Charles Stanford, a few years ago, published an edition from original manuscripts. There are four movements, two dealing with *Cork Reels*, while the others are

---

[15] 'Irish Music and Irish Enterprise / Petite Suite Irlandaise'; *The Irish Nation*, 11 September 1909.

[16] Donnchadh Ua Braoin: 'Swan Hennessy. An Irish Musician of To-day'; *Dublin Evening Telegraph*, 2 September 1922, p. 2.

[17] '[…] *une amusante et facile petite suite*', *S.I.M. Revue musicale mensuelle*, 15 January 1911, p. 95; '*Interessant und leicht spielbar* […]', *Allgemeine Musikzeitung*, 31 March 1911, p. 376.

[18] '*une sorte de petit régal à l'usage des gourmets*'; *Comoedia*, 1 June 1911, p. 2.

based on an *Ancient Clan March*, and the lovely air, *Sagaert tar teorach*. The characteristic themes are never lost sight of, but, indeed, by clever devices at times intensified.[19]

The earliest public performance of the *Petite suite irlandaise* appears to have taken place in Paris (Salle Érard), 23 April 1914, by Andrée Gellée and Paul Martineau. Paul Ladmirault, whose music may have inspired Hennessy's work (see above), wrote about it after this performance:

> Mr. Swan Hennessy's Suite irlandaise is [...] one of the most beautiful works of this skilful and fertile musician. All the capricious grace of the 'reels', the melancholy of Erin's old songs, come alive again in these delicate pages, adorned with discreet but penetrating harmonies and sober and clear developments.[20]

There is also a record of a live broadcast performance in Ireland from 2RN (the predecessor of today's RTÉ) on 12 September 1931, played by Frederick Stone and Edna Beaven. An arrangement of the *adagio* movement by one G. Meyer for cello and piano was a test piece at the Father Mathew Feis, Dublin, Easter 1923. In the United States, Victor Herbert arranged the suite for orchestra and conducted it at Carnegie Hall, New York, on 23 March 1913.[21]

* * *

The year 1912 was decisive in Swan Hennessy's career. Two developments contributed to it. One was the notion that, however hard he tried to be French, he did not receive the level of attention and success that he desired. Chapter 4 had shown how his musical language developed from a late Romantic to a contemporary French style, at which he firmly arrived around the year 1907. Chapter 5 showed him excel in that style with a prolific stream of works for the piano, particularly during 1911 and 1912. Reviews of these works were – with the typical disagreements in opinion – overwhelmingly positive, in France as well as in Germany and England. With regard to reviews, Hennessy certainly could not complain.

The decisive difference to most of his contemporaries in Paris was that his music was not performed (at least not at the time when it appeared). Obviously, the reviews did not prompt French pianists to buy the scores and include them in their recitals. The reviews certainly proved that it was not a matter of quality. So, what else was it?

One reason at least must be sought in the hidden presence that Swan Hennessy was until that time. He wrote in one of the letters to Schott (and Hugo Rasch

---

[19] *The Monthly Musical Record*, 1 June 1911, p. 148.
[20] '*La* Suite Irlandaise *de M. Swan Hennessy est* [...] *une des plus jolies œuvres de ce musicien habile et fécond. Toute la grâce capricante des "reels" la mélancolie des vieux chants d'Erin, revivent en ces pages délicates, parées d'harmonies discrètes mais pénétrantes et de développements sobres et clairs.*'; Paul Ladmirault in *La Revue musicale S.I.M.*, 1 January 1914, p. 58.
[21] Aaron C. Keebaugh: *Irish Music and Home Rule Politics, 1800–1922* (diss. Univ. of Florida, 2011), p. 192. See also Appendix 1B.

confirmed it in one of his reviews) that he lived in a withdrawn way; he apparently relied on his publishers to promote his music. He did not concertise, and it also seems that he did not mix a lot with the important performers of his time.

Another obstacle that may have impeded the contemporary reception of his music (and himself), perhaps until today, is that he does not seem to have been a member of one of the more prestigious musical societies in Paris: the Société Nationale de Musique de France, founded in 1871 by Romain Bussine and Camille Saint-Saëns and the Société Musicale Indépendante (SMI), founded in 1909 by Maurice Ravel, Paul Dukas, Charles Koechlin and others. As a foreign national, Hennessy may not have had access to the Société Nationale, which identified strongly with France for political and cultural reasons (and it would not have mattered that Hennessy did so, too). The SMI, on the other hand, at least invited foreign composers like Bartók, de Falla, Schönberg, and Stravinsky to have their works performed in France, but Hennessy may not have liked the organisation's Leftist and modernist stance.[22]

The Paris correspondent of the *Allgemeine Musikzeitung*, Heinrich Möller, nevertheless implied in early 1912 that these societies more or less excluded Hennessy:

> January brought an enormous swelling of the concert flood, but few events of importance. Multa non multum. For example, the artistic yield at the many concerts of exclusively modern French composers is very small. As gratifying as it may be that our neighbours, at least in their musical production, have not yet arrived at the two-children system and that the technical skills of the younger generation must be recognised, it would be advisable for those societies which are seeking the encouragement of up-and-coming talents, such as the Société Nationale, Société Musicale Indépendante, Société des Compositeurs, etc., to recommend a somewhat stricter selection in their programmes. Instead of bringing to light truly original talents still rejected by the big concert-giving societies (such are certainly not lacking, I would only mention the Irishman Swan Hennessy who lives here), they increasingly want to grow into party and clique organs and hotbeds of mediocre nerds. It is made too easy for certain composers to bring their half-baked works to the public. It is obvious that such flooding with modern mediocrity poisons the audience more than educates it, and only breeds snobbery and progressive philistry. I am not targeting composers such as Magnard, Turina, Ropartz, Sévérac, Albeniz, Aubert, who are among the more pleasing appearances in these circles.[23]

---

[22] See, for this aspect, Jane F. Fulcher: *The Composer as Intellectual. Music and Ideology in France* (New York: Oxford University Press, 2005), p. 32–4. The debates surrounding the *Société nationale* and SMI are also covered in depth in Michel Duchesneau: *L'Avant-garde musicale et ses sociétés à Paris de 1871 à 1939* (Sprimont: Mardaga, 1997) and Barbara L. Kelly: *Music and Ultra-Modernism in France. A Fragile Consensus, 1913–1939* (Woodbridge: The Boydell Press, 2013).

[23] *'Der Januar brachte ein gewaltiges Anschwellen der Konzertflut, aber wenige Veranstaltungen von Bedeutung. Multa non multum. Sehr geringfügig ist z. B. die künstlerische Ausbeute bei den vielen Konzerten ausschließlich moderner französischer Komponisten. So erfreulich es ist, daß unsere Nachbarn wenigstens in der musikalischen Produktion noch nicht beim Zweikindersystem angelangt sind und man das technische Können der jungen Generation anerkennen muß, so wäre den Gesellschaften, die sich die Ermutigung aufstrebender Talente angelegen sein lassen, wie der Société nationale, Société musicale indépendante, Société des Compositeurs usw. doch etwas strengere Auswahl bei ihrem Programmen zu empfehlen. Anstatt wirklich originale, von den großen Konzert-*

Hennessy also lacked the network that alumni of educational institutions enjoyed. He had neither studied at the Paris Conservatory nor at the Schola Cantorum, and he did not seek any private tuition from one of the more prominent composer-teachers in Paris, even if it had been for self-promoting reasons only, although he did not lack the necessary resources. Hennessy may have been the only graduate of the Stuttgart Conservatory active in Paris at the time. Nobody would have known this institution, and in terms of composition, it had no reputation.

The promoting role that a composers' or musicians' association could play should not be underestimated. It was probably even the decisive factor, as an association organised its own concert series, the members mutually supported each other in one way or another, and its activities were reported on in the relevant journals.

On the other hand, Hennessy did not live in private or artistic isolation. He was extremely well informed about contemporary music, read French, German and English journals with ease, bought scores, and was a frequent concert-goer. He knew what was going on, and as an intelligent observer, he must have recognised the situation he was in. But to the outside world (and at least until early 1912), he must have appeared as a composer who hid in his study, produced nothing but piano music that nobody performed, shied away from the modernists in the SMI, with seemingly no network of composer-colleagues and musician-friends that he would have had if he had studied in France.

The Association des Compositeurs Bretons

This is the situation, in which the other important 1912 development occurred. It was the founding of an organisation that must have had a liberating effect on Hennessy: l'Association des Compositeurs Bretons (ACB) – The Association of Breton Composers. It was with this association that Hennessy's reputation finally reached out beyond published criticism of his printed music into the recital hall.

It must have been Louis Vuillemin who brought Hennessy in contact with the association in the early months of 1912. Vuillemin has had a high opinion of Hennessy's qualities as a composer, as is very visible in his many positive, one might say enthusiastic, reviews of his work in the journal *Comoedia* (see Chapter 5). He would not have missed either that Hennessy had published a few works in an Irish style, the last in 1909. Vuillemin is the only member of the ACB who had been in contact with Hennessy prior to the founding of the group.

---

vereinen noch abgewiesene Talente ans Licht zu bringen (an solchen fehlt es sicherlich nicht, ich nenne nur den hier lebenden Iren Swan Hennessy), scheinen sie sich immer mehr zu Partei- und Cliquen-Organen und Brutstätten mittelmäßiger Streber auswachsen zu wollen. Es wird gewissen Komponisten zu leicht gemacht, ihre unausgegorenen Werke an die Oeffentlichkeit zu bringen. Daß eine solche Ueberschwemmung mit modernen Mittelmäßigkeiten das Publikum mehr vergiftet, als erzieht, und nur Snobismus und Fortschrittsphilisterei züchtet, liegt auf der Hand. Ich ziele hiermit nicht auf Komponisten wie Magnard, Turina, Ropartz, Sévérac, Albeniz, Aubert, die zu den erfreulicheren Erscheinungen in diesen Kreisen gehören.'; Heinrich Möller in *Allgemeine Musikzeitung* 39:8, 23 February 1912, p. 203–204.

The Association des Compositeurs Bretons was founded on 1 January 1912[24] by the five composers Maurice Duhamel (1884–1940), Paul Ladmirault (1877–1944) – the two chief intellectuals of the group –, Louis Vuillemin (1879–1929), Paul Le Flem (1881–1984), and the rather obscure Jean Laporte (life dates unknown), the latter appearing in the early months only. These five names clearly appear as founders of the association in the 8 February 1912 issue of *Comoedia*, as signatories to a long critique of the opera *La Lépreuse* by Sylvio Lazzari (1857–1944),[25] a work that had been written in 1899 but premiered as late as 7 February 1912. The opera had been based on an 1896 play of the same name by the librettist, Henry Bataille (1872–1922). *La Lépreuse* had a plot set in Brittany, and the five composers alleged that the story was largely based on texts of Breton folksongs collected in *Gwerziou Breiz-Izel / Chants populaires de la Basse-Bretagne* (1868) by François-Marie Luzel, hence lacking both literary originality and, in the opera, musical authenticity. It seems that the protest against *La Lépreuse* was the first reason to seek a public platform, before they even appeared as a group in any recital or other form.

A year after its foundation, the ACB also included – besides Duhamel, Ladmirault, Vuillemin, and Le Flem – Joseph-Guy Ropartz (1864–1955) as honorary president and Paul Martineau (1890–1915).[26] Whatever their early activities and (perhaps) problems were, they only gave their 'official' inaugural concert in Paris on 6 March 1913.[27] It seems, however, that a year before, on an unspecified date in March 1912, they had already organised a concert, perhaps in a private circle, to which the German music critic Heinrich Möller had access, probably through Hennessy. He wrote:

> A society of 'Celtic' composers has set itself the task of reforming French music, or rather of creating a truly national French music in the first place, by resorting to the one, racially pure autochthonous Celtic folk music. Habeant! As long as these enthusiasts perform such beautiful music as the Breton folk songs, the works of Ladmirault, Le Flem and above all the Irish suite by Hennessy, their endeavours can be no harm.[28]

---

[24] The founding date of the ACB and its motivation can also be found in Jean Laporte: 'L'Association des compositeurs bretons', *Revue française de musique*, 1 March 1912, p. 60–63. Bempéchat (see below) wrongly suggests 1910 as the year of the foundation and repeats it throughout his writings on the ACB, basing it on Philippe Gonin's study *Vie et oeuvre de Paul Le Flem* (Villeneuve d'Ascq: Presses universitaires de Septentrion, 2001), p. 346. Gonin copied it from Geneviève Bernard-Krauß: *Hundert Jahre französischer Musikgeschichte in Leben und Werk Paul Le Flems* (Frankfurt: Peter Lang, 1993), p. 33, where the initial mistake occurred.

[25] 'La première Lépreuse', *Comoedia*, 8 February 1912, p. 3.

[26] *La Revue musicale S.I.M.*, 15 January 1913, p. 58.

[27] Unmistakably described as such in *Ar Bobl*, 1 March 1913, p. 3; *Comoedia*, 6 March 1913, p. 2 & 13 March 1913, p. 2; and *La Critique indépendante*, 15 March 1913, p. 2. A reason for the delayed inaugural recital may have been the (unknown) circumstances of Jean Laporte's departure from the organisation.

[28] *'Eine Gesellschaft "keltischer" Komponisten hat es sich in den Kopf gesetzt, die französische Musik zu reformieren, oder vielmehr eine wahrhaft national-französische Musik erst zu schaffen, durch Zurückgreifen auf die eine, rassenreine autochthone keltische Volksmusik. Habeant! Solange diese Schwärmer so hübsche Musik vorführen, wie die bretonischen Volkslieder, die Werke von Ladmirault, Le Flem und vor allem die irische*

The role and activities of the Association des Compositeurs Bretons are not particularly well researched,[29] perhaps due to its short-lived existence: it was dissolved with the outbreak of World War I in mid-1914 (but succeeded after the War by the Société Artistique et Littéraire de l'Ouest). The only anglophone musicologist who appears to have studied it to some extent is the Harvard scholar Paul-André Bempéchat in his biography of Jean Cras (1879–1932) – the only prominent Breton composer who was *not* a member of the ACB – and in a dedicated research paper.[30]

Bempéchat rightly acknowledges the organisation's intellectual indebtedness to the 'Russian Five', which had been explained by Paul Ladmirault as late as 1928 in what Bempéchat called the 'artistic manifesto' of Breton composers, which had lost nothing of its momentum even though the ACB as such did not exist anymore by then.[31] In his article, Ladmirault explains the situation of the five Russian composers, also known in musical history as the 'Mighty Five' or 'The Mighty Handful' (Mily Balakirev, Cesar Cui, Modest Mussorgsky, Nikolai Rimsky-Korsakov, Alexander Borodin), who protested against the dominance of German and Italian music in mid-19th-century Europe. They sought to renew art music by recourse to national folklore including history, legends, and traditional music, demanding that works of art music should be inspired by the melodies and rhythms of native music. Ladmirault asked:

> Why, therefore, would a phenomenon so successful in Russia not be applicable to Brittany? [...] Because Brittany, like it or not, is hardly a province, but a nation: through its race, its language, its special mentality, its traditions, its admirable folklore, unrelated to France's, and its indigenous folk music.[32]

Bempéchat then also applied the concept of a group of five to the ACB and identified eight members, which – in relation to the Russian Five or perhaps even 'Les Six' – he now adapted as 'The Breton Eight' or 'Les Huit'. The eight members of the ACB

Suite von Hennessy, sind ihre Bestrebungen durchaus unschädlich.'; Heinrich Möller in *Allgemeine Musikzeitung* 39:12, 22 March 1912, p. 315. I checked this source twice to make sure there is no confusion with March 1913. No French journal reported about this event. There is a difference also in the works by Hennessy performed: in 1912 the 'Irish suite' may have been either the *Petite suite irlandaise*, Op. 29 for piano duet or the *Suite*, Op. 46 for string quartet; in 1913 it was the *Pièces celtiques*, Op. 45 for piano.

[29] It is not mentioned by any of the more prominent anglophone music historians of France, nor in Robert Marot: *Les Compositeurs Bretons. Les Sources de leur inspiration* (Nantes: CID Éditions, 1988) or Édith Weber's preface to Véfa de Bellaing: *Dictionnaire des compositeurs de musique en Bretagne* (Nantes: Ouest Éditions, 1992), p. 11–18. See, however, Yves Defrance: 'Un Bretonisme musical (1860–1980)', in: *Analyse musicale* no. 78 (December 2015), pp. 104–113.

[30] Paul-André Bempéchat: '*Allons enfants de *quelle* patrie?*' Breton Nationalism and the French Impressionist Aesthetic (Cambridge, Mass.: Harvard University, Center for European Studies Working Paper Series No. 106, 2003); and *Jean Cras. Polymath of Music and Letters* (Farnham, Surrey: Ashgate, 2009; reprint in paperback: London & New York: Routledge, 2017).

[31] Paul Ladmirault: 'L'Exemple des "Cinq" Russes / Skouer ar "Pemp" Rusiad', in: *Kornog* 1 (1928), p. 16–20; translated into English by Paul Bempéchat in *Allons enfants*, p. 14–17.

[32] Ladmirault as translated by Bempéchat, *Allons enfants*, p. 16.

were, in this calculation, Louis Aubert, Charles-Augustin Collin, Maurice Duhamel, Paul Ladmirault, Paul Le Flem, Paul Martineau, Guy Ropartz, and Louis Vuillemin.[33]

The original concert programmes to the events of the ACB, which are contained in the four volumes of 'Press Books' in possession of the Hennessy family, offer a different perspective. Since no official membership list of the ACB has yet come to light – if indeed such a list ever existed –, the composers represented at their concerts would have to be considered members. Thus, the list of members (see Table 6.1) would also include (in the order of their date of birth) Alice Sauvrezis, Léon Moreau, Lucien Haudebert, Jean Huré, Adolphe Piriou, Rhené-Baton, Roger Pénau, and – Swan Hennessy! These are the names that feature on the concert programmes of the association during 1913 and 1914 as well as in the reviews of these events in the contemporary press.[34]

Table 6.1: Members of the Association des Compositeurs Bretons in early 1914*
* as drawn from concert programmes and reviews of their events, in the order of the year of birth

J. Guy Ropartz (1864–1955)	Jean Huré (1877–1930)
Charles-Augustin Collin (1865–1938)	Paul Ladmirault (1877–1944)
Swan Hennessy (1866–1929)	Adolphe Piriou (1878–1964)
Alice Sauvrezis (1866–1946)	Rhené-Baton (1879–1940)
Léon Moreau (1870–1946)	Louis Vuillemin (1879–1929)
Raymond Hervé (1871–19??)	Paul Le Flem (1881–1984)
Jehan de Gibon (1873–1952)	Maurice Duhamel (1884–1940)
Louis Aubert (1877–1968)	Roger Pénau (1886–1961)
Lucien Haudebert (1877–1963)	Paul Martineau (1890–1915)

Hennessy was one of the older members of the group, and the only one who was neither Breton nor even French. But Paul Ladmirault described it as an organisation 'where integral Celts, Celts by inspiration and native Celts form a harmonious and varied community'.[35] Louis Vuillemin, on the other hand, seemed to quote from a programmatic statement of the group when he described their aims as:

> To encourage the study and dissemination of Celtic music; to bring together the various musicians who, through Breton birth, are likely to have natural affinities; to enrich Western music with elements derived from the Celtic tradition.[36]

---

[33] Bempéchat, *Allons enfants*, p. 10; *Jean Cras*, p. 167–8. Ladmirault mentions most of these in his 1928 'manifesto', excluding not only Swan Hennessy but many other members as well.
[34] Several members of the ACB were SMI members as well, such as (at least) Aubert and Huré. For further information on these composers (except R. Hervé), see de Bellaing (1992); the better known composers can also be found in the major musical encyclopaedias.
[35] *'où Celtes intégraux, Celtes d'inspiration et Celtes de naissance formaient un ensemble harmonieux et varié'*; *La Revue musicale S.I.M.* 10, 1 May 1914, p. 57.
[36] *'Provoquer à l'étude et à la diffusion de la musique celtique; grouper les différents musiciens susceptibles, de par la naissance bretonne, de posséder de naturelles affinités; enrichir la musique occidentale d'éléments dérivés de la tradition celtique.'*; Louis Vuillemin: 'La Semaine musicale', in: *Comoedia*, 13 March 1913, p. 2.

Hennessy's own connections with Brittany were tenuous – as explained in Chapter 2, his mother had died in a boating accident off Roscoff in 1880, and he often retreated to the region for a few summer weeks to compose. Yet certainly, his relationship to the group was rather that of, in Ladmirault's words, a 'Celt by inspiration'.

On the other hand, he seems to have been involved in an organising role at least once (and maybe more often) when he rented the Salle des Agriculteurs for the concert of the ACB on 26 November 1913, which included, as its final item, Hennessy's first string quartet, the *Suite*, Op. 46. This is documented in a June 1913 letter by Hennessy to Maurice Duhamel:

Paris, 25 June 1913

Dear Mr. Duhamel,
I have booked the Salle des Agriculteurs for the evening of <u>Wednesday, 26 November</u>. Please be kind enough to inform the members of the A.D.C.B.
Very cordially
Swan Hennessy[37]

Fig. 6.2: The Salle des Agriculteurs at the Sorbonne University in 1913 – an important chamber music hall in Paris, 1894–1925 (Source: gallica.bnf.fr / Bibliothèque Nationale de France)

---

[37] '*Paris, 25, 6, 13 / Cher Monsieur Duhamel, / J'ai réservé la salle des Agriculteurs pour la soirée de <u>Mercredi 26 Novembre</u>. Veuillez avoir la bonté de prévenir les members de l'A.D.C.B. / A vous très cordialement / Swan Hennessy*'; Bibliothèque de Rennes Métropole, MS 1636/42. Hennessy's 'A.D.C.B.' is the same as what I prefer to abbreviate as 'ACB'.

The ACB was the only formal group of composers in Paris with the culture of a geographical region as their focus of identity. A common denominator of the group was their frequent recourse to folk melody in compositions that were often coined as *'celtique'*, thereby creating a spiritual unity with other 'Celtic' nations including Ireland. Guy Ropartz and his fellow Bretons sought to establish a Breton identity in contemporary French music, respectively 'to acclimatise the Celtic muse in Paris'.[38] The techniques were largely the same as in works related to contemporary musical nationalism in other nations: the use of folk-song and dances (or their tonality) as thematic material in composition, settings of poetry relating to the region or from writers of the region, the use of dialects or minority languages in vocal works, historic legends as a common heritage in vocal or operatic music, etc.

In a special, albeit brief study of Breton composers and their influences, Robert Marot also refers to French compositional schools, identifying Ropartz, Cras, Piriou and Le Flem as adherents to the influence of César Franck, and Ladmirault and Vuillemin as pupils of a 'more French' school in the tradition of Gabriel Fauré.[39] In a grand *tour d'horizon*, Marot explains folkloristic schools across Europe since the mid-nineteenth century, but remains vague about the application of this idea to Brittany until, in conclusion, he asks whether there has been a Breton school of composition. While he acknowledges that all composers in question referred, in one way or another, to the great Breton folk music collections of the nineteenth century, notably the works of Luzel, La Villemarqué, and Bourgault-Ducoudray,[40] he still considers their aesthetic approaches too different to include all of them under a common headline of a 'Breton school of composition' – especially since this 'school' had no teacher. The actual teacher would have been, in Marot's view, d'Indy, but then, d'Indy was not Breton.

> In short: no real Breton school of 'enlightened' music; at most a vague *Armorican grouping* made up of elements that were insufficiently united and, moreover, dispersed.[41]

Given the common heritage of all the composers mentioned and their common aims expressed in their ACB membership, I would challenge that position. It can hardly be expected that such a large group of composers speaks exactly the same

---

[38] '[…] *cherche à acclimater à Paris la muse celtique* […]'; *La Revue musicale S.I.M.*, 15 January 1913, p. 58.

[39] Marot, *Les Compositeurs bretons*, p. 25. Only Ropartz had been a direct pupil of Franck. Cras came in via Henri Duparc; Piriou and Le Flem via Vincent d'Indy. Ladmirault and Vuillemin were direct pupils of Fauré at the Conservatoire. At a later point in his study, he also includes Aubert as a pupil of Fauré.

[40] Besides the already mentioned *Gwerziou Breiz-Izel* (1868) by Luzel, these would mainly include *Barzaz Breiz / Chants populaires de la Bretagne* (1839) by Théodore Hersart de La Villemarqué (1815–1895) and the *Trente Mélodies populaires de Basse-Bretagne* (1885) by Louis (-Albert) Bourgault-Ducoudray (1840–1910).

[41] '*En définitivement donc: pas de véritable École bretonne de musique "éclairée"; tout au plus un vague* groupement armoricain *constitué d'éléments insuffisamment soudés et, par surcroît, dispersés.*'; Marot, *Les Compositeurs bretons*, p. 115.

musical language, given the different biographical and educational backgrounds that every single person brought into the game. Yet, it is their roots, influences and concerns and, most of all, similar products in the form of music influenced by Breton traditional music that does justify speaking of a Breton school of ideas in music – and this ultimately found a sympathetic adherent in Swan Hennessy.

Marot is right, of course, in ascribing a pivotal influence of Vincent d'Indy in the formation of regionalist trends in French music that became increasingly audible since the closing years of the nineteenth century. D'Indy himself had written music adapting the folklore of various French regions, including Brittany, in his own music. A cofounder of his Schola Cantorum, Charles Bordes (1863–1909) likewise related to his native Basque region in his music. It is no coincidence that the better-known regionalist composers in France went through the Schola Cantorum, including Déodat de Séverac (1872–1921) who was so strongly influenced by the music of the Catalan respectively Languedoc region, and Joseph Canteloube (1879–1957) whose music is so deeply rooted in the Auvergne. Interestingly, although these are singular personalities, their music appears to be better known today than that of the much larger group of Breton composers working at the same time.

Thus, musical regionalism in France is a widely acknowledged aspect of French art music surviving far into the twentieth century, but scholarly attention has, curiously enough, not focused very much on Brittany.[42] Where regionalism has propped up in academic research, such as in the writings of Musk (1999) or Waters (2008),[43] the Breton side has never been covered.

Moreover, for many years, a majority of scholars seems to have consciously disregarded musical approaches they regarded as 'parochial', a term implying a negative connotation casting doubt on the relevance of such types of music for an international, discerning audience. Music with national or regional overtones was often viewed despicably, when one might just as well argue that regional influences make music more distinguishable, interesting, and even – because of the multitude of approaches – more individual.

Particularly in France, regionalism has a long history in all spheres of life. For a long period of modern history, there was widespread criticism over the central role that Paris occupied in politics, administration, education and not least in cultural life. In the context of music, Barbara Kelly wrote:

---

[42] Barbara L. Kelly's edited volume *French Music, Culture, and National Identity, 1870–1939* (Rochester, New York: University of Rochester Press & Woodbridge: Boydell & Brewer, 2008) contains a section on regionalism with essays by Katharine Ellis (on Dijon), Detmar Klein (on Alsace), and Didier Francfort (on Lorraine). Likewise, Ellis' article 'Paris and the Regions from the Revolution to the First World War' in *The Cambridge Companion to French Music*, ed. Simon Trezise (Cambridge: Cambridge University Press, 2015), p. 362–378, also ignores Breton music.
[43] Andrea N. Musk: *Aspects of Regionalism in French Music During the Third Republic: the Schola Cantorum, d'Indy, Séverac and Canteloube* (Oxford: Oxford University Press, 1999); Roger F. Waters: *Déodat de Séverac. Musical Identity in Fin-de-Siècle France* (Farnham, Surrey: Ashgate, 2008).

At the root of much of France's disunity was the issue of identity and what constituted the true France. This tension was apparent not only between Left and Right political polarizations but also over the issue of centralization.[44]

Therefore, what Kelly has termed the 'internal exotic' – the folk music of French regions – had a similar influence as the Spanish neighbour and even Asian music that received so much attention music since the Paris *Exposition Universelle* of 1889. Applying this term to Maurice Ravel's southern French and Spanish musical interests, she wrote:

> The 'internal exotic' is a useful term for musical and other products that focus on the periphery of France and attempts to capture the 'otherness' of that region through language, subject matter, instrumentation, and modal writing.[45]

There cannot be any doubt that the Breton composers of the time contributed to large extent to the 'internal exotic' of French musical life, even though this region has not yet attained the same level of academic attention as other parts of France.

* * *

It is not certain what the impact of the Association des Compositeurs Bretons on the French musical public really was beyond what can be deducted from published criticism. It was undoubtedly the First World War, which not only brought the activities of the ACB to a premature end but which also inhibited the sustainability of its impact. The programme of the inaugural public concert on 6 March 1913 in the Salle de l'École des Hautes Études Sociales (16 rue de la Sorbonne, Paris) consisted of:

Paul Martineau:	Sonatine, violin and piano
Louis Bourgault-Ducaudray:	*Mélodies gaéliques* (4), piano
Swan Hennessy:	*Pièces celtiques*, Op. 45, piano
Maurice Duhamel:	*Chansons bretonnes* (3), soprano and piano
Paul Ladmirault:	(2 excerpts from) *Dominical*, vocal quartet
Louis Vuillemin:	*Crépuscule*, vocal quartet and string quartet
J. Guy Ropartz:	*Air de Tual* (from Act 2 of *Le Pays*), soprano and piano
Louis Aubert:	*Sur le rivage*, from *Sillages*, Op. 27, for piano
Paul Ladmirault:	*Chemin creux* & *Minuit dans les clairières*, for piano
Paul Le Flem:	Piano Quintet

The long review article that Louis Vuillemin wrote about the event in *Comoedia* is for the most part concerned with justifying the event as such and with emphasising that the music of Breton composers does not necessarily need themes from Breton traditional music in order to sound Breton, because it is the spirit of this music that is more important:

---

[44] Kelly (ed.), *French Music*, 'Introduction', p. 1.
[45] Kelly (ed.), *French Music*, 'Introduction', p. 5.

Few people, not even musical people, have a feeling for Breton music. [...] With the exception of one man, Bourgault-Ducaudray, no composer ever dared to popularise the admirable folklore of Brittany. Even less to explain the meaning, the particularity, the richness and the relationships that ultimately exist between these natural songs and music. [...] The borrowing of a popular tune can be rewarding, if it is exceptional. However, we should prefer to study it. Let's listen to these songs. Let's enjoy them. Let's learn with what mysterious breath they come to life, with what secret fragrance they embalm us.[46]

In fact, while the songs by Bourgault-Ducaudray and Duhamel on the programme of the inaugural concert were arrangements of traditional songs and a majority of the other pieces were quite directly inspired by Breton traditional music, a work like Aubert's *Sillages*, Op. 27 (1912) evokes the spirit of the sea on the Breton coastline without any allusion to traditional music. Le Flem's Piano Quintet in E minor (1910), which had received its first performance at a 1910 concert of the Société Nationale, is strongly inspired by Breton folk music, particularly by the uneven rhythms and the pentatonic character of the themes, but does not quote any existing traditional tunes. Its Impressionist harmonic language quite obscures the ethnic allusions.[47]

A brief notice in the *Allgemeine Musikzeitung* also acknowledged the first concert of the ACB, emphasising the refreshing quality of music that is rooted in a type of traditional music that has not yet been exploited by too many musicians:

The Association of Breton Composers, of which as a 'Celt', i. e. Irishman, Swan Hennessy – great in the small forms – is also a member, presented in its last concert works by this master as well as by Ropartz, Ladmirault, Vuillemin, L. Aubert and Bourgault-Ducoudray; there is usually something healthy and fresh in this music, since it is rooted in a rich but still little exploited folk music.[48]

As a postscript to the issue of memberships in societies, it may be added here that Hennessy also became a member of the Union Syndicale des Compositeurs de Musique on the recommendation of his Breton colleagues Haudebert, Ladmirault, and Le

---

[46] '*Peu de gens dans le public, voire dans le public musical ont le sentiment de la musique bretonne. [...] À l'exception d'un seul homme, Bourgault-Ducaudray, nul compositeur ne s'avisa jamais de populariser l'admirable folklore de Bretagne. Encore moins d'en expliquer le sens, la particularité, la richesse et les rapports enfin qui existent entre ces chants naturels et la musique. [...] L'emprunt d'une mélodie populaire peut être heureux, s'il est exceptionnel. Il lui faut cependant préférer l'étude. Écoutons ces chants. Aimons-les. Sachons de quel souffle mystérieux ils s'animent ; de quel parfum secret ils embaument.*'; L. Vuillemin in *Comoedia*, 13 March 1913, p. 2.
[47] Bernard-Krauß, *Hundert Jahre Musikgeschichte*, p. 23. The author dates the work to 1905, but this is not supported by other sources. It was published in 1911.
[48] '*Der Verein der bretonischen Komponisten, dem als "Kelte", d. i. Irländer auch der im Kleinen große Swan Hennessy angehört, führte in seinem letzten Konzert Werke dieses Meisters und von Ropartz, Ladmirault, Vuillemin, L. Aubert und Bourgault-Ducoudray vor; es ist meist etwas gesundes und frisches in dieser Musik, da sie in einer reichen, aber noch wenig verwerteten Volksmusik wurzelt.*'; *Allgemeine Musikzeitung* 40:35/36, 5 September 1913, p. 1111.

Flem.⁴⁹ This, however, seems to have been more of a trade union than a lobbying organisation.

Pièces celtiques, Op. 45 (1912) for piano

Hennessy's *Pièces celtiques* received their first performance at the inaugural concert of the Association des Compositeurs Bretons on 6 March 1913 in Paris in a rendering by Antoinette Veluard, a noted pianist of the time specialising in contemporary French music. They were written in late 1912, perhaps in anticipation of the ACB event, and consist of three untitled movements (rather than pieces) that would add up to about seven minutes in performance. It is Hennessy's first composition with the epithet 'celtique', and it seems like an obvious choice that acknowledges the common 'Celtic' background of the works performed on this occasion.

The print does not bear any dedication, but two copies have survived with undated personal autograph dedications, one to Heinrich Möller, the Paris correspondent of the *Allgemeine Musikzeitung* (*'Meinem lieben Freunde Heinrich Möller, Swan Hennessy'*), and the other to the prominent French writer Romain Rolland (*'Monsieur Romain Rolland / Hommage d'admiration sincère / Swan Hennessy'*).⁵⁰ It is impossible to ascertain how stringently Hennessy pursued such marketing on his own behalf. In Möller's case, there was a personal friendship, with Hennessy probably enjoying the opportunity to practise his German. In Rolland's case, Hennessy was evidently aware of his writings on music; however, no source suggesting any personal acquaintance has been identified, although this cannot be excluded.

The first movement is in an A–B–A form, beginning and ending with eight-bar phrases in slow tempo and in a B flat major key that frame a considerably faster central section in C major. As usual, however, the key is but a relative indication of what really occurs in the music, and this becomes very evident in the unusual chordal progressions that accompany the 'Celtic' tune (Ex. 6.4):

The accompaniment to the 'tune', particularly as it passes through bars 5 and 6, is the clearest sign that the piece is not a mere harmonisation of a traditional melody. Indeed, the odd harmony is already preceded by an odd turn of phrase in the melody in bar 4 where the high B (not flattened) would never occur in a traditional tune in Ireland or Scotland. In fact, the geographic provenance Hennessy is aiming at is not entirely clear. The whole piece makes abundant use of the 'Scotch snap', which we had already observed in earlier works that Hennessy clearly placed in Ireland. Were it not for this small rhythmic device (the little semiquaver leaps upwards or downwards), the tune itself might well be located in Ireland.

---

⁴⁹ His undated membership application is in the Bibliothèque Nationale de France (Bibliothèque-Musée de l'Opéra/Magasin de la Réserve), call number 'LAS Hennessy (Swan)'.

⁵⁰ Thuringian State Music Archive, Weimar, Estate Heinrich Möller, call number NHM/2, Nr. 78; Bibliothèque Nationale de France (Dép. Musique/Richelieu), call number VMG 38175. Hennessy also used these words to Rolland in a copy of his Op. 46bis.

Ex. 6.4: *Pièces celtiques*, Op. 45, 1st movt, bars 1–8

Compared to earlier Irish-tinged works of his – even those of three years earlier at the beginning of this chapter – the harmonic language shows a marked development and now includes a number of passages in whole-tone sequences, particularly in the central part, that show how his French Impressionist works of the past few years have rubbed off – see, for example, the triplets starting from D♭ through E♭, F, and G (Ex. 6.5).

Ex. 6.5: *Pièces celtiques*, Op. 45, 1st movt, bars 30–43

The second movement is to be played *'dans l'esprit d'une légende'*. In an F major key, it begins in moderate tempo, featuring another clear melodic line to a very 'French' accompaniment, the only Irish aspect about it being the occasional snaps that are, however, less prevalent than in the first movement. It comes to a rather abrupt end in a second section marked *'mystérieux'* (♪ = 144), with heavily accentuated chords combining triadic with quartal harmony. The piece subsides silently with an allusion to the theme of the beginning, underlining its cyclic design.

In the third movement, Hennessy quotes the well-known Irish reel tune 'The Ewe with the Crooked Horn' that he found as no. 918 in the Petrie Collection. As before in the *Petite suite irlandaise*, Op. 29, he gives the Petrie Collection as his source (in the form of a small footnote in the score), but does not mention the name (or number) of the tune, leaving the proper identification to posterity. He facilitates the search, though, by resorting (again) to a tune from Cork – as such it has been designated by Petrie/Stanford. It seems like Hennessy had consciously searched the collection for tunes from his family's region. Hennessy transposes it from A minor (Petrie) to G minor.

Ex. 6.6: *Pièces celtiques*, Op. 45, 3rd movt, bars 1–15

The tune begins in bar 4, in the low registers of the left hand, and it occurs again later in the right hand. The piece remains in this mood (and the clear G minor tonality) for most of the duration of the piece except for a more abstract part in the central section where he plays with rhythmic elements of the tune that undergo some modest harmonic modulation. Hennessy has a light approach to the tune, not overburdening it with too sophisticated variations, and develops it further by using characteristic motivic elements from the tune and amalgamating these with his own creative ideas, with quite a felicitous result.

Writing about the performance at the ACB recital (to which he had himself contributed), Louis Vuillemin enigmatically described the work as 'bearing their quality in their very title'.[51] A German critic, hearing Hennessy perform this work himself a few months later in Berlin, was left unsatisfied. His words, however, suggest that his impression was only in part due to the unusual chordal progressions noted above but also to the melodic characteristics of the Irish tune in the third movement, which sounded 'wrong' to him:

---

[51] '*elles portent leur qualité dans leur titre même*'; L. Vuillemin, 'La Semaine musicale', p. 2.

The 'Celtic pieces', even if one takes the greatest possible consideration of the intended exotic character, do not satisfy because of their hair-raising chords and the conclusions that look like mischief. Obviously, the composer has a preference for the latter; they can also be found in other places.[52]

An unnamed French critic was particularly fond of the second movement, 'one of the most gentle evocations of naive art we have ever heard'.[53]

Portrait article in London

The *London Musical News* of 4 January 1913 carried the first ever portrait article about Swan Hennessy, a rather late event considering that Hennessy was already 47 years of age. The article contains some information that has not occurred in any previous review of a Hennessy composition, which is why the article is probably the result of an interview or a personal meeting between the (unnamed) journalist and the composer. This means that Hennessy is likely to have visited London in late December 1912 or during the very first days of January 1913. We know he was a frequent traveller to many places in Europe, but often it is not at all clear what he did on those journeys or whether they were motivated by pursuing his musical career. There is reason to believe that many of them had private or family reasons.

In this case, he at least partly used the journey to London to promote his music. The article is a short portrait of some 750 words, simply headed 'Mr. Swan Hennessy'.[54] It sounds much like a public relations exercise, designed to make the British public aware of his work so far. The promotional nature of the piece becomes clear from the very first paragraph:

> THE composer of real inspiration who has originality and an individuality of expression finds, through the spread of musical culture, a ready public for his works. This is especially true if they are cast in the lighter forms, as are those of Mr. Swan Hennessy, which have reached us from his publishers. They are mostly written for the piano, and have become very popular in France, and are gradually making their way in England. They well deserve this success, for their melodies have an attractiveness and distinction which gives them a charm quite their own. They are harmonized with an instinctive feeling for variety of tone and atmosphere which makes them grateful to the pianist and appealing to the music lover.

The assertion that his music has 'become very popular in France' is, as we know, quite an exaggeration, as are similar statements like that his very first work, *Ländliche Skizzen*, Op. 1 'made a hit' or that the Violin Sonata, Op. 14 'is a well-known favourite

---

[52] '[…] *befriedigen die "Keltischen Stücke", wenn man auch auf den beabsichtigten exotischen Charakter die größtmögliche Rücksicht nimmt, wegen ihrer haarsträubenden Akkordverbindungen und der wie Unfug aussehenden Schlüsse nicht. Offenbar hat der Komponist für letztere eine Vorliebe; sie finden sich auch an anderen Stellen.*'; Richard J. Eichberg in *Deutsche Tonkünstler-Zeitung*, 20 November 1913.
[53] '*Swan Hennessy présente ses Pièces Celtiques, dont la deuxième est une des plus suaves évocations d'art naïf que nous ayons entendues.*'; *La Revue musicale S.I.M.* 10, 1 February 1914, p. 68.
[54] Contained in vol. 1 of his Press Books (no page references).

in Paris'. Since nobody at the time in England could prove or disprove statements of this kind, he could simply maintain they were true, even though there is the possibility that these works received a certain measure of success that is not supported by the documented evidence.

The author names a few of the titles and subtitles of his descriptive piano music, adding, comprehensibly:

> Bearing in mind these descriptions one is able when listening to these selections to conjure up a vivid mental picture, but the test of their real value is found in the fact that the music per se, when the listener is not aware of these indications, still makes its appeal so potently that it affords rare pleasure.

The article mentions Hennessy's father by name, explains his American birth and Irish background, commenting 'it will be seen that he has the Gaelic temperament and rich musical endowment of his race', which had also given to the world composers such as Arthur Sullivan and Charles Villiers Stanford. This portrait is also the first source to name Hennessy's teacher of composition at Stuttgart, Percy Goetschius. In describing the years of travel during the 1890s, the writer makes the point of describing Hennessy's gift of observation, which so strongly informs his programme music, as a result of this period.

What follows is a list of his works up to the *Suite*, Op. 46 for string quartet and some of his publishers. It ends with the optimistic remark:

> His striving after an ideal has aroused wide interest in his compositions, and they will doubtless soon become as well known in London as they are now in the French capital.

Thus, while the article does contain some valuable information, not so far available elsewhere, its prime objective is to advertise himself. The article does not contain any critical examination or neutral assessment of his accomplishments. It should rather be understood as the gradual realisation on Hennessy's part that he could not rely on publishers alone to make a name for himself.

Two 1913 journeys to Berlin

Through his German education, Hennessy was acutely aware of the importance of the German market for the distribution and performance of his music. Besides works published in Germany (Schott and Breitkopf & Härtel), he also travelled to Berlin several times to perform (or have others perform) his music. He was, for instance, warmly received on 13 March 1913, just a week after the inaugural recital of the ACB, when Ella Jonas-Stockhausen gave the first performance of Hennessy's *Fêtes*, Op. 36, in the composer's presence. The programme also included works by Volkmar Andreae, Albert Bertelin, Théodore Dubois, Heinz Tiessen, and Charles-Marie Widor (see Chapter 5, p. 149).

Since this concert must have been planned well before the Breton event, he was not keen to have any of his (still small) oeuvre of 'Celtic' music included. But the remarkable fact about this recital is that here Swan Hennessy went all the way to Berlin to hear four minutes of his music performed by a prominent pianist and take a bow during the applause.

It seems like he also made arrangements for his next sojourn to Berlin, eight months later, when he rented the Choralionsaal on 12 November 1913, when he performed himself several of his piano works, also engaging the soprano Marguerite Sonntag for some of his songs accompanied by the Marix Loevensohn Quartet, which also gave the first performance of his *Suite*, Op. 46 for string quartet. The cellist Marix Loevensohn had already played some pieces (not by Hennessy) with Ella Jonas-Stockhausen at the event in March.

The event was announced as a '*Swan Hennessy-Abend*' (Swan Hennessy Evening), a bold undertaking for someone as unknown as he was. All he could build on were the positive reviews of his music in the German musical press and the celebrity of his co-performers aided, perhaps, by the confidence that his German language competence may have given him. It was also the first time ever that Hennessy performed his own works in public, at age 47! One might say, he used Berlin as an experimental field so that in case he would fail it would not harm his career in Paris.

The programme consisted of:

1. *Pièces celtiques*, op. 45[55]	the composer
2. Songs with string quartet accomp.[56]	Marguerite Sonntag with the
– *Lydia*, Op. 23 No. 1	Marix Loevensohn Quartet
– *Unter des Laubdach's Hut*, Op. 30 No. 1	
– *Epiphanie*, Op. 23 No. 2	
– *Annie*, Op. 26	
3.a) *Aus dem täglichen Leben* ('From Everyday Life')[57]	the composer
– *Basse-cour*, Op. 22 No. 3	
– *Dans une petite ville flamande le Dimanche*, Op. 40 No. 3	
– *Ouvriers allants à l'usine*, Op. 44 No. 1	
– *Petites scènes parisiennes: Montrouge le matin*, Op. 27 No. 4a	
– *Dans un atelier de couturiers*, Op. 47 No. 3	
b) *Sonatine*, Op. 43	the composer
4. *Suite* Op. 46 for String Quartet	Marix Loevensohn Quartet

---

[55] Announced as *Keltische Stücke*, op. 45 a) B-dur, b) F-dur, c) G-moll.
[56] Announced as '*Lieder mit Streichquartett-Begleitung*'. Some opus numbers have later been changed (see Table 4.1): *Lydia* became Op. 23 only (no separate numbers); *Unter des Laubdach's Hut* ('Under the Greenwood Tree') was withdrawn shortly afterwards; *Epiphanie* became Op. 26; and *Annie* Op. 31 No. 1.
[57] In the programme, they were announced in German translations: *Hühnerhof / In einem vlämischen Städtchen am Sonntag / Zur Fabrik ziehende Arbeiter / Pariser Vorstadt in der Frühe / In einem pariser Näherinnen-Atelier*.

There were quite a few reviews in the local as well as general musical press, naturally differing in their opinion about the merits of the music and the performances. A reviewer in the *Lokal-Anzeiger* wrote:

> In the Choralionsaal yesterday (Wednesday) the Parisian composer Swan Hennessy, an Irishman by birth, gave a well-attended composer evening in which he received a very warm success. Hennessy is a very likeable artist. Some small piano pieces, however, are, perhaps, more suited for dealing with them quietly in intimate circles rather than for the concert hall; pretty, distinctive ideas appearing in an abundantly aphoristic garb. Four songs with string quartet accompaniment performed in an appealing manner by the soprano Marguerite Sonntag contained the comparatively least of lasting value. But a Sonatina, Op. 43, which the composer – like all piano pieces – performed himself, and a Suite, Op. 46, for string quartet, which was helped by Loevensohn's chamber music association to an excellent sounding life, contained so much genuine, harmonious, sympathetically touching music that one can only wish that Hennessy would create much more of this kind. This is something that is lacking these days.[58]

Another very positive review also applauded Hennessy's pianistic talents and emphasised the qualities of songs when accompanied by a string quartet:

> The concert of Swan Hennessy's own compositions on Wednesday in the Choralionsaal offered a wealth of interesting musical pieces. Hennessy, a native Irishman who received his musical education in Germany, now lives in Paris and is therefore influenced by the younger French direction. He is a peculiar talent and has his own characteristics, which could be described as *'genre miniature'*. He also knows how to present his compositions excellently on the piano and achieved great applause with it. Miss Marguerite Sonntag sang four fine and atmospheric songs with an excellently beautiful, sonorous and well-educated voice. She was accompanied by the Loevensohn Quartet; one can only enjoy again and again the so rare combination of singing and quartet accompaniment. The quartet then played a very melodious suite for string quartet that best expresses the composer's individual talent with a very good tone and the most subtle nuances. All in all, a very remarkable evening.[59]

---

[58] *'Im Choralionsaale gab gestern (Mittwoch) der Pariser Komponist Swan Hennessy, von Geburt ein Ire, einen gut besuchten, von sehr warmem Erfolge begleiteten Komponistenabend. Hennessy ist ein sehr sympathischer Kleinkünstler. Einige kleine Klavierstücke allerdings mehr für die stille Beschäftigung damit in intimem Kreise als für den Konzertsaal geeignet, hübsche, aparte Einfälle treten in reichlich aphoristischem Gewande auf. Vier von der Sopranistin Marguerite Sonntag ansprechend vorgetragene Lieder mit Streichquartettbegleitung enthielten relativ am wenigsten von bleibendem Werte. Aber eine Sonatine, op. 43, die der Komponist, wie alle Klavierstücke, selbst vortrug, und eine Suite, op. 46, für Streichquartett, der die Loevensohnsche Vereinigung für Kammermusik ausgezeichnet zu tönendem Leben verhalf, enthalten so viel echte, klingende, sympathisch berührende Musik, daß man nur wünschen kann, Hennessy möge noch viel von dieser Art schaffen. Daran mangelt es in unseren Tagen.';* 'A. Sn.' in *Lokal-Anzeiger*, 13 November 1913.

[59] *'Das am Mittwoch im Choralionsaal gegebene Konzert eigener Kompositionen von Lwan Henessy* [sic!] *bot eine Fülle interessanter Musikstücke. Henessy, ein geborener Irländer, der seine musikalische Ausbildung in Deutschland erhalten hat, lebt jetzt in Paris und steht infolgedessen heute unter dem Einflusse der jüngeren französischen Richtung. Er ist ein eigenartiges Talent und hat sein eigenes Gepräge, das man als* genre

The critic in the *Deutsche Tonkünstler-Zeitung* did not agree with the positive judgement about Hennessy's pianistic abilities:

> As a pianist, Hennessy is not outstanding. One does not get the impression of an artist but of a schoolmaster.[60]

The *Allgemeine Musikzeitung* which had featured so many reviews of Hennessy's printed music in the past years had mixed feelings, applauding the characteristic piano pieces, including the *Sonatine*, but was less taken with the songs. The quartet suite raised hopes for more substantial pieces:

> There is no doubt that these specimens of Hennessy's works speak for a beautiful and promising talent from which the world can still expect many valuable offerings of a smaller format. The composer will still have to prove whether his creative powers are sufficient for works of a larger kind. At any rate, the Suite for string quartet contains hopeful indications in this direction.[61]

In this chorus of rather positive reviews, the outright negative one published in the newspaper *Der Reichsanzeiger* appears like the exception confirming the rule:

> All the pieces heard here had little invention, so that they could only be perceived as occasional music; nowhere a characteristic trait, a personal touch. Merely the works 'Aus dem täglichen Leben' (From Everyday Life) showed passable skills: small, meaningless piano pieces intended to illustrate the French worker, the seamstress, in her work. A sonatina and a string quartet seemed so weak that the performers had difficulty in giving them even the slightest success. The young singer's voice and skills were barely sufficient for the concert hall.[62]

---

miniature *bezeichnen könnte. Er weiß auch selbst seine Kompositionen am Klavier vorzüglich zur Geltung zu bringen und erzielte damit großen Beifall. Fräulein Marguerite Sonntag sang vier feine und stimmungsreiche Lieder mit hervorragend schöner, klangvoller und wohlgebildeter Stimme, sie wurde vom Loevensohnquartett begleitet; man kann nur immer wieder an der so seltenen Zusammenstellung von Gesang und Quartettbegleitung seine Freude haben. Die Quartettvereinigung spielte dann noch eine sehr wohlklingende und für das eigenartige Talent des Komponisten am meisten sprechende Suite für Streichquartett mit sehr guter Tongebung und subtilster Nuance. Alles in allem ein sehr beachtenswerter Abend.'*, 'K. H.' in *Norddeutsche Allgemeine Zeitung*, 16 November 1913.

[60] '*Als Pianist ist Hennessy nicht herausragend. Man hat bei seinem Spiel nicht den Eindruck des Künstlers sondern des Schulmeisters.*'; Richard J. Eichberg in *Deutsche Tonkünstler-Zeitung*, 20 November 1913.

[61] '*Aus den dargebotenen Proben Hennessyschen Schaffens spricht ohne Zweifel ein schönes und aussichtsreiches Talent, von dem die Mitwelt noch manch wertvolle Gaben kleineren Formats erwarten darf. Ob die Schöpferkraft auch für Werke größeren Stils ausreicht, das wird der Komponist noch nachzuweisen haben. In der Streichquartett-Suite finden sich jedenfalls hoffnungsvolle Ansätze dazu.*'; Paul Schwers in *Allgemeine Musikzeitung* 40:47, 21 November 1913, p. 1488.

[62] '*Sämtliche hier zu Gehör gebrachte Tondichtungen wiesen nur wenig Erfindung auf, sodaß man in ihnen eigentlich nur Gelegenheitsmusik erblicken konnte, nirgends ein charakteristischer Zug, eine persönliche Note. Leidliches Können zeigten die Werke „Aus dem täglichen Leben": kleine, wenig sagende Klavierstückchen, die den französischen Arbeiter, die Näherin in ihrem Tun illustrieren sollen. Eine Sonatine und ein Streichquartett*

Assisting Hennessy's sojourn to Berlin, it seems likely that it was Heinrich Möller who was consulted by Hennessy and who may have indicated to him that the Choralionsaal was a suitable location, perhaps even suggesting names of musicians. The German music critic was a friend of Hennessy's since at least 1909. A postcard dated 6 August 1913, preserved among Hennessy's papers in his family, is further proof of their close contact (Fig. 6.3). Apparently, around this time Möller had lent money from Hennessy and returned it now, writing to Hennessy's holiday address in the Breton coastal town of Pornichet.

Fig. 6.3: Postcard by Heinrich Möller to Swan Hennessy, 6 August 1913

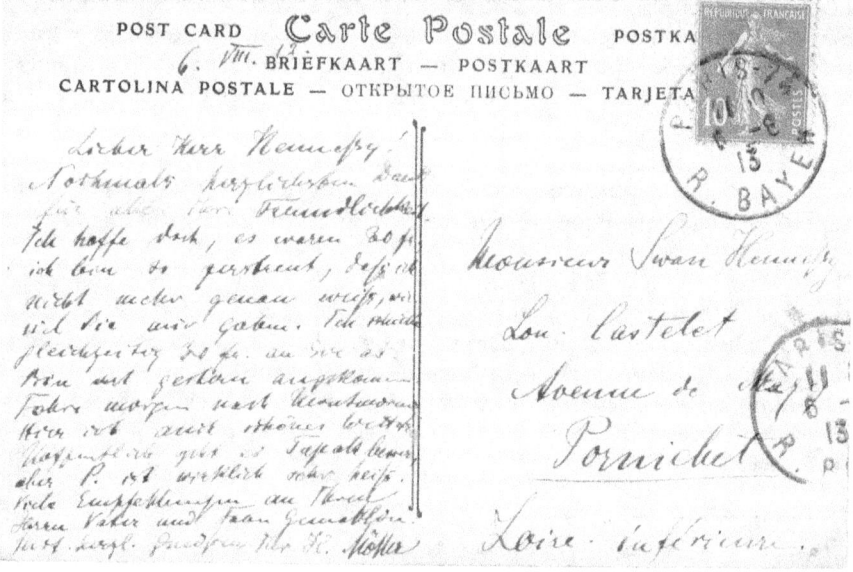

Dear Mr Hennessy!
Many thanks again for all your kindness. I hope it was 30 fr.; I am so absent-minded that I no longer know exactly how much you gave me. I am sending you 30 fr. at the same time. I only arrived yesterday. Will go to Montmorency tomorrow. Here, there is also nice weather. Hopefully there will be [days as better?], but P[aris] is really very hot. Best regards to your father and wife.
With cordial greetings, your H. Möller[63]

---

wirkten so schwächlich, daß die ausübenden Künstler Mühe hatten, ihnen auch nur einen Achtungserfolg zu verschaffen. Stimme und Gesangskunst der jugendlichen Sängerin war für den Konzertsaal kaum ausreichend.'; Der Reichsanzeiger, 18 November 1913.
[63] *'Lieber Herr Hennessy! Nochmals herzlichen Dank für alle Ihre Freundlichkeit. Ich hoffe doch, es waren 30 fr., ich bin so zerstreut, daß ich nicht mehr genau weiß, wie viel Sie mir gaben. Ich schicke gleichzeitig 30 fr. an Sie ab. Bin erst gestern angekommen. Fahre morgen nach Montmorency. Hier ist auch schönes Wetter. Hoffentlich [gibt es Tage als besser], aber P. ist wirklich sehr heiß. Viele Empfehlungen an Ihren Herrn Vater*

One of the papers Möller wrote for was the German-language *Pariser Zeitung* that catered for the German community in Paris. In one of his articles he remarked about the diversity of the Parisian concert scene of November 1913, singling out the second recital of the Association des Compositeurs Bretons that took place on the 26th in the Salle des Agriculteurs at the Sorbonne (see Fig. 6.2). Two weeks after the Swan Hennessy Evening in Berlin, this included the second performance of Hennessy's *Suite*, Op. 46 for string quartet. He wrote:

> The lack of space and the already beginning abundance of musical events forbid me to deal with the chamber music evenings of the Chaigneau siblings, the double quintet and the Société des Compositeurs Français, the choral concerts at the Sorbonne (with Handel's Messiah) and the Schola Cantorum (cantatas), and the last vocal evenings of Yvette Guilbert. I would only highlight the Suite for String Quartet by the Irishman Swan Hennessy and the arrangements of Breton folk music by Duhamel, Jean Huré and Sauvrezis from the interesting concert by the Breton composers with 'Celtic' music as significant new creations of racy beauty because of their folk influence.[64]

The programme of this ACB event consisted of:

1. J. Guy Ropartz — *Sonata* for Violin and Piano
   (Gaston Le Feuve, vn; Antoinette Veluard, pf)

2. Alice Sauvrezis
   a. *Détresse*, for cor anglais and piano
   b. *Allégresse*, for oboe and piano
   (Louis Bleuzet, c.a./ob; A. Sauvrezis, pf)

3. Louis Vuillemin — *Soirs armoricains*, Op. 21, for piano
   a. No. 1, *Au large des clochers*
   b. No. 3, *À l'ancre, en Sainte-Anne-la-Palud*
   c. No. 5, *Carillons dans la baie*
   (Maurice Dumesnil, pf)

4. Paul Ladmirault
   a. *Aubépine*, for soprano and piano
   b. *La Flûte*, for soprano and piano
   (Lucy Vuillemin, S; Ermend Bonnal, pf)

---

und Frau Gemahlin. Mit herzl. Grüßen, Ihr H. Möller'; postcard in Hennessy Family Collection, reproduced with permission. In the unreadable part, Möller probably omitted a word in error.
[64] '*Der Mangel an Raum und die schon beginnende Fülle der musikalischen Ereignisse verbieten es mir, auf die Kammermusikabende der Geschwister Chaigneau, des Doppelquintetts und der Societe des compositeurs français, die Chorkonzerte der Sorbonne (Messias von Händel) und der Schola cantorum (Kantaten), und die letzten Liederabende von Yvette Guilbert einzugehen. Nur aus dem interessanten Konzert der bretonischen Komponisten mit „keltischer" Musik seien als bedeutende Neuschöpfung von rassiger Schönheit die Suite für Streichquartett von dem Irländer Swan Hennessy und die Bearbeitungen bretonischer Volksmusik von Duhamel, Jean Hure [sic!] und Sauvrezis wegen ihres völkischen Gepräges hervorgehoben.*'; Heinrich Möller in *Pariser Zeitung*, 3 December 1913.

5. Paul Martineau *Petite suite sur des airs populaires nantais*, for pf duet
    (Jean Huré & Paul Martineau, pf 4-hands)

    – Break –

6. Maurice Duhamel (arr.) *Kanaouennou Breiz-Izel*, for voice and pf
    (*Chants populaires de Basse-Bretagne*)
    a. *An durzunel* (la tourterelle)
    b. *Silvestrik*

    (M. Nucelly, v; M. Duhamel, pf)

7. Paul Le Flem a. *Par landes*, for piano
    b. *Avril*, for piano

    (Maurice Dumesnil, piano)

8. Jean Huré *Chansons de Bretagne*, for soprano & piano
    a. *Belle, j'entends bien …*
    b. *La Petite lingère*
    c. *Le Petit cordonnier*

    (Lucy Vuillemin, S; J. Huré, pf)

9. Swan Hennessy *Suite*, Op. 46, for string quartet
    (Quatuor Le Feuve)

According to the programme, several pieces received their first performance, including Vuillemin's *Soirs armoricains*, Duhamel's *Kanaouennou Breiz-Izel*, and Hennessy's quartet, but at least for the Hennessy work we know that this was not the case. Remarkably, several of the works involving a piano featured the composers themselves, such as the works by Sauvrezis, Martineau, Duhamel, and Huré, making this concert an exceptionally interesting event.

The attractive concert had also aroused the interest of the well-known critic Émile Vuillermoz (1878–1960). He wrote in *Comoedia*:

> The concert of Celtic music should be given a special mention. To the difficult problem of the logical composition of a programme, the Association of Breton Composers has just provided a very ingenious solution: it is in the memories of their cradle, it is in their ethnic kinship, it is in a fraternally shared heritage, that these sons of Armor have discovered the precious secret of unity. Certainly, we must not let ourselves be induced into too easy generalisations borrowed from history or geography, and it is quite obvious that life has been responsible for clearly differentiating between the nine uprooted people who took us for confidants during this evening, but it is nevertheless true that some confessions characteristic of their sensitivities betray their nostalgia for the absent homeland. Their music is always homesick and this deaf pedal of melancholy that runs through their most disparate works brings them closer to each other and unites them like an invisible thread holding the pearls of a necklace. The same horizons, the same colours, the same visual and auditory impressions have educated their senses; all have the same sense of nature, all unintentionally paint the same landscape. They have similar hauntings: they hear eternal

bells as do the Flames, the powdery sound of carillons in the atmosphere, and we see in the transparency of their harmonies, as if they were escaping from the engulfed belfries of the city of Ys, the rising and blossoming of the Angelus.[65]

Unfortunately, apart from this flowery, yet sympathetic interpretation of the association's intention and common identity, Vuillermoz does not say much about the actual compositions performed on that evening, the only comment about the Hennessy quartet being that is was 'justly acclaimed' (*justement acclamé*).

At least Vuillermoz did not question the presence of Swan Hennessy in a programme of Breton composers, as did (apparently) the critic 'Santillane' (probably a pseudonym) in *Gil Blas*.[66] S/He listed the names of the eight Breton composers present on the programme, and dutifully ignored the ninth, the Irish-American. Apart from this *faux-pas*, s/he commented:

> It [the ACB] has just given a very remarkable and, in some respects, exceptional concert that allowed a large audience to applaud likeable, graceful and powerful music of undeniable originality. This was, as we hoped, very loyally dependent on Brittany, its harsh land, its stormy sea, and the so picturesque character of its customs. In the end, this is very sincere music, realised as works of art by gifted and very knowledgeable composers.[67]

---

[65] '*Il faut accorder au Concert de musique celtique une mention particulière. Au difficile problème de la composition logique d'un programme, l'association des compositeurs bretons vient, en effet, d'apporter une solution très ingénieuse : c'est dans les souvenirs de leur berceau, c'est dans leur parenté ethnique, c'est dans un héritage fraternellement partagé, que ces fils d'Armor ont découvert le précieux secret de l'unité. Certes, il ne faut pas se laisser entrainer à de trop faciles généralisations empruntées à l'histoire où à la géographie et il est bien évident que la vie s'est chargée de différencier tes nettement les neuf déracinés qui nous prirent pour confidents au cours de cette soirée, mais il n'en est pas moins vrai que certains aveux caractéristiques de leurs sensibilités trahissent leur commune nostalgie de la patrie absente. Leur musique a toujours le mal du « Pays » et cette sourde pédale de mélancolie qui traverse leurs œuvres les plus disparates les rapproche et les unit comme un fil invisible retient les perles d'un collier. Les mêmes horizons, les mêmes colorations, les mêmes impressions visuelles et auditives ont éduqué leurs sens ; tous ont le même sentiment de la nature, tous, sans le vouloir, peignent le même paysage. Ils ont des hantises semblables : ils entendent de cloches éternelles se grisent, comme des Flamands, de poudroiement sonore des carillons dans l'atmosphère et l'on voit dans la transparence de leurs harmonies, comme s'ils s'échappaient des beffrois engloutis de la ville d'Ys, monter et s'épanouir des angelus.*'; Émile Vuillermoz in *Comoedia*, 8 December 1913, p. 5.

[66] The seemingly female pseudonym 'Santillane' in *Gil Blas* refers to the original source of the journal's name. This is derived from the novel *Gil Blas de Santillane* by Alain-René Lesage (1668–1747). The pseudonym therefore may not be female at all, but could be any member of the journal's editorial team.

[67] '*Elle vient de donner un très remarquable et, à certains égards, un exceptionnel concert qui permit à un public nombreux d'applaudir des musiques aimables, gracieuses et puissantes, et des talents d'une incontestable originalité. Celle-ci est, comme on l'espérait, très loyalement tributaire de la Bretagne, de son âpre terre, de sa mer orageuse, et du caractère si pittoresque de ses mœurs. C'est là, finalement, de fort sincère musique, réalisée dans l'art par des compositeurs bien doués et très savants.*' This is followed by the list of composers, true in the way she introduces them: '*Les compositeurs bretons, c'étaient, à ce dernier concert, MM. Guy Ropartz, Louis Vuillemin, Paul Ladmirault, Jean Huré, Martineau, Paul Le Flem, Maurice Duhamel et Mlle Alice Sauvrezis.*'; 'Santillane' in *Gil Blas*, 10 December 1913, p. 5.

Heinrich Möller, writing for the *Allgemeine Musikzeitung*, criticised that Vuillermoz did not write more about Hennessy's quartet, which was, in his view, the most convincingly 'Celtic' work of the evening:

> A curious evening was the concert of the Breton composers with 'Celtic' music. The idea of combining composers of similar aims, inspired by the same sharply pronounced and not yet sufficiently exploited folk music, to form a group to oppose Parisian musical cosmopolitanism with a kind of homeland art and to refer French music to a healthy domestic breeding ground, is not so bad. But here, too, the personality and potency of the creator is more important than the material from which he draws. In the works of Guy Ropartz, for example, one searches in vain for local colour and Breton rhythm, the gifted Ladmirault, Paul Le Flem and others get stuck in the problematic, Duhamel, Sanorezis [*sic!*] and Jean Huré give their best in more or less happy folk song arrangements, not to mention others. And just as only the Tyrolean and Wagner pupil Sylvio Lazzari has so far succeeded in creating a great vivid work of art from Breton folk music in his 'Lépreuse', so not only the most mature and perfect in form, but also the most 'Celtic' piece of the Breton evening was the Suite for string quartet by the Irishman Swan Hennessy, which was recently also played in Berlin. Here, too, he received the recognition he deserved from the public and the press, with the exception of Mr Emile Vuillermoz in 'Comoedia', who wrote so many columns about his Breton compatriots that he left no room for the foreigner Hennessy.[68]

The critic, musicologist and philosopher Albert Bazaillas (1865–1924) chimed in with the characterisations of other French critics as to the peculiar spirit of Breton music while also devoting a few sentences to all the works, selectively quoted below. Bazaillas appears to have been impressed and fascinated by the melancholy character of the 'Celtic' music heard that evening. Although he seems to have enjoyed it, his review sounds as if there would have been nothing else apart from melancholy music (how good, then, that the Hennessy quartet ended on a joyful note):

---

[68] '*Ein eigenartiger Abend war das Konzert der Bretonischen Komponisten mit "Keltischer" Musik. Der Gedanke, durch Zusammenfassung gleichstrebender, von derselben scharf ausgeprägten und noch gar nicht genügend verwerteten Volksmusik inspirierter Komponisten zu einer Gruppe eine Art Heimatkunst dem Pariser musikalischen Kosmopolitismus entgegenzusetzen und die französische Musik auf einen gesunden heimischen Nährboden zu verweisen, ist nicht so übel. Aber es kommt auch hier mehr auf die Persönlichkeit und Potenz des Gestaltenden als auf das Material an, aus dem er schöpft. In den Werken von Guy Ropartz z. B. sucht man vergeblich nach Lokalfarbe und bretonischer Rhythmik, der begabte Ladmirault, Paul Le Flem u. a. bleiben im Problematischen stecken, Duhamel, Sanorezis, Jean Huré geben das Beste in mehr oder weniger glücklichen Volksliederbearbeitungen, von andern ganz zu schweigen. Und wie es bisher nur dem Tiroler und Wagnerschüler Sylvio Lazzari gelungen ist, in seiner "Lépreuse" aus der bretonischen Volksmusik ein großes lebendiges Kunstwerk entstehen zu lassen, so war nicht nur das reifste und formvollendetste, sondern auch das "keltischeste" Stück des Bretonenabends die Suite für Streichquartett von dem Irländer Swan Hennessy, die kürzlich auch in Berlin gespielt wurde. Auch hier fand sie die verdiente Anerkennung bei Publikum und Presse, mit Ausnahme des Herrn Emil Vuillermoz von der "Comoedia", der über seine bretonischen Landsleute so viele Spalten vollschrieb, daß er für den Ausländer Hennessy keinen Platz mehr übrig behielt.*'; Heinrich Möller in *Allgemeine Musikzeitung* 41:4, 23 January 1914, p. 100.

> The Breton composers recently gave a concert at the Salle des Agriculteurs, presenting a concert of first-rate artistic and ethnic character. The essential features of the poetry of the Celtic races were manifested in the choice of compositions, all marked by delicious sadness and reflecting popular inspiration with a scent of old legends and ancient beliefs. The beginning of Mr. Guy Ropartz's sonata is, in this respect, representative. [...] A sensation of the sky and sea of Brittany emerges with impressive clarity from the *Soirs armoricains* of Mr Louis Vuillemin. It is yet another mixture of bells and laments that we find in Mr Paul Martineau's Prelude, [...] And the same note of dreamy melancholy reappears, penetrating, in Swan Hennessy's new work. This character of religious gravity and sadness, by circulating in all these pieces, confers on them a kind of unity that is rooted in the race itself and in the conditions of Celtic sensitivity. These compositions remind us of the songs of the bards who cried more about their defeats than they celebrated victories. They form like a long lament that only speaks to us of exile, nostalgia, vertiginous rounds on the moors where the korrigans take us, leaks through the seas. They are not very cheerful. If they sketch a song of joy, it ends inevitably in elegy. There is nothing like their delicious sadness. Hence, the result for these musicians is an uninterrupted melody, with clearly an indefinite character, leading to sadness without purpose and without end.[69]

The closing of the concert with Hennessy's quartet suite was welcomed by the critic Jacques Pillois who also expressed his hope that the ideas of the ACB would gain ground in the future. His comment also suggests that the quartet was well received by the audience:

> As a conclusion to this long programme, the Le Feuve Quartet presented a *Suite* by Mr Swan Hennessy, with excellent quartet writing that features charming effects, uses the most beautiful samples of Irish folklore, and delights by its lightness, the happy proportion of its developments, and its picturesque tone. A bagpipe of four bows occurs in it, and it is [like] the Irish national anthem. The protagonists were applauded as appropriate and the

---

[69] '*Les compositeurs bretons donnaient récemment, à la salle des Agriculteurs, un concert présentant tout ensemble un caractère artistique et un caractère ethnique de premier ordre. Les traits essentiels de la poésie des races celtiques s'y sont manifestés dans le choix des compositions, toutes empreintes d'une délicieuse tristesse et reflétant l'inspiration populaire avec un parfum de vieilles légendes et d'antiques croyances. Le début de la sonate de M. Guy-Ropartz est, à cet égard, représentatif. [...] Une sensation de ciel et de mer de Bretagne se dégage avec une netteté impressionnante des Soirs armoricains de M. Louis Vuillemin. [...] C'est encore un mélange de cloches et de complaintes que nous retrouvons dans le Prélude de M. Paul Martineau, [...] Et la même note de mélancolie rêveuse reparaît, pénétrante, dans l'œuvre nouvelle de Swan Hennessy. Ce caractère de gravité religieuse et de tristesse, en circulant dans tous ces morceaux, leur confère une sorte d'unité qui tient à la race elle-même et aux conditions de la sensibilité celtique. Ces compositions nous rappellent les chants des bardes qui pleuraient plus de défaites qu'ils ne célébraient de victoires. Elles forment comme une longue complainte qui ne nous parle que d'exils, de nostalgies, de rondes vertigineuses sur les landes où nous emportent les korrigans, de fuites à travers les mers. Elles ne s'orientent guère vers la gaieté. Si elles ébauchent un chant de joie, il se termine bien vite en élégie. Rien n'égale leur délicieuse tristesse. De là devait résulter, chez ces musiciens, une mélodie ininterrompue, avec un caractère nettement indéfini, aboutissant à une tristesse sans objet et sans terme.*'; Albert Bazaillas in *La Renaissance*, 20 December 1913, p. 25.

author was called on to appear. The Association of Breton Composers has been endowed with a flowering health: let us hope for splendid growth.[70]

Even *The Times* of London reported about the event, but they sent an utterly conservative correspondent who seemed to object to anything that is new:

> A hearing of Breton composers in November brought forward a new suite for string quartet by Swan Hennessy, and the violin sonata, which dates from 1907, by Guy Ropartz. [...] The hearing of novelties such as these, however, though apt beforehand to excite agreeable curiosity, is seldom in the event keenly satisfactory, for new music is only too apt to be like new wine.[71]

after which the author continued with performances of works by Mozart and Beethoven.

Suite, Op. 46 (1912) for string quartet

Swan Hennessy's first string quartet is merely entitled 'Suite'. It was written in 1912 and published by Demets in the following year. The work is dedicated to the German Impressionist painter (and occasional composer) Carl Heffner (1849–1927), here called *'Monsieur le Professeur'*. Heffner was based in Berlin; he may have assisted in arranging the work's first performance in Berlin on 12 November 1913, but the dedication may also just mean an expression of personal friendship – an earlier work, *Fêtes*, Op. 36 (1910), had already been dedicated to Heffner's wife Betty. The scarcity of relevant sources does not shed any light on the nature of Hennessy's relationship to the Heffners.

Hennessy had written for string quartet before. It will be remembered that there have been several songs with string quartet accompaniment, some of which being arrangements of piano accompaniments, but others like *Lydia*, Op. 23 (1906) are original scores. But the *Suite* is his first proper quartet, a four-movement composition of about 15 minutes in performance, structured in four movements.

At a first hearing, the quartet is quite incoherent in terms of its stylistic language. And the impression of incoherence never quite fades, simply because it is based on fact: we are dealing with a work that features a first and a third movement, which reflect his musical environment in a light-hearted French style. In between comes a slow second movement that reminds of the German late-Romantics, and the fourth is very Irish, finishing with a boisterous finale on the basis of an Irish reel. It comes

---

[70] *'Comme conclusion à ce long programme, le quatuor Le Feuve fit entendre une* Suite *de M. Swan Hennessy, d'une excellente écriture de quatuor qui fourmille d'effets charmants, utilise les plus jolis échantillons du folklore irlandais et ravit, par sa légèreté, l'heureuse proportion de ses développements et son pittoresque. Une cornemuse à quatre archets la traverse, et c'est l'hymne national irlandais. Les protagonistes furent applaudis comme il convenait et l'auteur dut paraître. L'Association des Compositeurs Bretons est douée d'une santé florissante : attendons-nous à une belle croissance.'*; Jacques Pillois in *La Critique musicale*, 2 December 1913.
[71] 'Recent Music in Paris', *The Times*, 24 December 1913, p. 9.

across somewhat as the essence of the previous six years of his musical development, reflecting his search for artistic identity, but it comes all at once in one piece.

The first movement is an *Allegro* in 3/4 time and in a G minor tonality (with numerous modulations, mostly simply between the major and minor scales of G). Rhythmically, the movement is based on a one-bar motif consisting of a quaver, two semiquavers, two quavers and a crotchet. It first occurs in the first violin in bar 10 and the second violin in bar 11. It becomes a structural element from bar 15 when it occurs five times in the second violin, then five times in the cello (Ex. 6.7). This rhythmic element is applied with a great tonal flexibility – such as beginning on different pitches, being applied in major and minor tonalities –, but despite various alterations it still is a consciously repetitive device. Although there are variants as well, it is really this particular figure that is very striking throughout the movement. When it is over, after some four minutes, the listener has heard it exactly 71 times!

Ex. 6.7: *Suite*, Op. 46, 1st movt, bars 15–24

The movement is in classical sonata form, beginning immediately with the exposition of the two contrasting themes; the first occurrence of the rhythmic device observed above follows the first theme and a response, with a calm second theme following immediately in the first violin from bar 20, making a brief entry during letter B only. Much later, a second subject follows at letter F (bar 75ff.), before the recapitulation (theme 1 at letter G, response at H, theme 2 at I).

The second movement is an *Adagio* in D major, in Hennessy's words 'evoking a sweet summer night' (*'une évocation d'une douce nuit d'été'*).⁷² It is a movement of great lyrical beauty, with an expansive and very Romantic thematic gesture that reminds somewhat of the slow movement of Max Reger's last string quartet Op. 121 which, coincidence or not, had just appeared in the year before Hennessy's composition. Although the Reger work is much longer (and generally more substantial), the initial idea, the grand melodic gestures and the contrapuntal treatment are strikingly similar.

Ex. 6.8: *Suite*, Op. 46, 2nd movt, bars 1–13

An *Allegretto* in B minor takes over the role of the *scherzo* in the third movement. It is written in the somewhat unusual time signature of 5/4. With this quality it was included in a list of art music works in 5/4 time in Eaglefield Hull's 1914 harmony textbook.⁷³ For much of the time it is designed as an interplay of contrasting themes between the upper two and the lower two instruments that begin to mingle in the middle of the movement.

---

⁷² Anonymous work commentary in *Le Guide du concert*, 22 November 1913, p. 106–107, which also gives an overview of the principal themes of the quartet in Hennessy's handwriting. That the text is by Hennessy himself becomes clear in his own commented work-list, where the quotation be can be found in almost the same words. Apart from the remark about the summer night, he does not say anything else about the movement.
⁷³ A. Eaglefield Hull, *Modern Harmony*, p. 174.

In the fourth movement the thematic material is based on two tunes from the Petrie Collection of Irish traditional music. Hennessy re-uses two of the themes he had already deployed in the *Petite suite irlandaise*, Op. 29 for piano duet (1908), identifying these in a footnote on page 15 of the score merely as '*Sur des Airs irlandais anciens de la collection Petrie*' without indicating which. The movement begins in G minor with an *Andante sostenuto*, to be played '*très expressif*', on the tune '*Sagairt tar teorádh*'; this is number 1089 respectively 1247 in the Petrie Collection as edited by Stanford, with 'its note of sweet melancholy' ('*sa note de douce mélancolie*').[74] The second theme (*Vivacissimo*) is number 902 with Petrie/Stanford, a lively Irish reel better known as '*Molly on the Shore*', which provides a perfectly Irish *finale* full of bustling fiddles and temperament. Here, Hennessy turns to the tonic major. It enters in the first violin at bar 39, with viola and cello providing the drones of traditional Irish pipes (Ex. 6.9). In his own descriptive comment, Hennessy speaks of 'a kind of Irish jig' ('*l'éspèce de gigue irlandaise*'), but it is obviously not a jig (which is in ternary form) but a reel. Previously, in his Op. 29, he had correctly called the tune a 'Cork reel'.

Ex. 6.9: *Suite*, Op. 46, 4th movt, bars 39–42

The tune of '*Molly on the Shore*' had also been exploited around the same time by the Australian, English-resident composer Percy Grainger (1882–1961) whose several instrumental versions became incomparably more famous than Hennessy's. In fact, Hennessy publicly declared to have preceded Grainger, because he had also used it in the *Petite suite irlandaise*, Op. 29 in 1908. He must have noted the beginning popularity of the Grainger work, prompting him to write a letter to the editor of the *La Tribune musicale*.[75]

---

[74] Hennessy, ibid.
[75] '*Paris, 25 Mars 1914. / Monsieur, / Je viens d'apprendre que "Molly on the shore" de M. Percy Grainger, paru il y a deux ans, est écrit sur le même air populaire irlandais que le dernier mouvement de mon quatuor op. 46. Le dernier mouvement de mon quatuor est une transcription exacte du finale de ma Petite suite irlandaise publiée en 1909, ainsi que témoigne le copyright. / Oserai-je vous demander d'avoir la bonté d'insérer cette lettre dans votre estimable journal? / Avec mes remerciements anticipés, je vous prie d'agréer, Monsieur, mes meilleures salutations / SWAN HENNESSY.*'; *La Tribune musicale*, 1 April 1914.

Paris, 25 March 1914

Sir,

I have just learned that Percy Grainger's "Molly on the shore", published two years ago, is written to the same Irish folk tune as the last movement of my quartet Op. 46. The last movement of my quartet is an exact transcription of the finale of my *Petite suite irlandaise* published in 1909, as evidenced by the copyright date.

May I ask you to be so kind as to publish this letter in your esteemed journal? With my thanks in advance, please accept, Sir, my best regards.

SWAN HENNESSY

It is not quite clear what his intentions were in writing such a letter to a French journal, a rather unlikely place for Grainger to notice it. Besides, legally speaking, Hennessy was not correct in his copyright claim. First of all, there is no copyright at all on folk tunes, they can be used by any composer who wishes to write an arrangement of it; the arrangement, then, is under copyright, but Grainger did not use Hennessy's arrangement. Secondly, Grainger's arrangement (originally in two versions, one for string quartet and one for string orchestra), though published with Schott & Co., London, in 1911, seems already to have been written in July 1907.[76]

Despite the stylistic incoherence of the *Suite* and a few repetitive moments in the first movement, Hennessy himself was quite convinced of this quartet and promoted its performance until he died in 1929. Indeed, after those two early performances in Berlin and Paris in 1913, they were taken up again in the 1920s when the work was heard once more in Berlin, in several localities in France, and also in Dublin (1924). But their number dropped sharply after 1930 when Hennessy was no longer able to promote the work.

Most contemporary critics agreed with the composer's opinion. After the first German performance, one critic wrote the score contained 'so much real, sounding, sympathetically touching music that one can only wish that Hennessy would create much more of this kind. This is what is lacking in our days.'[77] Richard Eichberg thought of it: 'It is very characteristically worked out in its individual movements, with well thought-out contrasts and interesting musical ideas.'[78] Paul Schwers wrote in the *Allgemeine Musikzeitung*:

> The 'Suite for String Quintet' is distinguished by its beautiful treatment of the string instruments, its clear, skilful phrasing and its splendid musical sensitivity. Here the composer knows how to entertain his listeners in a way that is as simple as possible and pleasantly

---

[76] https://imslp.org/wiki/Molly_on_the_Shore_(Grainger%2C_Percy), accessed 26 December 2018.

[77] '[…] *so viel echte, klingende, sympathisch berührende Musik, daß man nur wünschen kann, Hennessy möge noch viel von dieser Art schaffen. Daran mangelt es in unseren Tagen.*'; *Lokal-Anzeiger*, 13 November 1913.

[78] '*Sie ist in ihren einzelnen Sätzen sehr charakteristisch herausgearbeitet, mit wohldurchdachten Gegensätzen und interessanten musikalischen Einfällen.*'; Richard J. Eichberg in *Deutsche Tonkünstler-Zeitung*, 20 November 1913.

deviates from the usual harmonic complexity of the modern French newtonians; indeed, in the nobly felt, expressive Adagio, the composer also strikes deeply inward tones.[79]

The printed score also received positive reviews. Eugen Segnitz appears to have been quite impressed, criticising only the brevity of the musical ideas:

> The four-movement G minor Suite (Op. 46) for string quartet by Swan Hennessy is much easier to comprehend than many of the piano pieces by this original tone poet. First and foremost, the conciseness of the general conception and the clarity of expression as well as the immediate transparency of the material are pleasing. Everything is ordered with sure aesthetic taste, light and shadow are effectively distributed. As characteristic as the formation of the parts is the intelligent use of the four string instruments and their timbres, very peculiar and, e.g. in the first Allegro, the strongly prominent chromatic element. A D major Adagio is of miraculous melodic intensity and such delicate instrumental melodiousness that there is only one thing to be reproached, namely the brevity of this only sketchy, rather than broadly interpreted musical mood.[80]

In the changed world of post-war 1920s Paris, a French critic could not close his eyes (or ears!) to the fact that the *Suite* was written in an all too Romantic style, but he acknowledged after a 1928 performance that it was 'perhaps not very current, but of an intense and sincere poetry' – which is a fair comment to make.[81]

* * *

Another concert of the Association des Compositeurs Bretons – a group, which in Paul Ladmirault's words, 'claims "home rule" for a musical nation unknown to some of our best geographers' – took place on 23 April 1914 at the Salle Érard.[82] The pro-

---

[79] *'Die "Suite für Streichquintett" zeichnet sich durch klangschöne Behandlung der Streichinstrumente, durch klaren, gewandten Satz und prächtiges musikalisches Empfinden aus. Auf denkbar einfache, von der üblichen harmonischen Kompliziertheit moderner französischer Neutöner wohltätig abweichende Art weiß hier der Komponist seine Hörer fesselnd zu unterhalten; ja im edel empfundenen, ausdrucksvollen Adagio schlägt der Komponist auch tiefinnerliche Töne an.';* Paul Schwers in *Allgemeine Musikzeitung* 40:47, 21 November 1913, p. 1488.

[80] *'Die viersätzige G-moll-Suite (op. 46) für Streichquartett von Swan Henessy ist inhaltlich dem Verständnis viel leichter zugänglich als viele Klaviersachen dieses originellen Tonpoeten. In erste Linie gefällt die Knappheit der allgemeinen Fassung und die Klarheit des Ausdrucks wie auch unmittelbare Uebersichtlichkeit des Gedankenmaterials. Mit sicher gehendem ästhetischen Geschmack ist alles geordnet, ist Licht und Schatten wirkungsvoll verteilt. Charakteristisch wie die Führung der Stimmen ist die klüglich verfahrende Ausnützung der vier Saiteninstrumente und ihrer Klangfarben, ganz eigenartig und, z. B. im ersten Allegro, das stark hervortretende chromatische Element. Ein D-dur-Adagio ist von wundersam wirkender melodischer Intensität und solch köstlich instrumentalem Wohlklang, daß man nur eins daran tadeln möchte, nämlich die Kürze dieses nur skizzenhaft angedeuteten, statt breiter ausgeführten musikalischen Stimmungsbildes.';* Eugen Segnitz in *Allgemeine Musikzeitung* 41:21, 22 May 1914, p. 818.

[81] *'peu actuel sans doute, mais d'une poésie intense et sincère';* P. Wolff in *La Liberté*, 15 June 1928.

[82] *'L'Association des Compositeurs Bretons qui revendique le "home rule" pour une nation musicale méconnue de quelques-uns de nos meilleurs géographes, nous conviait jeudi 23 avril, une nouvelle solennité, digne des*

gramme opened with the first public performance of Swan Hennessy's *Petite suite irlandaise*, Op. 29 (1908) for piano duet; the songs *Marine* and *Les Jardins* by Raymond Hervé, *Tout le long de la nuit* and *Lever d'Aube* by Guy Ropartz, and *Partance* and *Chanson de fou* by Paul Martineau; excerpts from the piano suites *En Bretagne* by Rhené-Baton and *Les Lutins* by Louis Aubert; excerpts from *Dominical* for vocal quartet and piano by Paul Ladmirault; the vocal octets *La Neige, La Procession,* and *Vray Dieu qui m'y confortera* by Paul Le Flem; the piano works *Esquisses bretonnes* by Léon Moreau as well as *Dimanche matin* and *Jabadao* by Maurice Duhamel; *Crépuscule* by Louis Vuillemin for vocal octet with string quartet; closing with the string quintet by Jean Huré.

According to Émile Vuillermoz, Aubert, Moreau and Rhené-Baton were new members of the Association, but at least for Aubert and Rhené-Baton this was not true; yet, his review is an interesting perspective on some of the composers on the programme:

> It would be necessary to describe in some detail the last concert of the Association of Breton Composers, always prosperous and vigorous. New members, their birth certificates in hand, demand the Celtic investiture. Louis Aubert, Rhené-Bâton and Léon Moreau eloquently presented their rights. The three new bards were acclaimed by the public. The founders were all here. There is Swan Hennessy and his melancholic and discreet *Suite irlandaise*, Maurice Duhamel and his joyfully colourful piano pieces, Paul Martineau, the SMI foal, and Mr Hervé, a young racy musician who does not wait to have a profession to prove that he has talent. There was the splendid *Quintet* by Jean Huré, a work so deeply lyrical and so generously musical, there was the *Crépuscule* by Louis Vuillemin, in which the author of Gabriel Fauré's monograph proves that we can honour in many ways the genius of a master we love, there were the delicious choral works of Le Flem where, for the first time, a musician of today seems to have understood the lesson of Debussy's *Trois Chansons*, and there was Ladmirault's *Dominical*, this admirable artist, a prodigious inventor of intoxicating harmonic perfumes, but a worried and tortured creator of scruples that paralyse him and prevent him from achieving his full potential in his current works.[83]

---

précédentes, [...] '; Paul Ladmirault in his review of the event in *La Revue musicale S.I.M.*, 1 May 1914, p. 57. 'Home Rule' was the established term for Irish self-government during the two decades before and after 1900. Ladmirault's application of this term for Brittany speaks for the parallels that Breton nationalists saw in the Irish situation.

[83] '*Il faudrait relater avec quelque détail le dernier concert de l'Association des Compositeurs bretons, toujours prospère et vigoureuse. De nouveaux adhérents, leur acte de naissance à la main, réclament l'investiture celtique. Louis Aubert, Rhené-Bâton et Léon Moreau y font valoir leurs droits avec éloquence. Les trois nouveaux bardes sont acclamés par le public. Les fondateurs sont tous là. Voici Swan Hennessy et sa* Suite irlandaise *mélancolique et discrète, Maurice Duhamel et ses pièces de piano si joyeusement colorées, Paul Martineau, poulain de la S.M.I., et M. Hervé, jeune musicien de race qui n'attend pas d'avoir du métier pour prouver qu'il a du talent. Voici le splendide* Quintette *de Jean Huré, œuvre si profondément lyrique et si généreusement musicale, voici le* Crépuscule *de Louis Vuillemin où l'auteur de la monographie de Gabriel Fauré prouve qu'on peut honorer de plusieurs façons le génie d'un maître qu'on aime, voici les délicieux chœurs de Le Flem où, pour la première fois un musicien d'aujourd'hui semble avoir compris la leçon des* Trois Chansons *de Debussy et voici le* Dominical *de Ladmirault, de cet artiste admirable, prodigieux inventeur de parfums harmoniques enivrants mais créateur inquiet et torturé de scrupules qui le paralysent et l'empêchent de se réaliser tout entier dans ses œuvres actuelles.*'; Émile Vuillermoz in *Comoedia*, 4 Mai 1914, p. 2.

The critic 'M. D.' seems to have been carried away by the atmospheric charm of the 'Celtic' programme, evoking images of fresh air and the sea:

> The round trip that was offered to their guests by the lyrical Celts did not lack charm, not even spice. It is a rugged country, very varied in its picturesqueness, as is this great musical Brittany. Wide maritime horizons are suddenly followed by small steep valleys, the burnt moors by plains covered with silken wheat, the low and cloudy skies by azure lights of unlimited dreams.[84]

applauding a programme 'full of attractions, and evocative of the best smells, the smells of holidays!'.

Notably, a critic in *Paris-Midi* drew the connection between the growing difficulties of large parts of the audience with the harmonic language and stylistic diversity of modern art music, praising the ACB for providing a solution in the form of musical regionalism:

> We know how reluctant music lovers are to put a little order, logic and clarity into their aesthetics. For them, any classification is an insult and a kind of attack on the freedom of art. This love of the jungle and this terror of the general idea have gradually transformed music into a shapeless chaos where it becomes difficult to find your way back without a lantern. So we must bless all those who are working hard to bring us a little more light and simplify our choice in this wonderful musical trade fair where the passer-by is beginning to lose his mind.
>
> The Association of Breton Composers is currently playing this beneficial role. It had the happy idea of grouping musicians by affinity of birth, by community of origin: regionalism is the solution they propose to the problem of the contemporary imbroglio. And they bravely set an example.[85]

A fourth and last concert of the ACB took place less than three weeks later, on 12 May 1914 at the Salle des Hautes Études Sociales of the Sorbonne University. It

---

[84] '*Le voyage circulaire offert à leurs invités par les Celtes lyriques ne manqua pas de charme, ni même de piquant. C'est un pays accidenté, très varié en pittoresque, que cette grande Bretagne musicale. Les larges horizons maritimes succèdent tout à coup aux petites vallées encaissées, les landes brûlées aux plaines couvertes de blés soyeux, les ciels bas et nuageux aux clartés azurées de rêve illimité.*' There follows a list of the pieces performed, closing with the remark '[…] *qui complétait si noblement le programme de cette soirée pleine d'attraits, et évocatrice des meilleurs parfums, des parfums de vacances!*'; M. D. in *La Critique musicale*, 5 May 1914.

[85] '*On sait la répugnance qu'éprouvent les mélomanes à mettre un peu d'ordre, de logique et de clarté dans leur esthétique. Tout classement est pour eux une injure et une sorte d'atteinte à la liberté de l'art. Cet amour de la forêt vierge et cette terreur de l'idée générale ont peu à peu transformé la musique en un chaos informe où il devient sort difficile de retrouver son chemin sans lanterne. Il faut donc bénir tous ceux qui s'appliquent à nous apporter un peu plus de lumière et à simplifier notre choix dans cette formidable foire à la musique où le passant commence à perdre la tête. / L'Association des Compositeurs Bretons joue en ce moment ce rôle bienfaisant. Elle a eu l'idée heureuse de grouper les musiciens par affinité de naissance, par communauté d'origine : le régionalisme est la solution qu'ils proposent au problème de l'imbroglio contemporain. Et ils ont donné bravement l'exemple.*'; 'Le Colleur d'Affiches' in: *Paris-Midi*, 23 April 1914, p. 2.

seems like this was a concert without the representation of Swan Hennessy – there is no programme and no review in his Press Books. Public announcements[86] mention the composers Louis-Albert Bourgault-Ducoudray, Charles-Augustin Collin, Maurice Duhamel, Jehan de Gibon, Paul Ladmirault, Paul Martineau, Roger Pénau, Adolphe Piriou, and an unknown composer named Permentier.

The reviews of the occasion name some but not all of the works performed. This time, Vuillermoz had no problem in ascribing to the music some of the qualities of Stravinsky's *Sacre du printemps*, almost suggesting that, in 1914, innovation comes from Brittany (NB.: 'Armor' is a lyrical name for Brittany):

> The Association of Breton Composers, always active, has brought us new Celtic harmonies. All the bards were there to be applauded: Mrs Lucy Vuillemin who deliciously detailed delightful folk songs by Duhamel and rich melodies by Piriou; Miss Coffer who gave a complete hearing of the five amusing and light *Esquisses bretonnes* of the same Duhamel already applauded; Louis Fournier in Roger Pénau's cello pieces, resolutely melodic pages that transported the audience; Nucelly who lend his generous voice to the splendid *Chant funèbre de Myrddhin* by Ladmirault, and Jean Huré performing with his pupil Martineau, who was the author, a *Suite sur des air nantais* that was highly acclaimed. And the Breton Bretons are delighted to have found in a Celtic festival, where the biniou was heard and the bombard unites their bracing and flickering sounds, the instrumental atmosphere so characteristic of the first bars of the *Sacre du Printemps*! It is from Armor today that the light comes to us![87]

Paul Dambly wrote:

> The Association of Breton Composers continues its propaganda. Among his latest revelations, we must remember the *Petite suite sur des airs populaires nantais* by Mr Martineau, whose fine musical sensitivity I have praised on several occasions, Mr Duhamel's *Esquisses bretonnes*, Mr Piriou's expressive *Heures d'été* and Mr Ladmirault's *Chant funèbre du Myrrdhyn*, which I hope will be presented some day on one of our operatic stages.[88]

---

[86] *Comoedia*, 9 and 12 May 1914, p. 5; *Gil Blas*, 9 May 1914, p. 5.

[87] *L'Association des Compositeurs bretons, toujours active, nous a fait entendre de nouvelles harmonies celtiques. Tous ses bardes étaient là pour applaudir : Mme Lucy Vuillemin qui détailla délicieusement de ravissantes chansons populaires de Duhamel et de riches mélodies de Piriou ; Mlle Coffer qui donna l'audition intégrale des cinq* Esquisses bretonnes, *amusantes et légères, du même Duhamel déjà applaudi ; Louis Fournier dans les pièces de violoncelle de Roger Pénau, pages résolument mélodiques qui transportent l'auditoire ; Nucelly qui prête sa voix généreuse au splendide chant funèbre du Myrddhin de Ladmirault et Jean Huré exécutant avec son élève Martineau, qui en était l'auteur, une* Suite sur des air nantais *qui fut très applaudie. Et les Bretons bretonnants se félicitent d'avoir retrouvé dans une fête celtique où l'on entendit le biniou et la bombarde unir leurs sonorités brasillantes et papillotantes, l'atmosphère instrumentale si caractéristique des premières mesures du* Sacre du Printemps! *C'est d'Armor aujourd'hui que nous vient la lumière !*'; Émile Vuillermoz in *Comoedia*, 18 May 1914, p. 3. The *'biniou'* is a Breton pipe instrument and the *'bombarde'* a Breton type of oboe.

[88] *'L'Association des compositeurs bretons poursuit sa propagande. Il faut retenir, parmi ses dernières révélations, la Petite suite sur des airs populaires nantais de M. Martineau, dont j'ai à plusieurs reprises loué la fine sensibilité musicale, les* Esquisses bretonnes *de M. Duhamel, les expressives* Heures d'été *de M. Piriou et le*

The last news items in the French musical press about the Association des Compositeurs Bretons are reports of its general assembly on 13 June 1914 at the Salle Rouart et Lerolle on Boulevard de Strasbourg.[89] Votes for the administrative council led to the election, for the next three years, of Louis Vuillemin as president, Paul Ladmirault as vice-president, Maurice Duhamel as general secretary, Paul Martineau as adjunct secretary, and Paul Le Flem as treasurer, with Guy Ropartz remaining president of honour. Swan Hennessy did not play any administrative role; modest as he was, he would always have given priority to the Bretons.

When war broke out at the end of July, and after the Germans declared war on France on 3 August 1914, all hopes for the future development of the ACB were crushed within a week. Most of the members, including Hennessy, were to reunite later under a different umbrella (see Chapter 8), but the modernity that came with the Celticity of the group of one Irish-American and seventeen Breton composers was history, for the time being.

* * *

Rapsodie celtique, Op. 50 (1914) for violin and piano

The last work that Swan Hennessy completed before the outbreak of the First World War was the *Rapsodie celtique*, Op. 50 for violin and piano. It was most certainly written with a prospective performance at an ACB event in mind. According to the list of works that he drew up in 1929, this piece dates from 1920, but in his manuscript, he indicates a copyright date of 1914, which may safely be regarded as the year of composition. Besides, the work was published with Demets in 1915, perhaps as one of the last things he organised before he went into his self-chosen exile in Switzerland in that year (Chapter 7).

This chamber work is set in three movements without descriptive titles. The first is an *Allegretto* in F sharp major, the second an *Andantino* in B flat major, the third an *Allegro appassionato* that returns to F sharp major. Probably owing to the circumstances at the time of writing, the work does not bear any dedication. Following the first performance in Paris at the Salle des Concerts Touche on 4 March 1922, with Ida Adam-Pineau and the composer, the work has had a number of performances in France, Germany, and England until 1941 when it shared the fate of most of Hennessy's works.[90]

As in the *Suite* for string quartet, there is a certain stylistic incoherency in his writing, albeit perhaps not as large. Here, the themes of all three movements are clearly derived from an Irish or Scottish background of traditional music, which does unite them to a common baseline. The incoherency (or diversity, perhaps) lies in the

---

Chant funèbre du Myrrdhyn de M. Ladmirault, qui tentera, je l'espère, quelque jour, une de nos scènes lyriques.'; Paul Dambly in *Le Petit journal*, 2 June 1914, p. 7.

[89] *Comoedia* and *Gil Blas*, each of 14 June 1914, p. 4.

[90] The third movement was recently performed in Dublin, Ireland, at the National Concert Hall, 5 April 2017, by Gillian Williams (violin) and Úna Hunt (piano).

difference between two rather simple first movements in technical and harmonic respects and an ambitious and demanding third movement. The *Rapsodie* would amount to about eleven minutes in performance.

The first movement is designed as a theme with four variations and an epilogue. Hennessy writes in a footnote in the score that the theme does not use any existing folk song. The theme is a 'conversation', with the 'tune' alternating between the violin and the piano (Ex. 6.10 shows the beginning).

Ex. 6.10: *Rapsodie celtique*, Op. 50, 1st movt, bars 1–3

After 16 bars, the first Variation sets in, which is for piano only and transforms the theme into a lively reel. The violin returns for Variation II (*Andante*); Variation III is a jig notated as triplets in 2/4 time. Variation IV repeats no. I, this time accompanied by the violin, which clearly gives priority to the piano. There follows a curious Epilogue in *Adagio*, which sits somewhat at odds with the rest of the piece (and the theme), melodically and harmonically.

The movement remains in F sharp major throughout and does so mostly in a very straightforward manner without any modulation. But there are three exceptions. One is in Variation II, bars 9 to 12, where the piano deviates from the main key with a chordal sequence including D major ninth, A sharp major, B major seventh, A sharp major augmented, etc. (Ex. 6.11).

Ex. 6.11: *Rapsodie celtique*, Op. 50, 1st movt, Var. II, bars 9–13

Bar 12 of Variation III features a similarly odd chordal progression, which would, like Example 6.11, not be so striking at all, would they not occur in an environment of unaltered F sharp major. The Epilogue, then, is a freely modulating passage of 16 bars, of which only the last four bars return to the initial theme of the movement. The easiest explanation for these deviations may be Hennessy's peculiar humour: he may have had fun inserting these brief chordal shifts and watching the reaction of the musicians.

The second movement is a very short *Andantino* with a theme of no necessary relationship to any Irish or Scottish traditional music, although the tune makes abundant use of the 'Scotch snap'. There are, in fact, two passages (bars 9–16 and 25–32) in which his piano writing reminds of a Russian turn-of-the-century type (Hennessy owned a large collection of late nineteenth- and early twentieth-century Russian piano music, which may have coloured off here), even though, admittedly, a Russian element in a Celtic rhapsody may sound a little far-fetched.

The most substantial part of the *Rapsodie celtique* is, no doubt, the third movement. As the instruction *Allegro appassionato* suggests, it is indeed a (for Hennessy) unusually passionate and complex score. Formally set in F sharp major, the score is much more modulatory than the previous two movements. Numerous sharps, double sharps and flats in a key with six sharps, played in rapid tempo and rich harmony makes this movement a technical challenge for the pianist (the violin part is considerably easier).

The movement is also of rhythmic interest, including frequent triplets and time signature changes between 3/4, 4/4, and 5/4. To underline a dramatic phrase of the violin, the piano often resorts to chordal triplets that apparently shocked some of the listeners in contemporary performances of the work in England (see below), even though their harmony is conventional (Ex. 6.12).

Ex. 6.12: *Rapsodie celtique*, Op. 50, 3rd movt, bars 19–26

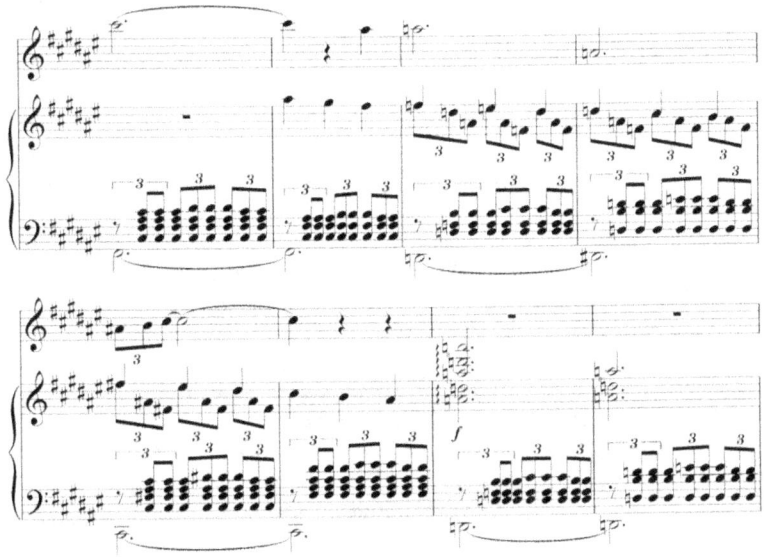

In his very short descriptive note about the movement in his list of works, Hennessy mentions *'rythmes de chevauchée'* – galloping rhythms – that he applied, and these occur briefly in bars 29 to 32 and 98 to 101. Since they are of no structural necessity, they may again be interpreted as an element of fun.

Melodically, there are interval leaps reminding of the folk music of the British Isles but they also occur in the second movement. For the uninitiated listener this would probably not be noticeable. The general impression is of a style with no obvious national overtones.

Since the publication of the piece happened during the War and the first performance did not take place before 1922, there were not many reviews. There was a comment of some 750 words in *Le Guide du concert*, undated in Hennessy's Press Books wand not traced so far, that probably appeared during the War.[91] Curiously, it deals with the first movement only and is not particularly informative. A 1921 review in the *Allgemeine Musikzeitung* recommends the work to the journal's readers:

> In a note, the composer protests against the possible supposition that his work should contain any folk melody, but that it is rather his own intellectual property. But the fine quiet theme of the first movement shows a very rare ability to adapt to the feelings and expressions of the folk soul. And the following four small variations, including the dreamy epilogue, are kept in the same spirit. Swan Hennessy's composition is characterised by a peculiar scarcity of form. Thus, the second movement, the sentimental B flat major Andantino, is not more than a sketch – as if the tone poet were not willing to say everything that fills and moves him. More passionate and almost capricious is the Allegro appassionato in the third movement, which, executed on a longer and wider scope, is particularly interesting for its well-founded alternation of measure and rhythm. One should pay much attention to Hennessy's beautiful composition.[92]

Another comment on this work can be found in a longer portrait article on Swan Hennessy by the prominent French music critic Henri Collet in his influential series *La Musique chez soi* in *Comoedia* (more about this article in Chapter 8). He wrote:

---

[91] It is pasted in between articles of May 1915 and September 1920. Presumably, Hennessy's copy arrived when he was not in Paris or did not have his Press Books at hand so that he could put a date on it.

[92] *'In einer Anmerkung verwahrt sich der Komponist gegen die etwaige Voraussetzung, daß sein Werk irgend eine Volksmelodie enthalte, sondern vielmehr völlig sein geistiges Eigentum sei. Aber das feine stille Thema des ersten Satzes bekundet doch ein ganz seltenes Anpassungsvermögen an das Empfinden und den Ausdruck der Volksseele. Und im gleichen Geiste sind die folgenden vier kleinen Variationen samt dem träumerisch erklingenden Epilog gehalten. Eine eigentümliche Knappheit der Form kennzeichnet Swan Hennessys Komposition. So ist auch der zweite Satz, das empfindungsreiche B-dur-Andantino, eigentlich nur eine Skizze – gleich als ob der Tondichter nicht alles auszusprechen gewillt sei, was ihn erfüllt und bewegt. Von leidenschaftlicherer und fast capriziöser Art ist das den dritten Satz bildende Allegro appassionato, das, länger und breiter ausgeführt, vor allem durch wohlbegründeten Wechsel von Takt und Rhythmus interessiert. Man sollte der schönen Komposition von Hennessy viel Aufmerksamkeit schenken.'*; Eugen Segnitz in *Allgemeine Musikzeitung* 48:43, 21 October 1921, p. 761.

The *Rhapsody*, solidly established in F sharp major, describes charming variations on a personal theme, and develops its elements in an *andantino*, then *allegro appassionato*. The relationship between the violin and the piano is one of imitation, of contrasts in augmentation, diminution, and rhythmic deformation. Nothing offensive but, on the contrary, a perfect balance and transparent fluidity.[93]

After the first performance, the Paris correspondent of the *The New York Herald* emphasised the 'Celtic' note of the work, without any comment on the arguably less Celtic third movement:

> American music is winning a foothold everywhere in Paris, from the Opéra-Comique and the symphony orchestras to the popular concert halls. Yesterday afternoon, Mr. Swan Hennessy's "Celtic Rhapsody" received its first audition at the Concert Touche, the famous popular concert hall in the boulevard de Strasbourg. Mr. Hennessy himself was heard at the piano and the violin part was interpreted by Mme. Adam-Pineau. The first movement of the new composition is Irish in its inspiration, the second Scotch, place thus being given for the expression of the spirit of two of the great branches of the Celtic race. The contrasting aspects of the Celtic personality, disposition of the reverie tinged with melancholy and eagerness for action, are developed in the principal themes. Despite the disadvantage of an inferior piano, the work made an impression which augurs well for its future success.[94]

After a 1928 performance in Exeter, England, a critic wrote:

> Perhaps the most attractive was Hennessy's "Rapsodie Celtique." It was the first time it had been played in England, but many will hope to hear it again very soon. This delightful blending of original Irish airs, with fascinating lilt, quickly appealed to all. The crashing, uncommon chords of the commencement of the second movement for the pianoforte may have astonished and slightly shocked the more sedate portion of the audience, but to the rest they were a sheer joy.[95]

Excursus: a 1913 ballet

A curious work shall bring this chapter to a close. It was found among Swan Hennessy's manuscripts, and it also appears in his list of works as a 22-minute piano work. However, it turns out to be music for a ballet, and the score reveals indications for a number of further instruments. Apart from the plot and stage directions, there are no

---

[93] '*La* Rhapsodie, *solidement établie en fa dièze majeur, décrit de charmantes variations sur un thème personnel, et en développe les éléments* andantino, *puis* allegro appassionato. *Les rapports du violon et du piano sont ceux de l'imitation, des oppositions par augmentation, diminution, déformation rythmique. Rien de heurté, mais au contraire le parfait équilibre et la fluidité transparente.*'; Henri Collet in *Comoedia*, 5 December 1921, p. 4 ('La Musique chez soi, XCVII: Œuvres de Swan Hennessy').
[94] 'American Music Successful'; *The New York Herald*, 5 March 1922.
[95] *Exeter and Plymouth Gazette*, 15 November 1928, p. 7. In his memory of the event, the critic must have mixed up the second and the third movement. The second movement does not contain any 'crashing, uncommon' chords at the beginning.

further documents about this work: no explanation, no performance (or any plans for one that survived), and no published print (although this was intended).

Les Noces du soldat de bois. **Ballet en un acte, Op. 37 (1913) for piano**

Another oddity of this work is its opus number: As Op. 37, it would normally have been written around 1909. By 1913, Hennessy had reached Op. 48 – should it therefore have been Op. 47? But the '37' is written in bold letters, and in his list of works it is clearly sorted between Op. 36 (*Fêtes*) and Op. 38 (*Introduction, XII variations et fugue sur un thème obligé*), works published in 1910 and 1911. Opus 47 was *Croquis parisiens*, written in 1912 and published in 1913. If this reflects another major reshuffle of his opus numbers, it is quite a puzzle which other works should have been affected. One explanation may be that he began work on this ballet as early as 1910, assigned an opus number before he was finished, and completed it in 1913. But this does not sound particularly convincing.

According to the manuscript, the piece was completed in July 1913 in Pornichet, the Breton coastal town in which Hennessy spent his summer holidays that year. It will be remembered that the German music critic Heinrich Möller wrote a postcard to Hennessy to this place dated 6 August 1913, which then turns out to have been just shortly after the work's completion.

All these dates suggest that the initial motivation to write a ballet must have come with the spectacular success of the Ballets russes, Sergei Diaghilev's famous ballet troupe, which first performed in Paris in May 1909. On 29 May 1913, the company produced Igor Stravinsky's *Le Sacre du printemps* to extraordinary (albeit controversial) public acclaim. It seems likely, then, that Hennessy went to one of the early performances of the work. The pagan ritual, the polyrhythmic and polytonal compositional elements, and the use of folk songs in parts of the score must have appealed to Hennessy and the circle of Breton composers.

On the other hand, Hennessy cannot seriously have expected that the Ballets russes would have performed his piece. By mid-1913, the ensemble had performed ballet compositions by French composers like Reynaldo Hahn (*Le Dieu bleu*, 13 May 1912), Claude Debussy (*L'Après-midi d'un faune*, 29 May 1912; *Jeux* 15 May 1913), Maurice Ravel (*Daphnis et Chloé*, June 1912), and Florent Schmitt (*La Tragédie de Salomé*, 12 June 1913), but these were clearly of a different calibre. Provided that Hennessy had specific performers in mind, it cannot have been this group, but he was certainly aiming to build on the momentum created by the ensemble.

The title of the work, *Les Noces du soldat de bois*, would translate as 'The Wood Soldier's Wedding'. All the characters in the plot appear to be wooden puppets or marionettes, the roles being distributed to

- *Le lieutenant des soldats de bois* (The lieutenant of the wooden soldiers),
- *Pierrot, son rival* (Pierrot, his rival),
- *La poupée brune, fiancée du lieutenant* (The brunette puppet, the lieutenant's fiancée),
- *La poupée blonde, sa rivale* (The blonde puppet, her rival),

- *Poupées, soldats de bois, deux carillonneurs mécaniques* (Puppets, wooden soldiers, two mechanical carilloneurs).

Fig. 6.4: Stage description including a sketch in Hennessy's hand

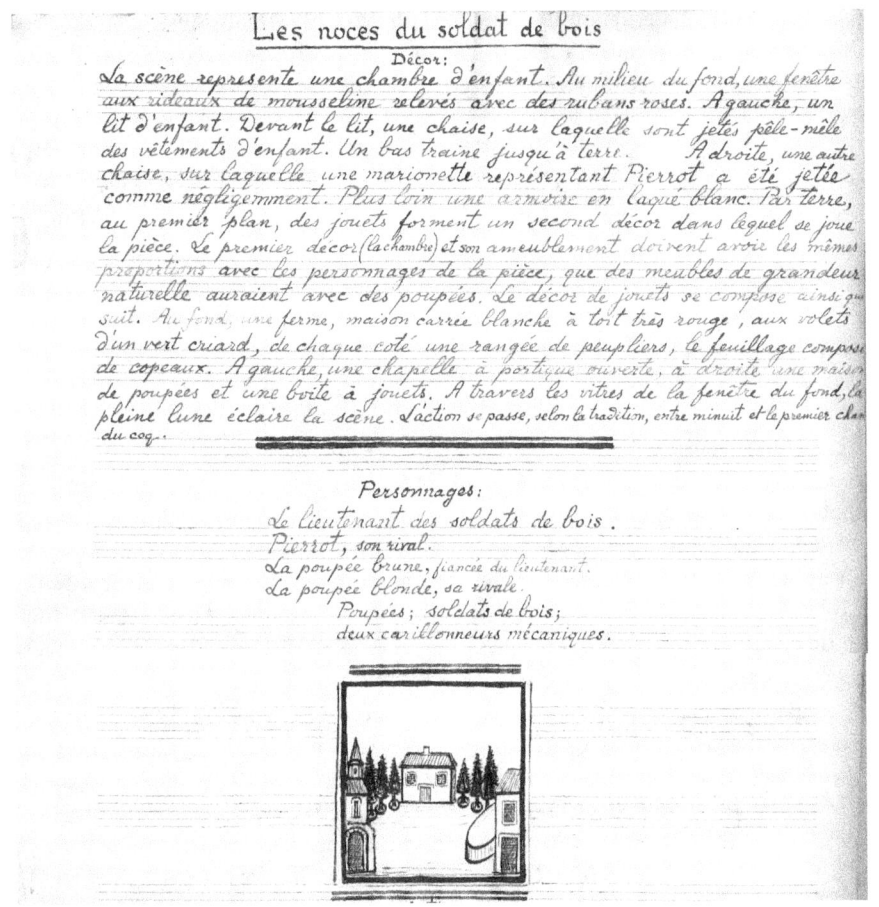

It seems, therefore, that there are influences or models in Tchaikovsky's *Nutcracker* (who usually resembles a wooden soldier) and Stravinsky's *Petrushka* (the heroine being a puppet and the story dealing with rivalries among puppets that come to life during a fair). The latter was premiered in Paris in June 1911 at the Théâtre du Châtelet by the Ballets russes. Vaslav Nijinsky's representation of Petrushka in this first performance resembled a punch – very close in appearance to Hennessy's Pierrot. Hennessy also certainly knew E.T.A. Hoffmann's modern fairy tale of *The Nutcracker and the Mouse King*, the basis of Tchaikovsky's ballet, which is even closer to Hennessy's story.

The plot, which seems to be Hennessy's own, is the following (Hennessy's French original in the left column, my translation in the right):

Décor

La scène représente une chambre d'enfant. Au milieu du fond, une fenêtre aux rideaux de mousseline relevés avec des rubans roses. À gauche, un lit d'enfant. Devant le lit, une chaise, sur laquelle sont jetés pêle-mêle des vêtements d'enfant. Une basse traine jusqu'à terre. À droite, une autre chaise, sur laquelle une marionnette représentant Pierrot a été jetée comme négligemment. Plus loin une armoire en laqué blanc. Par terre, au premier plan, des jouets forment un second décor dans lequel se joue la pièce. Le premier décor (la chambre) et son ameublement doivent avoir les mêmes proportions avec les personnages de la pièce, que des meubles de grandeur naturelle auraient avec des poupées. Le décor de jouets se compose ainsi que suit. Au fond, une ferme, maison carrée blanche à toit très rouge, aux volets d'un vert criard, de chaque côté une rangée de peupliers, le feuillage compose de copeaux. À gauche, une chapelle à portique ouverte, à droite une maison de poupées et une boite à jouets. À travers les vitres de la fenêtre du fond, la pleine lune éclaira la scène. L'action se passe, selon la tradition, entre minuit et le premier chant du coq.

Action

Bruits de carillon, le rideau se lève. À travers la porte de la chapelle on voit les carillonneurs qui sonnent pour annoncer le mariage du soldat de bois. Pierrot se redresse frotte se yeux et se laisse glisser à terre, par le pied de la chaise. Il montre le plus grand désespoir car il aime la poupée brune. Pantomime. La porte de la maison s'ouvre, la poupée brune et douze poupées rousses

Stage design

The scene represents a child's room. In the middle of the background, a window with muslin curtains raised with pink ribbons. On the left, a crib. In front of the bed, a chair, on which children's clothes are thrown in a jumble. A low end drags to the ground. On the right, another chair, on which a puppet representing Pierrot was thrown as if negligently. Further on, a white lacquered wardrobe. On the floor, in the foreground, toys form a second setting in which the piece is played. The first decoration (the bedroom) and its furnishings must have the same proportions with the characters in the room as natural-sized furniture would have with puppets. The toy decor is composed as follows. At the bottom, a farmhouse, a white square house with a very red roof, blinding green shutters, on each side a row of poplars, the foliage is made of wood chips. On the left, an open portico chapel, on the right, a puppet house and a toy box. Through the back window, the full moon lights up the scene. The action takes place, according to tradition, between midnight and the first rooster crow.

Action

Carillon sounds, the curtain rises. Through the door of the chapel you can see the carillonists ringing to announce the wedding of the wooden soldier. Pierrot straightens up, rubs his eyes and lets himself slide to the ground, along the foot of the chair. He shows the greatest despair because he loves the brunette puppet. Pantomime. The door of the house opens, the

(le corps de ballet) sortent en dansant gaîment et se forment en groupe. Pas seul de la poupée brune. Les poupées rentrent dans la maison. La poupée brune veut les suivre, mais Pierrot lui fait une déclaration brulante. Elle rit. Un clairon sonne ; c'est le lieutenant qui arrive avec ses soldats. La poupée brune est ravie. Pierrot rage. Elle rentre. Pierrot la suit. Au bruit de clairon, la boite à jouets s'est ouverte et la poupée blonde a regardé par l'entrebâillement du couvercle. Elle sort de sa boite et essaie de charmer le lieutenant en dansant lentement autour de lui. Il reste indifférent, et quand elle a fini sa danse, les soldats, par dérision, se mettent à danser en ronde autour d'elle. Elle sort furieuse, en menaçant le lieutenant qui hausse les épaules. Pas seul du lieutenant. Les poupées sortent de la maison toutes étincelantes et la poupée brune se jette dans les bras de son fiancé. En voyant cela, Pierrot, qui regardait par une fenêtre, s'arrache les cheveux de désespoir. La poupée blonde rentre en scène d'un pas furtif, et se cache. Autour des amoureux le corps de ballet danse une valse lente. Vers la fin de la valse, Pierrot, qui avait quitté la fenêtre, réapparait en se nouant une corde autour de cou et la poupée blonde s'étant glissée, armée d'un poignard, auprès de la poupée brune, lève le bras pour la frapper par derrière. À ce moment le chant de coq se fait entendre ; la poupée blonde laisse tomber son couteau ; Pierrot jette sa corde, et tous se précipitent pour reprendre la place qu'ils occupaient au début.

brunette puppet and twelve red puppets (the corps de ballet) come out dancing happily and form a group. Solo of the brunette puppet. The puppets are coming into the house. The brunette puppet wants to follow them, but Pierrot makes a passionate confession of love to her. She laughs. A bugle sounds; it is the lieutenant who arrives with his soldiers. The brunette puppet is delighted. Pierrot rages. She's going home. Pierrot follows her. At the sound of a bugle, the toy box opens and the blond puppet looks through the gap in the lid. She comes out of her box and tries to charm the lieutenant by dancing slowly around him. He remains indifferent, and when she finishes her dance, the soldiers, in derision, begin to dance in circles around her. She comes out furious, threatening the lieutenant who shrugs his shoulders. Solo of the lieutenant. The puppets leave the house all sparkling and the brunette puppet throws herself into the arms of her fiancé. When Pierrot sees this through a window and pulls his hair in despair. The blond puppet stealthily enters the scene, and hides. Around the lovers the corps de ballet dances a slow waltz. Towards the end of the waltz, Pierrot, who has left the window, reappears, knotting a rope around his neck and the blond puppet, armed with a dagger, slides near the brown puppet and raises her arm to stab her from behind. At that moment the rooster crow is heard; the blond puppet drops her knife; Pierrot throws away his rope, and everyone rushes back to the place they occupied at the beginning.

On the surface, it is a story for children, were it not for the open jealousy, the mildly macabre scene in which Pierrot is about to hang himself, and the brunette puppet intending to stab her rival. But Hennessy certainly speculates with a laugh from the audience at the end when everybody rushes back to their original place in order not to be caught by the human inhabitants of the house.

Ex. 6.13: *Les Noces du soldat de bois*, Op. 37 No. 1, bars 1–19 (author's transcription)

Musically, the one-act ballet consists of five numbers that illustrate the action on the stage. The manuscript score was apparently intended as a short score for an ensemble or even orchestral piece, with numerous indications like '*pizz.*' and '*arché*' for the strings, and cues for various instruments such as carillon (here a glockenspiel?), bugle or trumpet, drums, a cello solo, harp, and clarinet (see Fig. 6.5). No full score has survived (if it ever existed), but if it would have been realised this way it would have been Hennessy's largest score ever.

The manuscript also shows clear instructions to an engraver at a publishing company, with the following note: 'Engrave everything in one piece, linking the separate pieces. Write out the repetitions.' *('Graver tout d'une pièce en enchainant les morceaux séparés. Développer les reprises.')* Evidently, Hennessy wanted to have the piece published, and it is likely that the publisher (Demets?) dissuaded him from the idea as long as the work did not have any real prospect of a staging.

The passage from bar 9 reappears in the second number as the music for Pierrot's confession of love towards the brunette puppet. The third number begins with the brunette puppet's notion of the soldiers in the distance, her joy at seeing her fiancé, and the march accompanying the arrival of the soldiers. Number four begins with the blonde puppet's futile attempt at seducing the lieutenant, written in a line in the left hand from bar 2, which is intended for a cello (probably a solo cello). The amiable melody is contrasted with more dissonant material in the right hand, communicating the irritation on the lieutenant's part (Ex. 6.14).

Ex. 6.14: *Les Noces du soldat de bois*, Op. 37 No. 4, bars 1–22 (author's transcription)

The fifth number, eventually, features a waltz of the whole ensemble, during which Pierrot puts the rope around his neck, cut short by the sudden crow of the rooster and a silent fading out with indications of a harp and a clarinet.

Hennessy's ballet seems to deserve more attention than it can be afforded here in the context of a biographical overview. The story is interesting, and the score does make the impression of a piece fitting well into the context of its time. With its duration of approximately 22 minutes – which was Hennessy's estimation –, it would suit the contemporary practice of performing three or four ballets in one evening, and as an independent piece, it would be worth exploring (at least) by a group at one of today's academies of performing arts or an enterprising ballet company. In a workshop performance, the piano accompaniment alone might suffice; for any larger presentation, the construction of a full score on the basis of Hennessy's indications of various instruments would certainly be needed.

Fig. 6.5: End of the manuscript of the ballet Op. 37, showing the fall of the curtain with indications of a harp and a clarinet.

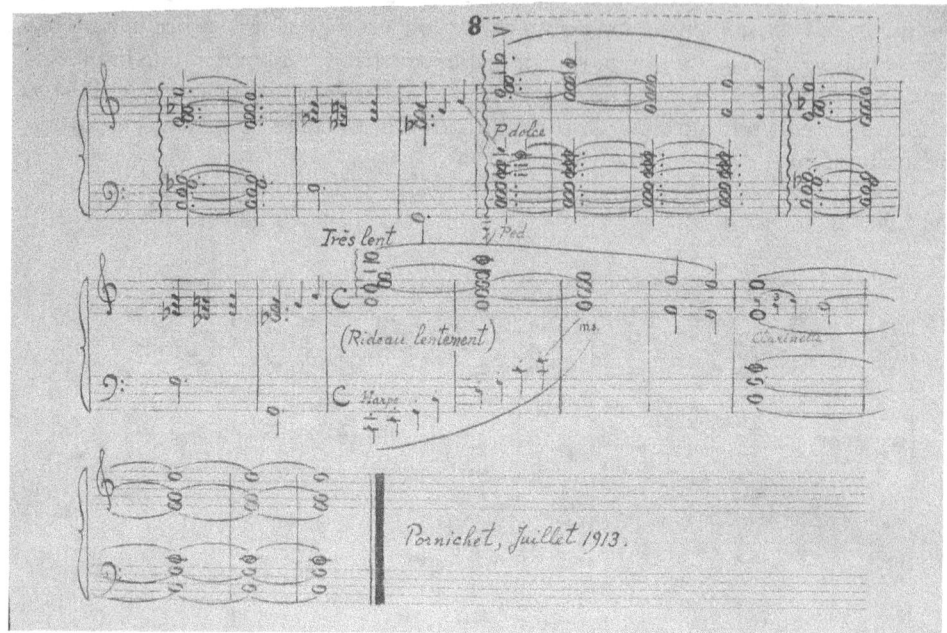

Chapter 7
Escape to Switzerland (1914–1919)

Sources are scarce that would help determine Swan Hennessy's activities and whereabouts after war broke out in the summer of 1914. On 21 August 1914, less than three weeks after the German declaration of war on France, he received a Certificate of Registration from the American Consul at Berne, Switzerland – although his residence was still at Paris. He may have gone there in order to prepare the later move of the whole family a year later. He showed this certificate (as his proof of US citizenship?) to the American Embassy in Paris on 12 December 1914 when he applied for an Emergency Passport for the purpose of 'going to England to bring my father back to Paris'. The document describes his outward appearance as age: 48 years; stature: 5 feet 7 inches [*c*1.70 m]; forehead: high; eyes: grey; nose: straight; mouth: moustache; chin: beard; hair: iron grey; complexion: ruddy; face: oval.

Another Emergency Passport Application, dated a week later, 19 December 1914, shows Michael Hennessy applying for a passport at the US Embassy in London, the stated purpose being 'returning to residence in France, coming to England + returning to the U.S. America'. It is also signed by Swan, giving witness to his father's identity. I have quoted this document before (Chapter 1, p. 23), since it is one of the key sources that describe the times and the route of Michael Hennessy's emigration from Ireland, his former position in Chicago, and the reasons why it was so difficult to prove his citizenship with all relevant documents burnt and destroyed.

Regarding his music, Hennessy still managed to have his *Rapsodie celtique*, Op. 50 for violin and piano published with Demets. It appeared in 1915, probably in the first half of the year.

And from then, the First World War put a temporary end to activities of this kind. It must have come as a shock for Hennessy and his family, and destroyed the plans that he and his Breton composer-friends had in further establishing a 'Celtic' note in the music of the French capital.

In August 1915, Hennessy and his father, wife and young son left Paris for five years. During these years they resided at Veytaux, a suburb of Montreux overlooking the eastern end of the Lake of Geneva in the French-speaking part of Switzerland. They lived in a house called Villa Bellevue, which they rented,[1] although it is unclear (and impossible to find out) since when exactly – whether, for instance, Swan arranged it when he had gone to Berne in August 1914. The house is no longer extant – presumably, it fell victim to the construction of the motorway A9 around 1970 that crosses Montreux as a viaduct on concrete stills high above residential areas before it enters a tunnel at Glion and for which some of the residential villas had to be demolished to make room for the stills.

---

[1] In a 1919 passport application, he submitted a 'lease of apartment and receipts from landlord'.

Fig. 7.1: Historical postcard of Veytaux

The family was obliged to report to the US consular agency at Lausanne each year, and their regular passport renewals can be found at familysearch.com today. They applied for the passports in order to be able to return to Paris, officially with the ultimate purpose of 'immediate return to the U.S.A.', which, of course, they had not the slightest intention to do in reality. They explained the necessity of the continued stay in Switzerland with the increasingly difficult medical situation of Michael Hennessy. In the application form dated 15 April 1918, for example, when Michael was 81 years of age, Swan explains (in a separate manuscript note pasted onto the form):

> I, Swan Hennessy, solemnly swear that whereas I am not only willing, but anxious to return to the United States, I am unable to leave my father Mr. Michael D. Hennessy whose ill health and great age make it impossible for him to undertake a journey at present.
> He may be obliged at any moment to undergo an operation which might endanger his life. A separation could be extremely painful, the more so as he only speaks English and is dependent on me as his interpreter. I therefore urgently beg the State Department to kindly grant me permission to stay in Switzerland.
> Swan Hennessy

In the same document, there is also a brief note by a Berne-based physician who certifies that Michael Hennessy was suffering from 'bladder-stones and cyolitis', confirming that '(t)ravelling would be quite out of question for him'. In another application, dated 16 October 1917, Swan Hennessy states that his father was 'an invalid, suffering from eleven stones in the bladder'.

Fig. 7.2: Photographs of the Hennessy family in wartime passport renewals[2]

Even if it is not very likely that Swan Hennessy, now aged around 50, would have been drafted to war, he may have been obliged to perform other, more civilian duties as an American citizen, at least after the United States officially entered the War in April 1917. In a way, therefore, he could be grateful to his father for his illness gave him a good, and probably true, reason to remain with the family. 'Between the lines', of course, we know that Switzerland was one of the few safe places in Europe at this time, and Michael Hennessy's illness protected the family at this difficult period while some of the most terrible battles of the twentieth century took place only a few hundred kilometres away.

It is unsure whether the Hennessys were aware that Igor Stravinsky lived very close by during these years. Stravinsky lived with his family in the suburb of Clarens between 1910 and 1915 (as much north of the centre of Montreux as Veytaux is south of it) and moved to Morges (closer to Lausanne) from 1915 to 1919. There is no record of any meeting, and it is not very likely since they would have had earlier (and later) opportunities to meet in Paris, which Hennessy took no avail of. Stravinsky lived there from the generosity of Swiss benefactors, while Hennessy still profited from the wealth accumulated by his father.

It may well be, on the other hand, that Hennessy met Romain Rolland during these years. The writer who received the 1915 Nobel Prize for Literature had also moved to Switzerland, working mainly from Geneva; he moved to Villeneuve, just south of Veytaux, in 1922. Hennessy had returned to Paris by this time, but he still frequently travelled to Switzerland. Since the two were in touch around 1913 (see Chapter 6), they may well have continued their contact, even though this must remain speculative.

Whether Hennessy sympathised with Rolland's pacifist views or whether he sided with any of the wartime opponents is not known either. It is not likely that he would have had any nationalist leanings, which would have been very difficult in his case, especially since the two countries he favoured for their musical life and in terms of

---

[2] Source: familysearch.com. Michael's photographs are too dark to be reproduced here.

performance and publication opportunities were now the strongest enemies: France and Germany. His American passport had its advantages, but otherwise, having left the United States at age twelve, never to return, it is highly unlikely that he would have identified as an American in any nationalist sense. Ireland, then, was in the process of liberating itself from its English oppressor – Hennessy's nascent Irish nationalism was of an exclusively cultural, respectively musical, nature; it would need a few more years to become more apparent. Thus, probably, the internationalist and pacifist views of someone like Rolland probably came nearest to his own views.

But Rolland's exile from France is symptomatic for the nationalist atmosphere which, understandably, perhaps, prevailed in French cultural life during the war years, with noticeable implications for music. These all but bypassed Hennessy – he may have received news from his French/Breton musical friends, but having left Paris behind for as long as five years resembled in many ways the ten years' absence from all musical life that he had already experienced during the 1890s. The two periods added up meant 15 years of a musical career wasted – unproductive and unsuccessful.

Being invisible in Paris during a time in which some French composers were able to demonstrate their patriotism did certainly not help. Jane Fulcher has shown how former rival factions of composers now joined forces in patriotic musical events, of which – following a few months of shock numbness – many resumed from about December 1914.[3]

> [...] composers previously associated with conflicting prewar schools or 'camps' were grouped together as 'the French school,' and thus assimilated to the same nationalist discourse.[4]

Hennessy, with his former (and still lingering) models in German (late-)Romanticism, would not have felt well in the anti-German musical climate of these years, during which several organisations excluded even historic composers of German birth from any concert programmes, not to speak of their influences.[5]

Organisations such as *L'Action française* (already founded before the war), *L'Œuvre fraternelle des artistes*, and the *Ligue nationale pour la défense de la musique française* with its journal *La Musique pendant la guerre* called upon French musicians and audiences to gather under the national flag with exclusively French programmes. Sitting between various national stools, this was not Hennessy's world.

In many of its reports and concert announcements, the journal *La Musique pendant la guerre* mentioned the current role in the war of the composers whose works were played or discussed. For example, in announcing the first *Festival de musique française* on 16 June 1916, one finds Hennessy's Breton composer-friends Paul Ladmirault and

---

[3] Jane Fulcher: *The Composer as Intellectual. Music and Ideology in France, 1914–1940* (New York: Oxford University Press, 2005), p. 27f.
[4] Fulcher, *The Composer as Intellectual*, p. 28.
[5] See, among many other contemporary sources, Camille Saint-Saëns' pamphlet *Germanophilie* (Paris: Dorbon aîné, 1916).

Roger Pénau as well as his personal friend Auguste Delacroix as *'mobilisé'* (Ladmirault and Pénau fought at Verdun); the composer Marcel Labey is mentioned as *'blessé'* (wounded) and Georges Krieger as *'disparu'* (missing).⁶ The youngest member of the Association des Compositeurs Bretons, Paul Martineau, died in 1915.

Several composers demonstrated their patriotism by writing music pertinent to their cause, including Claude Debussy with his *Berceuse héroïque*, Francis Casadesus with his *France lève-toi* and Lili Boulanger with her *Pour les funérailles d'un soldat*. While it may very well be that nobody expected Hennessy to write a work of this nature, the fact that he didn't was not to his advantage either.

In fact, Hennessy did not only write no patriotic piece of music during the war, he did not write anything at all. The years 1915 to 1919 are a total blank in his worklist. This is astonishing since one might think he had peaceful surroundings and ample leisure. But if he should have composed something it must have been withdrawn. More likely is he really did not compose.

There is a small exception, though, that appeared after careful screening of his manuscripts. During the late 1920s, Hennessy published five volumes of piano music with the collective title *À la manière de ...*, consisting of pastiche works in the styles of historical and contemporary composers. It seems like he already began the series in 1917. In the manuscripts, no. 6, *Anton Dvořák*, is marked 'Veytaux 1917' and no. 7, *Richard Strauss*, 'Veytaux, December 1917' (in English). Although these indications have been erased they are still legible. They were published as the last piece of volume 1 and the first piece of volume 2 with Max Eschig in 1927.

Death of Michael Hennessy

However, the likely reason for Hennessy's compositional silence during these years is the medical condition of his father who had become an invalid requiring constant care. In all likelihood, Hennessy spent these years mainly looking after his father with frequent travels to his doctor in Berne, also spending probably more time with his wife and young son than he might have done in Paris.

But old age and illness took its toll: Michael Hennessy died in Veytaux during the night of 15 to 16 August 1919, eight months after the end of the War. The fact that the family remained in Veytaux during this time and did not return to Paris as soon as it was possible underlines that Michael's need for care was at least an important reason to stay in Switzerland as the war.

The death certificate (Fig. 7.3) is archived at the civil registry office of canton Vaud at Moudon and reveals, besides the dates of birth and death of Michael Hennessy and his deceased wife Sarah Swan, also the names of Swan's Irish grandparents (David Hennessy and Mary Hayes).

---

⁶ *La Musique pendant la guerre* no. 7, 16 June 1916, p. 1.

Fig. 7.3: Death certificate of Michael D. Hennessy, Swan Hennessy's father (Courtesy: Centre administratif de l'état civil du Canton de Vaud)

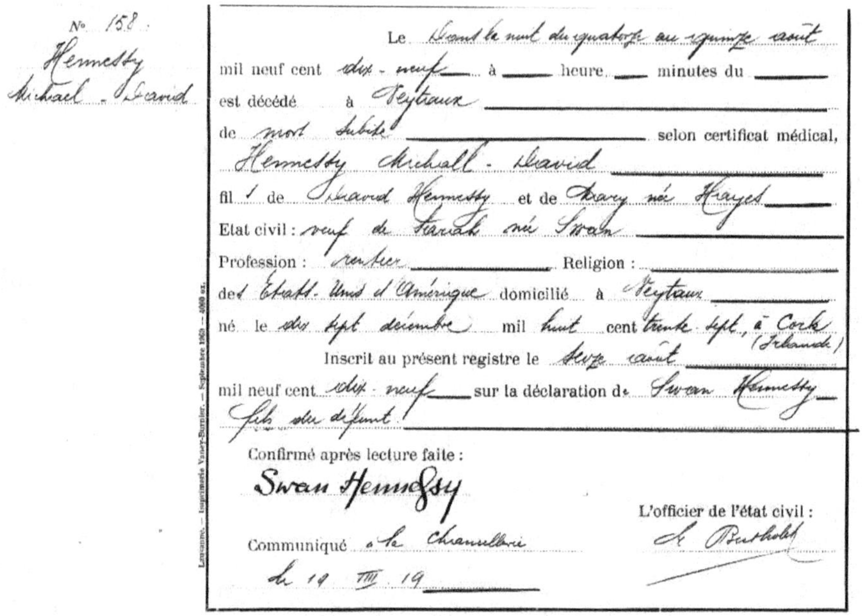
No 158
Hennessy
Michael David

Le Dans la nuit du quatorze au quinze août
mil neuf cent dix-neuf à heure minutes du
est décédé à Veytaux
de mort subite selon certificat médical,
Hennessy Michael David
fils de David Hennessy et de Mary née Hayes
Etat civil : veuf de Sarah née Swan
Profession : rentier Religion :
des Etats-Unis d'Amérique domicilié à Veytaux
né le dix sept décembre mil huit cent trente sept, à Cork (Irlande)
Inscrit au présent registre le seize août
mil neuf cent dix-neuf sur la déclaration de Swan Hennessy
fils du défunt.
Confirmé après lecture faite :
Swan Hennessy
L'officier de l'état civil :
Communiqué à la Chancellerie
le 19 VIII. 19

He was buried on a small cemetery in Territet which had been adjacent to the memorial of the Austrian empress Elisabeth ('Sissi'). The memorial is still (2019) at its place, now next to a small roundabout, but the cemetery right behind it has long since had to make room for private residences, the space between the lake and mountains being too small to let the precious ground be occupied by something as unprofitable as a cemetery.

* * *

Due to the war but no less due to Swan Hennessy's absence, no work of his was performed in France during the war years. At least this is what Hennessy's own Press Books suggest. However, they do reveal two performances of his violin sonata *'dans le style irlandais'*, Op. 14 in Egypt (!), apparently the war refuge of the Paris-based Greek violinist Alcibiade Anemoyanni. Today, the Athens born violinist (* 1866) is mainly known in connection with the first public concert by Manuel de Falla in Paris, who accompanied him in a recital on 7 May 1908. Anemoyanni had previously performed Hennessy's sonata in Paris (Salle Gaveau, 21 March 1914), and played it again, accompanied by one H. Félix, on 23 November 1915 at the Théâtre Alhambra in Alexandria, in a fund raising concert for the English Red Cross (the French programme flyer called it the *'Croix Rouge Anglaise'*) in a programme including other violin works by César

Franck and Henryk Wieniawski, and songs by Leo Delibes, Émile Paladilhe, Jules Massenet and Anton Rubinstein (performed by his wife, 'Mme' Coll-Anemoyanni). The concert ended on the *'Marseillaise'* and the English national anthem. A second performance of the same work took place half a year later, on 5 March 1916 at the Théâtre Cinéma Pathé in Cairo, accompanied by Jeanne Bouillard in a very similar programme. Needless to say, Hennessy was not present on those occasions, much as he perhaps would have liked to.

Similarly, the musical press was silent about him and his music during these years. His name does not appear again before a review of the *Rapsodie celtique*, Op. 50 in the 21 October 1921 issue of the *Allgemeine Musikzeitung*. On the same day, his portrait appeared on the cover of *Le Guide du concert*. By this time, he had sorted himself anew in the French capital, in a musical world that had considerably evolved.

Chapter 8
An Engagement with Ireland (1920–1924)

The war had ended in late 1918, Michael Hennessy had died in Veytaux in August 1919, and the family returned to Paris in September – the US consulate at Lausanne issuing Swan Hennessy an 'Amendment of Passport' on 9 September 1919. In this document (again traceable on familysearch.com), he indicated that he intends to travel to 'France (on my way to the Unites States)' for the purpose of 'settling up family affairs'. Next, he applied for a passport at the US embassy in Paris, 23 September, which was issued on 29 October 1919. From this time on, until he died almost exactly ten years later, Hennessy remained in France, occasional trips to neighbouring countries notwithstanding.

In the latter document, he mentioned his father as 'deceased', that he himself had last left the United States in 1907, with the bureaucratic form describing his intentions in Paris as 'residing for the purpose of "Composer of Music" on behalf of "Myself"'.

His legal address is given as 'Equitable Trust C.N.Y.', an investment trust in New York City where Michael Hennessy had invested all his money in and of which Swan was now the heir.[1] Interestingly, as his reference in the United States he gives 'The Honourable Lyman J. Gage, Guayamaca Club, St. Diego, Cal.'. Lyman J. Gage (1836–1927) was Secretary of the Treasury (the minister of finance in European terms) under presidents William McKinley and Theodore Roosevelt, becoming a banker in New York from 1902 before he retired to California. Was this merely presumptuous on Hennessy's part, or was he really personally acquainted with Gage? It seems hard to believe.

In any case, the income from those investments at the Equitable Trust Co. ensured that Swan Hennessy enjoyed financial independence for the rest of his life. This explains why the few biographical notes about Hennessy in musical reference works do not indicate any profession that he may have had – he had none (Hennessy, this should be clear, was not the only composer in such a comfortable situation: Ernest Chausson, Albéric Magnard and Francis Poulenc would be examples in France, Arnold Bax in England and, slightly later, Virgil Thomson in the United States).

At one time, Hennessy's extended absence from the United States required him to complete an 'Affidavit to Explain Protracted Foreign Residence and to Overcome Presumption of Expatriation'. In this very real threat of being expatriated, Hennessy explained his situation as follows:

> I came to France in 1907 to accompany my father, who was an invalid, and who died on August 15, 1919. I remained here in pursuance of my profession of musician, and for the

---

[1] A US journal reported in September 1920 that 'all persons having claims against Michael David Hennessy, late of Veytaud, Canton de Vaud, Switzerland, deceased, to present the same, with vouchers thereof' etc. to the attention of Swan Hennessy, Equitable Trust Co., 37 Wall Street, Manhattan, etc. This would not have been the first notice of this kind, because the original call was dated 5 March 1920; *School* 32:1, 2 September 1920, p. 10.

education of my child, Michael Patrick Hennessy. My wife, Mrs. Claire Hennessy, has remained with me in France since our marriage in 1909.[2]

He also clarified that he paid income tax at Baltimore, Maryland, and that he intended to return to the United States permanently within two years. It may well be that nowadays rules and regulations of this kind would be more strictly applied, but Hennessy's arguing seems to have convinced the American vice-consul at Paris. His statement reads:

> I am of the opinion that the facts recited constitute the true cause of the applicant's foreign residence and that they are sufficient under the established rules to entitle him to protection as an American citizen.

* * *

In a succinct summary, Michel Faure described the major changes in the development of art music in France after 1914 as:

> 1. A return to craftsmanship, i.e. the revaluation of the composer's craftsmanship as opposed to the artist's inspiration; 2. Mistrust of the new in the field of music, which manifested itself in a firm rejection of Schönberg; 3. Revaluation of tradition; 4. A commandment of serenity. Numerous compositions with a fleeting and euphoric character were created. […]; 5. The first French radio station, Radio Tour Eiffel, was put into operation in 1921.[3]

Apart from the fact that some of these statements would have to be put into perspective – for instance, Schönberg did have followers in France, too, and futurism, polytonality and other styles formed counterweights to the desire for tradition –, in all of these trends, Swan Hennessy appears like a true composer of his time. He has always advocated a high degree of craftsmanship in his music and has been acknowledged as such by many critics. He strongly opposed the aesthetics of Schönberg, as we have seen before and will see again. He also upheld tradition in many ways: while frequently experimenting with form in both his programmatic and his abstract music, he always remained attached to Romantic and late-Romantic formal models; he also consciously used techniques developed during the Baroque (fugues, in particular), as did several of his French contemporaries. He was a true propagator of the 'command-

---

[2] Appendix to passport application of 27 January 1921 (familysearch.com, accessed 28 June 2016).
[3] '1. Rückkehr zum Handwerk, d.h. die Aufwertung des handwerklichen Könnens des Komponisten im Gegensatz zur Inspiration des Künstlers; 2. Misstrauen gegenüber dem Neuen in der Musik, das sich in einer entschiedenen Ablehnung Schönbergs offenbart; 3. Aufwertung der Tradition; 4. Gebot der Heiterkeit. Es entstanden zahlreiche Kompositionen mit einem flüchtigen und euphorischen Charakter. […]; 5. Der erste französische Sender, Radio Tour Eiffel, wurde 1921 in Betrieb genommen.'; Michel Faure: 'Frankreich', 'VI. 1870 bis 1944', '2. 1914 bis 1944', in *Die Musik in Geschichte und Gegenwart (MGG)*, subject part, vol. 3 (Kassel: Bärenreiter, 1995), cc. 774–775.

ment of serenity' years before *Les Six* made it fashionable. Finally, as we shall see later, he also actively used the new medium of radio to make his music better known.

Barbara Kelly has also pointed out that a generational difference began to emerge, particularly after the death of Debussy, the appearance of Jean Cocteau's *Le Coq et l'arlequin* (both in 1918), and Henri Collet's famous identification of *Les Six* in 1920,[4] also singling out Georges Migot (1891–1976) as representing a new type of composer. For all his novel ideas during the 1920s, Migot clearly showed an intellectual or spiritual kinship with the much older Swan Hennessy, as we shall see in Chapter 9. Part of the reason for the 'generational gap' was that World War I had 'created a lost generation who are no longer there to defend themselves', having 'cut short the normal period a generation can expect to establish themselves and make their impact',[5] citing, in particular, the critic Émile Vuillermoz as one of several influential personalities who experienced difficulties in coming to grips with the developments after 1920.

The rise of neoclassicism is also mostly associated with French music of the interwar period of the 1920s and '30s. In fact, it would relate to three of the trends identified by Faure, namely the 'return to craftsmanship', the 'mistrust of the new' and the 'revaluation of tradition'. If it is interpreted as the return of order in reaction to the emotionalism of much of the music of the 'Impressionists', then it is indeed observable in the work of Swan Hennessy. However, this would not have started in 1920 but with Hennessy's association with the Bretons from 1912: his 'Celtic' works since then are in more traditional forms and a more traditional harmonic language than his very 'French' piano music of the period 1907 to 1912. Other elements of neoclassicism have always belonged to Hennessy and are therefore no new development, like the clarity of structures, the economy of means, a focus on counterpoint and an often expanded, yet generally tonal harmony. Again, one should think that Hennessy was now, perhaps stronger than ever, a truly contemporary composer.

* * *

The members of the Association des Compositeurs Bretons did not revive the organisation after the War. Perhaps, they lamented the loss of Paul Martineau who fell in 1915, perhaps they had other issues to worry about. Paul Ladmirault, who had fought four years on the front, withdrew from Paris and moved to rural Brittany for the rest of his life. Louis Vuillemin returned seriously wounded. There is no word about the ACB in the French press after mid-1914. Their ideas, however, were still vibrant and pertinent. In fact, most members of the group reassembled in the Société Artistique et Littéraire de l'Ouest, an organisation that had already been in existence before the

---

[4] See Henri Collet: 'La Musique chez soi (XII): Un livre de Rimsky et un livre de Cocteau – Les Cinq russes, les Six français et Erik Satie', in *Comoedia*, 16 January 1920, p. 2; and 'La Musique chez soi (XIII): 'Les "Six" français: Darius Milhaud, Louis Durey, Georges Auric, Arthur Honegger, Francis Poulenc et Germaine Tailleferre', in *Comoedia*, 23 January 1920, p. 2.
[5] Kelly, *Music and Ultra-Modernism*, p. 180.

ACB. Founded in 1889, the SALO[6] had a broader focus, including other art forms besides music and neighbouring regions bordering on Brittany such as Normandy and Pays de la Loire. They organised art exhibitions, poetry readings and concerts, all now organised by Alice Sauvrezis who had already been in the same function at the ACB and who had become president of the SALO in 1920.

Fig. 8.1: 270 boulevard Raspail, Paris, in June 2016 (author's photograph)

It turned out that Hennessy's apartment at 270 boulevard Raspail in the Montparnasse quarter of Paris was in a particularly fashionable area for artists of a wide spectrum. Apart from most members of *Les Six*, it was also the Paris home of a number of Breton composers. Just a few years into the 1920s, the artistic newspaper *Comoedia* described Montparnasse as 'Brittany in Paris', pointing out the concert hall and café 'Le Caméléon', which became a centre of their activity. Coincidentally, the building was situated diagonally opposite the boulevard from Hennessy's apartment.

> Brittany, in Paris, is bordered to the north by the Gare Montparnasse, to the west by the rue Lecourbe, to the south by the rue de Vouillé, and to the east by the boulevard Raspail. The *Caméléon*, therefore, finds itself in Brittany, and no locality could be better chosen in which to hear Celtic music. The atmosphere contributed greatly to the appreciation of the works that were offered to us, all by Celtic composers.[7]

---

[6] Like 'ACB', this is *my* abbreviation for the sake of brevity. In France at the time, the names of both organisations were always fully spelled out.

[7] *La Bretagne, à Paris, est limitée au nord par la gare Montparnasse, à l'ouest par la rue Lecourbe, au sud par la rue de Vouillé et à l'est par le boulevard Raspail. Le Caméléon se trouve donc en Bretagne et nul endroit*

An Engagement with Ireland (1920–1924)

Inspired by the legendary cultural café Le Chat noir on Montmartre, Le Caméléon was originally founded in 1921 on 146 boulevard Montparnasse, moving to 241 boulevard Raspail in November 1923, closing after 1,100 performances in 1927.[8] It was managed by Alexandre Mercereau (1884–1945), a symbolist poet and critic and an inspirational force in the development of Cubism in art. Apart from running a café, a concert venue and a gallery, Mercereau also organised his own *'Académie'* at Le Caméléon that was known to some at the time as *'Sorbonne montparnassienne'*. In fact, concert programmes in Swan Hennessy's Press Books show that the venue was also branded as *'Université Alexandre Mercereau (au Caméléon)'*. It was not only the Bretons who liked the venue: other composers associated with Le Caméléon included Honegger and Milhaud as well as the pianist Ricardo Viñes.

Despite the fact that Hennessy's musical *oeuvre* reflected the trends of his time, his post-war music is markedly different to most of what he wrote before 1914. For example, for the first half of the 1920s, the wit and humour of his pre-war compositions seems to be gone. The reasons may lie in the War itself (even though he was not directly involved in any of the battles), in the death of his father with whom he had shared so much of his life and travels, or indeed (and this is my assumption) in his discovery of his Irish heritage and the beginning success on the concert platform that was associated with it since he had joined the Association des Compositeurs Bretons in 1912. His musical humour is taking a break for the time being, with glimpses reappearing years later with *Banlieues*, Op. 69 (1926) and a few other works.

Instead, he now cultivated his 'Celtic' side and moved more into chamber music. Indeed, the majority of his pieces in a 'Celtic' style were published after 1920, and so were seventeen of his twenty-three pieces of chamber music. When Hennessy was asked by Lucien Chevaillier in 1929 how his 'Celtic' personality had revealed itself, he responded with what I would describe as a deliberate (and not very adroit) evasion of the truth:

> It is quite difficult for me to answer you. I have no drama, no story, not even an anecdote to tell you about this revelation. I just realised it one day. How it came about, I don't know. Some latent atavism was dormant within me. One fine day it arose, it imposed itself, and I had to accept the truth: I was a 'Celtic' composer. This Ireland I had seen so little of in my life stirred within me and guided my ideas. In fact, I have never stopped writing 'Celtic' music, and I acknowledged this explicitly by using the word 'Celtic' in many of my titles.[9]

---

n'était mieux choisi pour entendre de la musique celtique ; l'ambiance contribua pour beaucoup à goûter les œuvres qui nous étaient offertes, toutes de compositeurs celtes.', Comoedia, 7 November 1925, p. 2.

[8] Website *Ric's Métropole Paris*, http://www.metropoleparis.com/2000/539/539first.html (accessed 24 August 2018).

[9] *'Il m'est assez difficile de vous répondre. Je n'ai aucun drame, aucune histoire, pas même une anecdote à vous compter au sujet de cette révélation. Je me suis aperçu un jour que j'étais tel. Comment cela s'est-il fait, je n'en sais rien. Un atavisme sommeillait en moi, latent. Un beau jour il a surgi, il s'est imposé et je dus me rendre à la vérité: j'étais un compositeur "celte". Cette Irlande que j'ai si peu vue dans ma vie s'est agitée en moi et elle a conduit mes idées. De fait je n'ai plus cessé de faire de la musique "celte" et d'ailleurs je l'ai reconnu explicitement en accolant le mot "celtique" à un grand nombre de mes titres.'*; Chevaillier, 'Entretien', p. 792.

Of course, his 'Celtic' personality did not just fall from heaven 'one fine day'. The explanation that I have been offering in the course of Chapters 4 to 6 of this study is rather that the membership in the group of Breton composers and the performance opportunities that came along with it made him realise that this is the type of music that French audiences at the time wanted to hear. Equally important seems to be that his previous identification with French Impressionism and humourism was not appreciated as much by his French contemporaries. With his Irish surname, a 'Celtic' personality appeared a lot more credible to French audiences. As we shall see, they liked the 'Irish exoticism', paired with its Breton equivalent. And so, his 'Celtic' personality took its form based on supply and demand, and not on any heavenly inspiration.

* * *

Meanwhile in Ireland, although the country had not been a battle ground during World War I, the war years had also left their mark. Since the country was not independent yet, many Irishmen fought on the British side, not least in France (at the Somme, among other places). Moreover, revolutionary forces used the British distraction on the Continent to mount a rebellion in the form of the Easter Rising of 1916 in Dublin, brutally shot down with the execution of the Rising's leaders, which included poets like Patrick Pearse who subsequently became Irish heroes and martyrs. The War had barely ended when a Civil War broke out that lasted several years, ending in late 1922 with the partition of the country in the Irish Free State in the south and six counties in the north which became Northern Ireland, remaining a constituent of the United Kingdom.

The developments in Ireland were eagerly watched in France (which sympathised with the Irish), and particularly in Brittany, which had a rising number of people who might be willing to take up the Irish example on French soil. Jean Guiffan has shown how the Breton press has increasingly picked up on Irish topics since about 1870, and particularly since the question of Irish Home Rule was debated in the British Parliament, with legislative initiatives for a limited Irish self-government – commonly known as 'Home Rule Bills' – introduced in 1886, 1893, and 1912.[10] Guiffan quotes from an article in the bi-weekly Breton journal *Ar Bobl* of 20 April 1912, which first asserts that the British/Irish debate of Home Rule is about what is known in France as *'autonomie'* and *'régionalisme'*, then expresses its conviction that Wales and Scotland would most certainly want to follow the Irish example, which would then prepare the ground for the same in Brittany: *'À quand maintenant le* Home Rule *pour la Bretagne!'*[11] ('When will we see Home Rule for Brittany!'). When therefore the Easter Rising of 1916 seems to have taken the majority of French people by surprise, for the Bretons

---

[10] Jean Guiffan: 'La Presse bretonne et la "question d'Irlande" (1870–1914)', in: Yann Bévant and Laurent Daniel: *Bretagne/Irlande: quelles relations? / Brittany/Ireland: what relations?* (Rennes: Centre de Recherche Bretonne et Celtique, 2015), p. 83–101.

[11] *Ar Bobl*, 12 April 1912, p. 1, quoted after Guiffan, 'La Presse bretonne', p. 98.

it was the natural consequence of decades of British domination and of the political and cultural developments of the past decades.[12]

It can be taken for granted that Swan Hennessy, in his Swiss 'exile' and beyond, observed the Irish situation with keen interest, too – even though such an assertion cannot be backed up by any documented evidence. The clearest indication is the dedication of his second string quartet – or *Deuxième Quatuor à cordes*, Op. 49 – to the memory of Terence MacSwiney in the autumn of 1920 (see Fig. 8.2 including the first few unison bars of the Introduction).

Fig. 8.2: The dedication to Terence MacSwiney of Hennessy's quartet Op. 49

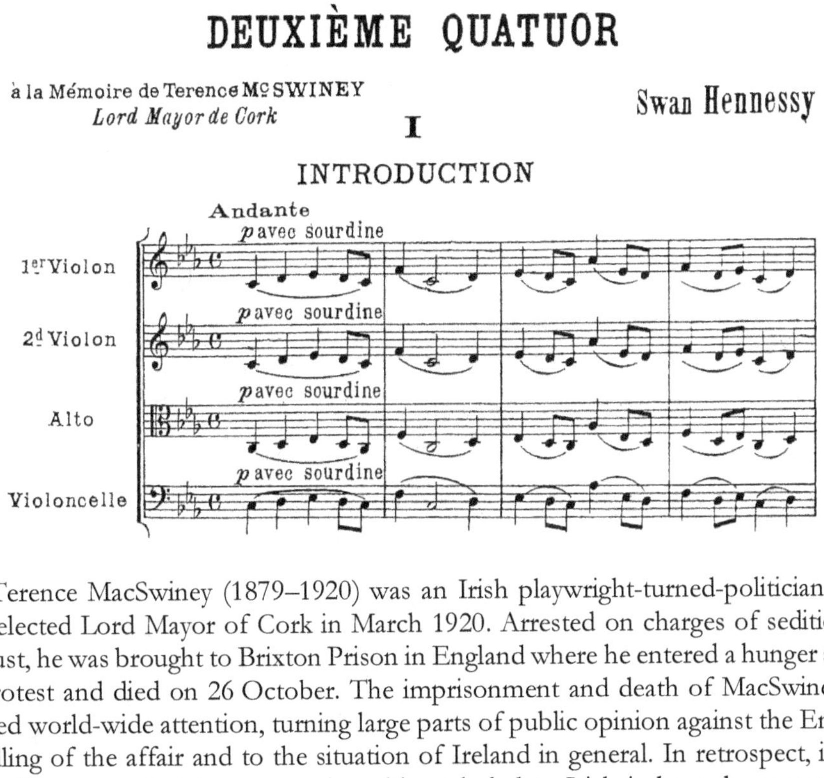

DEUXIÈME QUATUOR

à la Mémoire de Terence Mc SWINEY
Lord Mayor de Cork

Swan Hennessy

I

INTRODUCTION

Terence MacSwiney (1879–1920) was an Irish playwright-turned-politician who was elected Lord Mayor of Cork in March 1920. Arrested on charges of sedition in August, he was brought to Brixton Prison in England where he entered a hunger strike in protest and died on 26 October. The imprisonment and death of MacSwiney attracted world-wide attention, turning large parts of public opinion against the English handling of the affair and to the situation of Ireland in general. In retrospect, it was one of the most decisive events that ultimately led to Irish independence not long afterwards.[13]

It is likely that Hennessy and MacSwiney knew each other personally (see Chapter 6) so that there was a private side to the dedication of the quartet, too, in addition to Hennessy's interest in Ireland and ancestry in Cork. The personal dimension may

---

[12] Guiffan, 'La Presse bretonne', p. 101.
[13] In the absence of a proper academic biography of MacSwiney, interested readers are referred to Dave Hannigan: *Terence MacSwiney. The Hunger Strike that Rocked an Empire* (Dublin: O'Brien Press, 2010).

account for the fact that the quartet was written and (or at least finalised) as well as printed and published within a few weeks, before the end of 1920. It is somewhat confusing, though, that the score has a copyright date of 1920 on the first pages of both the score and parts, and of 1921 on the title page of the score. Maybe it was, after all, published in early 1921. In any case, the speed is astonishing and speaks for the spirit of sympathy and dismay in which the work was written.

The first thing that is striking about the quartet is its opus number – an opus 49 that apparently comes six years after opus 50! The five years in Switzerland notwithstanding, the reason is another group of works that Hennessy had withdrawn at some point, necessitating the renumbering of his work-list just in time before publication. Press reviews of performances of Hennessy's music help identify the missing pieces, and his manuscripts explain the change of opus numbers.

The manuscript to his *Trio*, Op. 54 in Hennessy's Manuscript Book IV features a catalogue of his chamber music to date in his own hand, with editorial changes by the publisher in blue crayon. These changes omit all opus numbers of the works on the list but, interestingly, these reveal an opus 53 for the second string quartet and an opus 55 for the *Petit trio celtique*. In the end, the second quartet stepped down four opus numbers to Op. 49 and the *Petit trio celtique* three numbers down to Op. 52.

Fig. 8.3: Portion of manuscript list of chamber music, showing deletions of opus numbers around 1920

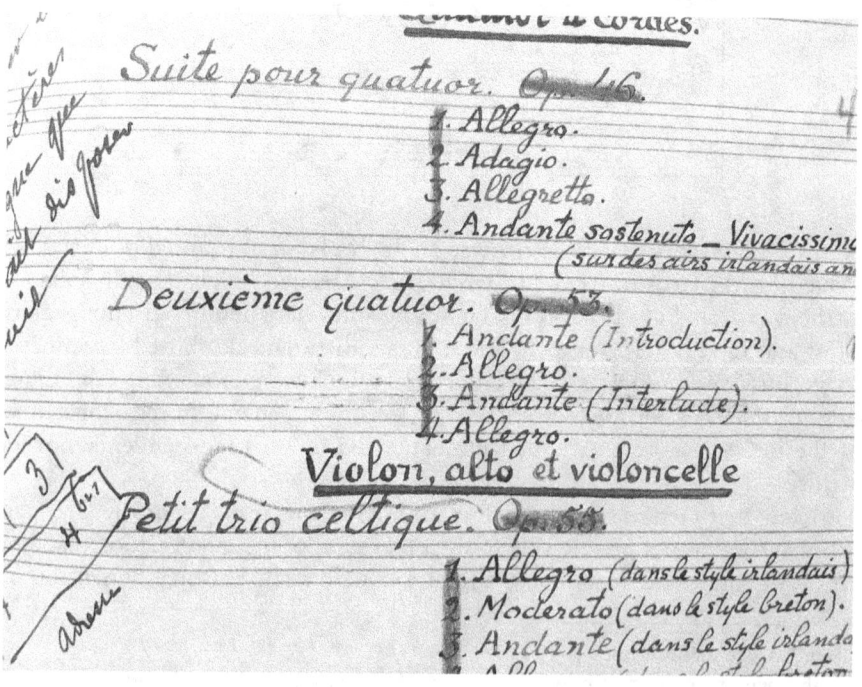

An Engagement with Ireland (1920–1924)

Of the missing works, not all can be identified. The original Opp. 51 and 52, for example, remain a mystery. But there are records of performances (in Berlin, 1922, more about which below), which reveal *Drei keltische Stücke*, Op. 53 for piano trio and a *Bretonische Rhapsodie*, Op. 55 for violin and piano. Table 8.1 also shows that the *Petit trio celtique*, Op. 52 for string trio was written *after* the Trio, Op. 54 for two clarinets and bassoon, both also in the last few weeks of 1920, like the second quartet.

'Op. 53' has been used three times: first for String Quartet No. 2, then for the *Drei keltische Stücke* for piano trio, and finally for the *Sonatine celtique* for piano (1923), which, so much may be revealed at this point, first saw life an *Irish Sonatina*, Op. 61 (!), published in London in 1924 and again with its final French title in Paris in 1929.

Table 8.1: Works Opp. 49–67 incl. opus number changes*

Title	instrumentation	composed	orig. op.	final op.
Rapsodie celtique	vn, pf	1914	50	50
??			51	
??			52	
~~*Drei keltische Stücke*~~	~~vn, vc, pf~~	(c.1919–20)	53	—
String Quartet No. 2	2vn, va, vc	1920	53	49
Trio	2cl, bn	1919–20	54	54
Petit trio celtique	vn, va, vc	1920	55	52
~~*Bretonische Rhapsodie*~~	~~vn, pf~~	(c.1920–1)	55	—
Trois Mélodies	v, pf	1921	56	56
Huit Pièces celtiques	pf	1922	57	51
Trois Pièces exotiques	pf	1922	57	57
~~*Deuxième Suite*~~	~~2vn, va, vc~~	(c.1922)	58	—
Variations sur un thème de 6 notes	fl, vn, va, vc	1922	58	58
Quatre Pièces celtiques	c.a., vn, va, vc	1923	59	59
Étude de concert	pf	1922–3	60	60
Sonatine celtique	pf	1923	61	53
String Quartet No. 3	2vn, va, vc	1922–3	61	61
Sonatine celtique	va, pf	1924	62	62
Epigrammes d'un solitaire	pf	1923	63	55
Rapsodie gaélique	vc, pf	1924	63	63
Douze Canons	pf	1924	64	64
Sérénade	2vn, va, vc	1924	65	65
Trois Mélodies	v, pf	1924	66	66
Rapsodie irlandaise	pf	1924	67	67

* Crossed-out works have been withdrawn; years in parentheses are uncertain.

This is Hennessy's last major reshuffling of opus numbers; from 1925 onward, no further changes occur. This is the basis for the present chapter, plus a brief look at the *Trois Chansons espagnoles*, Op. 42bis (1920), which is an exception in several ways.

Trois Chansons espagnoles, Op. 42bis (1920) for medium voice and piano

I will treat this composition as a brief excursus only, even though it was evidently one of Hennessy's more successful works in terms of public performances. Hennessy liked the Spanish idiom and applied it astonishingly well. But it remained a side aspect of his oeuvre and should therefore not be emphasised inappropriately.

The opus number is completely out of line with his more or less chronological series. It alludes to the piano work *Gitaneries*, Op. 42 (1911), his last 'Spanish' work to date – four brief pieces alluding to Bizet's opera *Carmen* – but apart from the Spanish colour there is no connection between Op. 42 and Op. 42bis. The songs are not, as one may have presumed, vocal adaptations of the piano pieces.

The words of the first of the *Trois Chansons espagnoles* are by Emmanuel von Geibel, those of the other two by Heinrich Heine. In fact, the songs have a German and a French text, with Hennessy providing the French translation himself. The songs are called 1. *Fluthenreicher Ebro (Sur les rives fleuries)*; 2. *Auf den Wällen Salamankas (Sur les murs de Salamanque)*; and 3. *Neben mir wohnt Don Henriquez (Mon voisin est Don Henriquez)*. The work also exists in a string quartet version dating from 1925.

The score features a year of publication of 1921, but the plate number E. 2083 D. rather speaks for a 1922 print (one of the last by Demets before he died in 1923). 1922 is probably more correct, and I presume that Hennessy may even have halted an earlier publication when prospects for a performance arose which allowed a dedication to the singer. This was done in favour of the American contralto Radiana Pazmor (1892–1986), then still in her early career. She gave the first performance together with Georg Vollerthun on piano at the Bechsteinsaal, Berlin, 23 November 1922, and a second one on 28 March 1923 at the Salle Beethoven in Paris, accompanied by the American pianist Ralph Lawton. She continued to sing them after her return to the United States, and they were also taken on by a number of other singers of the period, including Marthe Saisset, Lili Fabrègue, Éva Gauthier, Helia Wolska, and Mildah Polia. In fact, the event when the Canadian singer Éva Gauthier sang them, accompanied by Max Jaffe, at the Aeolian Hall in New York, 1 November 1923, made history because this also marked the first public appearance of George Gershwin in a 'classical' environment. Typical for the unknown status of Hennessy, these songs are often neglected when reference is being made to this famous recital. But they are briefly referred to in Alain Lacombe's and Howard Pollack's biographies of Gershwin.[14]

Reviews of both score and performances were positive throughout. Critics generally regarded them as not ambitious but entertaining. The *Allgemeine Musikzeitung* commented:

---

[14] Alain Lacombe: *George Gershwin. Une Chronique de Broadway* (Paris: Éditions Francis van de Velde, 1980), p. 61; Howard Pollack: *George Gershwin. His Life and Work* (Berkeley: University of California Press, 2007), p. 38.

Slightly tossed off, as if hummed to the mandolin, the songs in an undemanding, transparent setting and simple melodies quite gracefully meet a folksy tone of Spanish colour. In domestic music they will be more appropriate than in concert.[15]

The concert programme at the first performance in Berlin also included songs by Hugo Rasch and the Breton composer Lucien Haudebert – both friends of Hennessy's –, and a critic noted, '"Three Spanish songs by the Welshman Swan Hennessy […] were more lively. The best, "Auf den Wällen Salamankas", had to be repeated.'[16]

Despite the frequent performances in France (see Appendix 1), there are no French reviews. The programme of the 1923 New York performance was extraordinarily broad, reaching in six sections from the Renaissance into the present. There were sections devoted to Bartók, Hindemith and Schönberg; the three Gershwin songs appeared together with one each by Jerome Kern and Irving Berlin in an American section. The recital concluded with a group of French songs, including the *Chant de la nourrice* (from *Poèmes juifs*) by Darius Milhaud, *L'Alouette (du Baras)* by Maurice Delage, and ended with two of the three Hennessy songs from Op. 42bis, *Sur les murs de Salamanca* and *Mon voisin est Don Henriquez*.

Most of the American reviews focused on the variety of the programme and on the Gershwin appearance (who accompanied his own songs). Not many mentioned the Hennessy songs at all. An example is the following from *Musical America*:

> It was bound to happen. Sooner or later ragtime, or jazz – the pure stuff of Tin Pan Alley – was destined to make its way into the hallowed concert hall. Eva Gauthier, who loves a plunge against the icy current of musical convention, had the proper amount of conviction and the marriage to 'do it now,' with the result that her recital program at Aeolian Hall on the evening of Nov. 1 had an 'American' group by Messrs. Berlin, Kern, Donaldson, Gershwin, et al. A very large and expectant audience waited anxiously for this particular group, and getting it seemed vastly gratified. But all in its proper place. […]
>
> A group of new French songs by Milhaud, Delage and Swan-Hennessy – pallid pieces, cut to pattern, without life, fire or real inner movement – brought the program to a close. Mme. Gauthier's singing throughout the evening was invariably interesting and her voice often took on beautiful shades of color and meaning, she had a remarkable, although sometimes obtrusive, accompanist in Max Jaffe, who tossed off the terrifying difficulties of Bartok and Schoenberg as though playing from a volume of Czerny.[17]

Although Hennessy was American himself – how many critics or members of the audience would have been aware of that? – it was the 'jazzy' or Tin Pan Alley inspired works that stole the show.

---

[15] '*Leicht hingeworfen, gleichsam zur Mandoline geträllert, treffen die Liedchen in anspruchslosem durchsichtigen Satz und schlichter Melodik recht anmutig einen volkstümlichen Ton spanischen Kolorits. In der Hausmusik werden sie besser ansprechen als im Konzert.* […]'; Ludwig Misch in *Allgemeine Musikzeitung*, 51:41, 10 October 1924, p. 748.

[16] '*Drei spanische Liedchen des Wallisers Swan Hennesy* […] *schlugen lebhafter ein. Das beste, "Auf den Wällen Salamankas", mußte wiederholt werden.*'; *Deutsche Zeitung*, 5 December 1922.

[17] 'B. R.' in *Musical America*, 10 November 1923.

Fig. 8.4: Portrait of Swan Hennessy, around 1920 (© Boris Lipnitzky / Roger-Viollet)

Deuxième Quatuor à cordes, Op. 49 [String Quartet No. 2]

With Hennessy's second string quartet there came a more intense period of engagement with Ireland that lasted until 1924, with at least one visit to the country and some performances that introduced his name to a country in turmoil.

As explained above, the work was prompted by the death, by hunger strike, of the lord mayor of the southern Irish city of Cork – a symbol of the Irish struggle for independence.

Suiting the commemorative occasion, the work begins in C minor in a rather rugged melodic line in unison (see Fig. 8.2). The mute remains on for the duration of the first movement. The unison playing lasts for six bars only before the instrumental parts spread out towards Figure A (from bar 9). It is the falling interval of the fourth that permeates the whole movement (visible in Fig. 8.2, bar 2), undergoing numerous tonal transformations as it passes through modulations and from one instrument to the next. The way Hennessy applies this little thematic feature is particularly suited to express the painful and declamatory emotion that is at the core of this movement. Hennessy's counterpoint is faultless and very creative, and he does not feel bound by the C minor harmonic grid – and this assessment is not limited to this work. We have already encountered it in parts of the first quartet (the *Suite*, Op. 46), and we will see it in all of his 1920s chamber music. It is a clear difference to his pre-1914 piano music in which he mostly pursued a descriptive and programmatic style. With the exception of the third quartet (1923), all of his chamber music is abstract, and his approach is that of a tonally expanded counterpoint that centres around a fixed tonality in the tradition of the (late) Romantics.

The second movement is an *Allegro* in 3/4 time that remains in C minor and would resemble a *scherzo* if it was just a littler shorter. Starting from a phrase in the cello that moves in an imitative manner upwards through the four instruments of the quartet, Hennessy described the initial theme once from the point of view of its character as being 'full of sap'[18] and once from the hermeneutic perspective, that it 'expresses the joy of the sacrifice achieved' (i. e. MacSwiney's sacrifice).[19] The movement stands in classical sonata form, with a second subject in Figure D, both themes reappearing later in a full reprise. As a secondary theme, Figure E brings a very Romantic motif in the first violin that, with its spirited waltz character betrays Hennessy's German musical education and influences (Ex. 8.1). There are modest Irish influences as well, albeit not too plain and obvious, notably in the occasional use of the 'snap' and some intervallic constructions.

---

[18] '*L'allegro est bâti sur un thème plein de sève.*', quote from his short commentary on the work in his own list of works.

[19] '*Elle s'enchaine avec un allegro de forme classique assez développé qui exprime la joie du sacrifice accompli.*' ('It is followed by an allegro in a fairly developed classical form that expresses the joy of the sacrifice achieved.'); in *Le Guide du concert*, 12 December 1924, p. 286.

Ex. 8.1: String Quartet No. 2, Op. 49, 2nd movt., bars 57–68

As in the first quartet of nine years earlier, Hennessy again excels in the music for his slow movement – here it is an Interlude of just two pages in the score, set in A major. Beauty lays in the eye of the beholder, naturally (i. e. not everyone may agree in this assessment), but in these two pages that correspond to about 2'20 minutes in performance, Hennessy has created a little masterpiece in restrained melancholy, very economical in the means applied, and of timeless appeal. Hennessy described it as a meditation and *'d'une couleur très irlandaise'*[20] – and both is certainly true.

The thematic material is exposed in the first two bars, in a dominant line of the first violin that is accompanied by the viola (Ex. 8.2).

Ex. 8.2: String Quartet No. 2, Op. 49, 3rd movt., bars 1–2 (first violin)

This motif is used throughout the short movement in various guises, abbreviated and sketched forms, reaching a peak in bars 17–19 where the viola takes up the motif and the first violin retreats to a high-pitched accompaniment. This is a more than satisfying

---

[20] See previous two footnotes, the latter quote is in *Le Guide du concert*.

solution to the question of how to further develop the rather self-contained motif and bring it to a conclusion not long afterwards (Ex. 8.3).

Ex. 8.3: String Quartet No. 2, Op. 49, 3rd movt., bars 14–21

The *Finale* is the most Irish of the four movements. Set in C major, it clearly transforms the sorrow of the first movement, the 'joy of the sacrifice achieved' of the second, and the melancholy of the Interlude to a positive vision of what MacSwiney's sacrifice will mean for the struggle for independence in Ireland. This is why he closes a C minor quartet in C major, and why he is so Irish now in a work that was more ambiguous regarding its artistic provenance before.

I will yet come to Hennessy's opinion of the Irishness of the 'Scotch snap', but here we have it in abundance from the first system of the score (twice in bar 2, at the accent, see Ex. 8.4):

Ex. 8.4: String Quartet No. 2, Op. 49, 4th movt., bars 1–2 (first violin)

Hennessy declared that these two bars are his only quotations from existing traditional music, and that they derive from an (unidentified) Scottish tune.[21] In this context, of course, a 'Scotch snap' is perfectly appropriate, even though his vision here is an Irish one. But his interpretation is interesting, because his intention is 'evoking pan-Celtism', perhaps suggesting that Ireland's suffering was of common interest to the Celtic nations – something his Breton friends perceived so as well, as shown earlier.

This is followed by a (self-composed) jig tune to the accompaniment of pedal tones, reminding of bagpipes (Ex. 8.5).

Ex. 8.5: String Quartet No. 2, Op. 49, 4th movt., bars 9–12

The fourth movement is predominantly joyful, mainly played *allegro*, alternating with sorrowful passages that are marked *andante*. The ending is preceded by a forward-driving tune in the cello. Overall, Hennessy uses his thematic material quite economically, and mostly in an artistically convincing way, with the possible exception of some of the *andante* passages of the fourth movement that are, perhaps, somewhat dilated. But the purpose of the (dominating) brighter passages of the fourth movement is to celebrate Ireland, to communicate the positive message that the present suffering of the Irish will not be in vain, and also that there is a solidarity among the 'Celtic' nations.

The quartet was first performed in a festive evening programme of the 'World Congress of the Irish Race' that took place at the Hotel Continental, Paris, on

---

[21] '[…] *le final qui se compose d'une série de variations très libres sur un thème débutant par les deux premières mesures d'un air populaire écossais évoquant ainsi le panceltisme.*' ('[…] the finale, which consists of a series of very free variations on a theme starting with the first two bars of a Scottish popular tune, thus evoking panceltism.'; in *Le Guide du concert*, op. cit.

25 January 1922. The performers were an Irish quartet led by the prominent violinist Arthur Darley, with a young Terry O'Connor (violin, later the leader of the Irish String Orchestra), George H. Brett (viola) and Joseph Schofield (cello). The aim of the congress was to organise support for the effective setting up of the Irish Free State, with prominent politicians, businessmen and clergy from many countries present.[22]

The evening concert was attended by Éamon de Valera, Countess Markievicz and Mary MacSwiney, sister of the quartet's dedicatee – three of the most prominent Irish politicians of the time (Mary MacSwiney became an opponent to de Valera). The concert began with Hennessy's quartet, included a number of vocal items sung by Gerald Crofts, and concluded with another quartet, this one a medley of Irish folk tunes written by Henri Bast (1856–1907), a German-born cello professor at the Royal Irish Academy of Music.

In a review of the first performance, the Paris correspondent of the *New York Herald* characterised the work quite well:

> The outstanding feature of the first concert given last evening in connection with the Irish Congress at the Hotel Continental, Paris, was the initial audition of the string quartet by Mr. Swan Hennessy, of Rockford, Ill., one of the most interesting figures among contemporary American composers. The quartet, which is dedicated to the memory of Terence MacSweeney, Lord Mayor of Cork, who died on hunger strike while a political prisoner, begins slowly and sadly in a manner suggestive of the patriot's long self-imposed martyrdom. His gradual weakening and final death are indicated by a subtle progressive change of rhythmic values. In the three movements which follow the effort is to glorify Ireland, and both the more sombre and the gayer sides of the Celtic genius are indicated. There is a clever counterfeiting of the notes of the bagpipe, the occasional introduction of a bright theme from the popular ballads. The triumphant finale acclaims the glorious future of the new Ireland.[23]

The same Irish musicians performed the work about a week later, 2 February 1922, at the Engineer's Hall, 35 Dawson Street, Dublin. It can be deduced from the critic's remarks in *The Freeman's Journal* that he was less accustomed to this kind of music, arguing that what has been good enough for Paris cannot be bad for Dublin:

> Apart from its own intrinsic value as music, the quartet was heard with pleasure on account of the fact that it had earned much commendation at the recent proceedings in Paris, where its character and scope were sufficiently understood and appreciated.[24]

A bit more eloquent was the critic in *The Irish Times* who also pointed out the fact that an Irish work made such a favourable impression in Paris. It is worth being quoted here (almost) in its entirety for its interesting spotlight on Irish opinions:

---

[22] Dermot Keogh: 'The Treaty Split and the Paris Irish Race Convention, 1922, in *Études irlandaises* 12:2, 1987, p. 165–170; Gerard Keown: 'The Irish Race Conference, 1922, Reconsidered', in *Irish Historical Studies* 32:127, May 2001, p. 365–376.
[23] 'American Composer's Work Heard at Irish Concert'; *The New York Herald*, 26 January 1922.
[24] 'Good Programme at Concert in Aid of Teach Ultain'; *The Freeman's Journal*, 3 February 1922.

The string quartette, dedicated to Terence MacSwiney, by the Irish American composer, as well as being new, is a really beautiful work. It opens with an *Andante* noble and dignified rather than plaintive, though the mourning note permeates it, and it is kept at almost painful intensity through all the movement. The exhausting tension is accentuated by keenly delicate violin solo *motifs*, which give just the right sense of uplift.

This exquisite poise, though this time more of the playing than the writing, was also maintained in the "Interlude," which one could more fully enjoy freed from the painful association of the *Andante*.

The remaining movements were in great relief, though still on the same high musical level. They are, in a sense, descriptive, or, rather, suggestive of Ireland and its people.

The bagpipe's stirring note, straying melodies or idioms, and some fresh quick-stepping passages, are cleverly handled to a bright triumphant *finale* to typify a glorious future about to dawn.

Prophecy or no, it is extremely fine as music, and the players – Mr. Arthur Darley, Miss T. O'Connor (violins), Mr. George Brett (viola), and Mr. Joseph Schofield ('cello) – gave it with understanding, feeling, and artistic finish.

One is so accustomed to go to hear world-famed *virtuosos* from abroad that it was something of a novelty that these musicians should have returned from a similar welcome in Paris, and doubly gratifying when one heard in this work the impression they made there.[25]

On the basis of the printed score, the German *Allgemeine Musikzeitung* took a well-balanced view:

This is a kind of music one likes to write about. Their content is as dainty as these scores. First the (2nd) String Quartet in C minor. It is written with a fine pen, elegant and full of thoughts at the same time. […] And everything sounds because the dynamics of the string quartet have been cleverly exploited. […][26]

Understandably, perhaps, a reception of the quartet in England was barely noticeable. Hennessy's records do not show any performance in the country, and the only review of the score that has come to light is a remark in the *Musical Opinion* that reveals a rather superficial view with a touch of English snobbism:

[…] A *String Quartet* by the same musician is more ambitious, but hardly so successful. It is dedicated to the memory of Terence McSwiney. It is rather halting and patchy, and the elegiac vein does not seem in Mr. Hennessy's natural manner. […][27]

In France, there were comparatively few reviews. Perhaps, the 'World Congress of the Irish Race' was not perceived so much as a musical event. A short remark by

---

[25] 'Chamber Music / Irish American's work'; *The Irish Times*, 3 February 1922.
[26] '*Ueber solche Musik schreibt man gern. Zierlich wie diese Partituren ist auch ihr Inhalt. Zunächst das (II.) Streichquartett in c-moll. Es ist mit feiner Feder geschrieben, elegant und voller Gedanken zugleich. […] Und alles klingt, weil die Dynamik des Streichquartetts klüglich ausgenutzt wurde. […]*'; Eugen Segnitz in *Allgemeine Musikzeitung* 49:16, 21 April 1922, p. 343.
[27] *Musical Opinion*, February 1922.

An Engagement with Ireland (1920–1924)

Paul Le Flem, writing about a group of recitals that had taken place recently, mentioned it as 'a tasty quartet by Swan Hennessy, steeped in musical Celticism'.[28] In view of the discussion about pan-Celtism and Irishness, the opinion of Henri Collet should be interesting who regarded it as a rather French work:

> The Second String Quartet, dedicated to the memory of Terence Mac Swiney, Lord Mayor of Cork, exposed in muted unison an expressive and poignant phrase repeated at the end, after sketches put in opposition to plaintive chromatism. Rigorously fugato, the allegro makes a hieratic subject converse with a very personal lyrical phrase.
> The Interlude, a simple rhythmic presentation, is followed by the Finale, the theme of which, derived from the generating motif, is accentuated by distinct, loosely varied and colourful values. The work, without any picturesque ease, is lively, clear, evocative of a changing mood, of an almost French character.[29]

There were a number of sympathetic reviews of the Berlin performance that occurred not long afterwards, in May 1922. Most of them will be dealt with collectively further below, but here is one that concentrated on the second string quartet interpreting it as an expression of the peculiar political situation in Ireland and how it may affect the creative soul:

> Swan Hennessy is a real composer and a likeable one. Certain peculiarities of his sound-world, which could perhaps be pronounced as of Celtic origin, give his music its character. One of his best works is the second string quartet, Op. 49, written in memory of the Irish freedom fighter Terence Mc Swiney. The themes have a folk-song character, and the processing of the mostly delicate structures with their predominant minor harmony also endeavours to preserve this character, to which small phrases in bagpipe style also contribute. There is something original in this music. Nevertheless, the overall impression is not uniform, because these stylistic elements of the past and those of the present sometimes seem rather disconnected. However, these compositions delight in a strong love of the much-contested homeland with its austere beauties and the tranquillity of nature that leads to inner reflection and self-contemplation. We can be grateful to the ambitious Kulenkampff Quartet for this acquaintance, which shows us how music has a comforting and hopeful effect in this embattled corner of the earth.[30]

---

[28] '[…] *un savoureux* Quatuor *de Swan Hennessy imprégné de celtisme musical.*'; Paul Le Flem in *Comoedia*, 30 January 1922, p. 3.

[29] '*Le deuxième* Quatuor *à cordes, dédié à la mémoire de Terence Mac Swiney, lord mayor de Cork, expose en sourdine à l'unisson une phrase expressive et poignante reprise en fin du temps, après opposition de dessins au plaintif chromatisme. Rigoureusement fugué, l'*allegro *fait dialoguer un sujet hiératique avec une phrase lyrique bien personnelle. / A l'*Interlude*, simple exposé rythmique, succède le* Finale *dont le thème, issu du motif générateur, s'accentue en valeurs distinctes, souplement variées et colorées. L'œuvre, sans pittoresque facile, est vive, nette, évocatrice d'une humeur changeante, d'un caractère presque français.*'; Henri Collet: 'La Musique chez soi (xcvii): Œuvres de Swan Hennessy', in *Comoedia*, 5 December 1921, p. 4.

[30] '*Swan Hennessy ist ein wirklicher Komponist und ein sympathischer. Gewisse Klangeigentümlichkeiten, die man vielleicht als keltischen Ursprungs aussprechen könnte, geben seiner Musik das Gepräge. Zu seinen besten Arbeiten gehört das zweite Streichquartett, op. 49, dem irischen Freiheitskämpfer Terence Mc. Swiney zur Erinnerung geschrieben. Die Themen tragen volksliedmässigen Charakter, und auch die Verarbeitung der meist*

In an Irish context, Hennessy's String Quartet No. 2 is quite unique as one of the very few works by a 'classical' composer that directly responded to the political events that led to Irish independence. This is where this particular work could assume a level of national importance that is all but unknown in a culture that still struggles with its attitude to art music. It must be kept in mind that, in Ireland, during the two or three decades before and after the turn of the century, classical chamber music was mainly heard in social circles associated with the Protestant Anglo-Irish upper classes, in particular the members of the Royal Dublin Society. That art music – as any serious art – is (or at least, has been) associated with social class, more depending on income than on talent, is not new. But in a European comparison, the Irish peculiarity is that this class and its art forms were often regarded as foreign, as 'un-Irish', as an import from England, the historic invader and colonizer.

Hennessy then, was a Roman Catholic, albeit probably a non-practicing one. But the majority of Irish composers, contemporary to Hennessy, was Protestant. Nobody of them would have thought of dedicating a work of art music to an Irish rebel. It had to be an outsider who, in retrospect, assumed this potentially national role, because for many Irish composers of the time, political independence was a potential threat, at least it was a matter of uncertainty and anxiety. So we arrive at the fact that the major works of contemporary art music that refer to the struggle for Irish independence were written by sympathetic foreigners. Here we find the largest score in this regard being written by the Englishman Arnold Bax (1883–1953), whose orchestral piece *In memoriam* (1916) commemorates the death of Patrick Pearse following the Easter Rising. A similarly inspired work is his *Elegiac Trio* (1916) for flute, viola, and harp. The next major work, chronologically, is Hennessy's quartet.

Perhaps out of uncertainty or fear about what an independent Irish state might have in store for art music composers, the Irish composers of these years did not comment (musically) on their changing political and social environment. Some, like Carl Hardebeck (1869–1945) and Joseph Crofts (1886–after mid-1950s), wrote songs or ballads on revolutionary texts. Ina Boyle's (1889–1967) art songs *Sleep Song* (1923) and *A Mountain Woman* (1927) are settings of Pearse in a similar context, but came somewhat later. Later still, Hardebeck's *Spioraid na Saoirse 1916* for small orchestra was written in 1936 in commemoration of the events of 1916. In later decades, Irish composers contributed numerous works expressly upholding the memory of those revolutionary years between 1916 and 1923, but these were younger generations writing

---

zartgliedrigen Gebilde mit ihrer vorherrschenden Mollharmonik ist bestrebt, diesen Charakter zu wahren, wozu auch Sätzchen in Dudelsackpfeifer-Manier beitragen. Es steckt wohl Ursprüngliches in dieser Musik. Der Gesamteindruck ist zuletzt trotzdem kein einheitlicher, weil diese Stilelemente der Vergangenheit mit jenen der Jetztzeit zuweilen doch zu unverbunden nebeneinanderstehen. Es erfreut aber an diesen Kompositionen eine starke Liebe zur viel umkämpften Heimat mit ihren herben Schönheiten und jene Naturbeschaulichkeit, die zur Einkehr und Selbstbesinnung führt. Wir können dem strebsamen Kulenkampff-Quartett dankbar sein für diese Bekanntschaft, die uns zeigt, wie sich in jenem vielumstrittenen Erdenwinkel die Musik als Trösterin und Hoffnung auswirkt.'; Otto Steinhagen in *Signale für die musikalische Welt* 80:19, 10 May 1922, p. 642.

about events in the past that later turned out to be of historical importance.[31] Bax and Hennessy were the only ones who realised the importance of what was going on at the moment when it actually occurred.

In Ireland, the quartet was last heard at the Feis Doire Colmcille in Derry in April 1939 and remained forgotten until its first Cork performance on 5 November 2016[32] and its commercial CD release in April 2019 (see Appendix 7). This shows that it is sometimes a long way between potential and actual importance.

Trio, Op. 54 (1920) for two clarinets and bassoon

The woodwind *Trio*, Op. 54 may have been the first composition that Hennessy originally completed after his return from Switzerland in 1919. At least, among his manuscripts, there is a complete first version in pencil dated 1919, which has been revised during 1920, obviously after the String Quartet No. 2, Op. 49 (originally Op. 53) was finished, which must therefore have been around November of that year. There is also an arrangement for piano solo among Hennessy's manuscripts, which is dated 1919.

The two main differences between the 1919 and the 1920 versions are that an 'Intermezzo' has been added, placed between the second and the third movement, and that the whole work has been transposed one note up from G major to A major (this is for the transposing instruments; the sounding tonalities moved from F major to G major accordingly). The revised final score was published by E. Demets in 1921.[33] The work is dedicated to the Breton composer Paul Ladmirault (1877–1944).

The rather exotic instrumentation may have been an obstacle during Hennessy's lifetime: not more than five performances are recorded, the first in Berlin, three in Paris and one in Dublin. But today, ambitious chamber musicians on the lookout for original scores in unusual combinations have rediscovered Hennessy's *Trio*, and since about 2011, it is this composition (mainly) that has kept Hennessy's name in the concert repertory. A cursory internet search has revealed 26 performances between June 2011 and September 2018 – 15 of these by various ensembles in Germany, four in the United States, three in Italy, two in Austria and one each in France and China. In addition, it has appeared three times on commercial CDs (in 1999, 2002 and 2013; see Appendix 7), which is also a rarity in Hennessy's case.

---

[31] The conference 'Music in Ireland: 1916 and Beyond', which took place 22–24 April 2016 at the DIT Conservatory of Music and Drama, Dublin, highlighted some of these works and their background; see Wolfgang Marx's report about the conference in the *AIC New Music Journal* (online), http://www.aicnewmusicjournal.com/shorts/music-ireland-1916-and-beyond (accessed 10 March 2019).

[32] Performed by the RTÉ ConTempo Quartet on the occasion of Hennessy's 150th anniversary, suggested by the present author, in the presence of descendants of both the Hennessy and the MacSwiney families. It has since again been performed in Limerick (22 November 2018), Athenry Co. Galway (24 March 2019) and elsewhere.

[33] Still available from Durand-Salabert-Eschig. Since Hennessy's works entered the public domain, there have also been at least three reprints, available from two German and one American publisher; see Appendix 1.

Hennessy did not regard the Intermezzo as an independent movement, which it factually is, despite its brevity of just under one minute in performance – but this is part of a work that does not last longer than about nine minutes in its entirety.

The first movement in A major (sounding G major) is marked *Moderato con grazia*, another change in comparison to the 1919 version, where the same music was marked *Allegro*. The Intermezzo (*Andante sostenuto*) follows this tonality, but the second movement is an *Andante* in D major (sounding C major) and the third is marked *Vivace con spirito* (A minor, sounding G minor), ending on the parallel minor of the leading tonality. This is a similar process, albeit in a counter direction, as in the Quartet Op. 49, which began in C minor and ended on C major. Another parallel is that this *finale* is also the work's most 'Irish' movement, set predominantly in a lively jig rhythm, an Irish ending that we also encountered in the *Suite*, Op. 46. Contrary to the two quartets, however, there is neither a proper slow movement nor a classical *scherzo* in this *Trio*.

But the first movement is very classical insofar as it stands in perfect sonata form with two contrasting thematic subjects reached by modulation (Hennessy himself called them Haydenian[34], a development and a reprise. Rhythmically, the melodic material is contained in two groups of four quavers that spiral upwards and downwards with a great amount of alternation. Ever so often, there are 'breathing spaces' for a single instrument while another takes on its role or in instances when phrases end on a bar with two minims.

There are a number of interesting modulations in the work, for example, in the second movement at figure F where the (sounding) C major basic tonality briefly moves to A major, followed a short while later by several consecutive modulations at figure H. The main theme in this movement changes between the first clarinet and the bassoon. It is clearly derived from the first subject of the first movement.

After the pretty Intermezzo that reminds a little of an Irish narrative ballad, there follows the third movement, whose overtly Irish character derives from two 're-composed' or pastiche Irish jig tunes (a folkdance in 6/8 time, here notated as two groups of triplets in a 2/4 bar structure). The first of these may have been inspired by bagpipe music (in Ireland, the elbow-blown uilleann pipes). Here is, perhaps, where the reason for the work's dedication to Paul Ladmirault becomes apparent: in Ladmirault's *Rhapsodie gaélique* for piano duet there is a movement called *Limerick Pibroch* (a bagpipe tune from Limerick) which moves in similarly unusual interval pitches as Hennessy's tune with the striking E♭ in a (notated) A minor tune (see Ex. 8.6). As explained in Chapter 6, Hennessy's *Petite suite irlandaise*, Op. 29 for piano duet (1908) was most likely influenced by Ladmirault's work for the same instrumentation. It seems reasonable that the dedication and the presumed thematic allusion is a late expression of gratitude for an inspiration that was important to Hennessy in the formation of his 'Celtic' style, even though Hennessy's piano duet does not already contain such a thematic allusion.

---

[34] *Le Guide du concert*, 15 February 1924, p. 280. This brief anonymous analysis was most likely written by Hennessy himself.

An Engagement with Ireland (1920–1924)

Ex. 8.6: *Trio*, Op. 54, 3rd movement, bars 1–8

After a response in the bassoon, the second thematic subject of this movement, occurring in the first clarinet at figure L, sounds even more familiar, alluding to (without citing) several prototypical jig tunes of Irish provenance that one seems to recognise without being able to attach a title it. The 'pastiche' is revealed at the end of the eight-bar phrase: while an ending on repeated pitches is indeed a characteristic of Irish traditional music, this would not go beyond three notes; Hennessy elongates the phrase by extending it to six repeated pitches (Ex. 8.7).

Ex. 8.7: *Trio*, Op. 54, 3rd movement, bars 37–44

Compared to the second string quartet, the critical response to the *Trio*, Op. 54 was more modest. Interestingly, the earliest review appeared in the United States, but it disqualifies itself not only by its brevity but its polemic undertone. The whole 'review' in the *Musical Courier* of New York reads: 'Swan Hennessy, the Celtic composer, has just published a trio for two clarinets and bassoon. Why not for two piccolos and bass drum?'.[35] What is interesting about this comment is that Hennessy seems already to have been considered a 'Celtic' composer by 1921, when most of his Celticist works had not even been written. It is unlikely that this notice reflects a 'Celtic' reputation Hennessy would have had in the US; rather, it was probably written by a Paris correspondent of the journal who came across a recent issue of *Le Guide du concert* (21 October 1921), which featured a drawing of Hennessy's head on its title page accompanied by the line 'Swan Hennessy, the Celtic composer whose 2nd Quartet, a String Trio and a Trio for two clarinets and bassoon have just been released'.[36] Probably the 'reviewer' had not even seen the music; the cover page of the journal was quite enough.

Henri Collet reviewed the work for his 1921 portrait of Hennessy in *Comoedia*, focussing on the suitability of the woodwind instruments to express folkloristic music:

> […] the Trio for two clarinets and bassoon, with its fresh, green sound, makes the most of the instruments so wonderfully suited to evoking Celtic scenes or landscapes. Its three very short movements are a delight to the ear, and, passing from G major to G minor through an andante in C, bring about the essential musical diversity within the strong folkloristic unity.[37]

The first performance took place in the course of an event entirely devoted to music by Hennessy on 23 November 1922 at the Bechsteinsaal, Berlin, performed by Leonhard Kohl, Adolf Mützelburg, and Louis Scheiwein. Not all the (many) reviews of this event mentioned the *Trio*, but those that did were quite favourable, even though they acknowledged the modest proportions of the work. One critic wrote:

> A very charming trio for two clarinets and bassoon (Messrs Kohl, Mützelburg and Scheiwein) by Swan Hennessy […] was rightly applauded. This likeable Irishman, who by the way is in no way connected with the cognac company, once again says something pretty here in a small setting, with his own colouring in the last movement, and he gives the instruments interesting, stimulating tasks. What more do you want? Not all trees can grow into the sky, and wise self-restraint, which creates something so pleasant, is far more

---

[35] *Musical Courier*, 17 November 1921, p. 20.
[36] '*Swan Hennessy, le compositeur celtique dont le 2e Quatuor, un Trio à cordes et un Trio pour deux clarinettes et basson viennent de paraître.*'
[37] '*Enfin, le Trio pour deux clarinettes et basson, à la sonorité verte et fraîche, tire le plus savoureux parti des instruments si merveilleusement propres à évoquer des scènes ou des paysages celtiques. Ses trois temps, fort courts, sont un régal pour l'ouïe, et, passant de sol majeur à sol mineur par l'intermédiaire d'un andante en ut, réalisent l'indispensable diversité musicale dans la ferme unité populaire.*'; Henri Collet in *Comoedia*, 5 December 1921, p. 4.

sympathetic than the artificial inflation of the 'geniuses' running around in shock today, who hardly distinguish themselves through self-knowledge and personality.[38]

The critic in the *Allgemeine Musikzeitung* described it as a work,

> [...] in which technical dexterity, natural sense of sound, mind and mood combine to form excellent artistic harmony; in its own way, this original three-movement creation is a small masterpiece.[39]

Petit trio celtique, Op. 52 (1920) for violin, viola and cello

The cellist Joseph Schofield[40] who had been a member of the quartet that gave the first performance of Hennessy's quartet Op. 49 in Paris seems to have become quite a supporter of Hennessy's string music in Ireland, being involved in several performances of his chamber works. One of them was the first performance of the *Petit trio celtique*, Op. 52 for string trio, premiered on 30 March 1922 at the Engineer's Hall, Dawson Street, Dublin, together with John Moody (violin) and George H. Brett (viola).

It is the only first performance of a work by Hennessy in Ireland. But it is not entirely sure that Hennessy was aware of it. The performance was not announced as a first performance, and in Hennessy's records, the premiere is recorded as having taken place in January 1925 in the series of *Concerts Touche* in Paris. That, however, had only been the third performance, since there was a second one on 3 May 1922 in Berlin. Hennessy may not have been aware of the Dublin performance, if the musicians did not tell him, but he was present at the Berlin performance. It is a sign of how cautious one has to be in relying on a composer's information only.

Originally composed as Op. 55 in late 1920 (and therefore postdating the woodwind *Trio*, Op. 54), it was published with E. Demets in 1921. This piece turned out to be one of Swan Hennessy's most popular, i. e. most frequently performed, pieces during his own lifetime. There are 29 documented performances between 1922 and 1939 (16 of these before his death). Then it slumbered on shelves for decades, but – much like the *Trio*, Op. 54 – since about 2010 it has been rediscovered by chamber musicians and has seen performances in places as far apart as Spain and Australia.

---

[38] 'Ein sehr liebenswürdiges Trio für zwei Klarinetten und Fagott (die Herren Kohl, Mützelburg und Scheiwein) von Swan Hennessy [...] fand mit Recht viel Beifall. Dieser sympathische Ire, der übrigens mit der Kognak-Firma in keiner Weise zusammenhängt, sagt auch hier wieder in kleinem Rahmen Hübsches, im letzten Satze eigen Gefärbtes, und er stellt den Instrumenten interessante, anregende Aufgaben. Was will man mehr? In den Himmel können nicht alle Bäume wachsen, und weise Selbstbeschränkung, die so Liebenswürdiges schafft, ist weit sympathischer als die künstliche Aufblähung der heute schockweise herumlaufenden "Genies", denen nichts weniger eignet als Selbsterkenntnis und Persönlichkeit.'; Alfred Schattmann in Die Zeit, 2 December 1922.
[39] '[...] in dem sich satztechnische Gewandtheit, natürlicher Klangsinn, Gemüt und Laune zu trefflicher, künstlerischer Harmonie binden; in seiner Art ist diese originelle dreisätzige Schöpfung ein kleines Meisterstückchen.'; Paul Schwers in *Allgemeine Musikzeitung* 49:49, 8 December 1922, p. 907.
[40] For more information on Schofield see: https://riamarchives.wordpress.com/riam-cellists-and-composers/joseph-schofield-1886-1939/ (accessed 17 March 2019).

The *Petit trio celtique*, Op. 52 is in four movements, alternating between a movement *'dans le style irlandais'* and *'dans le style breton'*. The work is dedicated to Paul Le Flem (1881–1984), the Breton composer who was among Hennessy's closest friends in Paris. Hennessy gives clear regional backgrounds to his motivic ideas. But with one little exception he does not use themes from actual traditional music, and this is in the first of the two Breton movements where Hennessy used a theme he had received from Paul Le Flem.[41]

The main theme of the first movement in F major appears initially in a somewhat subdued form in the cello, risking to be drowned by the other instruments (Ex. 8.8), before it comes to the fore from bar 9 in the violin, at which point viola and cello withdraw in terms of dynamics.

Ex. 8.8: *Petit trio celtique*, Op. 52, 1st movt., bars 1–9

As in a number of earlier works in an Irish style, it is very clear how he interprets this: melodic contours that either move in plain diatonic scales (emphasising the folk-song qualities) or, as here in the cello, with the ubiquitous use of the 'Scotch snap', the little rhythmic upward or downward accentuation on the first beat of bars 2 to 6 in Example 8.8 (see below for a discussion of Hennessy's use of the 'snap').

A variant of this theme occurs at figure C which is continued in a more melancholic vein at figure D. This passage highlights a special role allotted to the viola in both of the Irish movements. While the melody often changes from the violin to the cello, it is the viola that keeps an overall tension by applying agitated ostinatos that deviate metrically from the – in comparison – more irregular violin and cello (Ex. 8.9).

---

[41] *'thème breton fourni par Paul Le Flem'*; *Le Guide du concert*, 21 March 1924, p. 362.

Ex. 8.9: *Petit trio celtique*, Op. 52, 1st movt., bars 74–81

Figure F sees a second thematic subject in 2/4 time with subdued violin and viola lines of alternating tones and a cantilena in the cello. It is a simple but quite effective idea, moving on into figure G and closing the first movement without any reprise of earlier ideas.

The second ('Breton') movement in A minor elaborates on Paul Le Flem's given motif, consisting of one bar in 5/8 with a decorative figure that Hennessy incorporates into a 3/4 metric structure (see Ex. 8.10), all to a melodic motif that might well have sprung from a Breton folkdance collection. There is a cello ostinato throughout almost the whole (brief) movement, with a melody running in parallel sixths in the other two instruments for much of the time.

Ex. 8.10: *Petit trio celtique*, Op. 52, 2nd movt., bars 1–8

The last movement in F minor, again in Breton style, is the most energetic part of the *Petit trio celtique*. It comes with a brisk approach in 5/4 time that is the basis of some Breton folkdances – an unusual time signature in Western European traditional music – evoking in Hennessy's words, 'some *Jabadao* from Trégunc or Pont-Aven, in a blatant light, and all in simple, heuristic, really popular movements'.[42] Again, the cello provides an ostinato grounding to staccato playing from the other two instruments and some virtuosic swirling 'fiddles' in several sections like that beginning in bar 5 of Ex. 8.11.

Ex. 8.11: *Petit trio celtique*, Op. 52, 4th movt., bars 1–6

The work convinces by its well-crafted counterpoint that is evident in all four movements. This comes with a music that is remarkably simple in technical terms (with the possible exception of the last movement).

In general, the two Irish movements come across as much smoother and more harmonious compared to the rougher, more edgy Breton parts. Hennessy's harmonic approach in most of his 1920s non-programmatic chamber music is that, despite a number of modulations, he remains, on the whole, in a straightforward diatonic language. As will be seen, there is a strong tendency in Hennessy's 'Celtic' works that he is somewhat less adventurous in harmonic terms in comparison to his pre-War piano

---

[42] *Le Guide du concert*, 21 March 1924, p. 362.

music. In the medium-paced third movement, for example, the composer strongly reminds of the contemporary pastoral style on the British Isles. While this is, of course, itself somewhat indebted to French Impressionism, this trio (and especially its 'Irish' movements) sounds rather British than French, and perhaps this was a key component in Hennessy's interpretation of musical Celticism.

Contemporary critics rather welcomed Hennessy's harmonic approach, although one must keep in mind that the early 1920s were a period of strong aesthetic divides. At least, the published criticism to this work (and to Hennessy's harmonic approach and technical facility generally) was rather positive. Comparing the *Rapsodie celtique*, Op. 50 for violin and piano, the String Quartet No. 2, Op. 49, and the *Petit trio celtique*, Op. 52, Henri Collet wrote:

> [...] there is always a subtle and meticulous simplicity, an elegant and fine implementation of original ideas, evocative because of their rhythm, their deep or naive, dreamy or ironic feelings towards green Ireland.

although he also balanced the work's expressiveness and technical simplicity by calling it an 'ingenious attempt and an undeniable success that confirms the difficulty overcome here of writing in a style that is simplified to the extreme.'[43]

A critic in *The Sackbut* aptly described the trio as 'a charming little work suitable for amateurs';[44] the *Allgemeine Musikzeitung* applauded the work's 'folkloristic sounding melodic idiom' as 'very pleasant'.[45] *The Irish Times*, reporting on the first performance in Dublin, considered it

> [...] extraordinarily rich in musical feeling and most definitively original. So much so that attention is gripped and held from start to finish. And it is not so much by the novelty – though that exists – but by the real music and character of the work.[46]

A 1922 American review is quite telling with regard to Hennessy's 'popularity' in the land of his birth. But the author's description of the various attitudes towards the value of simplicity versus complexity is fair enough:

> And again we find another unfamiliar name in Swan Hennessey, who at any rate, sounds Irish, though I have not been able to find out just where he hails from. Not such a young man, as the trio for violin viola and cello to hand is op. 53 [*sic*]. [...]. It has a decided charm, is not heavy (at least not in the pieces before me), and there is a purer melody than most musicians are writing today. To some, this will be a recommendation, to others quite

---

[43] '[...] *c'est toujours le même parti pris de simplicité subtile et minutieuse, de mise en œuvre élégante et fine d'idées originales mais évocatrices, par leurs rythmes, des sentiments profonds ou naïfs, rêveurs ou ironiques, de la verte Irlande.*'; *'Tentative ingénieuse et d'une réussite indéniable, que confirme la difficulté vaincue d'une écriture simplifiée à l'extrême.*'; Henri Collet in *Comoedia*, 5 December 1921, p. 4.
[44] *The Sackbut* 2:9, March 1922, p. 35.
[45] '*volkstümlich anmutende Melodik*' ... '*sehr erfreulich*'; Eugen Segnitz in *Allgemeine Musikzeitung* 49:16, 21 April 1922, p. 343.
[46] *The Irish Times*, 31 March 1922, p. 4.

the contrary, but, be it as it may, it has a spontaneity which is apparently sincere. [...] However, it is, after all, not the serious concert material, but rather a light trifle, excellently done.[47]

Hennessy and the 'Scotch snap'

Apart from melodic characteristics of traditional music of the British Isles (such as typical interval sequences), a main element of Swan Hennessy's 'Celtic' or Irish style is the 'Scotch snap', also known as 'Scots snap' or 'lombard rhythm'. As shown above, the *Trio*, Op. 54, the *Petit trio celtique*, Op. 52, and a number or earlier works use this little device. Since it is now at the centre of Hennessy's style, a brief look at this musical element and Hennessy's considerations for using it may be helpful.

In technical terms, the Scotch snap is a syncopated rhythmic element consisting of an accentuated semiquaver followed by a dotted quaver. It is a reversal of the much more frequent pattern in which the longer note value would precede the shorter one, which can be found in all types of music. The intervallic relationship of the two notes is of little importance: the second pitch may be higher or lower than the first, and all intervals between a minor third and a major sixth seem to be allowed.

As the term indicates, the original source of this element is to be sought in Scotland, existing there since the 18th century. It is a key component of the Scottish folk-dance called strathspey. Through migration and musical cross-fertilisation, this little musical element can today also be found in other parts of the English-speaking world, particularly in the Appalachia region of the eastern United States. It has also made its way into art music whenever an allusion to the traditional music of Scotland or, more generally, 'British' music is called for. Thus, it occurs, for example, in Dvořák's Symphony No. 9 'From the New World', to quote the perhaps best-known example.

Whenever Hennessy uses the Scotch snap in a work with the epithet *'celtique'*, it therefore sounds reasonable since this would include Scottish allusions. However, all too often he equates *'celtique'* with 'Irish', and this raises the question whether Hennessy has perhaps misunderstood something.

In the 1929 interview with Lucien Chevaillier in *Le Guide du concert* that was already quoted several times before, Hennessy was asked what it is that makes his music 'Celtic'. One of the elements that he singles out is the snap, but interestingly, he (probably) consciously avoids the 'Scotch' part of the term:

> For you, the readers of the *Guide* ... and for me, I would like to clarify the meaning of all these terms that are too often used wrongly and indiscriminately. I would like to ask Mr. Hennessy first of all, if it would be possible to characterise 'Celtic' music?
>
> – This is quite difficult, he replied. The material characteristics that I could try to discern are of little importance to the general character that resides in an atmosphere, in these essentially inexpressible impressions, but which nevertheless emerge from any music in an irresistible way.

---

[47] Rosalie Housman: 'Significant Music', in: *Pacific Coast Music Review* 42:21, 19 August 1922, p. 10.

> 'We often notice in the popular melodies of Ireland and Scotland the repetition of a terminal note, sometimes even in the middle of a phrase: I think it is quite special. A further specific character is called 'snap'. The 'snap' is not strictly speaking an appogiatura: it is an integral part of the melody and often of the harmony, is not as fast as the appogiatura and, particularly, is usually performed by a third – or even a fourth –. Moreover, as you know, the third plays a considerable role in Celtic music: England was the cradle of singing in thirds – the famous *gymel*. We find this interval used in all ways, and even the alternation of the major and minor third, producing frequent false relationships, is commonly used.'[48]

Judging from this, Hennessy appears to locate the snap equally to Ireland and Scotland, an idea many Irish traditional musicians would vehemently object to, pointing out that it is exactly the snap that (mainly) distinguishes Scottish from Irish traditional music.

However, the northern Irish province of Ulster has since the 16th century been populated by many Scottish settlers as part of the strategic colonisation of Ireland by its larger neighbour England, in the (successful) attempt to raise the Protestant proportion, loyal to the English Crown, of Ireland's population – the root cause of the Northern Irish conflict, which resulted in the partition of the country in 1923. In music, a result of this process was that the snap has found a firm foothold in Irish traditional music in northern Irish regions, particularly in fiddle music. Hennessy, therefore, is not wrong when he says the snap occurs in both Scotland and Ireland.

Hennessy then continues with how the snap is accentuated and is perfectly right about the origin of this rhythmic element in spoken (or sung) language:

> From a rhythmic point of view, I would like to highlight one more important point. The accent is on the first note of the snap and generally on the initial notes of the rhythms. This is a consequence of the language where many words have an accent on the first syllable. I remember that someone had accentuated the first syllable of 'Annie' for me: however, it was my critic who was wrong![49]

---

[48] *J'aimerais bien, pour vous lecteurs du* Guide… *et pour moi, préciser la signification de tous ces termes que l'on emploie trop souvent à tort et à travers. Je m'enquiers auprès de M. Hennessy tout d'abord, s'il serait possible de caractériser la musique "celte"? / – Cela est assez difficile, m'est-il répondu. Les caractères matériels que je pourrais essayer de discerner sont peu de chose auprès du caractère général qui réside dans une atmosphère, dans ces impressions essentiellement inexprimables mais qui cependant se dégagent de toute musique d'une façon irrésistible. / "On remarque assez souvent dans les mélodies populaires d'Irlande et d'Ecosse la répétition d'une note terminale, quelque fois même en cours de phrase: je crois que cela est assez spécial. Un caractère encore spécifique est ce qu'on appelle le 'snap'. Le 'snap' n'est pas à proprement parler une appogiature: il fait partie intégrante de la mélodie et souvent de l'harmonie, n'est pas aussi rapide que l'appogiature et, chose particulière, s'effectue la plupart de temps par tierce – ou encore par quarte – . D'ailleurs la tierce joue, vous le savez, un rôle considérable dans la musique celte: l'Angleterre a été le berceau du chant à la tierce – le fameux gymel. Nous retrouvons cet intervalle utilisé de toutes les façons, et même l'alternance de la tierce majeure et de la tierce mineure, produisant de fréquentes fausses relations, est d'un usage courant."*; Lucien Chevaillier: 'Un entretien avec … Swan Hennessy', in: *Le Guide du concert* 15:28, 12 April 1929, p. 791–793 [792].

[49] *'Au point de vue rythmique je vous signalerai encore un point important. L'accent tombe sur la première note du "snap" et en général sur les notes initiales des rythmes. Ceci est une conséquence de la langue où beaucoup de*

It is not entirely clear what he refers to in his last sentence. It is not just the female name of Annie that Hennessy has in mind here, although it does illustrate the snap's accent. Probably Hennessy refers to his own song *Annie* (No. 1 of *Trois Chansons écossaises*, Op. 31, 1906; see Chapter 4) and a critic's (now obscure) remark about it.

Since Hennessy saw the snap in both Scottish and Irish music, Chevaillier then asked him whether there were any differences in the traditional music of these countries – to which Hennessy replied:

> No doubt, but here again it is rather difficult to express! Scottish music is both more powerful and finer: Irish music is willingly melancholic, with a sadness that is a bit overwhelming. And when it is cheerful, it is with a rather down-to-earth cheerfulness, rather a kind of jovial exuberance and without purpose.[50]

Apart from the snap – and for the further discussion of Hennessy's Celticism further below – it should be kept in mind that it was not only analysable musical elements of style such as the snap that Hennessy was interested in. Being inspired by French Impressionism and musical thought, he also emphasised in his first quote above 'the general character that resides in an atmosphere, in these essentially inexpressible impressions', which he experienced as 'irresistible'.

* * *

The early 1920s were another period of intense, one might say, frantic work on new compositions, publications, and – for the first time – 'marketing' activity for Swan Hennessy. In the autumn of 1921, he turned 55 years of age, and he must have felt that it was time to make a name for himself. The five years lost through the Great War and his father's illness had further delayed these plans.

The membership in the Association des Compositeurs Bretons during 1912–4 had opened up the stylistic route he was going to take. If his French audience wanted him to sound 'Celtic', he would give it to them. He was confirmed in this idea by the increasing call for political independence in his ancestral home country, Ireland, resulting in the quick succession of his String Quartet No. 2, Op. 49, the *Trio*, Op. 54 and the *Petit trio celtique*, Op. 52, all written during the last quarter of 1920.

He had also learned his lesson from the exchange with the publisher Schott (see Chapter 5): from now on, he would not wait for a publisher to bring his works to the

---

mots ont l'accent sur la première syllabe. Je me souviens que quelqu'un m'avait accentué la première syllabe de "Annie": c'est cependant mon critique qui avait tort!'; Chevaillier, 'Entretien', p. 792. The same parallel between the snap and language has also been analysed in detail by Nicholas Temperley and David Temperley: 'Music–Language Correlations and the "Scotch Snap"', in *Music Perception* 29:1, September 2011, p. 51–63.

[50] *'Sans doute, mais encore ici combien difficile à exprimer! La musique écossaise est à la fois plus puissante et plus fine: l'irlandaise est volontiers mélancolique, d'une tristesse en peu accablée, à moins qu'elle ne soit gaie, mais d'une gaieté assez terre à terre, plutôt une sorte d'exubérance joviale et sans façon.'*; Chevaillier, 'Entretien', p. 792–793.

market. He realised that he had to be more active on his own behalf, and this insight made the 1920s the most outgoing phase in his career. This would include building up relationships with musicians, paying them for their services, organising concerts of his music, contacting music critics, placing advertisements of his publications in selected journals, performing his own (piano) music, doing radio broadcasts, etc.

His appearance on the cover of *Le Guide du concert* of 21 October 1921 (excerpt, Fig. 8.5) must be seen in this context. The Paris-based Dutch painter and illustrator Willem van Hasselt (1882–1963) had for some years designed the cover pages of the journal, portraying composers and musicians with current performances or other kinds of appearance in Paris, always entitled '*Les Musiciens du jour*'. Now Hennessy was included in the series, and under his name, the text called him a '*compositeur celtique*' and referred explicitly to his published Opp. 49, 54, and 52. Since his reputation as a 'Celtic' composer was still only in the making, this epithet was almost certainly his own wish, a conscious 'brand' he was now going to give to himself.

Fig. 8.5: Hennessy as 'Musician of the Day' in *Le Guide du concert* (1921)

Henri Collet's portrait of Hennessy

Next in line was Henri Collet's portrait article of Hennessy in the 5 December 1921 issue of the renowned arts daily *Comoedia*. It was part 97 (!) of Collet's series *'La Musique chez soi'* ('Music at home') – not meant as a series about *'Hausmusik'*, but in the sense of turning attention to music while reading at home, as opposed to listening while sitting in a concert hall.[51] In other words, Collet gave backgrounds, often very personal opinions rather than objective criticism, to contemporary music in France. The series had gained some notoriety as it was here that Collet coined the term *'Les Six'* for a barely connected group of six young composers protesting against Impressionism (in part 13, issue of 23 January 1920). Whether Collet approached Hennessy or rather the other way around will never be known for certain.

The article is designed as an introduction to Hennessy, explaining his geographical and musical background and influences, his context in France, and then turning to a number of his works with some critical comment on each of them. As in *Le Guide du concert*, the main idea of the article is Hennessy's Celticism, and the very first idea expressed by Collet is that Hennessy is not alone with this aesthetic – which is interesting for the fact that French/Breton Celticism in music has become such an unfamiliar topic in today's musical historiography in (or about) France.

Because this article is such an important (and rare) document in the bibliography about Hennessy, I will provide a translation of the first paragraphs, just until he gets into the description of the various pieces (these have already been used selectively before):

> A musician who came to us from the other side of the Channel, Swan Hennessy is in no way disoriented. Has he not even brothers on our shores: Ladmirault, Le Flem, Vuillemin, Martineau, Rhené-Baton? He is a Celtic musician among the Celts, and I would like him to be given a warm welcome.
>
> But Swan Hennessy deserves more than our sympathy. He brings us something new ... A fine poet's personality can be seen in various pages [of his music] from which all rhetoric is banished and which says just what is needed without borrowing of any kind from the current Parisian form.
>
> This is rare, at a time when our artists seem to doubt the inviolability of the ivory towers so dear to all true creators, and are eager to unite in renowned chapels whose patronage is the only one capable of supporting their very small fighting forces. Ah! the deceptive prestige of artistic friendships! Do you think that the public, as the only judge in the last resort, accepts your compromises, oh musicians who are interested? Do you think that it will not seek to discern in your dummy groups the really powerful personality, and therefore, will not condemn you with the most perfect contempt? Alas! I have seen some: die, young groups! on the ashes of which the eternal phoenix is reborn: the individual!
>
> Swan Hennessy does not belong to any group classified, labelled, catalogued by our musicologists, lovers of order. And that is why his work seems to me to be tasteful and precious. It is undoubtedly a little sketchy, but it is natural, it is expressive without effect,

---

[51] Henri Collet: 'La Musique chez soi, XCVII: Œuvres de Swan Hennessy', in *Comoedia*, 5 December 1921, p. 4.

without latent dramatism, it is pure and serene, it smells well of lavender, rosemary and rockrose.

It is mainly contrapuntal. And its undeniable harmonic interest comes from the lines only.

The form is perpetually new. Developments, certainly, and of an attractive musicality, but dictated by the artist's instinct, so sure of himself, in possession of a particularly flexible profession. Sometimes also, an astonishing conciseness, a brevity where all the elements of laborious and useless amplification are willingly cleaned up. Here the author is a master, indicating to us what one could do, but refusing to do it for his part, in order to preserve the freshness of his work and its folklore.

Because everything is there, in the possible architecture of a monument with a popular foundation ... I know too well myself what it costs to develop a form that is appropriate to our conceptions of an art with deep popular ties, so as not to admire the art with which Swan Hennessy has been able to create a musical oeuvre while remaining faithful to the land, and without his melodies losing their aroma in the skilful mixes prescribed by the current music.

This specifically Irish melody, which is his own, does not offer, like our Iberian melodies, infinite tonal possibilities. At most, it hesitates between maintaining or removing the sensitive. But it has the most flexible of all internal rhythms. I bet that a Georges Migot would like it for what it lends itself to the 'linear decorations' of its aesthetics. Swan Hennessy follows it with love, chisel, imitation, the multiplicity of affirmative unisons, expositions or conclusions. But he never mutilates it, he is not one of those who confuse *melody* and *leitmotiv*. [52]

---

[52] *'Musicien vers nous venu de l'autre côté de la Manche, Swan Hennessy ne se trouve nullement dépaysé. N'a-t-il point même sur nos rivages des frères: Ladmirault, Le Flem, Vuillemin, Martineau, Rhené-Baton? C'est un musicien celte parmi les Celtes, et je voudrais qu'il lui fût fait un cordial accueil. / Aussi bien Swan Hennessy mérite plus que notre sympathie. Il nous apporte du nouveau ... Une fine personnalité de poète se décèle en des pages diverses d'où toute rhétorique est bannie et qui disent juste ce qu'il faut sans emprunt d'aucune sorte au formulaire parisien courant. / Cela est rare, en ce temps où nos artistes semblent douter de l'inviolabilité des tours d'ivoire chères à tous les vrais créateurs, et s'empressent de s'unir aux chapelles renommées dont le patronage est seul capable de soutenir leurs forces bien peu combattives. Ah! le prestige trompeur des amitiés artistiques! Croyez-vous donc que le public, seul juge en dernier ressort, accepte vos compromis, ô musiciens que l'intérêt allie? Pensez-vous qu'il ne cherchera pas à discerner dans vos groupes factices la personnalité vraiment puissante, et dès lors, ne vous condamnera avec le plus parfait mépris? Hélas! que j'en ai vu: mourir, des jeunes groupes! sur les cendres desquels renaît le phénix éternel: l'individu! / Swan Hennessy ne relève d'aucun groupe classé, étiqueté, catalogué par nos musicographes, amoureux de l'ordre. Et c'est pourquoi son œuvre m'apparaît savoureuse et précieuse. Elle est sans doute un peu fruste, mais elle coule de source, elle est expressive sans effet, sans dramatisme latent, elle est pure et sereine, elle fleure bon la lavande, le romarin et les cistes agrestes. / Elle est surtout contrapontique. Et son indéniable intérêt harmonique ne lui vient que des lignes. / La forme en est perpétuellement neuve. Des développements, certes, et d'une séduisante musicalité, mais que dicte l'instinct si sûr de l'artiste en possession d'un métier particulièrement souple. Parfois aussi, une étonnante concision, une brièveté où se ramassent volontairement tous les éléments d'une laborieuse et inutile amplification. Ici l'auteur est maître, nous montrant ce qu'on pourrait faire, mais s'y refusant pour sa part, afin de conserver à son œuvre tou te sa fraîcheur folk-loresque. / Car tout est là, dans l'architecture possible d'un monument aux assises populaires ... Je sais trop moi-même ce qu'il en coûte d'élaborer une forme adéquate à nos conceptions d'un art aux profondes attaches populaires, pour ne pas admirer l'art avec lequel Swan Hennessy a su faire œuvre de musicien tout en demeurant fidèle au terroir, et sans que ses mélodies perdent leur arôme dans les malaxations habiles que*

And, following his discussion of some of Hennessy's more recent 'Celtic' works, Collet closes with the statement: 'Read and play Swan Hennessy: and you will better understand the Anglo-Irish problem.'

There are some extraordinary statements in these paragraphs that are worth highlighting. In the first two paragraphs he welcomes Hennessy as a 'a Celt among Celts' in France, naming members of the former association of Breton composers of which he was still a part. But then he does single out Hennessy, saying he brings something new that is not like 'the current Parisian form'.

Collet's third paragraph is a political statement directed against the French composers' and critics' tendency to group composers into factions according to their place of education, clearly alluding to the rivalry between the Conservatoire and the Schola Cantorum (hidden behind the term 'chapel'), with their 'prestige of artistic friendships' and their mutually supportive networks (NB.: from which Hennessy could not benefit), which he condemns as 'dummy groups' that the musical public is not interested in. That is a strong statement, and he does not leave it at that, because he closes that paragraph with alluding to groups of young composers – and who else can he have in mind here than his own creation, *Les Six*! – when he exclaims 'Alas! I have seen some: die, young groups! on the ashes of which the eternal phoenix is reborn: the individual!'

For Collet, Swan Hennessy is such an individual. He likes him because he does not fit the categories of the 'lovers of order', the critics and musicologists (*'musicographes'*). Unfortunately, one might add fatalistically, the musicologists' liking for groups and categories has not ended in the 1920s, resulting in a sometimes obsessive concentration on a group of six composers, too diverse to even count as a group, as the next stage of development in early 20th-century French music, to the effect that the individualists of the time that include Hennessy and Migot became forgotten. – Hennessy and Migot did actually become friends from the mid-1920s (see Chapter 9).

Suffice to add that Collet's concluding sentence may come as a surprise to readers with knowledge in Irish art music. Understanding the Anglo-Irish problem with the help of Hennessy's music is a daring idea. It suggests that Hennessy's use of Irish traditional musical material brings together an English and an Irish side in music that is rich in creative conflict (since he speaks of a 'problem'). This is not quite the case since Hennessy manages to find some very harmonic solutions. In hindsight, it is a fascinating idea when one considers the non-existing reputation of Hennessy in Ireland today and whether the Anglo-Irish conflict has played a role in that.

***

---

prescrivent les traites courantes. / Cette mélodie spécifiquement irlandaise qui est sienne, n'offre point, comme nos mélopées ibériques, des possibilités tonales infinies. Tout au plus hésite-t-elle entre le maintien ou la suppression de la sensible. Mais elle possède la plus flexible des rythmiques internes. Je gage qu'un Georges Migot l'aimerait pour ce qu'elle se prête aux "décors linéaires" de son esthétique. Swan Hennessy la suit avec amour, la burine, la contrepointe, l'imite, la multiplie en des unissons affirmatifs, d'exposition ou de conclusion. Mais jamais il ne la mutile, n'étant pas de ceux qui confondent mélodie *et* leitmotiv.*' […] 'Lisez et jouez Swan Hennessy: et vous comprendrez mieux le problème anglo-irlandais.'*; Collet, as above.

Trois Mélodies, Op. 56 (1921) for low voice and piano

Despite his focus on Celticism, from time to time Hennessy continued to write music without any national or regional overtones, except that, perhaps, one can discern a French provenance in the general character of his harmonic writing. Such a piece is the *Trois Mélodies*, Op. 56 for low voice and piano. Written in 1921, the little album consists of: 1. *Le Mort joyeux* to words by Charles Baudelaire (1821–1867); 2. *Les Grands jasmins épanouis*, text by Albert Samain (1858–1900); and 3. *Il était une fois*. Chansonnette, to a poem by Jean Ajalbert (1863–1947). The unifying idea about the three songs is the Symbolist nature of the poems – Samain was deeply influenced by Baudelaire, and Ajalbert – if not strictly a Symbolist – was another non-conformist poet and anarchist.

Baudelaire's poem is no. 72 in *Les Fleurs du mal* (1857), the extraordinary collection of poems that was so controversial at the time of its publication that it took a while before composers began to set them to music. Hennessy's first Baudelaire setting, the *c*.1907 music to *Le Revenant* (Op. 30 No. 2) came on a wave of such settings. The catalogue of the Bibliothèque Nationale de France has only one earlier printed setting of *Le Mort joyeux*, a probably pre-WW I piece by René Lenormand (1846–1932), *Les Fleurs du mal*, Op. 33 No. 4. There is also an earlier manuscript by Pierre Menu (1896–1919), *Les Fleurs du mal* (no. 2 of three songs dated 1919), then came the Hennessy, and there is also a 1924 manuscript by Raoul Laparra. Hennessy's also remained in manuscript until its posthumous publication by Eschig in 1932. It does not seem to have been performed in public. The song is dedicated to Jean Suscinio, pseudonym of the writer, singer and conductor Henri Texier (1884–1980) who at the time mixed with several composers from Hennessy's Breton circle including Ladmirault, Duhamel and Pénau.

Hennessy's version of 'The Happy Corpse' (as the poem is called in its English version[53]) is set in C minor and is – like his first series of French songs around 1906 – a very faithful and interesting setting of the poem, exploring numerous illuminating word–music relationships. In a very direct and pictorial language, the poems describes the protagonist's desire to be buried in a deep hole in 'rich land, fertile, replete with snails' and 'sleep unnoticed like a shark at sea'. Ex. 8.12 shows how the composer reaches the lowest tone of his melody, a B♭, just at the point where he reaches the 'sleep' ('*dormir*') and remains on this note for almost three bars before, by moving up two semitone steps, he ends the first stanza on the word '*onde*' ('wave', interpreted as 'sea' in the English translation. The chordal accompaniment here moves, barely noticeable, between a triad (B flat major) and a tetrad (D major seventh) above a low sustained B♭, resembling the slow wave movement at the bottom of the sea. It's as simple as it is genial. In contrast, he strongly expresses the protagonist's hate of testaments and epitaphs by reaching the song's highest pitch, a B♭ two octaves above the first, on both occurrences of the word 'hate' ('*hais*') at bars 12 and 13. This is followed in bar 16 by another high A♭ on the words '*vivant j'aimerais*', where the protagonist 'would, *alive, invite* the hungry crows' devour his carcass. This is impeccable, creative word painting in music.

---

[53] Charles Baudelaire: *The Flowers of Evil*, new translation by James McGowan (New York: Oxford University Press, 1993), p. 140–143 (with parallel French–English text).

Ex. 8.12: *Trois Mélodies*, Op. 56 No. 1, *Le Mort joyeux*, bars 6–11

We find the same qualities also in the other two songs from Op. 56. The poem of No. 2, *Les Grands jasmins épanouis* ('Large blooming jasmines'), is taken from Albert Samain's poetry collection *Au jardin de l'Infante* (1897) where it is poem no. 4 in the section *Heures d'été*. The song is dedicated to the American baritone Charles Hubbard who gave the first performance, accompanied by Madeleine d'Aleman, in the Salle des Agriculteurs at the Sorbonne on 10 January 1922. This recital contained no less than 40 songs grouped in four sections of ten songs each. Hennessy's was in the last section together with songs by Gustave Samazeuilh, Igor Stravinsky (2), Albert Roussel (2), Roland Manuel (2) and Claude Debussy. Other first performances in this recital, apart from Hennessy's, were *Chanson d'automne* by Darius Milhaud and *Tu te verras ton yvoire cresper* by Roland Manuel. Hubbard also performed Hennessy's song in the United States when he returned in the mid-1920s after some five years in Paris.

Les Grands jasmins épanouis is the brightest of the three songs, even though it is not the typical light summer song that one may expect. Set in F sharp major and to be played *'lent et très doux'* ('slow and very soft'), it is a very tender and delicate setting in 3/4 time (rather resembling 6/8) with numerous chromatic *arpeggios* under a rather simple and catchy melody. The poem is similarly rich in pictorial allusions compared to Baudelaire's, and Hennessy's setting is particularly moving in the middle section where the poem speaks of the beloved with her 'green eyes dreaming in the wide open' (*'tes yeux verts rêvent grands ouverts'*).

Song no. 3, *Il était une fois*, subtitled a *'chansonnette'*, is set to a poem by Jean Ajalbert, taken from his volume *Paysage de femmes* (1887). Like the Baudelaire song, it was not published before 1932, but it was performed, most likely for the first time, by Marthe Saisset, accompanied by the composer, at the Salle Majestic, Paris, on 1 December 1926. The song is dedicated to the French singer Marcelle Gerar who had also performed it at least once: as the opening item in a recital in April 1930 at the Salle Chopin,⁵⁴ the second half of which was dedicated to works by the Breton composer Jean Huré, who had recently died. The song is set in F minor and 6/8 time in quick tempo, resembling the symbolic idea (in the poem) of a heart setting out to cross the sea in a small boat. The uncertainty of the heart facing the waves in the third stanza is well expressed by changing the pattern of the accompaniment from six linear quavers per bar to full chords of dotted crotchets, played to a slower beat.

Two 1922 trips to Berlin

Two journeys that Swan Hennessy undertook in 1922 to Berlin show his continued interest in making a name for himself in Germany. It will be remembered (Chapter 5) that he already visited Berlin twice before the War, in March and November 1913. In the meantime, the German monarchy had fallen with the end of the War, and Hennessy now found himself in economically difficult times of the Weimar Republic. With the help of local concert agencies, he organised his own *'Keltischer Abend'* in May and returned for two events in November, the latter a *'Kompositionsabend'* of his own works. Between these two dates, the German currency was devalued by about one thousand percent and was galloping towards hyperinflation – not that this would have troubled Hennessy too much. But it may have been a convincing argument for the musicians he employed for the events, since he may have paid them in French francs or US dollars.

The first event was quite a success, judging from the press reviews that appeared afterwards in the very diverse landscape of daily newspapers and music journals in Berlin. The first took place in the Bechsteinsaal on 3 May 1922. The 'Celtic Evening' featured (in this order) his String Quartet No. 2, Op. 49; the early Violin Sonata, Op. 14; the *Petit trio celtique*, Op. 52, the *Rapsodie celtique*, Op. 50 for violin and piano, and the *Suite*, Op. 46 for string quartet. As performers Hennessy had commissioned some of the most prominent musicians of the time: the Kulenkampff Quartet and the pianist Michael Raucheisen. Georg Kulenkampff also played the two violin works.

Apart from a critical look at the pieces performed, the reviews are highly interesting for the general image that Hennessy presented to a critical audience used to hearing the latest developments in art music by a wide range of composers and styles. Most journals agreed that Hennessy's music represented lighter material of a less complex nature than what one was accustomed to from most of his contemporaries, an impression that was underlined by the comparative brevity of Hennessy's musical ideas. It is an approach that neither remained unnoticed nor uncommented upon. Most critics welcomed it, such as Alfred Schattmann who wrote in *Die Zeit*:

> [Hennessy] does not search for the unheard-of, he writes naturally and casually, but in a chosen and elegant way, even where he is consciously simple in the application of Celtic elements. Different chamber works [...] offered on the whole the same likeable picture.

---

⁵⁴ The programme (preserved in Hennessy's Press Books) announced this as the first performance, which is not correct.

Hennessy, who had already gained recognition here before the War, could probably be satisfied with the rendering of his charming works.⁵⁵

One critic applauded the 'emotional warmth and unconstrained melodic joy' of Hennessy's themes,⁵⁶ another considered them 'a little sketchy, but [showing] the echo of a healthy, arch-musical talent, from which one involuntarily demands to hear more'.⁵⁷

Several critics remarked on the Celtic theme of the evening, proving that Hennessy had the right instinct, namely that calling his programme 'Celtic' would arouse the curiosity of German critics. To some, it seemed fitting and interesting, others did not understand it. The *Allgemeine Musikzeitung* wrote:

> The national tone gave this concert, which was called 'Celtic Evening', its character and limitation. If one wants to do justice to Hennessy's music, which was offered this time, one cannot keep a sharp enough eye on it, that it wants to give as faithful and unaffected sound image as possible of Celtic folk music. This explains the occasional lack of ambition of the always refreshingly natural, warmly felt melodies, as well as the extremely concise, often laconic, even capriciously sketchy form of his compositions. […] Swan Hennessy's melodies, soothing in their simplicity and naturalness, are accompanied by a finely blended, intimate harmony. The transparent, genuinely chamber-musical sound testifies to the hand of a tasteful musician.⁵⁸

Negative criticism of the 'Celtic' idea concentrated mainly on the notion that five works of this type in one concert was a little too much, resulting in a certain monotony, and that it invariably leads to a degree of simplicity that is a little irritating. One critic wrote:

---

[55] 'Er sucht nicht nach Unerhörtem, er schreibt natürlich und zwanglos, dabei aber gewählt und vornehm, selbst wo er in der Anwendung keltischer Elemente bewusst einfach ist. Verschiedene dem Umfange nach wohltuend knappe Kammerwerke […] boten alle im Durchschnitt dieses selbe sympathische Bild. Hennessy, der hier schon vor dem Kriege Anerkennung gefunden hat, konnte mit der Aufnahme seiner liebenswerten Werke wohl zufrieden sein.'; Alfred Schattmann in *Die Zeit*, 10 May 1922. NB.: This paper is not the same as today's weekly paper of the same name.

[56] 'Gefühlswärme und unbefangene Melodienfreude'; anonymous critic in *Deutsche Tageszeitung*, 11 May 1922.

[57] 'ein wenig skizzenhaft gearbeitet, aber der Widerhall einer gesunden, erzmusikalischen Begabung, von der man unwillkürlich mehr zu hören verlangt'; anonymous critic in *Deutsche Zeitung*, 13 May 1922.

[58] 'Die nationale Note gab diesem Konzert, das sich als „Keltischer Abend" bezeichnete, Eigenart und Begrenzung. Will man der Musik Hennessys, welche diesmal geboten wurde, gerecht werden, so kann man nicht scharf genug im Auge behalten, daß sie ein möglichst getreues, unverkünsteltes Klangbild keltischer volkstümlicher Art geben will. Daraus erklärt sich die gelegentliche Anspruchslosigkeit der immer erquickend natürlichen, warm empfundenen Melodik, daraus auch die äußerst knappe, oft lakonische, ja kapriziös-skizzenhafte Form seiner Kompositionen, […] Die in ihrer Ungesuchtheit und Natürlichkeit wohltuenden Melodien Swan Hennessys werden von einer fein verästelten, intimen Harmonik untermalt. Das durchsichtige, echt kammermusikalische Klanggewand zeugt von der Hand eines geschmackvollen Musikers.'; Adolf Diesterweg in *Allgemeine Musikzeitung* 49:19, 12 May 1922, p. 402.

> Very tame and pale romanticism, the only advantage of which is that it emanates from Celtic folk song. Everything is neatly set in terms of craftsmanship, but the spark is missing. Why did the friends not stop Mr Hennessy from performing five of his works in a row? If there had only been two of them, one could speak of friendly music for domestic use if it were not technically quite tricky here and there.[59]

Another review was very similar, emphasising that even experienced musicians could not do much to dispel the notion of uniformity:

> He succeeds in everything – because he knows where his strengths are. He uses countless popular (Scottish) tunes, which results in a certain uniformity of melodic diction. He has splendid andante ideas, and his art of shaping forms has captivating charms of a genuine and untroubled beauty. But five works of this kind in one evening, that is a bit much, even if Raucheisen shines on the piano and Georg Kulenkampff-Post is a very pleasing violinist.[60]

Hennessy returned to Berlin in November of the same year for two events. One was another solo show on the 15th, now entitled 'Zweiter Kompositionsabend', the other a week later on the 23rd, when his *Trois Chansons espagnoles*, Op. 42bis and his *Trio*, Op. 54 for woodwind were included in a vocal recital of Radiana Pazmor.

The 'composition evening' at the Meister-Saal was Hennessy's last major representation in Berlin, and one wonders whether this had something to do with the chosen repertory and its reception. For anyone familiar with Hennessy's list of works, the recital contained several works in first performances that do not occur in his list, because they were withdrawn after this event. The programme consisted of

- *Drei keltische Stücke*, for piano trio (first performance)
- *5 Charakterstücke*, for piano
- *Bretonische Rhapsodie*, for violin and piano (first performance)
- *Drei exotische Bilder*, for piano (= Op. 57)
- *Zweite Suite*, for string quartet (first performance)

Drei keltische Stücke ('Three Celtic Pieces'), elsewhere numbered Op. 53, would have been his first piano trio after *Lieder an den Mond*, Op. 10 of 1888. The five 'character pieces' for piano were actually six or seven of his pre-War descriptive pieces – the programme, pasted into his Press Books, identify these in German translations) as Nos. 1, 3, and 5 of *Sentes et chemins*, Op. 44; *Dans un atelier de couturiers*, Op. 47 No. 3;

---

[59] 'Sehr zahme und blasse Romantik, deren einziger Vorzug ist, daß sie vom keltischen Volkslied ausgeht. Handwerklich ist alles ordentlich gesetzt, doch der zündende Funke fehlt. Warum haben die Freunde Herrn Hennessy nicht davon abgehalten, gleich fünf seiner Werke nacheinander vorzuführen. Wären es nur zwei gewesen, könnte man von freundlicher Gebrauchsmusik fürs Haus sprechen, wenn sie technisch nicht doch hier und da recht knifflich wäre.'; anonymous critic in *Der Reichsbote*, 11 May 1922.
[60] 'Ihm gelingt alles, – denn er weiß, was er kann. Er verwendet zahllose volkstümliche (schottische) Weisen, woraus sich eine gewisse Gleichförmigkeit der melodischen Diktion ergibt. Er hat prachtvolle Andante-Einfälle, und seine Formkunst hat bestechende Reize einer echten und unverkümmerten Schönheit. Doch fünf Werke solcher Art an einem Abend, das ist etwas viel, selbst wenn Raucheisen am Flügel glänzt und Georg Kulenkampff-Post sehr erfreulich geigt.'; anonymous critic in *Tägliche Rundschau*, 11 May 1922.

Fig. 8.6: Hennessy's advertisement for his 15 November 1922 Berlin recital

Champs de blé au clair de lune, Op. 40 No. 2; and both pieces of *Fêtes*, Op. 36. The *Bretonische Rhapsodie* ['Breton Rhapsody'], originally Op. 55, is now lost. *Drei exotische Bilder* is indeed the first performance of *Trois Pièces exotiques*, Op. 57 (more about which further below). And the *Zweite Suite* ['Second Suite'], the then Op. 58, has been a three-movement work for string quartet that later reappeared as three of the four movements of his String Quartet No. 3, Op. 61.

Again, Hennessy contracted some prominent musicians and evidently did not have the purpose to earn money with the event, because it was free for the audience. The quartet he commissioned was the renowned Deman Quartet, and the pianist was Bruno Eisner. It seems like Eisner stepped in at short notice, because a week earlier, the event was advertised in the *Allgemeine Musikzeitung* with the Munich-based pianist August Schmid-Lindner.[61] There is no explanation of or comment about this change in the press.

Hennessy's withdrawal of all of the three chamber works after the Berlin performance must have had something to do with the critics' response, which at this time was rather negative. One critic alleged that the musical style of the 'Three Celtic Pieces' for piano trio was outdated:

> Three 'Celtic Pieces' for trio showed good compositional structure, but their 'premiere' was meaningless because it could just as well have taken place 50 years ago.[62]

One devastatingly negative review appeared in the popular daily *B.Z. am Mittag*, not necessarily known for the quality of its music criticism – although it has to be said that the analysis of Hennessy as a composer leaning on Romanticism is not untrue.

> The American Swan Hennessy also composes. He also rents artists like Bruno Eisner and the Deman Quartet. What comes out of it? Frankly, I do. And as soon as possible. Whether Mr Hennessy composed in an old or new way is hard to say. Or rather: in the deepest sense, he is inclined to the old, to the folksy, to Romanticism. If he would only admit it! If he would only write cute little things! But no, he masks himself. And the more he does it, the more you feel that there's nothing behind it. His music, prepared with various ingredients, is absolutely indifferent.[63]

---

[61] Similarly, the announcements of the concert in *Führer durch die Konzertsäle Berlins* announced Schmid-Lindner in its issue no. 9 of 6 November and Eisner in issue no. 10 of 13 November.
[62] '*Drei "Keltische Stücke" für Triobesetzung zeigten gutes Satzgefüge, aber ihre "Uraufführung" war deswegen gegenstandslos, weil sie ebensogut vor 50 Jahren hätte stattfinden können.*'; anonymous critic in *Lokal-Anzeiger*, c.18 November 1922 (not dated in Hennessy's Press Books).
[63] '*Auch der Amerikaner Swan Hennessy komponiert. Auch er mietet sich Künstler wie Bruno Eisner und das Deman-Quartett. Was kommt dabei heraus? Offen gestanden ich. Und zwar so bald als möglich. Ob Herr Hennessy alt oder neu komponiert, ist kaum zu sagen. Oder vielmehr: er ist im tiefsten Grunde zum Alten, zum Volkstümlichen, zur Romantik gewandt. Wenn er's nur eingestände! Wenn er nur niedliche Kleinigkeiten von sich gäbe! Aber nein, er maskiert sich. Und je mehr er es tut, desto mehr spürt man, daß nichts dahinter steckt. Seine Musik, mit mancherlei Zutaten hergerichtet, ist absolut gleichgültig.*'; anonymous critic in *B.Z. am Mittag*, 20 November 1922.

Equally negative was a review in the *Morgenpost*, another daily newspaper with a large circulation:

> Swan Hennessy, some of whom claim to be American, others to be Irish, is by no means an important composer. His naivety and randomness outweigh the possible. How does a fine musician's head like Eisner and a quality violinist like Deman come to such music?[64]

Two of the main German music journals of the time, *Allgemeine Musikzeitung* and *Signale für die musikalische Welt*, offered more differentiated views, but they also emphasised Hennessy's artistic limitations. The *AMZ* wrote:

> We have already met in Berlin several times the natural, friendly talent of the Irish composer Swan Hennessy. Mr Hennessy has limited his creative field. He prefers to write chamber music in a smaller style based on Celtic or Breton melodies. The result is beautiful, sonorous genre pictures that are drawn with an amiable hand, that sound well and whose clean, free-from-pretension and therefore sincere emotional tone is sympathetically touching. [...] All in all, then, a friendly small and fine art that does not want to be and seem more than what it really is: a contemplative artistic creation that stands in noticeable contrast to our excited and overturning times.[65]

The critic in *Signale* missed profundity in Hennessy's music and diagnosed 'Celtic table confectionary':

> Swan Hennessy's second composition evening only confirmed, but did not deepen, the impressions of the first: wittily entertaining small paintings of an emphatically harmless and cheerful view of life. A musical illustrator without the detailed intentions of the programme musician. They are also character pieces, but depths are avoided, even contrasts do not touch them, not even in the Second Suite for String Quartet, [...]. Entertaining ripples on the surface. Celtic table confectionary.[66]

---

[64] '*Swan Hennessy, von dem einige behaupten, er wäre Amerikaner, die anderen, er sei Ire, ist keinesfalls bedeutsamer Komponist. Seine Naivität und Wahllosigkeit überwiegt das Mögliche. Wie kommt ein so feiner Musikantenkopf wie Eisner und ein Qualitätsgeiger wie Deman zu solcher Musik??*', anonymous critic in *Morgenpost*, 21 November 1922.

[65] '*Schon mehrfach haben wir in Berlin Proben von dem natürlichen, freundlichen Talent des irischen Tonsetzers Swan Hennessy kennen gelernt. Herr Hennessy hat sich sein Schaffensgebiet begrenzt. Er schreibt mit Vorliebe Kammermusik kleineren Stils und zwar unter Zugrundelegung keltischer oder bretonischer Melodien. Es entstehen so hübsche, klangfrohe Genrebildchen, die mit liebevoller Hand gezeichnet sind, sich wohl anhören und deren saubererer, von aller Prätension freier, darum aufrichtiger Gefühlston sympathisch berührt. [...] Alles in allem also eine freundliche Klein- und Feinkunst, die nicht mehr sein und scheinen will, als was sie in Wirklichkeit ist: ein beschauliches Kunstschaffen, das in merkbarem Gegensatz zu unserer aufgeregt und weltumstürzend sich geberdenden Zeit steht.*'; Paul Schwers in *Allgemeine Musikzeitung* 49:47, 24 November 1922, p. 870.

[66] '*Der zweite Kompositionsabend Swan Hennessys bestätigte nur, aber vertiefte nicht die Eindrücke des ersten: geistvoll kurzweilige Kleinmalereien einer betont harmlos-fröhlichen Lebensanschauung. Ein musikalischer Illustrator ohne die ausführlichen Absichten des Programm-Musikers. Sinds auch Charakterstücke, so werden doch Tiefen gemieden, selbst Kontraste rühren nicht daran, auch nicht in der erstmalig aufgeführten zweiten*

There were other, more positive reviews, but the general tone across the twelve reviews contained in Hennessy's Press Books about this second 'composition evening' is like that outlined above. His reception in Berlin had deteriorated within less than half a year, and this cannot have satisfied him. But since he did not intend to change his musical language in order to please Berlin critics, he must have decided to turn his back on Germany for the time being. This event at least had been a failure, and he took it seriously at least in part, since he withdrew the majority of his programme. And what was the use of all his deliberate expenses if his music neither impressed the musicians nor critical opinion? It was to be his last one-man show in Berlin; he never returned for a similar project.

Hennessy remained in Berlin for Radiana Pazmor's recital at the Bechsteinsaal and must have read the reviews of his previous concert with increasing frustration. The young American contralto was accompanied by Georg Vollerthun on piano, the programme ranging from Schubert and Brahms through Rachmaninov and Mussorgsky to contemporaries who happened to be friends of Hennessy's including Hugo Rasch and Lucien Haudebert. Both Haudebert's song cycle – five of the eight songs from *Dans la maison* (1920) – and Hennessy's *Trois Chansons espagnoles*, Op. 42bis (1921) were given as first performances; Hennessy's was dedicated to Pazmor.

The *Trio*, Op. 54 for two clarinets and bassoon was also given its first performance, by Leonhard Kohl and Adolf Mützelburg (clarinets) with Louis Scheiwein – the only piece the three musicians participated in that evening. Again, Hennessy allowed himself the luxury to have three prominent musicians appear for a roughly eight-minute performance.

Although most reviews concentrated on the performers, Hennessy's works were much warmer received than a week earlier (see further above in the discussions of Opp. 42bis and 54). Apparently one of the three Spanish songs had to be repeated by public demand.[67]

An Irish portrait article

In September 1922, the first portrait of Hennessy appeared in an Irish newspaper.[68] In it, the author, Donnchadh Ua Braoin – also known under his anglicised name Denis Breen (*c*.1886–1950) – includes many personal details about Hennessy that were not publicly available at the time. It seems like the article is a result of correspondence between Breen and Hennessy, since Breen cites from a letter he received.

The article appeared in the *Dublin Evening Telegraph* of 2 September 1922; a near copy, with minor updates, appeared in *The Leader* of 7 April 1923. This article has been quoted in parts before (Chapter 6), because it begins with recounting the author's

---

Suite für Streichquartett, [...]. *Unterhaltend kräuselts an der Oberfläche. Keltisches Tafelkonfekt.*'; Otto Steinhagen in *Signale für die musikalische Welt* 80:47, 22 November 1922, p. 1350.
[67] *Deutsche Zeitung*, 5 December 1922.
[68] D[onnchadh] Ua B[raoin]: 'Swan Hennessy. An Irish Musician of To-day', in: *Dublin Evening Telegraph*, 2 September 1922, p. 2; with the following quotes from this source.

astonishment on having first come across the name of Swan Hennessy in connection with the *Petite suite irlandaise*, Op. 29 (1908) for piano duo. Breen then mentions the May recital in Berlin, adding that 'the composer had to appear on the platform several times to acknowledge the plaudits of the audience'. This is an information that is not derived from any of the reviews of the event, in other words it must have come directly from Hennessy.

Breen continues with details of Hennessy's birth in the United States and his European education, before he turns to the composer's Irish interests:

> His Irish feeling must have been firmly fixed in his thoughts from early youth to survive so long and so well in a man who has never seen Ireland, living all his life in a circle and a society where Ireland was, perhaps, not more than a name. 'My great desire,' he writes, 'is to become known in Ireland, as it is the love of Ireland that has inspired my work, such as it is.'

Indeed, it would be interesting to know exactly where this inspiration came from, but he has never properly disclosed it. While there is no reason to doubt his awakening interest in the land of his father's birth, it has been speculated before that the desire to find a credible artistic identity in an increasingly complex musical environment and the beginning public success of this identity in France must have been motivating factors at least as great as family-related nostalgia.

Breen is of the opinion that an experienced composer like Hennessy could be a model for young Irish composers:

> Here, then, is an artist of note on the Continent, who deserves to be known and studied in Ireland, not alone for the purely Irish portion of his music, or simply for pseudo-patriotism, but also for the intrinsic beauty of his work, and because of the valuable help which he can give to young Irish composers and players.

Since Breen also quotes from the 1921 portrait of Henri Collet and a review by the German critic Eugen Segnitz, Hennessy must have given him copies or translations of these articles in addition to a number of recent scores, ending these paragraphs with the notion, 'Which makes one reflect that music which commands such respect in Berlin cannot be wholly unworthy of Cork or Dublin'.

Still, Breen appears to have some reservations about Hennessy's approach. He identifies French musical qualities in Hennessy's music that he describes as 'clearness and precision of form, certainty and unhesitating directness of expression, entire absence of cloudy or blurred outline, and absolute freedom from sentimentality', suggesting that these same characteristics can also be attributed to the music of the Irish harpers of the 17th and 18th centuries. But then he says:

> If there is a decided point of difference between Hennessy and the harpers, it is in the more binding restraint he imposes on himself. His music is always personal and distinctive, but sometimes seems to me a little too detached – not intimate enough: the expression of a nature not inclined to 'wear its heart upon its sleeve,' or even to trust itself to trace its

own thoughts to their fountain-head. Perhaps I do him an injustice here – for his violin sonata contains one movement of exquisite and sustained emotion – and I have never heard his string-music, and that may produce a new impression; but a glance over the scores hardly convinces me, and I shall be agreeably surprised if it turns out that I am mistaken.

* * *

Evidently, around this period, Hennessy was trying to make a name for himself not only in Germany but in Ireland as well. But it is noteworthy that he did not pursue the same strategy as in Berlin. The main reason should be that, at this time in 1922, Ireland was in a state of civil war that would, in 1923, lead to the partition of the country into an independent Irish Free State in the south and six counties in the north that remained part of the United Kingdom. Musical life suffered immensely under these conditions, and while concerts did take place, Hennessy would not know any details about the situation. Besides, in Berlin he had targeted the musical life of a European metropolis whereas little was known outside of Ireland about the musical life of Dublin, Belfast or Cork – and he would have been right in assuming that it was smaller.

But who would be his points of contact in Ireland? It is likely that Hennessy identified Breen because he had written about Hennessy before, namely about the Irish-style Violin Sonata, Op. 14 in the *Cork Examiner* of 22 April 1922 (see Chapter 4), which was performed by Liam O'Brady and Carl Hardebeck in a Gaelic League concert at the time. Hennessy had, most likely, made contact with Breen via the editorial office of the newspaper.

The social division in Ireland between adherents to the British influence and propagators of a stronger Irish cultural independence extended into the groups and individuals promoting art music in Ireland. This resulted in two competing musical festivals, both a combination of concerts and competitions, and both founded in 1896 with first series of events from 1897: on the one hand the Feis Ceoil, which had a stronger orientation towards the mainstream of European art music, with adjudicators coming mainly from England, and on the other hand An tOireachtas na Gaeilge, organised by the Gaelic League, which claimed a closer proximity to the Gaelic-speaking culture and its association with the traditional music of Ireland. Martin Dowling wrote:

> Though they seemed to have the same ideas about the programming of ancient Irish music, by 1904 it was clear that promotion of these cultural practices fell somewhere between the main priorities of the two organisations: the development of a national music on the one hand and the reinvigoration of the national language on the other. Furthermore, it became clear that these priorities were the responsibility of two separate and increasingly distant sections of society, with the Feis Ceoil in the hands of Protestant Anglo-Irish interests, and the Gaelic League, with the assistance and support of the clergy, the catholic petit bourgeois classes and peasantry.[69]

---

[69] Martin Dowling: *Traditional Music and Irish Society. Historical Perspectives* (Farnham: Ashgate, 2014, p. 168.

For outsiders, the difference is sometimes difficult to make, especially because the pool of experts that both organisations drew from was largely the same. The Feis Ceoil had the larger instrumental forces, more backing from the established institutions of musical education, and, in retrospect, the more influential competitions for composers and performers. But around 1922, clearly both festivals had competitions that resembled each other very much. It is a coincidence that through the April 1922 inclusion of a Hennessy work in a Gaelic League concert, his music was noticed first by a musician like Breen who leaned towards the Oireachtas side. Hennessy would know nothing about these differences, but as it happened, his contacts in Ireland developed closer ties with this organisation.

Other Irish musicians who knew Swan Hennessy personally included, of course, the members of the Irish string quartet who performed his Op. 49 in Paris in January 1922. This included Arthur Darley, one of the most prominent Irish musicians of the day and one the very few who moved effortlessly between the worlds of 'classical' and Irish traditional music – in his case, one might say, between the violin and the fiddle. Darley also recommended some of Hennessy's music as competitive repertory at the Father Mathew Feis – another organisation close to the Gaelic League and the Catholic clergy – in 1923, and Breen did the same for the Oireachtas festival that took place in Cork in May 1924.

The Cork-based Denis Breen seems to have been Hennessy's closest ally (or correspondent) for a while. There is a not particularly friendly characterisation of Breen by Aloys Fleischmann (1910–1992), then still a teenager, but later one of the most prominent Irish composers and musicologists of the twentieth century, founder of the Cork Symphony Orchestra and long-time Professor of Music at University College Cork (UCC). He wrote in his diary of 10 October 1926: 'Went to Mr. Corkery. The music on the wireless was very second-rate. Mr. and Mrs. Breen and Mr. Brady were there – all semi-musical musicians. Mr. Breen is a very rough fellow.'[70] This is accompanied by a footnote provided by the library of UCC:

> Denis Breen was a primary school teacher, a Gaelic Leaguer, a lover of music and a professed atheist. He had provided the music for the theatre founded by Corkery, Terence MacSwiney and others. Frank O'Connor describes him in *An Only Child* (Ch. 4, p. 152–3) as loud, emotional, intense, dogmatic. He reports that Breen had no time for Cork's German musicians, whose authority, like that of the clergy, he repudiated.

Breen therefore is another link between Hennessy and Terence MacSwiney, the dedicatee of his String Quartet No. 2, Op. 49 (about the possibility that Hennessy met MacSwiney, and perhaps Breen, as early as 1908 in the context of the Cork Dramatic Society see Chapter 6).

If Hennessy had merely corresponded with Breen up this point in autumn 1922, without having met him, Hennessy would know nothing about the 'very rough fellow'

---

[70] See Fleischmann Archive at UCC, online at http://fleischmanndiaries.ucc.ie/portfolio/october-1926-sunday-10/ (last accessed, 13 April 2019).

that Breen may have been. As a token of thanks for the portrait in the *Dublin Evening Telegraph*, Hennessy dedicated his *Huit Pièces celtiques*, Op. 51 for piano (1922) to Breen, but it appears like he was a second choice. Breen himself wrote in his article that this piece, originally entitled in English as *Eight Celtic Pieces* and carrying the opus number 57, was to be dedicated to the Irish politician Éamon de Valera[71] whom he may have met at the January 1922 performance of the quartet Op. 49 in Paris at the 'World Congress of the Irish Race'.

The *Eight Celtic Pieces* was a work that Hennessy originally intended to publish with the small Cork-based publisher Sullivan & Co. Breen wrote:

> That Swan Hennessy's expression of devotion to Ireland is not an empty phrase is shown by the fact that he has placed two of his latest compositions in the hands of an Irish publishing firm – Messrs. Sullivan, of Cork, viz. Eight Celtic Pieces for Piano, dedicated to E. de Valera, and a Celtic Trio for Piano, Violin and 'Cello.

Obviously, at this time, Hennessy's 'Celtic' piano trio, performed in Berlin in November 1922 and afterwards withdrawn, was already completed.

Another Irish musician was deeply involved in these proceedings: the today quite unknown pianist and composer Michael Kavanagh. He was the founder and honorary secretary of a short-lived 'Irish Society of Composers', with members including Joseph Crofts, Carl Gilbert Hardebeck, Geoffrey Molyneux Palmer, Robert O'Dwyer, and Annie Patterson.[72] It is well possible that Hennessy was asked to join as well.

Curiously, Kavanagh appears as the copyright owner of Hennessy's Opp. 51, 53, and 55[73], probably because he had a hand in the transferral of these works from Sullivan & Co. – which did not survive the Irish Civil War[74] – to the London publisher Evans & Co., where these works first appeared in 1924 (their French edition followed later).

The Irish Society of Composers was another ill-fated initiative that became a victim of the troubled times. It does not even seem to have survived the year 1921, when Kavanagh appeared in the press as leader of the 'orchestra' of the Pavilion Cinema,

---

[71] Éamon de Valera (1882–1975) was one of the most influential Irish politicians of the time. Initially a political rebel, he was President of the (unofficial) Irish Republic (August 1921 to January 1922), Taoiseach (prime minister; 1937–48, 1951–4, 1957–9), and President (1959–73).
[72] This organisation has been completely forgotten today. Its foundation was announced in a letter by Kavanagh to the editor of the *Freeman's Journal*, 5 March 1920, p. 3. An inaugural concert was held on 18 November (*Freeman's Journal*, 19 November 1920, p. 3). See also *The Musical Times*, 1 June 1920, p. 419; *Connacht Tribune*, 26 June 1920, p. 4.
[73] *Huit Pièces celtiques*, Op. 51, originally *Eight Celtic Pieces*, Op. 57; *Sonatine celtique*, Op. 53, originally *Irish Sonatina*, Op. 61; and *Épigrammes d'un solitaire*, Op. 55, originally Op. 63; see Table 8.1.
[74] The *Irish Examiner*, 1 September 1921, p. 8, wrote that he 'also founded a new and progressive publishing house for the works of native composers'. I presume that this was (to be) Sullivan & Co. in Cork. This article is the last time the society was mentioned.

Dublin.⁷⁵ Although the society appears to have dissolved around this time, Breen still expresses his desire for it in April 1923 and that Hennessy should join:

> His Irish nationality has procured him admission to the Society of Breton Musicians in France. Why not a Society of Irish Composers in Ireland, who would honour themselves and him by asking him to allow his name to stand among theirs?"⁷⁶

Breen may not have written this without Hennessy's consent.

Could it be, then, that Hennessy assigned the copyright to Kavanagh as an indirect means to contribute financially to such a society? By 1924, when Hennessy's three compositions were signed over to Evans & Co., Kavanagh had taken up a teaching post at the Guildhall School of Music, London – which would have facilitated the publication with a company in that city. It was to take until 1948, when in the form of the Composer's Group within the Music Association of Ireland, an Irish composers' society was eventually founded – to whose members both Swan Hennessy and Michael Kavanagh were not even names.

Huit Pièces celtiques, Op. 51 (1922) for piano

Originally completed as *Eight Celtic Pieces*, Op. 57 in 1922, this work consists of eight very short pieces in the Irish style. They are merely numbered, do not have descriptive titles, and only one of them (No. 5) is based on an existing Irish traditional melody, the revolutionary ballad 'The Wearing of the Green'. The playing indications read 1. *Allegro maestoso*; 2. *Andante*; 3. *Allegro*; 4. Andante sostenuto; 5. *Allegro*; 6. *Allegretto*; 7. *Allegro*; 8. *Allegretto*; followed by a short *Epilogue*. The work was originally published under its English title in 1924 in London with Evans & Co., with Michael Kavanagh's copyright – a second edition with the French title was part of Hennessy's *Album celtique* that appeared with Éditions Max Eschig in 1929.⁷⁷ The Eschig edition was newly set: for example, piece no. 2 is squeezed into one page in the Evans edition and has two pages with Eschig. The work is dedicated to Denis Breen.

While all the pieces are rather unpretentious – no piece exceeds two pages in the score, and all are in the technical reach of an amateur player – , some are striking for various reasons. No. 2, for example, repeats the same little figure of G – A – E – F in regular quavers unchanged for almost the whole piece (52 bars), only to slow down to crotchets for the last four bars – a really minimalist approach that leaves every melodic change and rhythmic variety to the left hand, which responds, quite flexibly, in both linear and chordal patterns (Ex. 8.13). In fact, Hennessy was lauded for this piece by Arthur Hoerée in a review of the *Album celtique* in *La Revue musicale*. After having noted

---

⁷⁵ *Irish Examiner*, 1 September 1921, p. 8.
⁷⁶ Writing as 'Craiftine' in *The Leader*, 'An Irish Musician of To-day'.
⁷⁷ All Eschig editions of the original Evans publications first retained the copyright notice. From a certain point in time (which is indeterminable), this was replaced by Eschig 'as legal successors of Michael Kavanagh'.

a conservative harmonic approach in these works (that, after all, extend over a period of twenty years), he continues:

> […] This does not in any way diminish the musical quality of these pages, particularly in the Sonatina and in the second of *Pièces celtiques*, where an ostinato design of the right hand constantly changes the perspective on the low-key tune.[78]

Ex. 8.13: *Huit Pièces celtiques*, Op. 51 No. 2, bars 1–12

Most of the pieces also remain in their assigned key but deviate from it in surprising modulations towards the end of a phrase or of the piece, such as the endings of No. 4 and 7. No. 8 is one of the few pieces that use an Irish dance form, with its borrowings from a jig. The piece is in A–B–A form, with the second A merely a repetition of the first. In the B part, the jig seems to move into a baroque gigue.

In his arrangement of the nineteenth-century Irish rebel song 'The Wearing of the Green' in No. 5, Hennessy made ample use of the 'Scotch snap', and it is well justified here, for the rhythmic emphasis of the words to the song provides numerous opportunities for its application. Still – Hennessy's piano version of the song does hide the melody well (Ex. 8.14), there are certainly more direct adaptations of the song in classical arrangements than this one.

---

[78] *'Ce qui n'empêche en rien la qualité musicale de ces pages, notamment dans la Sonatine et dans la deuxième de Pièces celtiques, où un dessin obstiné de la main droite modifie sans cesse la perspective du chant grave.'*; Arthur Hoerée in *La Revue musicale* 10:9, September/October 1929, p. 275.

Ex. 8.14: *Huit Pièces celtiques*, Op. 51 No. 5, bars 1–17 (representing the first half of the piece)

The *Huit Pièces celtiques*, Op. 51 are meant to be study pieces, not intended for the concert platform, and as such they may still be of good use, especially for teachers seeking original music with an Irish flavour that are simple but not simplistic. Yet, Hennessy's Press Books show two public performances of the whole set by the French pianist Marie-Antoinette Pradier in March 1930 and November 1931.

Trois Pièces exotiques, Op. 57 (1922) for piano

Despite their advanced opus number, the *Trois Pièces exotiques*, Op. 57 are Hennessy's next work in chronological order – because they survived the cuts the composer made to his work-list after the November 1922 recital in Berlin. They were first published with E. Demets in 1922 and reissued in a revised and corrected edition in 1924 by Max Eschig & Cie., the successor to Demets. The first performance has been briefly mentioned above; it took place on 15 November 1922 in Berlin, with Bruno Eisner. It also entered the repertory of the French pianist Maurice Servais.

It is funny that Hennessy calls the style of these three pieces 'exotic', since this work must rank as one of his most American compositions. Their rhythmic use of cakewalk, ragtime and other contemporary elements from early 1920s popular music, the harmonic treatment reminding of old-style jazz music, the subject matter – everything points to the southern states of the USA. This is certainly exotic, albeit not absolutely new, for French ears – and for Hennessy's as well because, after all, he has never spent any of his adult years in the US, and it is rather unlikely that he ever went to New Orleans as a child.

An Engagement with Ireland (1920–1924)

Hennessy was attracted to 'jazzy' popular music of an American style, in a tradition extending from Louis Moreau Gottschalk via (partly) Edward MacDowell to Scott Joplin, George Gershwin, and beyond. We have heard it before in parts of *Au village*, Op. 22 (1907; see Chapter 4) and in *L'Américain qui a bien dîné*, Op. 47 No. 2 (1912; see Chapter 5), and we will hear it again in the mid-1920s (Chapter 9).

It is a real interest, nothing to merely attract curiosity or to curry favour with parts of his audience who may expect an American in Paris to write in an American style. One of the very few bits we know about Hennessy's private interests is that he regularly frequented the Parisian cinemas with their largely improvised live music to silent movies. According to his son, he went almost every day to a cinema on Boulevard Montparnasse that had a removable roof.[79] The music he would have heard in such settings also influenced a composition like this.

The three pieces in the album are called (with his own translations given as subtitles in the publication) 1. *Fillettes brunes* ('Yellow Girls', 'Braune Mädchen'); 2. *Le Goût de la cannelle* ('The Taste of Cinnamon', 'Zimmtgeschmack'); and 3. *Nègre endimanché* ('Nigger in Sunday Clothes', 'Neger im Sonntagstaat'). Hennessy calls them 'light and humoristic sketches',[80] which is certainly true of the first and third piece.

Ex. 8.15: *Trois Pièces exotiques*, Op. 57 No. 3: *Nègre endimanché*, bars 1–12

---

[79] Information from Brigitte Hennessy.
[80] '*croquis légers et humoristiques*', in his commented work-list.

Fillettes brunes is an attractive piece in F major and 2/4 time that makes much use of lines and chords in *pizzicato*, frequently employing major seventh chords. *Le Goût de la cannelle*, despite its stated programme, is the most abstract and also the shortest piece in the set. It is a highly chromatic piece based on a C major key and written in 5/4 time that makes frequent use of whole-tone and minor seventh chords, probably intended to create a spicy, strangely sweetish harmonic 'taste'. *Nègre endimanché*, certainly a politically incorrect title nowadays, returns to the entertaining mood (and the tonality) of the first piece. Ex. 8.15 shows the beginning with a rhythmic bass motif in the left hand, joined from bar 5 by a buoyant melody much in the style of a contemporary cinema pianist.

The prominent Parisian music critic Émile Vuillermoz seemed to like the work when he heard it performed by Maurice Servais in 1925. He wrote:

> [...] three *Pièces exotiques* by Swan Hennessy, of skilful and delicious simplicity. His *Fillettes brunes* and his *Nègre endimanché* are very successful light sketches. And his *Goût de la cannelle* expresses a mystery of extremely curious synaesthesia.[81]

Variations sur un thème de six notes, Op. 58 (1922) for flute and string trio

The *Variations*, Op. 58 are a flute quartet, classically scored for flute, violin, viola, and cello. It is Hennessy's first quartet composition that is not a string quartet and his first work involving a flute. It was written in late 1922, probably after the second journey to Berlin. The parts were published by Max Eschig & Cie. in 1924, the score in 1925.

In a subline to the title on the first page of the score, Hennessy added 'H.B., E.B., C.H.'. These are indications of the pitches of the six notes to which the title refers, which he obviously read in the German way as H – B – E – B – C – H (in English: B – B♭ – E – B♭ – C – B). In a brief explanation in *Le Guide du concert* he solves the riddle with the words 'The letters H.B., E.B, and C.H. are the initials of three friends of the author to which this composition is dedicated'.[82] Unfortunately, these names could not be identified. The initials neither belong to any of the musicians who performed the work nor to any of his Breton composer-friends nor to any other person occurring in this study. Only 'C.H.' would fit Claire Hennessy, but he would not have called his wife a friend in the same sense as the other two. The fact that he used the German pronunciation of the pitches may point to the three friends being German. But this does not make it more conducive. We must therefore regard the three people as private friends from beyond his musical circles.

The work is written in one continuous movement, consisting of one page (in the score) exposing the theme (Ex. 8.16), followed by sixteen unnumbered variations

---

[81] '[...] trois Pièces exotiques, *de Swan Hennessy, d'une simplicité adroite et savoureuse. Ses* Fillettes brunes *et son* Nègre endimanché *sont de croquis légers fort réussis. Et son* Goût de la canelle *exprime un mystère de synesthésie extrêmement curieux.*'; Émile Vuillermoz in *Excelsior*, 9 March 1925.

[82] '*Les lettres H.B., E.B. et C.H. sont les initiales de trois amis de l'auteur auxquels cette composition est dédiée.*'; in *Le Guide du concert*, 9 May 1924, p. 458.

played without interruption, followed by a short epilogue. The duration is about eleven to twelve minutes.

Ex. 8.16: Theme of *Variations sur un thème de six notes*, Op. 58

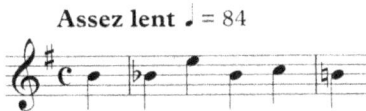

The theme is quite unusual, not suggestive of current melodies in a traditional sense, especially given the fact that Hennessy would have had other options of grouping the three pairs of letters/pitches together or of using octaves. The aural impression of the theme reminds of twelve-note-rows – although there are only four different pitches. Given Hennessy's sarcastic humour when it came to Schönberg, it would not be surprising if this would have been intended.

Hennessy uses a wide spectrum of techniques to vary his theme in a very creative manner. In the first variation (*'Beaucoup plus animé'*), which is largely played *staccato*, the theme moves to the viola and some of the tones are being played twice (Ex 8.17). There is a rhythmical change in variation 3 (*'Mouvt. de Gigue'*), a section in 9/8 where the theme first occurs in parallel octaves in the flute (Ex. 8.18) and the violin. Sometimes Hennessy uses techniques that are inspired by twelve-tone composition, such as variation 2, which not only uses a rhythmical variant but also, a few bars later, the retrograde of the theme in cello and viola (Ex. 8.19).

Ex. 8.17: *Variations*, Op. 58, variation 1, bars 1–4

Ex. 8.18: *Variations*, Op. 58, variation 3, bars 1–3 (flute, E minor)

Ex. 8.19: *Variations*, Op. 58, variation 2, bars 7–12

The ensemble writing is less canonical than in his previous quartets and trios, although imitative techniques still feature largely. The work is stronger than most of his chamber music dominated by a linear approach that gives the individual instruments a comparatively large degree of independence.

While some of the variations must be regarded as Hennessy's most abstract, perhaps his most modern, music, it is astonishing how even here he manages to include two variations of an 'Irish' character: variation 7 uses the 'Scotch snap' in a ballad-like movement in 2/4 time and a rather slow tempo, whereas variation 15 employs a jig rhythm in a much faster and animated section. In two variations only (nos 13 and 16) Hennessy moves away from the basic E minor tonality of the work. In no. 13 he switches to the tonic major, and in no. 16 he moves one tone down to D minor.

Part of the reason for the slight delay between composition and publication of the *Variations*, Op. 58 was the death of Hennessy's publisher Eugène Demets on 25 April 1923. The whole catalogue of Demets was taken over by the Czech-born Max Eschig (1872–1927) who had been active in Paris on a much lower business level since 1907. Max Eschig & Cie. grew in size and importance particularly after taking over Demets, followed by signing on the music of Manuel de Falla, Heitor Villa-Lobos and others.

It seems like Eschig was initially not certain how to deal with the works published by Demets. Maybe there were other business-related or legal reasons for the delay. Consequently, when Hennessy's Op. 58 was first performed in May 1924, it was in a series called 'L'Œuvre inédit', organised by the bi-weekly periodical *Le Guide du concert* in association with the impresario Francis Touche in the Salle des Concerts Touche on 25 boulevard de Strasbourg. The performers were an unidentified flutist, A. Trembelland, together with Émile Loiseau (violin), Robert Chantôme (viola), and Mathieu Barraine (cello).[83] Paul Le Flem wrote as music critic for *Comoedia* about the event,

---

[83] There is a letter in possession of the Hennessy family by Gaston Blanquart, first flutist of the Concerts Colonne, dated 25 September 1925, with the note 'Thank you for having sent me your *Variations on a theme of six notes* and for having given me the pleasure of reading a charming work whose ingenuity and musicality I already admire. So I look forward to deepening it through practice and I stand at your entire disposal for that.' *('Je vous remercie de m'avoir fait envoyer vos Variations sur un thème de Six notes et de m'avoir procuré ainsi le plaisir de lire une œuvre charmante dont*

describing the *Variations* as being 'of an exquisite colour; they seduce by the discreet charm of the lines and the extreme clarity of the writing'.[84]

Fig. 8.7: Hennessy's portrait for the publisher Max Eschig (1923, but probably ten years older)

In a review of the publication for *Die Musik*, the prominent German musicologist Wilhelm Altmann discovered the Irish themes in the score, even though he mistakenly took them as quotes from Irish traditional music. The review does not sound as if he had heard the name of Swan Hennessy for the first time:

---

j'admire déjà l'ingéniosité et la musicalité. Ainsi suis-je impatient de l'approfondir par l'exécution et je me tiens pour cela à votre entière disposition.'). However, there is no record of Blanquart ever having performed the piece. But he did perform in the *Trio*, Op. 70 (1925) for violin, flute and bassoon, which is partly dedicated to him.

[84] '[...] *sont d'une exquise couleur; elles séduisent par le charme discret de la ligne et l'extrême clarté de l'écriture*'; Paul Le Flem in *Comoedia*, 18 May 1924, p. 2.

With great art and also with not inconsiderable inventiveness, this very simple theme is modified; taste with regard to sound effects is also preserved; a lot of variety is achieved. The fact that the composer uses an Irish folk song in one of the variations will only surprise those who do not know that Hennessy uses every opportunity to emphasise his Irish nationality in his music.[85]

Quatre Pièces celtiques, Op. 59 (1923) for cor anglais and string trio

Despite its similar instrumentation – it is another quartet for a solo instrument and strings – the *Quatre Pièces celtiques*, Op. 59 is a very different work from the *Variations sur un thème de six notes*, Op. 58. And this is mainly due to its harmonic language. Again, it is observable that in a work of an overtly Irish/Celtic character, Hennessy's harmony becomes more diatonic and conventional, leaning strongly on a late Romantic sound world. Any experimental ideas are reduced to a minimum of structural ideas

The work was written in early 1923 with the cor anglais and oboe player Paul Brun in mind, to whom it is dedicated and who gave the first performance at the same *'L'Œuvre inédit'* event in May 1924 as the *Variations*, Op. 58. The string players were members of the Loiseau Quartet: Émile Loiseau, Robert Chantôme, and Robert Ladoux. Score and parts were published by Max Eschig & Cie. in early 1925. Brun played it for a about two years, before the work fell into a deep slumber, occasionally stirred by isolated performances in Switzerland, only to be woken up around the year 2009 in Germany by the Ensemble Più, which has given numerous performances since then.[86] It has also been heard in recent years in Finland, France, and Spain, contributing to the notion, expressed earlier, that Hennessy's reputation nowadays rests to a large degree on his early 1920s 'Celtic' chamber music.

The work consists of four very short numbered movements without descriptive titles, amounting to between eight and nine minutes in performance overall. It begins with an *Allegretto* (4/4) in F major, followed by an *Adagio* (3/4) in E minor, an *Allegro* (2/4) in F major that alternates with an *andante* section, and finally a faster *Allegro* (2/4) in the tonic minor (D minor). There is a strong melancholic note in the first two movements, which is lifted in the last two to make room for some exuberant 'Celtic' feeling.

In a brief note by Hennessy, which was published before the first performance in May 1924, he explains that the cor anglais may also be substituted by a clarinet (this is not mentioned in the score) and that he considers both instruments as qualified to

---

[85] *'Mit großer Kunst und auch mit nicht unbeträchtlicher Erfindungskraft ist dieses sehr einfache Thema abgewandelt; Geschmack in Bezug auf Klangwirkungen ist dabei auch gewahrt, viel Abwechslung dabei erzielt. Daß der Komponist zu einer Variation noch ein irländisches Volkslied heranzieht, wird nur den verwundern, der nicht weiß, daß Hennessy bei jeder Gelegenheit seine irische Nationalität in seiner Musik zu betonen pflegt.'*; Wilhelm Altmann in *Die Musik* 17:9, June 1925, p. 698.
[86] In addition, the Hungarian-born, German-resident oboist Lajos Lencsés recorded the work in 2005 for the German public broadcasting station SWR 2, together with Emily Körner (vn), Andra Darzins (va), and Zoltan Paulich (vc), which has occasionally been broadcast.

resemble a bagpipe in 'Celtic' art music.[87] He also adds that the work does not use existing traditional music except in the second movement, which is based on the Irish tune 'Last night I dreamt of my own true love', Petrie Collection no. 453 (Ex. 8.20).

Ex. 8.20: Tune no. 453 in the Petrie Collection, as edited by C. V. Stanford (1902)

Ex. 8.21: *Quatre Pièces celtiques*, Op. 59, 2nd movement, bars 1–4

Hennessy identifies the tune as 'Cette nuit j'ai rêvé', but there is no explanatory remark to this end in the score as he had done on previous occasions. He describes it thus: 'This tune, which perhaps dates back to the 17th century, is, through its tender nostalgia, one of the most characteristic of Irish folklore.'[88] In a later issue of the same journal, he maintains that the character of the third movement is rather Scottish than Irish, and it is here, indeed, that he makes the most of the 'Scotch snap'.[89] In the fourth movement he recalls some motivic ideas of the first and third movements.

---

[87] '*Le cor anglais et la clarinette, instruments souvent négligés, se prêtent, on ne peut mieux, à l'interprétation de la musique celtique et remplacent avantageusement la cornemuse et le biniou.*'; *Le Guide du concert*, 9 May 1924, p. 458 (anonymous article most certainly by S. H.).
[88] '*Cet air, qui remonte peut-être au XVII*ᵉ *siècle, est, par sa tendre nostalgie, un de plus caractéristiques du folklore irlandais.*'; ibidem. It is not sure what made Hennessy think that the tune was so old.
[89] *Le Guide du concert*, 6 February 1925, p. 509.

Étude de concert, Op. 60 (1922–3) for piano

In view of the first performance and the copyright year (1923), this virtuoso composition for piano must have been written in late 1922 and perhaps finalised very early in 1923, but more likely is a date of 1922. The first performance was on 15 February 1923, and if it was not arranged at short notice it must have been composed somewhat prior to that. Unfortunately, this is one of the comparatively few works for which no manuscript appears to have survived, which would perhaps have given a better indication. Yet, it is a work that has survived Hennessy's various changes of opus numbers, which means it was not withdrawn and must have had some value for the composer.

It is a very unusual work for Hennessy and one that should not detain us here too long. Hennessy has never before and again written a work to mainly satisfy the demands of a virtuoso. Perhaps, after he had occasionally received the feedback that many of his works were technically not very difficult, he had the desire to prove that he could write difficult music if needed. His descriptive comment in his own list of works consists of the three words 'De difficulté technique', which says 'something'.

The *Étude de concert* is in one movement written in F minor, with two *presto* passages framing a short middle section of a mere eleven bars in 3/4 time in B major marked *Meno mosso molto quasi adagio*. The contrast is not quite so strong, though, since Hennessy designs his 3/4 bars in three groups of semiquavers, keeping his score dense throughout. In the *presto* parts, the left hand mainly moves in octave parallels, accompanying a countermotion in (mainly) parallel sixths in the right hand. The whole work would last no longer than four minutes.

The piece was written for the French pianist Rachel Blanquer (1897–after 1957), one of the last pupils of Eraïm Miriam Delaborde (1839–1913) at the *Conservatoire*, where she had won a *Premier Prix* in 1914. In her recital at the Salle Érard[90] she began and ended her performance with Romantic works, beginning with Brahms, Chopin, and two songs by Wagner sung by Claire Croiza (the partner of Arthur Honegger), and ended on several works by Franz Liszt. The middle section had slightly more contemporary works, beginning with the first performance of Hennessy's *Étude*, followed by Blanquer's teacher's arrangement of the minuet from Bizet's *L'Arlesienne*, Charles-Valentin Alkan's *Quatre Chants* and another appearance of Claire Croiza in Maurice Ravel's *Cinq Mélodies populaires grecques*. With Alkan having been a friend of Chopin's and the father of Blanquer's teacher Delaborde, there were some nice inherent connections in the programme. Hennessy's composition in its Lisztian gestures and conservative harmonic approach contributed his own part in keeping the programme stylistically conform. In reviews of the event, Paul Le Flem regarded the Hennessy work as 'finely and skilfully written for the piano' and the critic 'L. H.' as 'admirably written for the instrument'.[91]

---

[90] Programme in Hennessy Press Book no. 3.
[91] '[…] *finement et adroitement écrite pour le piano*'; Paul Le Flem in *Comoedia*, 19 February 1923; '[…] *la très brillante* Etude de Concert *de Swan Hennessy admirablement écrite pour l'instrument.*'; L. H. in *Le Monde musical*, February 1923.

Sonatine celtique, Op. 53 (1923) for piano

The *Sonatine celtique*, Op. 53 for piano is Hennessy's second piano sonatina after the Ravel-inspired Op. 43 of 1911. Indeed – although it is not exactly decipherable in the manuscript – this work's title should probably have been *Deuxième Sonatine*. Since the composition coincided with the composer's reawakening interest in Ireland, another provisional title (and opus number) for this work was *Irish Sonatina*, Op. 61. Under this name it can be found in Hennessy's Manuscript Book II. The reason for the English title may be that Hennessy intended this work to be published in Cork with Sullivan & Co., alongside the *Eight Celtic Pieces* (*Huit Pièces celtiques*) and the withdrawn 'Celtic' piano trio.

Since these plans failed due to the Irish Civil War, Hennessy (respectively his copyright owner Michael Kavanagh) transferred the publication to Evans & Co. in London where it appeared in early 1924. As part of the *Album celtique* (1929) it was also published with Eschig in France. The work is dedicated to Lucien Haudebert, another of Hennessy's Breton composer-friends in Paris. Its three movements would add up to about eight minutes in performance.

The first two movements are written in F minor, which sometimes tends to be ambiguous, leaning on F major in some resolutions of phrases or, for example, in the ending of the first movement on an F major chord. The third movement, then, is clearly set in F major. The first movement (*Allegro*, which should not be taken too fast), is the technically most demanding part of the work. It makes frequent use of elements that Hennessy has described as Irish in the 1929 interview with Lucien Chevaillier such as the 'snap' and the ending of phrases on three repeated notes. There are also melodic contours recognisable from Irish traditional music.

Yet, overall the melodic appeal is less distinguished than in many other of Hennessy's compositions, and the harmonisation rather follows a German Romantic model than a contemporary French one. In his review, quoted earlier, of the *Album celtique* in *La Revue musicale*, Arthur Hoerée compared the harmonic approach to that of Schumann and Mendelssohn, adding that especially the latter had a long-lasting influence in England.[92] He seems to suggest here that Hennessy has a musical background in the British Isles, which may be forgivable. In Hennessy's case, of course, Schumann suggests himself rather than Mendelssohn, of whom Hennessy did not think very highly.

The second movement (*Andante*) is quite attractive, juxtaposing in an A–B–A–B form a contemplative melodic idea with an agitated section in *staccato* semiquavers that features an Irish-sounding tune in octaves of the right hand with a chromatic movement of thirds in the left (Ex. 8.22).

---

[92] *'Ces [œuvres] pourraient être contemporaines de Schumann ou Mendelssohn qui (surtout le dernier) ont laissé de longs échos en Angleterre.'*; Arthur Hoerée in *La Revue musicale*, op. cit.

Ex. 8.22: *Sonatine celtique*, Op. 53, 2nd movement, bars 47–54

The 6/8 rhythmic pattern of the third movement recalls an Irish or Scottish jig, with the tune moving through both hands – were it not for the melodic modulations that must sound weird and 'wrong' for a traditional musician. Here also, the notion of a German Romantic background to Hennessy's harmony disappears clearly in favour of a French approach, especially in the whole-tone dominated middle section from bar 53 (Ex. 8.23).

Ex. 8.23: *Sonatine celtique*, Op. 53, 2nd movement, bars 53–64

Yet, the overall impression of the work in contemporary France was that of a conservative approach, albeit one that was not necessarily negative. Lucien Chevaillier, who had interviewed him for the April 1929 issue of *Le Guide du concert*, wrote about the *Sonatine celtique* and the slightly later *Rapsodie irlandaise*, Op. 67, after he had heard them performed by Denyse Molié in June 1929:

> Full of natural music, ignoring the pressures of fashion and snobbery, disregarding any concern to put himself forward, he has quietly written a series of exquisite and scented works, which will be a comfort to musicians when they want to do a cure of detoxification that may be indispensable sooner or later.[93]

Troisième quatuor à cordes, Op. 61 [String Quartet No. 3] (1923)

Some reviews of the withdrawn *Deuxième Suite* for string quartet that was performed in November 1922 in Berlin show that this had three movements with programmatic titles, namely *Les Écossais*, *Les Fées*, and *Les Étudiants*. These now reappear in 1923 as three of the four movements of Hennessy's third string quartet. He moved *Les Étudiants* to the middle and added an Introduction that was probably written in early 1923. Since the original manuscript is not extant it cannot be determined whether there were any changes to the three original movements.

It took some three years before Eschig published the music in 1926. The four movements are individually dedicated to the members of the Quatuor Loiseau (Émile Loiseau, Adrien Fourment, Robert Chantôme, Robert Ladoux), who gave the first performance in the Salle des Agriculteurs of Sorbonne University on 14 October 1926.[94] Interestingly, this is the only documented performance of the work by the Loiseau Quartet – all later performances were by the Quatuor Krettly and (particularly) the Quatuor Calvet (see Appendix 1). Like all of Hennessy's string quartets, this work has not been publicly performed since the 1930s and only taken up very recently (and recorded for CD) by the RTÉ ConTempo Quartet in Ireland (see Appendix 7).

The Introduction – which is the longest of the four movements – borrows from the classical sonata form, with a first thematic subject in A major followed by a modulation from bar 33 to a Phrygian scale on A, that features a decidedly 'Celtic' melodic line (Ex. 8.24). This is followed by a second thematic subject in B flat major dominated by a cello line in quavers to a very calm accompaniment of the upper strings with occasional echoes of melodic snippets from the cello. Without a development section,

---

[93] '*Plein d'une musique naturelle, ignorant les pressions de la mode et du snobisme, négligeant à l'excès tout souci de se mettre en avant, il a écrit sans bruit une série d'œuvres exquises et parfumées, qui seront un réconfort pour les musiciens lorsqu'ils voudront faire la cure de désintoxication tôt ou tard indispensable.*'; Lucien Chevaillier in *Le Monde musical*, 30 June 1929.

[94] The programme consisted of (in this order) Brahms' Horn Trio, Op. 40 (Edouard Vuillermoz, Émile Loiseau and his [unnamed] wife; four songs by Eugène Cools (Marcelle Gerar, Janine Cools) incl. two first performances; Hennessy's 3rd quartet, Op. 61; two songs [*Deux Monodies*] by Georges Migot (Gerar, Migot); *Trois Chansons espagnoles*, Op. 42bis by Hennessy (Gerar, Quatuor Loiseau); and the Piano Quintet by Paul Le Flem (Mme Loiseau, Quatuor Loiseau).

the movement returns to A major for the recapitulation – Hennessy calls the movement *'un allegro de forme classique très concentrée'*.[95]

Ex. 8.24: String Quartet No. 3, Op. 61, 1st movt, bars 33–35

The following three movements keep to an extra-musical programme, making this work the most programmatic of Hennessy's quartets. In *'Les Écossais'* ('The Scots'), an *Allegro* in D minor, Hennessy uses elements of Scottish traditional music, emphasising that he is not utilising any traditional tune, but the strong chromatic harmonic shifts of the accompanying instruments prevent that this sounds similar to a folksong arrangement anyway. It appears clearest in a middle section where triplets briefly imitate a jig rhythm. In this attractive movement Hennessy demonstrates his contrapuntal qualities, taking traditional music as mere inspiration but not more.

'Les Étudiants' ('The Students') shows another side of Hennessy's folk music leanings: he is recalling his student days in Germany with intonations of a drinking song (Ex. 8.25) and brief allusions to hunting horns, describing it as 'a short evocation of the university life of a small German town in the late 19th century'[96] – and what else should he have in mind than his own student days in Stuttgart during the early 1880s!

Ex. 8.25: String Quartet No. 3, Op. 61, 3rd movt, bars 34–37 (cello)

There is also an emphatic passage in this movement that he has described variously as 'recalling the carefreeness of youth' or 'a passionate discussion' (Ex. 8.26).[97]

---

[95] In a notice on the work in *Le Guide du concert* 15:24, 15 March 1929, p. 714 (again, an anonymous short article most likely written by Hennessy himself).
[96] *'une courte évocation de la vie universitaire d'une petite ville allemande vers la fin du XIXe siècle'*, as above.
[97] *'l'insouciance de la jeunesse'*, in his work-list; *'une discussion passionnée'*, in *Le Guide*, as above.

Ex. 8.26: String Quartet No. 3, Op. 61, 3rd movt, bars 53–64

In the foreground there is a 'discussion' between the first violin and the viola, driven forward by the other instruments in bowed tremolos, but this represents the heated discussions among students, the drinking song and these discussions being two sides of Hennessy's experience during his studies in Stuttgart.

The fourth movement, 'Les Fées', is a light and vivid evocation in C major of Irish fairies dancing in the moonlight, put in contrast with a melancholic second subject that reminds the listener of the mysterious aspects that are also prevalent in fairy stories.

It turns out, therefore that this quartet has a programme that is to a large extent autobiographical. There is his Irish background, his German studies, and perhaps a Scottish experience, too, that may reach back to his first marriage in Edinburgh (although the latter is less likely; it is rather a pan-Celtic idea to resort to Scottish music).

In a short review of the 1926 concert when the quartet received its first performance, Jean Messager had the following to say about Hennessy's 3rd quartet:

> '[…] we had in a first audition, a *Quartet* by Mr Swan Hennessy, skilfully written, with a clear and subtle line. The musician whose melodic vein is very fresh, knows the art of exposing and uniting themes during which he sets his course with ease. The harmonic feeling is just right and the sound effect delightful. This Quartet was excellently played,

with delicate contrasts of designs by Mr Loiseau, Mr Fourment, Mr Chantôme and Mr Ladoux.[98]

In Ireland, 1924

Whenever Swan Hennessy spent time in Ireland, he did not leave any public trace. He did not give or participate in concerts and is not mentioned in reviews of events that he attended. Thus, the following is speculative, but there is good reason to assume that Hennessy was in Ireland at least once (in April 1924) and perhaps before, in 1923, also.

While Denis Breen's portrait article of Hennessy in the *Dublin Evening Telegraph* of 2 September 1922 and its updated version in *The Leader* of 7 April 1923 were likely the result of correspondence, the *Leader* article at least was timed to coincide with the Father Mathew Feis in Dublin. Here, two chamber works by Hennessy received several performances as test pieces on the 'chamber music day' of the festival, 6 April 1923: the early Violin Sonata, Op. 14, and the String Quartet No. 2, Op. 49. A critic wrote about the performance of the quartet:

> The quartet played was the composition of Swan Hennessy. It is not a difficult work, except patches where the intonation is not easy to preserve. It proved, however, a very useful test piece, as it was not too far beyond the scope of the players. The four ladies (Misses Murphy, Nolan, Reid, and Brady) have a good deal of musical feeling in their playing, and, if their attack was not always unanimous, I am inclined to attribute it to the fact that their desks were too high, and obscured the view of their colleagues.[99]

There is no word here about the composer being present, and it is not very likely, even though the perspective of hearing several performances of one's work may have been tempting.

The same goes for the performance of the violin sonata. But here, the critic is struck by the repeated presence of Hennessy's name on the programme and (probably justly) attributes it to the good contacts between the composer and the organisers of the Father Mathew Feis, who included Denis Breen and (particularly) Arthur Darley:

> In the opinion of Mr. Moody, the best instrumental performance of which he has had experience at this year's Feis was the performance of the sonata for violin and pianoforte given by Master R. Kieran and Master J. Doyle. The piece itself was a fairly easy sonata by Swan Hennessy, a composer who seems suddenly to have captured the fancy of those who are responsible for the selections. It has a nice opening movement, but, as in many modern sonatas, falls away in interest towards the end.

---

[98] '*Puis, nous eûmes en première audition, un* Quatuor *de M. Swan Hennessy, adroitement écrit, d'une ligne claire et subtile. / Le musicien dont la veine mélodique est des plus fraîches, connaît l'art d'exposer et d'unir des thèmes dont il règle le cours avec aisance. / Le sentiment harmonique est juste et l'effet sonore délicieux. Ce Quatuor fut excellemment joué, avec de délicates oppositions de plans par MM. Loiseau, Fourment, Chantôme et Ladoux.*'; Jean Messager in *Comoedia*, 20 October 1926, p. 2.

[99] S.R.W. in *The Irish Independent*, 7 April 1923, p. 10.

I have had occasion to comment favourably on the playing of both these young artists, especially Master Doyle, whose pianoforte technique and sense of tone, touch and rhythm are something quite remarkable. If Master Doyle preserves his interest in his work, hears all the music he can, and has his studies conducted on broad lines he will ultimately become a fine pianist.

Mr. Moody spoke very highly of the violin playing of Master Kieran, and both players gave a sympathetic rendering of the sonata. They were very punctilious in their observance of every mark of expression. If the performance had any fault it was that of respectability. It was too nicely dressed – not a speck of dust was to be seen. In the finale, a bustling movement, one would have welcomed a feeling of abandon. We wanted something more robust and dashing. The adjudicator had no hesitation in awarding silver medals to the players.[100]

Admittedly, even though Hennessy would probably have liked to argue about the missing 'feeling of abandon' in the violin sonata, it is not likely that he was there to defend his case. In March 1924, however, he was almost certainly in Dublin, and perhaps in May in Cork as well.

The immediate reason can be seen in two autograph dedications with signatures on two published scores (Fig. 8.8) that Hennessy must have given to Frederick May (1911–1985), then an aspiring young talent on the piano who had won his first prizes at the Feis Ceoil and who was, a decade later, on the way to fame as one of the most important twentieth-century composers in Ireland. Boxes with materials formerly belonging to May and now in possession of Trinity College Dublin,[101] include the scores of *Eight Celtic Pieces*, Op. 51 and *Épigrammes d'un solitaire*, Op. 55, both in their first 1924 editions with the London publisher Evans & Co. Both dedications are clearly written by Hennessy, but the handwriting differs nevertheless (see the capital F and M of May's name). The first reads *'Master Fred May. Le meas mór, S. H.'* and the other *'à Monsieur Fred May hommage sympathique. Swan Hennessy'*. Because of the different handwriting and language – in the first, Hennessy uses a greeting formula in Irish – I presume that the first was given to May when they met in Ireland and the second was sent later from Paris.

Fig. 8.8a+b: Dedications by Hennessy to Frederick May, 1924
(Courtesy: Library of Trinity College Dublin)

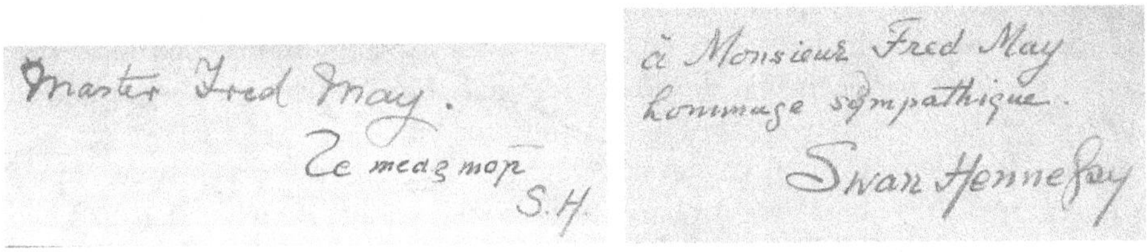

[100] S.R.W., as above. It is not clear which 'Mr Moody' the critic has in mind here.
[101] Uncatalogued, with sincere thanks to musicologist Dr Mark Fitzgerald for alerting me to these scores and to librarian Roy Stanley for providing me with copies.

May, who was born 9 June 1911, would have become 13 years of age in the course of 1924. Although these dedications do not bear a date, it is rather unlikely that a boy his age would have met Hennessy in Paris. These dedications therefore can be regarded as proof that Hennessy was in Ireland. But when and where exactly? The answer to these questions must be sought in performances of Hennessy's music in Ireland, and they be cannot have been before 1924, because the publication of the two works above dates from 1924.

It so happened that there was a concert at the United Arts Club, Dublin (then at 44, St Stephens Green), on 20 March 1924, by the 'Dublin String Quartette'. This was reported on as follows:

> Very enjoyable concert was held in the United Arts Club on Thursday evening last. The Dublin String Quartette, consisting of Mr. Arthur Darley (1st violin), Miss Rita Dowdall (2nd violin), Mr. George Hoyle (viola), Mr. Joseph Schofield (violincello) gave an excellent rendering of a fine historical piece by Swan Hennessy, heard in Dublin for the first time; also an appropriate selection of Irish airs by H. Bast. The vocalists – Miss Mary Maguire (Mrs. Joseph Schofield) and Mr. Joseph O'Reilly – were at their best, and delighted an appreciative audience. Miss Townsend accompanied on the harp with charming effect. Among the audience were – Mr. Dermod O'Brien, Mrs. Vanston, Miss O'Mara, Miss Dowdall, Mrs. May, Mr. and Mrs. Crofts, Mr. Barrett, Dr. Mervyn Crofton, Miss Macnie, Dr. Kennedy Cahill, Mr. Walsh, Mr. J. O'Reilly, and Mr. Chester Arthurs.[102]

This press notice would need several footnotes to correct and explain the names of those who were present on the occasion. The members of the quartet were, with one exception on the second violin, the musicians who had given the premiere of Hennessy String Quartet No. 2, Op. 49 in Paris in January 1922. The viola player is the first victim of misreading or misspelling: this must have been George H. Brett. 'Miss Townsend' is none other than Carrie Townshend who had cooperated with Hennessy in London about twenty years earlier. Mr Crofts is either the composer Joseph Crofts or his brother, the singer Gerald Crofts – Joseph had also been present in Paris in 1922. Mervyn Crofton was to become the librettist to the 'Celtic' operas of Geoffrey Molyneux Palmer and Staf Gebruers in the 1930s. And 'Mrs. May' could be Frederick May's mother, in which case young Fred would have accompanied her, and then Hennessy would have met him on this very occasion and given him the first of the two scores. The only irritating aspect is that, if members of the audience were mentioned by name, why not Hennessy also? But the explanation may be simply that the reporter of this society magazine did not recognise him or that Hennessy remained in the background, which would not be untypical for him.

As for Hennessy's work played on this occasion, the 'fine historical piece ... heard in Dublin for the first time' was probably not his second quartet (which has had two performances in Dublin prior to this event) but the first, the *Suite*, Op. 46 (1912).

Hennessy did probably not stay until the next performance of his works in Ireland about eight weeks later. But perhaps he did come again, because this would have been

---

[102] *Irish Society*, 22 March 1924, p. 5.

a trip to Cork, his father's birthplace, for the Oireachtas festival on 25 May 1924 in the Father Mathew Hall. This was again a competitive festival. Hennessy's Press Books contain cuttings from the programme of this event, which included performances of his Violin Sonata, Op. 14 (*c*.1904) and the *Variations sur un air irlandais ancien*, Op. 28 (1908) for piano. One of the organisers was Denis Breen.

Finally, the musical by-programme of the Tailteann Games, a large sports event in Dublin in August 1924, included Hennessy's *Trio*, Op. 54.[103]

Thus, there was a period in the early 1920s, when Hennessy enjoyed a number of performances in Ireland, coinciding with plans to have some of his music published in Ireland, potentially to support or join an Irish composers' society, and at least one actual journey to the country. We have dedications to Irish revolutionaries such as that of his second quartet to Terence MacSwiney and the intended, not realised, dedication of the *Eight Celtic Pieces* to Éamon de Valera. There is a clear mutual interest between Hennessy and Irish musicians of the time. Only the time itself was difficult, art music had a small following in Ireland and the situation of 'classical' musicians in these troubled times was fragile – a situation that was not to improve for many years.

In addition, the 1920s marked a generational change among Irish composers, too. The older generation died (O'Leary, Seymour, Jozé, Stanford, Wood, Flood, Esposito), younger ones withdrew (O'Dwyer, O'Brien, Harty, Palmer, Boyle, Coghill). The next generation were as yet teenagers (Fleischmann, May, Trimble, Boydell).[104] In retrospect, when Hennessy was – present or played – in Ireland, the vacuum was just opening, and when times began to improve during the 1940s, nobody remembered Swan Hennessy.

* * *

Sonatine celtique, Op. 62 (1924) for viola and piano

Not to be confused with the piano work (Op. 53) of the same title, this is a chamber work in three movements for viola and piano, of which there is also a transcription for violin and an arrangement (by René Laurent) for alto saxophone, both prepared in 1927. According to the manuscript, the work was written within three days, 22 to 24 July 1924. It was published with Eschig in the same year, mistakenly entitled *Sonate celtique*, but on the inside pages of the printed score, in most of the constituent manuscripts, and in programmes and reviews this work is mostly referred to as a *Sonatine*.[105]

---

[103] *Irish Examiner*, 11 April 1924, p. 10.
[104] I have developed this idea in 'Musik ohne Publikum. Die zwanziger Jahre in Irland' in Werner Keil (ed.): *Musik der zwanziger Jahre* (Hildesheim: Georg Olms, 1996), p. 166–185; and 'No State for Music', in: Michael Dervan (ed.): *The Invisible Art. A Century of Music in Ireland, 1916–2016* (Dublin: New Island, 2016), p. 47–68.
[105] Some library catalogues and reference works use the title *Sonate celtique*. The mistake may have been Hennessy's: it also occurs in his clean manuscript to the solo part of the violin version. The violin part contains more mistakes: in both manuscript and print, bars 44–49 do not match the number of corresponding bars in the score (two bars are missing). There is no full score to the arrangements, only their solo part is inserted into the full score for viola).

The work is dedicated to Robert Chantôme, the violist of the Quatuor Loiseau who not only gave the first performance (at the Salle des Quatuors Gaveau, Paris, 18 November 1924), but who also played it throughout his career (his last documented performance is in Rennes on 25 April 1938). The manuscript, however, has a crossed-out earlier dedication to Hennessy's son Patrice, accompanied by the somewhat enigmatic phrase (in English), "The bells are ringing / The devils are singing".

Formally, the work consists of three movements without programmatic titles. The first in E flat major begins *Allegro con brio*, the second is a short *Andante sostenuto* in the same tonality, and the third an *Allegro* in C major. The duration is approximately ten minutes.

The first movement is in an abridged sonata form, with a very energetic first subject, followed by a brief variant. A second subject marked *Andante* (from bar 21) appears in a considerably calmer mood and contains first hints to 'Celtic' traditional music in the form of some occurrences of the 'snap' and a melodic contour modelled after traditional music.

The exposition (from bar 32) makes the 'Celtic' (or more specifically Irish) character abundantly clear: this uses the Irish traditional tune 'St Patrick's Day in the Morning' as its theme, for which Hennessy changes from the 4/4 time structure to the jig rhythm in 6/8, making the *Sonatine celtique* one of the few works of his that use an existing traditional melody rather than a re-composed one. This begins in the form of a conventional arrangement of the tune to piano accompaniment and then develops further with first indications of contrapuntal treatment. The rhythmic charm of the piece is enhanced by the duplets Hennessy uses in the left hand of the piano (Ex. 8.27).

Ex. 8.27: *Sonatine celtique*, Op. 62, 1st movement, bars 52–61

Further contrapuntal treatment of this tune, including short harmonic excursions betraying his French background, lead to the brief recapitulation and a well-designed ending of the movement.

The second movement is a rather melancholic piece, divided into two sections, of which the second is repeated. Through its chordal treatment and the frequent use of suspended fourths it becomes a rather solemn hymn. The melodic use of the 'snap' ensures a vague Scottish/Irish feeling.

The last movement is a quick rondo that is the technically most demanding part for the viola. In stark contrast to the previous movement, it is also the rhythmically most diverse part and begins as the perhaps least 'Irish' of the three movements. Roughly in an A–B–A form, Irish elements in the strongly syncopated A part are reduced to occasional interval leaps that vaguely suggest an Irish background for those parts of an audience that have such a background (who would have been few in Hennessy's time, particularly in France). They come more to the fore in the B part, for which Hennessy changes (as in the first movement) from a binary rhythm (here 2/4) to a jig in 6/8, also moving to F major to heighten the contrast.

The *Sonatine celtique*, Op. 62 is a truly delightful and very well-made work for the viola (or violin or saxophone). As Hinson & Roberts wrote, it has 'tuneful writing with a strong Irish idiom',[106] and the outer movements have great rhythmic interest and variety. The calm second movement gives players and audience a rest from an at times quite agile score. Harmonically, it tends to be on the conservative side, despite some strong modulation, especially in the transitions between the structural sections. Despite its Irish interest, so far (writing in mid-2019) this work still awaits its first Irish performance.

Some of the extant reviews of the work are based on the printed score, others on performances. An Italian reviewer found:

> A tasteful sonatina of a rhapsodic character and easy to perform, remarkable for the fluidity of the musical discourse and for the vagueness of the melodic themes. The vague, Nordic-coloured harmony gives a special charm to this work, which belongs to one of the most difficult genres in music: the simple genre.[107]

After hearing Robert Chantôme play it, Maurice Imbert considered it a work 'where infinitely nostalgic expressions follow the scent of the landscape'.[108] When Henri Petit heard it in a concert together with the Viola Sonata (1920) by Arthur Honegger, he appeared to have favoured Hennessy's work:

---

[106] Maurice Hinson and Wesley Roberts: *The Piano in Chamber Ensemble. An Annotated Guide* (2nd edition, Bloomington, Indiana: Indiana University Press, 2006).

[107] '*Una gustosa sonatina di carattere rapsodico e di facile esecuzione, notevole per la fluidità del discorso musicale e per la vaghezza dei temi melodici. L'armonia vaga e di colore nordico infonde uno speciale charme a questo lavoro, che appartiene a un genere fra i più difficili in musica: il genere semplice.*'; *Mom-Mus*, 16 May 1929.

[108] '[…] *la* Sonate celtique *pour alto et piano – où à des expressions infiniment nostalgiques en succèdent fleurant bon le terroir –* […]'; Maurice Imbert in *Journal des débats*, 3 March 1931, p. 4.

Mr Robert Chantôme took great care in interpreting the *Sonata* for viola, which is not Honegger at his best, and to which we much prefer Mr Swan Hennessy's *Sonate celtique*. In this work, dedicated to him, Mr Chantôme could display all his musicality, which is remarkable; and with what a full and emotional sound he makes the *Andante* sing, a piece of such profound and fascinating charm.[109]

Épigrammes d'un solitaire, Op. 55 (1923) for piano

Originally completed as Op. 63 in 1923, this is the last of the three works that Hennessy intended to publish with Sullivan & Co. in Cork, with the copyright handed over to Michael Kavanagh, and which were then published with Evans & Co. in London in 1924, with a dedication to Kavanagh. It is an album of piano works whose original publication had eight constituent pieces. Numbers 7 and 8, entitled *Edvard Grieg* and *Richard Strauss*, were removed from the 1929 publication with Éditions Max Eschig. These pastiche works found their place in the first of Hennessy's five volumes of *À la manière de …* where they fit much better.

The remaining, 'actual', *Épigrammes d'un solitaire* are a highly underrated group of six programmatic works for the piano with which Hennessy continued, after an interruption of ten years, his series of descriptive and programmatic music. He had abandoned this type of music in favour of the 'Celtic' style, but this composition may be interpreted as his continued interest in the genre – and there will be a further work a little later in the form of *Banlieues*, Op. 69. As could have been expected, though, the *Épigrammes* remained just as neglected as his pre-War music. His recent success in a 'Celtic' line of works had not helped his reputation as a 'French' composer – his Parisian audience evidently wanted him to write in an Irish or 'Celtic' style. There was little interest in an Irish-American composer writing French music.

If this speculation is true, any conscious neglect by Eschig (for example) would have been caused by marketing considerations – the works not being in line with his 'Celtic' identity – and not for reasons of quality. It is in this light that one must see the title – 'Epigrams of a Solitary' or '… Loner' – Hennessy was well aware of his solitary position in France: it contributed to some wonderful compositions, like the ones in question here, but it did not make him many friends.

The work, in its final shape, consists of the six numbers 1. *La Forêt de Clamart à l'aube*; 2. *Un Jardin arabe*; 3. *Une Pagode indochinoise*; 4. *Un Berceau*; 5. *Un vieux cimetière*; and 6. *Un Souvenir lointain*. There was never a full performance of the whole work; numbers 1, 4, and 5 were first performed at the Guildhall School, London, 13 November 1924, by Leonard Reed. Other pieces were performed by Maurice Servais or Hennessy himself. Numbers 3 and 6 have never been performed in public (yet).

---

[109] '*M. Robert Chantôme apporte tous ses soins à traduire la* Sonate *pour alto qui n'est pas du meilleur Honegger et à laquelle nous préférons de beaucoup la* Sonate celtique *de M. Swan Hennessy. Dans cette œuvre, à lui dédiée, M. Chantôme peut déployer toute sa musicalité, qui est remarquable ; avec quel son plein et chargé d'émotion il en fait chanter l'*Andante, *cette page d'un charme si profond, si prenant.*'; Henri Petit in *Le Courrier musical*, 1 December 1931.

As the titles of the individual pieces suggest, most of the music owes its creation to places in urban landscapes such as the forest near the Paris suburb of Clamart, an old cemetery, objects found in Parisian parks such as an Arabian garden or an Indochinese pagoda,[110] or that remind of solitary occupations in a quiet home such as the cradle in No. 4 or the distant memory recalled in No. 6.

Each of the six works is extremely short, being real lessons in concentration and in focusing on the essential, on a brief moment, on an idea that is hinted at, not explored. None of the pieces exceeds two pages in the score, and four of them find space on a single page (*Un Berceau* is the only piece that contains a repetition). Hennessy's liking for short statements notwithstanding, this brevity and an at times ironic nature is the very meaning of an epigram as a poetic form that is interpreted here in music.

In terms of their subject matter and, indeed, partially their harmonic language, several of the pieces are, of course, a deep bow to Debussy, specifically to the *Arabesques* (c.1890) and the *Estampes* (1903), particularly *Pagodes* and *Jardins sous la pluie*. To these, Hennessy's *Épigrammes* may be seen as welcome additional repertory in a similar spirit. Initially, this may appear anachronistic, coming twenty or thirty years too late and at a time when *Les Six* & Co. had just declared Impressionism dead.

But first of all, Impressionism was not dead yet, and secondly, Hennessy did not just copy Debussy. While he indulges in the rich chromaticism of Impressionist harmony, Hennessy always places greater emphasis, compared to his French contemporaries, on melody and an expressiveness borrowed from late Romantic models. For example, a passage of slow triplets with a chordal base in *La Forêt de Clamart à l'aube* moves from a tonality of a whole-tone character based on D to a much clearer A minor, thereby moving subtly from a more 'French' to a more 'German' idiom (Ex. 8.28).

Ex. 8.28: *Épigrammes d'un solitaire*, Op. 55 No. 1 *La Forêt de Clamart à l'aube*, bars 16–19

---

[110] For example, there is an Indochinese pagoda in the Jardin d'agronomie tropicale, part of the Bois de Vincennes, in the 12th arrondissement, built around 1907.

A very similar process is at work at the beginning of *Un Jardin arabe*, which commences in a very French mood reminding of Debussy, assuming a very different, less obviously French character from bar 5 with the introduction of a *staccato* bass line at twice the speed of before (Ex. 8.29):

Ex. 8.29: *Épigrammes d'un solitaire*, Op. 55 No. 2 *Un Jardin arabe*, bars 1–6

In *Une Pagode indo-chinoise* Hennessy imitates a metallophone gamelan ensemble in a pentatonic phrase of parallel fourths and fifths. *Un Berceau* begins as a very conventional cradle song before the central (and repeated) section clearly leaves the idyll to make room for some irritating chromatic harmony to which the melody desperately tries to keep the homely spirit, succeeding only in the very end. *Un Vieux cimetière* is a very attractive piece, commencing in dark colours in the low registers before a change of mood brings about a more peaceful and relaxed scenario in rich, widely-spaced chords. The 'distant memory' in the last piece returns to the imaginary protagonist with force (in full, *fortissimo* chords) in the middle of the piece, yet keeps a strangely restrained passion, the whole now rather reminding of Brahms than of Debussy.

This album contains some exquisite music awaiting any pianist with an interest in early twentieth-century piano music with a French touch. There is a contemplative mood about the whole collection, yet the character of each piece is quite distinct. Even though some clichés are applied with regard to the exotic character of the second and the third piece, this is not clumsy or affected. Sometimes one would wish that the pieces would not be quite so short, but this is the nature of an epigram – it says all in two lines well put.

Rapsodie gaélique, Op. 63 (1924) for cello and piano

The *Rapsodie gaélique*, Op. 63 may have been the first piece that Hennessy wrote after his return from Ireland in April 1924. Judging from the numerous changes and corrections in the manuscript just until publication by Max Eschig & Cie. in 1925, it was not an entirely easy piece to write. The work is dedicated to the prominent French cellist, conductor and impresario Francis Touche (1872–1937), who performed it with Swan Hennessy at the Salle des Concerts Touche (!), Paris, 18 December 1925. The first performance, however was given by Robert Ladoux and Mme Loiseau at the Caméléon, 18 March 1925. The duration is about six minutes.

The score looks as if this was a work in one movement, but according to Hennessy's notes in his list of works, he regarded it as a work in two movements, with the second movement beginning without any break at the *Allegro* at the top of the sixth page of the score.

The first movement, then, begins *Moderato quasi andante* in C minor in 2/4 time with a sombre melody of the cello accompanied by simple arpeggiated chords. After a piano interlude of eight bars, a second thematic subject appears (from bar 27) that makes extensive use of the 'Scotch snap', and indeed Hennessy describes it as *'un sujet de couleur très écossaise'*. After the accompanimental pattern of the first theme reappears (bar 51 ff.) with a variant of the initial melody, the piano responds in a playful, contrapuntal manner to the cello.

Hennessy describes the second movement (bar 93 ff.) as *'une sorte de marche'*, and although he changes to a 4/4 time structure accordingly, this does not prevent him from introducing the odd bar of 7/4 (Ex. 8.30). The thematic material uses the same pitches as in the beginning of the first movement.

Ex. 8.30: *Rapsodie gaélique*, Op. 63, 2nd movt, bars 122–124

The harmonic writing is rather conservative, but it does contain some attractive and original writing. Laura Watson argued that the work 'was becoming dated as French images of Ireland changed'.[111] This image of Ireland in France, however, was perhaps not so much based on the country's music.

---

[111] Laura Watson: 'Ireland in the Musical Imagination of Third Republic France', in Una Hunt and Mary Pierse (eds.): *France and Ireland. Notes and Narratives* (Oxford etc.: Peter Lang, 2015), p. 97.

Douze Canons, Op. 64 (1924) for piano

The *Douze Canons à deux voix à tous les intervalles* ['Twelve Two-part Canons in all Intervals'], Op. 64 is a collection of twelve short piano pieces, each devoted to a different interval, with each hand representing one of the two parts. It is all too easy to dismiss these pieces as an irrelevant attempt to ridicule dodecaphony, even though this would not be untypical for Hennessy. Contemporary critics and performers did indeed ignore this publication: it was not reviewed in any journal anywhere, and it does not seem to have been performed in public. The work was written in 1924, published by Eschig in 1925, and it is dedicated to Hennessy's wife Claire.

The canons in all twelve pieces pursue a linear approach in both hands. There are no chords at all and all harmony is incremental, deriving from the meeting and crossing of melodic lines. They include 'harmony' only in places where, for example, a longer note in the right hand is held for the duration of several succeeding notes in the left. In addition to the twelve different intervallic treatments of the canons, there is also some variety in tonalities and rhythm. Each piece is in a different tonality, tempo and rhythmic approach.

On a closer look, Hennessy does not use all intervals at all, at least if one also counts the diminished and augmented versions of the intervals – and in such a case, twelve pieces would not be enough. There is one piece each for the unison (No. 10), second (No. 9), third (No. 4), fourth (No. 1), fifth (No. 7); sixth (No. 8), and seventh (No. 8) – applying to the major or perfect variant only. Then, there are five variants of a canon at the octave.

The intervals in question refer to the point of entry of the second part. This is very easy to see in No. 2, *Canon à l'octave, à une mesure de distance*, which begins with a downward scale of five semiquavers starting from a high C, followed in bar 2 by the same theme starting one octave lower. In No. 3, the responding theme of the octave follows in half a bar's distance. No. 5 is another canon at the octave where the responding part is *'en mouvement rétrograde'* – in other words, moving backwards. No. 11 is at an augmented octave, No. 12 at the diminished octave.

Piece No. 7 is another curiosity, a canon at an augmented seventh but this is written as a bitonal piece, the right hand is notated in A flat major, clashing with a left hand in A major.

Interestingly, there is a deleted but still visible note in the manuscript claiming that Numbers 4, 6, and 10 are based on Irish folksongs, and No. 5 (the retrograde canon at the octave) on a French one (all unidentified).

Technically, the pieces are undemanding and not really suited (or intended) as concert pieces. The manuscript shows that the original title of the work was *Canons à deux voix. 12 petites pièces très faciles pour piano*, the *'très'* being crossed out. The original sequence was in the numerical order of the intervals, underlining, perhaps, the study character of these pieces. The 'dodecaphonic ring' of a title promising 'twelve canons in all intervals' – a title that Hennessy did not choose himself and that he would have known was incorrect – was doomed to be disappointed. It was probably a marketing idea on Eschig's part that was bound to fail, and it did.

Sérénade, Op. 65 (1924) for two violins, viola and cello

The *Sérénade* is a short, one-movement work for string quartet that was written in 1924 and published by Eschig in the following year. It is dedicated to Émile Loiseau (1874–1966), the leader of the quartet that gave the first performance at the Caméléon concert hall in the Montparnasse quarter of Paris on 27 December 1925.

After a slow and somewhat sombre introduction that lasts less than a minute, the main part of the piece is a gay and very Irish *allegro* in bright G major with clear overtones of Irish traditional music, albeit with any quotation of a traditional tune and even without a clear Irish traditional dance rhythm. This is achieved by a typical melodic outline modelled on Irish tunes, with an ending on repeated notes, and a cello part that provides the drones of a set of bagpipes (Ex. 8.31).

Ex. 8.31: *Sérénade*, Op. 65, bars 12–15

The critic André Teissier wrote about the *Sérénade* in *La Revue musicale*:

> A pleasant ensemble of violins, where four fortunately independent parts sing with charm, imitate each other freely, reflect the themes at the right time, meet, cross paths, caress and collide temporarily, in a frank and natural effusion, albeit a little past of hue. It's what I would call, if it didn't seem half mocking, a fine lesson in sentimental counterpoint.[112]

---

[112] *Un agréable ensemble de violons, où quatre parties heureusement indépendantes, chantent toutes avec charme, s'imitent librement, se renvoient les thèmes à point nommé, se rencontrent, se croisent, se caressent et se heurtent passagèrement, dans une effusion franche et naturelle, quoique un peu passée de teinte. Ce que j'appellerais, si*

Trois Mélodies, Op. 66 (1924) for high voice and piano

The *Trois Mélodies sur des poésies d'André Delacour et de Leconte de Lisle*, Op. 66 – to give it its full title – unites three rather loosely connected poems. The songs were written between 1921 and 1924 for high voice and piano and assigned this opus number more or less for the purpose of its publication. The first two songs are based on poems by André Delacour (1882–1958), a fairly well-known writer and critic of the time and a personal friend of Hennessy's – *Si la distance nous sépare* and *Paysage* – , while the third poem is much older: *Jane* is one of the *Chansons écossaises* of Charles Leconte de Lisle (1818–1894). Hennessy's song *Jane* is, in fact, subtitled *Chanson écossaise*, but Eschig managed to omit the main title from their publication (1925) so that this song became known as *Chanson écossaise* only. This is also the oldest of the three songs; in the manuscript it was Op. 56 No. 3, dated 1921. Nos 1 and 2 are from 1924.

The work is dedicated to the soprano Marthe Saisset, one of the most important of Hennessy's interpreters and unfortunately just as forgotten as the composer is nowadays. Saisset gave the first performance of the whole opus at the Salle des Concerts Touche, Paris, on 18 December 1925, accompanied by the composer (this was actually preceded by a broadcast performance from Radio Tour Eiffel on the 7th).

These are three very short songs. The first is a lover's declaration that 'if distance separates us, it cannot disconnect us', and Hennessy's music (*andantino*, in a rather straightforward G major) builds up a marked climax where the parting lover assures his/her partner that his/her memory will always shine through even the most pallid horizons, with Hennessy supporting this affirmation by insistent chord repetitions marked *forte*.

In No. 2, *Paysage*, he picks up an earlier idea from the third piece in *Épigrammes d'un solitaire*, the gamelan imitation in *Une Pagode indo-chinoise*, by using a similar imitation of an Asian metallophone instrument in a phrase in the poem that speaks of 'splendours of the pagoda with its Japanese trinkets'. Having reached bar 12, the music then changes from F major to G major in parallel movements of scales in semiquavers that resemble the swelling of waves that themselves resemble the happy feelings of the protagonist. This modulation and its associated change of expression is quite unusual.

Jane, respectively the *Chanson écossaise*, is set in G flat major with hardly any notes foreign to the scale except in some very Romantic phrasing and suspended chords. As in previous settings from Leconte de Lisle's *Chansons écossaises* (see *Lydia*, Op. 23 and *Trois Chansons écossaises*, Op. 31 in Chapter 4), Hennessy is still the only composer in France who interprets these poems in a Scottish (or 'Celtic') musical style – with a melody leaning on folksong, including the occasional application of the 'snap' (Ex. 8.32). And he does so in a unique way that will never be confused with a folksong setting. This is art music of a national style that could be prototypical and of a kind that no Scottish or other composer has done. It is certainly set in a harmonic language of the late nineteenth century, but the fact remains that nobody wrote such music at

---

cela ne devait pas sembler à demi-railleur, une belle leçon de contrepoint sentimental.'; André Tessier in *La Revue Musicale* 7:4, 1 February 1926, p. 182.

An Engagement with Ireland (1920–1924)

that time. Like much of Hennessy's music – especially in his 'Celtic' style – this is extremely nostalgic, but highly individual music nevertheless.

Ex. 8.32: *Trois Chansons*, Op. 66 No. 3 *Jane*, bars 1–10

A brief description of the piece in *Le Courrier musical* that accompanies a music supplement of this piece, along with *Paysage*, acknowledges the Scottish musical idea, while maintaining that the simplicity of the accompaniment was a conscious effort on the part of the composer:

> Mr Swan Hennessy has enhanced the text with music inspired by a Scottish atmosphere, thus responding to the title chosen by the poet. The line is essentially vocal and the

accompaniment, while of great and appropriate simplicity, is fertile in full-bodied harmonies and always very tonal.[113]

The piece did not fail to have the desired effect on the French audience. In Maurice Imbert's view, this song was 'perfumed with the scents of the countryside and happily reminiscent of those Hebridian songs that had such an influence on Wagner at the time he wrote the Flying Dutchman'.[114]

Rapsodie irlandaise, Op. 67 (1924) for piano

A little-known piece in Hennessy's repertoire is the last piece that he wrote in an Irish style for piano solo, the *Rapsodie irlandaise*, Op. 67 (1924), dedicated to his then fourteen-year-old son Patrice.

Ex. 8.33: *Rapsodie irlandaise*, Op. 67, bars 93–104

---

[113] '*M. Swan Hennessy a rehaussé le texte d'une musique inspirée des atmosphère écossaises répondent ainsi au titre du poète. La ligne est essentiellement vocale et l'accompagnement, d'une grande simplicité voulue, est fertile en harmonies savoureuses et toujours très tonales.*'; 'Notre supplément musical', in *Le Courrier musical*, 15 November 1925, with an *erratum* relating to the title in the issue of 1 December.

[114] '[…] *parfumée de senteurs du terroir et rappelant heureusement ces chants des Hébrides qui exercèrent tant d'influence sur Wagner à l'époque où il écrivit* Le Vaisseau fantôme'; Maurice Imbert in *Journal des débats*, 1 March 1932, p. 4.

It was published a number of years later as part of the *Album celtique* (1929). As in several of his Irish works, the score contains a footnote to the effect that it contains no 'piece of folklore'.

Contrary to what the dedication to a teenager might suggest, this is not one of Hennessy's technically simple pieces, containing some quite demanding passages. Again, the 'Scotch snap' occurs more than once, but another rhythmic figure consisting of a dotted quaver, a semiquaver and quaver triplets is a more striking element, though not borrowed from traditional music. The most recognisably Irish-style melody appears twice in the piece, one of them towards the end where the harmony expands slightly beyond the predominant C major (Ex. 8.33).

* * *

Swan Hennessy has not been the first composer to explore images and influences from Ireland – musical, literary, cultural – in the art music of France. While the history of Franco-Irish musical connections reaches back to Henry Madin (1698–1748), the influence of Irish traditional music on French art music originated with the phenomenal success of the ten volumes of *Irish Melodies* (1808–32) by the Irish poet Thomas Moore and his musical collaborators and successors, perpetuated by the use of one of these melodies in the opera *Martha* (1846) by Friedrich von Flotow. These resulted in countless adaptations of Irish traditional airs in many genres of 'classical' music, from piano rondos to opera.[115] A sustained presence over one hundred years (1830s to 1930s) were also the four generations of musicians in the O'Kelly family in France.[116]

Laura Watson has explained several strands of influence in Third Republic France ranging from Hector Berlioz and Augusta Holmès, via the 'Celtic' cantatas *Alyssa* that were the subject of the *Prix de Rome* competition of 1903, including remarkable works by Maurice Ravel and Raoul Laparra, to the 1924 premiere of the opera *L'Appel de la mer* by Henri Rabaud.[117]

Arguably, the most wide-spread, vivid and creative mutual influences took place among the Breton composers of the early decades of the twentieth century, who had welcomed Swan Hennessy in their midst since the year 1912. Their common 'Celtic' spirit corresponded with Hennessy's ideas of pan-Celticism that included Irish, Scottish and Breton musical influences. It is from this circle that Hennessy's use of the term *'celtique'* stems, a term that was hardly ever used for this kind of music in Ireland itself, where musicians would rather have spoken of 'national' or 'folk music' influences. Musical Celticism in Ireland and Britain more specifically meant works that

---

[115] About this influence, which was particularly strong in France, see my survey '"All her lovely companions are faded and gone" – How 'The Last Rose of Summer' Became Europe's Favourite Irish Melody' and its accompanying appendix in Brian Caraher & Sarah McCleave (eds): *Thomas Moore and Romantic Inspiration* (London: Routledge, 2018), pp. 128–145 & 231–253.
[116] Axel Klein: *O'Kelly. An Irish Musical Family in Nineteenth-Century France* (Norderstedt: BoD, 2014).
[117] Watson, 'Ireland in the Musical Imagination', op. cit.

referred to obscure phases in Irish (pre-)history associated with the Celts and national legends stemming from this period. In music, in the two or three decades before and after 1900, these led to some remarkable large-scale works by composers of a 'Celtic' connotation including Granville Bantock, Rutland Boughton, John Foulds, and Arnold Bax in England or Michele Esposito, Robert O'Dwyer, and Thomas O'Brien Butler in Ireland. But this is not Hennessy's Celticism.

Fig. 8.9: Swan Hennessy at the piano, mid-1920s (© Boris Lipnitzky / Roger-Viollet)

An Engagement with Ireland (1920–1924)

Remarkably, Franco-Irish connections in music are still not part of the wider discourse of the various cultural strands that interconnect the two countries. A recent publication entitled *Paris. Capital of Irish Culture* ignores music almost totally.[118] Although it contains a list of 'Musicians and dancers in Paris, 1816–1939' and a section on 'Artists and Scholars', these do not include a single Irish musician.[119] The noteworthy statement, 'Celticism emerged out of the French/Catholic/Breton reaction against Parisian metropolitan modernity'[120] lacks the obvious conclusion of looking into the large quantity of Celticist works written during several decades by the Breton composer-friends of Swan Hennessy (and Hennessy's himself, for that matter).

It must be emphasised here that Hennessy's Celticist music and the musical influences he integrated from Ireland, Scotland and Brittany were part of a wider trend in French music of the first half of the twentieth century. Even the Association de Compositeurs Bretons of 1912 to 1914 did not come out of the blue but was a result of a long-gestating development that had many roots and causes. These included cultural and political movements, such as a dissatisfaction with French centralist politics, an emphasis on regional distinctiveness, a desire to identify with regional history and culture including vernacular musical traditions.

That group of Breton composers still existed and was at least as active as before the War, producing a significant corpus of music in all genres. To cite but a few: Louis Aubert (*Dryade*, 1924), Charles-Augustin Collin (*Rhapsodie bretonne*, 1922), Jean Cras (Piano Quintet, 1922), Lucien Haudebert (*Eglogue*, Op. 10, 1921; *Ma lande au grand soleil*, 1924; *Odes à la vie*, Op. 18, 1924), Jean Huré (String Quartet No. 2, 1921), Paul Le Flem (*Invocation*, 1920), Rhené-Baton (Cello Sonata, Op. 28, 1923; Piano Trio, Op. 31, 1923; *Danses paysannes*, 1924), Alice Sauvrezis (*Hymne orphique*, 1920), Louis Vuillemin (*En Kernéo*, Op. 23, 1922), etc. Works that were performed at the same events as Hennessy's included Louis Aubert's *Crépuscule d'automne* (Salle Beethoven, 28 March 1923), songs and chamber music by Lucien Haudebert (Concerts Touche, 16 February 1924), songs by Roger Pénau (Salle de la Fédération des Artistes, 6 November 1924), or Paul Le Flem's Piano Quintet with Hennessy's 2nd String Quartet (repeatedly; among others at the Salle Gaveau, 18 December 1924).

From these mutual musical cross-fertilisations, Yves Defrance deduces a greater influence of Swan Hennessy on the Breton part of French music than has so far been generally acknowledged. He writes:

> It is very likely that Ladmirault and other Breton composers of his time had access to Irish traditional musical sources through Swan Hennessy, an Irish-American musician based in Paris and well-known to Breton intellectual circles. […] We do not know if the publications of Petrie and his successors were in the hands of Breton musicians, but Swan Hennessy's legendary dynamism and humour probably left their mark on the minds of Breton

---

[118] Pierre Joannon & Kevin Whelan (eds): *Paris – Capital of Irish Culture. France, Ireland and the Republic, 1798–1916* (Dublin: Four Courts Press, 2017).
[119] ibid., p. 57–58.
[120] Ibid., p. 58.

culture and encouraged them to take Ireland into account in their Breton and Celtic musical approach.[121]

This flatly contradicts Irish musicologist Laura Watson's assessment that 'neither in general, nor in the specific evocations of Ireland was it [i. e. Hennessy's music] considered of major interest or novelty' in France.[122]

Still, there remains an irritating element of isolation about Hennessy as the Irish musical representative in France. It is remarkable that Hennessy did not seem to have sought contact with other Irish artists in Paris that he must have heard of. No contact, apparently, to James Joyce (1882–1941) who published his *Ulysses* in 1922 in Paris nor to Joyce's friend and sort-of-*protégé*, the Irish tenor John O'Sullivan (1877–1955) who sang at the Opéra between 1914 and 1922. Likewise, there is no source whatsoever suggesting contacts with other Irish writers in Paris such as James Stephens (1880–1950), who had lived in Paris before the War and visited Joyce in the late 1920s, or the young Samuel Beckett (1906–1989), a Paris resident for two years from October 1928. There also does not seem to have been any involvement with Paris-resident Irish revolutionaries Maud Gonne (1866–1953) and her son, Seán MacBride (1904–1988).

No contact also to those members of the Franco-Irish O'Kelly family who were still alive and publishing music, especially Henri senior (1859–1938) and junior (1881–1922). He evidently met the Irish-born composer (and wife of André Messager) Hope Temple (1859–1938),[123] but again, this does not seem to have led anywhere. The same applies to Irish painters who sought inspiration in Paris, including Roderic O'Conor (1860–1940), who even shared Hennessy's interest in Brittany, Paul Henry (1876–1958), Evie Hone (1894–1955), or Mainie Jellett (1897–1944).

Although Hennessy had opened up considerably since his withdrawn lifestyle of the 1910s, he still greatly enjoyed his privacy. His idea of Ireland was not developed further by seeking exchange with Irish men and women of note who happened to live on his doorstep. It was an imaginary Ireland, informed by traditional music in printed collections and by contacts to a handful of musicians in Cork and Dublin, neither of whom lived long enough to make his name survive into the 1940s or beyond.

---

[121] *'Il est très vraisemblable que l'accès de Ladmirault, et d'autres compositeurs bretons de son temps, au fonds musical traditionnel irlandais, se fit par le truchement de Swan Hennessy musicien irlando-américain installé à Paris et introduit dans les milieux intellectuels bretons. […] Nous ignorons si les publications de Petrie et de ses successeurs circulaient dans les mains des musiciens bretons mais le dynamisme et l'humour légendaire de Swan Hennessy marquèrent probablement les esprits cultivés bretons et incitèrent ceux-ci à prendre en compte l'Irlande dans leur approche musicale bretonne et celtique.'*; Yves Defrance: 'L'Irlande dans les musiques bretonnes actuelles', in Yann Bevant and Laurent Daniel (eds): *Bretagne/Irlande: quelles relations? / Brittany/Ireland: what relations?* (Brest: Centre de Recherche Bretonne et Celtique, Université de Bretagne Occidentale and Rennes: Université Rennes 2, 2015), pp. 159–196 [185, 187].

[122] She attributes this to '(t)he absence of Parisian press commentary on any of Hennessy's music'; this and the quote above in Watson, 'Ireland in the Musical Imagination', p. 97 (fn.). This assessment merely shows how unknown Hennessy is even among experts.

[123] They both participated in concerts where works of them were performed, see, for example, *Le Gaulois*, 7 November 1922, p. 2 and *Comoedia*, 9 November 1922, p. 2.

Chapter 9
Swan's Way: Hennessy in Search of Lost Time (1925–1929)

The last phase in Swan Hennessy's career is characterised by an ever-increasing impulse to make a name for himself in France, an impulse made the more urgent by the notion of increasing age and failing health. During these last five years of his life, he completed Opp. 68 to 81, which included a fourth string quartet (Op. 75), a trio (Op. 70) and several duos with piano. It is striking that his output for piano solo is considerably smaller compared to earlier periods of his creative life, at least in terms of opus numbers. But there is a quite successful series of pastiche works for the piano entitled *À la manière de …* which he did not assign an opus number to.

He also continues to write works in a 'Celtic' style, but cannot be reduced to it. There are works in which he responds to current musical trends in France like the increasing presence of jazz (Opp. 68 and 71), and there is also a last work in a descriptive, Impressionist style (Op. 69). His remarkable gift for the musical interpretation of poetic texts shows itself in three vocal albums (Opp. 72, 73, 79). And there is an unfailing interest in unusual instrumentations such as the *Trio*, Op. 70 for violin, flute, and bassoon, the *Trois Petits trios*, Op. 76 for unaccompanied soprano, mezzo, and contralto solo voices, and the *Sonatine*, Op. 78 for two solo violins.

But, his compositional activity aside, it is striking that he is now more outgoing than ever, even though he still does not mix with the Irish artistic community in Paris or the more prominent French composers of his time – except when they were Breton. The 'more outgoing' quality of these years manifests itself in 'festivals' of his own music, numerous letters to the French musical press, his participation in surveys on various current topics of concern to French musicians of the time, and in frequent performances in recitals and on radio. In other words, to quote very liberally from Marcel Proust, it was Hennessy's own unique 'Swan's Way', in an almost frantic 'Search of Lost Time'.

Swan Hennessy Festivals (1925)

With a 'Festival Swan Hennessy', organised at the Caméléon on 18 March 1925, Hennessy realised in France what he had done some years before in Berlin as a *'Kompositionsabend'* – a concert exclusively of his own compositions in a variety of genres and with the participation of several musicians who are now more and more part of his inner circle.

A festival celebrating a single composer is *per se* no novelty. The year 1895 saw such festivals in the names of Saint-Saëns, Massenet, and d'Indy. There were festivals in Lyon for Debussy (1909) and Ravel (1922), followed by several more in Paris and elsewhere in later years, Ropartz enjoyed his first in 1905, Dukas in 1921, to name but a few. Still – composers' festivals were usually held for personalities of greater reputation than Hennessy's. It was quite bold of him to organise his own festival given the comparatively low profile he had – and we can take it for granted that he organised this himself, including the payment of the musicians and the renting of a hall. He also did not intend to earn money with the event since it was advertised as an *'invitation pour plusieurs personnes'*. Concert goers were merely required to contribute the modest sum of 3 francs 50 centimes to cover taxes, as the programme outlined (Fig. 9.1).

Fig. 9.1: Programme card for the first 'Festival Swan Hennessy', 18 March 1925 (Courtesy: Hennessy family)

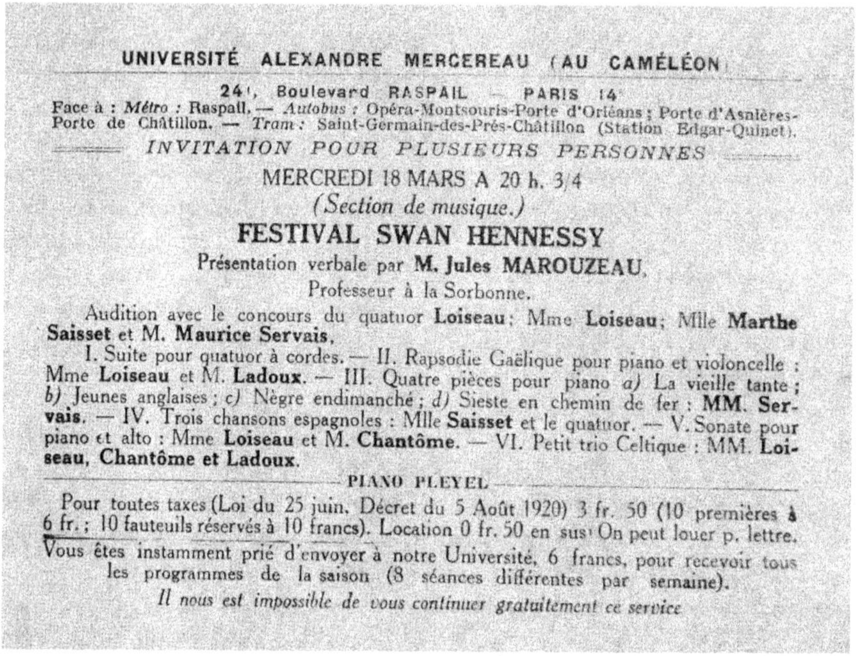

```
UNIVERSITÉ ALEXANDRE MERCEREAU (AU CAMÉLÉON)
          24, Boulevard RASPAIL  —  PARIS 14e
Face à : Métro : Raspail. — Autobus : Opéra-Montsouris-Porte d'Orléans ; Porte d'Asnières-
Porte de Châtillon. — Tram : Saint-Germain-des-Prés-Châtillon (Station Edgar-Quinet).
          INVITATION POUR PLUSIEURS PERSONNES
              MERCREDI 18 MARS A 20 h. 3/4
                  (Section de musique.)
              FESTIVAL SWAN HENNESSY
          Présentation verbale par M. Jules MAROUZEAU,
                  Professeur à la Sorbonne.
    Audition avec le concours du quatuor Loiseau ; Mme Loiseau ; Mlle Marthe
Saisset et M. Maurice Servais.
    I. Suite pour quatuor à cordes. — II. Rapsodie Gaëlique pour piano et violoncelle :
Mme Loiseau et M. Ladoux. — III. Quatre pièces pour piano a) La vieille tante ;
b) Jeunes anglaises ; c) Nègre endimanché ; d) Sieste en chemin de fer : MM. Ser-
vais. — IV. Trois chansons espagnoles : Mlle Saisset et le quatuor. — V. Sonate pour
piano et alto : Mme Loiseau et M. Chantôme. — VI. Petit trio Celtique : MM. Loi-
seau, Chantôme et Ladoux.
                    — PIANO PLEYEL —
    Pour toutes taxes (Loi du 25 juin, Décret du 5 Août 1920) 3 fr. 50 (10 premières à
6 fr. ; 10 fauteuils réservés à 10 francs). Location 0 fr. 50 en sus ! On peut louer p. lettre.
Vous êtes instamment prié d'envoyer à notre Université, 6 francs, pour recevoir tous
    les programmes de la saison (8 séances différentes par semaine).
        Il nous est impossible de vous continuer gratuitement ce service
```

The event included some of Hennessy's descriptive pre-War piano music, of which some received their first performance like *La Vieille tante* and *Jeunes anglaises* (from Op. 33, 1911) and the *Sieste en chemin de fer*, Op. 40 No. 5 as well as more recent chamber music. The full list with their performers is:

Suite, Op. 46 (strqu)	Quatuor Loiseau
Rapsodie gaélique, Op. 63 (vc, pf)	Robert Ladoux, Mme Loiseau
Four piano pieces:	Maurice Servais
– *La Vieille tante*, Op. 33 No. 3	
– *Jeunes anglaises*, Op. 33 No. 5	
– *Nègre endimanché*, Op. 57 No. 3	
– *Sieste en chemin de fer*, Op. 40 No. 5	
Trois Chansons espagnoles, Op. 42bis (S, strqu)	Marthe Saisset, Quatuor Loiseau
Sonatine celtique, Op. 62 (va, pf)	Robert Chantôme, Mme Loiseau
Petit trio celtique, Op. 52 (vn, va, vc)	E. Loiseau, Chantôme, Ladoux

These are, in fact, Swan Hennessy's most faithful interpreters: the Loiseau Quartet and their individual members, Émile Loiseau's wife (who never appears with her first name) on piano, the solo pianist Maurice Servais (another pianist, to complete the list, would have been Marthe Le Breton,), and the soprano Marthe Saisset. There were many other performers of Hennessy's music, for which Appendix 1 provides the evidence, but these names appear again and again over the course of many years, even after his premature death. In the course of time, all of them became dedicatees of Hennessy's compositions (see Appendix 4 for information on Hennessy's dedicatees).

A feature of these composers' festivals was that an expert of academic or journalistic background would provide a spoken commentary (*présentation verbale*). It is not clear whether this was in the form of an introduction at the beginning of the event or of short comments on the individual pieces. In this case it was given by Jules Marouzeau (1878–1964), professor of Latin at the Sorbonne, who seems to have taken an interest in this music. In most later events of this type, the speaker was the poet and journalist André Delacour (1882–1958). As a side note it may be added that Arthur Honegger also had his first own festival at the Caméléon, 8 November 1925.

Two reports of the event have surfaced in contemporary periodicals, one in *Comoedia* by Paul Le Flem, the other in *Le Monde musical* by Marcel Noël, and both are worth quoting. As a personal friend of Hennessy's, Le Flem, of course, knew the composer well. Noël had not so far written about Hennessy. Le Flem wrote:

> This week, the Caméléon organised a festival in honour of Mr Swan Hennessy, an Irishman of good stock and a musician dedicated to singing the praise of his country and his race. Swan Hennessy conveys a devout respect, a spontaneity of accent, a meritorious sincerity. Irish folklore has certainly enriched the music of this musician and in many places animates it with a picturesque and spicy touch. But these are not the only virtues of this composer who attracts the sympathies of the discerning listener thanks to his sober art, thanks also to his easy technique and good tone. He knows how to capture the object of his vision with a sharp stroke, without having to resort to noisy commentaries. Merits that everyone could see during the performance of a Quartet, Trio, Rhapsody, pieces for voice and piano. The interpreters were of the highest quality. I need only mention the Quatuor Loiseau, as well as Mme Loiseau, Mlle Saisset, and Messrs Servais, Ladoux, Chantôme.[1]

Noël focused his review on the individuality of the composer and the variety of the programme:

---

[1] '*Le Caméléon a organisé cette semaine un festival en l'honneur de M. Swan Hennessy, Irlandais de bonne souche et musicien appliqué à chanter son pays et sa race. Swan Hennessy y apporte un dévotieux respect, une spontanéité d'accent, une sincérité méritoire. Le folklore irlandais a certes vivifié la mélodie du musicien et l'anime, en maint endroit, d'un pittoresque piquant. Mais ce ne sont pas là les seules vertus de ce compositeur qui s'attire les sympathies des délicats grâce à son art sobre, grâce aussi à sa technique aisée et de bon ton. Il sait camper d'un trait vif l'objet de sa vision, sans avoir recours à de tapageurs commentaires. Mérites dont chacun put se rendre compte au cours de l'audition d'un Quatuor, d'un Trio, d'une Rapsodie, de pièces pour chant et pour piano. Les interprètes étaient de choix. Qu'il me suffise de citer le Quatuor Loiseau, ainsi que Mmes Loiseau, Saisset, MM. Servais, Ladoux, Chantôme.*'; 'Audition d'œuvres de Swan Hennessy', by Paul Le Flem, *Comoedia*, 20 March 1925, p. 2.

> Among the composers of our time, Mr Swan Hennessy stands out for his strong personality. His *Suite* for String Quartet, his *Rapsodie gaélique* for piano and cello, four pieces for piano, a *Sonata* for piano and viola, and a *Petit trio celtique*, gave a peremptory demonstration. These works, also interesting in their diversity, benefited from a first-rate performance by the Quatuor Loiseau, Mme Loiseau and Mr Maurice Servais (both excellent pianists). I will no less praise the talent of the singer and the beautiful voice of Mlle Marthe Saisset in three very evocative *Chansons espagnoles*, Mr. Hennessy has shown us that he has a precious quality of adaptation.
>
> Mr. Jules Marouzeau, who presented the composer, did so with infinite spirit and talent.[2]

Composers' festivals were even easier to organise in the new medium of the radio, a 'distribution channel', as we would say nowadays, that could reach out to a much larger number of listeners, even though these would have to cope with a poor sound quality. Hennessy participated in these very early days of French radio when music on the airwaves was, initially with no exception, presented live – here mostly from a studio of Radio Tour Eiffel in the middle of the Eiffel Tower. Another disadvantage was that no printed review could be expected and that media coverage would be reduced to a programme in small print in the rear of a daily newspaper.

Thus, several 'radio festivals' of composers took place during these years, often many more than proper concerts. The first devoted to Swan Hennessy was on 3 June 1925, repeated on 4 June, less than three months after the event at the Caméléon. It included an introduction by André Delacour (*'Un mot sur Swan Hennessy'*), followed by three compositions: the *Quatre Pièces celtiques*, Op. 58 (with Paul Brun on cor anglais and members of the Loiseau Quartet), a *Sonatine* for piano (probably the *Sonatine celtique*, Op. 53 rather than the *Sonatine*, Op. 43) performed by the composer, and the *Petit trio celtique*, Op. 52.[3]

The next 'Festival Swan Hennessy' was only six months away, on 27 December 1925, again at the Caméléon. Instead of organising it at 8:45pm as in March, it was now scheduled at 4pm in the afternoon, as in the case of the Honegger festival in November. It was probably deemed a better time for most members of the audience. This time, it was announced as being organised by one monsieur Marchessaux of the concert giving body (and orchestra) Concerts Rouge (founded in 1889 by Benjamin Rouge and in the meantime mainly organised by the cellist Francis Touche). A main

---

[2] *'Parmi les compositeurs de temps présent, M. Swan Hennessy se distingue par sa personnalité bien tranchée. Sa* Suite *pour quatuor à cordes, sa* Rapsodie Gaelique *pour piano et violoncelle, quatre Pièces pour piano, une* Sonate *pour piano et alto, et un* Petit trio celtique, *en donnerent une démonstration péremptoire. Ces œuvres, également intéressantes en leur diversité, bénéficiaient d'une interprétation de premier ordre par le Quatuor Loiseau, Mme Loiseau et M. Maurice Servais (excellentes pianistes tous les deux). Je ne louerai pas moins le talent de cantatrice et la belle voix de Mlle Marthe Saisset dans trois* Chansons espagnoles, *très évocatrices, M. Hennessy nous a montré par là qu'il possède une précieuse qualité d'adaptation. / M. Jules Marouzeau, que présentait le compositeur s'en acquitta avec infiniment d'esprit et de talent.'*; 'Au Caméléon / Festival Swan Hennessy', by Marcel Noël, in: *Le Monde musical*, 1 April 1925.

[3] *L'Homme libre*, 3 Juin 1925, p. 3 ; *Paris-soir*, 4 Juin 1925, p. 5.

difference compared to the first festival was that this time Hennessy participated himself – as an accompanist to songs performed by Marthe Saisset and Charles Hubbard, to duos with Paul-Louis Neuberth (viola) and René Laurent (alto saxophone), and as a solo pianist, again introducing several of his early compositions to a Paris audience for the first time. Like the radio festival in June, this event was introduced by André Delacour, followed by the following works:

Sérénade, Op. 65 (strqu) (1st perf.)	Quatuor Loiseau
Mélodies (I)	Marthe Saisset, S. H.
– *Si la distance nous sépare*, Op. 66 No. 1	
– *Paysage*, Op. 66 No. 2	
– *Jane. Chanson écossaise*, Op. 66 No. 3	
Mélodies (II)	Charles Hubbard, S. H.
– *Les Grands jasmins épanouis*, Op. 56 No. 2	
– *Nell*, Op. 31 No. 3	
Sonatine celtique, Op. 62 (va, pf)	Paul-Louis Neuberth, S. H.
Pièce celtique, Op. 68 No. 1 (a-sax, pf)[4]	René Laurent, S. H.
Piano works	S. H.
– *Valses*, Op. 32 No. 1 & 4	
– *Scènes d'enfants*, Op. 19[5]	
– *Montrouge le matin*, Op. 27 No. 4A	
– *Sérénade espagnole*, Op. 24 No. 1	
Petit trio celtique, Op. 52	Loiseau, Chantôme, Ladoux

Participation in public surveys

Part of Hennessy's strategy to become better known in Parisian musical circles was to have his name mentioned in the press as often as possible. A useful vehicle for this seemed to be the participation in public surveys ('*enquêtes*') of music periodicals, of which there were many in this period. These surveys invited composers to state their opinion on certain aspects of (presumed) importance to contemporary music. Several journals conducted such surveys, and with Hennessy's good relationship to *Le Guide du concert* (respectively its editor Gabriel Bender), he found a ready outlet for his statements there. Thus, in the next few years, we find Hennessy expressing his opinion on issues as diverse as music and sports, on immorality in music, on the living conditions of the (classical) musician, and on mechanical music; in addition, he contributed a

---

[4] Announced in the programme as *Romance irlandaise*.
[5] In the programme, the works were announced without opus numbers but with names of publishers. This piece is not exactly certain. The programme gives it as *Scènes d'enfants*, which would be the French version of *Aus dem Kinderleben*, Op. 19, published with Breitkopf & Härtel. But the publisher is here named as Schott, which had published the *Kinder-Album*, Op. 35. But the latter has 24 single pieces which makes it unlikely that they have been performed here. Rather, Hennessy mixed up the two German publishers.

statement to a 1929 special issue on chamber music of *Le Courrier musical*. These opinions are interesting in that they show us Hennessy's thoughts about current issues and how he indirectly explains his own aesthetics, making them important for the present study, since we do not have very many personal statements by the composer.

The first time his name appeared in such a context was the issue of 9 January 1925 of *Le Guide du concert*. The topic was whether sports can be a creative inspiration to composers, the editor of the journal having picked up on an earlier article by the French playwright André Obey (1892–1975) in *L'Impartial français*. Bender then invited composers to comment on the main thesis of Obey's article and apparently received some sixty responses ranging in length from a few lines to more than half a page. The series began with the issue of 17 October 1924 and ran through 13 March 1925. The first group of responses was introduced by the editor with a quote from Obey's original article:

> Prominent writers believe that sport will give birth to a New Art. 'What is this art? – writes Mr André Obey in "l'Impartial français". – He doubts that many people would know it. In joining the two words art and sport we sense a nebula of glimmer and harmony, vague also, but eager to harden, a sparkling nucleus. What fluids will condense to form this planet? What will the unknown star be? Mystery.' We have asked composers to unravel this 'mystery' if it is worth it to be 'unravelled', and the sixty or so letters we have received prove that they are not indifferent to the question.[6]

The first responses were written by (in this order) René Lenormand, Henry Woollett, Michel Maurice Levy, Léon Moreau, Gustave Samazeuilh, Marcelle Soulage, Reynaldo Hahn, Paul Pierne, Auguste Chapuis, Jean Huré, and Fernand Le Borne. Of the more prominent composers of the time there are responses from Alexandre Tansman (5 December 1924), Charles Koechlin, Maurice Ravel, Joaquín Nin, Paul Landormy, Alfredo Casella, Louis Vierne, and Alfred Bruneau (all in the issue of 2 January 1925), Swan Hennessy appeared on 9 January along with Roland-Manuel, Marcel Bernheim, and Sylvio Lazzari, followed by Georges Migot and others (16 January), Florent Schmitt and Joseph Canteloube (13 February), Raoul Laparra and Louis Aubert (20 February), Armande de Polignac and Jean Poueigh (13 March).

Most composers were unable to see any inherent link between music and sport, as could perhaps be expected from such a rather far-fetched connection, albeit with quite diverse shades of opinion and with ideas that reflect the personality of the composer. Ravel, for instance, thought sport could be, more or less, an extra-musical influence on composers like many other things in life as longs as music prevails:

---

[6] *'Des écrivains de valeur estiment que le Sport donnera naissance à un Art nouveau. 'Quel est cet art? – écrit M. ANDRÉ OBEY dans "l'Impartial français". – Nul ne le sait si beaucoup le pressentent. A joindre les deux mots Art et Sport nous sentons frémir comme une nébuleuse de lueurs, d'harmonies, vague encore, mais avide de durcir, un noyau étincelant. Quels fluides condenseront cette planète en travail? Que sera l'astre inconnu? Mystère.' Nous avons demandé aux compositeurs de percer ce 'mystère' s'il vaut la peine d'être 'percé' et la soixantaine de lettres que nous avons reçues prouvent que la question ne leur est point indifférente.'*; *Le Guide du concert*, 17 October 1924, p. 12.

Sport can be an abundant source of inspiration, just as love, death, the stars, the forest, the factory, the circus, the Métro; if it is only to be derived from pure music. Everything else, in fact, is just literature.[7]

Georges Migot insisted that it is the artist/composer who creates art from external influences, but that those externalities never constitute art themselves:

> Art in general is not driven by influences that are external to it. One can use them, of course, but there is no more an art of sports than an art of growing vegetables or a mechanical art. For the arts, all the phenomena of life and nature constitute no more than an immense vocabulary from which the creator can choose his words but where he alone is the master to assemble them according to relationships and syntactic rules that alone create a work of art.[8]

Other respondents were outright opponents of the idea that sport could inspire any music at all, rather it might even harm music. Quite succinct in this regard were Louis Vierne (first quote below) and Reynaldo Hahn (second quote):

> The sterile wiggling of the young people of these days, whether it is called tennis, golf, dance, or canoeing, has never inspired a single musical idea in me.[9]

> I don't care about sports, and the only idea that associates them, in my mind, with music, is the immense harm they have done to it, as, moreover, to all the arts.[10]

Hennessy, then, responded in quite a balanced way that would echo the majority of comments, essentially saying that it needed an artist to create art:

> I must admit that I have not yet perceived the shiver of which Mr. André Obey speaks; but since art can express so many things, why shouldn't sport have its share? However, I do not believe that sport alone can be enough as a source of artistic or even literary inspiration![11]

---

[7] '*Le sport peut être une source abondante d'inspiration, aussi bien que l'amour, la mort, les étoiles, la forêt, l'usine, le cirque, le métro; s'il ne doit en découler que de pure musique. Tout le reste, en effet, n'est que littérature.*'; Maurice Ravel, source as mentioned above.
[8] '*L'Art en général ne se conduit pas par des influences qui lui sont extérieures. Il peut les utiliser, certes, mais il n'y a pas plus d'art sportif que d'art maraîcher ou mécanique. Tous les phénomènes de la vie et de la nature ne constituent pour l'art qu'un immense vocabulaire où le créateur peut choisir ses mots mais où il est seul le maître de les assembler suivant des rapports et des règles syntaxiques qui créent seuls l'œuvre d'art.*'; Georges Migot, ibid.
[9] '*Le trémoussement stérile des jeunes gens de ce temps, qu'il se nomme Tennis, Golf, Danse, ou canotage, ne m'a jamais inspiré une seule idée musicale.*'; Louis Vierne, ibid.
[10] '*Je n'entends rien aux Sports et la seule idée que les associe, dans mon esprit, à la Musique, est celle du tort immense qu'ils lui ont fait, comme, d'ailleurs, à tous les arts.*'; Reynaldo Hahn, ibid.
[11] '*Je dois avouer que je n'ai pas encore perçu le frémissement dont parle M. André Obey; mais puisque l'art peut exprimer tant de choses, pourquoi le sport n'aurait-il pas sa part? Je ne crois pas, pourtant, que le sport puisse suffire à lui seul comme source d'inspiration artistique ou même littéraire!*'; Swan Hennessy, ibid.

Another extensive survey lasted from October 1925 to May 1926 on the issue of immorality in music, specifically in jazz. Gabriel Bender's enlightening introduction refers to the well-known prejudice that the American influence in European culture was a degenerating force, jazz being a prime example for it in music – at least in the eyes of some public authorities like the Parisian police:

> Last summer, the *Guide* sent the following letter to leading critics and composers: 'The Americans, continuing their moral cleansing campaign, are attacking music. They want to outlaw not only Jazz, which Mrs van Winckle, head of the female police force, considers to be "indecent music and music of crazy people" but all Music without words that Mr Hart, another police personality, declares "dangerously disturbing".' […] A focus is necessary. Different aspects of the question can be as follows: does music *itself* have a character of morality or immorality? Are the immoral effects of music – if any – not an aspect of *perception* and therefore extremely subjective? […][12]

The first issue of the journal documenting the responses appeared on 16 October 1925 with opinions by (in this order) Artur Honegger, Jean Déré, Samuel Rousseau, Jeanne Barbillion, and Marcel Bernheim. Hennessy's response followed in the next issue (23 October), along with Albert Roussel, Gabriel Grovlez, Jean-Marcel Lizotte, Alfredo Casella, Louis Aubert, Léon Moreau, and Pierre de Bréville.

Hennessy came straight to the point with his opinion:

> One of the puritan's specialities is to search everywhere for immorality, which in most cases exists in one's imagination only.
>
> No music can be immoral. Immorality, if it is immorality at all, is not in the music, but in the one who listens to it. Music can therefore only be 'dangerously disturbing' for the hysterical or dirty-minded. As for jazz, I would be very grateful to Mrs van Winkle, if she succeeded in eliminating it, not because of morality, but because of aesthetics, whatever Mr Wiéner may say![13]

It is interesting that Hennessy should present himself here as an opponent to jazz, albeit not from a moral standpoint. There are jazz influences in several of his com-

---

[12] '*Au cours de l'été dernier le Guide a adressé la lettre suivante aux principaux critiques et compositeurs: 'Les Américains, poursuivant leur campagne d'assainissement moral, viennent des attaquer à l'Musique. Ils veulent proscrire non seulement le Jazz que Mrs van Winckle, chef de la police féminine, considère comme une "musique indécente et de gens fous" mais toute la Musique sans paroles que M. Hart, autre personnalité policière, déclare "dangereusement troublante". […] Une mise au point est nécessaire. Les différents aspects de la question pourraient être les suivants: la musique en soi a-t-elle un caractère de moralité ou d'immoralité? Les effets immoraux de la musique – s'il en existe – ne sont-ils pas dans l'impression et par conséquent, extrêmement subjectifs? […]*'; 'La musique immorale', in: *Le Guide du concert*, 16 October 1925, p. 25.

[13] '*Une des spécialités du puritain c'est de rechercher partout de l'immoralité qui n'existe le plus souvent que dans son imagination. / Aucune musique ne peut être immorale. L'immoralité, si immoralité il y a, n'est pas dans la musique, mais dans celui qui l'écoute. La musique ne peut donc être "dangereusement troublante" que pour les grands hystériques ou les personnes à l'esprit impur. Quant au jazz, je serais très reconnaissant à Mme Van Winkle, si elle réussissait à la supprimer, non à cause de la morale, mais de l'esthétique, quoi qu'en dise M. Wiéner!*'; Swan Hennessy, in: *Le Guide du concert*, 23 October 1925, p. 46.

positions, but it seems that he allowed them as musical influences in art music but was less a friend of jazz proper. Contrary to some personalities in the Parisian police, however, he argued with the aesthetic quality, to which he apparently did not find an inner connection. The young Jean Wiéner (1896–1982), to whom Hennessy alluded here, was one of the strongest advocates of jazz influences in French music. Between 1920 and 1925 he also organised a series of concerts, promoting *Les Six* (particularly his friend Milhaud), Satie, and the Second Viennese School, even though this quote was before Wiéner founded his famous jazz duet with Clement Doucet. Unfortunately, Wiéner did not respond to the survey himself.

The debate is too diverse to be recounted here at any length, but Arthur Honegger's ironic comment may be interesting, welcoming immorality as an attraction for the audience:

> Your concerns about the campaign against 'immoral music' do not seem to me to be justified. Parliamentarians could never do less for music than they have done to date. On the contrary, I sincerely hope to see music classified as one of the immoral, indecent and disturbing pleasures.
>
> The day when the hearing of a Sonata has become a dangerous and perverse pleasure there will be crowds at concerts, and composers can hope to earn a living and occupy in our society a situation as honourable and respected as that of pleasure house owners.[14]

In the autumn of 1926, the *Guide* invited comments on the living conditions of musicians (and in particular composers), which were generally perceived as increasingly precarious. This survey ran between 22 October 1926 and 4 March 1927. The intention was 'to draw the attention of the public to the difficulties encountered by the representatives of French music',[15] to find remedies to solve the crisis, and to discuss whether occupations outside the field of composition can be one of the solutions.

It seems odd that a composer like Swan Hennessy should be invited to respond to this question, first of all, as a 'representative of French music', but also because he never had to make a living from his compositions. And indeed, his comment, published in the very first series of responses, reflected this problem:

> In my opinion, the situation of the composer has never changed. It is today what it was yesterday, because music is an art and not a profession. Art comes from the mind and the mind benefits less those who own it than those who exploit it. Can the composer have an

---

[14] '*Vos inquiétudes, en ce qui concerne la campagne contre la "musique immorale" ne me paraissent pas justifiées. Les parlementaires ne pourront jamais faire moins pour la musique qu'ils n'ont fait jusqu'à ce jour. Je souhaite, au contraire, vivement voir ranger la musique au nombre des plaisirs immoraux, indécents et troublants. / Le jour où l'audition d'une Sonate sera devenue une volupté dangereuse et perverse il y aura, foule aux concerts et les compositeurs de musique pourront espérer gagner leur vie et occuper dans notre société une situation aussi honorable et respectée que celle des tenanciers de maisons de jeu.*'; Arthur Honegger, in: *Le Guide du concert*, 16 October 1925, p. 25.

[15] '[…] *d'attirer l'attention du public sur les difficultés que rencontrent les représentants de la musique française,* […]'; 'La musique et la vie sociale. La condition du musicien', in: *Le Guide du concert*, 22 October 1926, p. 61.

occupation 'besides'? Why not. Inspiration is not a tool that is always at hand like a carpenter's hammer.¹⁶

To say that 'music is an art and not a profession' is, of course, totally ignorant of the fact that many, if not all, composers would very much like to make a living from writing music – except if one was born with the proverbial 'silver spoon in one's mouth' like Hennessy. It is hard to believe that he would not have been aware of it. But it seems to have been his experience that 'those who exploit it' (in other words, the music publishers and, perhaps, the concert organisers) would benefit more than the composer himself. He therefore had fundamental doubts that even a successful composer could become wealthy of his art alone.

The survey provoked further reactions from many composers including Hennessy's Breton friends Rhené-Baton (22 October) and Paul Ladmirault (29 October), also eliciting a very long response of two and a half pages from Georges Migot (5 November). Rhené-Baton, who (like Harty in Ireland) became known as an orchestral conductor, found nothing wrong in a profession outside composition as long as it was in music and finds, naturally, many examples in the past. He also appeared to suggest that even Paris was now too small to support many independent composers:

> There are more than 4 million inhabitants in Paris, and only 8 or 10,000 people go to concerts. This is the origin of the crisis. For my part, I have no problem with composers also having a second job … in music. Wagner was also a conductor, and so was Mendelssohn. Schumann held the pen of criticism. Brahms was a choir director, Bach was a cantor (!) and how many others divided their time between composition and teaching (!), example: César Franck. So what?¹⁷

French music after the War was also characterised by technical developments, of which the radio was but one – and one that was generally praised for the possibilities it offered to composers and musicians. Others were the gramophone and player pianos such as, in France, the Pleyela and other types of pianolas. Many composers and pianists recorded their music on gramophones or piano rolls, which still testify to the composers' original intentions and interpretations. Recordings were also (and are still) a huge opportunity for performing artists.

---

¹⁶ *'A mon avis, la situation de compositeur n'a jamais changé. Elle est aujourd'hui ce qu'elle était hier, car la musique est un art et non pas un métier. L'art relève de l'esprit et l'esprit profite moins à ceux qui le possèdent qu'a ceux qui l'exploitent. Le compositeur peut-il avoir une occupation "à côte"? Pourquoi pas. L'inspiration n'étant pas un outil qu'on a toujours sous la main comme le menuisier son marteau.'*; Swan Hennessy, ibid. Hennessy's statement became the subject of a short article about this debate under the headline of 'Music in France' in *The New York Times*, 14 November 1926, p. 10.

¹⁷ *'Il y a plus de 4 millions d'habitants à Paris, et 8 ou 10 000 personnes seulement qui vont au concert. Voilà l'origine de la crise. Pour ma part, je ne vois aucun inconvénient à ce que les compositeurs de musique exercent également un second métier … dans la musique. Wagner était également chef d'orchestre, Mendelssohn aussi. Schumann tenait la plume de critique. Brahms était directeur d'une chorale, Bach était cantor ! et combien d'autres partageaient leur temps entre la composition et le professorat ! exemple César Franck. Alors ?'*; Rhené-Baton, ibid.

On the other hand, the easy manner in which music could now be heard at home (by radio, gramophone, or pianola) also came with a risk – for piano manufacturers, many of whom were still struggling from the effects of the War (France nowadays has not a single manufacturer of pianos anymore), and for public tastes, favouring popular entertainment over the effort to learn an instrument and appreciate art in music. Scepticism as to where this trend would lead to was therefore understandable.

This was the background to the survey on mechanical music in *Le Guide du concert* of autumn 1928, in which we also find a statement by Swan Hennessy. It ran from 1 October to 7 December 1928. The period was somewhat shorter and the number of responses was – at under thirty – smaller as well, even though most of the responses were now longer compared to the first survey of 1925. But perhaps, the idea of composers' surveys was beyond its zenith now.

Hennessy's statement was in the same issue as responses from Marcel Delannoy, Rhené-Baton, Paul Ladmirault, Guy Ropartz, and Raoul Laparra. The statements differed greatly in their assessment whether mechanical music (as opposed to live music) was a good or a bad development. And this was not a matter of generations as, for instance, Guy Ropartz had no objections to technical trends, which he regarded as of inferior quality (and he was certainly right for the 1920s):

> The consequences of mechanical music will certainly not be fatal, neither for music nor for musicians. These means of musical diffusion can have their good side; they perfectly sustain direct hearing which is still something very different.[18]

Raoul Laparra was almost prophetic in his assessment that technical media would gain in importance the more they develop perfection in sound quality:

> I believe that mechanical music has a great future, if the broadcasts become clearer and less distort the sounds of the orchestra, whose contrasts of timbre are still being lost a lot. And I believe that if the programmes are being refined, it will be a powerful way to make the masses more musical […][19]

Hennessy was more on the sceptical side. He said he was not able to decide whether the loss of performance opportunities for musicians could be compensated by recordings, but he appeared to doubt it and rather saw the 'twilight of music' coming:

---

[18] '*Les conséquences de la musique mécanique ne doivent certainement pas être mortelles, ni pour la musique ni pour les musiciens. Ces moyens de diffusion musicale peuvent avoir leur bon côté; ils laissent parfaitement subsister l'audition directe qui est tout de même autre chose.*'; Guy Ropartz, in: *Le Guide du concert*, 12 Octobre 1928, p. 26.

[19] '*Je crois que la musique mécanique est d'un grand avenir, si les émissions arrivent à plus de clarté et altèrent moins les sonorités de l'orchestre, dont les contrastes de timbres se perdent encore beaucoup. Et je crois que si les programmes s'épurent, elle sera un moyen puissant de rendre les masses plus musiciennes …*'; Raoul Laparra, ibid.

> I think all artists are more or less threatened by mechanical music, and I don't feel competent to determine the extent to which they will be compensated by radio programmes and phonographic recordings. Can a musical work live without the performer's help? No doubt, but it's a dull life without ideals. It's the twilight of music.[20]

It was the last survey by *Le Guide du concert* in which Hennessy participated. Half a year before his death he was invited by *Le Courrier musical* to comment on trends in contemporary chamber music in a special issue devoted to this topic that appeared on 15 March 1929.[21] By this time, Hennessy had completed most of his major chamber music works including four string quartets and was evidently perceived as a major contributor to chamber music in France. The composers represented were (in this order) Paul Dukas, Gabriel Pierné, Guy Ropartz, Pierre de Bréville, Albert Roussel, Léo Sachs, Henry Woollett, Auguste Chapuis, Albert Bertelin, Marcel Labey, Joaquín Turina, Paul Bazelaire, Émile Trépard, Marc Delmas, Joaquín Nin, René de Castéra, Gustave Samazeuilh, Lazare Lévy, Louis Delune, Swan Hennessy, Alexander Tcherepnin, Alexandre Tansman, Jean Déré, Piero Coppola, Henri Collet, Madeleine Dedieu-Peters, and Simone Plé. Georges Migot is represented by a longer article entitled '*Réflexions sur la musique de chambre*'.[22]

In his introduction, Charles Tenroc did not ask the composers to respond to specific questions, even though it was thus understood by most of the respondents, but rather to a thesis, which sounds quite biased (and very flowery!):

> Thus, chamber music, such a pure branch of music, seems to us worthy of such a consultation with those who have dedicated themselves to protecting its health. It is because the Muse gives concern to lovers of its intimate graces and perennial virtues. It seems to suffer from an unease, which, undoubtedly, is the one that marks a transitional period in search of a balance between immortal laws and bold applications of an aesthetic on the way to renewal. May the opinions and assessments collected here contribute to the Muse's development and return to her that serenity, that simplicity, which gives her the profound and discreet charm of her conversation and the emotion of her confidential effusions – the Muse whose language is that of the very soul, in its innermost expression, the most deeply sensitive of her movements and meditations.[23]

---

[20] *Je pense que tous les artistes sont plus ou moins menacés par la musique mécanique et je ne me sens pas la compétence nécessaire pour déterminer dans quelle mesure ils seront dédommagés par les émissions radiophoniques et les enregistrements phonographiques. L'œuvre musicale peut-elle vivre sans le concours de l'interprète ? Sans doute, mais d'une vie terne et sans idéal. C'est le crépuscule de la musique.*'; Swan Hennessy, ibid.
[21] 'Enquête sur l'évolution et les tendances de la musique de chambre', introduced by Charles Tenroc, in *Le Courrier musical* 31:6, 15 March 1929, pp. 166–171.
[22] Ibid., pp. 173–174.
[23] '*Ainsi la Musique de Chambre, cette branche si pure de la musique, nous semble-t-elle digne d'une telle consultation auprès de ceux qui se sont voués à la protection de sa santé. C'est que la Muse donne des inquiétudes aux amateurs de ses grâces intimes et de ses vertus vivaces. Elle semble souffrir d'un malaise qui, sans doute, est celui dont souffre une période transitoire à la recherche d'un équilibre entre des lois immortelles et des applications hardies d'une esthétique en marche vers les renouvellements. Puissent les opinions et les ordonnances recueillies ici contribuer à l'épanouissement de la Muse et à lui rendre cette sérénité, cette simplicité qui fait le*

The bias lies in the intention to include only those composers 'who have dedicated themselves to protecting its [i. e. chamber music's] health' and in speaking of 'perennial virtues' and 'immortal laws', implying that chamber music that does not follow traditionally established rules would cause 'concerns', 'unease', and ultimately the demise of chamber music as it once was.

The survey, it can be taken for granted, targeted Arnold Schönberg and the Second Viennese School and therefore fell on fertile ground with Swan Hennessy who, by 1929, had become one of the most outspoken critics of Schönberg in France (as will yet be seen further below). He therefore seems to wholeheartedly support Tenroc's thesis, but joins in with his own arguments, which do go beyond a superficial criticism of Schönberg:

> This race to the abyss that we are witnessing, the break with all traditions, can it be called evolution?
> Isn't it more like a deviation from the evolutionary path? To get out of the impasse where it has gone astray, won't avant-garde music have to return, at least in part, to the traditions it has abandoned? I do not feel competent to answer these serious questions.
> What I regret most in today's chamber music is the tendency to write orchestral reductions for a limited number of instruments. Many quartets, for example, are more theatre than chamber music. I also deplore the current abuse of polytonality. Obviously, the latter can sometimes enrich the range of descriptive music, but it must be used with great discretion and skill. The same is true of the picturesque exotic, because, as captivating as oriental or African-American rhythms may be, they can be satisfied quite quickly, like whipped cream or caviar. After all, we are neither Cochin Chinese nor Negroes. Why look far away for what is often within reach.
> To return to evolution, are we sure it is a straight line and not a circle?[24]

While Hennessy here clearly criticises (Schönberg's) avant-garde for the 'impasse' it has created, demanding that those ultramodern composers return, 'at least in part', to more traditional means of expression, he also criticises the contemporary fashion

---

charme profond et discret de sa conversation et l'émotion de ses effusions confidentielles – la Muse dont le langage est celui de l'âme même, dans son expression la plus intérieure, la plus profondément sensible de ses mouvements et de ses méditations.'; ibid., p. 166.

[24] 'Cette course à l'abime qui a suivi, la rupture avec toutes les traditions peut-elle être appelée évolution? Ne serait-ce pas plutôt une déviation du chemin de l'évolution? Pour sortir de l'impasse où elle s'est fourvoyée, la musique d'avant-garde ne sera-t-elle pas obligée revenir, au moins en partie, aux traditions qu'elle a abandonnées? Je ne me sens pas la compétence nécessaire pour répondre à ces graves questions. Ce que je déplore surtout dans la musique de chambre actuelle, c'est la tendance à écrire pour un nombre restreint d'instruments des réductions d'orchestre. Beaucoup de quatuors, par exemple, relèvent plutôt du théâtre que de la musique de chambre. Je déplore aussi l'abus actuel de la polytonalité. Évidemment, cette dernière peut quelque fois enrichir la palette de la musique descriptive, mais il faut en user avec beaucoup de discrétion et d'habilité. Il en est de même du pittoresque exotique, car, aussi prenants que soient les rythmes orientaux ou américano-africains, on s'en rassasie assez vite, comme de la crème fouettée ou du caviar. Après tout, nous ne sommes ni des Cochinchinois ni de Nègres. Pourquoi chercher au loin de que l'on trouve souvent à la portée de la main. / Pour en revenir à l'évolution, est-on bien sûr que ce soit une ligne droite et non pas un cercle?'; Swan Hennessy, ibid., p. 169.

of polytonality and an excessive use of exotic influences.

First of all, he is clearly convinced that atonality is not the natural evolutionary path that music would have had to take sooner or later. He calls it a deviation from that path that has led to an impasse, in other words, once all traditional harmony is dissolved into dodecaphony, it cannot go further. While this is a perfectly understandable point of view, it does include the acknowledgement that music has to develop. But he argues for a smoother evolution, based on compositional traditions that would have to develop. Readers will perhaps remember that in 1911 he had already identified techniques used in descriptive music as a potential path for such a development and which he used extensively around that time.[25] And when he dismisses Asian and African-American influences in favour of 'what is often within reach', he alludes, of course, to European folk music influences – clearly an alternative for the evolution of contemporary art music in Hennessy's view.

Deux Petites pièces bi-tonales (1923) for piano

Speaking of polytonality, Hennessy clearly regarded it as unimaginative, making use of an all too simple tool – two or more parallel tonalities in one composition – to create harmonic friction. Since polytonality mostly manifested itself as bitonality, Hennessy showed what he meant in the form of two simple pieces that one can only describe as satirical: the *Deux Petites pièces bi-tonales* that appeared as a music supplement to *Le Guide du concert* of 26 January 1923. The satirical nature of the pieces is underlined by the fact that he did not give them an opus number; he merely wanted to clarify something.

The two little pieces are each one page long and simply headed '1' and '2'. No. 1 (*Andantino*) is written in the key of A major for the right hand and B major for the left. The right hand contains a simple tune in the manner of a nursery rhyme to which is added, from bar 7, a stomping bass line in a similar rhythmic outline as the right-hand tune. No. 2 (*Allegretto*) changes tonalities several times in the course of the short piece, beginning with a combination of D major/F major for 16 bars, followed by eight bars of G major/G minor and another eight bars of C minor/G minor before it returns to the combination of the beginning. Again, the 'tunes' sound like children's songs, carrying the message that bitonality is a little naïve, indirectly ridiculing composers who proclaim bitonality as a serious compositional technique (with whom he probably targets Milhaud and Koechlin as the two most conspicuous French composers in this regard, or perhaps even Stravinsky). He must have been aware that he was simplifying things, but this was essentially his opinion.

A month later, the editor of *Le Guide du concert* was able to report on numerous letters he received as a reaction to Hennessy's musical joke. Under the headline of '*La fièvre polytonale*' he wrote:

> The publication of Swan Hennessy's bitonal pieces has earned us a voluminous correspondence. Polytonal fever is common among our readers, but it manifests itself in very

---

[25] 'Sommes-nous à la veille d'une plus complète expression musicale?', in *La Revue musicale* 11:20, 15 October 1911, p. 421–422, cited in Chapter 5.

different ways. The letters received would be worthy of inclusion in a dossier of Musical Futurism, […] 'I didn't want to proclaim my conversion to complete polytonality', he [i. e. Hennessy] wrote to us, 'but only to demonstrate that we can effortlessly make polytonality more or less logical.' This is what one of our readers from Toulouse understood very well. Wanting to contribute to the bitonal movement, he offers us, inspired by the well-known adage: 'You who build, spare your mind', a small and completely original piece that we recommend to music lovers who want to 'train their ears'. There would be no need for written music, it is enough to perform the 4th figure of the Lancers' Quadrille (in D major) to the overture of William Tell (in E major). It's an irresistible effect.[26]

Hennessy and jazz

The discussion of jazz in the pages of *Le Guide du concert* between late 1925 and early 1926 showed Hennessy expressing his dislike of jazz 'not because of morality, but because of aesthetics'. This must be understood as the aesthetics of jazz bands and their improvisational nature to which he could find no relationship. As pointed out above, however, Hennessy did actually use harmonic and rhythmic elements of early jazz (ragtime and foxtrot) in several of his compositions when he was seeking expressions of the vernacular, respectively the popular, in music. Examples are *Au village*, Op. 22 (1907; see Chapter 4), the *Fête populaire dans la banlieue de Paris au XXme siècle*, Op. 36 No. 2 (1910), *L'Américain qui a bien dîné*, Op. 47 No. 2 (1912; the latter two in Chapter 5), and the *Trois Pièces exotiques*, Op. 57 (1922; see Chapter 8). In the mid-1920s, he worked with similar elements in two works for alto-saxophone and piano.

With an increasing number of 1920s' jazz-influenced compositions by members of *Les Six* (in particular, Auric, Milhaud and Poulenc) as well as Ravel, this style was now not as exotic anymore as it once was. Again, Hennessy appears like a precursor of *Les Six*, only that nobody seems to have noticed. He was certainly very open to jazz *as an influence*, in a similar way, perhaps, as Émile Vuillermoz described it at the time.[27]

---

[26] '*La publication des pièces bitonales de Swan Hennessy nous a valu un volumineux courrier. La fièvre polytonale sévit parmi nos lecteurs mais elle se manifeste de façon très différente. Les lettres reçues sont dignes de figurer au dossier du Futurisme Musical […] Je n'ai pas voulu proclamer ma conversion à la polytonalité intégrale, nous a-t-il écrit, mais seulement démontrer qu'on peut faire sans effort de la polytonalité plus ou moins logique.' C'est ce qu'a fort bien compris un de nos lecteurs de Toulouse qui, voulant apporter sa contribution au mouvement bitonal, nous offre, s'inspirant de l'adage connu: 'Toi qui bâtis, ménage tes méninges', un petit morceau tout à fait original et que nous recommandons aux mélomanes désireux de se 'faire les oreilles'. Point n'est besoin de musique écrite, il suffit d'exécuter la 4e figure du quadrille des Lanciers (en ré majeur) en l'accompagnant de l'ouverture de Guillaume Tell (en mi majeur). C'est d'un effet irrésistible.*'; Gabriel Bender: 'La fièvre polytonale', in *Le Guide du concert*, 23 February 1923.

[27] Jann Pasler has explained that 'Vuillermoz passionately defended jazz against those who only heard in it "the triumph of disorder". He saw it as the natural evolution of sound and a physicality that goes beyond the need for an orchestra.'; J. Pasler: '*Bleu-horizon* Politics and Music for Radio Listeners: *L'Initiation à la musique* (1935)', in Barbara L. Kelly and Christopher Moore (eds): *Music Criticism in France, 1918–1939. Authority, Advocacy, Legacy* (Woodbridge: Boydell Press, 2018, p. 100. Pasler cites from Vuillermoz's book *Musiques d'aujourd'hui* (Paris, 1923).

Deux morceaux, Op. 68 (1925) for alto-saxophone and piano

The *Deux morceaux*, Op. 68 were written in 1925 and dedicated to René Laurent, today a rather unknown saxophonist who was an early interpreter of both jazz and 'classical' works for his instrument. The work consists of two short pieces, No. 1 being entitled *Pièce celtique* (obviously no jazzy piece) and No. 2 merely *Jazz*. No. 1 had been performed when yet unpublished as *Romance irlandaise* on 27 December 1925 at the second 'Festival Swan Hennessy'. The first performance of both parts of Op. 68 was at the Salle Majestic, Paris, 22 January 1926 with René Laurent accompanied by the composer. The work was published in 1926 with Max Eschig & Cie.

Both pieces are short yet precise sketches that are very skilfully written. *Jazz* is a piece of just over one minute in duration that stands in an A – A' – B – A form and in the rhythm of a foxtrot. Part A consists of a theme of eight bars in the saxophone that follows a single introductory bar of the piano. In part A', the theme moves back and forth between the two instruments, with the saxophone pursuing the piano line in a parallel fashion a third apart. The piano is written in a style mixing an orchestrion at a funfair with the skills of a pianist accompanying silent movies. The indication for the pianist reads '*Très crapuleux*' ('Very villainous'). It is a very entertaining piece indeed, providing in its conciseness some very pleasant moments for both the musicians and the listener(s). Part B (if one may indeed interpret it as an independent thematic element or just as a funny interjection) underlines Hennessy's great sense of humour when he quotes for merely five bars from Stephen Foster's famous 'Swanee River' song to an eccentric variant of his accompanimental pattern (Ex. 9.1).

Ex. 9.1: *Deux Morceaux*, Op. 68 No. 2 *Jazz*, bars 16–20 (author's transcription with non-transposing saxophone part)

The contrast between *Jazz* and the *Pièce celtique* could not be greater (except that both pieces are notated in a related key: *Jazz* in A flat major and the *Pièce celtique* in F minor, merely ending on an A flat major chord). As a 'Celtic' piece with an *Andante sostenuto* indication that benefits from calm and sonorous *arpeggio* chords, it contrasts sharply with the lively, jazzy second piece of Op. 68. However, at second sight, with his concluding transition to A flat major and a saxophone line including – as 'blue notes', if one wants to see it that way – G♭ and F♭, Hennessy found an excellent solution to lead to the second piece, if a performer chooses to play both pieces in a set.

The *Deux Morceaux* were first performed in a *'Musique vivante'* concert at the Salle Majestic, Paris. This was a series organised by *Le Guide du concert*, introduced and moderated by Léon Vallas, which consisted of a mix of lectures and lecture recitals, panel discussions, spoken (i. e. read-out) music criticism, and actual performances, probably at least in part with an educational ojective. When the series had been started in late October 1925, its aims were described in *Le Ménestrel*:

> Under this title, our counterpart *Le Guide du Concert* organises evenings, which will become weekly, where, after a short hearing of early music, recent works will be heard, in a second audition; authors who so wish can prepare for the audition of their works, which will be given a first performance in the following week. Mr Léon Vallas, the 'game leader', will criticise the critics; finally, in a discussion in which the participants can take part, current controversies will be discussed. This is a copious programme that may be very difficult to keep up in two hours: its abundance is its only flaw.[28]

At this particular event on 22 January 1926, the topic of the day was jazz, and part of the discussion focused on whether jazz (or the term at least) was French, as Hennessy's friend Paul Le Flem wrote in a lengthy review of it for *Comoedia* ('Jazz – is it French?'):[29]

> Jazz has taken root everywhere. It has even become national in the same way as our anthem. It reigns in the music hall from where it came to us. It has acquired the right to be heard in the suburbs, in the palace, at the aperitif concert. It adjusts the choreographic movements of the humble and the more fortunate, throwing everywhere, on the fly, its frenzy, its solid rhythms, its mortifying and disparate timbres.
>
> Don't think that these are the only conquests of jazz, [...] Have we not seen talented composers scorn, in full glory, their own discoveries and humbly ask jazz for new precepts, unquestionably recognising some of its most earnest merits? [...]

---

[28] '*Sous ce titre, notre confrère le Guide du Concert organise des soirées, qui deviendront hebdomadaires, où, après une courte évocation de la musique ancienne, on fera entendre les œuvres récentes, en seconde audition; les auteurs qui le voudront bien prépareront à l'audition de leurs œuvres qui seront jouées pour la première fois la semaine suivante. M. Léon Vallas, le "meneur du jeu", procédera à la critique des critiques; enfin dans une discussion à laquelle les assistants pourront prendre part on traitera des controverses d'actualité. Voilà un programme copieux et qu'il sera peut-être bien difficile de faire tenir en deux heures: son abondance est son seul défaut.*'; Pierre de Lapommeraye in *Le Ménestrel*, 30 October 1925, p. 440.

[29] Paul Le Flem: 'Le jazz serait-il français?', in *Comoedia*, 25 January 1926, p. 1.

A perfect host, Mr Léon Vallas had therefore been very well inspired by submitting the question of jazz to a vote of his faithful regulars at his last session of spoken criticism. Sympathies were generated with pieces imported from America, perfectly reproduced on a phonograph, because of the absence of jazz and negroes. Mr Vallas warned the public against European jazz, which was only a caricature of American jazz, and quoted the opinion of Mr Schwerke, the sympathetic critic of the *Chicago Tribune*, that South Carolina should be considered the cradle of jazz.

According to Mr. Schwerke, *jazz* is a simple distortion of the French word *jase*, but spelled out in English. In the past, French black slaves enjoyed, during their meetings, to reproduce the thousand sounds of nature on small instruments that they had made themselves. They chatted, *jased*, and made music. So, is jazz of French descent?

Mr. Léon Vallas then proceeded to a penetrating analysis of the constituent elements of jazz. He distinguished *rag-time*, i. e. broken time, the syncope; *blue*, a harmonic element admitting the use of chords not recognised by traditional harmony textbooks; instruments, including the banjo, saxophone, trumpet, and trombone with their compulsory muted sounds, the violin; polyphony, very free; improvisation. [...]

René Laurent, the saxophone virtuoso, had previously shown, as a qualified expert, the merits of the instrument in charming and spiritual pieces by Swan Hennessy, who played the piano part.[30]

This may have been the first occasion – at least the first that is documented – when Hennessy met Léon Vallas and Irving Schwerke. The Lyon-based Vallas (1879–1956), of course, was well known for several years as a writer on music, both as author of books (he wrote influential biographies of Debussy) and as music critic. Irving

---

[30] *'Il s'est implanté un peu partout, le jazz. Il est même devenu national au même titre que notre hymne. Il règne au music-hall d'où il consentit à venir jusqu'à nous. Il a acquis droit de cité au faubourg, au palace, à l'apéritif-concert. Il règle les ébats chorégraphiques des humbles et des plus fortunés, jetant partout, à la volée sa frénésie, ses rythmes solides, ses timbres mordants et disparates. / Ne croyez pas que ce soient là les seules conquêtes du jazz. [...] N'a-t-on pas vu des compositeurs de talent dédaigner, en pleine gloire, leurs propres trouvailles et demander humblement au jazz des préceptes nouveaux et reconnaître sans discussion quelques-uns de ses plus sûrs mérites? / [...] Animateur parfait, M. Léon Vallas, avait donc été fort bien inspiré en soumettant au référendum de ses fidèles habitués à sa dernière séance de critique parlée, la question du jazz. Les sympathies furent acquises à des morceaux, importés d'Amérique, qu'un phonographe perfectionné reproduisit, à défaut de jazz et de nègres. M. Vallas ne manqua pas de mettre le public en garde contre le jazz européen qui n'est qu'une caricature du jazz américain et cita l'opinion de M. Schwerke, le sympathique critique de la* Chicago Tribune, *déclarant que la Caroline du Sud doit être considérée comme le berceau du jazz. / D'après M. Schwerke,* jazz *serait une simple déformation du mot français,* jase, *mais orthographié à l'anglaise. Jadis, les esclaves noirs français se plaisaient, au cours de leurs réunions, à reproduire les mille bruits de la nature sur de petits instruments qu'ils avaient eux-mêmes façonnés. Ils bavardaient,* jasaient, *tout en faisant de la musique. Le jazz serait donc d'ascendance française? M. Léon Vallas procède ensuite à une pénétrante analyse des éléments constitutifs du jazz. Il distingue le* rag-time, *c'est-à-dire le temps rompu, la syncope; le* blue, *élément harmonique admettant l'emploi d'accords non reconnus par les catalogues d'harmonie traditionnels; les instruments, parmi lesquels le banjo, le saxophone, la trompette et le trombone avec leurs obligatoires sons bouchés, le violon; la polyphonie, très libre; l'improvisation. / [...] / M. René Laurent, virtuose du saxophone, avait préalablement montré, en expert qualifié, les mérites de l'instrument dans de charmantes et spirituelles pièces de M. Swann* [sic !] *Hennessy qui tenait la partie de piano.'*; ibid.

Schwerke (1893–1975), in contrast, is lesser known today, but he wrote for a great variety of American newspapers and music journals on musical life in Paris. Hennessy remained in contact with both of them, as is evidenced by correspondence. Schwerke returned to the United States in 1942 in the course of the German occupation of Paris, with a 'Swan Hennessy File' among his papers (see Appendix 5.A and further on in this chapter).

Le Guide du concert also reported about the event, naturally, opening with a little drawing of some of the participants in the event, with Laurent and Hennessy on the right (Fig. 9.2).[31] The unsigned article quotes extensively from Le Flem's in *Comoedia*, but also mentions that the hall was packed to capacity and about 50 people had to be turned away.

Fig. 9.2: Hennessy as 'jazz accompanist' (Courtesy: Médiathèque Musicale Mahler)

Quatre Morceaux, Op. 71 (1926) for alto-saxophone/viola and piano

Briefly leaving the chronological account of Swan Hennessy's music, the *Quatre Morceaux*, Op. 71 should be included in the discussion of jazz influences in Hennessy's music, especially as this work was written for the same instrumentation as the *Deux Morceaux*, Op. 68 (however, as Op. 71bis, the alto-saxophone part may be substituted by a viola). Compared to Op. 68, this work is an exact duplication of the former, with two jazz-oriented pieces and two others going in a 'Celtic' direction constituting the album. They are called 1. *Foxtrot*; 2. *Tango*; 3. *Chanson de l'émigrant*; and 4. *Lever du soleil dans les Hébrides*.

The work was written in 1926 and published with Max Eschig in the following year. The manuscript reveals that the original title of the album was *Nouvelles pièces exotiques* (alluding to his Op. 57 for piano) and that it was limited to the first three

---

[31] On the left are the singer Pierrette Bonniol-Bondy and the pianist Jane Boulnois, performing a work by the composer Joseph Boulnois, according to the unsigned article in *Le Guide du concert*, 29 January 1926, p. 450. Also depicted is the gramophone player on which Vallas played American jazz records to the audience, with the caption '*Tous les jazz*'.

pieces. Taking for granted that the emigrant of the third piece was an emigrant to the United States, perhaps an Irish one, those three pieces would be unified by a musical idea of America and the creative influences gained from migration.

The four pieces are dedicated to the prominent viola player Paul-Louis Neuberth (1881–1959; nos 1 and 4), his wife Marthe (1884–1968; no. 3), and to Carol-Bérard (1881–1942), the composer and secretary of the French composers' union. There are several records of performances of the viola version (the first on 7 November 1927 by Paul-Louis Neuberth and the composer), but the saxophone version was considerably less successful, with only one documented performance of nos 3 and 4 in February 1932 by 'M. et Mme Roger Gely'. The *Chanson de l'émigrant* was once performed with viola and organ in September 1929 by Neuberth and the young Olivier Messiaen (see Appendix 1 for details).

The *Fox Trot* continues the stylistic line of *Jazz*, Op. 68 No. 2, but it is a little longer and more complex. Still, it remains an entertaining piece that resembles the style it alludes to rather than adapting it. In fact, in both Opp. 68 and 71 the main themes make one may wonder whether Hennessy was aiming at writing popular music proper or art music with a jazz appeal. They are certainly in a much more popular mood than, for instance, Georges Auric's foxtrot adaptation *Adieu, New York!* (1920). In comparison to Auric, Hennessy's music is much less dissonant. *Jazz* and *Fox Trot* (as well as *Tango* later on) remain in the popular mood, but their construction is different, somewhat more complex, more modulatory, and there is more contrapuntal/imitative interaction between the instruments. These elements make his music appear like an artistic improvement of jazz with the means of a 'classical' composer. Needless to say, there are no improvisatory elements (neither in Auric's or any other composer's jazz adaptations of the time), because that is where he clearly draws the line between what he likes about jazz and what he despised.

Ex. 9.2: *Quatre Morceaux*, Op. 71 No. 1 *Fox Trot*, bars 1–5

Harmonically, Hennessy works mainly with seventh chords (Ex. 9.2). *Fox Trot* is notated in F major, and the accompaniment to the main theme follows a sequence of F major, C major seventh (for two bars), F major sixth, F major seventh, followed by several chords with a seventh, which are ambiguous as to their genus for lack of a third. These introductory bars are followed in bars 8 and 9 by a chromatic rise in the piano from F major seventh, F sharp minor seventh, G minor seventh, A minor seventh before the saxophone commences with a side theme.

Tango is another excellent miniature, capturing the essence of the form with characteristic contemporary (popular) harmony and a rather oriental melodic theme. This shows another characteristic of this opus, the frequent change between major and minor modes. Set in G minor, the tango rhythm is mainly represented by reverse linear hand movements in the piano. As the first G minor passage dissolves in bar 16, there follow four bars of full-bodied chords in the tonic major including seventh chords (also major sevenths), with intermittent E minor and A minor chords (Ex. 9.3 is then followed by a reprise of the main theme).

Ex. 9.3: *Quatre Morceaux*, Op. 71 No. 2 *Tango*, bars 15–24

The *Chanson de l'émigrant* is the least distinctive piece of the album. 'Celtic' elements may only be detected with some benevolence, and neither melody nor harmony are very attractive. The simple accompaniment in regular crotchets remind of a chorale, and insofar Neuberth's or Messiaen's idea of performing it on the organ is not an inappropriate idea at all. In contrast, the 'sunrise on the Hebrides' (*Lever du soleil dans les Hébrides*) is quite a dramatic final piece, beginning in a calm mood in 6/8 time, accelerating in bars 13–16 where Hennessy notates 6/8 in the right hand to 4/4 with quavers in the left (he could have used semiquaver quadruplets instead) and then bursting in *doppio movimento* into a Scottish jig (four groups of quaver triplets in a bar) that grows in excitement as dynamically increasing tremolos bring the piece to an end.

There are a number of brief reviews of the publication and from performances, mostly appearing some four years later. One journal wrote: 'In these brief pages there is rhythm, fantasy, poetry, a very healthy musicality, a synthesis of Swan Hennessy's varied talent.'[32] A Swiss newspaper recommended the work for up and coming saxophonists: 'Simple and tasteful music, very charming. [...] Our saxophonists will be able to obtain deserved success with this music without any great technical difficulties.'[33] Another journal considered them 'very fine and very pleasant [...] Hennessy's style is clear; he does not seek difficulties of expression; he is accessible to everyone, and is true to his methods.'[34] In Tristan Klingsor's review of a 1930 performance of the viola version with Robert Chantôme, some three months after the composer's death, it is not entirely clear whether he speaks of Chantôme or Hennessy, except in his last sentence. It seems, though, that everything applies to Hennessy (as well):

> M. Chantôme triumphed with the *Quatre Pièces* and the *Sonat[in]e celtique* by the late Swan Hennessy: the penetrating sound of his instrument, the lightness of his bow, the accuracy of his interpretation highlighted these works full of poetry and colour; there was a musician who was hardly bothered by formulas, but whose heart was extremely sensitive and unfolded without pretension with a rare sincerity. Swan Hennessy was unintentionally personal, which is still the best way.[35]

Ravel and Gershwin

Swan Hennessy's obscurity and consequently his absence from almost all studies of recent French musical history have also concealed events that would be of interest to wider musicological circles. In connection with the foregoing aspects of jazz influences in his work, this includes Hennessy's meetings with George Gershwin and Maurice Ravel. The fact that these meetings are not mentioned in any biography of either composer does not prove necessarily that they did not take place. Every biographical study

---

[32] *'Il y a dans ces brèves pages du rythme, de la fantaisie, de la poésie, une très saine musicalité, une synthèse du talent varié de Swan Hennessy.'*; anonymous notice in *Revue internationale de la musique et de danse*, 15 August 1929.

[33] *'Musique simple et de bon goût, très charmante. [...] Nos saxophonistes pourront obtenir des succès mérités avec cette musique sans grandes difficultés techniques.'*; anonymous notice in *Tribune de Genève*, 3 January 1930.

[34] *'[...] très fins et très aimables. [...] Le style de Hennesy est clair; il ne recherche pas les difficultés d'expression; il est accessible à tout le monde, et garde une grande honnêteté de procédés.'*; anonymous notice in *I.M.I.*, 15 March 1930.

[35] *'M. Chantôme triompha avec* Quatre pièces *et une* Sonate celtique *du regretté Swan Hennesy: la sonorité pénétrante de son instrument, la légèreté de son archet, la justesse de son interprétation firent bien valoir ces œuvres pleines de poésie et de couleur; il y avait là un musicien qui ne s'embarrassait guère de formules, mais dont le cœur était extrêmement sensible et s'épanchait sans prétention avec une rare sincérité. Swan Hennessy était personnel sans le vouloir, ce qui est encore la meilleure manière.'*; Tristan Klingsor in *La Semaine à Paris*, 17 January 1930, p. 23.

is shaped by the sources on which it is based. And perhaps some potential sources were never consulted.

The source on which this information is based is Patrice Hennessy (1910–1973), son of Claire and Swan Hennessy. He passed the information on to his daughters Brigitte (* 1939) and Aline (* 1941) – it is a purely oral memory, never written down by anyone, never verified (and impossible to verify). And since no one has been interested in Swan Hennessy in the past decades, it has never come to light.

The exact date and the circumstances of the meetings are not part of the story. But for Patrice to remember them (or it) properly, they must have taken place in the second half of the 1920s, especially since they concern both Ravel and Gershwin, and Gershwin did not visit Paris before 1926. What connects Ravel and Gershwin in today's memory is the younger composer's request for tuition, with Ravel's denial and recommendation of Nadia Boulanger instead. And that is where our story sets in. Because before Boulanger came into this discussion, Ravel had apparently recommended Hennessy, probably on account of Gershwin's and Hennessy's common nationality and language. What Ravel probably did not know is that Hennessy never had any pupils and therefore would deny any such request, independent of who would have asked. And Gershwin may not have wanted it either, since he was interested in Ravel.

Fig. 9.3: Hennessy's grand piano, on which Ravel is supposed to have played[36]

---

[36] Hennessy owned a 19th-century German grand piano by the Kaps brand, bought probably while still at Stuttgart. It stood for many years in the Paris apartment of Hennessy's descendants and has been brought to a country house in southern Normandy in the mid-2000s where the photo was taken by the author in 2018.

Of course, this assumes that Ravel already knew Hennessy before. There would have been numerous occasions, mainly concerts in Paris, at which such a meeting may have occurred. Another option is correspondence, but Patrice clearly remembered that Ravel played on Hennessy's grand piano, in other words, such a meeting must have taken place in Hennessy's apartment on Boulevard Raspail. Gershwin, for his part, would know of Hennessy since the November 1923 recital in New York with Éva Gauthier described in Chapter 8.

Where- or whenever Ravel met (or knew of) Hennessy before the common encounter with Gershwin is impossible to ascertain. In previous chapters I have tried to explain that, of all contemporary French composers it was probably Ravel whom Hennessy admired most. Thus, an initial contact may have resulted from Hennessy sending Ravel some of his published compositions. In any case, their contact must have been (and remained) superficial. According to Ravel's biographer Arbie Orenstein, Hennessy is not even listed in Ravel's two personal telephone books.[37]

The Hennessy family also recalls that Hennessy met Gershwin in one of the bars on Boulevard Montparnasse that Gershwin went to on his travels to Paris in 1926 and/or 1928, most likely Le Select. However likely such a meeting is, Hennessy's jazz-influenced compositions of 1925 and 1926 show his keen interest in adapting elements of jazz in works of art music, and this may have been their topic of conversation. It is not likely, however, that Hennessy, the American dandy in Paris, would have been the model for Gershwin's *An American in Paris* – or would it?

As for Americans in Paris in general, Hennessy sought as little contact as with Irishmen, it seems. Paris in the 1920s was a magnet for American artists and intellectuals, with musicians like Gershwin, George Antheil, Virgil Thomson, Henry Cowell (whose first Paris concert in November 1923 was reviewed by two of Hennessy's Breton friends, Paul Le Flem and Louis Vuillemin),[38] and Cole Porter, writers like Djuna Barnes, T. S. Eliott, Scott Fitzgerald, Ernest Hemingway, and Ezra Pound, art collector Gertrude Stein, musicians' patron Winnaretta Singer, book publisher Sylvia Beach – it's a long list, but there is no evidence of any meeting or other kind of contact. One reason certainly was that Hennessy was financially independent, he did not need benefactors – he was rather a benefactor to others, especially to the musicians in his circle who performed his music. And there must have remained elements of that personal trait that had inhibited his career from the beginning: a mixture of modesty and reclusiveness, perhaps even shyness when it came to personal contacts – quite different, indeed, from the language, the directness, and the eloquence of his written forms of expression.

---

[37] E-mail from Orenstein to the author, 15 May 2017.
[38] Joel Sachs: *Henry Cowell. A Man Made of Music* (New York: Oxford University Press, 2012), p. 118.

Swan Hennessy's critique of Arnold Schönberg (2)

In the late 1920s, Hennessy also continues and intensifies his criticism of the musical avant-garde, as personified by Arnold Schönberg and the Second Viennese School, in a new series of letters and sarcastic comments in the press. This had begun with letters to English journals in late 1912 (see Chapter 5) and continued in ironic compositions (e. g., *Bébé prend sa médicine*, Op. 48 No. 6, 1913).

A new letter was published in *Le Guide du concert* in November 1921, responding to an unidentified letter by the composer Opol Ygouw (1871–1968)[39] that must have expressed the opinion that dissonance was omnipresent in contemporary urban life. Hennessy takes the opposite view, ending on a remark about Schönberg:

> Let me say, with regard to Mr. Ygouw's letter, that in the hubbub of a large city, even an industrial one, there is always some kind of harmony, some coherence of tone. You never find continuous dissonance anywhere.
>
> In my opinion, Arnold Schönberg and his imitators are as far from the truth as the excellent Mendelssohn was.[40]

The fact that, from 1928, another series of public comments appeared may have been caused by Hennessy's attending at least one of the two concerts comprising the 'Festival Arnold Schœnberg' in Paris: a concert including orchestral music on 8 December 1927 and a chamber recital on the 15th. It was the first time Schönberg came to Paris to conduct his own music. Both concerts featured his *Pierrot lunaire*, Op. 21 for reciter and small instrumental ensemble, written in 1912 in a freely atonal style, with a first Paris performance in January 1921. It is more likely, though, given the series of comments from 1928, that Hennessy attended the 1927 performance(s).

Astonishingly, Hennessy seems to have been quite fond, at least of *Pierrot lunaire*, as is evidenced by a letter from Paul Ladmirault to his wife that is archived in the Bibliothèque Nationale de France: He wrote:

> It seems that an innovative musician has been born, and he has a lot of talent. Hennessy who was very much warned against him returned quite enthralled by Schoenberg's *Pierrot lunaire*. Here comes a new star.[41]

---

[39] Pseudonym of Léopold Gouvy, nephew of Théodore Gouvy.
[40] '*Permettez-moi de dire, à propos de la lettre de M. Ygouw, que dans le brouhaha d'une grande ville, même industrielle, il y a toujours une espèce d'harmonie, de cohérence des sonorités. Vous ne trouverez nulle part une dissonance continue. / A mon avis, Arnold Schönberg et ses imitateurs sont aussi loin de la vérité que le fut l'excellent Mendelssohn.*'; in *Le Guide du concert*, 4 November 1921, p. 78.
[41] '*Il paraît décidément qu'un musicien novateur est né et il a beaucoup de talent. Hennessy qui était très prévenu contre lui est revenu séduit par le* Pierrot lunaire *de Schoenberg. Voilà le nouvel as.*', Paul Ladmirault, quoted after Marie-Claire Mussat: 'La Réception de Schönberg en France avant la Seconde Guerre mondiale', in *Revue de Musicologie* 81:1 (2001), p. 169. Mussat does not mention any exact source or shelf number of this letter.

Jane Fulcher has also shown that other composers/critics on a more conservative side, such as Paul Le Flem, Émile Vuillermoz and Gustave Bret also liked *Pierrot*, despite Schönberg coming from the Austro-Hungarian empire, the music of which was a taboo for many years after World War I, reminding of the Franco-German rivalry in music in connection with Wagner after the Franco-Prussian War fifty year earlier:

> Here their musical interests apparently overrode the ideological 'ban' so widely imposed in Paris on the performance of the former 'enemies" music.[42]

The recital on 15 December included the first Paris performance, by Eduard Steuermann, of the *Suite*, Op. 25 (1923) for piano – the earliest of Schönberg's works to employ a twelve-tone series. Even though Hennessy may have been 'enthralled' or 'seduced' by *Pierrot lunaire*, his criticism must have been sparked by other works on the programme including the *Suite*.

By the late 1920s, Hennessy's letters straddle between irony, sarcastic humour and desperation. In November 1928, he pre-empts the criticism he formulated again in 1929 in connection with the survey on contemporary chamber music in *Le Courrier musical* (see earlier in this chapter), namely that Schönberg had led music into a creative impasse. In this letter, which alludes to André Coeuroy's *Panorama de la musique contemporaine* (Paris: Éditions Kra, 1928) and a German review of it that he had read, Hennessy sounds truly worried:

> **Where are we going?**
> There has been a lot of talk lately about the disarray into which modern music has fallen. What to attribute it to? Some say, the War, but isn't it simply the weariness of influences that have been suffered for too long, especially those of Wagner and Debussy? It was necessary to find something new at any cost, and the easiest way was to break with tradition. This timidly initiated breakup soon became a real race to the abyss. Modern music is currently in a deadlock. Mr. Coeuroy tried very skilfully to square this vicious circle in his 'Panorama de la musique'. Talking about this book in the 'Allgemeine Musikzeitung', Mr Walter Dahms said that he finds consolation in realising that things are no better in France than they are in Germany and that the same nonsense is being said there. How will all this end?[43]

---

[42] Fulcher, *The Composer as Intellectual*, p. 161.

[43] '*Il a souvent été question, ces temps-ci, du désarroi dans lequel est tombé la musique moderne. A quoi l'attribuer? Quelques-uns disent la guerre, mais ne serait-ce pas tout simplement la lassitude d'influences trop longtemps subies, notamment celles de Wagner et de Debussy? Il fallait trouver du nouveau à n'importe quel prix et le moyen le plus facile était de rompre avec la tradition. Cette rupture commencée timidement devint bientôt une véritable course à l'abîme. Actuellement la musique moderne se trouve dans une impasse. M. Cœuroy a essayé très adroitement de faire la quadrature de ce cercle vicieux dans son "Panorama de la musique". En parlant de ce livre dans l'"Allgemeine Musik-Zeitung", M. Walter Dahms a dit qu'il trouve une consolation à constater que ça ne va pas mieux en France qu'en Allemagne et qu'on y dit les mêmes bêtises. Comment tout cela finira-t-il ?*'; 'Ou allons-nous?'; in *Le Guide du concert*, 9 November 1928, p. 154.

Partly repeating, and expanding, what he wrote above, he also contributed a letter to *Kornog*, a relatively new journal devoted to Breton cultural nationalism, to which Paul Le Flem contributed most articles relating to music. He must have been the one who gave Hennessy this forum. The article was given on a double page, with a version in Breton on the left and one in French on the right. The article/letter begins with two introductory paragraphs on Hennessy, where his music is described as influenced by Celticism and 'just modern enough that no one can blame him for ignoring anything of the achievements of his contemporaries'.[44] This is followed by Hennessy's words, in which he begins with a quote from an earlier (unidentified) article in *Le Guide du concert*:

The current musical disarray
A few years ago, during the first assault of the 'avant-garde', we said to ourselves: 'It is a temporary manifestation of weariness and powerlessness; let us wait for the reaction.' But the reaction did not come and we must face the facts: the avant-garde came to stay. We are told that its purpose is to destroy in order to rebuild. However, if the first part of this programme was easy to implement, the same cannot be said for the second part. There may be a certain fierce joy in trampling on the old principles, but replacing them with something else is hard, it's even so hard that it doesn't make fun at all anymore. It is from that first part that we got so many 'young geniuses'. The second part was not carried out. No masterpiece has replaced the old 'bullshit' that we wanted to remove. The avant-garde has thus remained solely destructive until now, and the 'firemen' are still masters of the battlefield. But the struggle has been hot and the losses are very heavy. Feeling has died; melody, harmony and counterpoint hold only by a thread, tonality has disappeared; only the rhythm is unscathed and doing well.

The above was published in the Guide du concert of 21 October 1927. Since then, much has been said about the disarray into which modern music has fallen. What to attribute it to? Some say the War, others say the awakening of Israel, but I believe (although these two things probably had a lot to do with it), that the main cause was the weariness of influences that had been suffered for too long (Wagner, Franck, Debussy). We needed something new at any cost. However, the safest and easiest way (alas) was to break with tradition. This break, timid and partial at first, then bolder, more complete, soon became a real race to the bottom. The avant-garde today finds itself in a dead end of travesty and incoherence. There is only one thing left for us to do, so as not to perish, and that is to retrace our steps.[45]

---

[44] '[…] *juste assez moderne pour que personne ne puisse lui reprocher d'ignorer quoi que ce soit des acquisitions de ses contemporains.*'; 'Ar strafuilh er sonerez bremañ / Le Désarroi musical actuel', in *Kornog* 1:2 (Winter 1928), pp. 43 (in Breton) and 44 (in French); most likely Le Flem's description.

[45] '*Il y a quelques années, lors du premier assaut de 'l'avant-garde', on s'était dit: 'C'est une manifestation passagère de lassitude et d'impuissance; attendons la réaction.' Mais la réaction n'est pas venue et nous devons nous rendre à l'évidence: l'avant-garde est venue pour rester. On nous dit que son but est de détruire pour reconstruire. Or, si la première partie de ce programme est de réalisation facile, il n'en est pas de même de la seconde. S'il y a une certaine joie féroce à piétiner les vieux principes, les remplacer par autre chose c'est dur, c'est même tellement dur que ce n'est plus du tout amusant. C'est cette première partie qui nous a valu un si grand nombre de 'jeune génies.' La seconde partie n'a pas été réalisée. Aucun chef-d'œuvre n'est venu remplacer les vieilles 'foutaises' qu'on voudrait supprimer. L'avant-garde est donc restée uniquement destructive jusqu'à présent,*

Here we are at the heart of what Hennessy criticised about the avant-garde: that it had killed (musical) feeling, that its effect was merely destructive without offering anything else of lasting value in its place,[46] that rhythm remained as the only basic elements of music after melody and harmony had died (although the persistence of rhythm may also be debated), and that it is therefore a creative impasse from which one has to return.

Another criticism that he expresses is the paucity of musical ideas that he perceived in music he perceived as 'incoherent':

Incoherence
How does one explain the ever-increasing fad of incoherence among certain composers of the avant-garde? It is simply the paucity of musical ideas.

It becomes more and more difficult to find something that has not already been said. Now, whereas the absence of ideas is cruelly felt in an orderly composition that respects principles that have hitherto prevailed, such absence of ideas cannot be perceived in an incoherent work, of that there can be no question.[47]

On the other hand, the revival of interest in Franz Schubert on the occasion of the centenary of his death in 1928, he (ironically?) describes as a 'reassuring symptom':

Reassuring symptom
What does all this hustle and bustle mean for Schubert? Never was a centenary celebrated as this one for the most Romantic of all Romantics! So, Romanticism is not the abominable thing one wants us to believe? Will we soon see the chameleons of the avant-garde

---

et les 'pompiers' sont encore maîtres du champ de bataille. Mais la lutte a été chaude et les pertes sont très lourdes. Le sentiment est mort; la mélodie, l'harmonie et le contrepoint ne tiennent plus que par un fil, la tonalité a disparu; seul le rythme est indemne et se porte bien. / Ce qui précède a paru dans le Guide du concert du 21 octobre 1927. Depuis lors on a beaucoup parlé du désarroi dans lequel est tombée la musique moderne. À quoi l'attribuer? Les uns disent la guerre, d'autres, le réveil d'Israël, mais je crois (quoique ces deux choses y sont sans doute pour beaucoup), que la cause principale fut la lassitude d'influences trop longtemps subies (Wagner; Franck; Debussy). Il fallait du nouveau à n'importe quel prix. Or, le moyen le plus sûr et le plus facile (hélas) c'était de rompre avec la tradition. Cette rupture, timide et partielle d'abord, ensuite plus hardie, plus complète, devint bientôt une véritable course à l'abîme. L'avant-garde se trouve aujourd'hui dans une impasse de pitrerie et d'incohérence. Il ne lui reste qu'une chose à faire, pour ne pas périr, c'est de revenir sur ses pas.'; ibid.

[46] Vincent d'Indy expressed a similar idea in two 1923 articles in *Comoedia*: '[…] he indicted the new musical procedures of youth as incapable of producing anything "substantial," and thus destined to self-destruct."; Fulcher, *The Composer as Intellectual*, p. 195.

[47] *'Quelle est l'explication de la vogue toujours croissante de l'incohérence chez certains compositeurs d'avant garde? C'est tout simplement la pénurie d'idées musicales. / Il devient de plus en plus difficile de trouver quelque chose qui n'a pas déjà été dit. Or, si l'absence d'idées dans une composition ordonnée et respectueuse des principes qui ont prévalu jusqu'à présent se fait cruellement sentir, cette absence d'idées ne saurait être aperçue dans une œuvre incohérente où il ne peut pas en être question.'*; 'L'Incohérence', in *Le Guide du concert*, 7 June 1929, p. 986.

offering us sweet romances without words in the manner of the immortal Felix? (There has always to be someone who does something in the manner of someone else).[48]

There is an element of fatalistic humour in this statement, and indeed, irony, ridicule and sarcasm were another way to deal with the (from Hennessy's perspective) frustrating developments. In this manner, he once devised a recipe for writing a modern sonatina:

Recipe for a modern sonatina (1929)
Take a melodic line as vulgar as possible. Have it harmonised by a child who has never studied music before. Sprinkle with unnecessary dissonance and serve hot.[49]

Composing music according to a system like the twelve-tone technique appeared to Hennessy like an automated, mechanical effort. In another statement against the contemporary background debate on 'mechanical music' (radio, gramophone, etc.) he suggested:

Call for inventors
Since the mechanical is on the agenda, why not invent a composing machine?
    As consonance, coherence and form are prohibited, there would be no disadvantage in referring to them randomly for the production of musical works. If chance turned out to be too reactionary, one could restart after pressing, pulling or turning something.
    What a saving of time and effort![50]

Of course, he is bordering on polemics with a statement like this, but it should be clear what his concerns were: he was clearly fearing that the level of quality and qualifications needed to become a composer was lowered to the extent that the mere use of a system without anything like inspiration and creativity would be enough to gain acceptance as a modern composer.

In addition to avant-garde composers, he also blamed the music journalists of his time for the crisis. In November 1927, he criticised music journalists by accusing them

---

[48] '*Que signifie tout ce remue-ménage pour Schubert? Jamais centenaire ne fut fêté comme celui du plus romantique des romantiques! Le romantisme n'est donc pas la chose abominable qu'on voulait nous faire croire? Verra-t-on bientôt les caméléons de l'avantgarde nous offrir de suaves romances sans paroles à la manière de l'immortel Félix? (Il faut toujours que ce soit à la manière de quelqu'un).*'; 'Symptôme rassurant', in *Le Guide du concert*, 7 December 1928, p. 299.

[49] '*Prenez une ligne mélodique aussi vulgaire que possible. Faites-la harmoniser par un enfant qui n'a jamais fait d'études musicales. Saupoudrez le tout de dissonances inutiles et servez chaud.*'; 'Recette pour faire une Sonatine moderne (1929)', in *Le Guide du concert*, 25 January 1929; also in the Italian journal *Mom-Mus*, 24 January 1929.

[50] '*Puisque la mécanique est à l'ordre du jour, pourquoi n'inventerait-on pas une machine à composer? / La consonance, la cohérence et la forme étant proscrites, il n'y aurait aucun inconvénient à s'en rapporter au hasard pour la facture des œuvres musicales. Si le hasard se montrait trop réactionnaire, on recommencerait après avoir pressé, tiré ou tourné quelque chose. / Quelle économie de temps et d'efforts!*'; 'Appel aux inventeurs', in *Le Guide du concert*, 26 April 1929, p. 862.

of not knowing enough about music, but of writing long articles with sham knowledge that made readers feel like experts, particularly when they try to be 'up to date'.

The enemies of music
Real music has many enemies: sport, literature, the virtuoso, the theatre – but the worst of all is the music journalist, who misleads the audience and maintains snobbery.
　The music journalist should not be confused with the music historian or the music critic. They contribute many valuable works. By music journalist I mean the man who indulges from noon to two o'clock in long and learned articles full of nonsense. Although these articles are rarely read and even less often understood, they impress. People think that a work must be of great value for so many things to be said. Instead of recognising the inconsistencies served to them in a cold manner, the public is sinking into comprehension, even enthusiasm, for fear of not appearing 'up to date'. Is there a cure? Unfortunately, I don't see any, unless music journalists are required to prove that they have some knowledge of the art on which they write.[51]

Finally, the 'young geniuses' of the avant-garde that he alluded to ironically in the 1928 issue of *Kornog* also found expression in a 'composition' that appeared in one of the five volumes of *À la manière de* … . Number 16 in volume 3 (1927) features a piece called *Jeune génie de l'avant garde* – it is the only piece that did not require any pastiche music and not even a composer to paraphrase; a verbal direction was quite enough:

Fig. 9.4: Hennessy's mockery of young avant-garde composers (1927)[52]

16

JEUNE GÉNIE DE L'AVANT GARDE

Mettez beaucoup de notes, n'importe lesquelles, sauf celles qu'il faut.

―――⬥―――

As understandable as Hennessy's position may be, his statements also show that he did not make the effort to see the modernity in Schönberg, something he could

---

[51] *'La musique pure a de nombreux ennemis: le sport, la littérature, le virtuose, le théâtre – mais le pire de tous c'est le musicographe, qui induit le public en erreur et entretient le snobisme. / Il ne faut pas confondre le musicographe avec l'historien ou avec le critique musical. On doit à ces derniers maintes œuvres précieuses. Par musicographe j'entends le Monsieur qui cherche midi à quatorze heures en de longs et savants articles truffés d'inepties. Quoique ces articles soient peu lus et encore moins souvent compris, ils impressionnent. Les gens se disent qu'une œuvre doit avoir une grande valeur pour que l'on en dise tant de choses. De sorte qu'au lieu de recevoir froidement les incohérences qu'on lui sert, le public singe la compréhension, voire même l'enthousiasme, de peur de ne pas paraître "à la page". Y a-t-il un remède? Hélas, je n'en vois pas, à moins que l'on exige des musicographes les preuves qu'ils ont quelques connaissances de l'art sur lequel ils écrivent.'*; 'Les ennemis de la Musique', in *Le Guide du concert*, 11 November 1927.
[52] 'Put in any old notes, no matter which, except the required ones.'

have done, for instance, by drawing a parallel to other art forms. Particularly in painting and sculpture, but also in other arts, there had for years been an ongoing trend towards abstraction and new forms, many of which were radical breaks with traditional ideas of beauty as well as the meaning and purpose of a work of art – if one compares naturalism in art with tonality in music. While Hennessy did not sacrifice his artistic integrity for the sake of modernity, neither did Schönberg sacrifice his own for the sake of comprehensibility.

And still, Hennessy's outspoken criticism, his cynicism and sarcastic humour, and his serious worries are more than just conservative reactionism. That would be something one might, perhaps, accuse a composer with who continued to write tonal music in the 1950s, 60s or beyond (and there were many), when another World War had occurred and the arts were yet further removed from traditional models. But Hennessy's verbal and artistic response to Schönberg in the 1910s and 20s is that of a concerned artist warning his contemporaries against developments that, in his view, were against human nature, against quality and craft as the basic means of artists, and against art as an expression of something else (as opposed to the idea of *l'art pour l'art*), etc. – Hennessy remained a firm believer in the expressiveness of music, be it in the form of descriptive, programmatic music or as an outlet for cultural identity.

In France generally, the musically literate public was as strongly divided about Schönberg and his impact as probably everywhere. Though an unlikely alliance, he had strong supporters in Ravel and *Les Six* (particularly Milhaud), to cite but the most prominent names, and critics in d'Indy and most (if not all) of the Breton group of composers, particularly Le Flem and Vuillemin. It is interesting (and troubling) that much of the critique toward the avant-garde is barely concealed anti-Semitism in an increasingly violent and racist language. Fulcher noted that the term '"[m]odernist" was still often used synonymously with undesirable cultural change and with "the Jewish" in this period'.[53] Vuillemin's equation of foreigners' music with bad taste and his implicitly expressed ideas of immigrant or visiting modern musicians and Jewish influence pre-empts much of what was still to come in the course of the 1930s.[54]

It is unlikely that, under such circumstances, Hennessy would still have been friends with Vuillemin as he was before the War. Not only was he a foreigner himself, he also had no fear of contact with the Germans, having studied there and still entertaining contacts with German musicians and the musical press. However, another former friend of Hennessy's, Hugo Rasch in Berlin, went in a very similar direction. An early member of the Nazi party (the NSDAP) and their paramilitary wing (the S.A.), he not only wrote for the *Allgemeine Musikzeitung* but was now also the music critic of the *Völkischer Beobachter* (the official news organ of the Nazis) and was a high-ranking officer in the music section of the Reichskulturkammer (from 1934) under Richard Strauss' direction.[55]

---

[53] Fulcher, *The Composer as Intellectual*, p. 381 (fn. 556).
[54] Louis Vuillemin: 'Concerts métèques', in *Le Courrier musical*, as reviewed by Jane Fulcher, *The Composer as Intellectual*, p. 196.
[55] Fred. K. Prieberg: *Handbuch Deutsche Musiker 1933–1945* (Kiel: the author, 2005), p. 5432–5.

It is very evident that musical nationalism (or, in France, regionalism) was no longer the innocent child of *fin-de-siècle* musical Romanticism that helped shape musical identity in so many countries. It was now increasingly interpreted as the 'healthy' alternative to an unhealthy international avant-garde under Jewish influence and instrumentalised to erect walls and borders.

Although Swan Hennessy has once ascribed the rise of the avant-garde to the aftereffects of the War and the 'awakening of Israel' (in *Kornog*, 1928, as above), this may well be interpreted as an observation only. Hennessy is very clear and succinct in his critique of the avant-garde, but he never employs anti-Semitic language in the manner of d'Indy or Vuillemin. On the contrary, he openly supported modern Jewish composers when the situation arose. An example is his promotion of the Jewish-Polish composer Joachim Mendelson (1892–1943) and his interpreters, the Hungaro-American Roth Quartet. Mendelson lived in Paris between 1929 and 1935 and must have been supported one way or another by Hennessy upon his arrival. Perhaps his Polish wife Claire intermediated. On 9 June 1928, the Roth Quartet performed Hennessy's early *Suite*, Op. 46, Mendelson's String Quartet Op. 7 as a world premiere, the first French performance of a quartet by Wladimir Vogel (1896–1984), a Jewish-Russian composer, closing with Schumann's Quartet Op. 41. Hennessy missed the American music critic Irving Schwerke in the audience and wrote to him the following day:

> I expected to see you at the salle des Agriculteurs last night. I should have liked you to hear my first quartett played by Roth – the more so as you did not seem to care about my second. [...]
> Joachim Mendelssohn's work is interesting and well written and that of Vladimir Vogel, tho' incoherent enough to satisfy the most advanced modernist, contains some clever writing.[56]

Whatever the exact nature of Hennessy's support for Mendelson, he recommended him here to a music critic. After Hennessy had died in October 1929, Mendelson wrote a Chamber Symphony that is dedicated '*à la mémoire de Swan Hennessy*' (published in Paris with Eschig, 1938).

It is also noteworthy that Hennessy found words of praise for the works of Mendelson and Vogel (the latter a dodecaphonic composition),[57] although the latter was clearly not his 'cup of tea'.

In his letter to Schwerke, he also expressed his sadness that the audience attendance was poor, saying:

---

[56] Letter to Schwerke, 10 June 1928; Library of Congress, Irving Schwerke Collection, not yet catalogued, see reference LCCN: 2014571130. See further below for more letters from Hennessy to Schwerke, also Appendix 5, A.5. 'Mendelssohn' is spelt here as in the original letter, but both this and the spelling in the programme ('Mendelshon') is incorrect.

[57] Vogel's quartet (1924) is now considered lost; see his entry in MGG II, biographical section vol. 17 (2007), c. 169.

It is a sad and significant thing that such men should only be able to half fill the salle des Agriculteurs, and will probably (unless you will say a word or two for them) be passed over in silence by the important critics.
I suppose the Parisian public reasons like the old lady who asked why she should be expected to pay 5 frs to hear four musicians when she could hear a full orchestra for the same money.

Fig. 9.5a+b: Front and back of the programme to the concert by the Roth Quartet, June 1928

SALLE DES AGRICULTEURS
8, RUE D'ATHÈNES

CENTRE INTERNATIONAL DE MUSIQUE
52, RUE JACOB, 6e · R. C. SEINE 224-429 · TÉL. : LITTRÉ 23-43

SAMEDI 9 JUIN 1928
A 21 HEURES

SIX CONCERTS

QUATUOR ROTH

ROTH - ANTAL - MOLNAR - VAN DOORN

SIXIÈME CONCERT

PRIX DES PLACES : 30 FR. - 20 FR. - 10 FR. (DROITS COMPRIS)

BILLETS : A LA SALLE — CHEZ DURAND, 4, PLACE DE LA MADELEINE — ROUART & LEROLLE, 40, BOULEVARD MALESHERBES — ROUDANEZ, 9, RUE DE MÉDICIS — AU B. M., 32, RUE TRONCHET — AU GUIDE-BILLETS, 20, AVENUE DE L'OPÉRA — AU C. I. M., 25, RUE JACOB — A LA SEMAINE A PARIS, 22, RUE DE CONDÉ — SÉNART — ESCHIG — HAMELLE — RICORDI — LAUDY — HEUGEL.

LE QUATUOR ROTH DONNERA, AU COURS DE LA SAISON 1928-29, UNE SÉRIE DE SIX CONCERTS

PROGRAMME

1. PREMIER QUATUOR OP. 46 · SWAN HENNESSY
ALLEGRO
ADAGIO
ALLEGRETTO
ANDANTE SOSTENUTO VIVACISSIMO

SWAN HENNESSY, d'origine irlandaise, est né en 1866 aux Etats-Unis d'Amérique. Sa musique a souvent un caractère celtique très prononcé, bien qu'il n'emploie que rarement des airs du folklore ; dans le Quatuor op. 46, on en retrouve seulement dans le final

2. QUATUOR OP. 7 ·· JOACHIM MENDELSSHON
(1re AUDITION, DÉDIÉ AU QUATUOR ROTH)
MODERATO MA CON SPIRITO
LARGO
ALLEGRO CON BRIO

JOACHIM MENDELSSOHN, né à Varsovie en 1890, a fait ses études dans cette ville avec Opienski. Ses œuvres comprennent des études symphoniques jouées par les Orchestres Philarmoniques de Berlin, de Varsovie, ainsi que par divers orchestres polonais, des pièces pour piano et ce Quatuor op. 7

3. QUATUOR .... WLADIMIR VOGEL
(1re AUDITION A PARIS, DÉDIÉ AU QUATUOR ROTH)
CORRENTE LENTO
GLISSANDO
PIZZICATO
FUGATO

WLADIMIR VOGEL, est né à Moscou en 1896, élève de Busoni. Ses œuvres sont d'une écriture tout à fait personnelle, qui a fait dire qu'il fallait « oublier tout ce qu'on était habitué à entendre pour s'accoutumer sans restriction à une manière nouvelle de s'exprimer en musique ». « Manière née de la poésie même de la matière du quatuor ». Ses œuvres comprennent entre autres : Suite pour orchestre à cordes et timbales - Quatuor à cordes (joué au Festival de la Société Internationale de Musique Moderne en 1927) - Simphonia fugata (jouée à Berlin 1928) - Chœurs pour chœurs mixtes, solistes et ensemble de saxophones, etc.....

4. QUATUOR OP. 41, N° 1·· ROBERT SCHUMANN
INTRODUZIONE ; ALLEGRO
SCHERZO
ADAGIO
PRESTO

MM. FERI ROTH ET ANTAL JOUENT DES VIOLONS "GALLICANNE"

The event was not 'passed over in silence' by the critics (Hennessy's press books has cuttings from *Le Gaulois*, *Le Courrier musical*, *Le Monde musical*, and *La Liberté*), but Schwerke did indeed pick up Hennessy's remarks, even using parts of his phrasing, writing a 'review' of a concert he did not attend for the *Chicago Tribune*:

> The Roth Quartet, which played Saturday evening, did not perform to the packed house these people deserve. The chances are the Parisian public reasons like the old lady who asked why she should be expected to pay five francs to hear four musicians, when she could hear a whole orchestra for the same money. However such considerations might be, the Roth Quartet gave an impeccable interpretation of Swan Hennessy's *Quartet op.* 46. Joachim Mendelsshon's (1890, Warsaw) *Quartet op.* 7 (1st audition) was similarly well-treated. In three movements, this work is interesting, reveals advanced workmanship, though one might desire more of the clarity and frankness that characterises the music of Joachim Mendelsshon's almost namesake, a certain Felix.[58]

We see from the way Swan Hennessy speaks or writes about Schönberg that he can be quite frank, does not hide his criticism behind diplomatic formulations, and can employ a very direct, at times polemic, and (in private) impolite language. His satirical compositions are ultimately aimed at ridiculing modern techniques such as polytonality and dodecaphony, even though he brilliantly and amusingly uses these techniques to show how easily they can be copied by any composer of average ability. And he has been similarly direct with regard to Max Reger and Erik Satie, as we have seen before, which clearly speaks against any potential assumption that his arguments may have been anti-Semitically motivated.

It seems, in fact, that Hennessy had a reputation for being all too frank, which may have been a reason why some French composers were not very interested in making his acquaintance. In a 1924 interview, the American contralto Radiana Pazmor remembered Hennessy whose *Trois Chansons espagnoles*, Op. 42bis she had premiered in Berlin in 1922. Her characterisation is quite enlightening:

> The songs of Swan Hennessy, an Irish-American, who has lived for years in Paris and is well known on the continent, were written for my Berlin debut and brought the house down by their delightful humor. Hennessy is what the French call a numero, which, being interpreted, means an extraordinary character. A big man, gray and jovial, with a real Irish wit and the Hibernian tendency to be 'agin' things, adored by his friends, and cordially hated by his enemies, of whom his weakness for saying just what he thinks has created him many.[59]

* * *

---

[58] *The Chicago Tribune*, 16 June 1928.
[59] *Pacific Coast Music Review* 46:24, 15 September 1924, p. 6.

Banlieues ... . **Six Petites pièces, Op. 69 (1925–9) for piano**

From about 1925, Hennessy's luck with his publisher began to wane. Although Hennessy seemed to have been on good terms with the new managing director at Eschig, the composer Eugène Cools, judging from a number of common recital appearances, they did not automatically accept everything that Hennessy offered. A first victim was *Banlieues ...*, Op. 69, originally consisting of three pieces and subtitled *Trois Petites pièces*. Hennessy published these himself in 1926 as *'Propriété de l'auteur'* – the first time he did such a thing since his Op. 13 in 1901. Maybe the little pieces were simply not substantial enough for Cools: a second edition with six pieces then appeared with Éditions Max Eschig (the new brand name from late 1927) in 1929. The Eschig publication still acknowledged Hennessy's copyright for the first three pieces. His manuscript for the second group of three pieces has a receipt stamp from SACEM, the French music rights organisation, of 27 June 1929. Still, it is likely that the completion of the second group rather dates to late 1928: Hennessy wrote a little explanatory note about the work for a January 1929 issue of *Le Guide du concert*.[60] Although the second group is therefore several years younger than the first, he did not change the opus number.

Hennessy was very much aware himself that *Banlieues ...* consisted of little, unpretentious pieces. Otherwise he would not have given them this subtitle. They are comparable to his *Épigrammes d'un solitaire*, Op. 55 of 1924 in that they are small but perfect genre paintings in an ideal Impressionist manner. In the present collection Hennessy's theme is the different character of Parisian suburbs, and in the aforementioned notice in *Le Guide du concert* he explains them thus:

> These 6 pieces are short impressions of the suburbs of Paris. Clamart (horticultural suburb); Aubervilliers (industrial suburb, dominated by the noise of factories); Meudon, bucolic suburb, home to lovers, birds and boy scouts); Robinson (popular and jovial suburb); Verrières (with solitary and mysterious woods) and Bourg-la-Reine. They are dedicated to Maurice Servais.[61]

He does not say much here about Bourg-la-Reine, but he does in a similar description in his commented list of works, which nicely complements the above:

> Clamart – souvenir of a walk in the woods – Aubervilliers, sad and dark – Meudon with its bird songs and passages of boy scouts – Robinson full of popular life – Verrières with its delicate charm – Bourg-la-Reine of a serious and sad character.[62]

---

[60] *Le Guide du concert* 15:17, 25 January 1929, p. 492.
[61] *'Ces 6 pièces sont de courtes impressions des banlieues de Paris. Clamart (banlieue horticole) ; Aubervilliers (banlieue laborieuse, dominée par le grondement des usines) ; Meudon, banlieue bucolique, repaire de amoureux, des oiseaux et des boy-scouts) ; Robinson (banlieue populaire et joviale) ; Verrières (aux bois solitaires et mystérieux) et Bourg-la-Reine. Elles sont dédiées à Maurice Servais.'.* This is the complete notice, anonymous, but as usual in this journal, most likely by Hennessy himself (op. cit.).
[62] *'Clamart – souvenir d'une promenade dans les bois – Aubervilliers triste et sombre – Meudon avec ses chants d'oiseaux et passages de boy-scouts – Robinson plein de vie populaire – Verrières d'un charme délicat – Bourg-la-Reine d'un caractère grave et triste.'*

In other words, there are three suburbs dominated by the beauty of nature, in particular, by woods (Clamart, Meudon, Verrières), two that make a rather sad impression, one of them on account of its industrial, built environment (Aubervilliers) and another for no specified reason (Bourg-la-Reine), and finally one that is rather lively and popular (Robinson). All except Aubervilliers were within easy reach from Hennessy's residence. Meudon and Clamart are neighbouring towns just east of Versailles in the south-western agglomeration of Paris. South of these is Robinson, and again bordering further south is Verrières(-le-Buisson). Bourg-la-Reine is also in the area, slightly to the east, situated between Sceaux and Villejuif. Aubervilliers, on the other hand, is just north of today's *Periphérique* around Paris, east of Saint Ouen. From his home in Montparnasse, passing through Montrouge, which has also previously played a role in his works (Op. 27 No. 4 and Op. 32), Hennessy would be in those five southern suburbs within a short time. He apparently associated the southern suburbs with green nature, the north with industry. Why Bourg-la-Reine was for him 'of a serious and sad character', remains his secret; perhaps he went there on a grey and rainy day.

And we can be sure that all six pieces result from personal experience, as is the case with all of Hennessy's descriptive piano music: he extensively explored his environment and took his experience as inspiration for his music. We also learn here that Hennessy preferred the southern suburbs to the northern and that he seems to have spent a lot of time hiking in the woods. Apart from bird calls, groups of boy scouts seem to have been commonplace in Parisian suburban woods at this period – he already included them in *Au bord de la forêt*, Op. 21 (1906). The woods of Clamart have also been a subject of his music before, in *La Forêt de Clamart à l'aube*, Op. 55 No. 1.

Clamart is written in 6/8 time in the key of A major, but this frequently modulates, including a phrase in E major in the middle of the A–B–A structure. The theme is at first treated canonically and often moves in parallel thirds, sixths and octaves. With the background of Hennessy's own interpretation, it creates are free walking movement, with interested looks left and right of the path, an interested observation in the middle section, concluding with a firm return to the initial idea. *Aubervilliers* is also in an A–B–A form, with the 'A' part suggesting the low rumbling noise of the machines in the town's factories (Ex. 9.4), accompanying a dreary theme in F minor.

Ex. 9.4.: *Banlieues* …, Op. 69 No. 2 *Aubervilliers*, bars 1–7

Still adhering to the A–B–A form (albeit now with a strongly abridged second 'A' that is but a short reminder of the first), *Meudon* is filled with 'external' musical influences that combine to make some jolly cacophony. If this was a piece of abstract music, it would probably be one of Hennessy's most modern. It begins with a syncopated countermovement of the two hands (the right hand in regular crotchets, the left shifted by a quaver, using crotchets and quavers), which is followed by a section B of irregular interjections of bird calls, mixing with a cornet (*clairon*) signal and a chant from a group of boy scouts in the distance, which form a curious melange of pitches (Ex. 9.5). In the last bar, the cacophony subsides to a peaceful D major seventh chord.

Ex. 9.5.: *Banlieues* …, Op. 69 No. 3 *Meudon*, bars 9–15

Robinson is the least Impressionist of the six pieces – written in a straightforward F major in quick allegro forming a hopping dance movement, befitting the good-tempered 'jovial and popular' character of this suburb. *Verrières*, to be played *lento con tenerezza*, returns to more contemporary music and is the least transparent piece in formal terms. Some elements have an improvisatory effect, like the interspersed bars with *appoggiaturas* and semiquaver triplets, and there are two reoccurrences of a cornet signal by the ubiquitous groups of boy scouts. At the beginning and end the melody runs through the left hand, which gives the piece a formal frame, but it is not such an obvious A–B–A form as previously. It is quite an attractive, somewhat mysterious piece. *Bourg-la-Reine* is in C minor, and the dreariness that Hennessy appears to have experienced there is expressed by a left hand in regular quavers in quartal harmony to a melody written in parallel octaves almost throughout. The music may have been inspired by Hennessy's large collection of late nineteenth-century Russian piano music.

Hennessy himself played the first three pieces of *Banlieues* ... in Paris in November 1927 and in Brussels in April 1928. The complete work in six pieces was first performed by the dedicatee, Maurice Servais, on 29 January 1929 at the Salle Érard.

Having heard the first three pieces in concert, the American music critic Irving Schwerke wrote about them, '(t)hey are full of piquant wit and withal quite atmospheric. The times they have been played in public have always been marked by success'.[63] Of Servais's first complete performance, Suzanne Demarquez wrote in *Le Courrier musical*:

> In the course of a programme ranging from Couperin to Swan Hennessy, this pianist could showcase the different sides of his talent to which, it seems to me, intimate pieces such as Swan Hennessy's *Banlieues*, a charming sequel where a dark melody expresses the grey skies in *Aubervilliers* while a cheerful rhythm, interrupted by cornet calls, recalls the popular joys of *Meudon* or *Robinson*. [...][64]

When they were performed in another 'Festival Swan Hennessy' after the composer's death, Maurice Imbert picked out the two pieces he liked best: 'the most evocative are "Robinson" – with its whirlwinds – and "Meudon" – which we heard as if being reflected in the water'.[65]

* * *

Mid-1920s compositions such as the jazz-inspired *Deux Morceaux*, Op. 68 and *Quatre Morceaux*, Op. 71 or the late-Impressionist *Banlieues* ..., Op. 69 should not hide the fact that Hennessy's actual focus in those years was on 'Celtic' music. Concerts by the Société Artistique et Littéraire de l'Ouest and other events featured his chamber music, with his Opp. 52, 54, 58, and 59 increasingly establishing themselves in the repertoire. He often participated in these himself (if they involved a piano) and in other cases he most certainly was present.

I have only found three instances of Hennessy performing works by someone else. The first was at a *'Concert de Musique Celtique'* organised by an Association des Étudiants Bretons à Paris, together with a mixed-voice choir from the Cercle Celtique de Paris that took place at the students' association's headquarters at 61 rue Madame on 12 December 1925 (6th arrondissement, just beside the Jardin de Luxembourg). This concert featured piano music by Rhené-Baton (played by Marthe Le Breton), arrangements in Breton language of Scottish and Irish traditional songs, art songs in a Breton

---

[63] *The Chicago Tribune*, 9 June 1928; reprinted in *The Musical Digest*, October 1928.

[64] '*Au cours d'un programme allant de Couperin à Swan Hennessy, ce pianiste sut faire valoir les différentes faces de son talent auquel conviennent mieux, me semble-t-il, les pièces de caractère intime comme les* Banlieues, *de Swan Hennessy, suite charmante où une sombre mélodie exprime les ciels gris à* Aubervilliers *tandis qu'un rythme allègre, coupé d'appels de clairon, évoque les joies populaires de* Meudon *ou de* Robinson. [...]'; Suzanne Demarquez in *Le Courrier musical* 15 February 1929.

[65] '[...] *les plus évocatrices sont "Robinson" – avec ses flonflons – et "Meudon" – qu'on entend comme se refléter dans l'eau.*'; Maurice Imbert in *Journal des débats*, 3 March 1931, p. 4.

style by Alice Sauvrezis, folk song arrangements by Maurice Duhamel, Louis-Albert Bourgault-Ducaudray, and the abbé H. Guillerm, Hennessy's *Petit trio celtique*, Op. 52 and finally Paul Ladmirault's *Airs de bibiou trécorois* for piano duet, performed by Alice Sauvrezis and Swan Hennessy.

The second was a *'Deuxième Séance de Musique Celtique Moderne'*, held at the Caméléon concert hall on 13 January 1926. This began with Hennessy performing the *Cinq Morceaux irlandais de Carolan (1670–1736)* by the Cork-based Irish composer Denis Breen, a work dedicated to Hennessy in a gesture of thanks for Hennessy dedicating his own *Huit Pièces celtiques*, Op. 51 to Breen. Hennessy took care that these arrangements of pieces by the Irish harper Turlough Carolan were published by Max Eschig in Paris. The concert also featured three art songs for voice, piano, and string quartet by Alice Sauvrezis, extracts from *En Bretagne* for piano by Rhené-Baton played by Marthe Le Breton, Hennessy's *Sérénade*, Op. 65 for string quartet, *Avril* for piano by Paul Le Flem, and *Ouverture, fugue et variation* for piano by Guy Ropartz, performed by one Mme Bleuzet. The quartet role was filled by the Quatuor Loiseau.

Hennessy performed the Breen piece again two weeks later, also at the Caméléon, at an Irish event on 1 February 1926 presided over by the Irish writer and fervent nationalist Lord Ashbourne, born William Gibson and also known as Liam Mac Giolla Bhride (1868–1942), a figure, converted to Catholicism, known at the time for always walking about Paris in a green Irish kilt. A speech by the Irish diplomat Leopold H. Kerney was followed by Hennessy's *Trio*, Op. 54 for two clarinets and bassoon, Irish songs arranged for violin, harp and piano by a trio of three sisters named Virginia, Frances, and Marguerite Morgan, Irish folk songs sung by 'Mme Paul Vulliaud O'Sullivan', accompanied by Hennessy, and Hennessy's rendering of Breen's Carolan pieces.

* * *

Trio, Op. 70 (1925) for violin, flute, bassoon

The *Trio*, Op. 70 is another of Hennessy's unusual chamber music combinations, written for violin, flute, and bassoon. Completed in or before September 1925,[66] the parts were originally published by Hennessy himself (*'Propriété de l'auteur'*), the score somewhat later by Max Eschig & Cie. in 1927 with the copyright assigned to Hennessy. The work is dedicated to the three musicians who gave the first performance at the Salle de Géographie of the Sorbonne University in November 1926, Émile Loiseau (leader of Hennessy's favoured string quartet), the prominent flutist Gaston Blanquart, and Gustave Dhérin, a later professor at the Conservatoire (from 1934).

As in the *Trio*, Op. 54, there is an 'Intermezzo' between the second and the third movement, which must be treated as a separate item, but Hennessy recognised that, with 30 bars only, it might not be generally regarded as a full movement. Hennessy gauged the overall duration of the work at about eight minutes.

---

[66] Gaston Blanquart thanked Hennessy for the (manuscript) score in a letter dated 25 September 1925 (see Appendix 5.A.6). This contradicts Hennessy's commentary in *Le Guide du concert* (5 November 1926, p. 135) that the work was written during the summer holidays 1926.

The different sound colours of the three instruments mix astonishingly well and at the same time guarantee the transparency and traceability of the score throughout. One bowed and two wind-blown instruments, of which one is a double reed, may initially sound exotic, but it is in fact an excellent choice. We have seen before that in his 'Celtic' music Hennessy sometimes uses Western classical instruments as a substitute for instruments used in traditional music. In this case, we have a lively gathering of a fiddle, a flute, and the nasal sound of a bagpipe.

The only irritating aspect about this approach is that Hennessy's music is, in fact, written as if it would resemble traditional music, played by 'classical' performers and arranged in a classical form. The work is diatonic in a very straightforward manner, the first movement is in A flat major (*'Moderato quasi allegretto'*) in his typical abridged sonata form, despite its clear modal modulations to a D Lydian scale in the development and G Locrian in a second subject; the second movement is a scherzo (*'Allegro, "bien rythmé"'*) in C minor with irregular metres borrowed from Breton traditional music; the Intermezzo stands in the preceding movement's parallel major, E flat major; and the final movement is a quick *Allegro* in an Irish reel rhythm that returns to A flat major – in other words, in a long-established classical form. The uniqueness of the work, therefore, does not lie in any formal, technical or harmonic experiments but in a rare application of a classical form to a Breton/Irish environment that has not seen so many original works of this kind in its art music history.

The only dissonant moments in the first movement occur in transitory bars of two minims between the formal sections of the sonata form. Ex. 9.6 shows the return from the Lydian mode to A flat major between the first development and the beginning of a side theme (see bars 17 and 19).

Ex. 9.6: *Trio*, Op. 70, 1st movt, bars 16–23

The second movement derives its interest from frequent bar changes, often for one bar only, beginning with 5/4, 7/4 (two bars), 6/4, 5/4, 7/4 (three bars) before a longer section in 6/4 begins from bar 9. In his commented list of works, Hennessy describes this first section as being influenced by Breton traditional music, followed by music in the Irish style. This reminds of the *Petit trio celtique*, Op. 52, which had alternating movements in a Breton and an Irish style. The short Intermezzo is not a slow movement, rather it has the character of a fanfare calling for attention. Despite its brevity, it tries various combinations of two-part writing between the three instruments.

The third (full) movement exploits the stylistic qualities of an Irish reel, ending the work with a lively Irish movement in the manner of his previous *Suite*, Op. 46 or the *Trio*, Op. 54. For this work he does not use any existing Irish tune, although it reminds of numerous tunes of its kind. The work begins with a theme in the violin to an accompaniment of the bassoon in (mainly) the alternating pitches A♭ and E♭; following an upbeat, from bar 9 the flute replaces the violin. Although notated in A flat major, from the middle of bar 5 Hennessy introduces a G♭ pitch and from bar 13 a C♭ as well. These are meant to give a modal flavour; they are no proper harmonic modulations to D flat major or even G flat major (Ex. 9.7).

Ex. 9.7: *Trio*, Op. 70, 4th movt, bars 1–6

A second motivic idea, in bars 19 to 28, imitates hunting horns – an idea that transports the scene to an Anglo-Irish hunting party in the distance that briefly distracts from the Irish festivities. A turbulent finale of all three instruments brings the work to a close.

It is through means like these that Hennessy creates his own alternative to the modernist trends of his time. Scales, melodic turns of phrase, and rhythms derived from the traditional music of Ireland and Brittany were still new and unusual in French art music. Clad in a traditional costume of classical conventions, his music builds on established formal models and would make him sound conservative to many French concert goers nevertheless. But he has undoubtedly found his own distinctive voice by looking neither towards Vienna nor to strange exoticisms, but by following his motto 'Why look far away for what is often within reach'.

The *Allgemeine Musikzeitung* considered the work …

> A simple three-movement little work with inserted intermezzo. Simple theme, free polyphonic arrangement. The small movements are pleasing and fresh. All in all, a very sympathetic work.[67]

Le Courrier musical was particularly taken by the balance between the three different instruments, calling it 'from beginning to end a wonder of sound balance'.[68]

Trois Chansons celtiques, Op. 72 (1926) for medium voice and piano

Hennessy's *Trois Chansons celtiques*, Op. 72 is a small cycle of songs on 'Celtic' themes. Though a little less pretentious than some earlier vocal music, this work is remarkable as another example of the composer's idea of pan-Celticism. Each of the three songs deal with a different Celtic region, No. 1, *La Chanson du rouet* to words by Charles Leconte de Lisle is designed as a Scottish song; No. 2, *Berceuse d'Armorique* on a poem by the Breton national poet Anatole Le Braz is about Brittany; and the third, *Le Départ des pêcheurs* is a setting of a poem by Pierre Scize to an Irish traditional melody. Only in the score of the third, Hennessy explains that the tune is borrowed from the Petrie Collection of Irish traditional music. But the musical character of the first two clearly betrays their Scottish and Breton influences. What's more, the first song is another of Hennessy's settings of one of the *Chansons écossaises* by Leconte de Lisle (and again with a clear Scottish musical character), while the choice of the poet for No. 2 and the use of uneven metrical structures in the music clearly define Brittany.

The work was composed in 1926 and published with Max Eschig & Cie. in 1927. The single pieces are dedicated to the music critic Henri Collet, the new Eschig director Eugène Cools, and the poet Pierre Scize respectively. The first performance took

---

[67] '*Ein einfaches dreisätziges Werkchen mit eingeschobenem Intermezzo. Schlichte Thematik, freie polyphone Bearbeitung. Die kleinen Sätze sind gefällig und frisch. Im ganzen eine sehr sympathische Arbeit.*'; Max Donisch in *Allgemeine Musikzeitung* 56:15, 12 April 1929, p. 440.

[68] '[…] *et ce Trio pour violon, flute et basson, qui est d'un bout à l'autre une merveille d'équilibre sonore.*'; Henri Petit in *Le Courrier musical*, 15 March 1931.

place in mid-December 1927 at the Salle du Guide de Concert, Paris, with Marthe Saisset and the composer.

La Chanson du rouet ('The Spinning Wheel Song') is a simple song in two stanzas set in F major. There is a short pre- and postlude and some chromatic transitions between some of the poetic lines, but otherwise he clearly remains in his chosen tonality. Hennessy makes ample use of the 'Scotch snap' to give the piece its Scottish imprint.

Through his earlier engagements with Breton traditional music, Hennessy had learned that uneven rhythms such as 5/4 and 7/4 frequently occur in this repertory, and these he has applied in the *Berceuse d'Armorique* ('Breton Lullaby'). This song is marked *'Lent et triste'* and set in C minor. There is, of course, an autobiographical reason for this utter sadness and it is revealed in Le Braz's text, which speaks of a storm that begins to rise with the moon over the see while a child, ignorant of the impending doom, falls asleep. This poem must have reminded Hennessy of his childhood experience when his mother drowned in a storm on the coast of Roscoff in Brittany in 1880 while the young composer was staying at home alone, perhaps sleeping. Normally, a lullaby would not need to express such sadness as here, but now we know why. The song in A–B–A form begins and ends in 6/8 time, changing to 5/4 for the parts of the text that conjure up the storm. There is some pretty imitative writing between voice and piano and a number of unusual major-minor inversions that attract attention; the piece ends on C major.

It would be interesting to know why Hennessy did not choose an Irish poet for the Irish song (that he may well have translated into French himself), *Le Départ des pêcheurs* ('The Fishermen's Departure'). To the best of my knowledge, Pierre Scize, artist's name for Michel-Joseph Plot (1894–1956) and better known as a dramatist and journalist, did not have any connection to Ireland. Hennessy indicated that the tune of the song is taken from the Petrie Collection. I was not able to identify it there, but found it instead in the second (1809) of the three collections of Irish traditional music by Edward Bunting[69] under the name of 'The Dawning of [the] Day'. There are several songs of this title in various collections, including the Petrie, but it is the Bunting version that comes closest.

For most of its duration, the song is a simple arrangement of an Irish folk song in F major and a standard nineteenth-century harmonisation, of which there are numerous examples in Ireland and Britain, the unusual element, certainly for Irish ears, being the French text. It begins with four bars of a piano introduction, followed by the first stanza of the song (Ex. 9.8). An extended piano postlude ends the piece. Bars 21 to 28, however, deviate strongly from the folk song arrangement idea, with a modulation to an F Phrygian scale and a denser piano accompaniment (Ex. 9.9).

---

[69] Edward Bunting (ed.): *A General Collection of the Ancient Music of Ireland* (London: Clementi & Co., 1809), p. 53; identified through Aloys Fleischmann (ed.): *Sources of Irish Traditional Music c.1600–1855* (New York: Garland Publishing, 1998), vol. 2, p. 900, tune no. 4958. I do not exclude that the tune is also in the Petrie Collection as edited by C.V. Stanford, a collection previously used by Hennessy.

Ex. 9.8.: *Trois Chansons celtiques*, Op. 72 No. 3, *Le Départ des pêcheurs*, bars 4–8

Ex. 9.9.: *Trois Chansons celtiques*, Op. 72 No. 3, *Le Départ des pêcheurs*, bars 21–25

The simplicity and conservativeness of the harmonic writing in this work was apparently regarded as appropriate at least by one of his target groups, the Breton community in Paris. Their central journal very warmly welcomed these songs:

> These poetic works, so delicious, win considerably with the appropriate harmonies, with which they have been piously surrounded by the admirable and wonderful composer, our friend Swan Hennessy.[70]

Fig. 9.6: Hennessy around 1925–6, portrayed by Boris Lipnitzky (Courtesy: Hennessy family)

---

[70] '*Ces œuvres poétiques, déjà délicieuses, gagnent considérablement avec les harmonies appropriés, dont les a pieusement entourées l'admirable et merveilleux compositeur qu'est notre ami Swan Hennessy.*'; in *La Bretagne à Paris*, 7 April 1928.

À la manière de ... (1926–7) for piano

The five volumes of *À la manière de ...* may have been Hennessy's biggest commercial success in terms of sales of his scores. Judging from the public echo, many musically literate people in contemporary France seem to have associated his name with either Celticism or with this series of pastiche works. Each volume contains six pieces named after a prominent European composer from the past and present. With an unmissable wink of the eye, volume 5 ends with a seventh piece, an *Appendice – Swan Hennessy*.

Three of the slim volumes appeared at once in early 1927 under the common title *À la manière de ... 18 Pastiches*. A fourth volume appeared in late 1927, and a fifth in early 1928 – all with Eschig. The series, which has no opus number, contains the following pieces:

- Vol. 1: 1. *Johannes Brahms*; 2. *César Franck*; 3. *Edvard Grieg*; 4. *Robert Schumann*; 5. *Gabriel Fauré*; 6. *Anton Dvořák*.
- Vol. 2 ('2e cahier'): 7. *Richard Strauss*; 8. *Stephen Heller*; 9. *Claude Debussy*; 10. *Benjamin Godard*; 11. *Max Reger et Paul Delmet*; 12. *Alexandre Borodine*.
- Vol. 3 ('3e cahier'): 13. *Félix Mendelssohn-Bartholdy*; 14. *Vincent d'Indy*; 15. *Muzio Clementi*; 16. *Jeune genie de l'avant garde*; 17. *Joaquin Turina*; 18. *Gioacchino Rossini*.
- Vol. 4 ('4e cahier'): 1. *Carl Maria von Weber*; 2. *Domenico Scarlatti*; 3. *Giuseppe Verdi*; 4. *Frédéric Chopin*; 5. *Emmanuel Chabrier*; 6. *Franz Liszt*.
- Vol. 5 ('5e cahier'): 1. *Franz Schubert*; 2. *Georg Friedrich Haendel*; 3. *Jules Massenet*; 4. *Johann Strauss II*; 5. *Maurice Ravel*; 6. *Hugo Wolf*; 7. *Appendice – Swan Hennessy*.

The origin of the first pieces dates back to 1917, but the work in earnest began in 1926. *Anton Dvořák* and *Richard Strauss* at least were written, probably as a pastime, during Hennessy's Swiss 'exile' during the War (see Chapter 7). *Robert Schumann* is identical with his own *Miniatures*, Op. 11 No. 1 of 1889. *Edvard Grieg* and *Richard Strauss* already appeared in the 1924 Evans edition of *Épigrammes d'un solitaire*, Op. 55.

The selection of composers does not necessarily reflect Hennessy's favourites, but it can probably be interpreted as his acknowledgement of 'influence' in one way or another. There are his heroes of the past (Schumann, Schubert, Mendelssohn, Brahms, except Bizet) but also baroque composers (Scarlatti, Handel, but no Bach), near-contemporaries (Fauré, Debussy, Reger, Delmet) and contemporaries (R. Strauss, d'Indy, Turina, Ravel). There is an indirect inclusion of Schönberg (vol. 3, no. 16) and, in volume 4, verbal explanations for the non-inclusion of Satie (see Chapter 5, p. 186) and Wagner.[71] On the other hand, if 'influence' was a criterion for him, the absence of Haydn, Mozart, Beethoven or of Mahler and Stravinsky is striking.

In his commented list of works, Hennessy (typeset by his widow) explained the motivation to write this series thus:

---

[71] '*Richard Wagner manque parce que plusieurs compositeurs contemporains l'ont si parfaitement imité que je ne pouvais pas espérer faire mieux.*' ('Richard Wagner is missing because several contemporary composers have imitated him so perfectly that I could not hope to do better.')

After reading Reboux and Muller's book, Swan Hennessy came up with the idea of rendering the compositional particularities of the following authors to music: [...][72]

Hennessy refers to a popular literary model, a series of short stories, also named *À la manière de* ..., by Paul Reboux and Charles Müller, which appeared in Paris in three volumes published 1908, 1910, and 1913. After the death of Müller in 1914, Reboux continued alone with a fourth (1925) and a fifth (1950) volume. Reboux and Müller had indeed applied the same technique: not directly copying, but adapting and exaggerating the styles of well-known writers.

Of course, in referring to this literary model, Hennessy consciously ignored earlier models in music. The earliest composer to adapt this idea is Alfredo Casella's volume of *À la manière de* ..., Op. 17, which comprised pastiches of Wagner, Fauré, Brahms, Debussy, R. Strauss, and Franck (1911). Maurice Ravel picked up the idea with his two works *À la manière de Borodine* and ... *Chabrier* (1913), which were published alongside two pastiches of d'Indy and Ravel by Casella in 1914. The idea was certainly *en vogue* around this time. The pianist and composer Ermend Bonnal (1880–1944) published in 1924, also with Eschig, *À la manière de* without naming anyone he intended to target. Also with Eschig in 1924 appeared *Trois Pièces à la manière d'Erik Satie* by Henri Cliquet-Pleyel (1894–1963), still in Satie's lifetime. Whether all these composers publicly referred to Reboux and Müller or not, they certainly did not invent the 'genre'. Hennessy must have been aware of Casella's and Ravel's musical adaptation of the idea anyway; it is unimaginable that he did not, even if he did not say so.

It should be clear that the idea of *À la manière de* ... was not just to copy the styles of other composers. While typical traits and manner(ism)s are being exposed and utilised, there is a strong element of parody, irony and satire in these adaptations. For those able to recognise them, this was what made this music so much fun and guaranteed their success. But there were bound to be misunderstandings. In a long review of more than two pages in the Dutch journal *De Muziek*, the composer and critic Willem Pijper (1894–1947) severely criticised Hennessy's approach:

> The pieces by Swan Hennessy [...] 'parody' seventeen authors, whose characteristics for him remained a closed book. As a rule, what he does is: add a few thirds and sixths, and this is called Brahms, take whole tones and major thirds: Debussy (!); a false modulation suggests d'Indy; an Alberti bass: Clementi; a three-four time: Turina; a quick alla-breve with tone repetitions: Rossini. Two scribbles seem to be one size fits all: Grieg and Dvòrak [sic!]. But we no longer call this pastiche, but quotations.[73]

---

[72] '*Après avoir lu le livre de Reboux et Muller, Swan Hennessy a eu l'idée de render en musique les particularités de composition des auteurs suivants:* [...]'.
[73] '*De stukjes van Swan Hennessy* [...] '*parodieeren*' *zeventien auteurs, wier kenmerken voor hem een gesloten boek bleven. In den regel doet hij maar wat: een paar tertsen en sexten, en dat heet het Brahms; wat heele tonen en groote tertsen: Debussy (!); een foute modulatie stelt d'Indy voor; een Albertijnsche bas: Clementi; een driekwartmaat: Turina; een vlug alla-breve met toonrepetities: Rossini. Twee krabbels lijken nog eenigermate: Grieg and Dvòrak. Maar dat noemen wij geen pastiches meer, doch citaten.*'; Willem Pijper: 'Namaak', in *De Muziek* 2 (1927–8), pp. 27–9 [28].

This remained an isolated opinion, though. In general, both the critical and the audience reception was much more positive. In one of his last reviews of a Hennessy publication, Hugo Rasch wrote:

> The creator of so many small, exquisite chamber music works and very remarkable piano music, already known and appreciated here, enters with four new volumes an area that would have to be described as delicate, if not dangerous, if the observer and listener of these piano pieces were not immediately disarmed both by the author's keen powers of observation and by his delicious humour, which is available to him in abundance as an Irishman of blood. As the title suggests, these sketches deal with the most diverse masters and their particular compositional peculiarities. In most cases, these are not caricatures, but rather portraits that have been seen aptly and with a wink of the eye [...], all with their particularly concise twists and turns, etc. Bringing Reger and Delmet together in one piece was an inspiration of a very special kind, which must make the expert laugh. Grieg, Mendelssohn, Schumann, Rossini and Stephen Heller must be regarded as particularly successful, while Richard Strauss, for example, even at his most tender age, may never have written so harmlessly.[74]

After the appearance of the fifth volume, Rasch continued his eulogy by briefly characterising the new pieces:

> Delicious is the clean technique of the experienced Handel, full of frightening sweetness the elegant Massenet, quite genuine the waltz by Johann Strauss, no less like Ravel's Tango. The best of the whole cycle, however, is the one page of Hugo Wolf; I can feel sorry for those who do not break out into liberated laughter in the almost ingenious comprehension of the character of this tone poet in just twenty-nine bars, in which we can find both the 'Spanish' and the Mörike-Wolf with their most typical twists.[75]

---

[74] '*Der Schöpfer so manch kleiner, exquisiter Kammermusikwerke und sehr beachtlicher Klaviermusik, auch bei uns schon gekannt und gewürdigt, betritt hier mit vorläufig vier neuen Heften ein Gebiet, das als heikel, wenn nicht gar gefährlich bezeichnet werden müßte, wäre der Betrachter und Hörer dieser Klavierstücke nicht sofort entwaffnet sowohl durch die sinnfällig scharfe Beobachtungsgabe des Autors als auch durch seinen köstlichen Humor, der ihm als Irländer von Geblüt ja in reichem Maße zur Verfügung steht. Denn diese Skizzen befassen sich, wie der Titel andeutet, mit den verschiedensten Meistern und ihren besonderen Kompositionseigenheiten. Und zwar sind es – in den meisten Fällen – keine Karikaturen, sondern treffend und mit einem lustigen Augenzwinkern gesehene Porträts, [...]. Reger und Delmet zusammen in einem Stück zu bringen, war eine Eingebung ganz aparter Art, die den Kundigen zum Lachen bringen muß. Als besonders gelungen müssen Grieg, Mendelssohn, Schumann, Rossini und Stephen Heller gelten, während beispielsweise Richard Strauß, selbst in zartestem Alter, doch nie so harmlos geschrieben haben dürfte.*'; Hugo Rasch in *Allgemeine Musikzeitung* 55:23, 8 June 1928, p. 759.

[75] '*Köstlich der handwerklich saubere Satz des Routiniers Händel, voll beängstigender Süßigkeit der elegante Massenet, ganz echt der Walzer von Johann Strauß, nicht minder wie Ravels Tango. Das beste des ganzen Zyklus aber ist die eine Seite Hugo Wolf; wer bei dem geradezu genialen Erfassen der Kompositionsweise dieses Tondichters im Rahmen von neunundzwanzig Takten, in denen sich sowohl der 'spanische' wie der Mörike-Wolf mit seinen typischsten Wendungen findet, nicht in befreites Lachen ausbricht, der kann mir leid tun.*'; Hugo Rasch in *Allgemeine Musikzeitung* 56:5, 1 February 1929, p. 117.

The American music critic Irving Schwerke was similarly convinced when he wrote:

> Each piece is an excellent parody, some going one better than the composer imitated. These *pastiches* are more than clever. They reveal uncommonly deep knowledge of the composers represented. Pianists will find in them material for study and for effective public presentation.[76]

There were no reviews of the publication in France, but a number of comments following performances. After a performance of several pieces from the collection by Marthe Le Breton in the northwestern French town of Laval, the local newspaper wrote: 'Mr Hennessy cheered up the audience with his *À la manière de ...*, which were particularly successful.'[77] A Paris recital acknowledged 'a 1st audition of *À la manière de ...* showed us Mr Hennessy, the spiritual and skilful pasticheur of Schubert, Handel, Massenet, J. Strauss, Clémenti, H. Wolf and ... Hennessy himself. He was nicely served by Marthe Le Breton's well-informed musical sense.'[78] Schwerke wrote another comment after a recital by the Polish pianist Richard Byk (the first three volumes are dedicated to Marthe Le Breton, the last two to Richard Byk):

> They are some of the most amusing that have been written in modern times, if it be well understood that parody is not merely facetious imitation but necessitates knowledge, – rarely possessed by would-be parodists! – of the composer thus caricatured.[79]

Still, the French critical response was sparse, which apparently did not impede its public success. In a letter to Schwerke of 24 March 1928, Hennessy contemplated inserting an advertisement in one of the American journals Schwerke wrote for, saying 'They are selling well here, but the sale of music is necessarily limited in Paris, whereas in America there would be a better, or at least a larger field.' (see below for more correspondence with Schwerke). Since about one third of the composers represented in *À la manière de ...* were French, did French critics consider this practice disrespectful, especially as they came from a foreigner? Hennessy sent the first group of three volumes to Léon Vallas, the influential author and biographer of Debussy in Lyon:[80]

---

[76] *The Chicago Tribune*, 9 June 1928 (reprinted in *Musical Digest*, October 1928).

[77] '*M. Hennessy dérida l'assemblée avec ses A la manière de ..., qui furent particulièrement réussis.*'; *Le Regional de l'Ouest*, 9 July 1928.

[78] '[...] *une 1re audition A la manière de ..., nous montra M. Hennessy spirituel et habile pasticheur de Schubert, Haendel, Massenet, J. Strauss, Clémenti, H. Wolf et ... Hennessy lui-même. Il fut joliment servi par le sens musical averti de Mme Marthe Le Breton.*'; Marcel Bernheim in *Le Courrier musical*, 1 January 1929.

[79] *The Chicago Tribune*, 14 May 1928.

[80] Bibliothèque Musicale de Lyon, Ms Vallas 203, pièce 59; see Appendix 5 section A.3 (p. 383, French original with my translation).

Fig. 9.7: Concert programme by Richard Byk including pieces from *À la manière de* ...[81]

Administration de Concerts A. DANDELOT & FILS, (fondée en 1898), 83, Rue d'Amsterdam

PLEYEL (Salle CHOPIN), 8, Rue Daru

Mercredi 16 Mai 1928, à 8 heures 45 du soir

RÉCITAL DE PIANO

Richard BYK

PROGRAMME

1. Trois Polonaises anciennes (1re audition) . . . . arr. par L. KAMIENSKI
   Trois Krakowiaks (1re audition) . . . . P. PERKOWSKI
   (Danses polonaises)
   Tantris le Bouffon (Extrait de *Masques*) . . . . K. SZYMANOWSKI
   Barcarolle, op. 60 . . . . CHOPIN

2. J'entends dans le lointain.. . . . . FLORENT-SCHMITT
   J'entends dans le lointain des cris prolongés de la douleur la plus poignante
   Mauresque. . . . . —
   La Tragique Chevauchée (Extrait de *Mirages*, 1re audition) . . . . —

3. Trois Pièces Celtiques (1re audition) . . . . S. HENNESSY
   A la manière de... . . . . —
   Weber — Mendelssohn — Schumann — Chopin —
   Borodine — Massenet — Clementi — Verdi
   La Soirée dans Grenade. . . . . Cl. DEBUSSY
   Le Chemin de l'Alhambra (Grenade) . . . . J. TURINA
   Miramar (Valencia) (Extraits des *Contes d'Espagne*) . . . . . . —

4. Rhapsodie Espagnole . . . . LISZT

PIANO PLEYEL

PRIX DES PLACES (Tous droits compris)

Parterre réservé : 30 fr. — Parterre : 20 fr. — Balcon : 10 fr.

BILLETS : à la SALLE PLEYEL, 252, Rue du faubourg Saint-Honoré ; chez M. DURAND, 4, Place de la Madeleine
au BUREAU MUSICAL, 32, Rue Tronchet ; au GUIDE-BILLETS, 20, Avenue de l'Opéra ;
chez MM. ESCHIG, ROUDANEZ, ROSSIGNOL, SENART, POULALION, au MAGASIN MUSICAL
et à l'Administration de Concerts A. DANDELOT & FILS, 83, Rue d'Amsterdam (Tél. Gut. 15-25).

---

[81] In section 3, the programme also announces a first performance of *Trois Pièces celtiques*. If these are to be the three *Pièces celtiques*, Op. 45 (1912), it cannot have been a first performance. He may have had three of the (eight) *Huit Pièces celtiques*, Op. 51 (1922) in mind, which had not yet been performed by April 1928.

Paris, 25 Juin, 1927

Cher Monsieur Vallas,

En même temps que cette lettre je me permets de vous envoyer mes À la manière de ... dans l'espoir que ces petits pastiches puissent vous amuser. [...]

D'après ce que vous en dites dans votre livre sur Debussy, je ne crois pas que cette petite rosserie soit pour vous déplaire, mais je vous demande bien pardon d'avoir enchaîné Debussy et Benjamin Godard ! [...]

Dear Mister Vallas,

At the same time as this letter I am sending you my À la manière de ... in the hope that these little pastiches can amuse you. [...]

From what you say in your book on Debussy, I don't think this little obscenity will displease you, but I apologise for connecting Debussy and Benjamin Godard! [...]

Ex. 9.10: *À la manière de ... Debussy*

Vallas' response, if there was one, is not known. Perhaps the scheme did not amuse him, perhaps he considered the Debussy–Godard connection too obscene. We will never know. The Debussy piece (Ex. 9.10) merely consists of one page of rising and falling scales and parallel fourths, perhaps inspired by Debussy's *Pagodes* (No. 1 of *Estampes*), and it is to be followed immediately by a piece 'about' Benjamin Godard (1849–1895), a waltz that is to be played in an *'élégant, pommadé'* manner, a remarkable contrast even though the scales are not dissimilar.

Deux Mélodies, Op. 73 (1927) for medium voice and piano

Compared to the *Trois Chansons celtiques*, Op. 72 of the previous year, the two songs of Op. 73 are in a much more contemporary style – as almost always in Hennessy's non-'Celtic' music. The two songs were written in 1927, published with Éditions Max Eschig in 1928 and consist of *Le Chasseur noir* to a poem by the Belgian writer Paul Gérardy (1870–1933)[82] and *La Chanson du vent de mer*, another setting of a poem by the Breton Anatole le Braz. The first performance of the work was given by Lili Fabrègue with the composer at the Lyceum de France, Paris, 11 January 1929; in an earlier broadcast from Radio Tour Eiffel on 8 July 1928, Marthe Saisset and Hennessy had already performed the first of the two songs.

Gérardy's poem is from the collection *Les Chansons naïves* (Liège, 1892), section 4 (*'Songes romantiques'*). In a very dark and evocative style, the poem tells the story of a black hunter with his equally black dog whose glowing eyes betray the demon he is. The music is set in E minor in a rocking 6/8 time (suggesting the hunter sits on a horse?), with dissonant material starting right in the four bars of piano introduction, preparing for the eerie atmosphere of the words. At the point where the demonic nature of the dog is revealed, the score gets particularly dense (Ex. 9.11).

Ex. 9.11: *Deux Mélodies*, Op. 73 No. 1 *Le Chasseur noir*, bars 17–21 (author's transcription)[83]

---

[82] Not by Paul Géraldy (1885–1983), as is suggested by the online catalogue of the Bibliothèque Nationale de France for settings of the same poem by Albert Bertelin (Paris: E. Demets, 1910) and Raoul Laparra (Paris: J. Hamelle, 1910), which are errors.
[83] This work is not listed in any library catalogue, incl. BnF and WorldCat, and has been transcribed here from the manuscript.

As in his *Berceuse d'Armorique* Op. 72 No. 2, Hennessy uses another sea- and wind-swept poem by Anatole Le Braz that may, like the former, have that autobiographical background relating to the death of his mother in a storm on the Breton coast. Only this time it is not a sad lullaby but a lively and excited piece in B flat minor (marked 'très animé'), which consists mostly of chromatic scales in counter movements of the pianist's hands, reaching a climax when the poem reads '*Souffle, souffle, grand souffle amer, / O roi des vents, o vent de mer!*' ('Blow, blow, great bitter blow; / O kings of the winds, o wind of the sea!') (Ex. 9.12).

Ex. 9.12: *Deux Mélodies*, Op. 73 No. 2 *La Chanson du vent du mer*, bars 25–34

* * *

It is possible that Swan Hennessy has always had some private network of friends and acquaintances in Brussels, one that may even date to beyond the 1903 event there when he first met his wife Claire. Perhaps it was even *her* network, not his. Unfortunately, the sparse information about Hennessy's private life does not give any further clue. In any case, he travelled there to participate in an evening exclusively of his own music that took place on 27 April 1928 at Le Lyceum de Belgique, probably an educational institution for girls, founded in 1923 by the Union Patriotique de Femmes Belges. The musicians included the soprano Elisabeth Miry, the violinist Francine Janssens, the violist Edmond Vanderborght, and the cellist (Elisa) Fernande Kufferath (who was the most prominent of the performers and probably the initiator of the event). The programme consisted of the following works:

Piano works:
   Banlieues, Op. 69 Nos 1–3 (pf)
   Croquis de femmes, Op. 33 Nos 1–5 (pf)
	S. H.

Rapsodie gaélique, Op. 63 (vc, pf)	F. Kufferath, S. H.

Songs:
   La Chanson du rouet, Op. 72 Nos 1
   Berceuse d'Armorique, Op. 72 No. 2
   Paysage, Op. 66 No. 2
	E. Miry, S. H.

Pièce celtique, Op. 74 (vc, pf)	F. Kufferath, S. H.
Trois Chansons écossaises, Op. 31	E. Miry, S. H.

À la manière de …
   Weber, Grieg, Schumann, Chopin, Godard,
   Massenet, Clementi, J. Strauss, Verdi, Rossini
	S. H.

Petit trio celtique, Op. 52	F. Janssens, E. Vanderborght, F. Kufferath

The most recent work on the programme was the *Pièce celtique*, Op. 74 for cello and piano. The work, dedicated to Fernande Kufferath, was given its first performance. According to a press report, the Belgian audience was numerous and seemed to like what they heard:

> The members of the Lyceum de Belgique had the good fortune to attend a very interesting performance of some of the works of the composer Swan Hennessy on Friday evening in their magnificent premises on the Place de l'Industrie.
>
>   A great protector of art and artists, Mr. Swan Hennessy is American, of Irish origin, and has lived in Paris for almost thirty years. He does not belong to any school. It is in the free and simple description of nature – sometimes transposed into psychological emotions, sometimes translated into the language of sounds – that makes the quality of his instrumental work, which is almost entirely devoted to the painting of the soul and the homeland of his ancestors. He has harmonic combinations that seem without rules, for so instinctive, but so charming and evocative are they of the country of musettes, bagpipes and all those naive instruments of the Gaelic and Breton countries! But he is above all a humourist and his 'Croquis de femmes' for piano, which he performed personally with a talent made of delicacy and feeling, are like little satires, fine, joyful, infinitely amusing. Also amusing are his spiritual piano pastiches entitled: 'À la manière de: Weber, Clementi, Chopin, Schumann, Strauss, etc.', although it takes the talent of Mr Swan Hennessy to reveal all of their finesse. […]

In short, a great audition, a large and informed audience, among which we noticed several musicians of great repute.[84]

Fig. 9.8: Swan Hennessy and the pianist Marthe Le Breton, pictured outside the 'Prieuré' in Fontenay-en-Vexin (southern Normandy) and published in *Le Courrier musical* of 1 October 1927. The accompanying text reads: 'Swan Hennessy spends his summer days (indicated in the calendar!) at the "Prieuré" in Fontenay-en-Vexin. This little snapshot shows him holding in his arms the son of Si-Mi, the well-known cat of the late publisher Demets; at his side, the charming artist Mrs. Marthe Lebreton [*sic*]'.[85]

---

[84] 'Les membres de Lyceum de Belgique ont eu la bonne fortune d'assister vendredi soir, en leur magnifique local de la place de l'industrie, à une audition fort intéressante de quelques œuvres du compositeur M. Swan Hennessy. / Grand protecteur de l'art et des artistes, M. Swan Hennessy est américain, d'origine irlandaise, et fixé à Paris depuis bientôt trente ans. Il n'appartient à aucune école. C'est dans la libre et simple description de la nature – tantôt transposée en émotions psychologiques, tantôt traduite par le langage de sons – que réside l'unité de son œuvre instrumentale, qui est presque entièrement consacrée à la peinture de l'âme et de la patrie de ces ancêtres. Il a des combinaisons harmoniques qui paraissent sans règles, pour ainsi dire instinctives, mais combien charmantes et évocatrices du pays des musettes, des cornemuses et de tous ces naïfs instruments des pays gaélique et breton ! Mais il est surtout humoriste et ses « Croquis de femmes », pour piano, qu'il a exécutés personnellement avec un talent fait de délicatesse et de sentiment sont comme de petites satires, fines, joyeuses, infiniment amusantes. Amusants aussi, ses spirituels pastiches pour piano intitulés : « A la manière de : Weber, Clementi, Chopin, Schumann, Strauss, etc. », encore qu'il faille tout le talent de M. Swan Hennessy pour en révéler toutes les finesses. […] / En somme, belle audition, public nombreux, averti, où l'on remarquait plusieurs musiciens de grande réputation.'; 'X.', in *L'Étoile Belge*, 29 April 1928.

[85] 'Swan Hennessy passe ses jours d'été (indiqués au calendrier !) au « Prieuré » à Fontenay-en-Vexin. Ce petit instantané l'a fixé tenant en ses bras le fils de Si-Mi le chat bien connu du regretté éditeur Demets ; à ses cotés, la charmante artiste Mme Marthe Lebreton.'

Pièce celtique, Op. 74 (1927) for cello or bassoon and piano

The *Pièce celtique*, Op. 74, first performed on 27 April 1928 in Brussels, is a very short work in one movement of under three minutes duration. It was written in late 1927, dedicated to the Belgian cellist Fernande Kufferath and published in 1928 by Éditions Max Eschig. It has had a few, but not many performances in Paris until the early 1930s,[86] including at least one with bassoon that is documented for August 1932 with Christian Dhérin and Marie-Antoinette Pradier on piano (see Appendix 1).

It is a very rhapsodic and tuneful work in E flat major, marked *Adagio*, with a theme whose Irish or Scottish provenance is difficult to distinguish – which may have been Hennessy's intention. The theme makes abundant use of the 'Scotch snap', but we have seen Hennessy using it in an Irish as well as a Scottish context before. It is accompanied by a two-part piano line with frequent parallel fifths and sixths that despite its chromatic movement does not appear modernist at all. An attractive feature are several short interjections of two bars in the solo piano in double tempo based on melodic contours frequently found in the traditional music of both Ireland and Scotland (Ex. 9.13).

Ex. 9.13: *Pièce celtique*, Op. 74, bars 1–5

Bars 15 to 18 are a cadenza in *Allegro* for solo cello in a jig rhythm, followed by eight bars of a piano response which is accompanied by a 'drone' on a low C in the cello in the manner of a bagpipe. A reprise of the previous material brings the work to a close.

---

[86] The work has had two recent performances in Dublin, Ireland, in January 2016 and April 2017, by Arun Rao (vc) and Una Hunt (pf).

Quatrième Quatuor à cordes Op. 75 [String Quartet No. 4] (1928)

During the last years of his life, Hennessy used to spend parts of the summer in Fontenay-en-Vexin, then as now a small village in southern Normandy (see Figs 9.8 and 9.9). In October 1928 he announced that he had completed his fourth string quartet there. Three journals brought the news;[87] *Le Courrier musical* again publishing a photograph with Hennessy and his cat (the 'son' of Eugène Demets' cat Si-Mi) writing: 'Mr Swan Hennessy has worked a lot during the holidays and particularly on his Fourth String Quartet, which he has just finished and which we will be hearing soon.' *Le Monde musical* had learned that the composer regarded this as his most important quartet so far: 'Mr S. Hennessy finished his 4th String Quartet, which, he tells us, was more important than the first three. The Andolfi, Loiseau and Roth Quartets will each play one in the coming season.'

Fig. 9.9: Hennessy outside the Prieuré in Fontenay-en-Vexin (*Le Courrier musical*, 1 Oct. 1928)

SWAN HENNESSY.

---

[87] *Le Monde musical*, 30 September 1928; *Le Courrier musical*, 1 October 1928; and the *Revue internationale de musique et de danse*, 15 October 1928.

The first performance occurred at a *'séance'* of the Société Artistique et Littéraire de l'Ouest at the Salle Debussy on 17 January 1929, which also included a Flute Sonata by Mel Bonis, the *Quatre Chants arabes* by Jean Déré, a poetry reading by Victor-Émile Michelet, and then came Hennessy's fourth quartet performed by the Quatuor Loiseau. There followed the piano works *Fontaines* by Jean Cras, *Le Vent est doux* by Guy Ropartz, and *Ronde des filles de Quimperlé*, a folk song arrangement by É. Vuillermoz (either the music critic Émile or the unrelated singer Édouard Vuillermoz), finally the *Poème* for cello and piano by Alice Sauvrezis – the typical 'mixed bag' of musical and literary items that characterised the programmes of this society. On later occasions the quartet has also been performed by the Quatuors Andolfi, Bastide, and Malézieux, but performances ceased with the outbreak of World War II.[88]

A short analysis appeared in *Le Guide du concert* in February 1931, shortly after the work was published posthumously by Eschig. Normally, Hennessy would have written these notices himself; now somebody else must have written it:

> Dedicated to the glorification of the Celtic genius, this quartet begins with a nostalgic introduction followed by a smoothly led *Allegro*. The *Andante*, very evocative, is linked to an *Allegretto*, spiritual and light, to which a ternary *molto vivace* rhythm gives the feeling of a folk dance. The theme in the viola brings back the nostalgic feeling of the beginning. A *pizzicato-scherzoso* frames the *Finale* in an amusing way, a kind of serenade written with verve in a warm tonality. The somewhat Schumannian character of the theme recalls, without creating anything disparate in the deliberately Celtic atmosphere, Swan Hennessy's particular sympathy for Schumann.[89]

There are parts of this description that are difficult to follow, firstly because, in this author's opinion, this quartet is probably the least 'Celtic' of Hennessy's quartets, and while Hennessy never quite shook off the profound influence of Schumann, it is not quite so apparent in the *Finale*.

Even less comprehensible, however, is the 'review' in *The Monthly Musical Record*, which maintained:

> THERE is not much to be said in favour of this quartet. Nowhere is there a really vital and interesting tune, and the whole is treated in the dullest of academic fashions. The counterpoint and general technique are amateurish.[90]

---

[88] The work is included in the CD of Hennessy's complete string quartets of April 2019, recorded by the RTÉ ConTempo Quartet; see Appendix 7. A fine reprint of score and parts is available from Musikproduktion Höflich (Munich, 2019).

[89] *'Consacré à la glorification du génie celte, ce quatuor débute par une introduction de caractère nostalgique que suit un* Allegro *mené rondement. L'*Andante, *très évocateur, se lie à un* Allegretto, *spirituel et léger, auquel un rythme ternaire molto vivace donne une allure de danse populaire. Le chant d'alto ramène le sentiment nostalgique du début. Un pizzicato-scherzoso encadre d'une amusante manière le* Final, *sorte de sérénade écrite avec verve dans une chaude tonalité. Le caractère un peu schumannien du thème rappelle, sans créer de disparate dans l'atmosphère volontairement celtique, a sympathie toute particulière de Swan Hennessy pour Schumann.'*; in *Le Guide du concert* 17:20, 20 February 1931, p. 571.

[90] *The Monthly Musical Record* 61:7, 1 July 1930, p. 212.

Without needing to defend this work 90 years later, the reviewer had certainly not heard the work performed and must have had a very superficial look at the score to come to the conclusion that 'nowhere is there a really vital and interesting tune' – and that about a work that is particularly tuneful from beginning to end, as everything that Hennessy has written (one might criticise Hennessy for his sketchiness and overall miniaturist approach, but certainly not for the lack of tunes).

The quartet is in four movements without any descriptive titles. The first is set in A flat major, with a lively *allegro* framed by an *andante* section at the beginning and the end of the A–B–A structure. The tuneful (!) theme in the *Andante* is carried by the two violins and accompanied in a quite chromatic manner by viola and cello (Ex. 9.14). There are cautious hints to Irish traditional element in parts of the *allegro*, particularly in the brief interplay between the upper and lower strings. But mostly the thematic material does not have any national overtones.

Ex. 9.14: *Quatrième Quatuor à cordes*, Op. 75, 1st movt, bars 1–5

Likewise, the second movement also benefits from the contrast between a hymn-like *andante* that appears with two reprises and two faster sections in between. The second of these is a very energetic *molto vivace* that, despite a basic tonality of D flat major, is quite chromatic in its tonal design. Yet, there is a certain structural weakness here when Hennessy merely repeats the A sections in an A–B–A–C–A format without much developing this part, even though the three sections are attractive in themselves. And exactly the same happens, structurally, in the third movement, which is a very entertaining *allegretto scherzoso* in F sharp major with extended *pizzicato* sections where the whole quartet joins in for fifteen bars. Even though its reoccurance as a third section is played *arco*, it is musically the same, and the third occurrence then is more than predictable. Still, it is fun to listen to and would probably make excellent TV music in a family comedy nowadays. Before the end of the movement comes a brief thematic reminder of the first movement. The concluding *allegro con brio* returns to the tonality of the first movement and is another showcase for Hennessy's contrapuntal skills that brings the work to a delightful *finale*.

Despite some chromatic scoring, the last movement (and the quartet on the whole) is very tonal and – I repeat – tuneful, particularly the *scherzo*. While this, of course, reflects Hennessy's dislike of the avant-garde of his time, one should not forget that this was still the mainstream of European art music. It was to take another two or three decades before this style was increasingly seen as outmoded. Hennessy's music is very entertaining and a pleasure to listen to.

Trois Petits trios pour voix de femmes, Op. 76 (1929) for soprano, mezzo-soprano, and alto solos

Swan Hennessy had a liking for unusual trios, but this setting for three unaccompanied female solo voices is certainly a curiosity. It is not sure whether he made any attempt at publishing the music since he must have been aware that there would be very few vocal trios in the world who would be waiting for this music. The work must have been a personal favour for the three vocalists who gave the first performance (of numbers 1 and 3 only) at the Salle Debussy, Paris, on 14 February 1929: G. (?) Molinier, Marthe Saisset, and Rachel Rialan, appearing under the name of 'La Triade Vocale'. The only documented performance of the complete work was by larger forces, which took place on 23 February 1939 by a women's choir named 'La Ménestrandise'. The score remained unpublished and was found among the manuscripts in the Hennessy family's collection. Because of this, members of this choir must also have been members of the original vocal trio in order to have access to the music.

The three pieces are *Il était une fois* to a text by Jean Ajalbert; *Panis angelicus*, the well-known religious text in Latin by St Thomas Aquinas; and the last is merely called *Vers traduits de Goethe* ['Verses translated from Goethe'], based on a translation of the famous Goethe poem *'Über allen Wipfeln ist Ruh'* into French by Louis de Ronchaud. The first two are dated July 1928, and the third has a date of 11 February 1929 – three days before the first performance. All three pieces are very short, without any repetitions, taking no longer than about three minutes to perform in their entirety.

If there is a common theme in those three very diverse texts, it may be the conscious and consecutive stringing together of a lonely heart risking its life on a deceivingly calm sea (*Il était une fois*), a poor soul asking God for forgiveness (*Panis angelicus*), and the serene search for a tranquil place beyond our earthly being (*Vers traduits de*

Goethe) – which one may interpret as a sense of finiteness and a desire to conclude with an arduous and exhausting life on Hennessy's part (at least at this period). As in the 'Bird of Time' quote that led to this book's title (see Introduction), which also originated at about this time, Hennessy felt that his health was failing and he might not have much time anymore. In a letter to Irving Schwerke of 15 April 1929 (see below), he wrote 'As for health, mine leaves much to be desired just now'. It may be an exaggerated interpretation, but it is a possibility.

Il était une fois is a 'choral' arrangement of Hennessy's song of the same name (*Trois Mélodies*, Op. 56 No. 3), set in G minor and in quick tempo. Although he had never worked in the vocal *a capella* genre before, his music is creative and well crafted. It contains sections of synchronous singing and others in which the lines of text are delayed or where certain phrases occur in one of the voices only. Ex. 9.15 shows this procedure, including a modulation to the tonic major in bars 17 to 19.

Ex. 9.15: *Trois Petits trios*, Op. 76 No. 1 *Il était une fois*, bars 17–24 (author's transcription)

Panis angelicus is Hennessy's only setting of a religious text in F minor, a short piece of 25 bars only. Alto and mezzo solos (in this order) begin in an imitative manner, while the soprano has a more independent part. The alto singer provides a kind of baseline with comparatively little movement, always circulating around the low C – for about six bars (4–9) it does not leave the C pitch at all while the other two voices move in chromatic steps downward, which has an interesting effect. The piece is one of several of Hennessy's works in a minor tonality that ends on its tonic major.

Vers traduits de Goethe is a piece in E major marked *'Lent, très doux'*. There is mainly polyphone, synchronous singing except where the ending is being prepared at the words *'Attends, et pour toi même, bientôt viendra la paix'* ('Wait, and for yourself, peace will come soon.'), the word *'Attends'* is lead consecutively through the three voices, which then re-unite for a final phrase. This is technically (or rather, musically) so well and appropriately done that one cannot but regret that the piece is so short.

After the 1939 choral performance, a critic wrote:

> We heard again, interpreted by the choir 'la Ménestrandise', pages by Swan Hennessy that made us deeply regret the death of this composer whose mind and heart knew so well how to come together to find a seductive expression.[91]

Deux Pièces celtiques, Op. 77 (1929) for viola and piano

Unfortunately, very little can be said about this duo work, because it was not published (neither by Eschig nor by Hennessy himself) and the manuscript score is lost. It consists of the two parts 1. *Danse écossaise* and 2. *Pièce celtique*. The only comment in Hennessy's own list of works is: *'Inédit'*.

It was first performed at the Salle Debussy, Paris, on 15 January 1929, by Robert Chantôme and the composer in a programme that included works by Artur Honegger and Tristan Klingsor, and there were three more documented performances until 1936. After a November 1931 performance, which again included the Viola Sonata by Honegger, a critic wrote:

> Mr. Chantôme's playing and his profound musicality give scores as different as Honegger's Sonata or such a finely musical score by Swan Hennessy's as the *Pièces celtiques* a powerful interest.[92]

a comment that does not say much about the music.

---

[91] *'Nous entendîmes encore, interprétées par la chorale "la Ménestrandise", de pages de Swan Hennessy qui nous font vivement regretter la disparition de ce compositeur dont l'esprit et le cœur savaient si bien s'accorder pour trouver l'expression séduisante.'*; Andrée Realtor in *L'Époque*, 2 March 1939.

[92] *'Le jeu de M. Chantôme et sa profonde musicalité donnent à des partitions aussi différentes que la Sonate d'Honegger et celle si finement musicale de Swan Hennessy, ou les Pièces celtiques du même auteur, un puissant intérêt.'*; Pierre Blois in *L'Européen*, November 1931 (quoted from Hennessy's Press Book IV, p. 155 which does not include a more exact date from this weekly journal (this month is not digitised in Gallica).

Sonatine, Op. 78 (1929) for two violins (or two groups of violins)

The *Sonatine*, Op. 78 is a short work in three movements for two violins, written in March 1929 for the pupils of Émile Loiseau, the leader of the quartet that gave almost all first performances of Hennessy's string quartets. A notice on the cover page of the manuscript indicating that the work is also suitable for two groups of violins suggests that it is not a particularly difficult work. It may be assumed that this score is rather aimed at young players and not at students at the Conservatoire where Loiseau also taught. It is for this background that Hennessy's notes do not contain any information about a public performance. While it is likely that the work received performances at semi-public student recitals, no professional performance is documented (and may not have been intended). It cannot have had any wider circulation, though, because the work was not published and any performance would have been from manuscripts handed out by Loiseau.

The work is in three movements entitled 1. *Allegro appassionato*; 2. *Allegro amabile*; and 3. *(d'après un air irlandais)*. The first movement is in D major in a quick 3/4 metre. This is an ambitious study in reading accidentals. There is a dominant rhythmic motif consisting of a dotted crotchet and three quavers, which is led through all sorts of chromatic shifts, sometimes resulting in quite harsh dissonances. Hennessy applies his typical abridged sonata form, and in the reprise the two violins change the roles they had at the beginning. Also typical, perhaps, albeit somewhat unexpected, appear two occurrences of the 'Scotch snap' in a short phrase reminding the listener of the composer's 'Celtic' interests. But these remain brief ideas that are not followed up on. Apart from the reading exercise, the score contains no other technical difficulties or unusual playing techniques – no *pizzicati*, no *flageolets*, no *glissandi* or other techniques that began to be associated with modern string music in the late 1920s.

Even more simple is the second movement in F major that stands roughly in an A–B–A form, with B and A being repeated. It is marked *'con grazia infantile'* ('with childish grace') and comes across as an all too simple piece, the second violin being clearly in second place with, in part A, a theme of four crotchets that is merely repeated eight times. This is something for the beginner on the instrument. As such, the second movement will bore the students who can manage the first and third movements.

In the third, Hennessy teaches young French violinists the art of Irish fiddling, with a reel tune borrowed largely from no. 917 of the Petrie Collection as edited by C. V. Stanford, the source he always uses in the not-so-frequent cases when he uses an actual traditional tune. Hennessy marked it *'Allegro molto'* but it is at a more appropriate tempo when played somewhat slower, at about 112 for the crotchet. From an Irish perspective, this is the most interesting movement, particularly because an Irish composer may have harmonised the dance tune, but Hennessy composed a second part, partly in simultaneous rhythm, partly in counterpoint. This procedure would not be unusual for Hennessy who had a strong interest in this traditional repertoire, but he dealt with it from an outside perspective that appears refreshingly disrespectful for Irish musicians (Ex. 9.16). Seen from this angle, the third movement would also make an excellent study for Irish students, not only those of Émile Loiseau.

Ex. 9.16a+b: *Sonatine* Op. 78, 3rd movt, bars 1–4 and 17–20

The work ends on a joke that proves how much fun the writing of this movement must have been for the composer. In bars 33 to 36 he quotes from another Irish tune, here the ballad 'The Dawning of the Day' that he already used in No. 3 of the *Trois Chansons celtiques*, Op. 72. It is not more than a brief reminder, which then joins forces with the reel tune to end the work on bar 40.

Deux Mélodies, Op. 79 (1929) for soprano and piano

This work consisting of two songs is the last vocal composition by Swan Hennessy. The manuscript notes a date of composition of April 1929, but the work was not published before 1932, probably on the initiative of his widow. The two songs are 1. *La Lune* (better known as 'La Lune blanche', a famous poem set to music by a large number of composers, written by Paul Verlaine (1844–1896) and originally published in the poet's collection *La Bonne chanson* (1870); and 2. *À Deux* to a poem by Prosper Blanchemain (1816–1879) from the volume *Poèmes et poésies* (1880). The idea to combine these two poems was an excellent one, since both conjure up images of a walk in the woods in the evening in an idyllic atmosphere imbued with nature and melancholy thoughts.

The work is dedicated to Marguerite Breitner, then a young composer and pianist who later gained a measure of fame as a performer on the Ondes Martenot. The reason for this dedication is unclear. She does not appear in connection with any of the documented public performances of this work, the first of these having been on 9 January 1930 at the Salle Chopin, Paris, with Marthe Saisset accompanied by Ludovic Bouserez.

La Lune is a very evocative song in a largely late-Romantic harmonic language. Notated in E major, Hennessy's modulations and harmonic ideas are always interesting and appropriate, albeit at times unusual. An example is at the point where the poem describes reflections in the water of a lake (Ex. 9.17) where he uses (from bar

11) a G major chord (certainly foreign to the scale of E major) and chords with augmented fifths but without a third, leaving their genus ambiguous.

Ex. 9.17: *Deux Mélodies*, Op. 79 No. 1 *La Lune*, bars 10–15

Between two stanzas, in bars 6 and 7, he even imitates the call of a nightingale, as he has previously done in some of his descriptive piano music.

The second song, *À deux*, fascinates by its utter simplicity. The music is reduced to the absolutely essential. It remains in a straightforward G major and a 2/4 measure throughout, the piano is limited to extended minims and crotchets, with a triplet appearing just twice. It is a conscious decision as we know that Hennessy can write in very complex way. It is also Hennessy's only strophic song (two stanzas). The six-bar piano interlude serves as the postlude as well. What's more, the music is in a clear 'Celtic' line, even though he does not say so, with a melody shaped after the model of countless Irish ballads and a piano line that picks up the idea of thrice repeating a pitch at the end of a phrase.

Deuxième Sonatine, Op. 80 (1929) for violin and piano

In calling this work his 'Second' Sonatina for violin and piano, Hennessy probably has the early Sonata, Op. 14 'in the Irish style' in mind – and not the *Sonatine celtique*, Op. 62 for viola that also exists in a violin version. Although it avoids any reference in the title to the Irish or 'Celtic' sound world, the work is, in fact, another specimen of this style, particularly in the first two movements. The movements have no titles and are merely marked 1. *Allegro*; 2. *Andantino*; and 3. *Allegretto*, which would add up to a duration of approximately nine to ten minutes in performance.

The work is dedicated to Suzanne Chevaillier, the prominent violinist, winner of a *Premier Prix* at the Conservatoire, and wife of the pianist, composer and journalist Lucien Chevaillier who had conducted the interview with Hennessy in the April 1929 issue of *Le Guide du concert*, which has frequently been quoted in this study. Ravel scholars know that Suzanne and Lucien Chevaillier had given the first performance of that composer's *Tzigane* in 1924, and the couple now also gave the premiere of Hennessy *Deuxième Sonatine*, Op. 80 at the Salle de l'École Normale de Musique, Paris, on 15 November 1929, about three weeks after the composer's unexpected death. Suzanne Chevaillier seems to have enjoyed the piece: Hennessy's (resp. his widow's) records show her performing the work at least until 1937 (her husband had died in 1932).

As several of Hennessy's last works, this sonatina, too, failed[93] to attract the interest of his long-standing publisher, Eschig. The last piece published by Eschig had been the short *Pièce celtique*, Op. 74 for cello and piano in early 1928, and 1929 only saw the publication of the expanded version of *Banlieues*, Op. 69 and the *Album celtique* with four older piano works. This included re-issues of the *Variations sur un thème original dans le style irlandais*, Op. 12 (originally by Augener, 1902) and *Huit Pièces celtiques*, Op. 51 (originally by Evans, 1924) as well as the first issues of the *Sonatine celtique*, Op. 53 (1923) and the *Rapsodie irlandaise*, Op. 67 (1924). After Hennessy's death, his widow Claire must have convinced (or payed) Eschig to publish the String Quartet No. 4 (in 1930) and several songs (in 1932). The *Deuxième Sonatine*, Op. 80 and the following *Sonatine*, Op. 81 for cello and piano were published by Hennessy himself (*'Propriété de l'auteur'*) in 1929 and were merely distributed by Eschig. Perhaps, these last two works, although fairly substantial for Hennessy, were not regarded by Eschig as modern enough, and Hennessy did not undertake the effort to have them published in London where this type of music still found publishers for many years.

If one disregards the work's conservative harmonic language, this *Deuxième Sonatine* is a very attractive work, full of creative ideas, technically polished yet approachable, and a really nice example of a late Romantic piece with recognisable Irish influences. As such, it should be of real interest to Irish musicians as well as any musicians on the lookout for works in this idiom. Harmonically, it might best be compared with a work by Brahms or Stanford (or more recent Irish composers such as Hamilton Harty and British composers such as some representatives of the 'English Musical Renaissance'), to which Hennessy adds a 'Celtic note'. Even though Stanford used an Irish idiom as well, he mainly used existing traditional Irish melodies (which Hennessy rarely did), and in the case of his violin sonat(in)as he does not apply the idiom.

The first movement in C sharp minor begins with a forceful theme in the violin that forms the core of the movement (Ex. 9.18). The falling fourth at the beginning, the interval steps of the quavers in bar 2, the rhythmical pattern and the descending

---

[93] At least I interpret it as a failure. There may also have been business considerations like being able to earn more from sales as a member of SACEM. But I think, in general, Hennessy was proud of being published by Eschig and would not have given it up lightly.

scale in bars 3 and 4, and the imitative handling of the themes between the two instruments – they all occur in various guises throughout the movement and also, occasionally, in the other movements.

Ex. 9.18: *Deuxième Sonatine*, Op. 80, 1st movt, bars 1–7

The second subject is a quote from an Irish traditional melody – described as such with an asterisk and a footnote in the score, but without naming the tune or its source. It appears that Hennessy adapted two almost identical tunes from the Petrie Collection as edited by C. V. Stanford, no. 322 ('Oh fair John my love') and no. 323 ('The enchanted valley'). Hennessy's tune is first stated in G minor in the piano (after an upbeat) in bars 23–26, followed by the violin (Ex. 9.19), and again shortly afterwards in bars 36–39 in C minor in the violin only. It fits amazingly well to his first subject, and the two are excellently combined in the development section. In the reprise, he even transforms the second subject into a jig (four quaver triplets in a bar) (bars 80–86).

Ex. 9.19: *Deuxième Sonatine*, Op. 80, 1st movt, bars 23–26

The second movement is in A major in the form of A–A'–B–A'–A, with the B part moving briefly to F major. The A part itself could be another Irish (or Scottish) folk tune with a 16-bar structure in phrases of A–A–B–A. The A' part of the primary structure starts at bar 17, with the tune of part A moving to the right hand of the pianist and the violin assuming an 'accompaniment' in a very easy-going manner in bowed *staccatos*, initially avoiding the first beat so as to resemble syncopated playing (which it is not really) (Ex. 9.20). This is immensely entertaining, almost creating the atmosphere of a traditional music session, an impression enhanced by the strictly diatonic accompaniment that contains no hint at all to late 1920s French art music (although, in fairness to Hennessy, it may be added here that this period in France was itself much more diverse than its reception history would make us believe).

Ex. 9.20: *Deuxième Sonatine*, Op. 80, 2nd movt, bars 17–19

The *Finale* begins with 26 bars in A minor before it returns to the C sharp minor tonality of the first movement. These initial phrases have a degree of drama through the agitated tremolo playing of the violin, combined with forceful chords with both hands on the main beats. Since Hennessy owned a large collection of late nineteenth and early twentieth-century Russian piano music, both melodic and harmonic writing may, at least subconsciously, stem from this background. This would also apply to the lighter dance-like music that follows with the return to the dominant key of this sonatina (and which also includes outings to the parallel E major).

With this second violin sonatina, Hennessy left one of his most mature scores in terms of form, dramatic conception, and thematic development. To count as a truly contemporary work on an equal footing with even modestly modern music of its time, it comes some 30 years too late. But that does not change the fact that we are dealing with a very attractive score that deserves to be performed again.

Sonatine, Op. 81 (1929) for cello and piano

A brief word about Hennessy's very last completed score shall bring this section to a close. The *Sonatine* Op. 81 is his first multi-movement work for cello and piano after two previous one-movement works of a rhapsodic character in Opp. 63 and 74. The three movements are marked, respectively called, 1. *Moderato assai*, which is set in F major and 3/4 time; 2. an *Allegretto à la manière de Johannes Brahms* in D flat major, again in 3/4 time; and 3. an *Allegro à la manière de Félix Mendelssohn Bartholdy* in 12/8 time.

At least in name, he alludes here, of course, to his own successful series of *À la manière de ...* for piano, but in the present case, we are not dealing with satirical works. In this opus, Hennessy really imitates the musical language of Brahms and Mendelssohn in his second and third movements, and perhaps of himself in the first movement with its very clear Irish-style melodic line. In the second movement, the German critic and musicologist Wilhelm Altmann even recognised thematic similarities with the middle movement of Brahms' own Cello Sonata, Op. 38.[94]

The *Sonatine*, Op. 81 is dedicated to the cellist Madeleine Monnier (1900–1984). Interestingly, she is not recorded as having performed the work. Monnier performed Hennessy's other cello works in an event in November 1928, but not this one. Was she not happy with the work? Instead, it received a first performance at the Lyceum de France, 31 January 1930, with Géo Dupuy and a Mlle. Rachmanoff. Two further performances are recorded for 1931 with Jacques Serres and Janine Cools.

* * *

The letters of Swan Hennessy to Irving Schwerke, 1928–9

An important contact in Hennessy's last years was the American music critic Irving Schwerke (1893–1975)[95] who was based in Paris for many years, writing for newspapers like *The Chicago Tribune* and *The New York Herald* as well as journals like *The Musical Digest* on musical life in France. According to the Library of Congress, which houses a large Irving Schwerke Collection, he wrote for 'more than 100 leading papers and magazines'.[96]

Hennessy and Schwerke probably got to know each other at the *Musique vivante* event about the influence of jazz on music in France, moderated by Léon Vallas, on 22 January 1926 described further above. Since then, a professional friendship seems to have ensued. Schwerke also entertained guests in his apartment and organised musical *soirées* on specific composers or topics. Hennessy benefitted from this at least twice: one event on 28 November 1928 was dedicated to works by Hennessy and Georges Migot (Fig. 9.10), another on 14 June 1929 exclusively to Hennessy.

Below I am documenting the letters Swan Hennessy wrote to Schwerke between March 1928 and May 1929, as collected in the 'Swan Hennessy File' of the Irving Schwerke Collection. The collection is uncatalogued[97] and does not contain copies of Schwerke's responses. The letters are all written in English with a number of French colloquial expressions and greeting formulas interspersed. As in the case of the Schott correspondence, I will briefly summarise the more poignant items of interest.

---

[94] *Allgemeine Musikzeitung*, 57:44, 31 October 1930, p. 1028.
[95] He is sometimes spelt Schwerké (with an accent on the E) to make clear that the name is to be pronounced with two syllables.
[96] http://memory.loc.gov/diglib/ihas/loc.natlib.scdb.200033739/default.html (last accessed, 26 July 2019).
[97] See Appendix 5., section A.5.

Fig. 9.10: Invitation by Irving Schwerke to a soirée on 28 November 1928 with Hennessy and Migot (Schwerke's handwriting in the middle, Hennessy's below (Courtesy: Hennessy family)

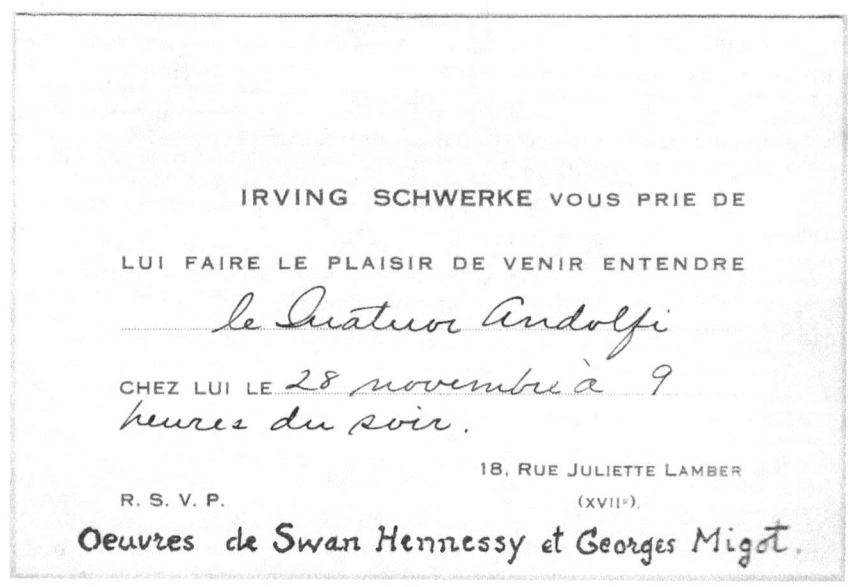

In letter no. 1 (24 March 1928), he expresses his interest to promote his music in the United States by way of financing an advertisement in *The Musical Digest*. This is interesting from two perspectives, a) that he is interested at all to be better known in the US, and b) that he finances the advertisement himself and not Eschig (the ad looks like one by Eschig). This is continued in letter no. 2 (2 April 1928).

Letter no. 3 (10 June 1928) has been quoted earlier. Here, he argues for the recognition of Joachim Mendelson and Wladimir Vogel as well the Roth Quartet.

In letter no. 4 (30 September 1928) he invites Schwerke to his own apartment for an audition of the Andolfi Quartet trying out the new String Quartet No. 4 – with the prospect of having this work performed at one of Schwerke's future *soirées*.

According to letter no. 5 (10 October 1928) the meeting seems to have taken place and they are now searching for a suitable date for the soirée. Hennessy suggests that Henri Collet should be invited (which proves the ongoing good contact between the two).

Letter no. 7 (5 November 1928) is interesting for its rare view into Hennessy's private affairs by him admitting to have only few of his original teeth left!

In letter no. 9 (4 January 1929) he invites Schwerke to a concert organised by the Société Artistique et Littéraire de l'Ouest, suggesting he might, if necessary, provide funding for Schwerke to cover the event in the *Musical Digest* and also that might 'get' the Loiseau or Roth Quartet to play the 4th quartet at one of the next soirées. This expresses quite clearly that, contrary to his pre-War practice, he now actively invested his private money into the promotion of his music.

On the other hand, he did not always do this. In letter no. 10 (23 February 1929), he says he would be 'greatly obliged' if Schwerke would review the *Album celtique*.

In letter no. 11 (4 April 1929) he proudly announces that six different string quartets will play his music this season in Paris and this should arouse the interest of the American musical public if this was known there (he is probably right, but of course he has himself not done much about his reputation in the US before his contact with Schwerke). He also mentions the possibility of Schwerke writing a longer article about him and asks what the status is. Furthermore, he describes his String Quartet No. 2, Op. 49, as 'the weakest' of his four quartets. Although he repeats this self-criticism later (letter no. 13), I think this must be interpreted primarily as his wish that Schwerke should come to hear his more recent.

Letter no. 12 (15 April 1929) deals with the upcoming second *soirée* of works by Hennessy at Schwerke's home, which seems to have been suggested by Schwerke. It also mentions his failing health.

In letter no. 13 (19 April 1929) he describes his second quartet at 'the poorest of my compositions' (see interpretation above at letter no. 11). This letter also contains the quote that has been used as the title of this book.

Letter no. 14 (13 May 1929) expresses Hennessy's joy at the prospect of being covered by a chapter in Schwerke's next book. Unfortunately, since Hennessy died five months later, this was never realised. The book in question must have been *Views and Interviews* (Paris, 1936), a book of 27 chapters in English including 14 musicians' portraits (among them Dukas, de Falla, Prokofieff, Migot, Lenormand etc.).

In letter no. 16 (22 May 1929) he suggests to invite two couples to the next *soirée* in June, among them the English composer John Foulds and his wife. Foulds had left England for Paris in 1927 and was trying to make a living as an accompanist for silent films. Hennessy may have met him on such an occasion since he was such an avid cinema goer. Foulds and Hennessy shared an interest in musical Celticism, although their respective artistic results are quite different.

Letter no. 1

Paris, March 24, 1928.

Dear Mr. Schwerke,

Many thanks for your kind note and the notice of the "Musical Digest".

I sent you three short piano pieces called "Banlieues" which Byk is going to play in his next concert. I hope you will like them. You will tell me when we next meet whether I have succeeded in giving the atmosphere of these places with which you are no doubt familiar.

Do you write in the "Musical Digest"? If so, I would willingly subscribe to the paper, tho' I must confess that I have a great distaste for musical papers as a general rule. Your articles will compensate me for the great quantity of rot which I shall have to swallow.

Commercially, I am convinced that the Musical Digest is valuable, and I should be much obliged if you would kindly tell me what it would cost to put in a permanent advertisement (for a year) of the following size:

It might be worth while to advertise my "pastiches." They are selling well here, but the sale of music is necessarily limited in Paris, whereas in America there would be a better, or at least a larger field.

Hoping to have the pleasure of seeing you again soon, I beg you to believe me
    Yours sincerely
        Swan Hennessy

Letter no. 2

Paris
[*printed on letter head:* 270 Boulevard Raspail, XIV]
April 2d, 1928

Dear Mr. Schwerke,

Please find enclosed a cheque for $60 and a model of my advertisement. I will see at the end of six months what the result is, and if it proves satisfactory, will renew. I will expect to see the first insertion in the May number.

With anticipated thanks and best regards.
    Yours sincerely
        Swan Hennessy

Letter no. 3

Paris, June 10th, 1928.

Dear Mr. Schwerke,

I expected to see you at the salle des Agriculteurs last night. I should have liked you to hear my first quartett played by Roth – the more so as you did not seem to care about my second (which, by the way was received with enthusiasm at Andolfi's concert at the salle Chopin on May 26).

Joachim Mendelssohn's work is interesting and well written and that of Vladimir Vogel, tho' incoherent enough to satisfy the most advanced modernist, contains some clever writing.

But the triumph was for Schumann's Op. 41 N°. 1. I have heard this work played by most of the celebrated quartetts, but not one of them came <u>anywhere near</u> these wonderful artists!

It is a sad and significant thing that such men should only be able to half fill the salle des Agriculteurs, and will probably (unless you will say a word or two for them) be passed over in silence by the important critics.

I suppose the Parisian public reasons like the old lady who asked why she should be expected to pay 5 frs to hear four musicians when she could hear a full orchestra for the same money.

I hope you will have very pleasant "vacances" and that we shall meet again at the "rentrée".

With best regards and anticipated thanks for any mention you will make of the Quatuor Roth,

believe me,
    Yours sincerely
    Swan Hennessy

<u>Letter no. 4</u>

Paris, 30 Sept., 1928.

Dear Mr. Schwerke,

You were so kind, some time ago, as to suggest my having one of my string quartets played at one of your "at homes".

Andolfi is coming in a few days to try over <u>the fourth</u>, which I have just finished.

Would you give me the pleasure of your company on this occasion? I should be happy to have your opinion, and we could arrange about the "audition" at your place. Before I fix a date with Andolfi for this "lecture", would you kindly, (in case you wish to come), name the days which w^d suit you (at about 5 o'clock) – between the 4th and 10th of October?

Hoping your "vacances" have been quite satisfactory, with best regards,
    Yours sincerely,
    Swan Hennessy

<u>Letter no. 5</u>

Paris, 10 Oct., 1928

Dear Mr. Schwerke,

Many thanks for your kind letter. Andolfi will write or telephone to you to fix a date. Any day will suit me except the 10th of November and the 6th of December. There is nobody whom I would suggest your inviting except perhaps Henri Collet (10 Avenue Kléber (XVIe)).

Looking forward to the pleasure of seeing you again soon, I beg you to believe me
>Yours sincerely
>>Swan Hennessy

Letter no. 6

Paris, Nov. 1, 1928.

Dear Mr. Schwerke,
Will you kindly tell me when I might call on you at your earliest convenience? There are several things I should like to ask you.

I hope you will go to hear Mme Helia Wolska sing my Spanish songs. She sings them remarkably well.

Dans l'attente de votre aimable réponse, with best regards,
>Yours sincerely
>>Swan Hennessy

Letter no. 7

Paris 5 Nov., 1928

Dear Mr. Schwerke,
I understand perfectly. Teeth are the most important part of life. I realize this all the better for having so few left!

I will call on you at 3.30 this afternoon (Tuesday 6th Nov.)
>Yours sincerely
>>Swan Hennessy

[with verso as 'envelope' marked "<u>Pneumatique</u>" and addressed to: Monsieur Irving Schwerke, 18 rue Juliette Lamber, <u>Paris</u> (17^e)]

Letter no. 8

Paris, 8 Nov., 1928.

Dear Mr. Schwerke,
Mr. Andolfi has written me that you have chosen the 28 of November for the performance of my quartett. This date will suit me perfectly.

I hope to have the pleasure of seeing you on Saturday. If not – "so long" until the 28th.
>With best regards.
>Yours sincerely
>>Swan Hennessy

Letter no. 9

Paris, Jan. 4, 1929

Dear Mr. Schwerke,

On the 17th of this month the S^{té} Artistique et Littéraire de l'Ouest is giving a séance at the salle Debussy (9 o'clock) at which the Quatuor Loiseau will play my fourth quartet. It is a concert "à bureaux fermés" and I will send you an invitation. I hope you will be able to come, as I am particularly anxious to know your opinion of this my last and most important work. Of course I shall be very glad to do all that is necessary with the Chicago Tribune (if you will kindly tell me how) to insure your presence.

If you like this quartet, and w^d care about it, I could get Loiseau or Roth to play it again at one of your "at homes".

With all best wishes and regards.
Yours sincerely
Swan Hennessy

Letter no. 10

Paris, 270 B^d. Raspail (14)
23 Février, 1929

Dear Mr. Schwerke

Simultaneously with this letter I am sending you my Album celtique which has just appeared.

You would greatly oblige me if you wd. write a criticism of it. The contents are quite characteristic of my style and extend over several periods (from op. 12 to 67!).

I called twice while you were away and wrote to you, but received no answer.

I was even asking myself whether I could have said or done anything to offend you, tho' nothing was further from my intention.

Please believe me, with all best greetings and regards,
Yours sincerely
Swan Hennessy

Letter no. 11

270 B^d. Raspail (14^e)
Paris April 4th, 1929.

Dear Mr. Schwerke,

You were so kind a few months ago as to offer to write a notice about me and my work for which I furnished you data and a photo. Was this notice intended for the Musical Digest? Mr. Pierre Key has on several occasions sent me hints to advertise. As the expense is considerable and no practical result followed my first effort, I have hesitated to do this – but if an article by you were to appear simultaneously, it might be worth while to advertise my chamber music. Quartetts of mine will have been played in Paris <u>this season</u> by Andolfi; Bastide; Calvet; Krettly, Loiseau and Roth! If this were known in America, it might excite curiosity. You only know one of my quartetts (N⁰. 2) – the weakest. I should like you to hear the others.

With best regards, cher ami, and anticipated thanks,
 Très cordialement vôtre,
  Swan Hennessy

Letter no. 12

Paris, 15 Avril, 1929.

 Très cher ami,
Merci pour votre lettre. Another soirée would be very nice.

You will find me at home any Sunday afternoon. As for health, mine leaves much to be desired just now, but it might be worse, so I won't complain.

Hoping to see you again soon,
With best wishes, and many thanks,
 Cordialement vôtre,
  Swan Hennessy

Letter no. 13

Paris April 19th, 1929.

 Cher ami,
Probably I shall not hear from you until after these pentacostal saturnalia.

I hope on the occasion of the soirée that you will do me the honour to write something in the Chicago Tribune + Musical Digest. If I am to become known before I die I must make haste, for the bird of time is on the wing.

You only know my second quartett, the poorest of my compositions, and of course the most often played. This time you will hear three of the best, by which I am ready to stand or fall in your opinion.

A bientôt, with all best wishes and regards,
 Yours cordially,
  Swan Hennessy.

P.S. What beastly cold weather for May – porca madonna! (to use a favourite expression of St Catherine of Sienna).

Letter no. 14

Paris, May 13, 1929.

 Cher ami,
Many thanks! I shall be much pleased and honoured by a chapter in your book. If you _really_ desire a soirée, I can furnish the quartett.

 A bientôt
  Cordialement vôtre,
   Swan Hennessy

Letter no. 15
19 – V – 29
                                                            Saturday evening.
    Cher ami,
Many thanks for your suggestion. The Quatuor Loiseau will be my interpreters on any of the following dates   1, 5, 8 or 14 June
Here is the programme I propose, subject to your approval.
    1   Petit trio (à cordes) Celtique
    2   2me Sonatine (op. 80) pour violon et piano
    3   Premier quatuor à cordes.
[durée de 35 à 40 m.]
    Please tell me at your earliest convenience which date you prefer.
        Cordialement vôtre,
            S. H

[with verso as 'envelope' addressed to: Monsieur Irving Schwerke, 18 rue Juliette Lamber, Paris (17e)]

Letter no. 16
                                                            Paris, 22, 5, 29.
    Cher ami,
    When you were so kind as to ask me whether I wished to invite anyone to your soirée on the 5th of June, I forgot two couples who would like to come and whom you would, I am sure, be glad to meet.
    Mr. & Mrs. Marten Cumberland
        20 rue Laugier (17e)
            and
    Mr. & Mrs. John Foulds
        45ter rue des Acacias (17e)
I would be much obliged if you w^d send them invitations.
    With all best greetings and thanks,
        Cordialement vôtre,
            Swan Hennessy

ENDS

Fig. 9.11: Portrait of Swan Hennessy, c.1928–9 (© Boris Lipnitzky / Roger-Viollet)

* * *

Swan's Way: Hennessy in Search of Lost Time (1925–1929)

In the interview in *Le Guide du concert* of 12 April 1929, Lucien Chevaillier begins by asking how well, and for what, Swan Hennessy is known in France – an interesting and pertinent question. After all, Hennessy had by now been living between 25 and 30 years in Paris, interrupted only by those five years in Switzerland during the War. It took a while for him to be acknowledged, and it began with favourable reviews of his Impressionist piano music, regular performances commencing only after his membership in the Association des Compositeurs Bretons and their circle. Not having been an alumnus of either the Conservatoire or the Schola Cantorum nor a member of the more prestigious musical societies, he did not have a large network of contacts, and as a miniaturist in small-scale genres he could not attract much attention. Still – given the originality and quality of much of his music, his reception has been remarkably modest. Did he go too far in his criticism of the avant-garde, was he, in Radiana Pazmor's words, really 'adored by his friends, and cordially hated by his enemies, of whom his weakness for saying just what he thinks has created him many' (see p. 366)?

In Chevaillier's introduction, this read thus:

> Swan Hennessy is often known for his short pieces for piano whose spiritual titles are not without analogy to those that made Erik Satie's fortune – but with a more balanced fantasy – : which may give such a misleading idea of his musical physiognomy, because, apart from this superficial analogy, there is really nothing in common between Swan Hennessy and the author of the 'Pieces in the Shape of a Pear', for whom he does not seem to have any exaggerated sympathy ...
>
> We also know Swan Hennessy through the volumes of *À la manière de ...* : but we would still have a very poor idea of him, if we limited ourselves to these pastiches full of fine observation and humour.
>
> We do not know enough about the full scope of his piano and chamber music works, but their clarity, frankness, conciseness, and natural charm are designed to seduce French ears in particular.
>
> So, I repeat: we know Swan Hennessy very little. [...][98]

Hennessy then explains his family background and the revelation at some point that he should be a 'Celtic' composer, gives details about his style and that it is not only the music of Ireland that he alludes to but that of Celtic regions in general – all largely quoted in this study.

---

[98] 'On connaît souvent Swan Hennessy par quelques pièces brèves pour le piano dont les titres spirituels ne sont pas sans analogie avec ceux qui firent la fortune d'Erik Satie – toutefois avec une fantaisie plus pondérée – : ce qui risque de donner de cette physionomie musicale si curieuse une idée assez fausse, car, en dehors de cette analogie superficielle, il n'y a vraiment rien de commun entre Swan Hennessy et l'auteur des morceaux En forme de poire, pour lequel il ne m'a pas semblé nourrir une sympathie exagérée ... / On connaît aussi Swan Hennessy par les recueils de A la manière de ... : mais l'on se ferait encore de lui une idée bien insuffisante, si l'on se bornait à ces pastiches pleins d'observation fine et d'humour. / On ne connaît pas assez toute l'étendue de son œuvre de piano et de musique de chambre dont cependant la clarté, la franchise, la concision, le charme naturel sont faits pour séduire particulièrement des oreilles françaises. / Donc, je le répète: on connaît très mal Swan Hennessy. [...]'; *Le Guide du concert* 15:28, 12 April 1929, p. 791–793 [791].

Chevaillier only indirectly asks why Hennessy has never written any large-scale scores for the stage or for orchestra, and Hennessy only responds to the 'theatrical part' of the question:

> – No orchestra, no theatre?
> – I can honestly admit that I do not feel at all gifted for the theatre: and this for the excellent reason that deep down ... I do not like the principle of it. I don't think that drama is appropriate for music. When the action is at its critical point, I much prefer that the protagonists use spoken language. Music could perhaps, in my opinion, find its place precisely when this action remains stationary or when it subsides: in short when the theatre is no longer theatre!
> – But this is the very formula of the Opéra-Comique with its alternation of spoken and sung words!
> – I'm not saying no,' smiles Mr Hennessy, 'so I do have a particular passion for *Carmen*!
> – What about Wagner?
> – I love his orchestra; the music is admirable and I am still waiting for the singers to keep quiet to listen to it at leisure.[99]

And then, of course, he is asked about his opinion of the avant-garde and why he is not influenced by it – and he is again very much to the point in his humorous (and yet serious) response:

> – I have sometimes tried – out of curiosity – to make 'modern' music, but what do you want, I can't do it! And besides, I don't see any point in it. I understand that Debussy has revealed unsuspected possibilities until now: this glory will not be taken away from him and we all benefit more or less from it. But I declare myself incompetent before the inventors of modern 'polytonality' – a word I prefer to that of atonality which means nothing –. Undoubtedly this superposition of different tones can enrich the palette of a descriptive composer, but it has been singularly abused, and this abuse is dangerous because it quickly leads to an unbearable monotony.

* * *

---

[99] '– *Ni orchestre, ni théâtre? / – Je vous avouerai franchement que je ne me sens aucunement doué pour le théâtre: et ceci par l'excellente raison qu'au fond ... je n'en aime guère le principe. Je ne trouve pas que le caractère dramatique convienne à la musique. Lorsque l'action est à son point critique, je préfère infiniment que les protagonistes se servent du langage parlé. La musique pourrait peut-être à mon sens trouver place précisément quand cette action reste stationnaire ou quand elle s'apaise: en somme lorsque le théâtre n'est plus du théâtre! / – Mais c'est la formule même de l'Opéra-Comique avec alternance du parlé et du chanté! / – Je ne dis pas non, sourit M. Hennessy, aussi ai-je une passion particulière pour* Carmen! */ – Et Wagner? / – J'adore son orchestre, la musique est admirable et j'attends toujours que les chanteurs se taisent pour l'écouter tout à loisir.*'; ibid, p. 793.

Swan Hennessy died in a hospital in Paris on 26 October 1929. Apparently, he had just spent fifteen days there following an (unspecified) operation and died suddenly from an embolism. The journals *Comoedia* and *Le Guide du concert* gave details:

> The composer Swan Hennessy has just died in a hospital after an operation that had yielded the best results. He had risen on Saturday for the first time in two weeks, on the doctor's instructions. Half an hour later, he died, in full consciousness, of an embolism.[100]

> Just a month ago, the composer Swan Hennessy came to the offices of the 'Guide' for a few moments before entering a hospital for surgery. He was smiling, witty and cheerful as usual. The operation was perfectly successful and the patient was already convalescing when, suddenly, last Saturday, he died of an embolism.[101]

There were obituaries (unsigned if not otherwise mentioned) in *Comoedia* (28 Oct.), *The Chicago Tribune* (30 Oct., by Irving Schwerke), *L'Européen* (30 Oct.), *Le Guide du concert* (1 Nov.), *La Semaine musicale* (1 Nov.), *Allgemeine Musikzeitung* (8 Nov.), *L'Esprit français* (8 Nov., by Georges Migot), *La Bretagne à Paris* (10 Nov., by Albert Robin), *The Irish Independent* (12 Nov.), *Le Courrier musical* (15 Nov.), *Le Monde musical* (?mid-Nov.,[102] by Lucien Chevaillier), *La Revue internationale de musique et de danse* (15 Nov., by 'C. B.'), and *The Irish Times* (21 Dec.) – see further down for excerpts – as well as short notices of his death in *Le Figaro* (29 Oct.), *Journal des arts* (30 Oct.), *Journal des débats* (30 Oct., 3 Nov.), *Le Ménestrel* (1 Nov.), *Le Journal de l'Ouest* (4 Nov.), and the *Neue Zeitschrift für Musik* (Dec. 1929).

The funeral service was held on 30 October at the Roman Catholic parish church of Saint-Dominique on Rue de la Tombe-Issoire in the 14th arrondissement. At the well-attended funeral on nearby Montparnasse Cemetery, where his grave is still extant, the composer Georges Migot gave a memorial speech. It seems like Migot and Hennessy had become quite close during the latter's last three or four years, a friendship that was probably based not only on personal liking but also the individualists' status that they both had among Parisian composers. Recently discovered autograph letters of 1929 give an idea of this relationship even though the image necessarily remains sketchy until more documents come to light in the future.[103]

---

[100] '*Le compositeur Swan Hennessy vient de mourir dans une maison de santé des suites d'une opération qui avait donné les meilleurs résultats. Il s'était levé samedi pour la première fois depuis quinze jours, sur les indications du médecin. Une demi heure après, il mourait, en pleine connaissance, d'une embolie.*'; in *Comoedia*, 28 October 1929, p. 3.

[101] '*Il y a un mois à peine, le compositeur Swan Hennessy était venu passer quelques instants aux bureaux du "Guide", avant d'entrer dans une maison de santé pour y subir une opération. Il était souriant, spirituel et gai comme à l'ordinaire. L'opération réussit parfaitement et le malade entrait déjà en convalescence lorsque, subitement, samedi dernier, il mourut d'une embolie.*'; *Le Guide du concert* 16:5, 1 November 1929, p. 123.

[102] Exact source and date not specified in Hennessy's Press Book no. 4.

[103] Part of a bulk of autograph letters by various musicians that was offered as lot 1411 in Catalogue 8 (June 2018) of the auctioneer Aguttes in Neuilly-sur-Seine. I acknowledge the generosity of the company in providing me with copies.

In a letter of 10 January 1929, Migot wrote to Hennessy:

> Dear friend
> I accept your kind and double proposal and thank you for it – I don't mind a night's outing, and it gives me pleasure to hear you in detail, and to hear only you – and then to share a meal – so to continue to find myself well with you, talking amongst each other about what is dear to us.
> Until Wednesday at Loiseau's and to you very cordially,
> Georges Migot[104]

There is no documented event on 'Wednesday at Loiseau's' (which would have been 16 January) in Hennessy's papers, but it may have been the last rehearsals of the Loiseau Quartet before their concert on the 17th, which was the SALO event at the Salle Debussy (see p. 390) – a concert without any work by Migot. They also looked forward to having dinner on that day and may have had common plans in mind, perhaps like the one by the Andolfi Quartet at the *Cercle Musical* of Bourg-la-Reine on 10 April 1929 when the programme included Brahms' Quartet in A minor Op. 51 No. 2, Migot's *Mouvements d'eau*, Hennessy's Quartet No. 2, Op. 49, and Ravel's Quartet.

The other letters are addressed to Hennessy's widow, the first written just after the funeral on 30 October:

> Dear Madam and friend,
> as you wished, I am hereby giving you today the very pages which I read this morning and that had to be said about my dear friend, gone –
> All my painful thoughts are with you and your son
> With all my heart
> Georges Migot[105]

A longer letter of 9 November is full of warm personal words of consolation that need not be quoted here. A separate, shorter letter of the same day, however, appears to be an accompanying letter to something that Migot sent to Claire Hennessy. He says here, 'here is a tribute to my dear departed friend – I have been allowed to testify publicly what I can know – it is only natural that I offer it to you, dear Madam, with my painful sympathy'.[106] He is probably attaching the obituary he wrote for the paper *L'Esprit français*, which appeared the day before (see below, p. 418).

---

[104] '*10 janv. 29 / Cher Ami / j'accepte votre aimable et double proposition et vous en remercie – cela ni évite une sortie nocturne, et cela m'écus de le plaisir de vous entendre en détail, et de n'entendre que vous – et puis de partager un repas – donc de continuer à me trouver bien avec vous, nous entretenant de ce qui nous est cher. / À mercredi chez Loiseau et à vous cordialement / Georges Migot*'.

[105] '*30 oct. 29 / Chère Madame et amie, / puisque vous le désirez, je tiens aujourd'hui même à vous donner les pages mêmes sur lesquelles j'ai lu ce matin ce qui devait être dit sur mon très cher ami, parti – / Toute me pensée douloureuse est avec vous et votre fils / De tout cœur / Georges Migot*'.

[106] '*9 nov. 29 / voici un hommage à mon cher ami disparu – il m'a été permis de témoigner publiquement ce que je peux sais – il est tout naturel que je vous l'offre, chère madame, avec ma douloureuse sympathie / Georges Migot*'.

The following is the funeral speech by Migot, which was printed on a simple sheet of paper for Hennessy's friends and acquaintances (taken from Press Book no. 4 of the Hennessy family), followed by a translation:

Sur la tombe de Swan Hennessy
30 Octobre 1929 ([1])

Couchées ou debout, dans la main de Dieu, nous sommes tous et chacun des parcelles d'une Éternité vers laquelle nous allons.

Mais à chacun de nous est réservé d'entrer dans cette Éternité à une heure qui n'est jamais la nôtre, ni celle de ceux que nous aimons et qui nous aiment.

Devant cette tombe d'un vrai ami, notre tristesse est grande.

Swan Hennessy portait en lui une âme belle, d'homme et de musicien.

Cette âme demeure.

Et nous devons en conserver le souvenir en nous, comme une preuve et un témoignage d'une humanité supérieure.

Tous ceux qui l'ont connu savent à quelle noble qualité d'homme il appartenait.

Nous ne devons pas plus oublier le musicien, car il a su chanter, librement et sans orgueil, de ses chants dont quelques-uns, soyez-en certains, demeureront, parce qu'ils sont sincères et qu'ils témoigneront, dans l'avenir, pour un des aspects de l'âme humaine.

Comme un barde d'Irlande accueilli par les troubadours et trouvères de France, Swan Hennessy semble avoir apporté de nouveaux chants au folklore éternel.

N'oublions pas cela, malgré les vaines agitations et surenchères qui troublent, en ces temps, la pensée de quelques-uns.

L'humble chant aux justes accents survit aux bruits de la cité.

Je n'ai pas craint d'affirmer que Swan Hennessy en a composé quelques-uns qui possèdent ce don de survivance.

Dans le souvenir, continuons à l'aimer et n'oublions pas le musicien auquel fut accordé de tracer quelques lignes sonores durables.

Au nom de ceux qui le connurent et l'apprécièrent, c'est ce que je voulais exprimer à celle qui fut son admirable compagne et à son fils.

Qu'il demeure, pour ce dernier, un exemple de noblesse humaine et artistique.

Non pas adieu, mais au revoir, mon cher Swan Hennessy, car nous avons la conviction que la vie continue par-delà la vie.

GEORGES MIGOT

(1) Nous sommes certains d'intéresser nos amis – qui furent par sympathie ceux de Swan Hennessy – en publiant ici les ultimes consolantes paroles que lui adressa Georges Migot au cimetière Montparnasse.

At the grave of Swan Hennessy

Lying or standing, in the hand of God, we are each and every one a fragment of an Eternity to which we are going.

But each of us is reserved to enter this Eternity at an hour that is never ours, nor that of those we love and who love us.

Before this grave of a true friend, our sadness is great.

Swan Hennessy carried within him a beautiful soul, as a man and a musician.

This soul remains.

And we must keep the memory of it in us, as proof and testimony of a higher humanity.

All those who knew him know to what noble quality of man he belonged.

We must not forget the musician either, for he knew how to sing, freely and without pride, his songs, some of which, be certain, will remain, because they are sincere and will testify, in the future, to one of the aspects of the human soul.

Like an Irish bard welcomed by the troubadours and trouvères of France, Swan Hennessy seems to have brought new songs to the eternal folklore.

Let us never forget that, despite the vain agitations and outbursts that are disturbing the thoughts of some people in these times.

The humble song with the right accents survives the sounds of the city.

I was not afraid to say that Swan Hennessy composed a few of them who have this gift of survival.

In our memory, let us continue to love him and let us not forget the musician to whom it was agreed to draw some lasting musical lines.

On behalf of those who knew and appreciated him, this is what I wanted to express to the woman who was his admirable companion and to his son.

May he remain, for the latter, an example of human and artistic nobility.

Not *adieu*, but *au revoir*, my dear Swan Hennessy, because we are convinced that life goes on beyond life.

Georges Migot

(1) We are sure that some of our friends – who were sympathetic to Swan Hennessy – will be interested in this publication of the last consoling words Georges Migot addressed to him at the Montparnasse cemetery.

* * *

The obituaries largely echoed what Migot said, but also pointed out what Hennessy was known for and what would – probably, hopefully – survive him. The pivotal argument seems to have been his uncompromising integrity as a composer, and his humour and generosity on a human level. Schwerke wrote:

> His music is a monument of sincerity and integrity. It will remain that which not a few have for years known it to be: – the testimonial of a creative artist who lived his life as a man and his life as a musician, on one indivisible plane of idealism, faith and conviction.[107]

The journal *L'Européen* emphasised the global citizen that Hennessy was, which led him to discover a source of inspiration in the music of Ireland:

> His cosmopolitanism had made him more aware of his personality and suggested that he go back to the roots of Irish folk music.
> It is, in fact, Celtic folklore, which he drew inspiration from to compose works of astonishing originality and flavour.
> He was, for the poetic Erin, what Albéniz and Manuel de Falla are for Spain; Déodat de Severac for the Cerdagne, and Joseph Canteloube for the Haute Auvergne and Quercy.
> This shows that a well-understood Europeanism, far from dispersing and losing an artist, actually allows him to find himself.[108]

Le Guide du concert, for which over the years he had written so many comments on his own music and his concerned letters on musical trends he disliked, wrote:

> His death was unanimously regretted because, through his frankness, spontaneity and kindness, he inspired the deepest sympathy to anyone who approached him.
> A sensitive and delicate musician, he leaves, especially in the field of chamber music, numerous and sincere works, characterised as much by their original and fine writing as by their delicious Celtic flavour. As he himself told Lucien Chevaillier, during an interview that will not be read without emotion, Swan Hennessy was an American citizen of Irish origin, even though he had long since made France his adopted homeland.

The *Allgemeine Musikzeitung* in Germany had also accompanied Hennessy's career through many years. It emphasised the individual route the composer had taken:

> With Hennessy, an unusually cultivated and emotionally sensitive artist has gone to his grave, a musician who had the courage to walk his own path in the midst of the confusion of our time, without passing by the signs of the present without understanding. One should not allow his artistic legacy to fall into oblivion, which is above all suited to adding genuine and original values to domestic music.[109]

---

[107] 'Funeral Services for Mr. Hennessy To Be Held Today'; *Chicago Tribune*, 30 October 1929.
[108] '*Son cosmopolitisme lui avait fait prendre une conscience pus claire de sa personnalité et lui avait suggéré de remonter aux sources de la musique populaire de l'Irlande. / C'est, en effet, du folklore celtique, qu'il s'est inspiré pour composer des œuvres d'une originalité et d'une saveur étonnantes. / Il a fait, pour la poétique Erin, ce qu'Albéniz et Manuel de Falla ont fait pour l'Espagne; Déodat de Severac pour la Cerdagne, et Joseph Canteloube pour la Haute Auvergne et le Quercy. / Comme quoi un européanisme bien compris, loin de disperser et de perdre un artiste, lui permet au contraire de se retrouver.*'; 'Le compositeur Swan Hennessy', in *L'Européen*, 30 Octobre 1929.
[109] '*Ein ungewöhnlich kultivierter und seelisch empfindsamer Künstler ist mit Hennessy ins Grab gestiegen, ein Musiker, der den Mut hatte, inmitten der Verwirrungen dieser Zeit seinen eigenen Weg zu wandeln, ohne dabei an den Zeichen der Gegenwart verständnislos vorüberzugehen. Man sollte seine künstlerische Hinterlassenschaft*

In his text for *L'Esprit français*, Georges Migot focused on Hennessy's 'Celtic' music and described this style as 'accents expressed in a simple and clear musical language, stripped of afflictions and lies'.

> This Irishman has been with us as one of us, because it was here that he found the enduring Celtic genius that is so essentially necessary in making us something other than Caesar's adopted children. He is the proof that, before Rome and Greece, we were already there. […][110]

Lucien Chevaillier wrote an excellent and emotional account of both the man and the musician, from which we learn something about Hennessy's appearance and reception. And he combines it with a strong critique of the contemporary French audience that refused to give an artist like Hennessy the recognition he deserved:

> The Celtic spirit lived in him with a strange vigour: he had understood it soon and had to remain steadfastly faithful to it until his last breath. A natural sensibility, discreet and somewhat melancholic, hidden badly under a disillusioned smile, sometimes letting himself go to a cheerfulness that was full of restraint, with a clear, simple expression, not backing away from naivety with always a tad shyness or modesty, respect for others and oneself: thus, one could try to define the essential characteristics of this 'Celticism', to which Hennessy had devoted the best of his activity. In our time, he was a remarkable and almost isolated case. While not leading a worldly existence, he was far from living apart, kept in perpetual contact with contemporary production, carefully read new works, frequented and received musicians, was long established in this Paris that he loved and where life seemed sweet to him: and yet he was never subject to any influence from this environment. In his latest productions, we would not find, a passage, a chord, a note, which owes something to our advanced aesthetics. Of Celtic inspiration and expression, first instinctively, then voluntarily, he was and remained so, without exception, without a second of hesitation, doubt or sagging.
>
> Independence is not the best way to glory. The artist who refuses to enlist himself, will find himself isolated. The groups conspire against him with silence: if they sometimes talk about him, it is to overwhelm him with rapid contempt, by which his qualities receive the names of their corresponding defects: sincerity becoming naivety, clarity becoming poverty, simplicity becoming platitude. The snobbish, fearful and deceived public does not dare to listen, does not dare to admire, wanting to be 'up to date', fearing sarcasm, believing omens. Thus, a whole body of luminous, melodic, and facile works has not reached the large mass of those who would rather let themselves be blindly led than to look at the pretty flowers that line the path. And yet, how many delicious and fragrant phrases would have been beneficial to them! How many pages of innate grace, directly accessible, never boring, would have softened their feverish minutes! …

---

nicht der Vergessenheit anheimfallen lassen, die vor allem geeignet ist, der Hausmusik echte und eigentümliche Werte zuzuführen.'; *Allgemeine Musikzeitung* 56:45, 8 November 1929, p. 1119.

[110] '[…] *accents exprimés en une langue musicale simple et claire, dépouillée d'afféteries et de mensonges* […] *Cet Irlandais fut chez nous comme un de nôtres, par ce qu'il retrouvait ici le génie celte perdurable et si essentiellement nécessaire pour faire de nous autre chose que des enfants adoptifs de César. Bien plus pour prouver qu'avant Rome et la Grèce nous étions déjà.* […]'; in *L'Esprit français*, 8 November 1929.

If it is true that beautiful works contain within them a mysterious force that saves them from death, justice will be done to those of Swan Hennessy, in which are reflected the rare qualities of this man whose fine, sometimes sharp mind did not hide the exquisiteness of the heart.[111]

A journey to the United States (1930)

The story of this book (almost) began in Rockford, Illinois as the place of Swan Hennessy's birth, and it shall (almost) end there. In 1930, Claire Hennessy and her son Patrice visited the United States, arriving by ship in New York on 1 July and staying at least until mid-September. Their trip included Boston and Gloucester, Massachusetts, arriving 'by motor' in September in Rockford to see Swan's birthplace. Claire had now inherited the well-invested wealth originally accumulated by Michael David Hennessy, and Patrice would be next in line. A local newspaper, the *Rockford Daily Republic*, reported about their visit and its reason:

> The approach of his [i. e. Swan's] son's twenty-first birthday brings the necessity for making an important decision, and it was for this reason that Mme. Hennessy brought her son to America, – in order that he might see his father's native land. Since Swan Hennessy remained an American citizen to the day of his death, his son is technically an American citizen also, although he had never seen this country until this summer. If he should decide to remain in France, there is the question of military service to be settled.

---

[111] '*Une sensibilité native, discrète et quelque peu mélancolique, s'abritant mal sous un sourire désabusé, parfois se laissant aller à une gaité d'ailleurs pleine de retenue, une expression nette, claire, simple, ne reculant point devant une naïveté avec toujours un tantinet de timidité ou de pudeur, le respect d'autrui et de soi-même : ainsi, pourrait-on essayer de définir les caractères essentiels de ce « celtisme », auquel Hennessy avait voué le meilleur de son activité. Il constituait à notre époque, un cas remarquable et presque isolé. Tout en ne menant pas une existence mondaine, il était loin de vivre à l'écart, se tenait en contact perpétuel avec la production contemporaine, lisait avec soin les œuvres nouvelles, fréquentait et recevait des musiciens, depuis longtemps fixé dans ce Paris qu'il aimait et où la vie lui semblait douce : et cependant jamais il ne subit de ce milieu, la moindre influence. Nous ne trouverions pas dans ses dernières productions, un passage, un accord, une note, qui dût quelque chose à nos esthétiques avancées. D'inspiration et d'expression celtes, instinctivement, puis volontairement, il le fut et le resta, sans une exception, sans une seconde d'hésitation, de doute, de fléchissement. / L'indépendance n'est pas le meilleur chemin vers la gloire. L'artiste qui refuse de s'enrégimenter, se trouve isolé. Les groupes font, contre lui, la conspiration du silence : s'ils en parlent parfois, c'est pour l'accabler d'un rapide mépris où les qualités reçoivent les noms des défauts correspondants, la sincérité devenant naïveté, la clarté, pauvreté, la simplicité, platitude. Le public snob, craintif et trompé, n'ose pas écouter, n'ose pas admirer, voulant être « à la page », redoutant les sarcasmes, croyant les augures. Ainsi, toute une théorie d'œuvres lumineuses, mélodiques, aisées, n'ont point atteint la grosse masse de ceux qui aiment mieux se laisser aveuglément conduire, que de regarder les jolies fleurs qui bordent le chemin. Et cependant, que de phrases délicieuses parfumées, leur eussent été bienfaisantes ! Que de pages d'une grâce innée, directement accessibles, jamais lassantes, leur eussent adouci les minutes enfièvres ! ... / S'il est vrai que les belles œuvres renferment en elles une force mystérieuse qui les sauve de la mort, on rendra justice à celles de Swan Hennessy, en qui se reflétaient les rares qualités de cet homme dont l'esprit fin, parfois acéré, ne dissimulait point l'exquisité du cœur.*'; 'Nécrologie / Swan Hennessy', in *Le Monde musical* (?), mid-November 1929 [the source is not exactly clear, quoted from Press Book no. 4, p. 93, pasted in by Hennessy's widow without clear reference].

Thus, there was apparently the option to move to the United States, and indeed Claire did buy property in New York where they travelled to frequently from Paris (which did remain their base). The 'question of military service' was solved by Patrice / Patrick remaining an American citizen.

The paper rightly considered their trip unusual, since there were far more Americans looking for their family's roots in Europe than the other way around:

> And thus the story of Patrick Hennessy, a young Frenchmen [*sic*] whose manners and moustache are as Parisian as his name is Irish, appealed to the imagination of a Republic reporter who chanced to meet Monsieur Hennessy and his mother today in Rockford.
>
> Mme. Hennessy and her son came to the United States from their home in Paris in July to see the sight of the old Holland house in Rockford, where Mme. Hennessy's late husband, Swan Hennessy, was born in 1866.
>
> In her musical Gallic English, Mme. Hennessy told the story of their visit. Swan Hennessy was the son of Mr. and Mrs. Michael Hennessy, who lived in Rockford for a time back in the nineteenth century, before the elder Mr. Hennessy, a lawyer, went to Chicago to practice. [...][112]

Another newspaper's report of the journey is fun to read, but full of inaccuracies, making Claire (who was Polish) French, Swan (who was American) Swedish, and Patrick (also American) French:

> Patrick Hennessy, a Frenchman from Paris, France, is in Rockford with his mother to visit the birthplace of his father, Swan Hennessy, who was born in the old Holland House, when his grandfather, Michael Hennessy, was a practicing lawyer in Rockford. Here's a study in names and nationalities. Michael Hennessy, Irishman, American; Swan Hennessy, a Swedish named Irish-American; Mrs. Swan Hennessy, pure French; Patrick Hennessy, French with an Irish name. They found the old Holland House gone, and a business block in its place, and the city like the place where Swan Hennessy was born in 1866.[113]

Also full of outright ridiculous mistakes is the story of Claire Hennessy's oil portrait, which the American painter Theresa Bernstein (1890–2002) made of her during this trip.[114] In a biography of her husband, William Meyerowitz, we read of a meeting with a certain Mr Boehland, apparently a schoolfriend of Swan's (probably in Chicago) whom Claire and the painter visited:

> I wrote to Mr Boehland and gave Mrs. Hennessy a letter of introduction. She got a wonderful reception from him. It turned out that Mr. Boehland was a school chum of her late husband Swan Hennessy. Swan Hennessy had left home at an early age to seek his fortune. He was a brilliant young man, and he became the partner of Edward McCormick of the

---

[112] 'M'sieu Hennessy Visits Father's Birthplace Here', in *Rockford Daily Republic*, 15 September 1930, p. 1–2.
[113] 'Presents a Study in Nationalities', in *Belvidere Daily Republican*, 17 September 1930, p. 5.
[114] This painting was on the market when this study was in its early stages, c. 2015. I saw it on an auction website at the time but it was not retraceable more recently.

National Harvester Company in Chicago. Hennessy told McCormick, 'When I make my first million, I'm going to retire.' That's what he did. He went to Paris and became the founder of the Three Stars Hennessy Company, a very successful distillery.[115]

Rarely was a biography decorated with more fanciful and absurd inventions.

On her return from the US, Claire Hennessy instigated a prize in memory of her husband. The newspaper *Paris-Midi* reported in October 1930:

> Mrs. Swan Hennessy founded an annual prize of 500 francs, reserved for Ms. Le Breton's piano students. In this way, she fulfils a wish expressed by the late composer.

It is not known what became of the prize, who was awarded, or for how long it was running. Marthe Le Breton had certainly been a faithful performer of Hennessy's piano music, and she remained that for many years.

Claire continued to promote the music of Swan Hennessy as best as she could. She had the String Quartet No. 4, Op. 75 published with Eschig in 1930, some of the early songs as well (1932), remained in touch with the small community of musicians associated with Swan, and continued to look after the Press Books, adding relevant concert programmes and their reviews.

Although she lived mainly in Paris, Claire Hennessy died in New York City in the summer of 1947. Her body was transferred to Paris and buried in the family plot in Montparnasse. While in the US, she extended the copyright on some of Swan's compositions, but in the meantime all is in the public domain, except for some vocal music.

Patrice Hennessy (1910–1973) was a very intelligent and talented young man. He was the painter of his father's oil portrait (an excerpt is on the cover of this book) in the mid-1920s, and he also wrote plays, of which *La Rude journée de la nouvelle scène* (1945) was published. But he became primarily known as an expert on the French Revolution, collecting an immense amount of documents, autographs and other sources relating to the personalities involved in this historical event in the course of several decades. In 1958, he sold a large part of his valuable collection, probably in temporal proximity to the financial crash that largely deleted Michael David Hennessy's invested fortunes. He apparently got involved in a risky real estate deal in the US, was cheated, and all the money was gone in an instant.

Patrice was married twice, both connections not lasting long. His first marriage with Simonne, née Broche, lasted from 1939 to 1946; Simonne was among the victims of the famous Air France plane crash on 28 October 1949 on the Azores that also killed the former World Champion boxer Marcel Cerdan, lover of Edith Piaf. The couple's daughters Brigitte and Aline carried on the family name and held Swan Hennessy's archive together. A second marriage to Monique, née Del Porto, was also divorced after four years in 1954. Patrice died at almost the same age as his father, on 29 April 1973.

---

[115] Theresa Bernstein Meyerowitz: *William Meyerowitz. The Artist Speaks* (Philadelphia: The Art Alliance Press, 1986), p. 56.

A last Swan Hennessy Festival (1931)

The Press Books of the Hennessy family with Claire's continuation show that Swan Hennessy's music continued to be performed for about ten years until the outbreak of World War II. There can be no doubt that the War contributed largely to the fact that his music was neglected and largely forgotten from then on. Claire lived until 1947 and would have continued to collect programmes and press notices if there had been any. As during World War I, Hennessy's music appears to have been music for peaceful times. And after 1945, the perception of twentieth-century Western art music had again changed drastically, with the effect that composers writing tonal music were regarded with suspicion and as utterly conservative.

However, before the devastations of the next war, this attitude was not at all common, and Hennessy's music was, in fact, quite frequently performed, as Appendix 1 gives ample evidence of. Hennessy's old musician-friends – the singer Marthe Saisset, the pianists Marthe Le Breton and Maurice Servais, the violists Robert Chantôme and Paul-Louis Neuberth – continued to perform his music, and so did younger musicians who only came to the fore during the late 1920s, including the singers Lili Fabrègue and Mildah Polia, the violinists Suzanne Chevaillier, Tina Manteufel, Odette Malézieux (also with her string quartet), and Léon Zighéra; the pianist Marie-Antoinette Pradier; the flutist Gaston Blanquart; and the bassoonist Gustave Dhérin.

These musicians also continued to organise 'Swan Hennessy Festivals' on radio and on the concert platform. Their names occur in the programme of a radio festival on 11 February 1930 with a mix of vocal and instrumental works on offer (see Fig. 9.12) that was organised by the newspaper *L'Européen*. It came with an article describing Hennessy without any modesty as the 'saviour of ancient Celtic melody':

> Swan Hennessy to whose music we dedicated our radio concert last night was the bard of Ireland; he resurrected the ancient Celtic melody. […]
>
> He restored to us this Irish melody which does not have the almost infinite tonal variety of Breton melodies, which oscillates between maintaining or suppressing the sensitive note, but whose sinuosity of line is admirable and which forms objects, attitudes, even feelings!
>
> Swan Hennessy also had the gift of sharp and brilliant irony; he was a humourist of a witty verve, whose hilarity was made up of both observation and invention, fantasy and psychology.[116]

---

[116] '*Swan Hennessy à la musique de qui nous avons consacré, hier soir, notre radio-concert aura été le barde de l'Irlande; il aura ressuscité l'ancienne mélodie celtique. / Il nous restitua cette mélodie irlandaise qui n'a pas les variétés tonales presque infinies des mélodies bretonnes, qui oscille entre le maintien ou la suppression de la note sensible, mais dont la sinuosité de ligne est admirable et qui dessine les objets, les attitudes, même les sentiments ! / Swan Hennessy eut également le don de l'ironie preste et brillante ; il fut un humoriste d'une verve drue dont la drôlerie était faite à la fois d'observation et d'invention, de fantaisie et de psychologie.*', A. D. [André Delacour?] in *L'Européen*, 12 February 1930, p. 3.

Fig. 9.12: Programme of the 1930 Swan Hennessy Festival on Radio Tour Eiffel[117]

LE POSTE DE LA TOUR EIFFEL

diffusera le

SÈPTIEME CONCERT

de

"l'européen"

LE MARDI 11 FÉVRIER 1930, à 19 h. 20

PROGRAMME

Festival des Œuvres de Swan HENNESSY

TRIO CELTIQUE .... Swan HENNESSY.
   par Mme Tina MANTEUFEL, Geo DUPUY et Paule BERTRAND.
TROIS CHANSONS ECOSSAISES ....
   chant par Mlle Marthe SAISSET.
TROIS VALSES ....
FETE DE VILLAGE AU XVIIIᵉ SIECLE....
   par Marthe LE BRETON, soliste des Concerts Colonne, Lamoureux et Pasdeloup.
PAYSAGE (poésie d'André Delacour) ......
LA-BAS (poème de Joséphin Soulary)
LA LUNE BLANCHE (poème de Paul Verlaine ....
A DEUX (poème de P. Blanchemin) ......
   chant par Mlle Marthe SAISSET.
SONATE, pour piano et violon ....
   par Mlle Tina MANTEUFEL et Mme Marie-Antoinette PRADIER.

---

[117] Unreferenced in Hennessy's Press Book no. 4, p. 114.

Arguably of more importance than the radio festival – because it created several reviews – was the 'physical' Festival Swan Hennessy that took place at the Salle Chopin (the chamber music venue beside the large Salle Pleyel) on 25 February 1931.

The programme consisted of the following works:

1. *Deuxième Sonatine*, Op. 80
   Suzanne Chevaillier (vn), Maurice Servais (pf)

2.a. *Madrigal*, Op. 27 No. 1
   b. *Banlieues*, Op. 69
   Maurice Servais (pf)

3. *Chansons espagnoles*, op. 42bis
   Marthe Saisset (S), Quatuor Andolfi

4. *Quatrième Quatuor*, Op. 75
   Quatuor Andolfi

5.a. *Sonatine celtique*, Op. 62
   b. Quatre Morceaux, Op. 71
   Robert Chantôme (va), Suzanne Astruc (pf)

6.a. *Valses*, Op. 32
   b. *Étude de concert*, Op. 60
   Maurice Servais (pf)

7. Mélodies:
   a. *Leise zieht durch mein Gemüth*, Op. 3 No. 1
   b. *La Lune*, Op. 79 No. 1
   c. *À deux*, Op. 79 No. 2
   d. *Jane. Chanson ecossaise*, Op. 66 No. 3
   Marthe Saisset (S), Suzanne Astruc (pf)

8. *Trio*, Op. 70
   Suzanne Chevaillier (vn), Gaston Blanquart (fl), Gustave Dhérin (bn)

It is a remarkably varied programme, ranging from one of the very early Heine songs (Op. 3) to the very recent violin sonata, Op. 80, including vocal, piano and chamber music.

In a long review for the *Journal des débats*, the critic and composer Maurice Imbert (1893–1981) took a retrospective view on the achievements of Swan Hennessy. Before he got to the discussion of the works performed, he described his impression and his memory of Hennessy in an introductory paragraph:

The memory of the late Swan Hennessy has remained vivid in the mind of all those who knew him. They enjoyed to remember how simple, how modest, how straight, how good he was; and to hear his music again, as melancholic as a lacustrine landscape in Scotland, or as animated as the cheerfulness that tempered his northern nature, his lips slightly wrinkled by a hardly ironic smile; always distinguished, even aristocratic, with manners evoking the gentleman farmer. All these distinctions of the man can be found in the composer's music: and we will have drawn a brief portrait of him when we add that, although born in America, Swan Hennessy was of Irish descent; had studied his art in Germany and although he had little knowledge of the country of his origins, his music is, instinctively, all embalmed with Celtic perfumes.[118]

Fig. 9.13: Advertisement for the third Hennessy Festival (in *Journal des débats*, 23 Feb. 1931)

Another warm personal memory was expressed by Eugène Cools in *Le Monde musical*:

It was, for all those who knew the excellent musician Swan Hennessy, a profound artist and a man of heart, a relaxing evening enhanced by the regrets of the untimely death of a remarkable, sensitive, modest but talented composer, whom his contemporaries may not always have appreciated at his true value. Swan Hennessy had studied very seriously and was well aware of the entire musical evolution of recent years. Under an apparent simplicity,

---

[118] '*Le souvenir du regretté Swan Hennessy est demeuré vivace en la mémoire de tous ceux qui l'ont connu. Ils se plaisent à se le rappeler si simple, si modeste, si droit, si bon; à le revoir, soit mélancolique tel un paysage lacustre d'Ecosse, soit animé de cette gaîté que tempérait sa nature nordique, soit la lèvre légèrement plissée par un sourire à peine ironique; distingué toujours, aristocratique même, avec cet on ne sait quoi dans les manières évoquant le gentleman farmer. Toutes ces distinctives de l'homme se retrouvent dans la musique du compositeur : et nous aurons tracé du celui-ci un portrait en bref quand nous aurons ajouté que, quoique né en Amérique, Swan Hennessy était de souche irlandaise; quoique ayant travaillé son art en Allemagne et connaissant peu son pays d'origine primitive, sa musique est, instinctivement, toute embaumée de parfums celtiques.*'; Maurice Imbert: 'Œuvres de Swan Hennessy', in *Journal des débats*, 3 March 1931, p. 4.

his works are full of unexpected turns and of his personality; I see no musician who can be compared to him in the evocation of Celtic folklore or in the poetry with which he exploits this music, which, I am sure, will survive many more modern works.[119]

> I leave Mr Hennessy deeply touched by his warm welcome,
> loaded with some precious scores that the Celtic Master offered me
> with the most charming good grace,
> and, back home, it is with delicate joy that I leaf through these
> delicious, clear, direct, varied pages on the piano,
> where everything flows from an abundant and pure source,
> true confidence, sweet consolation
> that we will always like to play again
> in morose days and at times of doubt and sadness.[120]

---

[119] '*Ce fut, pour tous ceux qui ont connu l'excellent musicien Swan Hennessy, profondément artiste et doublé d'un homme de cœur, une soirée reposante augmentée des regrets de la disparition prématurée d'un compositeur remarquable, sensible, modeste, mais plein de talent et que ses contemporains n'ont peut-être pas toujours apprécié à sa juste valeur. Swan Hennessy avait fait des études très sérieuses et il n'ignorait rien de toute l'évolution musicale de ces dernières années. Sous une apparente simplicité, ses œuvres sont pleines d'imprévu et de personnalité ; je ne vois aucun musicien qui puisse lui être comparé dans l'évocation du folklore celtique ou dans la poésie avec laquelle il exploite cette musique qui, j'en suis certain, survivra à quantité d'autres pages modernes.*'; Eugène Cools: 'Œuvres de Swan Hennessy', in *Le Monde musical*, (day?) March 1931 (no further references mentioned in Hennessy's Press Book no. 4, p. 141; this period of the journal is not in Gallica).

[120] This is the last paragraph from Lucien Chevaillier's interview with Swan Hennessy, op. cit., p. 793 – which I use here as my own farewell to Swan Hennessy. (*'Je quitte M. Hennessy profondément touché de son accueil plus que bienveillant, lesté de quelques précieux cahiers que le Maître Celte m'a offert avec la bonne grâce la plus charmante, et, revenu chez moi, c'est avec une joie délicate que je feuillette au piano ces pages savoureuses, limpides, directes, variés, où tout coule d'une source abondante et pure, vraies confidentes, douces consolatrices que nous aimerons toujours à relire dans les jours moroses, aux heures de doute et de tristesse.'*).

Afterword
Six National Perspectives on Swan Hennessy

As a composer who was American-born, German-educated, (briefly) English-resident, with an adopted home in France and a spiritual home in both Ireland and Brittany, Hennessy's biography and musical legacy is unusually diverse. This makes for an interesting musical *oeuvre* of many influences that can all be easily detected in his music.

The flipside of this versatility is that it has also hampered his perception. None of these nations or regions has unambiguously embraced Hennessy as 'one of their own'. For Hennessy's own time, this led to some confusion regarding his origins, which may have been obstacles in his quest for recognition. For the late twentieth century and our own times, he has fallen through the net of many ambitious musicians who would have been willing to explore rare repertory provided he had a clear national background, for instance in concert or recording programmes devoted to seldom heard music from a particular country. To questions like 'Is he American', 'Is he French', 'Is he Irish' one can (or must) reply 'yes' and 'no'. In a way, therefore, Hennessy's own epithet 'Celtic' is understandable, would it not disregard so much of his pre-WWI music (and sometimes beyond).

Thus, approaching Hennessy from six national or regional perspectives may be opportune. I will not go as far as including even more perspectives, such as an Italian (for his residence there for several years before 1903), Swiss (for his holidays and wartime residence there and some musical allusions), Belgian (for his travels before 1903 and contacts during the 1920s) or Spanish (for some of his music in a Spanish style). In the following six sketches my guiding question is: what is the connection, and why can Swan Hennessy be of interest to the musical public in these parts of the world?

1. The American Perspective

Through his birth in Rockford, Illinois, with a childhood and youth in Chicago, Hennessy benefitted from American citizenship. The Rockford Public Library is aware of him, and its website provides a little information. Very understandably, it is not much, but he is not ignored. On the other hand, few, if any, musically literate people of the United States are today aware of an American composer named Swan Hennessy. One may say, this is no wonder, as Hennessy has never spent any extended period of his adult life in the US, other than composers who spent only a period of their life in Paris and then returned. Hennessy had last seen the US in 1907 and then no more.

Hennessy had an extended family in the US on his maternal side, the family that gave him his putative first name, Swan. The once prominent Supreme Court judge Joseph Rockwell Swan was his father-in-law, and a relative who also practiced law supported the composer when he became divorced from his first wife in 1892–3.

In Stuttgart, Hennessy studied composition in an English-speaking composition class with the American teacher Percy Goetschius (1853–1943). Many years later, at age 80, when Hennessy had already died, Goetschius still remembered him as one of a handful of names he was able to recall.[1]

As the heir of his father's wealth, Hennessy lived all his life from the interest rates of investments at a Wall Street based investment trust – one of several advantages of his American passport, which also protected him during the war years in Switzerland. Through him, his wife Claire and son Michel Patrice (Michael Patrick) also gained American citizenship. Both frequently visited the US in later life, more often than Swan ever did, and Patrice lost most of the inherited money there in a real estate investment fraud during the 1950s.

In some musical compositions, Hennessy alludes to his American nationality: *L'Americain qui a bien diné*, Op. 47 No. 2 (1912), the *Trois Pièces exotiques*, Op. 57 (1922), the jazzy pieces of Opp. 68 (1925) and 71 (1926) – one may interpret these from a Parisian perspective, but one might do it at least as well from an American. The latter may perhaps have been inspired by his likely contact with George Gershwin.

There have not been particularly many performances of his music in the US, although I am hesitant to affirm this too strongly as it was not the scope of this study. Victor Herbert's orchestral arrangement of Hennessy's *Petite suite irlandaise*, Op. 29 was occasionally performed; there was the famous 1913 New York recital by Éva Gauthier, and a cursory internet search in American newspaper databases has revealed performances of Hennessy's chamber works Opp. 58 and 59 in the US between the 1950s and '70s. He also sought contact with the American singers David Bispham in the 1890s and Charles Hubbard in the 1920s.

Finally, an important contact was the music critic Irving Schwerke, Parisian correspondent to a number of American newspapers and journals, notably the *Chicago Tribune*. As shown in Chapter 9, they were on friendly terms, and had Hennessy lived but a few years longer, he would have been represented in Schwerke's volume of biographical essays, *Views and Interviews* (Paris, 1936).

There is every reason for American musicians and musicologists to explore the music of their forgotten compatriot, be it from an American, an Irish-American, or a research-based French angle: musicologists may want to study the 'American Impressionist', while Irish-Americans are presented with a new figure to examine, whom they have not been aware of previously. In my experience, though, while there is a large Irish Studies community at US universities that is strongly influenced by Irish-Americans, when it comes to music this is almost always confined to traditional music only – unthinkable if they would do the same in the study of literature or drama. It will be difficult but hopefully not impossible to establish Swan Hennessy as an important Irish-American composer, alongside Victor Herbert, Henry Cowell, and others. His 'Celtic' music should give more than enough evidence of his Irish identity.

---

[1] 'During these years, in my capacity as teacher, player and composer, I enjoyed many stimulating and delightful associations. There was Reginal de Koven (as pupil, but so briefly that I disclaim any responsibility); also, as pupils, John Carlowitz Ames, Harry Plunket-Greene (even a pair of Princesses), Swan-Hennessy and many more; [...]'; Percy Goetschius: 'Four Times Twenty Musical Years', in *The Etude*, March 1934, p. 158.

2. The German Perspective

We will never know exactly what made Swan Hennessy want to study music in Stuttgart, since hardly anything is known about his upbringing in Chicago and what may have brought him to music in the first place. Certainly, German music conservatories were very popular with American and British students of that time, as the research of E. Douglas Bomberger has impressively shown. Although he studied in an English-speaking class with the American Percy Goetschius, his piano teacher Edmund Alwens was German, and the seven years he spent in Stuttgart (1879–86) were enough to thoroughly inhale German language and culture. His education was conservative, deeply impregnated with German Romanticism, which is very evident in Hennessy's first compositions with publishers in Leipzig and Stuttgart, and in dedications to Clara Schumann and Theodor Kirchner.

Hennessy conversed fluently in both spoken and written German, and this opened doors for him when he successfully sought performance opportunities in Berlin in 1913 and 1922. Before the War, he also published a number of works with Schott in Mainz, even travelled there in April 1911, and the correspondence with Schott, documented in this study, speaks volumes with regard to his perception in Germany, the sympathies of Schott, and about Hennessy's attitude to the shared responsibilities of the composer and the publisher in terms of marketing. As a personal remark I may add here that because of this connection, it is a particular pleasure to have this book published by Schott so many years later.

The personal contacts he had in Germany (or with Germans) are not interconnected to the extent that one might speak of a network. The singer, critic and occasional composer Hugo Rasch wrote many supportive reviews, and it is such a disappointment to see him drifting off to the Nazis in the 1930s. Rasch intermediated with regard to the dedication of Hennessy's *Au village*, Op. 22 (1907) to Max Reger. Hennessy's attitude to Reger was ambiguous, though. The Paris-based music critic Heinrich Möller was a personal friend and sympathetic critic before the War, and similarly so the painter Carl Heffner and his wife.

Hennessy's music was very frequently reviewed by some of the leading German music journals, particularly the *Allgemeine Musikzeitung* and *Signale für die musikalische Welt*. Hopefully, these will become digitised in the near future (as in so many spheres, Germany is lagging behind international standards in terms of digitalisation).

Robert Schumann has been Hennessy's hero in his early music, and his spirit has never completely left him. He was also fond of Schubert and Mendelssohn as well as some aspects of the works of Reger. Unfortunately, we have no opinion by Hennessy of composers like Wagner, Brahms, Mahler, or Strauss, except that some of them appear in deliberately distorted form in his late 1920s' volumes of *À la manière de …* Heine and Geibel were German poets set to music by Hennessy.

Interestingly, German musicians are today among the most active performers of Hennessy's chamber music, particularly his Opp. 54, 58, 59. Long may it continue – and expand. This may be due to the rare instrumentation of these works and to the fact that many chamber ensembles – often offsprings of regional orchestras – are on the lookout for original works in their settings. Many German musicians have discovered that to distinguish oneself in the competition for attention, rare but attractive music helps, and this is a chance for Hennessy. Musicologists for their part may be drawn to the connections to Reger and Schott, quite apart from the broadening of the horizon, which goes hand in hand with the engagement with unknown composers beyond the established canon.

3. The English Perspective

It may very well be that, if there had not been the divorce in 1892–3, Swan Hennessy may never have left England (or the 'British Isles'). Initially, when he was sent to Europe for schooling in 1878, the destination was Oxford (not the university but an unidentified 'public' school). He did not stay longer than a year.

Immediately after his studies at Stuttgart in the summer of 1886 he returned to England, probably in the company of Lucy Roper, whom he may have met in Stuttgart. They lived in Southwark, London, and married in Edinburgh in December 1888, where Lucy's widowed mother lived with her sister. A daughter was born in London in 1889 whose 1920s photographic portrait as Lucie Mabel Henniker can be found on the website of the National Portrait Gallery, London. A son was born in Dublin in late 1890, as well. But the marriage failed early, and certainly not without Swan's fault. Lucy sought divorce in 1892, and it was granted a year later.

For some (unknown) reason, London remained attractive to Hennessy, but I failed to find a reason for the fact that his second marriage with the Polish woman Claire Przybyszewska took place in London in the summer of 1909, when both had already been living together in Paris for some years.

A number of his early works were published with Augener & Co. and Schott & Co. *The Monthly Musical Record*, an Augener publication, carried numerous reviews of Hennessy's publications, but these also include pre- and post-Augener publications. The fact that his Opp. 51, 53, and 55 were also published in London in 1924 is due to Michael Kavanagh, the Irish musician who initially attempted their publication in Cork, Ireland. There have also been some performances in England, but they were not many and they ceased many decades ago.

The pianist and composer Herbert Fryer was a friend for a few years, and he also met Carrie Townshend and Achille Simonetti in London, who all performed his music, notably the *Variations sur un thème original dans le style irlandais*, Op. 12 and the *Sonate en Fa (style irlandais)*, Op. 14. The various movements of *Miniatures*, Op. 11 were dedicated to English (private) friends, and the *Berceuse*, Op. 13 likewise to the English violinist Beatrice Langley.

The remarkable silence that befell Hennessy's reception in England after 1920 may be due to his visible siding with the revolutionary Irish in the form of the dedication of his String Quartet No. 2, Op. 49 to the hunger striker Terence MacSwiney. I have to say here, restrictively, that this is *my* interpretation in the absence of any available source that would give a different reason.

Why would Hennessy be of interest in England today? First of all, because of the connections outlined above and because of (hopefully) a more enlightened community of musicians, scholars and concert-goers today. But Hennessy's 'Celtic' music would also chime in nicely with contemporary approaches in England under the banner of the 'English Musical Renaissance', not because he would have been part of it (he wasn't), but because of stylistic affinities. Much of his music of the 1920s compares well with music by Granville Bantock, Rutland Boughton, Frank Bridge, or John Foulds and may be revived in their company.

4. The French Perspective

Swan Hennessy's reception in France has been extremely diverse, depending on the individual viewpoint of music critics, journals and musicians, ranging from the enthusiastic to the indifferent. His music was performed until the outbreak of World War II, his last propagators being his widow Claire who died in 1947 and some of the musicians with whom Hennessy had cooperated in his last decade. In other words, his music has not been performed in France for the last 80 years, with only very few exceptions since the copyright on most of his music expired in 1999.[2]

Hennessy settled in Paris around 1903 and died there in October 1929, thereby spending most of his professional life in France. It was a conscious decision, driven by the desire to be perceived in a French context. It was one of the longest periods of residence of any foreign composer in France around this time. Except for early works published in Germany and England, all of his music was published in France, mainly by E. Demets and his successor from 1923, Max Eschig, but some also with Hamelle.

From about 1906 until 1913, Hennessy produced a prolific stream of piano music and songs that clearly shows the increasing influence of his French environment. He has denied any strong influence of Debussy, but it can clearly be heard in much of his music. Without ever admitting it publicly, he was clearly influenced by Ravel at least in terms of formal models. He despised Satie who had produced more literature than music in Hennessy's eyes, but he has a very similar kind of childish, absurd humour in his titles and musical means. Compared to these three figures, Hennessy always places greater value on melody. But in his pre-War piano music, Hennessy is stylistically and technically fully up to date, never lagging behind. His descriptive, programmatic, humorous and Impressionist music compares well with that of his French contemporaries. Of this there can be absolutely no doubt, even though his music nearly always remains somewhat sketchy. I have also argued for Hennessy as a precursor of *Les Six*.

From the beginning, his music has received positive, sometimes enthusiastic reviews. But these did initially not lead to performances. It was only when he joined the group of Breton composers in 1912 that his music enjoyed more regular performances,

---

[2] His instrumental music is in the public domain, but there are still exceptions for some of his vocal music, which may still be under copyright depending on the date of death of the poet. In France, the general rule that a work loses its copyright 70 years after the death of its creator is expanded by the duration of the two world wars. In the case of a poet who died after May 1945, this may be up around ten years.

and after the War caused another interruption, there was only one decade left to make a name for himself. With his Irish name and a 'Celtic' style, he seems to have convinced French audiences more than with his pre-War attempts to be as French as possible. Unfortunately, this style often came at the expense of harmonic adventurousness. He was much more experimental in his non-'Celtic' music and was therefore now regarded as a conservative voice.

Hennessy's reputation suffered from a) the fact that he did not write any large-scale music, b) his general outspokenness, of which his published criticism of Schönberg and Satie has probably been only one aspect, and c) the fact that he had no alumni network in France, having neither studied at the Conservatoire nor at the Schola Cantorum and not being a member of the Société Musicale Indépendante.

Surely the sceptics among Hennessy's French contemporaries must have talked about him, perhaps more behind his back than in his face. They all must have seen his name in publishers' catalogues, on concert programmes, in the reviews. Did they consider him a weird American millionaire of no importance? Unless his name does appear in a French study in the future, we will never know what it was that prevented his breakthrough.

On the other hand, he did have a circle of committed performers, the Loiseau Quartet, the singer Marthe Saisset, the pianists Marthe Le Breton and Maurice Servais, the violist Robert Chantôme, the saxophonist René Laurent, and others. Apart from Breton composers, he was also cherished by another great individualist in France, Georges Migot. Renowned Paris music critics praised his music, including Henri Collet, Jules Combarieu, Émile Vuillermoz, and Lucien Chevaillier.

It has been Swan Hennessy's life-long desire to make a name for himself in France. Only half-fulfilled, his reputation evaporated with the outbreak of World War II. Will today's French musicians, musicologists, and the audience give him a second chance? I wished that the French would not say 'We have enough of our own composers to look after'. Here is a composer who can stand self-assuredly beside the better-known Impressionists and who also represented the 'Irish bard' among the regionalists of Brittany. 'Independence is not the best way to glory', wrote Lucien Chevaillier after Hennessy's death. Is it too much to hope that times have changed?

5. The Breton Perspective

The French will excuse me for including Brittany here as a 'nation'. A long separate history that lasted until the forced union under the French king François I. in 1532, during which Brittany was indeed independent (and then a French duchy until 1789), has shaped the way the Bretons see France and the French see Bretons. Of course, this is no longer the case, and the intense discussions in Brittany during Hennessy's lifetime and during Ireland's struggle for independence change nothing about it.

Yet, it was as part of a group of Breton composers seeking regional and cultural identity (and a degree of independence) that Hennessy began to be properly perceived by the French musical public. On account of what many at the time saw as a common, pan-Celtic identity, Hennessy came to be the Irish representative of 'Celtic' music in

France. Many years before this happened, the Hennessy family at least once spent their holidays on the northern coast of Brittany, when Swan Hennessy's mother died in that terrible boating accident near Roscoff in September 1880.

It is a pity that Hennessy is no longer perceived as a member of either the short-lived Association des Compositeurs Bretons or the Société Artistique et Littéraire de l'Ouest. More modern research or recording projects, themselves not many at all, do not include or even mention him, as if French society of the 1910s and 1920s had been more inclusive than today's. However, it may well be that Hennessy is simply too unknown to today's French musicians and the managers of recording companies, not to mention the representatives of French radio and music journals. For the record, therefore, this book served to demonstrate that Hennessy was part of a network that included composers such as Ropartz, Aubert, Ladmirault, Le Flem, Vuillemin, Haudebert, etc. (all except Jean Cras). Apart from a circle of devoted French musicians, it was the only network that he had.

The region and its traditional music were also significant sources of inspiration for Hennessy. The *Petite trio celtique*, Op. 52 as well as songs and small song cycles to poetry by Breton writers testify to this and may, together with similar influences from Scotland, form Hennessy's interpretation of pan-Celticism.

Brittany also played a role as a summer destination for Hennessy, where several of his works were written and performed. Slightly enlarging this regional focus, this would also include some parts of southern Normandy.

Breton musicians and musicologists may find in Swan Hennessy an important source linking the region with Ireland in the spirit of the still vibrant pan-Celtic idea.

6. The Irish Perspective

Swan Hennessy's father, Michael David Hennessy (1837–1919), was born in the city of Cork, and his paternal grandmother was from the Hayes family. Michael emigrated as a teenager during the last years of the Famine (1853) – it is unclear whether he did so all on his own, but it seems so. After a remarkable career in Chicago, Michael returned to Europe in his early sixties and died in Switzerland. Cork remained a focus for Swan, some of his contacts in Ireland were based there (Terence MacSwiney, Denis Breen) or came from there (Carrie Townshend), and he has been there at least once (in 1924) but probably more often.

Hennessy's first wife was from a family of former landowners in County Roscommon who was probably born in the locality of Ballygalda. Their second child, a son, was born in Dublin (or Sutton, near Howth, to be more exact) in December 1890, which must have been one of the occasions when Hennessy was in Ireland.

While in London in the early 1900s, Hennessy must have been an early customer of the Petrie Collection of Irish traditional music as edited by the Irish composer Charles Villiers Stanford. He has used tunes from it in his *Petite suite irlandaise*, Op. 29 (1908) for piano duet, the second of the *Pièces celtiques*, Op. 45 (1912) for piano, the fourth movement of the *Suite*, Op. 46 (1912) for string quartet, the third of the *Trois Chansons celtiques*, Op. 72 (1926) for voice and piano, the *Sonatine*, Op. 78 (1928) for two violins, the *Deuxième Sonatine*, Op. 80 (1929) for violin and piano, and a *Reel irlandais* (1928) for piano – in other words: in every composition in which he used an existing Irish traditional tune (rather than composing a tune in this style himself).

It took a while until Hennessy realised that his Irish heritage should become the core of his musical style. While there are early Irish-inspired works (cf. Opp. 12, 14, 28, 29, some pieces of Op. 35), it was only through his contact with Breton composers of a 'Celtic' persuasion from the year 1912 that he realised that this should be the route he was going to take. Interrupted by World War I and the death of his father, this could not be properly developed before 1920. But then it did.

'Celtique' as an epithet in his works' titles for Hennessy almost always means Irish, although there are exceptions when it explicitly includes Breton and Scottish influences. His music is *not* Celticist in the way that the music of Arnold Bax is (to take but one prominent example of British Celticism): Hennessy does not refer to any ancient Celtic legend, it does not portray landscapes. Hennessy recomposes tunes in an Irish style and uses them as thematic material in more or less tonal music, weaving these tunes into contrapuntal structures in a way that hardly another composer of the time did. This is an important achievement, and any accusation of conservativism must take second place.

It is difficult to determine how much real exposure to Ireland Hennessy had. Circumstantial evidence suggests his presence in Dublin in 1890, in Cork in 1908, and in Dublin and Cork in 1924. Apart from the aforementioned Townshend and Breen, other musicians he knew included the pianist Michael Kavanagh, the violinist Arthur Darley, the violist George H. Brett, and the cellist Joseph Schofield who performed Hennessy's music in Ireland in the early 1920s. He also met the young Frederick May in April 1924. His music was rather performed in the contexts of the Oireachtas and the Father Mathew Feis, not the Feis Ceoil, but this is a coincidence, being dependent on the musicians whom he knew. It still remains disturbing that none of his Irish visits is properly documented. He did not take part personally in Irish musical life in the form of concertising, interviews etc. In none of his vocal works did he use a text by an Irish poet. In Paris, too, he did not have any Irish network of contacts.

There was no reception or performances of Hennessy's music in Ireland after World War II (until the year 2016). The generation of modestly modern Irish composers that began to be active during the 1940s and '50s had never heard of him.

For Irish musical life of today, Hennessy's music has a great potential. So far, Irish composers writing in an Impressionist style were either arrangers of traditional music (Herbert Hughes), had a very small output (Rhoda Cghill) or came late (Joan Trimble). Hennessy's pre-War piano music (plus his 1920s Opp. 55 and 69) should be of huge interest to Irish pianists interested in French Impressionism. His wide range of Irish-influenced music for the piano, the duos with piano, his trios and quartets make available real discoveries of original chamber music with an 'Irish note'. It is a great resource to be studied in the academies, conservatories, and music schools, and it also makes attractive concert music and recording repertoire.

Appendix 1
List of works

The following is a list of Swan Hennessy's compositions sorted into the three types of genre (a) vocal music, (b) piano music, and (c) chamber music. They are represented by title (in *italics*), in the case of vocal music followed by the name of the text author, and opus number. Subtitles are not given in italics, independent of their language. They are followed by the titles or movements of the various pieces that make up a collection, and by the instrumentation. The documentation includes the (often approximate) date of composition, the publication (with publisher, year, and plate number), dedications (if applicable), selected advertisements, reviews of the publication and of performances, finally by contemporary performances before WW II, and broadcast performances (if no radio station is given, this applies to Paris, as broadcast from the Eiffel Tower). 'F.P.' indicates that the given date is without doubt the date of the *first* performance. When a score is available to download from the internet, this is included with a reference to either the Gallica website of the Bibliothèque Nationale de France (http://gallica.bnf.fr) and/or to the IMSLP Petrucci Music Library (http://imslp.org). In terms of libraries, the most significant ones with Hennessy holdings are in Paris (BnF), Berlin (StaBi), London (BL), and Washington D.C. (LoC).

In cases where a source for a performance or a review is given without a page reference, these are taken from one of the volumes of press books in the Hennessy Family Collection. These press books cite the names of journals and newspapers with their date, but without page numbers. When no source is mentioned at all, the information is from a programme leaflet of the event that was pasted into the press books.

The list combines the author's own research with registers in the Hennessy Family Collection. The latter feature opus numbers that in some cases are missing from the publications and also a handful of unpublished works. A few remaining obscure works (or sketches of works) are listed at the end of each section under 'See also'.

The Hennessy Family Collection

This refers to material in the possession of today's members of the Hennessy family in France (no direct relation to the cognac/brandy producing company, which is also of Irish origin). The collection is split into items located in the southern French city of Nimes and in a country house about 120 kilometres south-west of Paris. They comprise of six volumes of music manuscripts, bound in marbled cardboard and leather spines – here referred to as 'MS Book I' etc. – and four volumes of 'Press Books' covered in black cloth or cardboard.

The Press Books contain both clippings from the musical press and from newspapers of reviews of publications and recitals, as well as programme leaflets, all carefully pasted in and dated by hand (mostly Swan Hennessy's hand, after his death continued by his widow Claire). They begin in 1903, shortly after Swan Hennessy had met Claire, and extend into the mid- to late 1940s (his widow died in 1947), with a few late items inserted loosely, not pasted into the books.

Apart from the manuscript volumes and the Press Books, there are 15 volumes of printed music called (on the spine) 'École moderne – Piano', partly bound by Hennessy himself, in which he mixes his own music with that of contemporaries from France, Russia and Germany. Among those 15 volumes, one is exclusively devoted to songs by Hennessy, bound in brown leather and stamped 'C.H.' (probably for Claire Hennessy).

Finally, there is a list of works in Swan Hennessy's hand, with a typescript copy by his widow, which include selected brief commentaries about his compositional intentions or brief explanations.

Furthermore, the Collection also contains a volume of financial records of incomes and expenditures, both professional and private, meticulously recorded by Claire Hennessy.

There are no diaries or letters, but three hitherto unknown photographs, two rather early, private ones from the first decade of the twentieth century, two of Claire with their young son Patrice (probably dating from their Swiss 'exile'), a copy of the 1923 official Eschig portrait, and a mid-1920s portrait by Lipnitzki. As a highlight, there is an excellent framed oil portrait of Swan Hennessy painted by his teen-age son Patrice that probably dates from the mid to late 1920s.

I am extremely grateful for the trust that Brigitte Hennessy and her family showed towards me in that they allowed me to take these materials (except the oil portrait) to my home in Frankfurt and work with them at my leisure for the duration of writing the manuscript of this book (between June 2016 and September 2019). It has been a rare experience and an ideal situation for any musicologist to work in, free of any constraints about access, opening times of libraries, costs for reproductions, time pressure, and similar limitations. It was very helpful indeed to work with the music manuscripts; they revealed many dates of composition, unpublished pieces, variants, revisions, etc. Of the press books I made selective use, taking photographs or scans of the concert programmes and copying the majority of the review articles, except when I had already identified them in Gallica and other sources.

Considerations within the family as to where this material is to be archived at some point in time were not finalised by the time of completion of this book's manuscript, but it looks certain that it will be publicly accessible for research in an institutional library in due course.

Appendix

A. VOCAL MUSIC

***Vier Lieder,* Op. 3** (Heinrich Heine)
1. *Leise zieht durch mein Gemüth*; 2. *Die blauen Frühlingsaugen*; 3. *Mädchen mit dem rothen Mündchen*; 4. *Zum Schluss*.
For voice and piano.
Comp. *c*1885–6. MS missing. Pub. Stuttgart: G. A. Zumsteeg, 1886 (plate no. G.A.Z. 562^{a-d}). Dedication (no. 2 only): 'Fräulein Lucy Roper gewidmet'.
NB.: In the print, Nos. 3 and 4 have erroneously been numbered as Op. 3 No. 4 and 5 (i.e. either an error, or the collection had originally five pieces and No. 3 was not published).
Review in *The Monthly Musical Record* 17:197 (May 1887), 111.
Identified performances:
- Paris, Le Parthenon, 17 Jan. 1931, by Marthe Saisset and Maurice Servais (no. 1 only)
- Paris, Salle Chopin, 25 Feb. 1931, by M. Saisset and Suzanne Astruc (*Journal des débats*, 3 Mar. 1931; *Le Courrier musical*, 15 Mar. 1931)

***The Blackbird has a Golden Bill,* Op. 5.1** (Swan Hennessy)
For mezzo-soprano and piano.
Comp. 1886. MS missing. Pub. Stuttgart: G. A. Zumsteeg, 1886 (plate no. G.A.Z. 587). Dedication: 'To Miss I. C. Ross'.
Advertised in *The Musical Times* (1 Mar. 1887), 186. Review in *The Monthly Musical Record* 17:197 (May 1887), 111.
NB.: The work was published in a 'Second Edition' as 'Op. 5 No. 1'. No first edition or other parts of Op. 5 have come to light. In his own work-list, drawn up in 1929, this song merely appears as 'Op. 5', suggesting that Hennessy discarded other parts of the composition that may once have existed.

***Lydia,* Op. 23** (Charles Leconte de Lisle)
For high voice and string quartet.
Comp. 1906. MS missing. Unpublished. Like the piano version (below) probably dedicated to Hugo Rasch.
Identified performances:
- (F.P.) Berlin, Sing-Akademie, 16 Oct. 1906, by Hugo Rasch with Karl Klingler (vn), Joseph Rywkind (vn), Fritz Rückward (va), Arthur Williams (vc) (*Vössische Zeitung*, 17 Oct. 1906)
- Berlin, Choralion-Saal, 12 Nov. 1913, by Marguerite Sonntag with the Marix Loevensohn Quartett.

Version for high voice and piano
Comp. 1906, MS Book IV no. 1. Pub. Paris: J. Hamelle, 1906 (plate no.: J. 5489 H.). Second edition as no. 1 of *Quatre Mélodies*, Paris: J. Hamelle, 1908 (same plate no. as before). Third edition, Paris: E. Demets, 1913 (plate no. E. 1244 D.). Online score at Gallica. Dedication: 'à mon ami Hugo Rasch'.

Reviews (of *Quatre Mélodies*) in *La Revue musicale* 8:10 (15 May 1908), 306; *Allgemeine Musikzeitung* (22 Sep. 1911); *Lydia* also briefly in *Comoedia* (17 Aug. 1911), 2.

Identified performances (*Lydia*):
- Paris, Salle Majestic, 20 Nov. 1925, by Marthe Saisset and Maurice Servais
- Paris, Lyceum de France (17 rue de Bellechasse), 31 Jan. 1930, by Mme. Kotlaroff and Mlle. Rachmanoff
- Paris, Salle de la Société de Géographie, 9 May 1931, by Mme. J.-L. van Weydeveldt and Mlle. E. Talayrach
- Paris, Salle Debussy, 8 Jun. 1931, by Anne Valencin and Georges Hugon
- Paris, Salle de la Revue musicale, 26 Feb. 1934, by William Gwin and Ivan Markovitch
- Paris, Salle de concert de la Revue musicale, 9 Dec. 1934, by Jeanne Eudes and Valentin Pavlovski
- Paris, Salle Debussy, 7 May 1935, by Jane Herault-Harlé and Nilda Cazes-Novello
- Paris, Salle du Conservatoire Russe, 23 Jun. 1936, by Alice Milet and Jeanne Knoertzer

Broadcast performances:
- 13 Mar. 1928, by Marthe Saisset and S. H. (*Paris-soir*, 14 Mar. 1928)
- 30 Jun. 1929, by M. Saisset and S. H. (*La Croix*, 30 Jun. 1929, 7; *Hebdo*, 30 Jun. 1929)

Épiphanie, Op. 26 (José-Maria de Heredia)
For high voice and organ or piano.
Comp. 1906, originally as Op. 25, MS Book IV no. 4. Pub., Paris: J. Hamelle, 1907 (plate no.: J. 5501 H.). Second edition (without opus no.), as no. 2 of *Quatre Mélodies* (see Op. 23 & 31), Paris: J. Hamelle, 1908 (same plate no. as before). Third edition, Paris: E. Demets, 1913 (plate no. E. 1245 D.). Online score at Gallica. Dedication: 'à Mademoiselle Marie Stark'.

Review in *S.I.M. Revue musicale mensuelle* 7:1 (15 Jan. 1911), 93.

Identified performances:
- Paris, École de Chant Challet-Vicq, 4 Nov. 1922, by Gaëtane Challet-Vicq and S. H.
- Paris, Salle Majestic, 20 Nov. 1925, by Marthe Saisset and Maurice Servais
- Paris, Lyceum de France, 11 Jan. 1929, by Lili Fabrègue and S. H.
- Paris, Salle Debussy, 14 Feb. 1929, by M. Saisset and S. H.
- Paris, Salle Brunin, 23 May 1929, by Denise Groult and Mizzi de Mallen

- Paris, Salle Chopin, 9 Jan. 1930, by M. Saisset and Ludovic Bouserez
- Paris, Lyceum de France (17 rue de Bellechasse), 31 Jan. 1930, by Mme. Kotlaroff and Mlle. Rachmanoff
- Paris, Salle de la Revue musicale, 26 Feb. 1934, by William Gwin and Ivan Markovitch
- Paris, Salle Debussy, 7 May 1935, by Jane Herault-Harlé and Nilda Cazes-Novello
- Paris, Salle du Conservatoire Russe, 23 Jun. 1936, by Alice Milet and Jeanne Knoertzer

Broadcast performances:
- 26 Apr. 1925, by Marthe Saisset and Mme Esrabat-Eytmin (*Paris-soir*, 27 Apr. 1925)
- 7 Dec. 1925, by M. Saisset and S. H. (*Le Ouest-Éclair*, 7 Dec. 1925, 7)
- 1 Jul. 1929 (*La Croix*, 30 Jun. 1929, 7).

Version with string quartet accompaniment:
- Berlin, Choralion-Saal, 12 Nov. 1913, by Marguerite Sonntag and Marix Loevensohn Quartett (as Op. 23 No. 2).

Deux Mélodies, Op. 30

1. *Là-bas!* (Joséphin Soulary); 2. *Le Revenant* (Charles Baudelaire).
For low voice and piano.

Là-bas! comp. 1906 as *Deux Mélodies*, Op. 26 No. 2 (!), MS Book IV no. 3. *Le Revenant* comp. c1907, MS Book IV no. 5. Pub., without opus number, Paris: E. Demets, 1907 (plate nos. E. 1246 D. and E. 1247 D.). Second ed., as nos 3 and 4 of *Quatre Mélodies* (see Op. 23 & 26), Paris: J. Hamelle, 1908 (plate nos.: J. 5506 H. and J. 5656 H.). Online score at Gallica. Dedications: 1. 'à mon Ami Gino Sartoni'; 2. [none].
Identified performances:
- Paris, Salle Chopin, 5 Mar. 1931, by Jean Suscinio and Marcel Raby

(no. 1 only):
- (F.P.) Paris, Salle Majestic, 20 Nov. 1925, by Marthe Saisset and Maurice Servais
- 7 Dec. 1925, by M. Saisset and S. H. (*Le Ouest-Éclair*, 7 Dec. 1925, 7)
- 13 Mar. 1928, sung by M. Saisset (*Paris-soir*, 14 Mar. 1928)
- 11 Feb. 1930, by M. Saisset and Marie-Antoinette Pradier
- Paris, Salle Debussy, 23 Jun. 1932, by M. Saisset and Madeleine Dupré

(no. 2 only):
- Paris, Salle Majestic, 1 Dec. 1926, by M. Saisset and S. H.

Broadcast performances
- 30 Jun. 1929, by M. Saisset and S. H. (*La Croix*, 30 Jun. 1929, 7; *Hebdo*, 30 Jun. 1929)

***Trois Chansons écossaises*, Op. 31** (Charles Leconte de Lisle)
1. *Annie*; 2. *La Fille aux cheveux de lin*; 3. *Nell*.
For high voice and piano.

    1. *Annie* comp. 1906 as *Deux Mélodies*, Op. 26 No. 1 (!), MS Book IV no. 2. Pub. (as Op. 31 No. 1), Paris: J. Hamelle, 1907 (plate no. J. 5505 H.) and Paris: E. Demets, 1907 (plate no. E. 1286 D.). Also published as music supplement to *La Revue musicale*, no. 52 (1911). Dedication: 'à son ami Hugo Rasch' (Demets edition only).

    2. *La Fille aux cheveux de lin* comp. *c*1907, MS Book IV no. 6. Pub. Paris: E. Demets, 1920 (plate no. E. 2006 D.). Online score at Gallica. Dedication: 'à Madame Delorme Jules Simon'.

    3. *Nell*, comp. *c*.1906–9 (? or *c*.1921). MS missing. Pub. Paris, E. Demets, 1922 (plate no. E. 2037 D.). Dedication: 'à Charles Hubbard'.

    NB.: The typed work-list that Hennessy's widow prepared in the early 1930s claims that these three songs were composed in 1909. But this is is most certainly not true: the first two are older, and the third may date from as late as 1921.

    Reviews of no. 1 in *S.I.M. Revue musicale mensuelle* (15 Jan. 1911), 93; *Comoedia* (17 Aug. 1911), 2; *Allgemeine Musikzeitung* (23 Sep. 1911), 907; of no. 2 in *Musical Opinion* (Feb. 1922).

Identified performances:
- Paris, Salle Pleyel, 27 May 1922, by Mlle. E. Pellion and S. H.
- Paris, École de Chant Challet-Vicq, 4 Nov. 1922, by Gaëtane Challet-Vicq and S. H.
- Paris, Salle de la Fédération des Artistes, 6 Nov. 1924, by Marthe Saisset and Paulette Mayer
- Paris, Salle Majestic, 1 Dec. 1926, by M. Saisset and S. H.
- Brussels, Le Lyceum de Belgique, 27 Apr. 1928, by Elisabeth Miry and S. H. (*L'Étoile Belge*, 29 Apr. 1928)
- Paris, Salle Debussy, 8 Jun. 1931, by Anne Valencin and Georges Hugon (*Le Monde musical*, 30 Jun. 1931; *Le Courrier musical*, 1 Aug. 1931)
- Paris, Salle des Concerts de Montparnasse, 7 Jun. 1932, by Marie-Louise Labayle and unnamed pianist

(no. 1 only):
- Poitiers, late Nov. 1929, by Simone Bottrel and unnamed pianist (*L'Avenir de la Vienne et de l'Ouest*, 1 Dec. 1929)
- Paris, Salle Chopin, 23 Feb. 1932, by Mona Sangor and Denise Cools (*Journal des débats*, 1 Mar. 1932; *Comoedia*, 4 Mar. 1932; *Le Courrier musical*, 15 Mar. 1932; *Le Monde musical*, 31 Mar. 1932)
- Paris, Salle des Quatuors Gaveau, 22 Mar. 1933, by Simone Kaskevitz and Marguerite Papin
- Paris, Théâtre Albert I, 28 May 1933, by Marie-Louise Labayle and Mme. P. M. Jamet-Mottet
- Paris, Salle de la Revue musicale, 26 Feb. 1934, by William Gwin and Ivan Markovitch

- Paris, Salle Debussy, 7 May 1935, by Jane Herault-Harlé, Nilda Cazes-Novello

(nos 1 & 3 only):
- Paris, Salons Mustel, 27 Jan. 1929, by S. Bottrel and S. H.
- Paris, Maison des Arts et des Oeuvres, 17 May 1929, by S. Bottrel and Pierrette Bonniol-Bondy
- Chalon-sur-Saône, Théâtre, 17 Oct. 1929, by S. Bottrel and Lilette Besset

(no. 2 only)
- Paris, Salle Brunin, 23 May 1929, by Denise Groult and Mizzi de Mallen
- Paris, Salle Chopin, 5 Mar. 1931, by Jean Suscinio and Marcel Raby

(no. 3 only):
- Paris, Caméléon, 27 Dec. 1925, by Charles Hubbard and S. H.
- New York, 66 Fifth Avenue Playhouse, 21 Apr. 1926, by Ch. Hubbard and Josef Adler

Broadcast performances:
- 11 Feb. 1930, by Marthe Saisset and Marie-Antoinette Pradier

(no. 2 only)
- 13 Mar. 1928, by M. Saisset and Paul Géraldy

Version of no. 1 for high voice and string quartet
- Berlin, Choralion-Saal, 12 Nov. 1913, by Marguerite Sonntag and Marix Loevensohn Quartett

Trois Chansons espagnoles, Op. 42bis

1. *Fluthenreicher Ebro / Sur les rives fleuries* (Emmanuel von Geibel); 2. *Auf den Wällen Salamankas / Sur les murs de Salamanque* (Heinrich Heine); 3. *Neben mir wohnt Don Henriquez / Mon voisin est Don Henriquez* (H. Heine). French translations by Hennessy.
For medium voice and piano.

Comp. 1920, MS Book IV nos 7–9. Pub. Paris: E. Demets, 1921 (plate nos E. 2083 [1–3] D.). Second ed., Paris: Max Eschig & Cie., 1923 (plate nos E. 2083 [1–3] D.). Online score at Gallica and IMSLP. Dedication: 'à Mademoiselle Radiana Pazmor'.

Review in *Allgemeine Musikzeitung* (Oct. 1924).

Identified performances:
- (F.P.) Berlin, Bechsteinsaal, 23 Nov. 1922, by Radiana Pazmor and Georg Vollerthun (*Führer durch die Konzertsäle Berlins* 10, 13–26 Nov. 1922, 64; *Allgemeine Musikzeitung*, 8 Dec. 1922)
- Paris, Salle Beethoven, 28 Mar. 1923, by R. Pazmor and Ralph Lawton
- London, Guildhall School of Music, 13 Nov. 1924, by Adelaide Rind and Michael Kavanagh
- Paris, Salle Majestic, 20 Nov. 1925, by Marthe Saisset and S. H.
- Paris, Salle des Concerts Touche, 18 Dec. 1925, by M. Saisset and S. H.

- Laval, Hôtel de l'Ouest, 1 Jul. 1928, by M. Saisset and S. H. (*Le Regional de l'Ouest*, 9 Jul. 1928)
- Bourg-la-Reine, Salle de la Mairie, May 1931, by Lili Fabrègue and Georges Hugon
- Sceaux (Dép. Hauts-de-Seine), May 1931, by L. Fabrègue and G. Hugon
- Paris, Maison de la Mutualité (24 rue Saint-Victor), 16 Feb. 1932, by M. Saisset and Mme. Ferail
- Paris, Salle Debussy, 2 Dec. 1933, by Mme Anssono and Lucy Gard

Broadcast performances:
- 26 Apr. 1925, by Marthe Saisset and Mme Esrabat-Eytmin (*Paris-soir*, 27 Apr. 1925)
- 23 May 1927, by M. Saisset and S. H. (*Le Gaulois*, 22 May 1927, 5)
- 8 Jul. 1928, by M. Saisset and S. H. (*Radio-Magazine*, 8 Jul. 1928)

(nos 2 & 3 only)
- New York City, Aeolian Hall, 1 Nov. 1923, by Éva Gauthier and Max Jaffe (*Musical America*, 10 Nov. 1923)
- San Francisco, Scottish Rite Auditorium, 16 Sep. 1924, by R. Pazmor and Charles Hart (*Pacific Coast Music Review*, 15 Sep. 1924, p. 6)
- Oakland, California, Berkeley Playhouse, 16 Jul. 1926, by R. Pazmor and Elizabeth Alexander (*Oakland Tribune*, 11 Jul. 1926, p. S 5)

<u>Version for voice and string quartet.</u> Arranged from piano version, 1925. MS missing. Pub. [parts only] Paris: Max Eschig & Cie. (1926) (plate no. E. 2083 D.). Review in *Le Guide du concert* (9 Nov. 1928), 167.

Identified performances:
- (F.P.) Paris, Caméléon, 18 Mar. 1925, by Marthe Saisset and Quatuor Loiseau
- Paris, Salle des Quatuors Gaveau, 25 Feb. 1926, by M. Saisset and Quatuor Loiseau (Comoedia, 28 Feb. 1926, 2)
- Paris, Salle des Agriculteurs, 14 Oct. 1926, by Marcelle Gérar and Quatuor Loiseau
- Paris, Salle Majestic, 14 Mar. 1928, by Helia Wolska and Quatuor Loiseau
- Paris, Salle Chopin, 10 Nov. 1928, by H. Wolska and Quatuor Loiseau (*Le Courrier musical*, 1 Dec. 1928)
- Paris, Salle Chopin, 25 Feb. 1931, by M. Saisset and Quatuor Andolfi (*Journal des débats*, 3 Mar. 1931; *Le Courrier musical*, 15 Mar. 1931)
- Paris, Salle Chopin, 22 Apr. 1931, by Lili Fabrègue and Quatuor Andolfi
- Paris (unnamed location), 18 Mar. 1933, by L. Fabrègue and quartet of Mmes. Guellette, Blanche, Marc, Estignard
- Paris, Salle Debussy, 7 Jan. 1936, by L. Fabrègue and the Quatuor Malézieux (*L'Art musical*, 3 Jan. 1936, 201 [ann.] & 17 Jan. 1936)
- Paris, Salle Chopin, 13 Feb. 1937, by Mildah Polia and the 'Cordes du Quintette de Paris' (Lucienne Royer, Paulette Mélicourt, Cécile Blottière, Pierre Ruyssen) (*L'Art musical*, 12 Feb. 1937, 456)

- Paris, Students' Atelier Reunions (65 quai d'Orsay), 7 Mar. 1937, by M. Polia and the 'Cordes du Quintette de Paris'
- Paris, Salle Chopin, 13 Feb. 1938, by M. Polia and the 'Cordes du Quintette de Paris'
- Paris, 16 Avenue Henri-Martin, 22 Mar. 1939, by M. Polia with Jean Fuchs, M. Fuchs-Barbazanges, C. Blottière, P. Ruyssen.

Broadcast performance:
- 9 Mar. 1936, by M. Polia with unnamed quartet (*Le Peuple*, 9 Mar. 1936, 2)

Trois Mélodies, Op. 56

1. *Le Mort joyeux (Dans une terre grasse et plein d'escargots)* (Charles Baudelaire); 2. *Les Grands jasmins épanouis* (Albert Samain); 3. *Il était une fois. Chansonnette* (Jean Ajalbert). For low voice and piano.

Comp. 1921. 1. MS missing. Pub. Paris: Éditions Max Eschig, 1932 (plate no. M.E. 3692); 2. MS Book IV no. 10. Paris: Max Eschig & Cie., 1925 (plate no. M.E. 1564); 3. MS missing. Paris: Éditions Max Eschig, 1932 (plate no. M.E. 3693). Dedications: 1. 'à Jean Suscinio'; 2. 'à Charles Hubbard'; 3. 'à Marcelle Gerar'.

Identified performances:

(no. 2 only):
- (F.P.) Paris, Salle des Agriculteurs, 10 Jan. 1922, by Charles Hubbard and Madeleine d'Aleman (*The Chicago Tribune*, 10 Jan. 1922; *Comoedia*, 16 Jan. 1922, 4)
- Paris, Caméléon, 27 Dec. 1925, by Ch. Hubbard and S. H.
- New York City, 66 Fifth Avenue Playhouse, 21 Apr. 1926, by Ch. Hubbard and Josef Adler

(nos 2 & 3 only):
- Paris, Salle Majestic, 1 Dec. 1926, by Marthe Saisset and S. H.

(no. 3 only):
- Paris, Salle Chopin, 7 Apr. 1930, by Marcelle Gerar and Madeleine d'Aleman (announced as 1st performance)

Trois Mélodies sur des poésies d'André Delacour et de Leconte de Lisle, Op. 66

1. *Si la distance nous sépare* (André Delacour); 2. *Paysage* (A. Delacour); 3. *[Jane] Chanson écossaise* (Charles Leconte de Lisle). For high voice and piano.

Comp. 1921–4. No. 1 (*Si la distance ...*), MS Book IV no. 11. No. 2 (*Paysage*), MS Book IV no. 13. No. 3 (*Chanson écossaise*), as Op. 56^C, MS Book IV no. 12. Pub. Paris: Max Eschig & Cie., 1925 (plate no. M.E. 1631). Nos 2 and 3 also issued as a supplement to *Le Courrier musical*, 15 Nov. 1925. Dedication: 'à Mademoiselle Marthe Saisset' (in the MS, no. 3 is dedicated 'À mon fils Patrice').

NB.: In the MS, No. 3 is called *Jane*. '*Chanson écossaise*' is merely the subtitle. The title *Jane* has been omitted from the print.

Identified performances:
- (F.P.) Paris, Salle des Concerts Touche, 18 Dec. 1925, by Marthe Saisset and S. H.
- Paris, Caméléon, 27 Dec. 1925, by M. Saisset and S. H.
- Paris, Cercle Internationale de Musique, 23 Apr. 1928, by Denise Groult and S. H.
- Laval, Hôtel de l'Ouest, 1 Jul. 1928, by M. Saisset and S. H. (*Le Regional de l'Ouest*, 9–Jul. 1928)

(nos 1 & 3 only):
- Paris, Salle Brunin, 23 May 1929, by Denise Groult and Mizzi de Mallen

(no. 2 only):
- Brussels, Le Lyceum de Belgique, 27 Apr. 1928, by Elisabeth Miry and S. H.
- Paris, Salle Chopin, 9 Jan. 1930, by Marthe Saisset and Ludovic Bouserez

(no. 3 only):
- Paris, Salle du Guide de Concert, 28 Nov. 1927, by Denise Groult and S. H.
- Paris, Salle Debussy, 14 Feb. 1929, by M. Saisset and S. H.
- Paris, G.L.D.F.R.L. 439 'Droit & Devoir', 27 Feb. 1929, by D. Groult and Émile Carasso
- Paris, Le Parthenon, 17 Jan. 1931, by M. Saisset and Maurice Servais
- Paris, Salle Chopin, 25 Feb. 1931, by M. Saisset and Suzanne Astruc (*Journal des débats*, 3 Mar. 1931; *Le Courrier musical*, 15 Mar. 1931)
- Paris, Salle Debussy, 8 Jun. 1931, by Anne Valencin and Georges Hugon (*Le Monde musical*, 30 Jun. 1931; *Le Courrier musical*, 1 Aug. 1931)
- Paris, Salle Chopin, 23 Feb. 1932, by Mona Sangor and Denise Cools (*Journal des débats*, 1 Mar. 1932; *Comoedia*, 4 Mar. 1932; *Le Courrier musical*, 15 Mar. 1932; *Le Monde musical*, 31 Mar. 1932)
- Paris, Salle des Concerts de Montparnasse, 7 Jun. 1932, by Marie-Louise Labayle and unnamed pianist
- Paris, Salle Debussy, 7 May 1935, by Jane Herault-Harlé, Nilda Cazes-Novello

Broadcast performances:
- 7 Dec. 1925, by Marthe Saisset and S. H. (*Le Ouest-Éclair*, 7 Dec. 1925)
- 23 May 1927, by M. Saisset and S. H. (*Le Ouest-Éclair*, 23 May 1927, 3)

(nos 1 & 3 only):
- 8 Jul. 1928, by M. Saisset and S. H. (*Radio-Magazine*, 8 Jul. 1928)
- 11 Feb. 1930, by M. Saisset and Marie-Antoinette Pradier (no. 2 only)

(no. 2 only):
- 14 Feb. 1939, by Yvonne Aubert and unnamed pianist (*Le Peuple*, 14 Feb. 1939, 5)

Trois Chansons celtiques, Op. 72
1. *La Chanson du rouet* (Charles Leconte de Lisle [Écosse]); 2. *Berceuse d'Armorique* (Anatole le Braz [Bretagne]); 3. *Le Départ des pêcheurs* (Pierre Scize [Irlande]).
For medium voice and piano.

Comp. 1926, MS Book IV nos 14–16. Pub. Paris: Éditions Max Eschig, 1927 (plate no.: M.E. 2115). Dedications: 1. 'à Henri Collet'; 2. 'à Eugène Cools'; 3. 'à Pierre Scize'.

Reviews in *La Bretagne à Paris*, 7 Apr. 1928; *La rassegna musicale* 1 (Aug.–Sep. 1928), 501; *La Semaine à Paris* (4 Jan. 1929).

NB. The tune of no. 3 is 'd'après un air irlandais de la collection Petrie'. I have not identified this tune in the Petrie Collection but found it in the first Bunting collection (1796) as 'The Dawning of Day'.

Identified performances:
- (F.P.) Paris, Salle du Guide de Concert, mid-Dec. 1927, by Marthe Saisset and S. H. (*Comoedia*, 12 Dec. 1927, 3)
- Paris, Salle Mustel, 17 Dec. 1927, by M. Saisset and S. H.

(nos 1 & 2 only):
- Brussels, Le Lyceum de Belgique, 27 Apr. 1928, by Elisabeth Miry and S. H.
- Paris, Salons Mustel, 27 Jan. 1929, by Simone Bottrel and S. H.

(nos 1 & 3 only):
- Paris, Salle de concert de la Revue musicale, 9 Dec. 1934, by Jeanne Eudes and Valentin Pavlovski

(nos 2 & 3 only):
- Paris, Lyceum de France, 11 Jan. 1929, by Lili Fabrègue and S. H.
- Paris, Salle de la Société de Géographie, 9 May 1931, by Mme. J.-L. van Weydeveldt and Mlle. E. Talayrach

(no. 3 only):
- Paris, Le Parthénon, 7 Feb. 1929, by L. Fabrègue and Christiane Maizier
- Paris, Salle Chopin, 23 Feb. 1932, by Yvon Le Marc'Hadour and Denise Cools (*Journal des débats*, 1 Mar. 1932; *Comoedia*, 4 Mar. 1932; *Le Courrier musical*, 15 Mar. 1932; *Le Monde musical*, 31 Mar. 1932)
- Paris, Salle Debussy, 17 Jan. 1933, by L. Fabrègue and Viviane Demolière

Deux Mélodies, Op. 73

1. *Le Chasseur noir* (Paul Gérardy); 2. *La Chanson du vent de mer* (Anatole Le Braz)
For medium voice and piano.

Comp. 1927, MS Book IV nos 17 & 18. Pub. Paris: Éditions Max Eschig, 1928 (plate nos: M.E. 2249 & M.E. 2250).

Identified performances:
- Paris, Lyceum de France, 11 Jan. 1929, by Lili Fabrègue and S. H.
- Paris, Maison de Balzac (Passy), 1 Feb. 1929, by Marthe Saisset and S. H.

(no. 1 only):
- Paris, Salle des Concerts de Montparnasse, 7 Jun. 1932, by Marie-Louise Labayle and unnamed pianist

(no. 2 only):
- Paris, Le Parthénon, 7 Feb. 1929, by L. Fabrègue and Christiane Maizier

- Paris, Salle Debussy, 17 Jan. 1933, by L. Fabrègue and Viviane Demolière

Broadcast performances (no. 1 only):
- Paris, Tour Eiffel, 8 Jul. 1928, by Marthe Saisset and S. H. (*Radio-Magazine*, 8 Jul. 1928)
- Paris, Salle Chopin, 23 Feb. 1932, by Mona Sangor and Denise Cools (*Journal des débats*, 1 Mar. 1932; *Comoedia*, 4 Mar. 1932; *Le Courrier musical*, 15 Mar. 1932; *Le Monde musical*, 31 Mar. 1932)

Trois Petits trios pour voix de femmes, Op. 76

1. *Il était une fois* (Jean Ajalbert); 2. *Panis angelicus* (St Thomas Aquinas); 3. *Vers traduits de Goethe* (Louis de Ronchaud).
For soprano, mezzo-soprano, and alto (solo voices).
   Comp. July 1928 (Nos 1 and 2), 11 February 1929 (No. 3). MS in Hennessy Family Archive (unbound). Unpublished.
NB.: No. 1 is an arrangement of Op. 56 No. 3.
Identified performance:
- (F.P., of nos 1 & 3) Paris, Salle Debussy, 14 Feb. 1929, by La Triade Vocale (G. Molinier, Marthe Saisset, Rachel Rialan)
- (no. 2 only), Jun. 1932 [unspecified location, date and performers, typescript programme in Hennessy's Press Book No. 4, p. 167]

Choral performance (complete):
- Paris, Salle Debussy, 23 Feb. 1939, by La Chorale 'La Ménestrandise' (*L'Époque*, 2 Mar. 1939)

Deux Mélodies, Op. 79

1. *La Lune* (Paul Verlaine); 2. *À Deux* (Prosper Blanchemain).
For soprano and piano.
   Comp. Paris, Apr. 1929, MS Book IV nos. 19 & 20. Pub. Paris: Éditions Max Eschig, 1932 (plate no. M.E. 3694). Dedication: 'A Mlle. Marguerite Breitner'.
Identified performances:
- Paris, Salle Chopin, 9 Jan. 1930, by Marthe Saisset and Ludovic Bouserez
- Paris (unidentified location), early Mar. 1930, by M. Saisset and Edouard Mignan
- Paris, Le Parthenon, 17 Jan. 1931, by M. Saisset and Maurice Servais
- Paris, Salle Chopin, 25 Feb. 1931, by M. Saisset and Suzanne Astruc (*Journal des débats*, 3 Mar. 1931; *Le Courrier musical*, 15 Mar. 1931)

(no. 1 only)
- Paris, Salle Chopin, 23 Feb. 1932, by Mona Sangor and Denise Cools (*Journal des débats*, 1 Mar. 1932; *Comoedia*, 4 Mar. 1932; *Le Courrier musical*, 15 Mar. 1932; *Le Monde musical*, 31 Mar. 1932)

(no. 2 only)
- Paris, Salle des Quatuors Gaveau, 22 Mar. 1933, by Simone Kaskevitz and Marguerite Papin
- Paris, Salle Debussy, 7 May 1935, by Jane Herault-Harlé and Nilda Cazes-Novello

Broadcast performance:
- 11 Feb. 1930, by Marthe Saisset and Marie-Antoinette Pradier

SEE ALSO:

Nur wer die Sehnsucht kennt. **Lied von Goethe in Musik gesetzt von Swan Hennessy, Op. 14.**
For voice and piano.
Manuscript, 1894, listed in: Otto Edwin Albrecht: *A Census of Autograph Music of European Composers in American Libraries* (Univ. of Pennsylvania Press, 1953), 145: "4 leaves 30 x 24 cm. Music on recto only. Song with piano accpt. Dedicated to David Bispham. New York Public Library." – Lost, according to information from NYPL.[1]
NB.: Opus 14 has later been ascribed to a different piece (see CHAMBER MUSIC).

Songs from 'As You Like It' (Shakespeare), **Op. 30**
1. *Under the Greenwood Tree / Unter des Laubdach's Hut*; 2. *Blow, Blow, thou Winter Wind*; 3. *It was a Lover and his Lass*.
For soprano and piano, with a version for string quartet.
Comp. *c*1909, MS Book IV no. 14. Unpublished and withdrawn. Dedications: 1. 'To Herr Heinrich Möller'; 2. 'To Mlle. Marie Stark', 3. 'To Miss Annabel McDonald'.
NB.: In Hennessy's own list of works, Op. 30 is ascribed to *Deux Mélodies* (1906, pubd 1908). For the German translation, his remark in the MS reads "Deutscher Text frei nach Schlegel und Tieck", suggesting that they are by Hennessy freely using the translations by Friedrich (von) Schlegel and Ludwig Tieck.
Identified performances:
- London, Bechstein Hall, 7 May 1909, by Annabel McDonald and Madeleine Booth (*The Morning Post*, 8 May 1909)
  (no. 1 in German translation, with string quartet accompaniment):
- Berlin, Choralion-Saal, 12 Nov. 1913, by Marguerite Sonntag (S), Marix Loevensohn Quartett.

---

[1] E-mail from NYPL dated 24 March 2017 indicating that after much searching and consulting with curatorial staff, the piece could not be located.

B. PIANO MUSIC
(piano solo, except Op. 29)

Ländliche Skizzen, Op. 1

1. *Am Bache (Andantino)*; 2. *Waldvöglein (Un poco vivace)*; 3. *Ländler (Moderato – Legato – [unmarked] – meno mosso)*; 4. *Ringellied (Allegretto)*; 5. *Legende (Lento quasi adagio)*; 6. *Die Sägemühle (Non troppo allegro)*.

Composed 1884. MS missing. Published Leipzig: Breitkopf & Härtel, 1885 (plate no. 17120); no. 6 published separately, London: Grosvenor, 1886 (*The Grosvenor Series* [...]; plate no. B. No. 5). Dedication: 'Seinem Freund und Lehrer Herrn Professor Percy Goetschius gewidmet'.

Advertised in *Musikalisches Wochenblatt* (8 Oct. 1885), 519; *Musikalisch-literarischer Monatsbericht* (Sep. 1885), 244; *Neue Zeitschrift für Musik* 52/81:40 (2 Oct. 1885), 408; (as *Rustic Sketches*) *The Musical Times* (1 Nov. 1885), 686.

NB.: There is also a copyright indication for G. Schirmer, New York, 1885.

Review in *Signale für die musikalische Welt* 43:73 (1885) 1154; *The Monthly Musical Record* 17:197 (May 1887), 111; also mentioned in *The London Musical Courier* (4 Jan. 1913).

Identified performance:
(no. 6 only):
- (as *Scierie dans la forêt*) Paris, Maison Gaveau (Salle des Quatuors), 21 Mar. 1930, by Marthe Le Breton
- Paris, Le Parthenon, 17 Jan. 1931, by Maurice Servais

Ein Spinnerliedchen, Op. 2

Comp. 1885. MS missing. Pub. Stuttgart: G. A. Zumsteeg, 1886 (plate no. G.A.Z. 564).

Announcements (as *A Spinning Song*) in *The Musical Times* (1 Aug. 1886), 495; *Musikalisch-literarischer Monatsbericht* (Sep. 1886), 297. Review in *The Monthly Musical Record* 17:197 (May 1887), 111.

Identified performance:
- (F.P.) Paris, Salle de la Société de l'Encouragement, 24 May 1908, by Mlle. Lucienne A. (pupil of Gabrielle Pineau)

Two Studies, Op. 4

1. *Staccato*; 2. *Legato*.

Comp. 1886. MS missing. Pub. London: Augener & Co., 1886; rev. ed. 1902. No. 2 published as *Study (legato)* (Augener & Co., and New York: G. Schirmer, 1890; plate no. 7241, published in a series called *Perles musicales*, no. 9); also published in *The Monthly Musical Record* 22:253 (Jan. 1892), 11–4. Rev. edition: "New Edition revised by the Composer, with fingering by Miss Carrie Townshend". Online score of the 1890 Schirmer print of Op. 4.2 at IMSLP.

Appendix 449

Advertised in *The Monthly Musical Record* 16:182 (Feb. 1886), 48. Reviews in *The Monthly Musical Record* 16:184 (Apr. 1886), 88–9; *The Monthly Musical Record* 32:384 (Dec. 1902), 230–1. The publication of no. 2 in the *Perles musicales* series was reviewed briefly in *The Monthly Musical Record* 20:240 (Dec. 1890), 274 & 22:253 (Jan. 1892), p. 9; likewise of the Schirmer print of no. 2 in *The Times* (26 Dec. 1890), 2.

Carneval-Studien, **Op. 6** (2 volumes).
Erste Folge: 1. *Moderato, con espressione caricata*; 2. *Thema. Un poco più mosso*; 3. *Prestissimo*; 4. *Energico*; 5. *Papillon. Molto vivace*; 6. *Prestissimo possibile – Agitato*; *O.J.I.D.L.Y.S!*. Zweite Folge: 7. *Velocissimo*; 8. *Thema. Andante molto*; 9. *Alice. Listesso tempo*; 10. *Finale (alla "G.")*. *Non troppo vivace; G! Prestissimo, giocoso – Precipitandosi*.

Comp. 1886–7. MS missing. Pub. Stuttgart: G. A. Zumsteeg, vol. 1, 1886 (plate no. G.A.Z. 591); vol. 2, 1887 (plate no. G.A.Z. 617). Dedication: 'Seinem Freunde Herrn Ernest Longley gewidmet'.

Announcement in *Musikalisch-literarischer Monatsbericht* (Oct. 1887), 469. Review of 1st vol. in *The Monthly Musical Record* 17:197 (May 1887), 111; of 2nd vol. in *The Monthly Musical Record* 17:202 (Oct. 1887), 235.

NB.: This work does not appear in Hennessy's own list of works, suggesting it has been withdrawn.

Im Gebirg (In the Mountains). **4 Klavierstücke, Op. 7**
1. *Mittagsstille / Noon (Andantino)*; 2. *Zwiegespräch / Canon (Lento)*; 3. *Abendnähe / Twilight (Ondeggiante)*; 4. *Träumerei / Dreaming (Lento con tenerezza)*.

Comp. 1887. MS missing. Pub. London: Augener & Co., 1887 (plate no. 7671); nos. 1–3 also published as a music supplement to *The Monthly Musical Record* 17:200 (Aug. 1887), with introduction on p. 178. Dedication: 'An Herrn Theodor Kirchner'.

Advertised in *The Monthly Musical Record* 17:198 (Jun. 1887), 144 & 17:199 (Jul. 1887), 168. Reviews in *The Monthly Musical Record* 17:199 (Jul. 1887), 153–4; *The Musical World* 65:39 (24 Sep. 1887), 752; *The Monthly Musical Record* 20:240 (Dec. 1890), 272.
Identified performance:
(no. 1 only):
- Paris, Salle de la Société de l'Encouragement, 24 May 1908, by Mlle. Elise I. (pupil of Gabrielle Pineau).
- Paris, Le Parthenon, 17 Jan. 1931, by Maurice Servais

Album Leaves (Albumblätter), **Op. 8**
1. *Lento*; 2. *Leggiero, con grazia*; 3. *Andante*; 4. *Vivace, giocoso*; 5. *Andantino*.

Comp. 1887. MS missing. Pub. London: Augener & Co., n. d. [1887] (plate no. 7672). Dedication: 'To Frau Clara Schumann'.

Advertised in *The Monthly Musical Record* 17:199 (Jul. 1887), 168.

Étude-Fantaisie, Op. 9
Comp. *c*1887–8. MS missing. Pub. London: Augener & Co., 1888 (plate no. 7902).
Advertised in *The Monthly Musical Record* 18:206 (Feb. 1888), 48; *Musikalisch-literarischer Monatsbericht* (Jul. 1888), 268. Review in *The Monthly Musical Record* 18:208 (Apr. 1888), 89.

Miniatures. Cinq petites pièces, Op. 11
1. *Vivace*; 2. *Moderato (più tosto vivace)*; 3. *Andantino*; 4. *Andante (legatissimo)*; 5. *Con brio assai*.
Comp. 1889. MS missing. Pub. Paris: Durand & Schoenewerk, 1889 (plate no. D.S. 4043). Dedications: 1. 'à Lucie'; 2. 'à Lambert Zegers Veeckens'; 3. 'à Miss Katie Lewis'; 4. 'à Gretchen Gœtschius'; 5. 'à William T. Scott Barber'.
Review in *The Monthly Musical Record* 19:222 (Jun. 1889), 130.
NB.: Withdrawn (no. 1 reappears as *Robert Schumann* in *À la manière de* …, vol. 1 no. 4 of 1926).

Variations sur un thème original dans le style irlandais, Op. 12
Theme of eight bars, followed by eight variations: 1. *Maestoso*; 2. *Allegretto con grazia*; 3. *Canon*; 4. *Fairies Dance. Vivacissimo molto leggiero*; 5. *Jig. Vivace*; 6. *Con tenerezza*; 7. *Moderato*; 8. *Fughetta. Allegro ma non troppo*.
Comp. *c*.1902. MS missing. Pub. London: Augener & Co. 1902 (plate no. 1287). Revised edition as *Variations on an Original Theme in the Irish Style* [published without opus number] London: Augener & Co., 1903 (plate no. 1287α). Second ed. as part of the *Album celtique*. Paris: Éditions Max Eschig, 1929 (plate no. M.E. 2319). Dedication: 'à Mlle Carrie Townshend'; in the rev. Augener edition: 'To Miss Carrie Townshend'.
Identified performances (see also *Album celtique*):
- (F.P.) London, Bechstein Hall, 2 Feb. 1903, by Carrie Townshend (*Daily Telegraph*, 3 Feb. 1903; *The Times*, 3 Feb. 1903)

Deux Études (en ut mineur) pour la main gauche seul, Op. 15
1. *Moderato, sempre molto legato*; 2. *Allegretto, più tosto sostenuto*.
For the left hand only.
Comp. 1905, MS Book I no. 1. Pub., without opus number, Paris: J. Hamelle, 1906 (reprinted, 1927) (plate no. J. 5405. H.). Online score at IMSLP.
Reviews in *La Revue musicale* (1 Jan. 1911), 18; *Monthly Musical Record* (1 Mar. 1911), 62; *Allgemeine Musikzeitung* (25 Apr. 1913), 610.
Identified performance:
- Paris, Salle de la Société de l'Encouragement, 24 May 1908, by Mlle. Georgette H. and Odette S. (pupils of Gabrielle Pineau)

Praeludium & Fuga, Op. 16

Comp. 1906, MS Book I no. 2. Pub. Paris: J. Hamelle, 1906 (plate no. J. 5340. H.), repr. 1927.

Reviews in *Monthly Musical Record* (1 Oct. 1910), 226; *Allgemeine Musikzeitung* (25 Apr. 1913).

Identified performance:
- (F.P.) Paris, Salle Debussy, 13 Jun. 1932, by Marthe Le Breton

Mazurka et Polonaise, Op. 17

1. *Mazurka*; 2. *Polonaise*.

Comp. 1906, MS Book I no. 3. Pub. for the composer, London: Augener & Co., 1906 (plate no. 1360α). Dedication: 'à Mlle. Claire Przybyszewska'.

Petit album, Op. 18

1. *Fussreise* / *En route* / *On the Road*; 2. *Das Wirthshaus* / *L'Auberge* / *The Inn*; 3. *Vorüberziehende Kinder* / *Enfants qui passent* / *Passing Children*; 4. *Aus der alten Zeit* / *Aux temps passés* / *From Old Times*, a. *Fughetta*, b. *Menuet*; 5. *Tänzerin auf der Bühne* / *Danseuse sur la scène* / *Balletgirl on the Stage*; 6. *Sonatine*; 7. *Scherzetto*.

Comp. 1905, MS Book I no. 4. Pub. London: Schott & Co., n. d. [1907] (plate no. 27919). No dedication in the print; in MS: 'à Mlle. Claire Przybyszewska'.

Reviews in *Allgemeine Musikzeitung* (31 Mar. 1911); *Comoedia* (20 Jul. 1911), 2; *Signale für die musikalische Welt* 71:38 (17 Sep. 1913), 1364.

Identified performance:
(no. 3 only)
- Paris, Le Parthenon, 17 Jan. 1931, by Maurice Servais

Aus dem Kinderleben. 6 kleine Tonbilder (*Scènes d'enfants* / *Scenes from Child Life*), Op. 19

1. *Puppenwiegenlied* / *Berceuse de la poupée* / *The Doll's Cradle Song*; 2. *Puppentanz* / *Danse de la poupée* / *The Doll's Dance*; 3. *Im Wald* / *Dans les bois* / *In the Wood*; 4. *Erster Walzer* / *Premier valse* / *The First Waltz*; 5. *Schläfriges Kind* / *Envie de dormir* / *The Sleepy Child*; 6. *Auf Wiedersehen!* / *Au revoir* / *Goodbye*.

Comp. 1904, MS missing. Pub. Leipzig: Breitkopf & Härtel, 1905 (plate no. Klav. Bibl. 24931).

Reviews in *Der Klavier-Lehrer* 29 (1906), 187; *Allgemeine Musikzeitung* (31 Mar. 1911).

Identified performances:
- (F.P.) Cannes, Villa Florence, 13 Jan. 1905, by S. H. (*New York Herald*, 14 Jan. 1905)
- Paris, Salle de la Société de l'Encouragement, 24 May 1908, by Mlle. Gabrielle I., Mlle. Alice P., Mlle. Marcelle van G. (pupils of Gabrielle Pineau)
- Paris, Caméléon, 27 Dec. 1925, by S. H.

Au bord de la forêt, Op. 21

Comp. 1906, MS missing. Pub. Paris, E. Demets, n. d. [1907] (plate no. E. 1267 D.). Dedication: 'à Mademoiselle Claire Przybyszewska'.

Au village. **Petite suite caractéristique, Op. 22**

1. *Noce campagnarde*; 2. *Fillettes*; 3. *Basse-Cour*; 4. *Sur l'herbe*; 5. *Au bord du ruisseau*.

Comp. 1906–7, MS Book I no. 5. Pub., without opus number, Paris: E. Demets, 1907 (plate nos. E. 1293 D.; E. 1294 D.; E. 1295 D.; E. 1296 D.; E. 1297 D.). Dedication: 'à Max Reger'.

Reviews in *Le Guide musical* (3 Nov. 1907); *La Revue musicale* 7:22 (15 Nov. 1907), 523–4; *Monthly Musical Record* (1 Mar. 1911), 62; *Comoedia* (1 Jun. 1911), 2.

Identified performances:

(nos 1 & 5 only):

- Paris, Salle de la Société de l'Encouragement, 24 May 1908, by Mlle. Madeleine R. and Mlle. Odette S. (pupils of Gabrielle Pineau)

(no. 1 only):

- Tarbes (Hautes-Pyrenées), (illegible date), 37bis rue Larrey, by P. Quijoux (pupil of Jean Clarens)

(no. 3 only)

- (as *Hühnerhof*) Berlin, Choralion-Saal, 12 Nov. 1913, by S. H. (*Allgemeine Musikzeitung*, 21 Nov. 1913)
- Paris, Le Parthenon, 17 Jan. 1931, by Maurice Servais

Eaux fortes, Op. 24

1. *Sérénade espagnole*; 2. *Bergérie*; 3. *Petite mazurka*.

Comp. 1906, MS Book I no. 6. Pub. Paris: E. Demets, 1908 (plate nos. E. 1387 [I–III] D.). Online score at IMSLP. No dedications in the print, but in MS only: 1. 'à Mlle. Gabrielle Pineau'; 2. 'à Monsieur Auguste Adam'; 3. 'à Mlle. Claire Przybyszewska'.

Review in *Comoedia* (1 Jun. 1911), 2.

Identified performances:

- (F.P.) London, Aeolian Hall, 5 Mar. 1910, by Herbert Fryer (*The Times*, 5 Mar. 1910, 14; *Daily Telegraph*, 6 Mar. 1910; *The Morning Post*, 6 Mar. 1910)
- Paris, Salle Pleyel, 12 Mar. 1910, by H. Fryer

(no. 1 only):

- Paris, Caméléon, 27 Dec. 1925, by S. H.

Broadcast performance:

(no. 1 only):

- 30 Jun. 1929, by S. H. (*La Croix*, 30 Jun. 1929, 7; *Hebdo*, 30 Jun. 1929)

Étude, Op. 25

Comp. 1906, MS Book I no. 7. Pub. Paris: E. Demets, 1907 (plate no. E. 1271 D.). Second ed., Paris: Max Eschig & Cie., n. d. [1923] (plate no. E. 1271 D.). Dedication: 'A Monsieur E. Demets'.

Reviews in *La Revue musicale* 10:19 (1 Oct. 1910), 428–9; *Signale für die musikalische Welt* (23 Nov. 1910); *Monthly Musical Record* (1 Dec. 1910), 271; *Comoedia* (1 Jun. 1911), 2; see also *Harvard Musical Review* 3:5 (Feb. 1915), 8.

Nouvelles feuilles d'album, Op. 27

1. *Madrigal*; 2. *Canon*; 3. *Style irlandais*; 4. *Petites scènes parisiennes*: a) *Montrouge le matin*; b) *Sortie de midinettes*.

Comp. 1907, MS Book I no. 8. Pub. Paris: E. Demets, 1908 (plate no. E. 1346 [I–IV^B] D.). Dedication: 'À mon ami Auguste Delacroix'.

Reviews in *La Revue musicale* 10:21 (1 Nov. 1910), 479; *Monthly Musical Record* (1 Jan. 1911), 17; *Allgemeine Musikzeitung* (31 Mar. 1911), 376; *Comoedia* (1 Jun. 1911), 2.

Identified performances:

(no. 1 only):
- Paris, Salle Chopin, 25 Feb. 1931, by M. Servais (*Journal des débats*, 3 Mar. 1931)
- Paris, 29 avenue de Suffren, 28 Nov. 1934, by Jules Fache
- Paris, Salle des Fêtes du 'Journal', 2 Dec. 1935, by J. Fache

(no. 4 a & b only):
- (as *Pariser Vorstadt in der Frühe*) Berlin, Choralion-Saal, 12 Nov. 1913, by S. H.
- (with French title) Paris, Caméléon, 27 Dec. 1925, by S. H.
- Paris, Le Parthenon, 17 Jan. 1931, by Maurice Servais

(nos 1 & 4a):
- Paris, Salle du Guide de Concert, 28 Nov. 1927, by S. H.

Variations sur un air irlandais ancien, Op. 28

Theme with twelve variations.

Comp. May 1908, MS Book I no. 9. Pub. Mainz: B. Schott's Söhne, 1908 (plate no. 28388). Online score at IMSLP.

Reviews in *La Revue Musicale* 8:22 (15 Nov. 1908), 609; *Monthly Musical Record* (1 Nov. 1910), 249; *Allgemeine Musikzeitung* (31 Mar. 1911).

NB.: The source of the Irish traditional tune is the Petrie Collection as edited by C. V. Stanford, corresponding to no. 1177.

Identified performances:
- Cork, Father Mathew Hall, 25 May 1924 (Oireachtas Festival), by Treasa Nic Ruaidhrí

***Bláithfhleasg bheag, d'fhonnaibh arsa Gaedhealacha as leabhar Petrie. / Petite suite irlandaise, d'après des airs anciens de la collection Petrie*, Op. 29**
1. *Ancient Clan March*; 2. *Cork Reel*; 3. *Sagairt tar teorach*; 4. *Cork Reel.*
For piano 4-hands.

Comp. 1908, MS Book I no. 10. Pub., without opus number, Paris: E. Demets, 1909 (plate no. E. 1409 D.).

Reviews in *The Irish Nation* (11 Sep. 1909); *S.I.M. Revue musicale mensuelle* (15 Jan. 1911), 95; *Allgemeine Musikzeitung* (31 Mar. 1911); *Comoedia* (1 Jun. 1911), 2; *Monthly Musical Record* (1 Jun. 1911), 148.

NB. 1: The source of the Irish traditional tunes is the Petrie Collection as edited by C. V. Stanford, corresponding to the numbers 983; 903; 1089/1247 (identical); and 902.

NB. 2: There have been several other instrumental versions of this piece, probably unpublished, including one for orchestra (arranged by Victor Herbert)[2] and one for wind instruments.[3] In 1936, no. 3 was performed 'by a little group of strings (members of the Arbourfield Players)' in Dublin.[4]

Identified performances:
- Paris, Salle Érard, 23 Apr. 1914, by Andrée Gellée and Paul Martineau (*La Revue musicale S.I.M.*, 1 May 1914, 58; *Comoedia*, 4 May 1914, 5; *La Critique musicale*, 5 May 1914; *Le Monde musical*, 15 May 1914)
- Laval, Hôtel de l'Ouest, 1 Jul. 1928, by Marthe Le Breton and S. H. (*Le Regional de l'Ouest*, 9 Jul. 1928)

Broadcast performance:
- 2RN (Dublin), 12 Sep. 1931, by Frederick Stone and Edna Beaven (*Irish Examiner*, 12 Sep. 1931, 7)
- Radio Éireann, 2 Jul. 1937 (no performers mentioned; *Evening Herald*)

(Victor Herbert's orchestral arrangement)
- Radio Wien (Austria), 20 Mar. 1929, by Wiener Konzertorchester, Max Geiger (cond.) (*Radio-Wien*, 15 Mar. 1929, 8)

Arrangement of no. 3: *Sagairt tar teorach. Adagio de la 'Petite suite irlandaise'*
For cello and piano, arr. by G. Meyer.

Pub. Paris: E. Demets, 1913 (plate no. E. 1783 D.).

Advertised in *The Musical Times* (1 Nov. 1913), 775; review in *Allgemeine Musikzeitung* (22 May 1914).

---

[2] Performed New York, Carnegie Hall, 23 March 1913; a concert programme is in one of the Press Books in the Hennessy Family Collection. See also Aaron C. Keebaugh: *Irish Music and Home Rule Politics, 1800–1922* (diss. Univ. of Florida, 2011), 192.

[3] Performed as *Little Irish Suite*, New York, Guild Theater, March 1930 in 'Barrere Little Symphony' series; see *Brooklyn Daily Eagle*, 31 March 1930, 18. Also radio broadcast on Radio Wien (Austria), 20 March 1929, by Wiener Konzertorchester Max Geiger, *Radio-Wien* (15 March 1929), 36.

[4] *The Irish Press*, 9 January 1936, 9.

Identified performances:
- Dublin, Easter 1923, test piece in Father Mathew Feis
- Paris, Salle de l'École Normale de Musique, 11 Mar. 1931, by Jacques Serres and Janine Cools
- Dublin, Engineers' Hall, 17 Jul. 1931, by J. Serres and Fred Stone

Broadcast performances:
- Rome (441,2 m), 14 Oct. 1931 (in an 'Irish National Evening', no performers mentioned; *Irish Press*, 14 Oct. 1931, 3; *Radio-Wien*, 14 Oct. 1931, 63)
- Radio Éireann (Athlone; relayed from Engineers' Hall, Dublin), 8 Jan. 1936, by Joseph Schofield w/ unnamed pianist (*Irish Press*, 8 Jan. 1936, 5)

Valses, Op. 32

1. [no descriptive title] (*Allegro*); 2. *Espagne*; 3. *Suisse*; 4. [no descriptive title] (*Mesto*).

Comp. 1909, MS Book I no. 12. Pub. Paris: E. Demets, 1909 (plate no. E. 1448 D.); repr. by Max Eschig & Cie. (*c*.1923, with Demets plate no.). Dedication: 'à Mlle. Claire Przybyszewska'.

Reviews in *La Revue musicale* 10:12 (15 Jun. 1910), 302–3; *Signale für die musikalische Welt* (23 Nov. 1910), 1787; *S.I.M. Revue musicale mensuelle* (15 Jan. 1911), 94; *Allgemeine Musikzeitung* (31 Mar. 1911), 376; *Comoedia* (1 Jun. 1911), 2; *Monthly Musical Record* (1 Aug. 1911), 204.

Identified performances:
- Laval, Hôtel de l'Ouest, 1 Jul. 1928, by Marthe Le Breton (*Le Regional de l'Ouest*, 9 Jul. 1928)
- (nos. 1 and 4 only):
- Paris, École de Chant Challet-Vicq, 4 Nov. 1922, by M. Le Breton
- Paris, Caméléon, 27 Dec. 1925, by S. H.
- Paris, Salle Chopin, 25 Feb. 1931, by Maurice Servais

(no. 2 only):
- Paris, École de Piano Marthe Le Breton, 26 Jun. 1927, by (Mlle.) A. Charaitecher

(no. 3 only):
- Paris, Salle du Guide de Concert, 28 Nov. 1927, by S. H.
- Paris, Salle Chopin, 17 Nov. 1928, by Maurice Servais
- Paris, Salle des Fêtes du 'Journal', 3 May 1935, by Jules Fache

(three pieces from this collection):
- Paris, Le Parthenon, 17 Jan. 1931, by Maurice Servais
- Paris, Salle Chopin, 25 Feb. 1931, by M. Servais (*Journal des débats*, 3 Mar. 1931; *Le Courrier musical*, 15 Mar. 1931)
- Paris, Salle Chopin, 23 Feb. 1932, by M. Servais (*Journal des débats*, 1 Mar.1932; *Comoedia*, 4 Mar. 1932; *Le Courrier musical*, 15 Mar. 1932; *Le Monde musical*, 31 Mar. 1932)

Broadcast performance:
- 8 Jul. 1928, by Marthe Le Breton (*Radio-Magazine*, 8 Jul. 1928)

Croquis de femmes, Op. 33

1. *Au couvent*; 2. *Bavardes*; 3. *La Vieille tante*; 4. *Mondaine*; 5. *Jeunes anglaises*; 6. *Dans les jardins du sérail*; 7. *Charmeuse de serpents*.

Comp. *c.*1910–11, MS Book III no. 2. Pub. Paris: F. Durdilly, Ch. Hayet, successeur, 1911 (plate no. C. 6254 H.). Dedication: 'à Monsieur Jules Combarieu, Hommage sympathique et reconnaissant'.

Reviews in *Monthly Musical Record* (1 Apr. 1911), 92; *La Revue musicale* 11:8 (15 Apr. 1911), 173; *Signale für die musikalische Welt* (24 May 1911); *Comoedia* (25 May 1911), 2; *Allgemeine Musikzeitung* (16 Jun. 1911), 672.

Identified performances:
(nos 2 & 5 only):
- Paris, Maison Gaveau, 26 May 1930, by Marie-Antoinette Gaveau (*Le Monde musical*, 1 Jun. 1930; *Journal des débats*, 4 Jun. 1930)

(nos 3 & 5 only):
- Paris, Caméléon, 18 Mar. 1925, by Maurice Servais
- Paris, Le Parthenon, 17 Jan. 1931, by M. Servais

(no. 5 only):
- Paris, Salle du Guide de Concert, 28 Nov. 1927, by S. H.

(nos 1–5 only):
- Brussels, Le Lyceum de Belgique, 27 Apr. 1928, by S. H. (*L'Etoile Belge*, 29 Apr. 1928)
- Paris, Salle Gaveau, 6 Jun. 1929, by Denyse Molié (*Journal des débats*, 10 Jun. 1929; *La Semaine à Paris*, 14 Jun. 1929, *Le Courrier musical*, 1 Jul. 1929)

Broadcast performance (nos 2 & 5 only):
- 4 Jul. 1931, by unnamed performer (*La Croix*, 3 Jul. 1931, 7)

Petite suite sur les notes Mi Do Mi Fa Si Mi, Op. 34

1. *Allegretto*; 2. *Andante semplice*; 3. *Finale; Fuga*.

Comp. in Zweisimmen, Switzerland, August 1909 (on the last page of the Schott print, it reads 'Septembre 1909'), MS Book I no. 13. Pub. Mainz: B. Schott's Söhne, 1911 (plate no. 29378). Dedication: 'à mon cher ami E. Demets' (in the MS: 'À mon ami Eugène Demets, en souvenir de son chat et ses chiens: "Mi-Do", "Mi-Fa" et "Si-Mi"', with pencil note *"fällt weg"* ['to be deleted']). NB.: On the cover page, the pitches of the title are rendered as musical notes.

Announcement in *Musikalisch-literarischer Monatsbericht* (Jan. 1912), 10. Reviews in *Allgemeine Musikzeitung* (20 Oct. 1911), 1058; *La Revue musicale* 11:22 (15 Nov. 1911), 451; *Comoedia* (23 Nov. 1911), 3; *Monthly Musical Record* (1 Dec. 1911), 323; *La Revue musicale S.I.M.* (15 Jan. 1912), 76; *Signale für die musikalische Welt* (28 Feb. 1912).

Identified performance:
- Paris, Salle des Agriculteurs, 25 Nov. 1922, by Maurice Servais

Kinder-Album. **24 kleine Präludien in verschiedenen Ton- und Taktarten, Op. 35**

1. *Morgenliedchen*; 2. *Gesichterschneiden*; 3. *Mietzi's Schlummerlied*; 4. *Langweilige Geschichte*; 5. *Der lustige Irländer* (in MS: '*Irisher Tanz*'); 6. *Einzug des Prinzen Charmant mit seinem Gefolge*; 7. *Heute kommt der Lehrer nicht!*; 8. *Aus der Heimath*; 9. *Annie*; 10. *Begräbniss eines Bleisoldaten* (in MS: '... *Blechsoldaten*'); 11. *Erwartung*; 12. *Pfeifender Handwerksbursch*; 13. *In der Kirche*; 14. *Hübsch fleissig!*; 15. *Auf der Schaukel*; 16. *Puppen-Menuet*; 17. *Nach dem Regen*; 18. *Im Dunkeln*; 19. *Sonntags*; 20. *Der Sandmann kommt!*; 21. *Zerbrochene Puppe*; 22. *An den Mond*; 23. *Ländler*; 24. *Zum Schluss.*

Comp. 1909, MS Book III no. 1. Pub. Mainz: B. Schott's Söhne, 1910 (plate no. 28824). Dedication: 'Meinem lieben Vater gewidmet'.

Announcement in *Musikalisch-literarischer Monatsbericht* (Jun. 1910), 147. Reviews in *La Revue musicale* 10:12 (15 Jun. 1910), 300–2; *The Monthly Musical Record* (1 Jul. 1910), 153; *Signale für die musikalische Welt* (23 Nov. 1910), 1787; *Allgemeine Musikzeitung* (31 Mar. 1911), 376; *S.I.M. Revue musicale mensuelle* 7:7 (15 Jul. 1911), 90; *The Musical Standard* (13 Apr. 1912), 234; *The Musical Times* 53:836 (Oct. 1912), 654.

Identified performances:

(no. 7, as *Le Professeur ne veut pas*; no. 10, as *Enterrement d'un soldat de plomb*; no. 15, as *Sur la balançoire*; no. 18, as *Dans l'obscurité*):
- Paris, Maison Gaveau (Salle des Quatuors), 21 Mar. 1930, by Marthe Le Breton

(no.7, as *Le Professeur ne vient pas aujourd'hui*; no. 11, as *Attente*; no. 15, as *Sur la balançoire*):
- Bourg-la-Reine, Salle de la Mairie, Nov. 1931, by M. Le Breton
- Sceaux (Dép. Hauts-de-Seine), Nov. 1931, by M. Le Breton

Fêtes. **Deux Morceaux descriptifs, Op. 36**

1. *Fête de village au XVIIIme siècle*; 2. *Fête populaire dans la banlieue de Paris au XXme siècle.*

Comp. Paris, July 1910, MS Book I no. 14 Pub. Mainz: B. Schott's Söhne, 1911 (plate no. 29379). Dedication: 'à Madame Betty Heffner, Hommage sympathique' (in MS: 'Frau Professor Heffner gewidmet').

Announcement in *Musikalisch-literarischer Monatsbericht* (Jan. 1912), 10. Reviews in *Allgemeine Musikzeitung* (20 Oct. 1911); *Monthly Musical Record* (1 Dec. 1911), 323; *La Revue musicale* 12:1 (1 Jan. 1912), 4–5 *La Revue musicale S.I.M.* (15 Jan. 1912), 76; *Comoedia* (25 Jan. 1912), 3; *Signale für die musikalische Welt* (28 Feb. 1912).

NB. At the first performance in Berlin the collective title of the work was *Impressions*.

Identified performances:
- (F.P.) Berlin, Harmoniumsaal, 13 Mar. 1913, by Ella Jonas-Stockhausen (*Berliner Lokal-Anzeiger*, 16 Mar. 1913; *Vossische Zeitung*, 17 Mar. 1913; *Berliner Tageblatt*, 19 Mar. 1913; *Signale f. d. mus. Welt*, 19 Mar. 1913; *Allgemeine Musikzeitung*, 21 Mar. 1913; *Die Musik*, 1st Apr. issue 1913)
- Paris, École de Chant Challet-Vicq, 4 Nov. 1922, by Marthe Le Breton

- Berlin, Meister-Saal, 15 Nov. 1922, by Bruno Eisner (*Lokal-Anzeiger*, 18 Nov. 1922; *Der Tag*, 22 Nov. 1922)

(no. 1 only):
- Paris, École de Piano Marthe Le Breton, 26 Jun. 1927, by (Mlle.) A. Blin

(no. 2 only):
- Paris, Salle Debussy, 8 Jun. 1931, by Janine Cools (*Le Monde musical*, 30 Jun. 1931; *Le Courrier musical*, 1 Aug. 1931)

Broadcast performance:
- 11 Feb. 1930, by Marthe Le Breton

Les Noces du soldat de bois. Ballet en un acte, Op. 37

Comp. in Pornichet (Bretagne), July 1913, MS Book I no. 15. Unpublished.

NB.: The date can be found on the last page of the MS score. See, however, for another (unpublished) Op. 37 under 'See also' at the end of this section of the work-list.

Introduction, XII Variations et fugue sur un thème obligé, Op. 38

Introduction; *12 Variations*: 1. *Listesso tempo, espressivo*; 2. *Allegro molto*; 3. *Tempo primo*; 4. *(brillante)*; 5. *Lento sostenuto*; 6. *(Choral) Tempo primo*; 7. *Adagio*; 8. *(Polka) Allegretto*; 9. *(Style irlandais) Lento*; 10. *(Valse) Tempo di Walzer*; 11. *Andante*; 12. *(Carillon) Adagio*; *Fugue (à 2 voix), Moderato*.
For the left hand only.

Comp. 1909, MS Book II no. 1. Pub., published without opus number, Paris: E. Demets, 1910 (plate no. E. 1487 D.). Dedication: 'à mon ami Hugo Rasch'.

Reviews in *La Revue Musicale* 10:9 (1 May 1910), 237; *Monthly Musical Record* (1 Aug. 1910), 178; *Signale für die musikalische Welt* (23 Nov. 1910); *La Revue musicale S.I.M.* (15 Jan. 1911), 94; *Allgemeine Musikzeitung* (31 Mar. 1911); *Comoedia* (25 May 1911), 2.

NB.: The publication also includes, in the same volume, further variations about the same theme by the following composers:
- Hugo Rasch (1873–1947): *VIII Variations sur le thème obligé*, Op. 6. Dedication: 'à mon ami Swan Hennessy'; four pages (plate no. E. 1488 D.).
- Georges Loth (1880–1949): *2 Variations*: 1. *Bébé s'endort*; 2. *Bébé s'éveille – Joie*. Dedication: 'À ma petite Madeleine et à sa Maman'; fourteen pages (E. 1489^{I} + ^{II} D.).
- Auguste Delacroix (1871–1936): *Mazurka sur un thème obligé*. Dedication: 'à mon ami Swan Hennessy'; six pages (E. 1490 D.).
- Herbert Fryer (1877–1957): *Variations (sur un thème obligé)*. Dedication: 'à mon cher ami Swan Hennessy'; six pages (E. 1491 D.).

Incunabula, Op. 39

1. *Berceuse*; 2. *Bébé dort*; 3. *Croquemitaine*.

Comp. June 1911, MS Book II no. 2. Pub. Paris: E. Demets, 1912 (plate nos. E. 1614[1–3] D.). Online score at IMSLP. Dedication: 'à Tupac'.

Reviews in *The Monthly Musical Record* (1 Feb. 1912), 45; *La Revue musicale S.I.M.*, 15 Apr. 1912, 71; *Die Musik* 11:17 (1st June issue 1912); *The Musician* 27:4 (Apr. 1922), 25.

Broadcast performance (nos. 1 & 2 only):

- 30 Jun. 1929, by S. H. (*Hebdo*, 29 Jun. 1929; *La Croix*, 30 Jun. 1929, 7)

En passant … (Études d'après nature), Op. 40

1. *Petit pâtre sur les hauts pâturages*; 2. *Champs de blé au clair de lune*; 3. *Dans une petite ville flamande le dimanche*; 4. *Cîmes neigeuses*; 5. *Sieste en chemin de fer*.

Comp. Sep. (no. 5: Oct.) 1911, MS Book II no. 3. Pub. Paris: E. Demets, 1912 (plate no. E. 1615$^{(1)-(5)}$ D.). Online score at IMSLP.

Review in *Comoedia* (25 Jan. 1912), 3; *The Monthly Musical Record* (1 Feb. 1912), 45; *Il Mondo del Arte*, 12 Apr. 1912; *La Revue musicale S.I.M.*, 15 Apr. 1912, 71; *Die Musik* 11:17 (1st June issue 1912); *Allgemeine Musikzeitung* (25 Oct. 1912).

Identified performances:

(nos 1 & 5):

- Paris, Salle Debussy, 8 Jun. 1931, by Janine Cools (*Le Monde musical*, 30 Jun. 1931; *Le Courrier musical*, 1 Aug. 1931) – F.P. for no. 1

(no. 2 only):

- (as *Kornfeld im Mondschein*) Berlin, Meister-Saal, 15 Nov. 1922, by Bruno Eisner (*Der Tag*, 22 Nov. 1922)
- (with French title) Paris, Salle du Guide de Concert, 28 Nov. 1927, by S. H.

(nos 2 & 5):

- Paris, Salle Chopin, 23 Feb. 1932, by Maurice Servais (*Journal des débats*, 1 Mar. 1932; *Comoedia*, 4 Mar. 1932; *Le Courrier musical*, 15 Mar. 1932; *Le Monde musical*, 31 Mar. 1932)

(nos 2, 3, 5 only):

- Paris, Salle Majestic, 20 Nov. 1925, by M. Servais

(no. 3 only):

- (as *In einem vlämischen Städtchen am Sonntag*) Berlin, Choralion-Saal, 12 Nov. 1913, by S. H. (*Die Post*, 17 Nov. 1913)

(no. 5 only):

- Paris, Caméléon, 18 Mar. 1925, by Maurice Servais
- Paris, Salle Gaveau, 6 Jun. 1929, by Denyse Molié (*Journal des débats*, 10 Jun. 1929; *La Semaine à Paris*, 14 Jun. 1929)
- Paris, Maison Gaveau, 26 May 1930, by Marie-Antoinette Gaveau (*Le Monde musical*, 1 Jun. 1930)
- Paris, Le Parthenon, 17 Jan. 1931, by M. Servais

Broadcast performances:
- 23 May 1939, by Mlle. G. Lacroix (*Le Peuple*, 23 May 1939, 5)
- (of nos 1–3 only): 30 Jun. 1929, by S. H. (*La Croix*, 30 Jun. 1929, 7; *Hebdo*, 30 Jun. 1929)
- (no. 5 only): 4 Jul. 1931, by unnamed performer (*La Croix*, 3 Jul. 1931, 7)

Valses caprices, Op. 41

1. *Valse rustique*; 2. *Valse canaille*; 3. *Valse distraite*; 4. *Valse boîteuse*; 5. *Valse érotique*; 6. *À la Reger*; 7. *Encore une valse*.

Comp. Oct. 1911 (nos 1, 2, 3, 4, 6) and Nov. 1911 (nos 5 & 7), MS Book II no. 4. Pub. Paris: E. Demets, 1912 (plate no. E. 1664 D.). Online score at IMSLP.

Reviews in *Comoedia* (21 Nov. 1912), 3; *L'Echo musical* (Dec. 1912); *La Revue musicale S.I.M.* (15 Dec. 1912), 67; *The Monthly Musical Record* (Jan. 1913), 19–20; *Die Musik* 12:8 (2nd Jan. issue 1913), 108; *Allgemeine Musikzeitung* (7 Mar. 1913), 326; *The Times* (13 May 1913), 9; *Signale für die musikalische Welt* (4 Jun. 1913), 912; *Musica* (Jun. 1913).

Identified performances:
- ('*4 valses*', perhaps from this collection) Vierzon, Hotel des Messageries, 6 Jun. 1926, by Jacqueline Adam

Broadcast performance:
- ('*Trois Valses*', perhaps from this collection) 11 Feb. 1930, by Marthe Le Breton

Gitaneries, Op. 42

1. *Carmen*; 2. *Mercédès*; 3. *Jacinta*; 4. *Manuelita*.

Comp. 1911, MS Book II no. 5. Pub. Paris: E. Demets, 1912 (plate no. E. 1678 D.). Dedication: 'à la mémoire de Bizet'.

Reviews in *La Revue musicale S.I.M.* (15 Jan. 1912), 67; *The Monthly Musical Record* (Jan. 1913), 19–20; *The Times* (13 May 1913), 9; *Signale für die musikalische Welt* (4 Jun. 1913, 912); *Musica* (Jun. 1913).

Identified performance (no. 1 only):
- Paris, École de Piano Marthe Le Breton, 26 Jun. 1927, by (Mlle.) G. Courant

Sonatine, Op. 43

1. *Allegro appassionato*; 2. *Tempo di menuetto*; 3. *Vivace ma non troppo*.

Comp. late 1911, MS Book II no. 6. Pub. Paris: E. Demets, 1912 (plate no. E. 1674 D.). Online score at IMSLP. Dedication: 'à mon ami Heinrich Möller'.

Reviews in *Comoedia* (21 Nov. 1912), 3; *The Monthly Musical Record* (Jan. 1913), 19–20; *Die Musik* 12:8 (2nd Jan. issue 1913), 108; *Allgemeine Musikzeitung* (7 Mar. 1913), 326; *The Times* (13 May 1913), 9; *Signale für die musikalische Welt* (4 Jun. 1913), 912.

Identified performance:
- Berlin, Choralion-Saal, 12 Nov. 1913, by S. H. (*Berliner Lokal-Anzeiger*, 13 Nov. 1913; *Der Reichsanzeiger*, 18 Nov. 1913; *Allgemeine Musikzeitung*, 21 Nov. 1913, 1488–9)

Sentes et chemins (Nouvelles études d'après nature), Op. 44

1. *Ouvriers allants à l'usine*; 2. *Promenade du philosophe*; 3. *A travers bois*; 4. *Cornemuse en tête*; 5. *Sur la route d'Amalfi*; 6. *Sentier de Meudon au printemps*; 7. *Par la pluie*.

Comp. June to September 1912, MS Book II no. 7. Pub. Paris: E. Demets, 1912 (plate no. E. 1726 D.). Dedication: 'À mon Père'.

Reviews in *Allgemeine Musikzeitung* (7 Mar. 1913), 326; *Le Guide du concert* (6 Dec. 1913), 130; *La Revue musicale S.I.M.* 10 (1 Feb. 1914), 68; *Die Musik* 13:13 (1st April issue 1914), 45; *The Musician* 27:4 (Apr. 1922), 25.

Identified performances:
(no. 1 only):
- (as *Zur Fabrik ziehende Arbeiter*) Berlin, Choralion-Saal, 12 Nov. 1913, by S. H. (*Die Post*, 17 Nov. 1913)

(nos 1, 3 & 5 only):
- (no. 1, as *Arbeiter auf dem Wege zur Fabrik*; no. 3 as *Im Walde*; no. 5 as *Auf der Strasse nach Amalfi*) Berlin, Meister-Saal, 15 Nov. 1922, by Bruno Eisner (*Lokal-Anzeiger*, 18 Nov. 1922; *Der Tag*, 22 Nov. 1922; *Signale f. d. mus. Welt*, 22 Nov. 1922, 1350)

(no. 2 only):
- Paris, Salle du Guide de Concert, 28 Nov. 1927, by S. H.

(nos 2 & 5 only):
- Paris, Salle Debussy, 8 Jun. 1931, by Janine Cools (*Le Monde musical*, 30 Jun. 1931; *Le Courrier musical*, 1 Aug. 1931)
- Paris, Salle Chopin, 23 Feb. 1932, by Maurice Servais (*Journal des débats*, 1 Mar. 1932; *Comoedia*, 4 Mar. 1932; *Le Courrier musical*, 15 Mar. 1932; *Le Monde musical*, 31 Mar. 1932)

(no. 3 only):
- Paris, École de Piano Marthe Le Breton, 26 Jun. 1927, by (Mlle.) M. Fouquerière

(no. 5 only):
- Paris, École de Piano Marthe Le Breton, 26 Jun. 1927, by (Mlle.) S. Fouquerière

Pièces celtiques, Op. 45

1. *Assez lent – Beaucoup plus vite – Premier mouvement*; 2. *Modéré, dans l'esprit d'une légende*; 3. *Très animé*.

Comp. 1912, MS Book II no. 8. Another MS in Médiathèque Musicale Mahler, Paris (Fonds Paul Le Flem). Pub. Paris: E. Demets, 1912 (plate nos. E. 1727 D.). Online score at IMSLP.

Reviews in *Allgemeine Musikzeitung* (7 Mar. 1913), 326; *Deutsche Tonkünstler-Zeitung* (20 Nov. 1913); *Vossische Zeitung* (9 Dec. 1913); *La Revue musicale S.I.M.* 10 (1 Feb. 1914), 68; *Die Musik* 13:13 (1st April issue 1914), 45.

NB 1: The Bibliothèque Nationale de France is in possession of a copy personally inscribed to Romain Rolland: *"Monsieur Romain Rolland / Hommage d'admiration sincère / Swan Hennessy"* (see also Op. 46bis below).

NB 2: In the third movement, Hennessy quotes the Irish reel tune 'The Ewe with the Crooked Horn', no. 918 in the Petrie Collection as edited by C. V. Stanford.

Identified performances:
- (F.P.) Paris, Salle de l'École des Hautes Études Sociales, 6 Mar. 1913, by Antoinette Veluard (*Comoedia*, 13 Mar. 1913, 2; *Allgemeine Musikzeitung*, 22 Mar. 1913)
- Berlin, Choralion-Saal, 12 Nov. 1913, by S. H.
- Paris, Salle du Guide du concert, Nov. 1927 by unknown pianist (Hennessy work-list)
- Paris, Maison Gaveau, 2 Apr. 1938, by Marcelle de Lacour

(no. 3 only)
- Dublin, test piece in Father Mathew Feis, Easter 1923

Adagio et allegretto du quatuor à cordes, Op. 46bis
1. *Adagio*; 2. *Allegretto*.

Comp. 1912, MS Book II nos. 10 & 11. Pub. Paris: E. Demets, 1912 (plate no. E. 1732 D.).

Review in *The Musician* 27:4 (Apr. 1922), 25.

NB.: The *first* movt. of the quartet (*Allegro*) was also arranged for piano, but not published (MS Book II no. 9). The Bibliothèque Nationale de France is in possession of a copy personally inscribed to Romain Rolland: *"Monsieur Romain Rolland / Hommage d'admiration sincère / Swan Hennessy"* (see also Op. 45 above).

Croquis parisiens, Op. 47
1. *Promenade matinale au Jardin du Luxembourg*; 2. *L'Américain qui a bien dîné*; 3. *Dans un atelier de couturiers*.

Comp. 1912, MS Book I no. 11. Pub. Paris: E. Demets, 1913 (plate no. E. 1747 D.). Dedication: 'à Louis Vuillemin'.

Reviews in *La Revue musicale S.I.M.* 10 (1 Feb. 1914), 68; *The Musical Standard* (28 Feb. 1914); *Die Musik* 13:13 (1st April issue 1914), 45.

Identified performances:
- (no. 3 only, as *In einem pariser Näherinnen-Atelier*): Berlin, Choralion-Saal, 12 Nov. 1913, by S. H. (*Die Post*, 17 Nov. 1913; *Die Volks-Zeitung*, 19 Nov. 1913; *Deutsche Tonkünstler-Zeitung*, 20 Nov. 1913; *Allgemeine Musikzeitung*, 21 Nov. 1913, 1488)

- (no. 3 only, as *In einem Schneiderinnenatelier*) Berlin, Meister-Saal, 15 Nov. 1922, by Bruno Eisner (*Lokal-Anzeiger*, 18 Nov. 1922)

Impressions humoristiques, Op. 48

(Prologue) *Dédicace: Aux Amis de Russie (Un peu lent, triste)*; 1. *Tupac-Polka (Gai, pas trop vite)*; 2. *"Das Fräulein stand am Meere / Und seufzte lang und bang" (Heine) (Lent, rêveur)*; 3. *Napolitains (Vite, malicieux)*; 4. *En regardant une ronde de jeunes filles (Gentiment)*; 5. *Chanteuse de beuglant (Vif, gauche et aussi canaille que possible)*; 6. *Bébé prend sa médicine (Modéré)*.

Comp. 1913, MS Book III no. 3. Pub. Paris: E. Demets, 1913 (plate no. E. 1794 D.); US copyright renewed on 8 Oct. 1941.

NB.: In the MS, piece no. 4 is called *Ronde d'ivrognes tristes*. Also, no. 6 carries a footnote to the title that was not published: "Malgré les apparences, l'enfant n'habite pas Vienne", alluding to Schönberg.

Identified performance:
- Paris, Jun. 1929, by Denyse Molié (*Journal des débats*, 10 Jun. 1929, 4)
- Paris, unidentified location, May 1930, by Marie-Antoinette Pradier (*Le Monde musical*, 1 Jun. 1930)

Huit Pièces celtiques, Op. 51 (originally: *Eight Celtic Pieces*)

1. *Allegro maestoso*; 2. *Andante*; 3. *Allegro*; 4. *Andante sostenuto*; 5. *Allegro* [on *The Wearing of the Green*]; 6. *Allegretto*; 7. *Allegro*; 8. *Allegretto*; *Epilogue*.

Comp. 1922 as *Eight Celtic Pieces*, Op. 57 (!), MS missing. Pub. London: Evans & Co., 1924 (plate no. S. & Cº. 31) ('Copyright MCMXXIV by Michael Kavanagh'); pub. as *Huit Pièces celtiques* in *Album celtique*, Paris: Éditions Max Eschig, 1929 (plate no. M.E. 2320); copyright notice in later reprints: "© Éditions Max Eschig as legal successor of Michael Kavanagh". US copyright claimed on 18 Dec. 1924; last renewed on 20 Feb. 1952. Dedication: 'To Denis Breen' (in Eschig edition: 'à Denis Breen').

NB.: This work was initially to be published with the Cork, Ireland, based publisher Sullivan, which ran into financial difficulties in the course of the Irish Civil War. No. 2 reappears in 1928 as vol. 5 no. 7 of *À la manière de ...* .

Identified performances (see also under *Album celtique*):
- Paris, Le Club musical/Studio des Agriculteurs (8, rue d'Athènes), 8 Mar. 1930, by Marie-Antoinette Pradier
- Paris, Salle Chopin, 17 Nov. 1931, by M.-A. Pradier (*L'Européen*, Nov. 1931; *Comoedia*, 19 Nov. 1931, *Le Courrier musical*, 1 Dec. 1931)

Performance of three unidentified pieces from this collection:
- Paris, Salle Chopin, 16 May 1928, by Richard Byk

Sonatine celtique, Op. 53
1. *Allegro*; 2. *Andante*; 3. *Vivace*.

    Comp. 1923 as *Irish Sonatina*, Op. 61 (*sic!*) in MS Book II no. 12. Pub. London: Evans & Co. 1924 (plate no. S. & C°. 41) ('Copyright MCMXXIV by Michael Kavanagh'); also in *Album celtique*, Paris: Éditions Max Eschig, 1929 (plate no. M.E. 2321); copyright notice in later reprints: "© Éditions Max Eschig as legal successor of Michael Kavanagh". US copyright claimed on 20 Dec. 1924; last renewed on 25 Sep. 1952. Dedication: 'A mon cher ami Lucien Haudebert' (in MS and in the Eschig edition: 'à Lucien Haudebert').

Identified performances:
- Paris, Salle des Concerts Touche, 7 Mar. 1925, by Marthe Le Breton
- Paris, Salle Gaveau, 6 Jun. 1929, by Denyse Molié (*Journal des débats*, 10 Jun. 1929, 4; *La Semaine à Paris*, 14 Jun. 1929; *Le Monde musical*, 30 Jun. 1929; *Le Courrier musical*, 1 Jul. 1929)

Broadcast performances:
- (as *Sonatine*): 3 Jun. 1926, by S. H. (*Le Gaulois*, 2 Jun. 1926)
- (with full title) 8 Jul. 1928, by S. H. (*Radio-Magazine*, 8 Jul. 1928)

Épigrammes d'un solitaire, Op. 55
1. *La Forêt de Clamart à l'aube*; 2. *Un Jardin arabe*; 3. *Une Pagode indochinoise*; 4. *Un Berceau*; 5. *Un vieux cimetière*; 6. *Un Souvenir lointain*; [7. *Edvard Grieg*; 8. *Richard Strauss*].

    Comp. 1923 as Op. 63 (!) in MS Book II no. 13. Pub. London: Evans & Co., 1924 (plate no. S. & C°. 40) ('Copyright MCMXXIV by Michael Kavanagh'); new edition with nos 1–6 only, Paris: Max Eschig & Cie., 1929 (plate no. M.E. 2322); no. 1 also 'Supplement au *Courrier Musical* du 15 Mars 1929'. Dedication: 'à Michael Kavanagh'.

    NB.: Movements 7 and 8 of the first issue re-appeared in 1927 as nos 3 and 7 of *À la manière de …* (see below).

Identified performances:
- (F.P.) (of nos 1, 4, 5 only): London, Guildhall School of Music, 13 Nov. 1924, by Leonard Reed

(nos 1 & 5 only):
- Paris, Salle Majestic, 20 Nov. 1925, by Maurice Servais

(no. 1 only):
- Paris, Salle Chopin, 17 Nov. 1928, by M. Servais

(no. 2 only):
- Paris, Salle du Guide de Concert, 28 Nov. 1927, by S. H.

Trois Pièces exotiques, Op. 57
1. *Fillettes brunes*; 2. *Le Goût de la cannelle*; 3. *Nègre endimanché*.

Comp. 1922, MS missing. Pub. Paris: E. Demets, 1922 (plate no. E. 2070 D.). *'Edition revue et corrigé par l'Auteur'*, Paris: Max Eschig & Cie., 1924 (plate number E. 2070 D.). US copyright claimed on 20 Oct. 1924, last renewed on 20 Feb. 1952.
Identified performances:
- (F.P.) Berlin, Meister-Saal, 15 Nov. 1922, by Bruno Eisner (*Berliner Börsenzeitung*, 17 Nov. 1922; *Allgemeine Musikzeitung*, 24 Nov. 1922; *Signale f. d. mus. Welt*, 27 Nov. 1922)
- Paris, Salle de la Société de Géographie, 6 Mar. 1925, by Maurice Servais (*Excelsior*, 9 Mar. 1925)
- Paris, Salle Debussy, 2 Dec. 1933, by M. Servais

(no. 3 only):
- Paris, Caméléon, 18 Mar. 1925, by M. Servais (*Le Monde musical*, 1 Apr. 1925)

Broadcast performances:
- 7 Dec. 1925, by S. H. (*Le Ouest-Éclair*, 7 Dec. 1925, 7; *L'Intransigeant*, 7 Dec. 1925, 6)

(no. 3 only):
- 25 Feb. 1925, by unnamed performer (*Le Figaro*, 25 Feb. 1925, 5)

Deux Petites pièces bi-tonales
1. Andantino; 2. Allegretto

Comp. 1922–3, MS missing, no opus number. Pub. as a music supplement to *Le Guide du concert* 9:16, 26 January 1923.
Identified performance:
- Paris, early 1923, in the course of '*Mercredis musicaux*' on Champs Elysees, unknown performer (S. H.?), according to the title page of the journal

Étude de concert, Op. 60
Comp. 1923, MS missing. Pub. Paris: Max Eschig & Cie., 1924 (plate no. M.E. 1262). US copyright claimed on 1 July 1924, last renewed on 20 Feb. 1952. Dedication: 'à Mademoiselle Rachel Blanquer'.
Identified performances:
- (F.P.) Paris, Salle Érard, 15 Feb. 1923, by Rachel Blanquer (*Comoedia*, 19 Feb. 1923; *Le Monde musical*, Feb. 1923)
- Paris, Salle Érard, 29 Jan. 1929, by Maurice Servais (*Le Courrier musical*, 15 Feb. 1929)
- Paris, Le Club musical / Studio des Agriculteurs (8, rue d'Athènes), 22 Mar. 1930, by M. Servais
- Paris, Salle Chopin, 25 Feb. 1931, by M. Servais (*Journal des débats*, 3 Mar. 1931; *Le Courrier musical*, 15 Mar. 1931)

Broadcast performance:
- 8 Jul. 1928, by Marthe Le Breton (*Radio-Magazine*, 8 Jul. 1928)

***Douze Canons à deux voix à tous les intervalles*, Op. 64**
1. *Canon à la quarte*; 2. *Canon à l'octave, à une mesure de distance*; 3. *Canon à l'octave, à une demie-mesure de distance*; 4. *Canon à la tierce*; 5. *Canon à l'octave, en movement rétrograde*; 6. *Canon bitonal, à la septième augmentée*; 7. *Canon à la quinte*; 8. *Canon à la sixte*; 9. *Canon à la seconde*; 10. *Canon à l'unisson*; 11. *Canon à l'octave, en augmentation*; 12. *Canon à l'octave, en diminution*.

Comp. 1924, MS Book II no. 15. Pub. Paris: Max Eschig & Cie., 1925 (plate no. M.E. 1563). Dedication: 'à ma femme'.

***Rapsodie irlandaise*, Op. 67**

Comp. 1924, MS Book II no. 16; another in MS Book V no. 14. Pub. Paris: Éditions Max Eschig, 1929 (plate no. M.E. 2264); US copyright last renewed on 17 Feb. 1956. Dedication: 'à mon fils Patrice'.
Identified performance:
- Paris, Salle Gaveau, 6 Jun. 1929, by Denyse Molié (*Journal des débats*, 10 Jun. 1929, 4; *La Semaine à Paris*, 14 Jun. 1929, *Le Courrier musical*, 1 Jul. 1929)
- Paris, Salle Chopin, 17 Nov. 1931, by Marie-Antoinette Pradier (*L'Européen*, Nov. 1931; *Comoedia*, 19 Nov. 1931, *Le Courrier musical*, 1 Dec. 1931)

Broadcast performance:
- Rome (441 m), 14 Oct. 1931 (in an 'Irish National Evening', no performers mentioned; *Irish Press*, 14 Oct. 1931, p. 3)

***Banlieues ... . Six Petites pièces*, Op. 69**
1. *Clamart*; 2. *Aubervilliers*; 3. *Meudon*; 4. *Robinson*; 5. *Verrières*; 6. *Bourg-la-Reine*.

Comp. 1925, MS Book II no. 18. Pub. of first three numbers, subtitled 'Trois Petites pièces', Paris: Propriété de l'auteur, 1926; the complete set, Paris: Éditions Max Eschig, 1929 (plate no. M.E. 2410). Copyright notice, nos 1–3: © 1926 by Swan Hennessy; nos 4–6: © 1929 by Éditions Max Eschig. SACEM stamp in MS Book II dated 27 June 1929. No. 1 also published as a music supplement to *Le Monde musical*, 31 Mar. 1926. Dedication: 'à Maurice Servais'.

Reviews in *The Chicago Tribune* (9 Jun. 1928); *Le Guide du concert* (25 Jan. 1929), 492.
Identified performances:
- Paris, Salle Erard, 29 Jan. 1929, by Maurice Servais (*Le Courrier musical*, 15 Feb. 1929)
- Paris, Salle Chopin, 25 Feb. 1931, by M. Servais (*Journal des débats*, 3 Mar. 1931; *Le Courrier musical*, 15 Mar. 1931)

(nos. 1–3 only):
- Paris, Salle du Guide de Concert, 28 Nov. 1927, by S. H.
- Brussels, Le Lyceum de Belgique, 27 Apr. 1928, by S. H.
- Paris, Le Club musical / Studio des Agriculteurs (8, rue d'Athènes), 22 Mar. 1931, by M. Servais

- Paris, Salle de la Revue musicale, 26 Feb. 1934, by Édouard Wronsky

À la manière de ... 18 Pastiches

Vol. 1 ('1er cahier'): 1. *Johannes Brahms*; 2. *César Franck*; 3. *Edvard Grieg*; 4. *Robert Schumann*; 5. *Gabriel Fauré*; 6. *Anton Dvořák*.

Vol. 2 ('2e cahier'): 7. *Richard Strauss*; 8. *Stephen Heller*; 9. *Claude Debussy*; 10. *Benjamin Godard*; 11. *Max Reger et Paul Delmet*; 12. *Alexandre Borodine*.

Vol. 3 ('3e cahier'): 13. *Félix Mendelssohn-Bartholdy*; 14. *Vincent d'Indy*; 15. *Muzio Clementi*; 16. *Jeune génie de l'avant garde*; 17. *Joaquin Turina*; 18. *Gioacchino Rossini*.

Comp. 1917–26, MS Book II no. 19. Pub. Paris: Éditions Max Eschig, 1927 (plate nos. M.E. 1781, M.E. 1782, M.E. 1783). Dedication(s): 'à Marthe Le Breton'.

NB.: Footnote in vol. 1 no. 3 (Grieg) and vol. 2 no. 7 (Strauss) remark that these pieces had already appeared as nos 7 and 8 in *Epigrammes d'un solitaire*, Op. 55. However, these are contained in the 1924 Evans edition only, not in the 1929 Eschig edition, which has just six numbers. Vol. 3 No. 16 ('Jeune génie ...') does not contain music but merely the remark *"Mettez beaucoup des notes, n'importe lesquelles, sauf celles qu'il faut."*.

À la manière de ... 6 Nouveaux pastiches

Vol. 4 ('4e cahier'): 1. *Carl Maria von Weber*; 2. *Domenico Scarlatti*; 3. *Giuseppe Verdi*; 4. *Frédéric Chopin*; 5. *Emmanuel Chabrier*; 6. *Franz Liszt*.

Comp. 1926, MS Book II no. 20. Pub. Paris: Éditions Max Eschig, 1927 (plate no. M.E. 1986). Dedication: 'à Richard Byk'.

Preparation announced in *Le Guide du concert* (19 Jun. 1926), 990.

NB.: This volume closes with Hennessy's remark that he considered including pastiches of Erik Satie and Richard Wagner and why he did not proceed (see Chapters 5 and 9).

À la manière de ...

Vol. 5 ('5e cahier'): 1. *Franz Schubert*; 2. *Georg Friedrich Haendel*; 3. *Jules Massenet*; 4. *Johann Strauss II*; 5. *Maurice Ravel*; 6. *Hugo Wolf*; 7. *Appendice – Swan Hennessy*.

Comp. 1927, MS Book II no. 21. Pub. Paris: Éditions Max Eschig, 1928 (plate no. M.E. 2251). Dedication: 'à Richard Byk'.

Announced in *Le Guide du concert* (6 Jan. 1928), 370.

NB.: No. 7 carries the footnote *"Ce morceau a déjà paru dans 'Eight Celtic Pieces' (op. 51)"*. It is, in fact, no. 2 of that collection.

Reviews of *À la manière de ...*:
– *De Muziek* 2 (1927–8), 27–9
– *Allgemeine Musikzeitung* (8 Jun. 1928 & 1 Feb. 1929)
– *The Chicago Tribune* (9 Jun. 1928)

Performances of pieces from *À la manière de ...* :[5]

- *Richard Strauss*, London, Guildhall School of Music, 13 Nov. 1924, by Leonard Reed
- F.P. of full vol. 1 (in the order *Franck, Brahms, Grieg, Schumann, Dvorák, Fauré*) and *Debussy/Godard, Borodine*: Laval, Salle des Fêtes de l'Hôtel-de-Ville, 6 Jan. 1927, by Marthe Le Breton
- *Franck, Grieg, Schumann, Fauré, Debussy/Godard, Borodine, Mendelssohn, Clementi, Rossini*: Paris, École de Piano Marthe Le Breton, 26 Jun. 1927, by Marthe Le Breton
- *Clementi, Grieg, Godard, Rossini, Weber, Chopin*: Paris, Salle Mustel, 17 Dec. 1927, by S. H.: Paris, Salle Mustel, 17 Dec. 1927, by S. H.
- *Grieg, Schumann, Fauré, Godard, Verdi, Chopin, Clementi, Rossini*: Paris, Salle du Parthénon, 24 Mar. 1928, by S. H.
- *Weber, Grieg, Schumann, Chopin, Godard, Massenet, Clementi, J. Strauss, Verdi, Rossini*: Brussels, Le Lyceum de Belgique, 27 Apr. 1928, by S. H. (*L'Etoile Belge*, 29 Apr. 1928)
- *Weber, Mendelssohn, Schumann, Chopin, Borodine, Massenet, Clementi, Verdi*: Paris, Salle Chopin, 16 May 1928, by Richard Byk (*Chicago Tribune*, 14 May 1928)
- (undisclosed pieces, but *"redemandé"*), Paris, Salle du Parthénon, 9 Jun. 1928, by S. H.
- *Weber, Scarlatti, Chopin, Mendelssohn, Heller, Haendel, Massenet, Verdi*: Laval, Hôtel de l'Ouest, 1 Jul. 1928, by S. H. (*Le Regional de l'Ouest*, 9 Jul. 1928)
- *Mendelssohn, Schumann, Chopin, Borodine, Massenet, Clementi, Verdi*: Begnins (Vaud, Switzerland), 8 Jul. 1928, by R. Byk (*Gazette de Lausanne*, 16 Jul. 1928)
- *Weber, Schumann, Chopin, Massenet, Clementi, Verdi*: Paris, Students Atelier (Blvd. Montparnasse), 28 Oct. 1928, by R. Byk (*The New York Herald*, 27 & 30 Oct. 1928)
- *Schubert, Haendel, Massenet, J. Strauss, Ravel, Wolf, Hennessy*: Paris, Salle Debussy, 6 Dec. 1928, by Marthe Le Breton (*Le Courrier musical*, 1 Jan. 1929)
- *Chopin, Fauré*: Paris, Salle Erard, 29 Jan. 1929, by Maurice Servais
- *Schumann, Fauré, Clementi, Rossini, Weber, Verdi, Chopin, Massenet, J. Strauss*: Paris, Lyceum de France (17 rue de Bellechasse), 31 Jan. 1930, by Marie Erdsieck
- *Grieg, Schumann, J. Strauss, Massenet, Borodine*: Paris, American Women's Club, 25 Oct. 1931, by M. Le Breton
- *Fauré, J. Strauss, Dvorak, Borodine*: Bourg-la-Reine, Salle de la Mairie, Nov. 1931, by M. Le Breton
- *Fauré, J. Strauss, Dvorak, Borodine*: Sceaux (Dép. Hauts-de-Seine), Nov. 1931, by M. Le Breton

---

[5] A first performance of volume 4 was announced for Paris, Salle du Guide du Concert, 28 Nov. 1927, by the Polish pianist Richard Byk (*Le Guide du concert*, 18 Nov. 1927), but had to be cancelled due to an accident of the pianist (ibid, 25 Nov. 1927). See instead the date 16 May 1928.

Appendix

Broadcast performances:
- 13 Mar. 1928: *Grieg, Schumann, Fauré, Godard, Clementi, Chopin, Verdi, Rossini,* by S. H. (*L'Echo,* Angoulême, 12 Mar. 1928)
- (Frankfurt radio) 10 Oct. 1929: *Schumann, Chopin, Massenet, Clementi, Verdi,* by Richard Byk

***Allegretto du quatrième quatuor à cordes,* Op. 75bis**
Comp. June 1928, MS Book II no. 17. Unpublished.

SEE ALSO:

(six short untitled works)
1. *Allegretto*; 2. *Andantino*; 3. *Vivace non troppo*, 4. *Allegretto*; 5. *Andante*; 6. *Adagio non troppo*.
Undated MS (*c.*1909–13), MS Book I no. 17.

***2 Orientales,* Op. 37**
1. *Odalisque*; 2. *Nubienne*.
Undated MS (*c*1911–13), MS Book I no. 16.
NB.: In Hennessy's own list of works, Op. 37 is his unpublished ballet *Les Noces du soldat de bois*. The latter is dated July 1913, but it comes between Op. 36 (1910) and Op. 38 (1909). These *2 Orientales* are based on pieces from *Croquis de femmes,* Op. 33 (1911).

***Trio,* Op. 54**, arranged for piano solo
Comp. 1919, MS Book V no. 6. Unpublished.

***Reel Irlandais* (de la collection Petrie), arrangé par Swan Hennessy**
Pub. in *Le Guide du concert* (6 Jan. 1928), 380–1.
NB.: Published as a photostat print of Hennessy's handwriting. Hennessy had used this tune before, in the third movement of the *Sonatine,* Op. 78 for two violins. It is no. 917 in the Petrie/Stanford Collection.

Album celtique
Consists of the following four pieces: *Variations sur un thème original dans le style irlandais*, Op. 12; *Huit Pièces celtiques*, Op. 51; *Sonatine celtique*, Op. 53; *Rapsodie irlandaise*, Op. 67.
 Pub. Paris: Éditions Max Eschig, 1929 (plate nos. M.E. 2319, 2320, 2321, 2264).
 Reviews in *Mom-Mus* (21 Mar. 1929); *La Revue musicale* 10:9 (Sep.-Oct. 1929), 275; *Le Guide du concert* (4 Oct. 1929); *Tribune de Genève* (3 Jan. 1930); *I.M.I.* (15 Mar. 1930); *Allgemeine Musikzeitung*, 57:49, 5 Dec. 1930, p. 1140.
 Identified performances (of whole *Album*):
- Paris, Salle de Concert de la Revue musicale, 9 Dec. 1934, by Valentin Pavlovski
- Paris, Salle du Conservatoire Russe, 23 Jun. 1936, by Jeanne Knoertzer

C. CHAMBER MUSIC

Lieder an den Mond. Romantische Stücke, Op. 10
1. *Um Mitternacht*; 2. *In der Frühe*; 3. *Am Abend*.
For piano trio (vn, vc, pf).
 Comp. *c*1887–8, MS missing. Pub. London: Augener & Co., 1888 (plate no. 7942).
 Announcement in *Musikalisch-literarischer Monatsbericht* (Jul. 1888), 263; Reviews in *The Monthly Musical Record* 18:209 (May 1888), 106; *The Morning Post*, 8 Sep. 1888, 2; *The Musical Standard* 36:1277 (19 Jan. 1889), 46.
 NB. This piece is missing from Hennessy's own list of works, which could mean that he withdrew it.
Identified performances:
- Edinburgh, Music Hall of Philosophical Institution, 22 Dec. 1903, by 'Madame' Drechsler Hamilton, David Millar Craig, Paul della Torre (*Edinburgh Evening News*, 23 Dec. 1903, 2)
- Edinburgh, 16 Nov. 1905, by David Bayne, D. Millar Craig, Colin Mackenzie (*The Musical Times*, Dec. 1905, 813)

Berceuse, Op. 13
For violin and piano.
 Comp. 1900, MS missing. Pub., without opus number, Paris: Enoch & Cie., 1901 (plate no. E. & C. 4658). Dedication: 'à Madame Béatrice Langley'.
 Listed among pieces 'Received for review' in: *The Monthly Musical Record*, 33:394 (Oct. 1903), 193.

Sonate en Fa (style irlandais), Op. 14
1. *Allegro, ma non troppo*; 2. *Vivace capriccioso*; 3. *Andante – Allegro*.
For violin and piano.

Comp. c1902–4, MS in Bavarian State Library, Munich, Schott Production Archive (archived under plate no. 27497). Pub. London: Schott & Co., 1904; second ed. Mainz: B. Schott's Söhne, n. d. [1905] (plate no. 27497). On p. 1 of the second edition, the work's title is '1ʳᵉ. Sonate'. Dedication: 'à son ami A. Simonetti'.

Reviews in *Le Guide du concert*, 21 Mar. 1914; *Cork Examiner*, c.22 Apr. 1922; briefly mentioned in *The London Musical Courier* (4 Jan. 1913).

Identified performances:
- (F.P.) Cannes, Villa Florence, 14 Jan. 1905, by Achille Simonetti and S. H.
- Paris, Palais des Beaux Arts, 7 May 1907, by Auguste Delacroix and (first name?) de Bruyne (*Le Figaro*, 7 May 1907, 5; *Le Guide musical*, 19 May 1907; *Le Monde musical*, 30 May 1907)
- Paris, Salle de la Société de l'Encouragement, 24 May 1908, by Ida Adam-Pineau and S. H.
- Paris, Salle Gaveau, 21 Mar. 1914, by Alcibiade Anemoyanni and Mme Lavello-Stiévenard (*Le Guide du concert*, 21 Mar. 1914; *La Critique musicale*, 30 Mar. 1914)
- Alexandria (Egypt), Théâtre Alhambra, 23 Nov. 1915, by A. Anemoyanni and H. Félix
- Cairo (Egypt), Théâtre Cinéma Pathé (Avenue de Boulac), 5 Mar. 1916, by A. Anemoyanni and Jeanne Bouillard
- Cork, Opera House (Gaelic League concert), 23 Apr. 1922, by Liam O'Brady and Carl Hardebeck (*Cork Examiner*, 26 Apr. 1922, 2)
- Berlin, Bechstein-Saal, 3 May 1922, by Georg Kulenkampff-Post and Michael Raucheisen
- Paris, Salle Pleyel, 27 May 1922, by Ida Adam-Pineau and S. H.
- Paris, École de Chant Challet-Vicq, 4 Nov. 1922, by I. Adam-Pineau and S. H.
- Dublin, 6 April 1923 (Father Mathew Feis, test piece), by R. Kieran and J. Doyle etc. (*Irish Independent*, 7 Apr. 1923, 10)
- Cork, Father Mathew Hall, 25 May 1924 (Oireachtas Festival), by Máire Nic Uidhir and Eibhlín Ní Uaidh
- Paris, Salle de l'École Normale de Musique, 1 Mar. 1930, by Tina Manteufel and Marie-Antoinette Pradier (*Comoedia*, 26 Feb. 1930, 2; *La Semaine à Paris*, 14 Mar. 1930; *Le Courrier musical*, 15 Mar. 1930)
- Paris, Hotel Majestic, 4 Dec. 1931, by M.-A. Pradier and Léon Zighéra
- Paris, Salle des Concerts du Conservatoire, 14 Nov. 1933, by T. Manteufel and Suzanne Lecointe
- Paris, Villa Montmorency, 3 Dec. 1935, by Monique Haas and L. Zighéra

(movt. 1 only):
- Cork, Lecture Hall, Castle Street, 19 Jan. 1926, by Miss C. Bresnan and Miss G. O'Shea or Mr. R. Shermann

Broadcast performances:
- 11 Feb. 1930, by Tina Manteufel and Marie-Antoinette Pradier
- 15 Jan. 1935, by André Pascal and M.-A. Pradier (*Le Peuple*, 14 Jan. 1935, 2)

***Tarantelle*, Op. 20**
For violin and piano.
   Comp. *c*1905, MS missing. Unpublished.

***Suite pour quatuor à cordes*, Op. 46** [String Quartet No. 1]
1. *Allegro*; 2. *Adagio*; 3. *Allegretto*; 4. *Andante sostenuto (Sur des Airs irlandais anciens de la collection Petrie)*.
For string quartet (2vn, va, vc).
   Comp. 1912, MS Book VI, nos 1–11. Pub. Paris: E. Demets, 1913 (plate no. E. 1784 D.). Reprints: London: Merton Music, 1996 (plate no. MM 112 [score] and MM 4507 [parts]); Munich: Musikproduktion Höflich, 2019 (plate no. 5281). Online score and parts at IMSLP. Dedication: 'à Monsieur le Professeur Carl Heffner'.
   Reviews in *Le Guide du concert* (22 Nov. 1913), 106–7; *Die Musik* 13:13 (1st April issue 1914), 45; *Allgemeine Musikzeitung* (22 May 1914), 818; *Le Guide du concert* (1 Jun. 1928), 965; *Mom-Mus* (13 Jun. 1929).
   NB.: The last movement is based on two tunes from Petrie/Stanford Collection, no. 1089 resp. 1247 (*'Sagairt tar teorádh'*) and no. 902 (*'Molly on the Shore'*). They have already been used as nos. 3 and 4 in Hennessy's *Petite suite irlandaise*, Op. 29 (1908). – The Fonds Paul Le Flem in the Médiathèque Musicale Mahler, Paris, contains a copy of the miniature score of the printed work, signed and dedicated to Paul Le Flem by Swan Hennessy as follows: "à mon cher ami Le Flem / souvenir du 5 Nov. 1913 / Swan Hennessy".
Identified performances:
- (F.P.) Berlin, Choralion-Saal, 12 Nov. 1913, by Marix Loevensohn Quartett (Louis van Laar, vn; G. Kutschka, vn; David Hait, va; Marix Loevensohn, vc) (*Lokal-Anzeiger*, 13 Nov. 1913; *Norddeutsche Allgemeine Zeitung*, 16 Nov. 1913; *Der Reichsanzeiger*, 18 Nov. 1913; *Deutsche Tonkünstler-Zeitung*, 20 Nov. 1913; *Allgemeine Musikzeitung*, 21 Nov. 1913 & 23 Jan. 1914; *Vossische Zeitung*, 9 Dec. 1913)
- Paris, Salle des Agriculteurs, 26 Nov. 1913, by Quatuor Gaston Le Feuve (*La Critique musicale*, 2 Dec. 1913; *Comoedia*, 8 Dec. 1913, 5; *La Renaissance*, 20 Dec. 1913, 25; *La Revue musicale S.I.M.* 10:1 (Jan. 1914), 58)
- Berlin, Bechstein-Saal, 3 May 1922, by Kulenkampff-Quartett (*Allgemeine Musikzeitung*, 12 May 1922)
- Paris, École de Piano Marthe Le Breton, Feb. 1924, by Quatuor Loiseau (*Comoedia*, 21 Feb. 1924, 2; *Le Courrier musical*, 1 Mar. 1924)
- Dublin, United Arts Club, 20 Mar. 1924, by Dublin String Quartet (Arthur Darley, Rita Dowdall, George H. Brett, Joseph Schofield) (*Irish Society*, 22 Mar. 1924, 5)
- Nevers, Salle du Ciné-Parc, 30 Apr. 1925, by Quatuor Loiseau
- Paris, Caméléon, 18 Mar. 1925, by Quatuor Loiseau

- Paris, Salle des Agriculteurs, 9 Jun. 1928, by Quatuor Roth (*La Liberté*, 15 Jun. 1928; *The Chicago Tribune*, 16 Jun. 1928; *Le Gaulois*, 17 Jun. 1928, 5; *Le Monde musical*, 30 Jun. 1928; *Le Courrier musical*, 1 Jul. 1928)
- Paris, Salle Chopin, 10 Nov. 1928, by Quatuor Loiseau (*Le Courrier musical*, 1 Dec. 1928)
- Paris, Salle de la Lune Rousse, 15 May 1929, by Quatuor Bastide
- Brest, Salle des Arts, Feb. 1930, by Quatuor Calvet

Orchestral arrangement of 4th movt. by Leigh Henry
- Swansea, National Eisteddfod, 26 Jul. 1926

Deuxième Quatuor, Op. 49 [String Quartet No. 2]

1. *Introduction – Andante*; 2. *Allegro*; 3. *Interlude – Andante*; 4. *Allegro*.
For string quartet (2vn, va, vc).

Comp. 1920 (as Op. 53, written after the *Rapsodie celtique*, Op. 50, which follows below), MS Book VI, nos 2–2d. Pub. Paris: E. Demets, 1920 (plate nos. E. 1994 D. [parts] and E. 1994bis D. [score]); date on dust cover: 1921, date on first music page and on instrumental parts: 1920. Reprint: Munich: Musikproduktion Höflich, 2019 (plate no. 5282). Online score at IMSLP. Dedication: 'à la Mémoire de Terence McSWINEY, *Lord Mayor de Cork*'.

Reviews in *Comoedia* (5 Dec. 1921), 4; *Musical Opinion* (Feb. 1922); *Allgemeine Musikzeitung* (21 Apr. 1922), 343; *Il pianoforte* 3:10–12 (Oct.–Dec. 1922), 256; *Le Guide du concert* (12 Dec. 1924), 286.

NB.: An arrangement of movts 3 & 4 as *Irish Fantasy* for saxophone quartet by Robert Stevens, Saxpress, undated (plate no. SKU 1129-4).

Identified performances:
- (F.P.) Paris, Hotel Continental, 25 Jan. 1922 by Arthur Darley, Terry O'Connor, George H. Brett, Joseph Schofield (vc) (*The New York Herald*, 26 Jan. 1922; *Comoedia*, 30 Jan. 1922, 3)
- Dublin, Engineer's Hall, 35 Dawson Street, 2 Feb. 1922, by A. Darley, T: O'Connor, G. H. Brett, J. Schofield (*The Freeman's Journal*, 3 Feb. 1922; *The Irish Times*, 3 Feb. 1922)
- Berlin, Bechstein-Saal, 3 May 1922, by Kulenkampff-Quartett (*Berliner Börsen-Courier*, 7 May 1922; *Deutsches Tageblatt*, 9 May 1922; *Die Zeit*, 10 May 1922; *Signale f. d. mus. Welt*, 10 May 1922, 642; *Allgemeine Musikzeitung*, 12 May 1922, 402)
- Dublin, 6 April 1923 (Father Mathew Feis, test piece), by 'Misses Murphy, Nolan, Reid, and Brady' (*Irish Independent*, 7 Apr. 1923, 10)
- Paris, Salle des Quatuors Gaveau, 18 Dec. 1924, by Quatuor Loiseau
- Paris, Caméléon, 4 Nov. 1925, by Quatuor Loiseau
- Paris, Salle Chopin, 26 May 1928, by Quatuor Andolfi
- Marseille, Société de Musique de Chambre, 23 Nov. 1928, by Quatuor Andolfi
- Bourg-la-Reine, Salle de la Mairie, 10 Apr. 1929, by Quatuor Andolfi

- Paris, Maison de la Mutualité (24 rue Saint-Victor), 16 Feb. 1932, by string musicians from an unnamed orchestra cond. by J. Jemain
- Paris, Palacio de la Madeleine, 27 Apr. 1932, by Quatuor Odette Malézieux
- Derry, Apr. 1939, test piece at 'Feis Doire Colmcille' (*The Derry Journal*, 14 Apr. 1939, 16)

Broadcast performances:
- 28 Apr. 1929, by Quatuor Russe (*Le Journal*, 28 Apr. 1929, 6; *Radio Magazine*, 28 Apr. 1929)
- (excerpts): Dublin (Radio Éireann), 25 Oct. 1935, by station ensemble (MacSwiney commemoration) (*Irish Press*, 25 Oct. 1935, 5)

Rapsodie celtique, Op. 50

1. theme (*Allegretto*), four variations and epilogue; 2. *Andantino*; 3. *Allegro appassionato*. For violin and piano.

Comp. 1914, MS Book V nos 1–5. Pub. Paris: E. Demets, 1915 (plate no. E. 1825 D.). Online score at IMSLP.

Advertised in *The Musical Times* 58:895 (Sep. 1917), 431. Reviews in *Le Guide du concert* (undated in Press Book, *c*1915–7); *Allgemeine Musikzeitung* (21 Oct. 1921, 761); *Comoedia* (5 Dec. 1921), 4.

NB. According to Hennessy's own list of works, this piece dates from 1920, but in the MS he gives a copyright date of 1914.

Identified performances:
- (F.P.) Paris, Salle des Concerts Touche, 4 Mar. 1922, by Ida Adam-Pineau and S. H. (*The New York Herald*, 5 Mar. 1922)
- Paris, Salle Saint-Georges, 11 Mar. 1922, by I. Adam-Pineau and S. H. (*Comoedia*, 20 Mar. 1922, 2)
- Berlin, Bechstein-Saal, 3 May 1922, by Georg Kulenkampff-Post and Michael Raucheisen (*Allgemeine Musikzeitung*, 12 May 1922)
- Paris, École de Chant Challet-Vicq, 4 Nov. 1922, by I. Adam-Pineau and S. H.
- Quimper (at Congrès Panceltique), 9 Sep. 1924, by 'Mlle. M.' and 'Mme. G.'
- London, Guildhall School of Music, 13 Nov. 1924, by Adelaide Lane and Michael Kavanagh
- Exeter, Maynard School Hall, 14 Nov. 1928, by Miss Ethel Bankart and Mrs. Huth (*Exeter Express & Echo*, 14 Nov. 1928; *Exeter and Plymouth Gazette*, 15 Nov. 1928, 7; *The Musical Times* 70:1031, Jan. 1929), 73
- Exeter, Barnfield Hall, 12 Dec. 1928, by E. Bankart and Mrs. Huth (*Exeter and Plymouth Gazette*, 13 Dec. 1928, 2; *The Musical Times*, 1 Jan. 1929, 73)
- Paris, Salle Debussy, 23 Jan. 1929, by Tina Manteufel and S. H.
- Paris, Salle Chopin, 15 May 1931, by T. Manteufel and Sophie Stivel
- Paris, Institut Musical Marthe Le Breton, 7 Jul. 1941, by Odette Malézieux and Madeleine Dupré

Broadcast performances:
- 7 Dec. 1925, by Odette Malézieux and S. H. (*Le Ouest-Éclair*, 7 Dec. 1925, 7; *L'Intransigeant*, 7 Dec. 1925, 6)
- 9 Dec. 1928, by Tina Manteufel and S. H. (*Le Journal*, 9 Dec. 1928, 6)

Petit trio celtique, Op. 52
1. *Allegro (dans le style irlandais)*; 2. *Moderato (dans le style breton)*; 3. *Andante (dans le style irlandais)*; 4. *Allegro (dans le style breton)*.
For string trio (vn, va, vc).

Comp. 1920, originally as Op. 55, MS Book IV nos 24–27. Pub. Paris: E. Demets, 1921 (plate no. E. 2002 D. [parts] & E. 2002bis D. [score]). Second ed., Paris: Éditions Max Eschig, *c.*1928 (plate no. E. 2002 D.). Reprints: London: Merton Music, *c.*2009 (Demets' plate no., plus on title page: 3336); Munich: Musikproduktion Höflich, 2019 (plate no. 5285). Online score at IMSLP. Dedication: 'à mon ami Paul Le Flem'.

Reviews in *Comoedia* (5 Dec. 1921), 4; *Musical Opinion* (Feb. 1922); *The Sackbut* 2:9 (Mar. 1922), 35; *Allgemeine Musikzeitung* (21 Apr. 1922); *Le Guide du concert* (21 Mar. 1924), 362.

Identified performances:
- (F.P.) Dublin, Engineer's Hall, Dawson Street, 30 Mar. 1922, by John Moody, George H. Brett, Joseph Schofield (*The Irish Times*, 31 Mar. 1922)
- Berlin, Bechstein-Saal, 3 May 1922, by Georg Kulenkampff-Post, Karl Glaser, Ursula Hildebrand (*Allgemeine Musikzeitung*, 12 May 1922)
- Paris, Salle des Concerts Touche, 10 Jan. 1925, by Lucien Bellanger, Georges Drouet, Francis Touche
- Auxerre, Sélect Cinema Théâtre, 27 Jan. 1925, by Émile Loiseau, Robert Chantôme, Robert Ladoux
- Paris, Univ. Sorbonne (Amphithéâtre de Chimie), 21 Feb. 1925, by E. Loiseau, R. Chantôme, R. Ladoux (*La Bretagne à Paris*, 28 Feb. 1925)
- Paris, Caméléon, 18 Mar. 1925, by E. Loiseau, R. Chantôme, R. Ladoux
- Paris, Caméléon, 4 Nov. 1925, by E. Loiseau, R. Chantôme, R. Ladoux (*Comoedia*, 7 Nov. 1924, 2; *Le Courrier musical*, 1 Dec. 1925)
- Paris, Association des Étudiants Bretons à Paris (61 rue Madame), 18 Dec. 1925, by E. Loiseau, R. Chantôme, R. Ladoux
- Paris, Caméléon, 27 Dec. 1925, by E. Loiseau, R. Chantôme, R. Ladoux
- Paris, Salle des Quatuors Gaveau, 25 Feb. 1926, by E. Loiseau, R. Chantôme, R. Ladoux (*Comoedia*, 28 Feb. 1926, 2)
- Paris, Salle des Agriculteurs, 14 Oct. 1926, by E. Loiseau, R. Chantôme, R. Ladoux (*Comoedia*, 20 Oct. 1926, 2)
- Saint-Dié, Théâtre Municipal, 23 Apr. 1927, by Mlle. Cécile Roussel, R. Chantôme, Maurice Roussel
- Paris, Salle du Guide de Concert, mid-Dec. 1927, by E. Loiseau, R. Chantôme, R. Ladoux (*Comoedia*, 12 Dec. 1927, p. 3)

- Brussels, Le Lyceum de Belgique, 27 Apr. 1928, by Francine Janssens, Edmond Vanderborght, Fernande Kufferath (*L'Étoile Belge*, 29 Apr. 1928)
- La Londe (Seine-Maritime), Église Notre Dame, 23 Sep. 1928, by Mme. Raoul Logeart, Marguerite Hauser, Georgette Hauser
- Paris, Salle Chopin, 31 May 1929, by Trio Pasquier (*La Semaine à Paris*, 9:365 [24–31 May 1929], 84)
- Paris, Lyceum de France (17 rue de Bellechasse), 31 Jan. 1930, by Tina Manteufel, Paule Bertrand, Géo Dupuy
- Paris, Maison de la Mutualité (24 rue Saint-Victor), 16 Feb. 1932, by MM. A. Jacob, Terrade, Cambo
- Dublin, Gate Theatre, 6 Mar. 1932, by Messrs Tracey, Etherington, Joseph Schofield (*The Irish Press*, 7 Mar. 1932, 4; *The Irish Times*, 7 Mar. 1932, 4)
- Paris, Salle Chopin, 6 May 1933, by Alfred Loewenguth, Jack W. George, Jacques Neilz
- Paris, Students' Atelier Reunions (65 quai d'Orsay), 17 Dec. 1933, by Odette Malézieux, F. Lemaire, Mme. V. Blanchon-Mialin
- Paris, Salle de Conférences de la Société Industrielle, 15 Mar. 1935, by O. Malézieux, Jacques Boucher, V. Blanchon-Mialin
- Paris, chez Alfred Loewenguth, 16 & 18 Mar. [mid-1930s], by A. Loewenguth, Gaston Despiau, Roger Loewenguth
- La Flèche (Dép. Sarthe / Loire), 16 May 1935, by O. Malézieux, J. Boucher, V. Blanchon-Mialin (*Journal Flèchois*, 22 May 1935, 2)
- Paris, Société Industrielle, 15 Oct. 1935, by O. Malézieux, J. Boucher, V. Blanchon-Mialin
- Boulogne-sur-mer, Chambre de commerce, 6 Dec. 1936, by O. Malézieux, J. Boucher, V. Blanchon-Mialin
- Paris, Le Triptyque (blvd. Raspail), 24 Feb. 1938, by by Jean Fuchs, Cécile Blottière, Pierre Ruyssen
- Paris, chez Madame Cluzel, 10 Mar. 1939, by J. Fuchs, C. Blottière, P. Ruyssen
- Paris, 16 avenue Henri Martin, 22 Mar. 1939 by J. Fuchs, C. Blottière, P. Ruyssen

Broadcast performances:
- 21 Feb. 1925, by Émile Loiseau, Robert Chantôme, Robert Ladoux (*Paris-soir*, 22 Feb. 1925)
- 3 Jun. 1926, by an unnamed string trio (*Le Gaulois*, 2 Jun. 1926)
- 11 Feb. 1930, by Tina Manteufel, Paule Bertrand and Géo Dupuy

Trio, Op. 54

1. *Moderato, con grazia*; 2. *Andante*; *Intermezzo – Andante sostenuto*; 3. *Vivace con spirito*.
For two clarinets and bassoon.

Comp. 1919–20, MS Book IV nos 28–31. Pub. Paris: E. Demets, 1921 (plate no. E. 2001 D.). Reprints, Munich: Edition diewa, 2005 (plate no. dw 75); Warngau:

Accolade, 2010 (plate no. ACC 1306); Ham Lake, Minnesota: Jeanné, Inc., 2011 (plate no. JP 5056). Online score and parts at IMSLP. Dedication: 'à mon ami Paul Ladmirault'.

Reviews in *Musical Courier*, 17 Nov. 1921, 20; *Comoedia* (5 Dec. 1921), 4; *Musical Opinion* (Feb. 1922); *Allgemeine Musikzeitung* (21 Apr. 1922); *Le Guide du concert* (15 Feb. 1924), 280.

Identified performances:
- (F.P.) Berlin, Bechsteinsaal, 23 Nov. 1922, by Leonhard Kohl, Adolf Mützelburg, Louis Scheiwein (*Die Zeit*, 2 Dec. 1922; *Allgemeine Musikzeitung*, 8 Dec. 1922)
- Paris, Salle des Concerts Touche, 16 Feb. 1924, by Louis Cahuzac, Maximilien Riol, Henri-Eugène Bretenaker (*Comoedia*, 21 Feb. 1924, 2)
- Dublin, Apr. 1924, test piece in Tailteann Games (*Irish Examiner*, 11 Apr. 1924, 10)
- Paris, Caméléon, 24 Nov. 1925, by Louis Cahuzac, Jean (?) Bailly, Gustave Dhérin
- Paris, Caméléon, 1 Feb. 1926, by L. Cahuzac, J. Bailly, G. Dhérin
- Perf. with clarinet, alto-saxophone and bassoon: Paris, Salle Debussy, 13 Mar. 1934, by messieurs Doreau, René Laurent, Dufrenne

Broadcast performance:
- 15 Dec. 1925, by L. Cahuzac, J. Bailly, G. Dhérin (*Le Gaulois*, 15 Dec. 1925, 5)

Arrangement for piano solo:
Comp. 1919 (!), MS Book V no. 6. Unpublished.

Variations sur un thème de six notes, Op. 58

In one movement, with 16 variations.
For flute, violin, viola, cello.

Comp. 1922, MS of full score missing, except last page in MS Book VI, no. 6d; parts: ibidem, nos 6a–6d. Pub. Paris: Max Eschig & Cie., 1924 (plate no. M.E. 1315^a [parts]) and 1925 (plate no. M.E. 1315^b [score]). Dedication: the print does not bear any dedication, but Hennessy wrote in *Le Guide du concert*, 9 May 1924, p. 458, referring to the German names of the notes of the theme H–B–E–B–C–H: *"Les lettres H.B., E.B. et C.H. sont les initiales de trois amis de l'auteur auxquels cette composition est dédiée"*. The names of these friends have not been identified yet.

Reviews in *Le Guide du concert* (9 May 1924), 458; *Die Musik* 17:9 (1925) 698.

NB.: On the first page of the (miniature) score the work has a copyright date of 1925, on the cover it is 1924 (as in the publication of the parts).

Identified performances:
- (F.P.) Paris, Salle des Concerts Touche, May 1924, by (monsieur) A. Trembelland, Émile Loiseau, Robert Chantôme, Mathieu Barraine (*Comoedia*, 18 May 1924, 2)

- Paris, Salle de la Fédération des Artistes, 29 Jan. 1925, by A. Trembelland, Odette Malézieux, Alice Quintin, Aristodème Vrassy
- Paris, Salle des Concerts Touche, 28 Feb. 1925, by Lucien Lavaillotte, Lucien Bellanger, Georges Drouet, Francis Touche
- Paris, Salle Debussy, 29 Nov. 1932, by A. Trembelland, Odette Malézieux, Jacques Boucher, V. Blanchon-Mialin
- Kingston, New York, Maverick, 20 Jun. 1937, by Georges Barrère, Pierre Henrotte, Henri Michaux, Horace Britt (*Kingston Daily Freeman*, 18 Jun. 1937)

Quatre Pièces celtiques, Op. 59

1. *Allegretto*; 2. *Adagio*; 3. *Allegro*; 4. *Allegro*.
For cor anglais, violin, viola, cello.
Comp. 1923, MS for a reduction to cor anglais and piano: MS Book V no. 8. Pub. Paris: Max Eschig & Cie., 1925 (plate no. M.E. 1430); reprinted in early 1950s. Reprint as *Vier keltische Stücke (Four Celtic Pieces):* Warngau: Accolade, 2009 (plate no. ACC 1303). Online score at IMSLP. Dedication: 'à M. Paul Brun'.
Reviews in *Le Guide du concert* (9 May 1924), 458; *ibid.* (6 Feb. 1925), 509; *Il pianoforte* 6:12 (Dec. 1925), 360.
Identified performances:
- (F.P.) Paris [unnamed location], May 1924, by Paul Brun, Émile Loiseau, Robert Chantôme, Robert Ladoux (*Comoedia*, 18 May 1924, 2)
- Paris, Salle des Quatuors Gaveau, 10 Feb. 1925, by P. Brun, É. Loiseau, R. Chantôme, R. Ladoux (*Comoedia*, 13 Feb. 1925, 2)
- Grenoble, during Exposition de la Houille Blanche et du Tourisme, 28 Jul. 1925, by P. Brun, André Le Métayer, (monsieur) Lagardère, (monsieur) Moyse
- Paris, Caméléon, 4 Nov. 1925, by P. Brun, É. Loiseau, R. Chantôme, R. Ladoux (*Comoedia*, 7 Nov. 1925, 2)

Broadcast performance:
- 3 Jun. 1926, by Paul Brun and an unnamed string trio (*Le Gaulois*, 2 Jun. 1926)

Troisième Quatuor à cordes, Op. 61 [String Quartet No. 3]

1. *Introduction*; 2. *Les Écossais*; 3. *Les Étudiants*; 4. *Les Fées*.
For string quartet (2vn, va, vc).
Comp. 1922–3, MS Book VI, no. 3 (score only, parts missing). Pub. Paris: Max Eschig & Cie., 1926 (plate no. M.E. 1719 [score], M.E. 1719ᵇ [parts]). Reprint: Munich: Musikproduktion Höflich, 2019 (plate no. 5283). Dedications: 1. 'à Émile Loiseau'; 2. 'à Adrien Fourment'; 3. 'à Robert Chantôme'; 4. 'à Robert Ladoux'.
Reviews in *Le Guide du concert* (1 Feb. 1926), 13; *Le Guide du concert* (15 Mar. 1929), 714.
NB. The piece is a reworking of a 1922 *Deuxième Suite* (*Zweite Suite für Streichquartett*) in three movements that was first performed in Berlin, Meister-Saal, 15 Nov. 1922, by

the Deman Quartet. Here, the movement *Les Étudiants* had been the final movt. (*Berliner Börsenzeitung*, 17 Nov. 1922; *Tageblatt*, 18 Nov. 1922; *Börsen-Courier*, 22 Nov. 1922; *Allgemeine Musikzeitung*, 24 Nov. 1922; *Signale f. d. mus. Welt*, 27 Nov. 1922).
Identified performances:
- (F.P.) Paris, Salle des Agriculteurs, 14 Oct. 1926, by Quatuor Loiseau (*Comoedia*, 20 Oct. 1926, 2; *Le Gaulois* (24 Oct. 1926), 2;)
- Paris, Salle Érard, 22 Feb. 1929, by Quatuor Krettly
- Paris, Salle Chopin, 20 Mar. 1929, by Quatuor Krettly
- Lille, Salle Odéola, 8 Nov. 1929, by Quatuor Calvet
- Nantes, 5 Jan. 1930, by Quatuor Calvet
- Saint Nazaire, Salle des Arts, 6 Jan. 1930, by Quatuor Calvet
- Redon, Salle des Fêtes du Collège St-Sauveur, 7 Jan. 1930, by Quatuor Calvet
- Pontivy, 8 Jan. 1930, by Quatuor Calvet
- Vannes, Salle des Clissons, 10 Jan. 1930, by Quatuor Calvet (*L'Avenir du Nord*, 18 Jan. 1930)
- Quimper, Théâtre Municipal, 13 Jan. 1930, by Quatuor Calvet
- Brest, Salle des Arts, 14 Jan. 1930, by Quatuor Calvet
- Paris, Salle Érard, 5 Feb. 1930, by Quatuor Calvet
- Paris, Hôtel Majestic, 12 Feb. 1930, by Quatuor Calvet (*Le Monde musical*, 28 Feb. 1930; *Le Courrier musical*, 1 Mar. 1930)

Broadcast performances:
- (movts. 1, 2, and 3) Radio-Paris, 21 Oct. 1929, by Quatuor Calvet

Sonatine celtique, Op. 62
1. *Allegro con brio*; 2. *Andante sostenuto*; 3. *Allegro*.
For viola and piano.

Comp. 22–24 July 1924, MS Book III no. 4 (movts 1 & 2 only), MS Book V no. 10 (movt 3); MS Book V no. 9 (va part). Pub. (as '*Sonate celtique*') Paris: Max Eschig & Cie., 1924 (plate no. M.E. 1425); reprinted Paris: Éditions Max Eschig, c.1930, 1945 and 1974 (with correct title). Online score at IMSLP. Dedication: 'à Robert Chantôme'.

Reviews in *Le Guide du concert* (14 Nov. 1924), 157; *ibid.* (8 Mar. 1929); *ibid.* (20 Feb. 1931), 571; *Mom-Mus* (16 May 1929). See also Hinson/Roberts 2006 (bibliography).
Identified performances:
- (F.P.) Paris, Salle des Quatuors Gaveau, 18 Nov. 1924, by Robert Chantôme and Mme. Loiseau
- Paris, Caméléon, 18 Mar. 1925, by R. Chantôme and Mme. Loiseau
- Paris, Le Choral Moderne, 29 Mar. 1925, by R. Chantôme and Mme. Loiseau
- Paris, Caméléon, 27 Dec. 1925, by Paul-Louis Neuberth and S. H.
- Saint-Dié, Théâtre Municipal, 23 Apr. 1927, by R. Chantôme and Paul Gentilhomme
- Paris, Salle Mustel, 17 Dec. 1927, by Mlle. Brulé and S. H.
- Calais, Crystal-Palace, 9 May 1928, by Nathalie Séménova and Robert Buérick

- Auxerre, Théâtre Municipal, 24 Apr. 1929, by R. Chantôme and Paul Berthier
- Paris, Salle Chopin, 9 Jan. 1930, by R. Chantôme and Alexandre Cellier (*La Semaine à Paris*, 17 Jan. 1930, 23; *Le Monde musical*, 31 Jan. 1930)
- Paris, Salle Chopin, 25 Feb. 1931, by R. Chantôme and Suzanne Astruc (*Journal des débats*, 3 Mar. 1931, 4; *Le Courrier musical*, 15 Mar. 1931)
- Paris, Salle Chopin, 17 Nov. 1931, by R. Chantôme and S. Astruc (*L'Européen*, Nov. 1931; *Comoedia*, 19 Nov. 1931, *Le Courrier musical*, 1 Dec. 1931)
- Tours, Foyer Municipal, 9 May 1936, by R. Chantôme and M. Alavoine
- Paris, Hotel des Deux-Mondes (Maison des Intellectuels), 6 Jun. 1936, by R. Chantôme and Marcelle Fossier-Brillot
- Paris, Conservatoire Russe (26, avenue de Tokio), 15 Jun. 1936, by Mlle. Y. Goujeon and Raymond Belinkoff (*L'Art musical*, 12 Jun. 1936, 759)
- Paris, Le Triptyque (Blvd. Raspail), Jul. 1936, by Y. Goujeon and R. Belinkoff (*Eschig-Informations*, Jul. 1936, 1)
- Rennes, Tour d'Auvergne, 25 Apr. 1938, by R. Chantôme and Mme. Latapi (*Le Ouest-Éclair*, 15 Apr. 1938)
- Paris, Salle Debussy, 23 Feb. 1939, by Suzanne Paris and Louise Paris

Broadcast performances:
- 1 Jul. 1929, by unnamed performers (*Comoedia*)
- Radio Prague, 9 Mar. 1936, by unnamed performers (*Eschig-Informations*, Mar. 1936, 1)

Arrangement for alto saxophone and piano (by René Laurent)

Comp. *c.*1927, MS missing. Pub. Paris: Éditions Max Eschig, 1927 (plate no. [a-sax part] M.E. 1889).

Identified performances:
- Paris, Salle du Guide de Concert, 7 Nov. 1927, by René Laurent and S. H.
- Compiègne (exact location unknown), 7 Feb. 1928, by R. Laurent and Germaine Bedenne
- Paris, Salle Gaveau, 18 Dec. 1929, by R. Laurent and Yvonne François (*Revue Internationale de Musique et de Danse*, 15 Jan. 1930)
- Dijon, Conservatoire National de Musique, 20 Apr. 1932, by Louis Duchesne and unnamed pianist

Arrangement for violin and piano (by S. H.)

Comp. *c.*1927, MS Book V no. 11 (vn part only). Pub. Paris: Éditions Max Eschig, 1927 (plate no. [vn part] M.E. 1919).

Identified performance:
- Paris, Salle Chopin, 16 Mar. 1929, by Tina Manteufel and S. H.

Broadcast performance:
- 28 Apr. 1929, by Tina Manteufel and S. H. (*Le Journal*, 28 Apr. 1929, 6; *Radio Magazine*, 28 Apr. 1929)
- 30 Jun. 1929, by Hélène Arnitz and S. H. (*Hebdo*, 29 Jun. 1929)

Rapsodie gaélique, Op. 63
For violoncello and piano.

Comp. 1924, MS Book V nos 12 & 13. Pub. Paris: Max Eschig & Cie., 1925 (plate no. M.E. 1447). Dedication: 'à Francis Touche'.

Reviews in *Le Guide du concert* (13 Mar. 1925), 669; *Il pianoforte* 6 (Aug.–Sep. 1925), 265.

Identified performances:
- (F.P.) Paris, Caméléon, 18 Mar. 1925, by Robert Ladoux and Mme. Loiseau
- Paris, Salle de la Fédération des Artistes, 30 Apr. 1925, by Odette Malézieux and S. H.
- Paris, Salle des Concerts Touche, 18 Dec. 1925, by Francis Touche and S. H.
- Brussels, Le Lyceum de Belgique, 27 Apr. 1928, by Fernande Kufferath and S. H. (*L'Etoile Belge*, 29 Apr. 1928)
- Paris, Salle Debussy, 15 Nov. 1928, by Madeleine Monnier and Richard Byk (*Le Courrier musical*, 1 Nov. 1928; *Le Monde musical*, 30 Nov. 1928)
- Paris, Salle Debussy, 5 Feb. 1929, by Robert Ladoux and S. H.
- Paris, Salle Gaveau, 13 Mar. 1932, by Colette Carlioz and Henriette Roget

Broadcast performance:
- Rome (441,2 m), 14 Oct. 1931 (no performers mentioned) (*Radio-Wien*, 14 Oct. 1931, 63)

Sérénade, Op. 65
For string quartet (2vn, va, vc).

Comp. 1924, MS Book VI nos 5a–5d (parts only, full score missing). Pub. Paris: Max Eschig & Cie., 1925 (plate nos. M.E. 1525 [parts] and M.E. 1525^b [score]). Reprint: Munich: Musikproduktion Höflich, 2019 (plate no. 5286). Online score (parts only) at IMSLP. Dedication: 'à Émile Loiseau'.

Review in *La Revue musicale* 7:4 (1 Feb. 1926), 182.

Identified performances:
- (F.P.) Paris, Caméléon, 27 Dec. 1925, by Quatuor Loiseau
- Paris, Caméléon, 13 Jan. 1926, by Quatuor Loiseau (*La Bretagne à Paris*, 23 Jan. 1926)[6]
- Pittsburgh, Hotel Schenley, 26 Nov. 1933, by Shapiro Quartet (Max Shapiro, William Loesel, Francis Kleyle, Samuel Kliachko)
- Boulogne-sur-mer, Chambre de commerce, 6 Dec. 1936, by Quatuor Malézieux
- Paris, Salle Debussy, 23 Feb. 1939, by Quatuor Malézieux

Broadcast performance:
- (Lyon P.T.T.) 29 May 1934, by an unnamed quartet (*Comoedia*, 29 May 1934, 5)

---

[6] At the same occasion, Hennessy performed the *Cinq morceaux irlandais de Carolan*, by Denis Breen.

***Deux morceaux*, Op. 68**
1. *Pièce celtique*; 2. *Jazz*.
For alto saxophone and piano.

Comp. 1925, MS Book V nos 15–18. Pub. Paris: Max Eschig & Cie., 1926 (plate no. M.E. 1637). Online score at Gallica and IMSLP. Dedication: 'à M. René Laurent'.
Identified performances:
- (F.P.) Paris, Salle Majestic, 22 Jan. 1926, by R. Laurent and S. H. (*Comoedia*, 25 Jan. 1926, 1; *Le Guide du concert*, 29 Jan. 1926, 450)
- Paris, Salle Majestic, 1 Dec. 1926, by R. Laurent and S. H.
- Berlin, Stern'sches Konservatorium, 21 Feb. 1930, by Max Salomonsohn and unnamed pianist

(no. 1 only)
- (as an as yet unpublished) *Romance irlandaise*, Paris, Caméléon, 27 Dec. 1925, by René Laurent and S. H.
- Berlin, Stern'sches Konservatorium, 11 Apr. 1930, by Kurt Petzelt and unnamed pianist

***Trio*, Op. 70**
1. *Moderato quasi allegretto*; 2. *Allegro*; *Intermezzo*; 3. *Allegro*.
For violin, flute, bassoon.

Comp. 1925, MS Book IV no. 32 (score only). Pub. (parts) Paris: Propriété de l'auteur, 1926 (no plate no.); (score) Paris: Max Eschig & Cie. ('Copyright by Swan Hennessy'), 1927 (print says incorrectly 1926; plate no. M.E. 1985); also available as a *'Nouvelle édition revue et corrigée par l'auteur'* of the same year (plate no. M.E. 1985[A] [parts] and M.E. 1985[B] [score]). Reprint, Warngau: Accolade, 2010 (plate no. ACC 1307). Dedication: 'A mes amis Emile Loiseau, Gaston Blanquart et Gustave Dhérin' (missing in score).

Reviews in *Le Guide du concert* (5 Nov. 1926), 135; *Allgemeine Musikzeitung* (12 Apr. 1929); *Le Guide du concert* (20 Feb. 1931), 571.
Identified performances:
- Paris, Salle de Géographie (Sorbonne), early Nov. 1926, by Émile Loiseau, Gaston Blanquart, Gustave Dhérin (*Comoedia*, 10 Nov. 1926, 2)
- Paris, Salle Debussy, 6 Dec. 1928, by É. Loiseau, G. Blanquart, G. Dhérin
- Sidmouth, Manor Hall, 12 Feb. 1929, by H. G. McWhinnie, Ethel Bankart, W. Evins
- Paris, chez Mme. Domange (Mel Bonis), 21 blvd. Berthier, 2 Mar. 1929, by É. Loiseau, G. Blanquart, G. Dhérin
- Paris, Salle Chopin, 25 Feb. 1931, by Suzanne Chevaillier, G. Blanquart, G. Dhérin (*Journal des débats*, 3 Mar. 1931; *Le Courrier musical*, 15 Mar. 1931)
- Paris, Maison de la Mutualité (24 rue Saint-Victor), 16 Feb. 1932, by M. Bonne, Paulette Souvignet, M. Gaspariantz

- Paris, Maison Gaveau (Salle des Quatuors), 3 Dec. 1932, by S. Meynieu, A. Trembelland, A. Péronne (vc!)
- Paris, Académie des Lanturelus, 9 May 1933, by Jan Merry, Gaston Hamelin (cl!), G. Dhérin
- Paris, Société Artistique et Littéraire des Agents de la Compagnie P.L.M., 26 May 1934, by Léon Zighéra, G. Blanquart, G. Dhérin
- Paris, Villa Montmorency, 17 Dec. 1935, by L. Zighéra, G. Blanquart, G. Dhérin

Brodacast performance:
- 20 Sep. 1933, by Léon Zighéra, Gaston Blanquart, Gustave Dhérin

***Quatre Morceaux*, Op. 71** (a-sax) and **Op. 71bis** (va)
1. *Fox Trot*; 2. *Tango*; 3. *Chanson de l'émigrant*; 4. *Lever du soleil dans les Hébrides*.
For alto saxophone or viola and piano.
  Comp. 1926, MS Book V nos 19–21. Pub. Paris: Éditions Max Eschig, 1927[7] (plate no.: M.E. 1941). Dedications: 1. 'à Paul-Louis Neuberth'; 2. 'à Carol-Berard'; 3. 'à Madame Neuberth'; 4. 'à Paul-Louis Neuberth'.
  Reviews in *Revue internationale de la musique et du danse* (15 Aug. 1929), *Tribune de Genève* (3 Jan. 1930), *I.M.I.* (15 Mar. 1930).
  NB.: Originally comprising the first three pieces only and entitled *Nouvelles pièces exotiques* (alluding to Op. 57 for pf).
Identified performance:
(nos 3 & 4 only):
- Paris, Maison de la Mutualité (24 rue Saint-Victor), 16 Feb. 1932, by 'M. et Mme Roger Gely'

Op. 71bis:
Identified performances:
- (F.P.) Paris, Salle du Guide de Concert, 7 Nov. 1927, by Paul-Louis Neuberth and S. H.
- Paris, Salle Debussy, 15 Jan. 1929, by Robert Chantôme and S. H. (*La Semaine à Paris*, 11 Jan. 1929, 84)
- Auxerre, Théâtre Municipal, 24 Apr. 1929, by R. Chantôme and Paul Berthier
- Morat/Murten, Switzerland, Salle des Concerts, 17 Nov. 1929, by P.-L. Neuberth and Fred Hay
- Paris, Salle Chopin, 9 Jan. 1930, by R. Chantôme and Alexandre Cellier (*La Semaine à Paris*, 17 Jan. 1930, 23; *Le Monde musical*, 21 Jan. 1930)

---

[7] The plate number belongs to the year 1927, but in the author's copy of the print Eschig claims its copyright as 1929, in a second line also stating 'Copyright 1929 assigned to Associated Music Publishers Inc. New York'. I interpret this as an original 1927 edition by Eschig and a second edition of 1929.

- Sceaux (Dép. Hauts-de-Seine), Jun. 1936, by P.-L. Neuberth and Marcelle Soulage

(no. 2 only):
- Mons, Salle Académique de l'Institut Supérieure de Commerce, 17 March 1931, by P.-L. Neuberth and Marguerite Lestrade
- Paris, Salle Chopin, 30 Nov. 1932, by P.-L. Neuberth and Marthe Le Breton

(nos. 3 & 4 only)
- Paris, Salle Debussy, 23 Feb. 1939, Suzanne Paris and Louise Paris

Version of no. 3 for viola and organ:
Comp. *c*.1927–9, MS missing, unpublished, withdrawn.
Identified performance:
- Tencin (Isère), Église Saint Jean, 15 Sep. 1929, by Paul-Louis Neuberth and Olivier Messiaen (under the title *Plainté de l'émigrant*)

Pièce celtique, Op. 74
For violoncello or bassoon and piano.
Comp. 1927, MS Book V no. 22. Pub. Paris: Éditions Max Eschig, 1928 (plate no. M.E. 2252). Online scores at Gallica and IMSLP. Dedication: 'à Madame Fernande Kufferath'.
Identified performances:
- (F.P.) Brussels, Le Lyceum de Belgique, 27 Apr. 1928, by Fernande Kufferath and S. H. (*L'Etoile Belge*, 29 Apr. 1928)
- Paris, Salle Debussy, 15 Nov. 1928, by Madeleine Monnier and Richard Byk (*Le Courrier musical*, 1 Nov. 1928)
- Paris, Salle Debussy, 5 Feb. 1929, by Robert Ladoux and S. H.

Broadcast performances:
- 12 Sep. 1931, by Roger Boulmé (vc) and unnamed pianist (*Le Peuple*, 11 Sep. 1931, 2)
- 16 Aug. 1932, by Christian Dhérin (bassoon) and Marie-Antoinette Pradier (*Comoedia*; *Le Journal*)

Quatrième Quatuor à cordes Op. 75 [String Quartet No. 4]
1. *Andante con moto*; 2. *Andante*; 3. *Allegretto scherzoso*; 4. *Allegro con brio*.
For string quartet (2vn, va, vc).

Comp. 1928, MS Book VI nos 4a–4h. Pub. Paris: Éditions Max Eschig, 1930 (plate nos. M.E. 2463 [score] and 2464 [parts]). Reprint: Munich: Musikproduktion Höflich, 2019 (plate no. 5284).

Completion announced in *Le Monde musical* (30 Sep. 1928), *Le Courrier musical* (1 Oct. 1928), and *Revue internationale de musique et de danse* (15 Oct. 1928). Reviews in *Monthly Musical Record* 61:7 (Jul. 1930), 212; *Le Guide du concert* (20 Feb. 1931), 571.

Appendix

Identified performances:
- (F.P.) Paris, Salle Debussy, 17 Jan. 1929, by Quatuor Loiseau (*Le Courrier musical*, 1 Feb. 1929)
- Paris, Salle Chopin, 25 Feb. 1930, by Quatuor Andolfi (*Daily Mail*, 1 Mar. 1930; *Le Courrier musical*, 15 Mar. 1930)
- Paris, Salle Chopin, 25 Feb. 1931, by Quatuor Andolfi (*Journal des débats*, 3 Mar. 1931; *Le Courrier musical*, 15 Mar. 1931)
- Paris (unnamed location), 28 Feb. 1931, by Quatuor Bastide
- Paris, Salle de la Lune Rousse (58 rue Pigalle), 10 Mar. 1931, by Quatuor Bastide (announced as F.P.)
- Paris, Salle Debussy, 9 Mar. 1938, by Quatuor Malézieux

Deux Pièces celtiques, Op. 77
1. *Danse écossaise*; 2. *Pièce celtique*
For viola and piano.
   Comp. 1928, MS missing. Unpublished.
Identified performances:
- (F.P.) Paris, Salle Debussy, 15 Jan. 1929, by Robert Chantôme and S. H. (*La Semaine à Paris*, 11 Jan. 1929, 84)
- Vernon (Dép. Eure), Salle des Répétitions, 29 Jan. 1930, by Paul-Louis Neuberth and Marcel Labey (*Journal de Vernon*, 25 Jan. 1929)
- Paris, Salle Chopin, 17 Nov. 1931, by R. Chantôme and Suzanne Astruc (*L'Européen*, Nov. 1931; *Comoedia*, 19 Nov. 1931, *Le Courrier musical*, 1 Dec. 1931)
- Paris, Hotel des Deux-Mondes (Maison des Intellectuels), 6 Jun. 1936, by R. Chantôme and Marcelle Fossier-Brillot

Sonatine, Op. 78
1. *Allegro appassionato*; 2. *Allegro amabile*; 3. *(d'après un air irlandais)*.
For two violins (or two groups of violins).
   Comp. March 1929, MS Book V no. 7. Unpublished.
   NB: Title according to MS: *Sonatine pour deux violons*[NB] *composée pour les élèves de M. Emile Loiseau Professeur au Conservatoire*. NB ou deux groups de violons.
   NB 2: The Irish traditional tune in the third movement is No. 917 ('Reel') from the Petrie Collection. Towards the end he also quotes briefly from 'The Dawning of Day' (see Op. 72 No. 3).

Deuxième Sonatine, Op. 80
1. *Allegro*; 2. *Andantino*; 3. *Allegretto*.
For violin and piano (also a transcription for viola and piano).

Comp. 1929, MS Book V no. 23. Pub. Paris: Proprieté de l'auteur, 1929 (distributed by Éditions Max Eschig) [no plate no.]. Dedication: 'A Suzanne Chevaillier'.
Reviews in *Le Petit Havre* (11 Oct. 1929); *Allgemeine Musikzeitung* (31 Oct. 1930). Also mentioned in *Le Guide du concert* (11 Oct. 1929).
Identified performances:
- (F.P.) Paris, Salle de l'École Normale de Musique, 15 Nov. 1929, by Suzanne and Lucien Chevaillier
- Paris, Le Parthenon, 17 Jan. 1931, by S. Chevaillier and Maurice Servais
- Paris, Salle Chopin, 25 Feb. 1931, by S. Chevaillier and M. Servais
- Paris, Salle de l'École Normale de Musique, 7 May 1932, by Argéo Andolfi and Christiane Maizier (*Le Courrier musical*, [?] May 1932; *Le Monde musical*, [?] May 1932)
- Paris, 25 Nov. 1932, by S. Chevaillier and Julieff Melmeister
- Paris, Salle des Concerts de Montparnasse, 29 Dec. 1932, by S. Chevaillier and Marguerite Papin
- Paris, Salle Debussy, 2 Dec. 1933, by Julien Villain and M. Servais
- Paris, Club des Champs-Élysées (35 av. Victor-Emmanuel III), 23 Feb. 1937, by S. Chevaillier and Julia Efron (*L'Art musical*, 19 Feb. 1937, 490).

Transcription for viola and piano
Comp. 1929, MS missing. Pub. Paris: Proprieté de l'auteur, 1929 (distributed by Éditions Max Eschig) [no plate no.].

Sonatine, Op. 81
1. *Moderato assai*; 2. *Allegretto à la manière de Johannes Brahms*; 3. *Allegro à la manière de Félix Mendelssohn Bartholdy*.
For violoncello and piano.
Comp. 1929, MS Book V nos 24 & 25. Pub. Paris: Proprieté de l'auteur, 1929 (distributed by Éditions Max Eschig). Dedication: 'À Madeleine Monnier'.
Reviews in *Le Petit Havre* (11 Oct. 1929); *Allgemeine Musikzeitung* (31 Oct. 1930); briefly mentioned in *Le Guide du concert* (11 Oct. 1929).
Identified performances:
- Paris, Lyceum de France (17 rue de Bellechasse), 31 Jan. 1930, by Géo Dupuy and Mlle. Rachmanoff
- Paris, Salle de l'École Normale de Musique, 11 Mar. 1931, by Jacques Serres and Janine Cools
- Paris, Salle Debussy, 8 Jun. 1931, by J. Serres and J. Cools (*Le Monde musical*, 30 Jun. 1931; *Le Courrier musical*, 1 Aug. 1931)

Appendix

SEE ALSO:

Trois Pièces Celtiques (Drei keltische Stücke), Op. 53
For piano trio (vn, vc, pf).
    Comp. 1922, MS missing. Withdrawn after first performance at Berlin, Meister-Saal, 15 Nov. 1922, by Rudolf Deman, Carl Dechert, Bruno Eisner (*Lokal-Anzeiger*, 18 Nov. 1922; *Der Tag*, 22 Nov. 1922; *Deutsche Allgemeine Zeitung*, 28 Nov. 1922).
    This work was to be published with the Cork, Ireland, based publisher Sullivan which ran into financial difficulties in the course of the Irish Civil War.

Rapsodie breton (Bretonische Rhapsodie), Op. 55
For violin and piano.
    Comp. 1922, MS missing. Withdrawn after first performance at Berlin, Meister-Saal, 15 Nov. 1922, by Rudolf Deman and Bruno Eisner.

Deuxième Suite (Zweite Suite für Streichquartett), Op. 58
For string quartet (2vn, va, vc)
    Comp. 1922, MS missing. Withdrawn after first performance at Berlin, Meister-Saal, 15 Nov. 1922, by Deman Quartet, and merged into String Quartet No. 3, Op. 61; see for details there.

Pièce celtique d'après un vieil air écossais
For cello and piano.
    Comp. 1928, MS missing. Unpublished.
    Identified performance:
- Paris, Salle Debussy, 15 Nov. 1928, by Madeleine Monnier and Richard Byk (*Le Courrier musical*, 1 Nov. 1928; *Le Monde musical*, 30 Nov. 1928).

Appendix 2
List of works in opus numbers

The following is a list of Swan Hennessy's works sorted after opus numbers (final opus number sequence only). For more details of the pieces, see Appendix 1.

Ländliche Skizzen, Op. 1 (1884)
For piano. Leipzig, 1885.

Ein Spinnerliedchen, Op. 2 (1885)
For piano. Stuttgart, 1886.

Vier Lieder, Op. 3 (*c*1885–6)
For voice and piano. Stuttgart, 1886.

Two Studies, Op. 4 (*c*1886)
For piano. London & New York, 1890.

The Blackbird Has a Golden Bill, Op. 5.1 (1886)
For mezzo-soprano and piano. Stuttgart, 1887.

Carneval-Studien, Op. 6 (*c*1886–7)
For piano. Stuttgart, 1887.

Im Gebirg (In the Mountains). 4 Klavierstücke, Op. 7 (*c*1887)
For piano. London, 1887.

Album-Blätter (Album Leaves), Op. 8 (1887)
For piano. London, 1887.

Étude-Fantaisie, Op. 9 (1888)
For piano. London, 1888.

Lieder an den Mond, Op. 10 (1888)
For piano trio. London, 1888.

Miniatures. Cinq Petites pièces, Op. 11 (1889)
For piano. Paris, 1889.

Variations sur un thème original dans le style irlandais, Op. 12 (*c*1902)
For piano. London, 1902.

Berceuse, Op. 13 (1900)
For violin and piano. Paris, 1901.

Sonate en fa (style irlandais), Op. 14 (c1902–4)
For violin and piano. London, 1904.

Deux Études (en ut mineur) pour la main gauche seule, Op. 15 (1905)
For piano. Paris, 1906.

Praeludium et fuga, Op. 16 (1906)
For piano. Paris, 1906.

Mazurka et Polonaise, Op. 17 (1906)
For piano. London, 1906.

Petit album, Op. 18 (1905)
For piano. London, 1907.

Aus dem Kinderleben. 6 kleine Tonbilder, Op. 19 (1904)
For piano. Leipzig, 1905.

Tarantelle, Op. 20 (1906)
For violin and piano. Unpublished.

Au bord de la forêt, Op. 21 (1906)
For piano. Paris, 1907.

Au village. Petite suite caractéristique, Op. 22 (1906–7)
For piano. Paris, 1907.

Lydia, Op. 23 (1906)
For high voice and string quartet; version with piano. String quartet original: unpublished; piano version: Paris, 1908.

Eaux fortes, Op. 24 (1906)
For piano. Paris, 1908.

Étude, Op. 25 (1906)
For piano. Paris, 1907.

Epiphanie, Op. 26 (1906)
For high voice and organ or piano. Paris, 1908.

Nouvelles feuilles d'album, Op. 27 (1907)
For piano. Paris, 1908.

Variations sur un air irlandais ancien, Op. 28 (1908)
For piano. Mainz, 1908.

Bláithfhleasg bheag, d' fhonnaibh arsa Gaedhealacha as leabhar Petrie. / Petite suite irlandaise, d'après des airs anciens de la collection Petrie, Op. 29 (1908)
For piano 4-hands. Paris, 1909.

Deux Mélodies, Op. 30 (1906)
For low voice and piano. Paris, 1908.

Trois Chansons écossaises, Op. 31 (c.1906–9)
For high voice and piano. Paris, 1906–22.

Valses, Op. 32 (1909)
For piano. Paris, 1909.

Croquis de femmes, Op. 33 (1911)
For piano. Paris, 1911.

Petite suite (sur les notes mi do mi fa si mi), Op. 34 (1909)
For piano. Mainz, 1911.

Kinder-Album. 24 kleine Präludien in verschiedenen Ton- und Taktarten, Op. 35 (1909)
For piano. Mainz, 1910.

Fêtes. Deux Morceaux descriptifs, Op. 36 (1910)
For piano. Mainz, 1911.

Les Noces du soldat de bois. Ballet en un acte, Op. 37 (1913)
For piano. Unpublished.

Introduction, XII variations et fugue sur un thème obligé, Op. 38 (1909)
For piano. Paris, 1910.

Incunabula, Op. 39 (1911)
For piano. Paris, 1912.

En passant ... (Études d'après nature), Op. 40 (1911)
For piano. Paris, 1912.

Valses caprices, Op. 41 (1911)
For piano. Paris, 1912.

Gitaneries, Op. 42 (1911)
For piano. Paris, 1912.

Trois Chansons espagnoles, Op. 42bis (1920)
For medium voice and piano. Paris, 1921.

Sonatine, Op. 43 (1911)
For piano. Paris, 1912.

Sentes et chemins (Nouvelles études d'après nature), Op. 44 (1912)
For piano. Paris, 1912.

Pièces celtiques, Op. 45 (1912)
For piano. Paris, 1912.

Suite pour quatuor à cordes, Op. 46 [String Quartet No. 1] (1912)
For string quartet. Paris, 1913.

Adagio et allegretto du quatuor à cordes, Op. 46bis (1912)
For piano. Paris, 1912.

Croquis parisiens, Op. 47 (1912)
For piano. Paris, 1913.

Impressions humoristiques, Op. 48 (1913)
For piano. Paris, 1913.

Deuxième Quatuor, Op. 49 [String Quartet No. 2] (1920)
For string quartet. Paris, 1920.

Rapsodie celtique, Op. 50 (1914)
For violin and piano. Paris, 1915.

Huit Pièces celtiques, Op. 51 (1922)
For piano. London, 1924.

Petit trio celtique, Op. 52 (1920)
For string trio. Paris, 1921.

Sonatine celtique, Op. 53 (1923)
For piano. London, 1924.

Trio, Op. 54 (1919–20)
For two clarinets and bassoon. Paris, 1921.

Epigrammes d'un solitaire, Op. 55 (1923)
For piano. London, 1924.

Trois Mélodies, Op. 56 (1921)
For voice and piano. Nos. 1 & 3: Paris, 1932, no. 2: Paris, 1925.

Trois Pièces exotiques, Op. 57 (1922)
For piano. Paris, 1922.

Variations sur un thème de six notes, Op. 58 (1922)
For flute quartet. Paris, 1924.

Quatre Pièces celtiques, Op. 59 (1923)
For cor anglais quartet. Paris, 1925.

Étude de concert, Op. 60 (1923)
For piano. Paris, 1924.

Troisième Quatuor à cordes, Op. 61 [String Quartet No. 3] (1923)
For string quartet. Paris, 1926.

Sonatine celtique, Op. 62 (1924)
For viola and piano. Paris, 1924.

Rapsodie gaélique, Op. 63 (1924)
For violoncello and piano. Paris, 1925.

Douze Canons à deux voix à tous les intervalles, Op. 64 (1924)
For piano. Paris, 1925.

Sérénade, Op. 65 (1924)
For string quartet. Paris, 1925.

Trois Mélodies, Op. 66 (1921–4)
For high voice and piano. Paris, 1926.

Rapsodie irlandaise, Op. 67 (1924)
For piano. Paris, 1929.

Deux morceaux, Op. 68 (1925)
For alto saxophone and piano. Paris, 1926.

Banlieues …. Six Petites pièces, Op. 69 (1925)
For piano. Paris, 1926 (1–3) & 1929 (4–6).

Trio, Op. 70 (1925)
For violin, flute, bassoon. Paris, 1926.

Quatre Morceaux, Op. 71 (1926)
For alto saxophone (or viola) and piano. Paris, 1929.

Trois Chansons celtiques, Op. 72 (1926)
For medium voice and piano. Paris, 1927.

Deux Mélodies, Op. 73 (1927)
For medium voice and piano. Paris, 1928.

Pièce celtique, Op. 74 (1927)
For violoncello (or bassoon) and piano. Paris, 1928.

Quatrième Quatuor à cordes Op. 75 [String Quartet No. 4] (1928)
For string quartet. Paris, 1930.

Allegretto du quatrième quatuor à cordes, Op. 75bis (1928)
For piano. Unpublished.

Trois Petits trios pour voix de femmes, Op. 76 (1928)
For soprano, mezzo-soprano, alto (solos). Unpublished.

Deux Pièces celtiques, Op. 77 (1928)
For viola and piano. Unpublished.

Sonatine, Op. 78 (1929)
For two violins. Unpublished.

Deux Mélodies, Op. 79 (1929)
For soprano and piano. Paris, 1932.

Deuxième Sonatine, Op. 80 (1929)
For violin and piano (version with viola). Paris, 1929.

Sonatine, Op. 81 (1929)
For violoncello and piano. Paris, 1929.

Works without opus-numbers

Deux Petites pièces bi-tonales (1923)
For piano. Paris, 1923.

À la manière de ... 18 Pastiches (3 volumes) (1917–26)
For piano. Paris, 1927.

À la manière de ... Six Nouveaux pastiches, 4e cahier (1926)
For piano. Paris, 1927.

À la manière de ... 5e cahier (1927)
For piano. Paris, 1928.

Appendix 3

Publishers' plate numbers

The following tables show the plate numbers used by Swan Hennessy's publishers for his publications, with the year of publication in the second column. The list is revealing in terms of the order of publication as opposed to the chronology of opus numbers and as to how Hennessy succeeded in finding a new and ultimately a regular publisher. The overall order follows the chronology of the first published piece of the respective publishers.

Breitkopf & Härtel (Leipzig)

Plate no.	Year	Title / Op.
17120	1885	*Ländliche Skizzen*, Op. 1
24931	1905	*Aus dem Kinderleben. 6 kleine Tonbilder*, Op. 19

G. A. Zumsteeg (Stuttgart)

Plate no.	Year	Title / Op.
G.A.Z. 562[a–d]	1886	*Vier Lieder*, Op. 3
G.A.Z. 564	1886	*Ein Spinnerliedchen*, Op. 2
G.A.Z. 587	1886	*The Blackbird has a Golden Bill*, Op. 5.1
G.A.Z. 591	1886	*Carneval-Studien*, Op. 6 (Vol. 1)
G.A.Z. 617	1887	*Carneval-Studien*, Op. 6 (Vol. 2)

Augener & Co. (London)

Plate no.	Year	Title / Op.
7241	1886	*Two Studies*, Op. 4
7671	1887	*Im Gebirg (In the Mountains). 4 Klavierstücke*, Op. 7
7672	1887	*Album Leaves (Albumblätter)*, Op. 8
7902	1888	*Étude-Fantaisie*, Op. 9
7942	1888	*Lieder an den Mond. Romantische Stücke*, Op. 10
1287	1902	*Variations sur un thème original dans le style irlandais*,
1287α	1903	Op. 12 (w/rev. ed.)
1360α	1906	*Mazurka et Polonaise*, Op. 17

Durand & Schoenewerk (Paris)

Plate no.	Year	Title / Op.
D.S. 4043	1889	*Miniatures. Cinq petites pièces*, Op. 11

Enoch & Cie. (Paris)

Plate no.	Year	Title / Op.
E. & C. 4658	1901	*Berceuse*, Op. 13

Schott & Co. (London) &
B. Schott's Söhne (Mainz)

Plate no.	Year	Title / Op.
27497	1905	*Sonate en Fa (style irlandais)*, Op. 14
27919	1907	*Petit album*, Op. 18
28388	1908	*Variations sur un air irlandais ancien*, Op. 28
28824	1910	*Kinder-Album*. 24 kleine Präludien in verschiedenen Ton- und Taktarten, Op. 35
29378	1911	*Petite suite sur les notes Mi Do Mi Fa Si Mi*, Op. 34
29379	1911	*Fêtes*. Deux Morceaux descriptifs, Op. 36

J. Hamelle (Paris)

Plate no.	Year	Title / Op.
J. 5340. H.	1906	*Praeludium & Fuga*, Op. 16
J. 5405. H.	1905	*Deux Études (en ut mineur) pour la main gauche seul*, Op. 15
J. 5489 H.	1906 (²1908)	*Lydia*, Op. 23
J. 5501 H.	1907 (²1908)	*Épiphanie*, Op. 26
J. 5505 H.	1907 (²1908)	*Annie* Op. 31 No. 1 (orig. Op. 26 No. 1)
J. 5506 H.	1908?	*Là-bas!*, Op. 30 no. 1 (orig. Op. 26 No. 2)
J. 5656 H.	1908	*Le Revenant*, Op. 30 No. 2

E. Demets (Paris)

Plate no.	Year	Title / Op.
E. 1244 D.	1907	*Lydia*, Op. 23 (reprinted 1913, but not delivered until 1917)
E. 1246 D.	1907	*Là-bas!*, Op. 30 no. 1 (orig. Op. 26 No. 2)
E. 1247 D.	1907	*Le Revenant*, Op. 30 No. 2
E. 1267 D.	1907	*Au bord de la forêt*, Op. 21
E. 1271 D.	1907	*Étude*, Op. 25
E. 1286 D.	1907	*Annie* Op. 31 No. 1 (orig. Op. 26 No. 1)
E. 1293 D.	1907	*Noce campagnarde*, Op. 22 No. 1
E. 1294 D.	1907	*Fillettes*, Op. 22 No. 2
E. 1295 D.	1907	*Basse-Cour*, Op. 22 No. 3
E. 1296 D.	1907	*Sur l'herbe*, Op. 22 No. 4
E. 1297 D.	1907	*Au bord du ruisseau*, Op. 22 No. 5
E. 1346 [I–IV] D.	1908	*Nouvelles feuilles d'album*, Op. 27
E. 1387 [I–III] D.	1908	*Eaux fortes*, Op. 24
E. 1409 D.	1909	*Petite suite irlandaise, d'après des airs anciens de la collection Petrie*, Op. 29
E. 1448 D.	1909	*Valses*, Op. 32
E. 1487 D.	1910	*Introduction, XII Variations et fugue sur un thème obligé*, Op. 38

Appendix

E. 1614[1–3] D.	1912	*Incunabula*, Op. 39
E. 1615(1)–(5) D.	1912	*En passant ... (Études d'après nature)*, Op. 40
E. 1664 D.	1912	*Valses caprices*, Op. 41
E. 1674 D.	1912	*Sonatine*, Op. 43
E. 1678 D.	1912	*Gitaneries*, Op. 42
E. 1726 D.	1912	*Sentes et chemins (Nouvelles études d'après nature)*, Op. 44
E. 1727 D.	1912	*Pièces celtiques*, Op. 45
E. 1732 D.	1912	*Adagio et allegretto du quatuor à cordes*, Op. 46bis
E. 1747 D.	1913	*Croquis parisiens*, Op. 47
E. 1783 D.	1913	*Sagairt tar teorach. Adagio de la 'Petite suite irlandaise'* [Op. 29]
E. 1784 D.	1913	*Suite pour quatuor à cordes*, Op. 46
E. 1794 D.	1913	*Impressions humoristiques*, Op. 48
E. 1825 D.	1915	*Rapsodie celtique*, Op. 50
E. 1994 D. E. 1994bis D.	1920	*Deuxième Quatuor*, Op. 49
E. 2001 D.	1921	*Trio*, Op. 54
E. 2002 D. E. 2002bis D.	1921	*Petit trio celtique*, Op. 52
E. 2006 D.	1920	*La Fille aux cheveux de lin*, Op. 31 No. 2
E. 2037 D.	1922	*Nell*, Op. 31 No. 3
E. 2070 D.	1922	*Trois Pièces exotiques*, Op. 57
E. 2083 [1–3] D.	1921	*Trois Chansons espagnoles*, Op. 42bis

F. Durdilly, Ch. Hayet, successeur (Paris)

Plate no.	Year	Title / Op.
C. 6254 H.	1911	*Croquis de femmes*, Op. 33

Max Eschig & Cie. and
Éditions Max Eschig (Paris)

Plate no.	Year	Title / Op.
M.E. 1262	1924	*Étude de concert*, Op. 60
M.E. 1315	1924	*Variations sur un thème de six notes*, Op. 58
M.E. 1425	1924	*Sonatine celtique*, Op. 62
M.E. 1430	1925	*Quatre Pièces celtiques*, Op. 59
M.E. 1447	1925	*Rapsodie gaélique*, Op. 63
M.E. 1525	1925	*Sérénade*, Op. 65
M.E. 1563	1925	*Douze Canons à deux voix à tous les intervalles*, Op. 64
M.E. 1564	1925	*Les Grands jasmins épanouis*, Op. 56 No. 2
M.E. 1631	1925	*Trois Mélodies*, Op. 66 1. *Si la distance nous sépare* 2. *Paysage* 3. *Chanson ecossaise* (orig. Op. 56 No. 3)
M.E. 1637	1926	*Deux Morceaux*, Op. 68
M.E. 1719	1926	*Troisième Quatuor à cordes*, Op. 61
M.E. 1781	1927	*À la manière de ... 6 Pastiches* (Vol. 1)

M.E. 1782	1927	*À la manière de* ... 6 Pastiches (Vol. 2)
M.E. 1783	1927	*À la manière de* ... 6 Pastiches (Vol. 3)
M.E. 1889	1927 (print says 1924)	*Sonatine celtique*, Op. 62 (alto-saxophone arrangement)
M.E. 1919	1927 (print says 1924)	*Sonatine celtique*, Op. 62 (violin arrangement)
M.E. 1941	1927 (print says 1929)	*Quatre Morceaux*, Op. 71
M.E. 1985	1927 (print says 1926)	*Trio*, Op. 70 (rev. ed., score and parts)
M.E. 1986	1927	*À la manière de* ... 6 Nouveaux pastiches (Vol. 4)
M.E. 2115	1927	*Trois Chansons celtiques*, Op. 72 1. *Le Chanson du rouet* 2. *Berceuse d'Armorique* 3. *Le Départ des pêcheurs*
M.E. 2249	1928	*Le Chasseur noir*, Op. 73 No. 1
M.E. 2250	1928	*La Chanson du vent de mer*, Op. 73 No. 2
M.E. 2251	1928	*À la manière de* ... (Vol. 5)
M.E. 2252	1928	*Pièce celtique*, Op. 74
M.E. 2264	1929	*Rapsodie irlandaise*, Op. 67 (in *Album celtique*)
M.E. 2319	1929	*Variations sur un thème original dans le style irlandais*, Op. 12 (in *Album celtique*)
M.E. 2320	1929	*Huit Pièces celtiques*, Op. 51 (in *Album celtique*)
M.E. 2321	1929	*Sonatine celtique*, Op. 53 (in *Album celtique*)
M.E. 2322	1929	*Épigrammes d'un solitaire*, Op. 55
M.E. 2410	1929	*Banlieues* .... *Six Petites pièces*, Op. 69
M.E. 2463	1930	*Quatrième Quatuor à cordes* Op. 75 (score)
M.E. 2464	1930	*Quatrième Quatuor à cordes* Op. 75 (parts)
M.E. 3692	1932	*Le Mort joyeux*, Op. 56 No. 1
M.E. 3693	1932	*Il était une fois*, Op. 56 No. 3
M.E. 3694	1932	*Deux Mélodies*, Op. 79 1. *La Lune* 2. *À Deux*

Evans & Co. (London)

Plate no.	Year	Title / Op.
S. & Cº. 31	1924	*Eight Celtic Pieces*, Op. 51 (= *Huit Pièces celtiques*)
S. & Cº. 40	1924	*Épigrammes d'un solitaire*, Op. 55
S. & Cº. 41	1924	*Sonatine celtique*, Op. 53

Propriété de l'auteur (= self published)

Plate no.	Year	Title / Op.
—	1926	*Banlieues* .... Trois Petites pièces, Op. 69 (later six pieces, see Eschig M.E. 2410)
—	1926	*Trio*, Op. 70 (parts)
—	1929	*Deuxième Sonatine*, Op. 80
—	1929	*Sonatine*, Op. 81

Appendix 4
Dedications and Dedicatees

This section is in two parts. Part A gives brief information about the people Hennessy dedicated some of his music to. Part B does the same for composers who dedicated their works to Hennessy. Each section is in alphabetical order, beginning in each case with the title of the piece, its date, and the exact wording of the dedication, followed by the personal information. Years of birth and death are given only when identified with certainty.

Part A: Dedicatees of Hennessy's compositions

Auguste Adam
- *Bergerie*, No. 2 of *Eaux fortes*, Op. 24 (1906): 'à Monsieur Auguste Adam'.

Not identified; probably a personal friend of the Hennessys in Paris (see Gabrielle Pineau below).

William T. Scott Barber
- *Con brio assai*, No. 5 of *Miniatures. Cinq petites pièces*, Op. 11 (1889): 'à William T. Scott Barber'.

Not identified, probably a personal friend during Hennessy's time in England.

David Bispham (1857–1921)
- *Nur wer die Sehnsucht kennt*, Op. 14 (1894) (withdrawn work).

American operatic baritone, born in Philadelphia, died in New York City. His first professional appearance was in 1891 in a London performance of André Messager's *La Basoche*, and he remained in London probably until 1896, therefore this is where Hennessy must have seen or met him. He later worked mainly in New York, specialising in Wagner roles (Wikipedia).

Georges Bizet (1838–1875)
- *Gitaneries*, Op. 42 (1911): 'à la mémoire de Bizet'.

Well-known French composer, of whose opera *Carmen* (1875) Hennessy was very fond.

Gaston Blanquart (1877–1962)
- *Trio*, Op. 70 (1925) for violin, flute and bassoon: 'A mes amis Emile Loiseau, Gaston Blanquart et Gustave Dhérin'

French flutist, born in Raismes, Département Nord, died in Clichy near Paris. He studied in Valenciennes and at the Paris Conservatory (with Paul Taffanel), with a *Premier Prix* in 1898. He joined the Concerts Colonne in 1900 and was its first solo flutist, 1905–39. He participated in important performances of works with a prominent flute part by composers including Debussy, Ravel, Stravinsky, Schönberg, and others. He also taught at the Schola Cantorum, the Institut Berlioz, and privately.

Rachel Blanquer (1897–after 1957)
- *Étude de concert*, Op. 60 (1923): 'à Mademoiselle Rachel Blanquer'.

French pianist, born in Paris, studied at the Conservatoire with E.-M. Delaborde, winner of a *Premier Prix* in 1914, later a prominent concert pianist in the series of Colonne, Lamoureux, Pasdeloup, and in Monte Carlo.

Denis Breen (*c.*1886–1950)
- *Huit Pièces celtiques*, Op. 51 (1922): 'à Denis Breen'.

Irish music teacher, pianist and composer/arranger, based in Cork, also known as Donnchadh Ua Braoin. Active for the Gaelic League and the Oireachtas Festivals (particularly the one in Cork, 1924). For twenty years from 1932, he was the 'Organising Inspector of Musical Instruction' at the Department of Education. See also Part B below.

Marguerite Breitner
- *Deux Mélodies*, Op. 79 (1929): 'A Mlle. Marguerite Breitner'.

Not properly identified. Composer, pianist and performer on the Ondes Martenot.

Paul Brun
- *Quatre Pièces celtiques*, Op. 59 (1923): 'à M. Paul Brun'.

Cor anglais player in France in the early decades of the twentieth century. Studied at the Conservatoire (*Premier Prix*, 1897); active as a chamber musician, also appeared as soloist with Concerts Colonne.

Richard Byk[8]
- *À la manière de …*, vols 4 (1926) & 5 (1927): 'à Richard Byk'.

Polish pianist and composer who studied in Vienna with Theodor Leschetizky. He subsequently established a successful international performing career, making his U.S. debut in New York in 1925. In the 1930s, after being forced into exile and finding refuge in the United States, Byk settled in Southern California. Here he became known above all for his inspired teaching and for incorporating indigenous American themes in compositions such as the Fantasia for piano. See also Part B below.

Carol-Bérard (1881–1942)
- *Tango*, No. 2 of *Quatre Morceaux*, Op. 71 (1926): 'à Carol-Berard'.

Also spelled 'Carol Bérard', pseudonym of Charles-Louis Bérard, music critic and composer, born in Marseille, died in Paris. A pupil of Albéniz, he was influential as secretary of the French composers' union (Union Syndicale des Compositeurs de Musique). As a composer, he attracted attention for incorporating industrial and other sounds into his music such as in his *Symphonie des forces mécanique* (1908).

---

[8] Source: Karl Weigl Foundation, http://www.karlweigl.org/?page_id=136 (accessed 25 June 2018).

Robert Chantôme (1890–1960)[9]
- *Les Étudiants*, 3rd movt. of *Troisième quatuor à cordes*, Op. 61 (1923): 'à Robert Chantôme'.
- *Sonatine celtique*, Op. 62 (1924): 'à Robert Chantôme'.

Viola player, born in Paris, died in Civray, Département Cher. Studied at the Conservatoire (*Premier Prix*, 1910). Chantôme was a member of the Quatuor Loiseau and in this capacity participated in several first performances of Hennessy's string quartets and the *Petit trio celtique*, Op. 52 and played in numerous performances of the quartets and other works involving his instrument, including many performances after Hennessy's death. He also premiered the *Deux Pièces celtiques*, Op. 77 (1928).

Suzanne Chevaillier
- *Deuxième Sonatine*, Op. 80 (1929): 'À Suzanne Chevaillier'.

French violinist, recipient of a *Premier Prix* from the Paris Conservatory, mainly performing contemporary French repertory. In December 1924, she gave the first performance of Ravel's *Tzigane*, together with her husband, the composer, pianist and journalist Lucien Chevaillier (1883–1932) whom she survived by at least six years. She gave the first performance of Hennessy's Op. 80 on 15 November 1929. She also participated in the February 1931 'Festival Swan Hennessy'.

Henri Collet (1885–1951)
- *Le Chanson du rouet*, No. 1 of *Trois Chansons celtiques*, Op. 72 (1926): 'à Henri Collet'.

One of the best-known Parisian music critics (and a composer, too). Among other things, he wrote the influential series 'La Musique chez soi' in *Comoedia*, in the course of which he coined the term *Les Six* (1920) and also portrayed Swan Hennessy (1921).

Jules Combarieu (1859–1916)
- *Croquis de femmes*, Op. 33 (1911): 'à Monsieur Jules Combarieu, Hommage sympathique et reconnaissant'.

Prominent French music critic and musicologist. Founder (in 1901) of the *Revue d'histoire et de critique musicales*, which became *La Revue musicale* in 1904 and *La Revue musicale S.I.M.* in 1912. Hennessy always fared well in these journals.

Eugène Cools (1877–1936)[10]
- *Berceuse d'Armorique*, No. 2 of *Trois Chansons celtiques*, Op. 72 (1926): 'à Eugène Cools'.

French composer, critic and music publisher of Belgian origin, born in Paris and died in L'Isle-Adam (Val d'Oise). He had studied at the Paris Conservatory with Gedalge, Fauré and Widor and was Gedalge's teaching assistant between 1907 and

---

[9] Source: https://data.bnf.fr/17021318/robert_chantome/ (accessed 21 February 2019).
[10] Denis Havard de la Montagne: 'Eugène Cools (1877–1936)', *Musica et Memoria*, http://www.musimem.com/cools_eugene.htm (accessed 4 August 2018).

1923. From 1919 he also taught harmony at the École Normale de Musique and wrote reviews for *Le Monde musical*. After Max Eschig's death in September 1927 he succeeded him at the top of his publishing company (which had taken over E. Demets in 1923), which was transformed into a publicly listed company and rebranded 'Éditions Max Eschig' from November 1927. Cools remained the company's director until his death on 5 August 1936. Two of his daughters were also involved in performances of Hennessy's music: the pianist Janine Cools and the musician and writer Denise Cools.

Auguste Delacroix (1871–1936)
- *Nouvelles feuilles d'album*, Op. 27 (1907): 'À mon ami Auguste Delacroix'.

French composer and pianist, born in Louviers, Département Eure (Normandy). See also in Part B below.

Jeanne-Charlotte Delorme-Jules Simon († 1933)[11]
- *La Fille aux cheveux de lin*, No. 2 of *Trois Chansons écossaises*, Op. 31 (c1907): 'à Madame Delorme Jules Simon'.

French writer, winner of the 1917 *Prix Littéraire* (*Prix Montyon*) of the Académie Française; granddaughter of the philosopher and politician Jules Simon (1814–1896). Famous for her novels reflecting World War I experiences. According to the 1922 *Annuaire International des Lettres et des Arts* she lived at the same address as Swan Hennessy (270 boulevard Raspail). The dedication was probably added to the 1921 publication.

Eugène Demets (1858–1923)
- *Étude*, Op. 25 (1906): 'A Monsieur E. Demets'.
- *Petite suite sur les notes Mi Do Mi Fa Si Mi*, Op. 34 (1909): 'à mon cher ami E. Demets'.

Paris-based music publisher, operating between 1899 and his death in 1923. Hennessy published his first work with him in 1907; from 1911 he became his exclusive publisher. After his death, his catalogue was taken over by Max Eschig & Cie. (see also Eugène Cools).

Gustave Dhérin (1887–1964)[12]
- *Trio*, Op. 70 (1925) for violin, flute and bassoon: 'A mes amis Emile Loiseau, Gaston Blanquart et Gustave Dhérin'.

French bassoonist (and oboist). Studied at the Paris Conservatory (*Premier Prix*, 1907) and taught there, 1934–57. Known for performances of contemporary music by, among others, Nadia Boulanger, Eugène Bozza, André Jolivet, Francis Poulenc, Igor Stravinsky, etc. Frequently performed Hennessy's Opp. 54 and 70, including the latter work's first performance.

---

[11] Short obituary in *Paris-soir*, 4 April 1933, p. 3.
[12] Michael Burns: 'Music Written for Bassoon by Bassoonists: An Overview', in: *Double Reed* 24:2 (2001), p. 51–65 [58].

Adrien Fourment
- *Les Écossais*, 2nd movt of String Quartet No. 3, Op. 61 (1923): 'à Adrien Fourment'.

Second violinist in the Quatuor Loiseau, which premiered the 3rd string quartet and other quartet compositions by Hennessy.

Marcelle Gerar (1891–1970)[13]
- *Il était une fois*, No. 3 of *Trois Mélodies*, Op. 56 (1921)

Pseudonym of Marcelle Regerau. Belgian-born French singer, born in Brussels, died in Paris. She studied privately with Ninon Vallin and later taught at the École Normale de Musique, Paris. A number of French composers dedicated songs to her, including Honegger, Huré, Ibert, Milhaud, Ravel, Roussel, and Schmitt. After Ravel's death she edited a collection of her correspondence with him.

Gretchen Goetschius
- *Andante*, No. 4 of *Miniatures*, Op. 11 (1889): 'à Gretchen Gœtschius'.

Probably the daughter of Percy Goetschius, Hennessy's teacher of composition at Stuttgart (his wife had a different name).

Percy Goetschius (1853–1943)
- *Ländliche Skizzen*, Op. 1 (1885): 'Seinem Freund und Lehrer Herrn Professor Percy Goetschius gewidmet'.

Hennessy's professor of composition at Stuttgart. American-born Goetschius taught at Stuttgart (1878–92), the New England Conservatory, Boston (1892–1905), and the Institute of Musical Art, New York (1905–25).

Lucien Haudebert (1877–1963)[14]
- *Sonatine celtique*, Op. 53 (1923): 'A mon cher ami Lucien Haudebert' (in MS); 'à Lucien Haudebert' (in Eschig edition).

French (Breton) composer. Born in Fougères, Département Ille-et-Vilaine (Brittany), he first studied at Laval for a business degree, following his father's wishes, and then went to Paris where he was a private pupil of Gabriel Fauré. Although he created a large oeuvre of orchestral and chamber music, his vocal and choral music are regarded as his main achievement. His greatest success was the oratorio *Dieu vainqueur* for vocal soloists, mixed chorus, organ and orchestra, given with 600 participants in December 1927 at Mannheim, Germany. He was awarded the *Prix Paul Dukas* in 1945.

---

[13] https://de.wikipedia.org/wiki/Marcelle_Gerar (German only; accessed 8 April 2019).

[14] Gérard Leclerc: 'Haudebert, Lucien', in Véfa de Bellaing (ed.): *Dictionnaire des compositeurs de musique en Bretagne* (Nantes: Ouest Éditions, 1992), p. 114–117.

Carl [or Karl] Heffner (1849–1925/7)[15]

- *Suite pour quatuor à cordes*, Op. 46 (1911): 'à Monsieur le Professeur Carl Heffner'.

Painter and (minor) composer (published a number of songs in Bavarian dialect), born in Würzburg, died in Berlin. He first studied music in Munich, and was self-educated as a painter, with several journeys to England, France, and Italy. Lived first in Dresden (from 1894), then in Freiburg and Berlin. Apparently one of the earliest and most successful impressionist painters in Germany.

Elisabeth 'Betty' Heffner

- *Fêtes*. Deux Morceaux descriptifs, Op. 36 (1910): 'à Madame Betty Heffner, Hommage sympathique'; in the MS: 'Frau Professor Heffner gewidmet'.

The wife of Carl Heffner, see above. No further information available.

Claire Hennessy; see Claire Przybyszewska

Michael David Hennessy (1837–1919)

- *Kinder-Album*, Op. 35 (1909): 'Meinem lieben Vater gewidmet'.
- *Sentes et chemins (Nouvelles études d'après nature)*, Op. 44 (1912): 'À mon Père'.

Swan Hennessy's father, born in Cork, Ireland, emigrated to Chicago, became President of the Chicago City Railways and a successful lawyer, returned to Europe around 1890 to live with his son and his family. Died in Veytaux, near Montreux, Switzerland.

Patrice Hennessy (1910–1973)

- *Chanson écossaise*, No. 3 of *Trois Mélodies sur des poésies d'André Delacour et de Leconte de Lisle*, Op. 66 (*c*1921): 'À mon fils Patrice'.
- *Rapsodie irlandaise*, Op. 67 (1924): 'à mon fils Patrice'.

Swan Hennessy's son, born and died in Paris, known mainly as 'Patrice', but also as 'Michel Patrice' or 'Michael Patrick'. Multitalented from early youth, he painted Swan Hennessy's oil portrait while still in his teens, wrote plays (of which *La Rude journée de la nouvelle scène*, 1945, was published), and was an avid collector of historical documents about the French Revolution. This made him one of the most acknowledged experts on this period in French history and a household name in the collectors and auction scene of his time and as an *'homme de lettres'*.[16] In this regard, he wrote *L'Autograph. Valeur de placement*, a text bound together with Michel Vaucaire's *Le Livre. Valeur de placement* (published Paris: Le Prat, 1970).

---

[15] Wikimedia Commons; wuerzburgwiki.de; accessed 21 August 2017.

[16] In 1958, he sold a large part of his collection via the Parisian auction house Drouot, see *Catalogue de lettres autographes et de documents historiques sur la Révolution française faisant partie de la collection de M. Patrice Hennessy dont la vente aura lieu, Hôtel des commissaires-priseurs, Drouot..., les 6 et 7 mai 1958 ... par M. Jacques Arnna* (Paris: Drout, 1958).

Charles Hubbard

- *Nell*, No. 3 of *Trois Chansons écossaises*, Op. 31 (c1921): 'à Charles Hubbard'.
- *Les Grands jasmins épanouis*, No. 2 of *Trois Mélodies*, Op. 56 (1921): 'à Charles Hubbard'.

American tenor who performed in Paris frequently during 1921–5. His programmes included mainly contemporary French composers, but he was also the first to introduce the music of Aaron Copland to a European audience (in 1921 accompanied by Nadia Boulanger, in 1922 by Madeleine d'Aleman). He gave the first performances of both Hennessy works dedicated to him and also sang them in the United States (at least once, in New York, 1926).

Michael Kavanagh

- *Épigrammes d'un solitaire*, Op. 55 (1923): 'à Michael Kavanagh'.

Irish pianist and occasional composer with whom Hennessy was in contact during 1922–24. Probably cooperated with the small, Cork-based music publisher Sullivan or responsible for the publication of three Hennessy works with Evans & Co. of London: *Huit pieces celtiques*, Op. 51, *Sonatine celtique*, Op. 53 and *Épigrammes d'un solitaire*, Op. 55, the copyright of which Hennessy assigned to Kavanagh in 1924. In that year, Kavanagh began to teach at the Guildhall School of Music, London. Before that, he led a short-lived attempt to establish an 'Irish Society of Composers' from early 1920, which failed during the Civil War years (see Chapter 8), and led the 'orchestra' of the Pavilion Cinema, Dublin (1921).

Theodor Kirchner (1823–1903)

- *Im Gebirg (In the Mountains)*. 4 Klavierstücke, Op. 7 (1887): 'An Herrn Theodor Kirchner'.

German composer in the Romantic tradition, born at Neukirchen near Chemnitz, studied in Leipzig, taught at Leipzig, Winterthur, Zurich, Würzburg, and Dresden, died in Hamburg. Friend of Robert and Clara Schumann and Johannes Brahms.

Fernande Kufferath (1875–?)

- *Pièce celtique*, Op. 74 (1927): 'à Madame Fernande Kufferath'.

(Élisa Marie Joséphine) Fernande Kufferath – Belgian cellist, born in Schaerbeek, Brabant, date and place of death unknown. She studied at the Brussels Conservatory with Edouard Jacobs, gaining a first prize in 1894. She performed, both as a chamber musician and as soloist in orchestral music, in Belgium, the Netherlands, England and Germany. In April 1928 she gave the first performance in Brussels of Hennessy's Op. 74 with the composer.

Paul Ladmirault (1877–1944)

- *Trio*, Op. 54: 'à mon ami Paul Ladmirault'.

French (Breton) composer and music critic, born in Nantes, died in Camoël, Département Morbihan. Studied at the Paris Conservatory with Gabriel Fauré. He participated in World War I and afterwards withdrew to rural Britanny. Admired by Claude Debussy and Florent Schmitt, much of his work is imbued with a Breton (Celtic) spirit. He is strongly associated with Breton cultural nationalism, being nominated a druid by the Gorsedd (a meeting of modern-day bards) of Brittany in 1908. He wrote operas, orchestral and chamber music, some piano music and art songs.

Robert Ladoux (1899–after 1963)[17]
- *Troisième Quatuor à cordes*, Op. 61 [String Quartet No. 3], 4th movement: 'à Robert Ladoux'.

French cellist, studied at the Paris Conservatory (*Premier Prix*, 1924) and was a member of the Société des Concerts du Conservatoire, 1929–60. Member of the Loiseau Quartet, which gave numerous (first) performances of Hennessy's string quartets. He also performed the *Petit trio celtique*, Op. 52 numerous times, the *Quatre Pièces celtiques*, Op. 59, the *Pièce celtique*, Op. 74, and he gave the first performance of the *Rapsodie gaélique*, Op. 63 in March 1925.

Beatrice Langley (1872–1958)[18]
- *Berceuse* Op. 13 (1900): 'à Madame Béatrice Langley'.

English violinist, born in Chudleigh, Devonshire, and died in Teignmouth. Private studies with the Joachim-pupil Joseph Ludwig and with August Wilhelmj. First public appearance at an 1882 recital in Dublin, official debut in London, November 1893, in Max Bruch's Violin Concerto and a *Capriccio* by Niels Gade. Already quite popular around the turn of the century, she founded the chamber music series 'Thursday Twelve O'Clocks' at the Aeolian Hall, London, that lasted about thirty years from 1906.

René Laurent
- *Deux morceaux*, Op. 68: 'à M. René Laurent'.

French alto-saxophonist, no biographical information available. Gave the first (and several later) performance of Op. 68; also arranged the viola work *Sonatine celtique*, Op. 62 for alto saxophone (1927).

---

[17] D. Kern Holoman, website accompanying his study *The Société des Concerts du Conservatoire (1828–1967)*, https://www.hector-dkh.com (accessed 20 April 2019).
[18] Silke Wenzel: 'Beatrice Langley', *MUGI. Musikvermittlung und Genderforschung: Lexikon und multimediale Präsentationen*, ed. Beatrix Borchard & Nina Noeske, Hochschule für Musik und Theater Hamburg, 2003ff., as of 19 December 2017. URL: http://mugi.hfmt-hamburg.de/Artikel/Beatrice_Langley (accessed 13 January 2018).

Marthe Le Breton
- *À la manière de …* (1917–27), vols 1–3: 'à Marthe Le Breton'.

French pianist, no biographical information available. According to the Gallica database of the BnF, she performed between about 1905 and 1943, initially as an accompanist only (for singers as well as instrumentalists, incl. Georges Enescu), and later as soloist performing in the series of Concerts Colonne, Lamoureux and Pasdeloup. She also ran her own piano school since the 1920s which was later called L'Institut Musical Marthe Le Breton, with locations in Paris (Rue Franklin), Laval, Poitiers, Romorantin, and Vierzon. In 1940, she appeared as the general secretary of L'Union des Femmes Artistes Musiciennes (*Le Matin*, 26 June 1940, p. 2). She has been one of the most frequent performers of Hennessy's music.

Paul Le Flem (1881–1984)[19]
- *Petit trio celtique*, Op. 52: 'à mon ami Paul Le Flem'.

French (Breton) composer, born in Radon, Département Orne (Normandy), grew up in Lézardrieux (Côtes-d'Armor, Brittany), which he has always regarded as his native village. He studied initially for three years at the Conservatoire with Charles-Marie Widor and Albert Lavignac (1899–1902), took courses in philosophy with Henri Bergson at the Sorbonne, and then changed to the Schola Cantorum to study with Vincent d'Indy, Albert Roussel, and Charles Bordes (1903–09). World War I caused a long break in his creative output, he only recommenced composition in 1936. Initially influenced by Debussy, he developed an individual voice through his involvement in Breton folk culture and, like Hennessy and other members of the Breton group of composers in Paris, developed a 'Celtic' identity in his music. Le Flem wrote in all genres including opera and orchestral music.

Katie Lewis
- *Andantino*, No. 3 of *Miniatures. Cinq petites pièces*, Op. 11 (1889): 'à Miss Katie Lewis'.

Not identified, probably a London friend of Hennessy and/or his wife.

Émile Loiseau (1874–1966)[20]
- 'Introduction' to *Troisième quatuor*, Op. 61 (1923): 'à Émile Loiseau'.
- *Sérénade*, Op. 65 (1924) for string quartet: 'à Émile Loiseau'.
- *Trio*, Op. 70 (1925) for violin, flute and bassoon: 'A mes amis Emile Loiseau, Gaston Blanquart et Gustave Dhérin'

---

[19] Geneviève Bernard-Krauß: *Hundert Jahre französischer Musikgeschichte in Leben und Werk Paul Le Flems* (Frankfurt: Peter Lang, 1993); Philippe Gonin: *Vie et oeuvre de Paul Le Flem (1881–1984)* (Villeneuve-d'Ascq: Presses universitaires du Septentrion, 2001 [diss. Univ. Lyon, 1998]).

[20] Source: Bibliothèque Nationale de France, http://data.bnf.fr/15015975/emile_loiseau/ (accessed 22 February 2018). See also Jean-Michel Roudier, Nicolas Brocq: *Le Legs Loiseau: la peinture moderne au Musée de la Loire de Cosne-sur-Loire* (Cosne-sur-Loire: Musée de la Loire de Cosne-sur-Loire / Musées de la Nièvre, 2004).

Violinist, founder and leader of the Quatuor Loiseau, born 31 December 1874 in Briare (Loiret), died 27 March 1966 in Cosne-en-Loire (Nièvre). Before he founded his own quartet, he was the second violinist in the Quatuor Parent (before WW I). He taught violin and viola at the Conservatoire and was concert master in its orchestra. The Loiseau Quartet gave most of the premieres of Hennessy's string quartets. In October 1942 he retired to Cosne-en-Loire. During his time in Paris, he was also an art collector; he bequeathed his important collection to the Musée de la Loire in his home town (he is not identical with the sculptor of the same name, who lived 1861–1927).

Ernest Longley (1866–1889)
- *Carneval-Studien*, Op. 6 (2 vols, 1886, 1887): "Seinem Freunde Herrn Ernest Longley gewidmet".

A promising Canadian pianist, born in Maitland, Ontario, fellow student of Hennessy's at Stuttgart. His premature death of 'consumption' in Stuttgart on 5 December 1889 was reported in *Monatshefte für Musikgeschichte* (1890), 96; and *The Dominion Illustrated* (11 January 1890), p. 26.

Terence MacSwiney (1879–1920)[21]
- *Deuxième quatuor à cordes*, Op. 49 (1920): 'à la Mémoire de Terence McSwiney, Lord Mayor de Cork'

Irish dramatist and politician, born in Cork, died of hunger strike in Brixton Prison, Lambeth (England). In 1908 he was a co-founder, with Daniel Corkery, of the Cork Dramatic Society, for which he wrote a number of plays. In 1913, he was a co-founder of the Cork Brigade of the Irish Volunteers, a paramilitary revolutionary organisation, and was involved in the Easter Rising of 1916. Following the murder of his predecessor, he was elected Lord Mayor of Cork on 20 March 1920, was arrested on 12 August for possession of revolutionary material and sentenced to two years imprisonment. He immediately went on hunger strike, which gained worldwide attention the longer it took. The hunger strike and his death on 25 October 1920 drew the world's attention to the situation in Ireland and was one of the decisive factors leading eventually to Irish independence in 1923. – It is possible that Hennessy and MacSwiney knew each other personally, probably in connection with the Cork Dramatic Society.

Annabel McDonald
- *It was a Lover and his Lass*: no. 3 of *Songs from 'As You Like It' (Shakespeare)*, Op. 30 (*c.*1909; withdrawn): 'To Miss Annabel McDonald'.

English soprano who can be traced on British song recital programmes from the mid-1900s to the early 1920s.

---

[21] Dave Hannigan: *Terence MacSwiney. The Hunger Strike that Rocked an Empire* (Dublin: O'Brien Press, 2010).

Heinrich Möller (1876–1958)[22]
- *Under the Greenwood Tree / Unter des Laubdach's Hut;* no. 1 of *Songs from 'As You Like It' (Shakespeare)*, Op. 30 (c.1909; withdrawn): 'To Herr Heinrich Möller'.
- *Sonatine*, Op. 43 (1911): 'à mon ami Heinrich Möller'.

German music critic and editor, born in Breslau (today Wroclaw in Poland), died in Naumburg/Saale (German Democratic Republic). Briefly studied medicine in Jena, then (from 1897) German, philosophy and musicology in Leipzig (with Hugo Riemann and Hermann Kretzschmar) and Berlin (with Max Friedländer). After his studies he went to Paris as a correspondent and critic for (mainly) the *Allgemeine Musikzeitung* and the German-language *Pariser Zeitung*. With the outbreak of World War I, he went to New York, and thereafter to Norway and Denmark before returning to Germany in the early 1920s, where he began editing a multiple-volume series of international folksongs called *Das Lied der Völker* (with Schott, until early 1930s), a series applauded by Thomas Mann and Romain Rolland but criticised by Bela Bartók. From 1935 to 1945 he taught European folksong at the university of Jena. In his retirement he translated the libretti of Russian operas by Borodin, Rimsky-Korsakoff and Tchaikowsky. Today, his papers are kept at the Thüringisches Landesmusikarchiv, Weimar, among them many compositions by Swan Hennessy.

Madeleine Monnier (1900–1984)
- *Sonatine*, Op. 81 (1929): 'À Madeleine Monnier'.

French cellist, born in Paris, performing mainly baroque and contemporary music. Among other works, she premiered the *Improvisations* by André Caplet (Feb. 1924), the *Cello Concerto* by Jacques Ibert (February 1926), and some of the *Chansons bretonnes*, Op. 115 by Charles Koechlin (May 1932), etc. There is no record of her having premiered or performed Hennessy's *Sonatine*, Op. 81, but she did play the *Rapsodie gaélique*, Op. 63, the *Pièce celtique*, Op. 74 and the withdrawn *Pièce celtique d'après un vieil air écossais* in November 1928 (with Richard Byk). She married the Italian violinist Adolfo Betti (1875–1950) in 1936.

Marthe Neuberth (1884–1968)
- *Chanson de l'émigrant*, No. 3 of *Quatre Morceaux*, Op. 71: 'à Madame Neuberth'.

French pianist and clavicinist, teacher of French at the Lycée Lakanal. Wife of Paul-Louis Neuberth (below).

Paul-Louis Neuberth (1881–1959)
- *Foxtrot* and *Lever du soleil dans les Hébrides*, Nos 1 and 4 of *Quatre Morceaux*, Op. 71: 'à Paul-Louis Neuberth'.

French performer/arranger on the viola and viola-alta, particularly active during the 1920s. He also transcribed many works for the viola that were originally written

---

[22] Otto Löw: 'Vergessenes aus der Jenaer Musikgeschichte: Das Wirken von Heinrich Möller', 20 July 2009; https://www.tabularasamagazin.de/vergessenes-aus-der-jenaer-musikgeschichte-das-wirken-von-heinrich-moeller/ (accessed 3 August 2018).

for violin by composers such as Albeniz, Canteloube, Ibert, d'Indy, Pierné, Ravel, Roussel and others (see BnF and WorldCat). Hennessy's work was not the only one written for him: examples are Henri Collet's *Rapsodie castillane*, Op. 73, for viola and orchestra (1924) and Alexander Winkler's *Deux Morceaux*, Op. 31 (c1935).

Radiana Pazmor (1892–1986)[23]

- *Trois Chansons espagnoles*, Op. 42bis (1921): 'à Mademoiselle Radiana Pazmor'.

Artist name for Harriet Horn Pasmore, American contralto, teacher and music therapist, born in San Francisco, died in Sonoma, California. She gave the first performance of Op. 42bis in the Bechsteinsaal, Berlin, 23 November 1922, also singing them in Paris, Salle Beethoven, 28 March 1923, Oakland, CA, 16 July 1926, and probably elsewhere.

Gabrielle Pineau

- *Sérénade espagnole*, No. 1 of *Eaux fortes*, Op. 24 (1906): 'à Mlle. Gabrielle Pineau'.

Not properly identified. French pianist, and one of the earliest friends of Claire and Swan Hennessy in Paris. She operated a private music school in Paris; her sister (?) Ida Adam-Pineau was probably the wife of Auguste Adam (see above).

Claire Przybyszewska, married Claire Hennessy (1883–1947)

- *Mazurka et Polonaise*, Op. 17 (1906): 'à Mlle. Claire Przybyszewska'.
- *Petit album*, Op. 18 (1905): 'à Mlle. Claire Przybyszewska'.
- *Au bord de la forêt*, Op. 21 (1907): 'à Mademoiselle Claire Przybyszewska'.
- *Petite mazurka*, No. 3 of *Eaux fortes*, Op. 24 (1906): 'à Mlle. Claire Przybyszewska'.
- *Valses*, Op. 32 (1909): 'à Mlle. Claire Przybyszewska'.
- *Douze Canons à deux voix à tous les intervalles*, Op. 64 (1924): 'à ma femme'.

Second wife of Swan Hennessy (married London, 1909), born in Płużnica, Poland, grew up in Brussels, lived most of her life in Paris, died near New York, buried in Paris, Montparnasse Cemetery.

Hugo Rasch (1873–1947)[24]

- *Lydia*, Op. 23 (1906): 'à mon ami Hugo Rasch'.
- *Annie*, Op. 31 No. 1 (1906; orig. Op. 26 No. 1): 'à son Ami Hugo Rasch'.
- *Introduction, 12 Variations et fugue sur un thème obligé*, Op. 38 (1909): 'à mon ami Hugo Rasch'.

German music critic, tenor, voice coach (he gave the first performance of Hennessy's *Lydia*, Op. 23, in 1906), occasional composer, and (later) civil servant. Studied singing with Resz, Garsó and Sabatini (Milan) and composition with Frank Limbert

---

[23] *Grove America*; Nancy Eagle Lindley: *Singer Radiana Pazmor and American music: The Performer as Advocate* [Ph. D. thesis, University of Maryland at College Park, 1993].
[24] Fred. K. Prieberg (ed.): *Handbuch Deutsche Musiker 1933–1945* (CD-ROM, Kiel: Prieberg, 2004), 5432–5435; H. J. Moser: *Musik-Lexikon* (Berlin: Max Hesse, 1935), 664.

and Berthold Knetsch. Born and died (by his own hand) in Munich, lived for many years in Berlin, as music critic for the *Allgemeine Musikzeitung* (and during the Nazi period for the *Völkischer Beobachter*). In 1907, Rasch arranged Max Reger's permission for Hennessy's dedication of his Op. 22 to Reger (see Chapter 4, and below). Later a convinced Nazi, member of the NSDAP (since April 1931) and the S.A. (since July 1933; S.A. = 'Sturmabteilung', a paramilitary wing of the Nazi Party), and an employee of Richard Strauss in the music section of the Reichskulturkammer (since 1934).

Max Reger (1873–1916)
- *Au village*. Petite suite caractéristique, Op. 22 (1906–7): 'à Max Reger'.

German late Romantic composer. Reger was teaching in Leipzig since March 1907, when he agreed to Hugo Rasch's request whether he would accept Hennessy's dedication (in a postcard dated Leipzig, 4 August 1907; see Chapter 4).

Lucy Roper, married Lucy Hennessy (c.1868–19??)
- *Vier Lieder*, Op. 3 (1886): 'Fräulein Lucy Roper gewidmet'
- *Vivace*, No. 1 of *Miniatures. Cinq petites pièces*, Op. 11 (1889): 'à Lucie'.

Swan Hennessy's first wife (Dec. 1888 to Oct. 1893), born in Ballygalda, County Roscommon (Ireland), remarried with Alexander Stuart (London, 1903). Her date and place of death are unknown.

Isabella C. Ross
- *The Blackbird has a Golden Bill*, Op. 5 (1886): 'To Miss I. C. Ross'.

Not properly identified. Daughter of Alexander and Isabella Ross in London, personal friends of Hennessy during the mid- to late 1880s.

Marthe Saisset
- *Si la distance nous sépare* and *Paysage*, Nos 1 & 2 of *Trois Mélodies sur des poésies d'André Delacour et de Leconte de Lisle*, Op. 66 (1924): 'A Mademoiselle Marthe Saisset'.

French mezzo-soprano, no biographical information available. She was a pupil of Rose Caron, probably during the period the latter taught at the Conservatoire (1902–09). The Gallica database of the BnF records performances of her between about 1904 and 1932. She sang almost exclusively contemporary French repertory, both in concert and on radio, appearing with numerous artists of her time including Nadia Boulanger. In the late 1920s she also formed a vocal trio, La Triade Vocale, for which Hennessy wrote his *Trois Petis trios*, Op. 76. Saisset has been the most frequent vocalist associated with Swan Hennessy, giving several first performances including the *Trois Mélodies*, Op. 66 and the *Trois Chansons celtiques*, Op. 72.

Gino Sartoni
- *Là-bas*, No. 1 of *Deux Mélodies*, Op. 30 (1906): 'à mon Ami Gino Sartoni'.

Not identified. Perhaps a friend from Hennessy's time in Italy in the 1890s.

Pierre Scize (1894–1956)[25]

- *Le Départ des pêcheurs*, No. 3 of *Trois Chansons celtiques*, Op. 72: 'à Pierre Scize'.

French poet, journalist, theatre, music and cinema critic, pseudonym of Michel-Joseph Piot, born in Pont-de-Chéruy, Département Isère, died accidentally in Melbourne, Australia.

Maurice Servais

- *Banlieues* … . Six Petites pièces, Op. 69 (1925): 'à Maurice Servais'.

French pianist, author and impresario, who frequently performed in Hennessy's piano and chamber music during the 1920s and beyond. Apart from his own pianistic career, he organised the 'Concerts Servais' in Paris, was author of the series 'Le Coin du pianiste' in *Le Guide du concert* during 1930–1, and was the director of the 'École de Piano du Champ-de-Mars'.

Clara Schumann (1819–1896)

- *Album-Blätter (Album Leaves)*, Op. 8 (1887): 'To Frau Clara Schumann'.

German pianist, composer, and pedagogue, née Wieck, born in Leipzig, died in Frankfurt am Main. She married Robert Schumann (1810–1856) in 1840. Hennessy dedicated his very schumannesque *Album-Blätter* to the widow, and she appears to have appreciated it (Chevaillier, 'Entretien').

Achille Simonetti (1857–1928)[26]

- *Sonate en Fa (style irlandais)*, Op. 14 (c1902–4): 'à son ami A. Simonetti'.

Italian violinist resident in England and Ireland. Born in Turin, he studied in Turin, Milan, Genoa and Paris, with teachers including Francesco Bianchi, Camillo Sivori, and Charles Dancla, also studied composition in Paris with Jules Massenet. He lived in London from 1891, was best known as a chamber musician, and was a member of the first London Trio (1901–12). From 1912 to 1919, he taught at the Royal Irish Academy of Music, Dublin, which instituted an Achille Simonetti Scholarship in 1951. He died in London.

Marie Stark

- *Épiphanie*, Op. 26 (1906): 'à Mademoiselle Marie Stark'
- *Blow, Blow, thou Winter Wind*, No. 2 of *Songs from 'As You Like It' (Shakespeare)*, Op. 30 (c.1909; withdrawn): 'To Mlle. Marie Stark'.

Soprano, probably English or English-resident, who performed with the English pianist Herbert Fryer at the Salle Gaveau in Paris on 27 January 1908. The review of the recital in *Comoedia* (7 February 1908, p. 4) does not mention their programme (only the solo piano pieces that Fryer played). It may well be that *Épiphanie* was performed on that occasion. However, the performance of the Shakespeare songs in London on

---

[25] https://fr.wikipedia.org/wiki/Pierre_Scize (last accessed, 21 May 2019).
[26] Pine, Richard & Charles Acton (eds.): *To Talent Alone. The Royal Irish Academy of Music, 1848–1998* (Dublin: Gill & Macmillan, 1998), 460–1.

7 May 1909 was not by Stark, despite the dedication. On other occasions in England, she performed with her sister, the violinist Meta Stark.

Jean Suscinio (1884–1980)[27]
- *Le Mort joyeux*, No. 1 of *Trois Mélodies*, Op. 56 (1921): 'à Jean Suscinio'.

Jean Suscinio is the pseudonym of the writer and singer Henri Texier, later also active as a conductor with his own salon orchestra, which made gramophone recordings in the 1940s. Documents show his involvement with several composers from Hennessy's Breton circle including Paul Ladmirault, Maurice Duhamel and Roger Pénau through whom they must have come into contact. There is no documented performance by Suscinio of the song in question, but he may have sung it in private or semi-public emvironments.

Francis Touche (1872–1937)[28]
- *Rapsodie gaélique*, Op. 63 (1924): 'à Francis Touche'.

Prominent French cellist, conductor and impresario, born in Toulouse, died in Paris, whose 'Concerts Touche' was one of the most active concert-giving organisations in Paris for many years. Hennessy's *Rapsodie gaélique*, Op. 63 was not premiered by Touche, but he did perform it together with Hennessy in 1925. He was also involved in several chamber music performances of other works by Hennessy.

Carrie Townshend (1870–1951?)[29]
- *Variations sur un thème original dans le style irlandais*, Op. 12 (*c.*1902): in 1903 London edition: 'To Miss Carrie Townshend'; in 1929 Paris edition: 'à Mlle Carrie Townshend'.

Irish pianist and harpist, probably born in (County) Cork: possibly in August 1870 in Clonakilty. She studied with Giuseppe Buonamici in Florence and was mainly active in England since about 1890. She gave the first performance of Hennessy's Op. 12 in London, February 1903. Also provided the fingering for the second edition of Hennessy's *Two Studies*, Op. 4 (1902). She lived for many years at Glandore, County Cork, and in more advanced age moved to Dublin. Larchet-Cuthbert (1975) asserts, 'She was interested in everything Irish, the language, culture, music, and taught the Irish Harp to anyone interested, […] She always wore dresses in Celtic designs and large Celtic brooches'. She taught prominent Irish harpists including Máirín and Róisín Ní Sheaghda (O'Shea). She is also documented as one of the very few Munster members

---

[27] See https://data.bnf.fr/de/13841019/jean_suscinio/ (accessed 6 April 2019).
[28] See https://data.bnf.fr/fr/16909534/francis_touche/ (accessed 6 April 2019).
[29] Sheila Larchet-Cuthbert, *The Irish Harp Book* (Cork: Mercier Press, 1975), p. 238, where she is listed as 'Miss Caroline Townshend'. The official Irish genealogy website www.irishgenealogy.ie (church records section) identifies only one possible person, a Caroline Townsend [sic!], baptised at Clonakilty, County Cork, on 15 August 1870. In the civic records section, there is a Caroline Mary Townshend, spinster, died in Dublin aged 91 (!) on 12 May 1951. The age indication may be a mistake.

of the Feis Ceoil Association (1920s and 30s) to which she sponsored the Townshend Cup (now integrated into the 'Dr. Annie Patterson Medal').

Tupac
- *Incunabula*, Op. 39 (1911): 'à Tupac'.

Not identified.

Lambert Zegers Veeckens
- *Moderato*, No. 2 of *Miniatures. Cinq petites pièces*, Op. 11: (1889): 'à Lambert Zegers Veeckens'.

Not identified. Since Hennessy spent some time in Brussels, probably a Belgian friend.

Louis Vuillemin (1879–1929)[30]
- *Croquis parisiens*, Op. 47 (1912): 'à Louis Vuillemin'.

French (Breton) composer and music critic, born in Nantes, died in Paris. He studied at the conservatories of Nantes and Paris (where he was pupil of Gabriel Fauré and Xavier Leroux). He was a founding member of the Association des Compositeurs Bretons. Severely wounded in a gas attack during WWI, this is thought to have cut short his life. Wrote numerous works influenced by his native Brittany. As a music critic, he wrote numerous reviews for *Comoedia, Musica, Le Courrier musical, Paris-soir, La Lanterne*, etc. as well as brief biographical monographs of Louis Aubert, Gabriel Fauré, and Albert Roussel for the music publisher A. Durand et fils.

Part B: Works dedicated to Hennessy

Denis Breen (*c*1886–1950)
- *Six Irish pieces of the XVIIth and XVIIIth centuries (Six morceaux irlandais des XVIIe et XVIIIe siècles)* (Paris: Max Eschig & Cie., 1924). Contains: 1. *Concerto*; 2. *The Princess Royal*; 3. *Planxty O'Donnell*; 4. *Miss Goulding*; 5. *The Lark in Clear Air*; 6. *Nancy McDermott*: "To Swan Hennessy".

Irish music teacher, pianist and composer/arranger, based in Cork, also known as Donnchadh Ó Braoin (or Ua Braoin); see part A.

Auguste Delacroix (1871–1936)
- *Deux Variations* (*c*1909; see Hennessy, Op. 38): 'à mon ami Swan Hennessy'

French composer and pianist, born in Louviers, Département Eure (Normandy); see part A.

---

[30] De Bellaing, *Dictionnaire* (1992), p. 250–1.

Herbert Fryer (1877–1957)
- *Variations* for piano (*c*1909; see Hennessy, Op. 38): 'à mon cher ami Swan Hennessy'.

English pianist and composer, born in Hampstead (London), pupil of Oscar Beringer at the Royal Academy of Music (RAM), taught piano at the RAM (1905–14), and at the Royal College of Music (1917–47), where Constant Lambert, Cyril Smith and Richard Bonynge were among his students. One of the most widely travelled English pianists of his time. Gave the first performance of Hennessy's *Eaux fortes*, Op. 24, in London, March 1910.

Joachim Mendelson (1892–1943)
- *Chamber Symphony* (*c*.1929–30; published 1938): 'à la mémoire de Swan Hennessy'.

Polish composer. Born in Warsaw, Mendelson lived in Paris from 1929 (when he came in contact with Hennessy) to 1935, when he returned to Warsaw. He was forced to live in the ghetto where he was killed in 1943. The year 1938 is the year of publication of this work at Max Eschig, Paris; it was probably composed considerably earlier (1929?).

Appendix 5
Sources

This appendix deals with the primary sources relating to Swan Hennessy, with most of the space being devoted to the kind and the location of the music manuscripts. Other primary material such as autograph letters is comparatively scarce, and for that reason the appendix begins with these.

A. Letters

Very few of Swan Hennessy's letters appear to have survived. That he must have been an active letter writer is suggested by the fact that the Irving Schwerke Collection at the Library of Congress in Washington D.C. alone has 16 autograph letters from Hennessy to Schwerke. Another 12 letters written to the music publishing company Schott are preserved in Berlin (see below). In addition, some 18 published letters survive in English and French journals, and these have been documented in this study. All this suggests that there are probably more letters to be found at some time. For the time being, however, there are five sources of autograph letters in public archives (listed here in chronological order of the letters).

A.1: Staatsbibliothek Berlin, Stiftung Preußischer Kulturbesitz (Berlin, Germany)
Call number: Not definite, as yet. The letters are part of the 'Safe Archive' within the Schott Archive that the Staatsbibliothek Berlin partially acquired from the publishing company B. Schott's Söhne (Mainz, Germany). The huge archive was acquired by six German research libraries, with the bulk of material going to the state libraries at Berlin and Munich. A common research platform with digitised scores and correspondence is to be made available within the next few years. At the time of writing (2018) the twelve letters by Hennessy and nine responses from Schott are archived according to a preliminary list in files no. 44614 and nos. 56040 to 56050. In the future online research platform these will receive a new registration resp. catalogue number. In the course of the cataloguing work, the library does not exclude that more correspondence may come to light. Hennessy published six works with Schott in the years 1902, 1904, 1908, 1910, and 1911 (2). All letters are in German and demonstrate Hennessy's excellent command of this language.

The letter in file no. 44614 dates from 13 November 1885, files no. 56040 to 56050 from April 1911 to February 1912. The 1885 letter, written about ten days before the composer's 18th birthday when he was still a student at Stuttgart, offers some piano works (*'einige kleine Klavierstücke'*) for publication, which he apparently attached but did not list in his letter. It is written on a letterhead of a hotel in Switzerland.

The 1911–12 correspondence is about piano works Hennessy offered for publication. They describe the publication process for the *Petite suite (sur les notes mi do mi fa si mi)*, Op. 34 and *Fêtes. Deux Morceaux descriptifs*, Op. 36, as well as the proposal and denial of *Incunabula*, Op. 39, *En passant ... (Études d'après nature)*, Op. 40, and *Valses caprices*, Op. 41. All Schott letters were written by the company's director, Ludwig

Strecker senior (1853–1943); Hennessy addresses him as 'Herr' or 'Herr Geheimrath'. Since the files in the Schott archive are not chronological, the following is a chronological list of the exchange.

Date	File no.	Content
13 Nov 1885	44614	Hennessy to Schott, written from the Maloja Hotel in Switzerland. Offers some piano works for publication (unsuccessful). Small note on verso that the letter was replied to on 17 Nov. (no copy).
4/5 Apr 1911	56043	Hennessy to Schott. Had been visiting Schott in Mainz, but Strecker was not there. Sends pieces that he had intended to play to him.
21 Apr 1911	56050 / 2	Schott to Hennessy. Is delighted about Opp. 34 and 36, agrees to publishing them. Suggests a different title for Op. 34. In PS, regrets not to have met Hennessy in Mainz, but says that his son had been there.
23 Apr 1911	56042 / 1	Hennessy to Schott. Delighted about the interest. Agrees to different title for Op. 34 and publishing conditions. Hopes to meet him and his son in Paris some time.
14 Jun 1911	56044	Hennessy to Schott. Announces he will be away from Paris all summer. Asks when he can expect proofs of the prints of Opp. 34 and 36 so that he can give Schott an address.
16 Jun 1911	56050 / 3	Schott to Hennessy. Apologises for long silence and explains it with busy schedules. Asks for Hennessy's summer address.
17 Jul 1911	56045	Hennessy to Schott. Says that if the proofs have not already been sent to Andermatt, they shall now be sent to a hotel in Lungern (Obwalden), Switzerland.
16 Sep 1911	56046	Hennessy to Schott (from a hotel in Vittel, French Alps). Sends corrections to the proofs of Opp. 34 and 36 (with a pencil note by Schott that proofs have been corrected by 1 Oct.).
29 Sep 1911	56048	Hennessy to Schott (from Paris). Sends MSS of Opp. 39 and 40, asking for publication. Includes some recent reviews.
3 Oct 1911	56050 / 4	Schott to Hennessy. Thanks for the MSS but rejects publication, because he considers the programmatic effects in the scores unsuitable for the piano. Announces the imminent completion of Opp. 34 and 36.
4 Oct 1911	56047	Hennessy to Schott. Is disappointed about rejection. Complains that Schott does not advertise enough, that it is not the quality of music but their advertising that decides about the success, that a certain modernist [he probably implies Schönberg] is successful only for his advertising.
5 Oct 1911	56050 / 5	Schott to Hennessy. Forwards suggestions by 'their common friend' Hugo Rasch for Opp. 34 and 36 and has halted the printing process until Hennessy's decision.

1/3 Nov 1911	56049	Hennessy to Schott. Complains that he is now waiting for 7 months for the music, that those little tempo markings by Rasch would merely take half a day. Alleges little interest on Schott's part in his music.
3 Nov 1911	56042 / 3	Schott to Hennessy. Sends 20 printed copies of each of the two works, apologises for the delay, but that this was a 'dead time' [summer months?] in which nothing would be reviewed. Denies lacking interest, on the contrary, but that Hennessy should listen to his advice about 'permissible harmonies and rhythms'.
6/7 Nov 1911	56050 / 1	Hennessy to Schott. Briefly thanks for the prints and hopes that they will be as successful as earlier pieces.
6 Dec 1911	56042 / 2	Schott (not Strecker) to Hennessy. Detailed invoice of production costs for Opp. 34 and 36.
7 Dec 1911	56041 / 1	Hennessy to Schott. Sends cheque over 75% of the costs. Complains that Schott used the backs of the covers to advertise other composers' works and hopes that they pay for it.
9 Dec 1911	56041 / 2	Schott to Hennessy. Acknowledges receipt of cheque – and of the complaint. Would have liked to avoid it, but this is company policy now. Hopes Hennessy will not object when he appears on the back of other composers' works.
16 Jan 1912	56040 / 1	Schott to Hennessy. Rejects (again; see 3 Oct. 1911) to publish Opp. 39 and (revised) 40, with similar reasons as before.
2 Feb 1912	56040 / 2	Hennessy to Schott. Sends MS of *Valses caprices*, Op. 41 and asks for publication.
7 Feb 1912	56040 / 3	Schott to Hennessy. Briefly rejects Op. 41; he likes the work but does not foresee commercial success.

A.2: Bibliothèque de Rennes Métropole, Les Champs Libres (Rennes, France)
Call number: Ms 1636/42. Part of the Fonds Véfa de Bellaing (Ms 1633 to 1636).

Autograph letter (in French) from Swan Hennessy to Maurice Duhamel, dated 25 June 1913, one page; in ink, on Hennessy letter head, with hand-addressed envelope (see chapter 4).

Maurice Duhamel (1884–1940) was a Breton composer, founder-member of the Association des Compositeurs Breton in 1912. In the letter, Hennessy confirms (in French) that he has booked the Salle des Agriculteurs for a concert of the Association on 26 November 1913.

Geneviève ('Véfa') de Bellaing (1909–1998) was a Breton writer and activist who edited the *Dictionnaire des compositeurs de musique en Bretagne* (Nantes, 1992) which has a short entry on Hennessy.

The Fonds Véfa de Bellaing also has a file on Hennessy, compiled by de Bellaing, consisting of research material she used for the *Dictionnaire*, including newspaper cuttings of reviews, notes, photocopies, and correspondence; call number Ms 1633/181.

A.3: Bibliothèque Municipale de Lyon (Lyon, France)
Call number: Ms Vallas 203, pièce 59. Part of the Fonds Léon Vallas / Correspondance / Diverse, 1902–1966 / Correspondance diverse, classée par ordre alphabétique des correspondants, 1876–1948, Cote: 59.

Autograph letter (in French) from Swan Hennessy to Léon Vallas, dated 25 June 1927, two-sided sheet, with hand-addressed envelope.

Léon Vallas (1879–1956) was a prominent Lyon-based music critic, founder of *La Revue musicale de Lyon* (in 1903) which became the *Revue française de Musique* in 1912. He also taught music history at Lyon university and the Conservatoire National de Musique de Lyon (until 1931). Most importantly in the present context is Vallas' role as biographer of Debussy.[31] Apparently, Hennessy had attached the first three volumes of *À la manière de …* (not preserved) and briefly explained the series, announcing the imminent completion of vol. 4, referring to his pastiches of Satie, Debussy and Godard, and hoping that the scheme will amuse Vallas.

A.4: Yale University Library (Irving S. Gilmore Music Library) (New Haven, CT, USA)
Call number: MSS 56 (John Kirkpatrick Papers), Box 16, Folder 188.

Autograph letter (in French) from Swan Hennessy, dated [not in Hennessy's hand] 5 September 1927. The letter was not written from Paris but from 'Le Prieuré / Fontenay-en-Vexin / Eure' (in Normandy, where Hennessy often spent summer months). The addressee is unclear (Hennessy addresses the letter to 'Monsieur'). As part of the John Kirkpatrick Papers, all letters would have been addressed to the pianist and scholar Kirkpatrick (1905–1991). However, Kirkpatrick would have been rather young, so he may have acquired the letter from someone else in later years. It is also not very likely that Hennessy would have addressed a fellow American in French.

In the short, one-sided letter, Hennessy writes that he was asked by the publisher Max Eschig to provide the postal address of the Cork-based pianist and teacher Denis Breen, which Hennessy does, giving Breen's address in Irish. It is curious that Hennessy wrote the letter in French if the addressee was American, but perhaps he did so because the original request for Breen's address was in French.

A.5: Library of Congress (Washington D.C., USA)
Call number: none, as yet; reference is made to 'Irving Schwerke Collection – Unrecorded'. LCCN: 2014571130.

16 autograph letters (in English, with occasional greetings and set phrases in French) from Swan Hennessy to Irving Schwerke, Paris, 24 March 1928 to 22 May 1929, plus a two-page autobiographical sketch with a list of published and manuscript works.

---

[31] *Debussy (1862–1918)* (Paris: Plon, 1926); *Les Idées de Claude Debussy, musicien français* (Paris: Librairie de France, 1927), Engl. as *The Theories of Claude Debussy* (London: Oxford University Press, 1929); *Claude Debussy et son temps* (Paris: Félix Alcan, 1932), Engl. as *Claude Debussy. His Life and Works* (London: Oxford University Press, 1933); *Achille-Claude Debussy* (Paris: Presses Universitaires de France, 1944).

This 'Swan Hennessy File' forms part of the Irving Schwerke Collection (83 boxes resp. 13 linear feet of material dating 1919 to 1973). Schwerke (1893–1975) was a Jewish American music critic who was based in Paris for many years. He wrote for more than 100 newspapers and journals in the United States, but also England and Italy. He returned to the U.S. in 1942 in the course of the German occupation of Paris.

The letters are dated: 24 March 1928; 2 April 1928; 10 June 1928; 30 September 1928; 10 October 1928; 1 November 1928; 5 November 1928; 8 November 1928; 4 January 1929; 23 February 1929; 4 April 1929; 15 April 1929; 19 April 1929; 13 May 1929; 19 May 1929; 22 May 1929 (see Chapter 9 for a full documentation).

A.6: Select correspondence in possession of Hennessy family
Hennessy did not make copies of his outgoing correspondence so what is preserved in the family's possession is correspondence addressed to Hennessy, but not letters by him. It is surprisingly little; paragraph c) below suggesting that someone may have given correspondence away at some point (Claire or Patrice Hennessy?).

a) A postcard from the German music critic Heinrich Möller, written in German, dated 6 August 1913, addressed to Hennessy's hotel in Pornichet, a coastal village near Saint Nazaire and traditionally in southern Brittany, now Département Loire-Atlantique. He returns 20 francs that Hennessy had lent him, announces his impending holidays, and sends greetings to Hennessy's father and wife (see Chapter 5 and D.1 below).

b) A short autograph letter by the French flutist Gaston Blanquart (in French), dated 25 September 1925; blank verso. He thanks Hennessy for having sent the *Variations sur un thème de six notes*, Op. 58, and expresses his appreciation of the work; also for the *Trio* Op. 70, and that he is sure it will find its way (see Chapter 8).

c) Five autograph letters by Georges Migot of autumn 1929 to Swan Hennessy and, after he had died, to his wife. These letters came up for auction in Paris in June 2018 but were not sold. My attempts to buy them afterwards or to receive copies for this study were not successful – one of the very few sad and incomprehensible aspects of my research.

B. Reviews and concert programmes

Thanks to the digitisation of many newspapers and music journals at the Bibliothèque Nationale de France, consultable on Gallica (gallica.bnf.fr), a large number of reviews of concerts and printed music can easily be researched online. In addition, the British Newspaper Archive (www.britishnewspaperarchive.co.uk) and the Irish Newspaper Archive (www.irishnewsarchive.com) also offer digitised newspapers containing reviews.

Most but not all of these reviews, along with a large number of concert programmes, are preserved in four big volumes of 'Press Books' (a term used in French) by the Hennessy family. They commence in 1903, have been carefully pasted into the books and annotated by Swan Hennessy himself. After his death, his widow Claire continued the collection until the mid-1940s, the last ones merely loosely inserted into the fourth of these books. Vols 1 to 3 have been made available to me during a visit to Paris at which I took numerous photographs (not complete). Vol. 4, commencing in February 1928, was lent to me to work with in Frankfurt for a period of about two years. Hennessy and his widow did not include page references when annotating the press clippings. If these journals and newspapers have also been digitised at Gallica etc., I took down the page numbers, and I did the same with the German *Allgemeine Musikzeitung* and *Die Musik* in the university library at Frankfurt. But in a number of cases, pages references are still missing.

The concert programmes are, of course, of particular value as they show the context in which Hennessy's music was performed and which is often not fully included in concert reviews.

C. Music Manuscripts

At the time of publication of this book, the majority of the music manuscripts are in the hand of the Hennessy family in France (here called the 'Hennessy Family Collection'). One manuscript is located in the Bavarian State Library (Munich) and two more used to be in the United States, one in the New York Public Library and one in the Library of Congress (both still lost at the time of publication of this book). They are sorted below in chronological order, with the larger family archive coming last.

<u>C.1: New York Public Library, Music Division</u>
Nur wer die Sehnsucht kennt; subtitled *Lied von Goethe in Musik gesetzt von Swan Hennessy*, Op. 14 (1894).
For voice and piano.

Listed in: Otto Edwin Albrecht: *A Census of Autograph Music of European Composers in American Libraries* (Univ. of Pennsylvania Press, 1953), 145: "4 leaves 30 x 24 cm. Music on recto only. Song with piano accpt. Dedicated to David Bispham. New York Public Library."

The 1953 source can be found online on archive.org, the manuscript itself is not listed in the online catalog of NYPL. On request, the library communicated that the piece is lost. It is listed here in the hope that the piece might resurface some time.

<u>C.2: Bavarian State Library (Bayerische Staatsbibliothek, BSB), Schott Archive</u>
Sonate en Fa (Style Irlandais), Op. 14 (*c.*1903).
For violin and piano.

In December 2014, the Bavarian State Library acquired the production archive of Schott, the German music publisher which for many years had subsidiaries in London, Paris and Brussels. Of the six pieces by Hennessy that appeared with Schott, Opus 14 is the only one with a MS in this archive (the others are in the Hennessy Family Collection). Because of the sheer number of over 42,000 items, this collection does not have proper library call numbers yet, as it is still (2018) in the process of being catalogued. So far, the ordering system follows the Schott plate numbers. In this case, the full citation is 'Bavarian State Library, Munich, Schott Production Archive, plate no. 27497'.

Physical description: single loose leaves; title on a separate leaf, second title starts with music on the back side, namely the violin part, p. 1; violin part has 6 pages – apart from p. 1 all on separate leaves. Score begins with a p. 2 and runs to p. 29, written on both sides of the paper; numerous corrections in the form of crossed-out bars (p. 20 completely crossed out), pasted-in systems and very occasional minor corrections in pencil in a different hand.

Further remarks: a) on the first title page (a leaf with blank verso) the dedication originally read 'A mon ami …' – the 'm' in 'mon' is corrected in pencil to 's' ('A son ami …', in Hennessy's hand); b) the title originally was '1ère Sonate' (in a red box), below this title, in ink: '(Style Irlandais)', underneath, in pencil '(Dans le style irlandais)' – impossible to say which was written earlier; c) this page also has Hennessy's address at the time, '4 Rue Chalgrin / 16me Arr. / Paris'; d) a second title page features a pencil remark in the upper left-hand corner: '6 Frei Ex / (Autor nimmt 50 Ex.)',[32] here also the title 'Première Sonate / pour / piano et violon / par / Swan Hennessy' in a red box, to the right of this box in the first line 'en Fa', below this 'Style irlandais' (consulted on location, 16 December 2016).

C.3: Hennessy Family Collection

The following is a detailed overview of the contents of the Hennessy Family Collection (see introduction in Appendix 1). Besides the 'Press Books' (books with newspaper clippings and concert programmes carefully pasted into folio-size books, annotated mainly in Swan Hennessy's hand and continued by his widow after his death), the collection includes several large bound volumes of music manuscripts that are explained below.

The manuscripts represent his clean copies as given to the publisher's engraver. With very few exceptions, these are not sketches.

C.3.1: MS Book I: Piano music, 1905 to 1913

Physical description: Bound with brown leather spine, reading 'SWAN HENNESSY' in gilt letters, with brown-green marbled paper boards. Measurements: 35.2 cm high x 28.0 cm wide, approx. 2.4 cm thick. Paper size: 34.5 x 26.5 cm, except when otherwise noted in the table below. Contains pages that have been cut at the upper edges to fit into the binding, sometimes cutting off parts of the handwriting of the titles.

These are manuscripts of Hennessy's opus numbers (in this order) 15 to 18, 24, 25, 27, 28, 47, 32, 34, 36, 37, 37 (different piece), and a collection of six short works without any title.

All pieces are in Hennessy's hand in black ink. Some contain colour markings in pencil or red and blue crayon by the engravers, which point out line and page breaks, and similar technical hints to producing the prints. Some also contain the publisher's

---

[32] "6 free copies / author takes 50 copies".

plate numbers (written by another hand), the intended paper format, etc. Some of the manuscripts have a date.

List of Contents:

1. Title: Deux Etudes / en ut mineur / pour la main gauche / seul / par / Swan Hennessy / Op. 15
Pages: Title page ornamented by Hennessy, a blank page, 6 pages of music.
Date: –
Remarks: On the bottom of the first music page, publisher's plate number J. 5405 H.

2. Title: PRÆLUDIUM / Swan Hennessy Op. 16 / FUGA / Swan Hennessy Op. 16
Pages: (no title page), 3 pages Præludium, 3 pages Fuga, all on one side only, leaving verso blank.
Date: –
Remarks: Smaller paper size: 28.3 cm x 24.2 cm. On the bottom of the first page, publisher's plate number J. 5340 H.

3. Title: à Mlle. Claire Przybyszewska / Mazurka / et / Polonaise / pour piano / par / Swan Hennessy / Op. 17 / N°. 1 / Mazurka […] N°. 2 / Polonaise
Pages: Title page, 3 pages of music, new title page with 'Polonaise', 3 pages of music.
Date: –
Remarks: On the bottom of the title page, publisher's plate number 1360[a]. Last page ends with 6 bars of music in pencil (not an alternative ending).

4. Title: à Mlle. Claire Przybyszewska / PETIT ALBUM / POUR / PIANO / par / Swan Hennessy / Op. 18 / I. En route. / II. L'auberge. / III. Enfants qui passent. / IV. Aux temps passes 1. Fughetta. 2. Menuet. / V. Danseuse sur la scène. / VI. Sonatine. / VII. Scherzetto.
Pages: Title page, 14 pages of music, one blank page.
Date: 'S. H. 1905' on p. 14.
Remarks: On the bottom of the title page, publisher's plate number 27919. Title of 7th piece pasted on the page, concealing an 8th piece, partly loose revealing '… *vivacissimo*'. Title page glued together with a blank staff page; last page glued together with a page of music manuscript, partly visible, that conceals parts of 3 lines from the 8th piece.

5. Title: A MAX REGER / AU VILLAGE / petite suite caractéristique / pour piano / par / Swan Hennessy
Pages: Title page, a blank page, 16 pages of music, 2 blank pages (1 leaf).
Date: –
Remarks: This is Op. 22. Continuous plate numbers at beginning of each movement. Corrections pasted on p. 2 (3 systems, 17 bars), amending the end of movt. 1. Pp. 7 & 8 glued together, with music underneath. Pp. 9–16 loose. Last (blank) page with 5 bars in pencil. No opus number.

Appendix

6 Title: EAUX FORTES / petits morceaux pour piano / par / Swan Hennessy / Op. 24 / ~~Cahier 1~~ / No. 1. Sérénade espagnole / 2. Bergerie / 3. Petite Mazurka / ~~Cahier 2~~ / ~~4. Kermesse / 5. Paysage / 6. Petite Valse~~
Pages: Title page 1, 2 pages of music, a blank page, title page 2, 2 pages of music, a blank page, title page 3, 2 pages of music, a blank page.
Date: –
Remarks: Obviously, a 2nd vol. was planned. The three dedications in red ink on each first page of music (not in the published version). Title page glued together 3-fold. No sign of any pieces no. 4 to 6.

7 Title: à Monsieur E. Demets / Etude / en ut majeur / Op. 25 / pour piano / par / Swan Hennessy.
Pages: Title page, 4 pages of music, 3 blank pages (the last one without staves).
Date: (Copyright date in MS: 1907)
Remarks: –

8 Title: A / mon ami / Auguste Delacroix / Nouvelles / feuilles / d'Album / pour piano / par / Swan Hennessy / Op. 27 / 1. Madrigal. / 2. Canon. / 3. Style irlandais. / 4. Petite Scènes Parisiennes. / A. Montrouge le matin. B. Sortie de Midinettes.
Pages: Title page, 7 pages of music.
Date: (Copyright date in MS: 1908)
Remarks: Slightly smaller paper size (32.3 x 24.8 cm). Pp. 5–6 glued together, concealing what lies behind no. 3 ('*Style irlandais*'); what is partly visible is *not* no. 4A.

9 Title: Variations / sur / un air irlandais / ancien / pour piano / par / Swan Hennessy / Op. 28 / (Mai 1908)
Pages: Title page, a blank page, 8 pages of music, a loose leaf with one side of music in pencil, 2 blank pages (1 leaf).
Date: 'Mai 1908', on title page.
Remarks: The word '*ancien*' has clearly been added later (different type of ink & squeezed in). The loose page in pencil is the sketch of variation XII (finale).

10 Title: ~~No. 1 Ancient Clan March.~~ / ~~No. 2. Cork Reel.~~ / ~~No. 3 Sagairt tar teorach (Priests over the border).~~ / ~~No. 4 Cork Reel.~~ / Preceded by pencil note (in German): "*Für den Stecher: Als Partitur zu stechen wie Verl.-N: 1379. Es sind Trennungsstriche // zwischen jedes der durch eine Klammer verbundenen zwei Systeme zu stechen. Drei Klammern (zu je vier Systemen) auf eine Seite. Kopftitel mit kleiner Schrift, der Titel zur linken und der Autorenname zur rechten Seite.*" Under the crossed-out titles the instruction "*Zum Stich*".
Pages: Title page, a blank page, 14 pages of music.
Date: –
Remarks: This is the *Petite suite irlandaise*, Op. 29 for piano 4-hands. Slightly smaller paper size (30.2 x 23.0 cm). The long note in German is a formal instruction to the engraver (the Paris-based company C. G. Röder seems to have employed Germans).

11 Title: à Louis Vuillemin / Croquis Parisiens / Op. 47 / Cahier I / No. 1 Promenade matinale au jardin du Luxembourg. / – 2 L'Américain qui a bien dîné. / – 3 Dans un atelier de couturiers.
Pages: Title page, 7 pages of music.
Date: (copyright date 1913)
Remarks: Small paper size, as no. 10 above.

12 Title: Swan Hennessy / Valses / Op. 32 / a Mlle. Claire Przybyszewska / Swan Hennessy / Valses / pour piano / Op. 32
Pages: Title page with blank verso. Title page, blank verso, 11 pages of music.
Date: Montrouge 1909. (also copyright date in MS: 1909)
Remarks: Extensive corrections in movts. 1 & 2.

13 Title: A mon ami Eugène Demets / en souvenir de son chat et ses chiens: 'MI-DO' / 'MI-FA' et 'SI-MI'. / Sonatine / 'Petite suite sur le Thème / [the six notes in music]' / par / Swan Hennessy / Op. 34 / I. Allegretto. / II. Andantino semplice. / III. FINALE. Vivace, ma non tanto _ Moderato (FUGA). / [with plate number and Hennessy's address in Paris]
Pages: Title page with blank verso, 9 pages of music, the last of which with blank verso.
Date: Zweisimmen, Août 1909.
Remarks: The MS title 'Sonatine' is missing from the printed edition, which is called *Petite suite sur les notes Mi Do Mi Fa Si Mi*, Op. 34, with pitches in notation. The words 'Petite suite' and the pitches are written in pencil, the rest in blank ink. The print also gives Sep. 1909 as date. Larger corrections on pp. 3 and 8.

14 Title: Frau Professor Heffner / gewidmet. / Fêtes / 2 morceaux descriptifs pour piano / par / Swan Hennessy / Op 36 / N°. 1 Fête de Village au XVIIIme siécle [sic!] / N°. 2 Fête populaire dans la banlieu de Paris au XXme siècle / [with plate number]
Pages: Title page of light blue paper, glued on music paper, which is p. 1 of the music; 3 pages of music. Title page (on music paper) with blank verso, exactly as first title, but now with N°. 1 underscored, 3 pages of music, 3 blank pages.
Date: Paris, Juillet 1910.
Remarks: Minor corrections in the *Fête populaire*, but p. 1 of the *Fête de Village* is glued together with p. 2, partly revealing different music for p. 2.

15 Title: Swan Hennessy. / "Les noces du soldat de bois," / ballet en un acte. / Op. 37 / Compte rendu. / Introduction et Pantomime / de Pierrot. / [in red] NB. Graver tout d'une pièce en enchainant les morceaux séparés. Dévelloper les reprises.
Pages: Complete contents:] / p. 1: title page [left] / p. 2: Description of stage decoration, personages, small stage drawing, action. / p. 3: Action continued, 2 music systems. / p. 4: 3 music systems. / p. 5: Piece no. 2, title page. / pp. 6–8: Music. / p. 9: Piece no. 3, title page. / p. 10–11: Music. / p. 12: blank. / p. 13:

Piece no. 4, title page. / p. 14–16: Music. / p. 17: Piece no. 5, title page. / p. 18–22: Music.
Date: Pornichet, Juillet 1913.
Remarks: Obviously intended for publication by a French company but never realised. Also, apparently intended as a short score for an ensemble (orchestral?) piece, with numerous indications of differences between 'pizz.' and 'arché' for the strings, carillon, clarion, tambours, violoncelle, harpe, clarinette.

16 Title: Swan Hennessy / Op. 37 / 2 / ORIENTALES / pour / Piano
Pages: Title page consisting of three sheets glued upon each other, 2 pages of 'Odalisque', 2 pages of 'Nubienne', the second of which is glued on a different sheet. Verso with a printed list of H.'s works, with additions in MS.
Date: –
Remarks: Another Op. 37 (!). Unpublished.
The upper sheet of the title is loose, revealing handwriting mentioning Op. 33, 'paru en 1911', and the publisher Hayet on Blvd. Haussmann.

17 Title: [six short untitled piano pieces] / No. 1 Allegretto; No. 2 Andantino; No. 3 Vivace non troppo; No. 4 Allegretto; No. 5 Andante; No. 6 Adagio non troppo.
Pages: 2 pages in landscape format (35 x 27 cm), folded in order to fit into the volume, blank verso each, with three pieces on each sheet.
Date: –
Remarks: Unpublished. Not identified.

C.3.2: MS Book II: Piano music, 1909 to 1929
Physical description: Bound with brown leather spine, reading 'SWAN HENNESSY' in gilt letters, with brown-green marbled paper boards. Measurements: 35.2 cm high x 28.0 cm wide, approx. 2.5 cm thick. Paper size: 34.5 x 26.5 cm, except when otherwise noted in the table below. Contains many pages that have been cut at the upper edges to fit into the binding, sometimes cutting off parts of the handwriting of the titles.
   These are manuscripts of Hennessy's opus numbers (in this order) 38 to 45, 46bis, 53, 55, 57, 64, 67, 75bis, 69, and the five volumes of *À la manière de* ....
   All pieces are in Hennessy's hand in black ink. Like in MS Book I, they contain numerous colour markings in red and blue by the engravers, which sometimes point out minor mistakes, line and page breaks, and other technical hints to producing the prints. For the Demets pieces, they also contain the publisher's plate numbers (written by hand), the intended paper format, etc. Some of the manuscripts have a date.
   List of Contents:

1 Title: Introduction, XII / VARIATIONS et Fugue / pour la main gauche seule / Sur le thème obligé: / [4 bars of music] / par / Swan Hennessy
Pages: Title page on faded blue paper, a blank page, 7 pages of music, a blank page.
Date: (Copyright date in MS: 1909)
Remarks: This is Op. 38. Extensive corrections on p. 6.

2. Title: Swan Hennessy / Incunabula / pour piano / Op. 39 / 1. Berceuse / 2. Bébé dort / 3. Croquemitaine
Pages: Title page, 5 pages, 2 blank pages.
Date: Paris, Juin 1911 Copyright date in MS: 1911)
Remarks: Title page includes dedication on: *'A TUPAC'*. Title is followed by the titles of the three movements, publishing details, and the remark *"à graver en format Peters"*.

3. Title: En Passant ... / 4 / Etudes d'après / Nature / par / Swan Hennessy / Op. 40 / 1. Petit pâtre sur les hauts pâturages / 2. Champs de blé au clair de lune / 3. Dans une petite ville flamande, le dimanche / 4. Cîmes neigeuses / 5. Sieste en chemin de fer
Pages: Etude 1: Title page, 2 pages of music, a blank page; / Etude 2: title page, 1 page of music, 2 blank pages; / Etude 3: title page, 2 pages of music, 1 page of music, 2 blank pages; / Etude 4: title page, 1 page of music, 2 blank pages; / Etude 5: title page, 4 pages of music, 3 blank pages.
Date: Paris, Oct 1911. (Copyright date in MS: 1911). NB: Hennessy already sent nos. 1–4 to Schott in Sep. 1911.
Remarks: Title *'En Passant ...'* later added in pencil (the rest is in ink). Title of Etude 1 was changed from *Petit vacher montagnard sur les hauts pâturages*. Remark on title page: *"à graver en format Peters"*. The 4 etudes are followed by a 5th one (*Sieste en chemin de fer*). This comes after the crossed-out title *Impressions de Voyage. Etudes d'après Nature Op. 40 No. 5, En Chemin de Fer*.

4. Title: Swan Hennessy / VALSES-CAPRICES / Op. 41 / (4 pieces with Roman numbers without the descriptive titles of the printed work). /MS vs. Print / I I. Valse rustique / II II. Valse canaille / III III. Valse distraite / IV IV. Valse boiteuse / V (corrected to VI) (à la Reger) VI. À la Reger / Missing in the MS: V. Valse érotique, and VII. Encore une valse.
Pages: Title page, 7 pages of music.
Date: Paris, Nov. 1911. (Copyright date in MS: 1912)
Remarks: Here, the publishing details are at the bottom of p. 1 of the music. Extensive corrections pasted in throughout. The printed work consists of 7 pieces, nos. V and VII of the print are missing. Piece no. IV originally had a different ending, pasted over by two systems (8 bars) of different music, ending with the date *"Paris, Oct. 1911."*. Pieces V to VII must have been added until Nov. 1911.

5. Title: Gitaneries / pour piano / par / Swan Hennessy / Op. 42 (4 numbered pieces without the descriptive titles of the printed work)
Pages: Title page, 6 pages of music in small format, followed by a blank page, 2 pages in large format for piece no. 4.
Date: (Copyright date in MS: 1912)
Remarks: Pieces 1 – 3 on smaller paper (30 x 23 cm), then piece 4 on the volume's size.

6   Title: Swan Hennessy / SONATINE / pour piano / op. 43
    Pages: Title page, a blank page, 7 pages of music for movts. I and II, a blank page, 4 pages of music for movt. III, 2 blank pages.
    Date: (Copyright date in MS: 1912)
    Remarks: Publishing details at the bottom of p. 1 of the music. Some crossed-out corrections in movt. II (8 bars after bar 27).

7   Title: A mon Père / Sentes et Chemins / (Nouvelles etudes d'après nature.) / pour piano / par / Swan Hennessy / Op. 44 / 1. Ouvriers allant à l'usine / 2. Promenade du Philosophe / 3. A travers bois / 4. Cornemuse en tête / 5. Sur la route d'Amalfi / 6. Sentier du Meudon au printemps / 7. Par la pluie
    Pages: Title page, a blank page, 14 pages of music, 2 blank pages.
    Date: Juin – Septembre 1912 (Copyright date in MS: 1912)
    Remarks: Smaller paper size (30 x 23 cm) Title page with large blue remark: *"ne pas oublier les textes en haut de chaque pièce"*. First two pages glued together, indicating that p. 2 has been substituted.

8   Title: Swan Hennessy / Pièces Celtiques / Op. 45
    Pages: Title page, 5 pages of music, 2 blank pages.
    Date: (Copyright date in MS: 1912)
    Remarks: Title page with large blue remark: *"Format Peters inutile que les N^{os} commencent en tete d'un page, gravez tout à la Suite. Attention pour le N° 2 qui n'est pas à sa place"* (in the order I, III, II).

9   Title: Swan Hennessy / Op. 46 / Premier Mouvement du Quatuor / à Cordes / Op. 46 / Transcription pour piano / II. Allegro
    Pages: Title page, a blank page, 5 pages of music, a blank page.
    Date: –
    Remarks: This arrangement for piano of the <u>first</u> movt. of the String Quartet was <u>not</u> published. Smaller paper size (30 x 23 cm). No publishing details, no dates.

10 Title: Swan Hennessy / Adagio et Allegretto / du ~~Premier~~ Quatuor à cordes / (op. 46) / Arrangement pour piano par l'auteur / No. 1 Adagio
    Pages: Title page, 2 pages of music, a blank page.
    Date: (Copyright date in MS: 1912)
    Remarks: Smaller paper size (30 x 23 cm).

11 Title: Swan Hennessy / Adagio et Allegretto / du / ~~Premier~~ Quatuor / à cordes / (Op. 46) / Arrangement pour piano par l'auteur / No. 2 Allegretto
    Pages: Title page, a blank page, 5 pages, a blank page.
    Date: –
    Remarks: Even smaller paper size (27.4 x 18.2 cm). No publishing details, no dates.

12 Title: Swan Hennessy / IRISH SONATINA / Op. 61 / I. Allegro / II. Andante / III. Vivace
    Pages: Title page, 9 pages of music, 2 blank pages.
    Date: –

Remarks: Op. 61 actually is the 3rd String Quartet. This work was published as *Sonatine celtique*, Op. 53. Text on title page: "NB. This composition contains no popular airs." Title page with a small drawing of a spider. No publishing details, no dates.

13. Title: Swan Hennessy / EPIGRAMMES / D'UN / SOLITAIRE / Op. 63 / ~~SUR~~ LA FÔRET (*sic!*) DE CLAMART A L'AUBE / ~~SUR~~ UN JARDIN ARABE / ~~SUR~~ UNE PAGODE INDO-CHINOISE / ~~SUR~~ UN BERCEAU / ~~SUR~~ UN VIEUX CIMETIÈRE / ~~SUR~~ UN SOUVENIR LOINTAIN
    Pages: Title page, 6 pages of music, a blank page.
    Date: See Remarks.
    Remarks: This work was published as Op. 55 in 1929. Pencil note at bottom of 1st page of music: "Copyright MCMXXIV (1924) by Michael Kavanagh on each 1st plate". The first 3 of the 6 leaves are glued together, suggesting extensive corrections underneath.

14. Title: TROIS PIÈCES EXOTIQUES / Op. 57 / 1. Filettes brunes / 2. Le gout de la cannelle / 3. Nègre endimanché
    Pages: [no title page], 4 pages of music.
    Date: –
    Remarks: No publishing details, no dates.

15. Title: Swan Hennessy / Canons à deux voix / 12 petites pièces ~~très~~ faciles pour piano / Op. 64 / 1. Canon à la quarte / 2. Canon à l'octave à une mesure de distance / 3. Canon à l'octave à demie mesure des distance / 4. Canon à la tierce / 5. Canon à l'octave en movement retrograde / 6. Canon bitonal à la septième augmentée / [7.] Canon à la quinte / 8. Canon à la sixte / 9. Canon à la seconde / 10. Canon à l'unison / 11. Canon à l'octave en ~~élargissement~~ [unreadable] / 12. Canon à l'octave en ~~rétrécissement~~ diminution
    Pages: Title page, page with table of contents, 10 pages of music.
    Date: –
    Remarks: Smaller paper size (31 x 24 cm). Title page is followed by a page with table of contents (*"Table des matières"*), crossed out incl. remark *"Supprimer"*. This list has a different order, following the order of intervals. Under the suppressed table of contents is a glued-over remark (readable against the light): *"NB. Les numeros 1, 3 et 7 sont d'après des airs populaires irlandais et le numero 10 d'après un air francais."* (this refers to the order above). First page of music with dedication: *"A MA FEMME"*. Pencil corrections in 1st piece. No publishing details, no dates.

16. Title: Swan Hennessy / Rapsodie Irlandaise / (Op. 67) / pour piano
    Pages: 'Half' title page with 8 bars of music at bottom, 3 further full pages of music.
    Date: –
    Remarks: 1st page with footnote: *"NB. Cette oeuvre ne contient aucun air du folk-lore."* Some corrections pasted into the score. No publishing details, no dates.

Appendix 531

17 Title: Allegretto du quatrième quatuor a cordes / Transcription pour piano / Swan Hennessy / Op. 75bis
Pages: [no title page] 4 pages of music.
Date: Paris, Juin, 1928
Remarks: (unpublished)

18 Title: First title: Swan Hennessy / Banlieues / 6 petites pièces pour Piano / Second title: À Maurice Servais / Banlieues … / 3 petites pièces pour piano / par / Swan Hennessy / Op 68 (*sic!*) / Third title: A Maurice Servais / Banlieues / Six petites pièces pour / piano / par / Swan Hennessy / Op. 69 / 1. Clamart / 2. Aubervilliers / 3. Meudon / 4. Robinson / 5. Verrières / 6. Bourg-la-Reine
Pages: <u>Cardboard title page</u> from original print with 3 pieces, the back of which with a printed list of Hennessy's chamber music; <u>title page no. 2</u> on paper, a blank page, 3 pages of music (pieces I to III), 3 blank pages; <u>title page no. 3</u>, 3 pages of music (pieces IV to VI).
Date: Third title page with SACEM stamp dated "27 Juin 1929".
Remarks: Originally, 3 works of 1926; 3 more works added for the 1929 publication, which is Op. <u>69</u>. First title page of light green cardboard taken from a publication, printed letters, no. '6' corrected manually, probably to hide the '3' beneath. Remark at bottom of page 1: *"Copyright 1926 par Swan Hennessy / Proprieté de l'auteur"*. Corrections in no. 3 (*Meudon*) for bars 5 & 6 and 13 to 15. Minor corrections (1 bar each) in no. 5 (*Verrières*) and no. 6 (*Bourg-la-Reine*). No publishing details.

Inserted grey cardboard of title page of the Trio Op. 70, blank verso.

19 Title: À Marthe Le Breton / Swan Hennessy / À la manière de ….. / I. Johannes Brahms / II. César Franck / III. Edvard Grieg / IV. Robert Schumann / V. Gabriel Fauré (1re manière) / VI. Anton Dvořák / VII. Richard Strauss / VIII. Stephen Heller / IX. Claude Debussy / X. Benjamin Godard / XI. Max Reger et Paul Delmet / XII. Alexandre Borodine / XIII. Félix Mendelssohn-Bartholdy / XIV. Vincent d'Indy / XV. Muzio Clementi / XVI. Jeune genie de l'avantgarde / XVII. Joaquin Turina / XVIII. Gioacchino Rossini
Pages: Title page, 23 pages of music.
Date: Two pieces with erased (but still legible) dates: VI. "Veytaux, 1917, …" and VII. "Veytaux, December 1917".
Remarks: The first pieces appear in the following order: II, III, I, IV, then correct ordering from IV onward. No. IV (*Robert Schumann*) taken *verbatim* from the print of *Miniatures*, Op. 11 No. 1; not a manuscript but a page from the 1889 print of Op. 11. Corrections in nos. 9 (*Debussy*); pages with pieces 16 & 17 glued together. No publishing details.

20 Title: Swan Hennessy / A la manière de … / 4e cahier / dédié à Richard Byk / I. Carl Maria von Weber / II. Domenico Scarlatti / III. Giuseppe Verdi / IV. Frédéric Chopin / V. Franz Liszt / VI. Emmanuel Chabrier
Pages: Title page, 11 pages of music.
Date: –

Remarks: Pieces were originally numbered XIX to XXIV, then changed with a pencil note at the head of piece I: *"numeroter les morceaux de I a VI au lieu de XIX à XXIV"*. Corrections in the last line of no. III (*Verdi*), extensive ones on no. IV (*Chopin*) and V (*Liszt*); last page of *Liszt* and first of *Chabrier* glued together. No publishing details, no dates.

21 Title: À Richard Byk / Swan Hennessy / à la manière de ..... / 5me cahier / I. Schubert / II. Haendel / III. Massenet / IV. Johann Strauss / V. Maurice Ravel / VI. Hugo Wolf.
Pages: Title page, 8 pages of music.
Date: –
Remarks: Pencil note on title page: *"1ere Semaine Mars"*. Last page of *Schubert* and first of *Handel* glued together, likewise *Massenet* and first pages of *Strauss*, extensive corrections in *Strauss*. No publishing details, no dates.

22 Title: Appendice / ~~Epilogue~~ / Swan Hennessy[1] / [1] Ce morceau a deja paru dans "Eight Celtic Pieces" (op. 51)
Pages: One page.
Date: –
Remarks: This is the appendix to vol. 5 of *À la manière de* ... The music is <u>not</u> in manuscript; small format (18 x 15 cm) of printed music pasted onto larger page.

C.3.3: MS Book III: Piano music, 1909 to 1913; plus 2 movts. of Op. 62 f. va & pf (1924)
Physical description: Bound with red leather spine, reading 'SWAN HENNESSY KINDER-ALBUM' in gilt letters, with red-blue-yellow marbled paper boards. Measurements: 28 cm high x 19.5 cm wide, approx. 1.5 cm thick, making this the smallest and shortest of the manuscript books. Paper size: 27 x 17 cm (pieces 1 and 2) and 27.5 x 18.4 cm (pieces 3 and 4).

These are manuscripts of Hennessy's opus numbers (in this order) 35, 33, 48 (for piano), and 62 (for viola and piano, first two movements only).

All pieces are in Hennessy's hand in black ink, the *Kinder-Album* with some additions in red (mainly expression marks). Some also contain the publisher's plate numbers (written by hand). Some of the manuscripts have a date.
List of Contents:

1 Title: KINDER-ALBUM / 24 / Kleine / Präludien / in verschiedenen Tonarten / und Rhytmen [sic!] / für / Klavier / componirt / von / Swan Hennessy / Op. 35
Pages: Volume opens with 5 blank pages. Title page with blank verso, contents page ('Inhalt') with blank verso, 31 numbered pages of music (pp. 3–33), 3 blank pages.
Date: Paris 1909.
Remarks: A number of corrections, particularly in pieces no. 2 and 17. Pages glued together, suggesting further revisions: pp. 5/6, 7/8, 19/20, 23/24, 25/26. Some pieces have a different title than in the printed edition.

Appendix

2   Title: CROQUIS / DE / FEMMES / 7 petits morceaux caracteristiques pour piano / par / Swan Hennessy / Op. 33 / 1 Bavardes / 2 La Vieille Tante / 3 Au Couvent / 4 Mondaine / 5 Jeunes Anglaises / 6 Dans les Jardins du Serail / 7 Charmeuse de Serpents
    Pages: Title page of blue paper with music paper attached to verso (= p. 1 of the music), 14 numbered pages of music, one blank page.
    Date: –
    Remarks: Page 1 of the music contains the dedication to Jules Combarieu. In the printed edition, *Au couvent* is in 1st place. Pages 8/9 glued together. Some of the titles seem to have been changed at the last minute (glued on the paper).

3   Title: Swan Hennessy / IMPRESSIONS / HUMORISTIQUES / pour piano / Op. 48 [followed by publishers' details incl. plate number]
    Pages: Title page, 7 pages of music.
    Date: 1913.
    Remarks: In the print, the *Dédicace* comes first, here it is the last piece. No. 4 has a different title in the print. No. 6 is written in blue ink.

4   Title: Swan Hennessy / Sonatine Celtique / pour / Piano et alto / Op. 62 / ~~A mon fils Patrice / Paris 22 – 24 Juillet / 1924~~ / ~~"The bells are ringing / The devils are singing".~~
    Pages: Title page, 10 numbered pages of music (score), 1 blank page.
    Volume closes with 7 blank pages.
    Date: (Paris 22 – 24 Juillet 1924).
    Remarks: Third movement is missing here; no separate part for the viola (both included in MS Book V).

C.3.4: MS Book IV: Songs, 1906–1929, and trios (1921, 1926)
Physical description: Bound with brown leather spine, reading 'SWAN HENNESSY MANUSCRITS MELODIES TRIOS' in gilt letters, with brown-yellow-blue marbled paper boards. Measurements: 35.2 cm high x 28.0 cm wide, approx. 2 cm thick. Paper size: approx. 34.5 x 26.5 cm, except when otherwise noted in the table below.
   These are manuscripts of songs to Hennessy's opus numbers (in this order) 23, 26, 25, 30.2, 42.2, 56.2, 66.1, 56.3, 66.3, 72, 79, plus a different Op. 30, also the chamber music trios Opp. 54 and 70.
   All pieces are in Hennessy's hand in black ink. Some contain markings in pencil by the engravers. Some also contain the publisher's plate numbers (written by hand). Some of the manuscripts have a date.
   List of Contents:

1   Title: A son ami Hugo Rasch. / Lydia / (Leconte de Lisle) / Romance pour tenor / avec accompagnement / de piano ou quatuor / a cordes / par / Swan Hennessy / Op. 23 [also indication of vocal compass, paper format (in German): "4o Pag 3–5 gr. Zwischenformat", and the number 74622 in blue crayon]

Pages: Title page with blank verso and (German) commentary: "Alle Achtel ausstechen", 3 pages of music, 3 blank pages.
Date: –
Remarks: Piano version of the piece. On the bottom of the first music page, publisher's plate number J. 5489 H. (Hamelle).

2. Title: Deux Mélodies / pour chant / et piano / par / Swan Hennessy / Op. 26 N°. 1: "Annie", (paroles de Leconte de Lisle.) [in pencil: Chanson Ecossaise] / N°. 2: "La-bas", (paroles de Joséphin Soulary.) / Du même auteur: "Lydia", (paroles de Leconte de Lisle) / "Epiphanie", (paroles de J. M. de Heredia).
Pages: Title page, 2 pages of music, 1 blank page.
Date: 1906
Remarks: In the print edition, *Annie* is Op. 31 No. 1. For Op. 26 see below.

3. Title: Deux Mélodies / pour chant / et piano / par / Swan Hennessy / Op. 26 / N°. 1: "Annie", (paroles de Leconte de Lisle.) / N°. 2: "La-bas", (paroles de Joséphin Soulary.) / [same note as above re. 'Du même auteur']
Pages: Title page, 2 pages of music, 1 blank page.
Date: 1906
Remarks: In the print edition, *Là-bas* is Op. 30 No. 1. For Op. 26 see below.

4. Title: Epiphanie / (José-Maria de Heredia, Les Trophées) / pour chant / et orgue ou piano / par / Swan Hennessy / Op. 25 / [also indication of vocal compass and a note (in French) to the engraver]
Pages: Title page, 2 pages of music, 1 blank page.
Date: –
Remarks: In the print edition, this is Op. 26. On the bottom of the title pages: publisher's plate no. 5501 (Hamelle).

5. Title: Swan Hennessy / "Le Revenant" / (paroles de Baudelaire) / [beneath, in smaller print:] / —> Quatre Melodies / pour chant et piano / par / Swan Hennessy / 1. Lydia (Tenor). Paroles de Leconte de Lisle. / 2. Epiphanie (Tenor ou Soprano). Paroles de J. M de Heredia. / 3. Le Revenant (Baryton). Paroles de Baudelaire. / 4. Là-bas (Baryton ou mezzo-soprano).[NB] Paroles de Josephin Soulary. / NB. J'ai fait un petit changement dans cette dernière mélodie de sorte que sa portée sera maintenant B – e [in pitches].
Pages: Title page, 3 pages of music
Date: –
Remarks: No opus number mentioned, but this one is Op. 30 No. 2. On the bottom of the music page: publisher's plate no. J. 5656 H. (Hamelle). First music page also includes the source of the poem (*Les Fleurs du mal*) and the publisher's permission.

6. Title: à Madame Delorme Jules Simon / LA FILLE AUX CHEVEUX DE LIN / Chanson Ecossaise / Paroles par Leconte / De Lisle / Musique par / Swan Hennessy [also publisher's details, incl. plate no., in a different hand]

Pages: Title page, 3 pages of music.
Date: (Originally c.1907; copyright date in MS: 1920)
Remarks: Smaller paper size: 30.3 x 22.5 cm. First music page titled 'Chanson écossaise' only. Published as Op. 31 No. 2 with Hamelle; this is the MS for the Demets edition.

7 Title: N°. 1 / "Fluthenreicher Ebro" / (Geibel) / Lied / für Mezzo Sopran / mit Klavier Begleitung / von / Swan Hennessy / Op. 42^{Bis} / N°. 1 [followed by the words of the poem in French]
Pages: Title page, 3 pages of music (with German text)
Date: –
Remarks: –

8 Title: N°. 2 / "Auf den Wällen Salamanca's." / (Heine) / Lied für Mezzo-Sopran / mit / Klavierbegleitung / von / Swan Hennessy / Op. 42^{Bis} N°. 2 [followed by the words of the poem in French]
Pages: Title page, 3 pages of music (with German text)
Date: –
Remarks: Smaller paper size: 31.6 x 23.5 cm.

9 Title: N°. 3 / "Neben mir wohnt Don Henriquez" / (Heine) / Lied für Mezzo-Sopran / mit Klavierbegleitung / von / Swan Hennessy / Op. 42^{Bis} / N°. 3 [followed by the words of the poem in French]
Pages: Title page, 7 pages of music (with German text)
Date: –
Remarks: Smaller paper size: 30.2 x 22.5 cm.

10+11 Title: à Charles Hubbard / "Les grands Jasmins épanouis …" / Poésie d'Albert Samain / mise en musique / par / Swan Hennessy / Op. 56^B / à Mlle Marthe Saisset / "Si la distance nous separe." / Poésie d'André Delacour / Op 66^A
Pages: Title page, 2 pages of music with Op. 56 No. 2, 1 page of music with Op. 66 No. 1 (written on verso of 2nd page of the preceding piece).
Date: –
Remarks: Smaller paper size: 31.5 x 26.5 cm. Despite the difference in opus numbers, both pieces written in or around 1921. They were published in 1925 and 1926 respectively.

12 Title: À / mon fils Patrice / JANE / Chanson Écossaise. / Paroles de Leconte de Lisle. Musique de Swan Hennessy / Op. 56^C
Pages: Title page, 2 pages of music, 1 blank page.
Date: –
Remarks: In the print edition, this is Op. 66 No. 3.

13 Title: A Mademoiselle Marthe Saisset. / PAYSAGE. / Paroles d'André Delacour. Musique de Swan Hennessy. / Op. 66^B
Pages: Title page, 2 pages of music, 1 blank page.
Date: –

    Remarks: –

14 Title: A Henri Collet / Swan Hennessy / La Chanson du Rouet / mélodie pour voix moyenne / Op. 72 N°. 1
    Pages: Title page, 2 pages of music, 1 blank page.
    Date: –
    Remarks: –

–   Title: Trois Chansons / Celtiques / par / Swan Hennessy / Op. 72 / 1 (Écosse) La Chanson du Rouet (Leconte de Lisle.) /2 (Bretagne) Berceuse d'Armorique (Anatole Le Braz.) / 3 (Irlande) Le Départ des Pêcheurs (Pierre Scize.)
    Pages: Title page with blank verso only (intended as a cover for pieces 14 to 16).
    Date: –
    Remarks: Main title written on gray paper and pasted onto music paper. Verso contains the following crossed-out note: ~~NB. La troisième de ces chansons est une adaptation d'un air irlandais ancien de la collection Petrie. Les deux autres ne contiennent aucun thème du folk-lore proprement dit.~~

15 Title: A Eugène Cools / Swan Hennessy / Berceuse d'Armorique / mélodie pour voix moyenne / Op. 72 N°. 2
    Pages: Title page, 3 pages of music.
    Date: –
    Remarks: Some corrections, particularly on p. 3.

16 Title: À Pierre Scize / Swan Hennessy / Le Départ des Pêcheurs / mélodie pour voix moyenne / Op. 72 N°. 3
    Pages: Title page w/ blank verso, 4 pages of music
    Date: –
    Remarks: Some corrections, particularly on p. 2. On the first music page, the word 'Chant' is pasted above an earlier note 'Une ou plusieures voix'.

–   Title: DEUX MÉLODIES / pour une voix moyenne / par / Swan Hennessy / Op 73 / N°. 1 Le Chasseur Noir (Paul Gérardy) / N°. 2 La Chanson du Vent de Mer (Anatole Le Braz)
    Pages: Title page with blank verso only (intended as a cover for pieces 17 & 18).
    Date: –
    Remarks: –

17 Title: Swan Hennessy / Le Chasseur Noir / mélodie pour voix moyenne / Op. 73 N°. 1 / (Paroles de Paul Gérardy)
    Pages: Title page, 3 pages of music.
    Date: –
    Remarks: –

18 Swan Hennessy / La Chanson du Vent de Mer / mélodie pour voix moyenne / Op. 73 N°. 2 / (Paroles d'Anatole Le Braz)
    Pages: Title page, 3 pages of music, 2 blank pages.

Date: –
Remarks: Crossed-out dedication (on title page and first music page): ~~À ma femme~~.

19+20 Title: Deux Mélodies / pour une voix de soprano / par / Swan Hennessy / Op. 79
Pages: Title page, 3 pages of music (the 2nd piece written on verso of 2nd page of the preceding piece).
Date: Paris, Avril, 1929.
Remarks: These are the pieces *La Lune* (Paul Verlaine) and *À deux* (Prosper Blanchemain).

21–23 Title: SONGS / from / "AS YOU LIKE IT" / (Shakespeare) / by / Swan Hennessy / Op. 30 / N°. 1 "Under the greenwood tree." / N°. 2 " Blow, blow, thou winter wind." / N°. 3 "It was a lover and his lass." / Deutscher Text frei nach Schlegel und Tieck
Pages: Title page, 2 pages of music (for No. 1), 1 blank page; title page, 2 pages of music (for No. 1), 1 blank page;
Date: –
Remarks: Unpublished (written c.1909). Op. 30 was later assigned to a different piece. No. 1 with full German translation, nos. 2 & 3 with some indications in German only. Coloured paper for the title pages.

24 Title: à mon ami Paul Le Flem / PETIT / TRIO / CELTIQUE / pour / Violon, alto et violoncelle / par / Swan Hennessy / Op. / 52 / (1920) [also publisher's details, incl. plate no., in a different hand]
Pages: Title page, 15 pages of music (score).
Date: 1920
Remarks: Smaller paper size: 29.4 x 26.5 cm. Score in the order of movements 1, 2, 4, 3.

25 Title: Violon / à mon ami Paul Le Flem / Swan Hennessy / Petit / TRIO CELTIQUE / pour violon, alto et violoncelle. / Op. 52 [also publisher's details, incl. plate no., in a different hand]
Pages: Title page, 5 pages of music (violin part).
Date: –
Remarks: In the order of movements 1, 2, 4, 3. On the 2nd page of movt. 1, there is a little pencil sketch of an encircled moustached male face with the initials J. G., probably originally with a hat (erased), c.5 cm in diameter.

26 Title: Alto / à mon ami Paul Le Flem / Swan Hennessy / Petit / TRIO CELTIQUE / pour violon, alto et violoncelle. / Op. 52
Pages: Title page, 5 pages of music (viola part).
Date: –
Remarks: In the order of movements 1, 2, 4, 3.

27 Title: Violoncelle / à mon ami Paul Le Flem / Swan Hennessy / Petit / TRIO CELTIQUE / pour violon, alto et violoncelle. / Op. 52

Pages: Title page, 4 pages of music (cello part), 3 blank pages.
Date: –
Remarks: In the order of movements 1, 2, 4, 3.

28 Title: à mon ami Paul Ladmirault / Trio / pour / ~~Basson et~~ deux clarinettes et Basson / par / Swan Hennessy / Op. 54 [also publisher's details, incl. plate no., in a different hand]
Pages: Title page, 13 pages of music (score), 1 page with a catalogue of chamber music, 1 blank page.
Date: (Copyright date in MS: 1920)
Remarks: The catalogue of Hennessy's chamber music is most interesting. The publisher removed opus nos. in blue crayon, but it reveals that the 2nd string quartet (Op. 49) was originally Op. 53 and the *Petit trio celtique*, Op. 52, originally Op. 55.

29 Title: à mon ami Paul Ladmirault / Swan Hennessy / Trio (style irlandais) / pour / Basson et deux clarinettes / Op 54 / (1919) [all in pencil]
Pages: Title page in pencil w/ verso containing one system of music in black ink, 10 pages of music in (neat) pencil (score).
Date: (1919)
Remarks: The pencil date 1919 is confusing and contradicts the date in the parts.

30 Title: à mon ami Paul Ladmirault / Trio / pour deux Clarinettes et Basson / Swan Hennessy
Pages: (no title page!) 4 pages of music in ink (1st clarinet).
Date: (Copyright date in MS: 1920)
Remarks: –

31 Title: à mon ami Paul Ladmirault / Trio / Swan Hennessy
Pages: 4 pages of music in ink (bassoon).
Date: –
Remarks: –

32 Title: Swan Hennessy / TRIO / pour violon, flûte et basson / Op. 70 [includes plate no. ME 1985[B] in blue crayon, diff. hand]
Pages: Title page, 13 pages of music (score).
Date: –
Remarks: –

C.3.5: MS Book V: Chamber music, 1914 to 1929, and one piano piece

Physical description: Bound with green leather spine (faded to brown), reading 'SWAN HENNESSY – MANUSCRIT – PIANO VIOLON ALTO SAXOPHONE' in gilt letters, with green-brown marbled paper boards. Measurements: 35.5 cm high x 28.0 cm wide, approx. 3 cm thick. Paper size: 34.8 x 27 cm, except when otherwise noted in the table below.

Appendix 539

These are manuscripts of Hennessy's opus numbers (in this order) 50, 54 (arr.), 78, 59, 62, 63, 67, 68, 71, 74, 80, and 81.

All pieces are in Hennessy's hand in black ink. Some contain pencil markings by the engravers. Some also contain the publisher's plate numbers (written by hand), the intended paper format, etc. Some of the manuscripts have a date.
List of Contents:

1. Title: Swan Hennessy / Rapsodie Celtique / pour piano et violon / Op. 50 / I
   Pages: Title page w/blank verso, 6 pages of music (score), 8 blank pages.
   Date: (Copyright date in MS: 1914)
   Remarks: The piece was not published in 1914 but in 1915. Pages 5 & 6 glued together, partly revealing different music underneath.

2. Title: Swan Hennessy / Rapsodie Celtique pour Piano et Violon. / Op. 50 / II & III
   Pages: Title page, 17 pages of music (score), 1 blank page.
   Date: –
   Remarks: Smaller paper size: 27 x 17 cm. Movt. III precedes movt. II. Extensive corrections on pp. 6, 7 & 12, pp. 10 & 11 glued together.

3. Title: <u>Violon</u> / Swan Hennessy / Rapsodie Celtique / pour piano et violon / Op. 50 / I
   Pages: Title page, 2 pages of music (violin), 1 blank page.
   Date: –
   Remarks: Corrections (one system) on p. 1.

4. Title: Violon / Swan Hennessy / Rapsodie Celtique / pour Piano et Violon / Op. 50 / II
   Pages: Title page, 1 page of music (violin).
   Date: –
   Remarks: Smaller paper size: 30.3 x 22.5 cm.

5. Title: Violon / Swan Hennessy / Rapsodie Celtique / pour piano et violon / Op. 50 / III
   Pages: Title page, 3 pages of music (violin).
   Date: –
   Remarks: Smaller paper size: 27 x 17 cm. Some crossed-out bars.

6. Title: Swan Hennessy / Trio / pour / ~~Violon, alto et violoncelle / ou /~~ Basson et deux Clarinettes / Op. 54 / (1919) / Arrangement pour piano
   Pages: Title page, 10 pages of music (score), 1 blank page.
   Date: (1919)
   Remarks: Slightly smaller paper size: 34 x 25 cm. Both the title page and the first music page reveal an originally intended alternative instrumentation. Although titled an arr. for piano, the left hand is depicted in two systems in treble clef.

7 Title: Partition / Swan Hennessy / Sonatine pour deux violons[NB] / composée pour les elèves / de / M. Emile Loiseau / Professeur au Conservatoire. / NB ou deux groups de violons
Pages: Title page, 6 pages of music (score), 1 blank page.
Date: Paris, Mars 1929.
Remarks: Unpublished. 'Op. 78' appears on first music page only.

8 Title: Swan Hennessy / 4 / Pièces Celtiques / pour / Cor anglais ou clarinette, / violon, alto et violoncelle / Op. 59 / Réduction pour cor anglais / et piano.
Pages: Title page, 12 pages of music (score), 1 blank page.
Date: –
Remarks: This piano arrangement unpublished. First music page contains dedication: 'A Monsieur PAUL BRUN'. In the order 1, 4, 3, 2. Pages 8 & 9 and 12 & 13 glued together, partly revealing different music underneath.

9 Title: <u>Alto</u> / Swan Hennessy / Sonatine Celtique / pour piano et alto / Op. 62
Pages: Title page, 4 pages of music (viola), 1 blank page.
Date: –
Remarks: Smaller paper size: 30.4 x 22.8 cm.

10 Title: Swan Hennessy / Sonatine Celtique / pour piano et alto / Op. 62 / III / (Finale)
Pages: Title page, 5 pages of music (score), 2 blank pages.
Date: –
Remarks: Smaller paper size: 25.2 x 22.7 cm

11 Title: <u>Violon</u> / Swan Hennessy / Sonate Celtique Op. 62 / pour alto et piano / Transcription pour saxophone par René / Laurent. / Transcription pour violon par l'auteur. / Cotage M. E 1919
Pages: Title page, 5 pages of music (violin), 2 blank pages.
Date: –
Remarks: This is the composer's violin arrangement of the viola piece (vn part only). Note the wrong title 'Sonate'.

12 Title: à Francis Touche / Swan Hennessy / Rapsodie / Gaélique / pour violoncelle et piano / Op. 63
Pages: Title page w/ blank verso, 11 pages of music (score), 1 blank page.
Date: –
Remarks: Smaller paper size: 28.4 x 23.4 cm. Extensive corrections on pp. 4, 5 and 7, pp. 4 & 5 glued together.

13 Title: Swan Hennessy / Rapsodie Gaélique / pour violoncelle et piano / Op 63.
Pages: Title page, 2 pages of music (cello), 1 blank page.
Date: –
Remarks: Smaller paper size: 31.2 x 23.4 cm. Some corrections.

14 Title: Swan Hennessy / Rapsodie Irlandaise[NB] / (Op. 67) / pour piano
Pages: (No title page, piece begins in bottom two systems) 4 pages of music

Date: –
Remarks: Page 1 contains dedication 'A mon fils Patrice' and the note, also in the print, that the piece does not contain any piece of folklore. Page 2: two systems crossed out. Page 4: also three isolated bars of piano music.

15 Title: À M. René Laurent. / Swan Hennessy / Deux Morceaux / pour / Saxophone-alto et piano / Op. 68 / <u>N°. 1 Pièce celtique</u> / N°. 2 Jazz
Pages: Title page, 2 pages of music (score), 1 blank page
Date: –
Remarks: –

16 Title: À M. René Laurent. / Swan Hennessy / Deux Morceaux / pour / Saxophone-alto et piano / Op 68 / N°. 1 Pièce celtique / <u>N°. 2 Jazz</u>
Pages: Title page, 3 pages of music (score).
Date: –
Remarks: –

17 Title: À M. René Laurent. / Swan Hennessy / Deux Morceaux / pour / Saxophone-alto et piano / Op. 68
Pages: Title page, 1 page of music (sax.).
Date: –
Remarks: No. 1 (*Pièce celtique*) only.

18 Title: À M. René Laurent. / Swan Hennessy / Deux Morceaux / pour / Saxophone-alto et piano / Op 68 / N°. 1 Pièce celtique / <u>N°. 2 Jazz</u>
Pages: Title page, 1 page of music (sax.).
Date: –
Remarks: No. 2.

– Saxophone / Swan Hennessy / Nouvelles pieces exotiques / Op. 71
Pages: Title page w/ blank verso only.
Date: –
Remarks: –

19 Title: Swan Hennessy / Quatre Morceaux / ~~Nouvelles pièces exotiques~~ / pour saxophone alto ou pour / viola alta et piano / Op. 71 / 1. Fox trot. / 2. Tango. / 3. Chanson de l'emigrant. / 4. Lever du soleil dans les Hébrides.
Pages: Title page, 9 pages of music (score).
Date: –
Remarks: Original title (that alluded to the piano work Op. 57) changed. Piece no. 4 probably added later, after renaming (slightly different colour of ink on title page; see no. 21 below). Dedication of no. 2 changed from 'à Paul-Louis Neuberth' to 'à Carol Berard', of no. 3 from 'à Paul-Louis Neuberth' to 'à Madame Neuberth'. Pages 6 & 7 glued together (i.e. new 2nd page for no. 3). A number of corrections in no. 4.

20 Title: Saxophone / Swan Hennessy / Nouvelles pièces exotiques / Op. 71
    Pages: Title page, 3 pages of music (sax.).
    Date: –
    Remarks: Piece no. 4 missing.

21 Title: Viola alta / Swan Hennessy / Nouvelles pièces exotiques / Op. 71
    Pages: Title page, 4 pages of music (viola), 1 blank page.
    Date: –
    Remarks: All 4 pieces. Two versions of no. 4, on pp. 3 and 4, the scond with clearer indications of the piano part.

22 Title: Swan Hennessy / Pièce Celtique / pour / Violoncelle / ou / Basson et piano / Op. 74
    Pages: Title page, 2 pages of music (score), 1 blank page.
    Date: –
    Remarks: –

23 Title: SWAN HENNESSY / Deuxième Sonatine / pour / Alto et piano / ou / Violon et piano / Op. 80 [title crossed out in pencil]
    Pages: Title page w/ blank verso, 14 pages of music (score).
    Date: –
    Remarks: 2nd movement follows the 3rd. Corrections on pp. 1, 4, 5, 10, 13.

24 Title: A Madeleine Monnier / Swan Hennessy / Sonatine / pour piano et violoncelle / Op. 81 [in smaller font:]
    Propriété de l'auteur / 270 B^d Raspail, Paris (14e). / Copyright 1929 by Swan Hennessy /Tous droits etc. / Envoi franco / Prix 15 frs. Majoration comprise / NB Graver le titre pareil à celui de la sonatine op. 80
    Pages: Title page, 10 pages of music (score), 5 blank pages.
    Date: (Copyright date: 1929)
    Remarks: Minor corrections throughout, major ones on p. 9.

25 Title: Violoncelle / A Madeleine Monnier / Swan Hennessy / Sonatine / pour piano et violoncelle / Op. 81
    Pages: Title page, 3 pages of music, 4 blank pages.
    Date: –
    Remarks: –

C.3.6: MS Book VI: Quartets
Physical description: Bound with reddish-brown leather spine, reading 'SWAN HENNESSY – MANUSCRITS – QUATUORS' in gilt letters, with red-black marbled paper boards. Measurements: 37 cm high x 29.0 cm wide, approx. 3.5 cm thick. Paper size: 35.4 x 27 cm, except when otherwise noted in the table below.

These are manuscripts of Hennessy's string quartets Opp. 46, 49, 61, 75, the *Sérénade*, Op. 65, and the flute quartet Op. 58.

Appendix

All pieces are in Hennessy's hand in black ink. Some contain pencil markings by the engravers. Some also contain the publisher's plate numbers (written by a different hand), the intended paper format, etc. There are no dates.

List of Contents:

— Volume begins with 7 blank pages

1. Title. à Monsieur le Professeur Carl Heffner / Swan Hennessy / SUITE pour QUATUOR à CORDES / Op 46
   Pages: Title page w/blank verso, 20 pages of music (score), 2 blank pages.
   Date: (Copyright date: 1913)
   Remarks: Clean copy, no corrections.

1a. Title: Premier violon / Swan Hennessy / Quatuor Op. 46 / Premier violon / N°. 1 Allegro.
   Pages: Title page, 2 pages of music, 1 blank page.
   Remarks: Smaller paper: 24 x 31.5 cm. One crossed out line on p. 1. Page 2 glued upon another page.

1b. Title: Premier violon / Swan Hennessy / Quatuor Op 46 / Premier violon / N°s. 2 et 3 Adagio et Allegretto.
   Pages: Title page, 2 pages of music, 1 blank page.
   Remarks: Paper size as 1a. Page 2 glued upon another page. With erased (but still legible) additions to tempo markings: 'Très lent, avec tendresse' (Adagio) and 'Gentiment, & pas trop vite' (Allegretto).

1c. Title: Premier violon / Swan Hennessy / Quatuor Op 46 / Premier violon / N°. 4 Finale (sur des airs de la collection Petrie).
   Pages: Title page, 2 pages of music, 1 blank page.
   Remarks: Even smaller paper size: 22.5 x 30.5 cm. Some added performance directions in red ink.

1d. Title: Deuxième violon / Swan Hennessy / Quatuor Op. 46 / Deuxième violon / N°. 1 Allegro
   Pages: Title page, 2 pages of music, 1 blank page.
   Remarks: Paper size as 1a.

1e. Title: Deuxième violon / Swan Hennessy / Quatuor Op. 46 / Deuxième violon / N°s. 2 et 3 Adagio et Allegretto.
   Pages: Title page, 2 pages of music, 1 blank page.
   Remarks: Paper size as 1a. With erased additions to tempo markings (illegible).

1f. Title: Deuxième violon / Swan Hennessy / Quatuor Op 46 / Deuxième violon / N°. 4 Finale (sur des airs de la collection Petrie).
   Pages: Title page, 2 pages of music, 1 blank page.
   Remarks: Paper size as 1a. Some added performance directions in red ink.

1g Title: Alto / Swan Hennessy / Quatuor Op. 46 / Alto / N°. 1 Allegro
Pages: Title page, 2 pages of music, 1 blank page.
Remarks: Paper size as 1c.

1h Title: Alto / Swan Hennessy / Quatuor Op. 46 / Alto / N°s. 2 et 3 Adagio et Allegretto.
Pages: Title page, 2 pages of music, 1 blank page.
Remarks: Paper size as 1c. Title page and first music page glued together.

1i Title: Alto / Swan Hennessy / Quatuor Op. 46 / Alto / N°. 4 Finale (sur des airs de la collection Petrie).
Pages: Title page, 2 pages of music, 1 blank page.
Remarks: Paper size as 1c. Some added performance directions in red ink.

1j Title: Violoncelle / Swan Hennessy / Quatuor Op. 46 / Violoncelle / N°. 1 Allegro.
Pages: Title page, 2 pages of music, 1 blank page.
Remarks: Paper size as 1c.

1k Title: Violoncelle / Swan Hennessy / Quatuor Op. 46 / Violoncelle / N°s. 2 et 3 Adagio et Allegretto.
Pages: Title page, 2 pages of music, 1 blank page.
Remarks: Paper size as 1c. Title page and first music page glued together.

1l Title: Violoncelle / Swan Hennessy / Quatuor Op. 46 / Violoncelle /
Pages: Title page, 2 pages of music, 1 blank page.
Remarks: Paper size as 1c. Some added performance directions in red ink.

2   Title: Swan Hennessy / Deuxième / Quatuor / Op. 49
Pages: Title page w/blank verso, 23 pages of music, 1 blank page, 3 pages of music (= Interlude), 1 blank page, 8 pages of music (all in score).
Date: (Copyright date: 1920)
Remarks: Paper size: 22.5 x 30.5 cm. Page 6 (= end of Introduction) crossed out completely (16 bars w/ a different ending). Page 7 (beginning of 2nd movt) with 3 crossed-out bars; initially headed 'I' (crossed out with pencil). Pp. 12/13 with 12 crossed-out bars. Pages 17 and 20 with corrections. Interlude looks like put in separately. 4th movt initially headed 'II' (crossed out with pencil).

2a Title: 1er Violon. / Swan Hennessy / Deuxième Quatuor / [in box:] NB pour le graveur. Ordre des morceaux: / 1) Introduction / sans interrup / 2) Allegro / 3) Interlude / 4) Allegro
Pages: (no extra title page) 10 pages of music (all movts).
Remarks: 'Deuxième Quatuor' written on a square piece of light blue paper glued upon a piece of beige paper glued upon the music paper. 'I' crossed out in blue crayon. The beige paper covers a variant of the title ('Deuxième Quatuor [Ut mineur] / pour Quatuor à / cordes / Op. 49') and 3 bars of music. NB. This is the complete part for violin 1, with second Allegro from p. 6, Introduction on p. 8, Interlude on p. 10. Corrections on pp. 3, 5, 9. Pages 5 & 6 glued together.

Appendix

2b Title: 1ᵈ Violon. / Swan Hennessy / Deuxième Quatuor
    Pages: (no extra title page) 9 pages of music, 1 blank page (all movts).
    Remarks: NB: 2a – 2d return to large paper size. Design as in 2a, except Interlude on p. 9.

2c Title: Alto / Swan Hennessy / Deuxième Quatuor
    Pages: (no extra title page) 9 pages of music, 1 blank page (all movts).
    Remarks: Design as in 2b.

2d Title: Cello / Swan Hennessy / Deuxième Quatuor
    Pages: (no extra title page) 9 pages of music, 1 blank page (all movts).
    Remarks: Design as in 2b.

3   Title: Pour le Quatuor Loiseau / Swan Hennessy / 3ᵉ / Quatuor à cordes / Op. 61
    Pages: Title page indicating movts I and II, 11 pages of music, title page for movt III w/blank verso, 5 pages of music, 2 blank pages, title page for movt IV, 7 pages of music (all score).
    Date: –
    Remarks: Movt III with slightly smaller paper (25.5 x 35 cm) and some corrections. NB.: The parts for the 3rd quartet are missing.

4a Title: Swan Hennessy / 4ᵉ / QUATUOR / Op. 75 / PARTITION / Premier mouvement
    Pages: Title page, 12 pages of music (score), 1 blank page.
    Date: –
    Remarks: Corrections throughout, mostly as glued-over staves. The leaf for pp. 6/7 consists of 3 leaves glued upon each other, hiding corrections.

4b Title: Swan Hennessy / 4ᵉ / QUATUOR / Op 75 / PARTITION / Second mouvemᵗ
    Pages: Title page, 11 pages of music (score), 2 blank pages.
    Remarks: Clean copy.

4c Title: Swan Hennessy / 4ᵉ / QUATUOR / Op. 75 / PARTITION / Troisième mouvement
    Pages: Title page, 9 pages of music (score), 4 blank pages.
    Remarks: Clean copy.

4d Title: Swan Hennessy / 4ᵉ / QUATUOR / Op. 75 / PARTITION / Quatrième mouvement
    Pages: Title page, 14 pages of music (score), 1 blank page.
    Remarks: Pages 10/11 and 12/13 glued together, hiding corrections; otherwise clean copy.

4e Title: Premier violon / Swan Hennessy / 4ᵉ / QUATUOR / Op. 75
    Pages: Title page, 9 pages of music, 2 blank pages.
    Remarks: –

4f Title: Deuxième violon / Swan Hennessy / 4e / QUATUOR / Op. 75
    Pages: Title page, 8 pages of music, 3 blank pages.
    Remarks: –

4g Title: Violoncelle / Swan Hennessy / 4e / QUATUOR / Op. 75
    Pages: Title page, 9 pages of music, 2 blank pages.
    Remarks: –

4h Title: Alto / Swan Hennessy / 4e / QUATUOR / Op. 75
    Pages: Title page, 9 pages of music, 2 blank pages.
    Remarks: –

5a Title: Premier violon / A Emile Loiseau / Swan Hennessy / Sérénade / pour / Quatuor à cordes / Op. 65 [with Eschig plate number]
    Pages: Title page, 2 pages of music, 1 blank page.
    Remarks: NB.: The full score of the Sérénade is missing.

5b Title: Second violon / A Emile Loiseau / Swan Hennessy / Sérénade / pour / Quatuor à cordes / Op. 65
    Pages: Title page, 2 pages of music, 1 blank page.
    Remarks: Title page and 1st music page glued together.

5c Title: Vionloncelle [sic!] / A Emile Loiseau / Swan Hennessy / Sérénade / pour / Quatuor à cordes / Op 65
    Pages: Title page, 2 pages of music, 1 blank page.
    Remarks: –

5d Title: Alto / A Emile Loiseau / Swan Hennessy / Sérénade / pour / Quatuor à cordes / Op. 65
    Pages: Title page, 2 pages of music, 1 blank page.
    Remarks: –

6   Title: Swan Hennessy / Variations sur un thème de six notes / pour / Flûte, violon, alto et violoncelle / Op. 58 [with Eschig plate number]
    Pages: Title page w/ blank verso, 12 pages of music (score).
    Date: –
    Remarks: Extensive corrections on pp. 4, 5, 8.

6a Title: V celle / ~~Suite / pour / Flûte, violon, alto et violoncelle~~ / Variations / ~~celtiques~~ / sur un thème de six notes; / ~~Adagio; Souvenir de la vie d'étudiant.~~ / Op. 58 / Swan Hennessy
    Pages: Title page, 7 pages of music.
    Remarks: After the ending, the MS contains the cello part of an Irish air (in *Adagio*) that is named 'One night I dreamed'. However, it neither resembles the Irish-style tune in the piece (which is in the flute) nor is it the cello part to that tune.

6b Title: Alto / ~~Suite / pour / Flûte, violon, alto et violoncelle~~ / Variations / ~~celtiques~~ / sur un thème de six notes; / ~~Adagio; Souvenir de la vie d'étudiant.~~ / Op. 58 / Swan Hennessy

Pages: Title page, 7 pages of music.
Remarks: The additional Irish tune from 6a is missing here.

6c Title: Violon / ~~Suite / pour / Flûte, violon, alto et violoncelle~~ / Variations / ~~celtiques~~ / sur un thème de six notes; / ~~Adagio; Souvenir de la vie d'étudiant.~~ / Op. 58 / Swan Hennessy
Pages: Title page, 7 pages of music.
Remarks: With a number of corrections. The additional Irish tune from 6a is missing again.

6d Title: Flûte / ~~Suite / pour / Flûte, violon, alto et violoncelle~~ / Variations / ~~celtiques~~ / sur un thème de six notes; / ~~Adagio; Souvenir de la vie d'étudiant.~~ / Op. 58 / Swan Hennessy
Pages: Title page, 9 pages of music. This is followed by the last page only of the full score.
Remarks: Ends on the last 25 bars of the full score (rest is missing).

C.3.7: Single unbound manuscripts, correspondence and ephemera

In July 2018, further single manuscripts were found by the family, along with some printed music and correspondence (the latter is described above under A.6). These are not bound in the style of the others and are mostly earlier drafts of some of the music listed above. These consist of the following items:

- A version of Op. 34 (Petite Suite …), here called *Variations en forme de Sonatine*, underneath the alternative title *Sonatine & Prelude et fugue / sur les themes /* [written in notation] $E – C\sharp – E – F\sharp – B – E$ et $E – C\natural – E – F\natural – B – E$. The variant with the dissolved accidentals does not occur in the final publication. The opus number has been changed from 33 to 34. This manuscript is divided between a booklet of eight (movts 1, 2, 3) and four (movt 4) pages.
- A booklet of four pages, which contains *Aubervilliers* and *Meudon* from *Banlieues*, Op. 69 (in black ink) on three pages and the fourth page with excerpts from the Introduction to String Quartet No. 3, Op. 61 (pencil sketch).
- *Trois Petits trios* pour voix de femmes, Op. 76: six pages on three leaves of paper; No. 2 is dated 'Paris, Juillet 1928' (which probably also applies to No. 1), No. 3 is dated 'Paris, Février 11, 1929'.
- Printed publications of *Vier Lieder*, Op. 3, the *Sonate en fa (style irlandais)*, Op. 14, and *Là-bas*, Op. 30 No. 1.
- A manual transcript by William Gwin of Herbert Hughes' song *Monday, Tuesday* with the dedication *'Pour Mme Swan Hennessy en aimable souvenir'* (undated).

Correspondence, consisting of:
- Postcard from Heinrich Möller to Swan Hennessy at Pornichet, 6 Aug. 1913, in German (see Chapter 6)
- Manuscript letter from Gaston Blanquart to Swan Hennessy, 25 September 1925, thanking him for the scores of Opp. 58 and 70, expressing his admiration and that he is waiting for an opportunity to perform them.

- Typed and signed letter from SACEM (Société des Auteurs, Compositeurs et Éditeurs de Musique), Service International, unidentified person (*'P. le Directeur Adjoint'*) to 'Madame Swan Hennessy', dated 18 Oct. 1939, in French. Sender acknowledges receipt of two 'copyright receipts' (*'récépisses des copyright'*) namely Opp. 80 and 81. Attached are two cards from the copyright office of the Library of Congress, which must be copies.
- Typed and signed letter with envelope from George F(rederick) McKay, letter head of University of Washington, School of Music, Seattle, to Swan Hennessy, dated 30 Oct. 1939, in English; envelope addressed to publisher Max Eschig, re-addressed to 270 blvd. Raspail, further re-addressed to 15 rue de Chilly, Longjumeau (south of Paris, where Hennessy's widow must have lived at the time). McKay wants to include him in 'a special study of contemporary composers' with a focus on piano music, asks for a list of titles with bibliographic details.
- Typed and signed letter with envelope from Gabriel Reuillard, *Chef du Service de la Documentation artistique*, Ministère de l'Information Radiodiffusion Française, dated 9 Nov. 1944, in French, addressed to 'Madame Swan Hennessy' at 8 rue du Douanier, Paris 14e. The sender thanks for her response of the 6th inst., saying that it was still time to include her information for a planned *'catalogue général des musiciens don't nous voudrions voir leur repertoire entrer à la Radio'*.
- Typed and signed letter with envelope, as above, dated 23 Jan. 1945. Now Reuillard thanks Claire Hennessy for her letter with the attached list of *'oeuvres de votre mari'*, announcing that he would soon return to her with a selection of works he would like to have the scores of, with a view to future broadcasts.

D. Swan Hennessy's music collection

Also currently in the family's possession, there are a number of bound volumes of printed music that once belonged to Swan Hennessy. It is unlikely that this is all that he possessed (there must once have been more), as the collection does not include any British or Irish music that he must have had also. There are about five thick (3–4 cm) volumes of German classics and romantics and fifteen slightly more slim volumes imprinted at the spine as 'École moderne – Piano'. These contain piano music by his French, German and Russian contemporaries, often containing annotations in red ink and pencil. These mostly pertain to stylistic complaints (regarding, for example, Reger, Schönberg, d'Indy) and misprints he found and corrected in the scores.

D. Mixed items

D.1: Estate Heinrich Möller, Thuringian State Music Archive, Weimar
Call number: NHM/2, Nr. 64–82.

The 'Nachlass Heinrich Möller' at the Thüringisches Landesmusikarchiv at Weimar, Germany, is dedicated to the work of the German music critic and folk music editor Heinrich Möller (1876–1958), a good friend of Hennessy's during his time as Paris correspondent of the *Allgemeine Musikzeitung* (from c.1909 to the outbreak of

World War I in summer 1914) (see also A.6.a above). Möller's importance today rests with his multi-volume series of *Das Lied der Völker*, published during the 1920s and early 1930s with Schott, which forms the core of the Weimar collection. However, there are also 19 publications of works by Swan Hennessy, some of them in three or four copies, and several of them with autograph dedications by Hennessy, mostly reading *'Meinem lieben Freunde Heinrich Möller'* ('To my dear friend …') with his signature and often a place and date.

The finding aid to this part of the estate is structured as follows, using the item numbers 64 to 82 in roughly alphabetical order:

- 64: *Adagio et Allegretto du Quatuor à cordes* [Op. 46bis]. Ded. *'Meinem lieben Freunde Heinrich Möller. Swan Hennessy'*.
- 65: *Au village* [Op. 22].
- 66: *Au bord de la Forêt* [Op. 21].
- 67: *Croquis de femmes*, Op. 33 (in MS: *'Dr. Heinrich Möller, Paris 1911, Dedié v. Hennessy'*).
- 68: *Croquis parisiens*, Op. 47. Ded. *'Meinem lieben Freunde Heinrich Möller. Swan Hennessy'*.
- 69: *Eaux fortes* [Op. 24]. (stamp: *Dr. Heinrich Möller / 3, Rue Montenotte / Paris XVIIIa*).
- 70: *Étude*, Op. 25 (stamp: *Dr. Heinrich Möller / 3, Rue Montenotte / Paris XVIIIa*).
- 71: *Fêtes* [Op. 36 No. 1]. Three copies.
- 72: *Fêtes* [Op. 36 No. 2]. Four copies, one of them ded. *'Au Docteur Möller hommage sympathique. Swan Hennessy'*.
- 73: *Im Gebirg*, Op. 7.
- 74: *Incunabula*, Op. 39. Ded. *'Meinem lieben Freunde Heinrich Möller, Swan Hennessy'*.
- 75: *Ländliche Skizzen* [Op. 1].
- 76: *Petit album*, Op. 18 (in MS: *'Dr. Heinrich Möller, Paris 1912'*).
- 77: *Petite suite sur les notes Mi Di Mi Fa Si Mi*, Op. 34.
- 78: *Pièces celtiques*, Op. 45. Ded. *'Meinem lieben Freunde Heinrich Möller, Swan Hennessy'*.
- 79: *Praeludium et fuga*, Op. 16 (stamp: *Dr. Heinrich Möller / 3, Rue Montenotte / Paris XVIIIa*).
- 80: *Sentes et Chemins*, Op. 44. Ded. *'Meinem lieben Freunde Heinrich Möller, Swan Hennessy'*.
- 81: *Sonatine*, Op. 43.
- 82: *Valses caprices*, Op. 41. Ded. *'Meinem lieben Freunde Heinrich Möller, Swan Hennessy. Paris, 1912'*.

Appendix 6
Bibliography

1. Dictionary entries

Basso, Alberto (ed.): *Dizionario Enciclopedico Universale della Musica e dei Musicisti* (Turin: Unione Tipografico – Editrice Torinese [UTET], 1986), vol. 3, p. 553.

Bellaing, Véfa de: *Dictionnaire des compositeurs de musique en Bretagne* (Nantes: Ouest Éditions, 1992), p. 262.

Blume, Friedrich (ed.): *Die Musik in Geschichte und Gegenwart* (MGG), first edition, vol. 6 (Kassel: Bärenreiter, 1957), pp. 152–153 (article by Guy Ferchault).

Frank, Paul & Altmann, Wilhelm (eds.): *Kurzgefasstes Tonkünstler-Lexikon* (Regensburg: Gustav Bosse, 1936).

Gurlitt, Wilibald (ed.): *Riemann Musik Lexikon*, vol. 1 (Mainz: B. Schott's Söhne, 1959), p. 769.

Honegger, Marc (ed.): *Dictionnaire de la musique* (Paris: Bordas, 1970–76; also editions of 1986 and 1993), p. 565 (in 1993 ed.).

Robijns, Jozef & Zijlstra, Miep (eds.): *Algemene Muziek Encyclopedie* (Haarlem: De Haan, 1979–84).

Schmidl, Carlo (ed.): *Dizionario universale dei musicisti*; supplement volume (Milan: Sonzogno, 1938).

Slonimsky, Nicolas [& Kuhn, Laura Diane] (ed.): *Baker's Biographical Dictionary of Musicians*, 6th edition (New York: Schirmer, 1978), p. 729; similarly in 7th ed. (1984), 8th ed. (1992), 9th ed. (2001).

2. Books and articles
a. Contemporary

(anon.): *Festschrift für das fünfundzwanzigjährige Jubiläum des Konservatoriums für Musik in Stuttgart* (Stuttgart, J. B. Metzler, [1882]).

(anon.), 'Mr. Swan Hennessy', in: *The London Musical Courier*, 4 January 1913.

Aulich, Bruno & Heimeran, Ernst: *The Well-Tempered String Quartet* (New York: H. W. Gray, 1938). English translation, with additions by David Millar Craig, of German original: *Das stillvergnügte Streichquartett* (Munich: Ernst Heimeran Verlag, 1936). Numerous later editions in both languages.

Chevaillier, Lucien: 'Un Entretien avec Swan Hennessy', in: *Le Guide du concert*, 12 April 1929, pp. 791–793; available online: http://lmhsbd.oicrm.org/media/ART-CHL-1929-10.pdf (accessed 16 March 2018).

Collet, Henri: 'La Musique chez soi – XCVII. Œuvres de Swan Hennessy', in: *Comoedia*, 5 December 1921, p. 4.

'Craiftine': 'An Irish Musician of To-day', in: *The Leader*, 7 April 1923, pp. 208–210 [see also Ua Braoin 1922].

Dumesnil: René: *La Musique contemporaine en France* (Paris: Librairie Armand Collin, 1930; revised and enlarged edition, 1949); two volumes.

Goetschius, Percy: *The Material Used in Musical Composition. A System of Harmony Designed and Adopted for Use in the English Harmony Classes of the Conservatory of Music at Stuttgart* (Stuttgart: G. A. Zumsteeg, 1882; sixth edition: New York: G. Schirmer, 1903).

Hull, Arthur Eaglefield: *Modern Harmony. Its Explanation and Application* (London: Augener Ltd. & Boston: Boston Music Co., n. d. [1914]).

Ladmirault, Paul: 'L'Exemple des "Cinq" Russes / Skouer ar "Pemp" Rusiad', in: *Kornog* 1 (1928), p. 16–20.

O'Brien, Grace: 'Synge at the Paris Opera – Franco-Irish Musical Associations', in: *The Irish Press*, 10 November 1931, p. 5.

Pijper, Willem: 'Namaak', in: *De Muziek* 2 (1927–8), pp. 27–29.

Reboux, Paul and Müller, Charles: *À la manière de ...* (Paris: Bernard Grasset; 3 vols: 1908, 1910, 1913); vols 4 and 5 (1925, 1950) by Paul Reboux only.

Ua Braoin, Donnchadh: 'Swan Hennessy. An Irish Musician of To-day', in: *Dublin Evening Telegraph*, 2 September 1922, p. 2 [see also 'Craiftine' above].

Woollett, Henry: 'Hennessy, Swan', in: Cobbett, Walter Wilson and Mason, Colin (eds): *Cobbett's Cyclopedic Survey of Chamber Music* (London: Oxford University Press, 1929; ²1963); vol. 1: pp. 550–551.

b. Modern

Bayreuther, Rainer: 'Komponieren als akademische Disziplin. Von den Anfängen bis zur Gründung des Elektronikstudios', in Kremer & Schmidt (2007), pp. 299–329.

Bempéchat, Paul-André: 'Toward a Breton Musical Patrimony. Symbiosis and Synthesis of the Folkloric, the Classical and the Impressionistic', in *Proceedings of the Harvard Celtic Colloquium* 22 (2002), pp. 1–38.

— : '*Allons enfants de *quelle* patrie?*' *Breton Nationalism and the French Impressionist Aesthetic* (Cambridge, Mass.: Harvard University, Center for European Studies Working Paper Series No. 106, 2003) (expanded version of above).

— : *Jean Cras. Polymath of Music and Letters* (Farnham: Ashgate, 2009; reprint in paperback, London & New York: Routledge, 2017).

Bernard-Krauß, Geneviève: *Hundert Jahre französischer Musikgeschichte in Leben und Werk Paul Le Flems* (Frankfurt am Main: Peter Lang, 1993) (= *Europäische Hochschulschriften*, series 36 [musicology], vol. 93).

Bickhoff, Nicole: *Im Takt der Zeit. 150 Jahre Musikhochschule Stuttgart* (Stuttgart: Landesarchiv Baden-Württemberg, 2007).

— and Koch, Elke: 'Abgebrannt und umgezogen: Zur Überlieferung der Staatlichen Hochschule für Musik und Darstellende Kunst Stuttgart'; in: Kremer & Schmidt (2007), pp. 61–82.

Bodlore-Penlaez, Mikael and Ripoche, Aldo: *Musique classique bretonne / Sonerezh klasel breizh* (Spézet: Éditions Coop Breizh, 2012); with CD.

Bomberger, E. Douglas: *The German Musical Training of American Students, 1850 to 1900* (unpublished Ph.D. thesis, University of Maryland, 1991).

Brennan, Marjorie: 'Swan Song for One of Cork's Revolutionary Heroes', in: *Irish Examiner*, 31 October 2016, p. 15.

Cooper, David (ed.): *The Petrie Collection of the Ancient Music of Ireland* (Cork: Cork University Press, 2002).

Defrance, Yves: 'L'Irlande dans les musiques bretonnes actuelles', in: Yann Bevant, Laurent Daniel (eds): *Bretagne/Irlande: quelles relations? / Brittany/Ireland: what relations?* (Brest: Centre de Recherche Bretonne et Celtique, Université de Bretagne Occidentale and Rennes: Université Rennes 2, 2015), pp. 159–196.

— : 'Un Bretonisme musical (1860–1980)', in: *Analyse musicale* no. 78 (December 2015), pp. 104–113.

Dervan, Michael: 'Swan Hennessy: Ireland's Great Lost Composer', in *The Irish Times*, 27 March 2019.

Dibble, Jeremy: *Charles Villiers Stanford. Man and Musician* (Oxford: Oxford University Press, 2002).

— : *Hamilton Harty, Musical Polymath* (Woodbridge: The Boydell Press, 2013).

Dowling, Martin: *Traditional Music and Irish Society: Historical Perspectives* (Farnham: Ashgate, 2014; reprint in paperback, London & New York: Routledge, 2016).

Fitzgerald, Mark and O'Flynn, John (eds): *Music and Identity in Ireland and Beyond* (Farnham: Ashgate, 2014).

Fulcher, Jane F.: *The Composer as Intellectual. Music and Ideology in France, 1914–1940* (Oxford: Oxford University Press, 2005).

Hinson, Maurice and Roberts, Wesley: *The Piano in Chamber Ensemble. An Annotated Guide* (2nd edition, Bloomington, Indiana: Indiana University Press, 2006).

— : *Guide to the Pianist's Repertoire* (4th edition, Bloomington, Indiana: Indiana University Press, 2013), p. 499.

Joannon, Pierre & Whelan, Kevin (eds): *Paris – Capital of Irish Culture. France, Ireland and the Republic, 1798–1916* (Dublin: Four Courts Press, 2017).

Kelly, Barbara L.: (ed.) *French Music, Culture, and National Identity, 1870–1939* (Rochester, New York: University of Rochester Press & Woodbridge: Boydell & Brewer, 2008).

— : *Music and Ultra-Modernism in France. A Fragile Consensus, 1913–1939* (Woodbridge: Boydell Press, 2013).

— and Moore, Christopher (eds): *Music Criticism in France, 1918–1939. Authority, Advocacy, Legacy* (Woodbridge: Boydell Press, 2018).

Klein, Axel: 'An Irish-American in Paris: Swan Hennessy (1866–1929)', in: *Journal of the Society for Musicology in Ireland* 13 (2017–18), pp. 47–78.

— : 'Swan Hennessy', CD booklet notes to *Swan Hennessy: Complete String Quartets 1–4 , Sérénade and String Trio* (Limerick: RTÉ lyric fm CD 159, 2019).

Kremer, Joachim and Schmidt, Dörte (eds.): *Zwischen bürgerlicher Kultur und Akademie. Zur Professionalisierung der Musikausbildung in Stuttgart seit 1857* (Schliengen: Edition Argus, 2007).

Larchet-Cuthbert, Sheila: *The Irish Harp Book. A Tutor and Companion* (Cork: Mercier Press, 1975; R/Dublin: Carysfort Press, 2013).

Llano, Samuel: *Whose Spain? Negotiating 'Spanish Music' in Paris, 1908–1929* (New York: Oxford University Press, 2013).

Londeix, Jean-Marie: *125 ans de musique pour saxophone* (Paris: Leduc, 1971).

Marot, Robert: *Les Compositeurs bretons. Les Sources de leur inspiration* (Nantes: CID Éditions, 1988).
Metzner, Günter: *Heine in der Musik. Bibliographie der Heine-Vertonungen* (Tutzing: Hans Schneider, 12 vols, 1989–94), vol. 5: *Komponisten G–J* (1989), pp. 304–305.
Meyerowitz, Theresa Bernstein: *William Meyerowitz. The Artist Speaks* (Philadelphia: The Art Alliance Press, 1986).
Mussat, Marie-Claire: 'La Réception de Schönberg en France avant la Seconde Guerre mondiale', in: *Revue de Musicologie* 87:1 (2001), pp. 145–186.
Newman, William S.: *The Sonata Since Beethoven* (3rd edition, New York: W. W. Norton, 1983), p. 551.
Pollack, Howard: *George Gershwin. His Life and Work* (Berkeley: University of California Press, 2007).
Roudier, Jean-Michel and Brocq, Nicolas: *Le Legs Loiseau: la peinture moderne au Musée de la Loire de Cosne-sur-Loire* (Cosne-sur-Loire: Musée de la Loire de Cosne-sur-Loire / Musées de la Nièvre, 2004).
Ryan, Isadore: *Irish Paris* (Paris: the author, 2011).
Schipperges, Thomas: 'Musikausbildung und ihre Träger. Von der privaten Musikschule über das Königliche Konservatorium zur Staatlichen Hochschule für Musik', in: Kremer & Schmidt (2007), pp. 83–113.
Waters, Roger F.: *Déodat de Séverac. Musical Identity in* Fin de Siècle *France* (Farnham: Ashgate, 2008; reprint in paperback, London & New York: Routledge, 2016).
Watson, Laura: 'Ireland in the Musical Imagination of Third Republic France', in: Una Hunt and Mary Pierse (eds.): *France and Ireland. Notes and Narratives* (Oxford etc.: Peter Lang, 2015), pp. 91–109.
White, Harry: *The Keeper's Recital. Music and Cultural History in Ireland, 1770–1970* (Cork: Cork University Press, 1998).

3. Writings by Swan Hennessy

a. Articles

'Sommes-nous à la veille d'une plus complète expression musicale?', in: *La Revue musicale* 11:20 (15 October 1911), p. 421–422.
'Ar strafuilh er sonerez bremañ / Le Désarroi musical actuel', in: *Kornog* 1:2 (Hiver 1928), pp. 43–44 [p. 43 in Breton, p. 44 in French].

b. Published letters

1. *The Musical Standard*, 5 October 1912
    Themes: critique of avant-garde – Arnold Schönberg
2. *The Musical Standard*, 7 December 1912
    Themes: critique of avant-garde – Arnold Schönberg
3. *La Tribune musicale*, 1 April 1914
    Themes: Percy Grainger's *Molly on the Shore*, copyright

4. *Le Guide du concert*, 4 November 1921
   Themes: critique of avant-garde – Arnold Schönberg
5. *Le Guide du concert*, 22 October 1926, pp. 61–62
   Themes: response to survey about the social condition of musicians
6. *Le Guide du concert*, 11 November 1927
   Themes: critique of music journalism / music critics
7. *Le Guide du concert*, 2 December 1927
   Themes: criticises the contemporary completion of Schubert's Unfinished Symphony
8. *Le Guide du concert*, 17 February 1928
9. *Le Guide du concert*, 2 March 1928
   [with a response by Charles Monnier, 24 February 1928]
   Themes: the theories and influence of Henri Bergson
10. *Le Guide du concert*, 12 October 1928
    Theme: response to survey about *'musique méchanique'*
11. *Le Guide du concert*, 9 November 1928
    Theme: critique of avant-garde – the direction of modern music
12. *Le Guide du concert*, 7 December 1928
    Theme: critique of avant-garde – romanticism vs. avant-garde
13. *Le Guide du concert*, 25 January 1929
    Theme: critique of avant-garde – recipe for writing a modern sonatina
14. *Le Courrier musical* (chamber music special issue), 15 March 1929
    Theme: critique of avant-garde – challenges in writing chamber music
15. *Le Guide du concert*, 26 April 1929
    Theme: critique of avant-garde – suggestion to invent a composing machine
16. *Le Guide du concert*, 7 June 1929
    Theme: critique of avant-garde – lack of creative imagination
17. *Le Guide du concert*, 4 October 1929
    Theme: critique of avant-garde – pseudo Jazz and Viennese school
18. *Le Guide du concert*, 1 November 1929
    Theme: complains about the poor quality of a Scottish tune in a previous issue

Appendix 7
Discography

A. Recorded works by Swan Hennessy

If evidence was needed for the almost total neglect of Swan Hennessy in the past decades, this page shows all works that have ever been commercially recorded so far. The 2019 CD of the complete string quartets and the string trio was suggested by the present author and contains his booklet notes. A CD of selected piano music by the German pianist Moritz Ernst is currently in preparation.

***Suite*, Op. 46** for string quartet [String Quartet No. 1]
– Performed by the RTÉ ConTempo Quartet (Bogdan Sofei, vn; Ingrid Nicola, vn; Andreea Banciu, va; Adrian Mantu, vc): RTÉ lyric fm CD 159 (CD, 2019)

***Deuxième quatuor*, Op. 49** [String Quartet No. 2]
– Performed by the RTÉ ConTempo Quartet (as Op. 46): RTÉ lyric fm CD 159 (CD, 2019)

***Petit trio celtique*, Op. 52** for string trio
– Performed by members of the RTÉ ConTempo Quartet (Bogdan Sofei, vn; Andreea Banciu, va; Adrian Mantu, vc): RTÉ lyric fm CD 159 (CD, 2019)

***Trio*, Op. 54** for two clarinets and bassoon
– Performed by Trio d'Ance di Bolzano (Roberto Gander, cl; Bruno Righetti, cl, Giuseppe Settembrino, bn): Rainbow RW 98107 (CD, 1999)
– Performed by Calamus Trio (Josias Just, cl; Martin Imfeld, cl; Martin Zimmermann, bn): M&S Edition 5031/2 (CD, 2002)
– Performed by Trio Pleyel (Johannes Gmeinder, cl; Matthias Höfer, cl; Richard Morschel, bn): bremen radiohall records brh CD 1305 (CD & downloads, 2013)

***Quatre Pièces celtiques*, Op. 59** for cor anglais, violin, viola, violoncello
– (arrangement for cor anglais and organ)
Performed by Manfred Hoth (cor anglais) and Ulrich Leykam (organ): K&M Records, CD (1990s)
– (arrangement for cor anglais and string orchestra)
Performed by Rachel Tolmie (cor anglais), Bourbaki Ensemble: Wirripang Wirr 018 (CD, 2008)
– studio recording for broadcast, recorded 14 November 2008 by SWR 2 (Stuttgart, Germany), production number 1000076, first broadcast on 11 May 2010, performed by Lajos Lencsés (c.a.), Emily Körner (vn), Andra Darzins (va), Zoltan Paulich (vc)

***Troisième quatuor,* Op. 61** [String Quartet No. 3]
– Performed by the RTÉ ConTempo Quartet (as Op. 46): RTÉ lyric fm CD 159 (CD, 2019)

***Sérénade,* Op. 65** for string quartet
– Performed by the RTÉ ConTempo Quartet (as Op. 46): RTÉ lyric fm CD 159 (CD, 2019)

***Quatrième quatuor,* Op. 75** [String Quartet No. 4]
– Performed by the RTÉ ConTempo Quartet (as Op. 46): RTÉ lyric fm CD 159 (CD, 2019)

B. Related repertoire

To form a picture of the aural world Hennessy lived in and of the aesthetics he followed, it can be helpful to listen to music by Hennessy's Breton composer-friends. With few exceptions (like Guy Ropartz or Jean Cras) they, too, suffer from widespread neglect on the part of the recording industry. The following list is a non-exhaustive overview of some interesting repertoire that is currently available. It focuses on chamber and piano music as genres that Hennessy used as well, disregarding the composers' operatic, choral, or orchestral music.

Louis Aubert: Oeuvres pour violon et piano
Azur Classical AZC 166 (CD, 2018), performed by Stéphanie Moraly (vn) and Romain David (pf).
    CD includes: Violin Sonata (vn, pf); *Caprice* (vn, pf); *Berceuse de la Suite brève*, Op. 6 (vn, pf); *Sillages*, Op. 27 (pf); *Aubade* (vn, pf); *Lutins*, Op. 11 (pf); *Romance* (vn, pf), *Trois Esquisses*, Op. 7 (pf); *Romance*, Op. 2 (vn, pf); *Madrigal*, Op. 9 No. 1 (arr. f. vn, pf); *Sur deux noms* (vn, pf).

Jean Cras: Oeuvres pour piano
Timpani 1C1087 (CD, 2004), performed by Alain Jacquon.
    CD includes: *Danze, Paysages, Poèmes intimes*.

Jean Cras: Cello Sonata, Trio, Largo
Timpani 1C1151 (CD, 2008), performed by Philippe Koch (vn), Alexandr Khramouchin (vc), Alain Jacquon (pf).
    CD includes Cello Sonata, Piano Trio, *Largo* (vc, pf).

Jean Cras: Ma famille bien-aimée
Timpani 1C1200 (CD, 2013), performed by Philippe Graffin (vn), Mélanie Boisvert (S), Lionel Peintre (Bar), Alain Jacquon (pf), François Kerdoncuff (Pf), Laurent Wagschal (pf), Colette Cras-Tansman (pf), Orchestre Radio-Symphonique de Paris, Eugène Bigot (cond).

CD includes: *Âmes d'enfants*, *Quatre Pièces pour violon et piano*, *Trois Chansons bretonnes*, Piano Concerto.

Jean Huré: Les trois sonates pour violoncelle et piano
daphénéo 9812 (2002), performed by Raphaël Chrétien (vc), Maciej Pikulski (pf).
CD includes: *Sonate en fa majeur; Sonate en fa♯ mineur; Sonate en fa♯ majeur.*

Jean Huré: Sonate violon-piano, quintette
Timpani 1C1166 (2009), performed by Philippe Koch (vn), Quatuor Louvigny, Marie-Josèphe Jude (pf).
CD includes Violin Sonata and Piano Quintet.

Charles Koechlin: Chansons bretonnes
Hänssler Classics CD 98.258 (2006), performed by Peter Bruns (vc) and Roglit Ishay (pf).
CD includes all three volumes of the *Chansons bretonnes*, Op. 115 (1931) for cello and piano, plus cello sonatas by Koechlin (Op. 66, 1917) and Debussy (1915).

Paul Ladmirault: Intégrale des sonates
Skarbo DSK 4952 (1995), performed by Roland Daugareil (vn), Yvan Chiffoleau (vc), Jacques Lancelot (cl), Robert Plantard (pf).
CD includes Violin Sonata; Violoncello Sonata; Clarinet Sonata.

Paul Ladmirault: Quatuors, trios, fantaisie
Skarbo DSK 4001 (2000), performed by Quatuor Liger and Louis-Claude Thirion (pf).
CD includes *Quatuor* (string quartet); *Fantaisie* (vn, pf); *La Chevauchée. Fantaisie sur des reels écossais* (vn, vc, pf); *Romance* (strqu).

Paul Le Flem: Quintette & Sonate
Timpani 1C1077 (2004), performed by Philippe Koch (vn), Alain Jacquon (pf), Quatuor Louvigny.
CD includes Piano Quintet and Violin Sonata.

Paul Le Flem: Complete Piano Works
Grand Piano GP 695 (2016), performed by Giorgio Koukl.
CD includes *Avril; Vieux calvaire; Par landes; Par grèves; Le Chant des genêts; Sept Pièces enfantines; Les Korrigans – Valse bretonne; Pour la main droite; Mélancolie; Éponine et Sabinius; Pavane de mademoiselle (Style Louis XIV); Émotions.*

Rhené-Baton: Mélodies
Maguelone MAG 111.121 (1998), performed by Sonia de Beaufort (Mez) & Bruno Schweyer (pf).
CD *includes Chansons douces*, Op. 7; *Heures d'été*, Op. 14; *Cinq Mélodies*, Op. 16; *Dans un coin de violettes*, Op. 20; *Chansons bretonnes*, Op. 21.

Ropartz / Rhené-Baton: Trios avec piano
Atma Classique ACD2 2542 (2007), performed by Trio Hochelaga
 CD includes Guy Ropartz, Piano Trio in G minor (1918), and Rhené-Baton, Piano Trio, Op. 31 (1923).

Guy Ropartz: Piano Music
Toccata Classics TOCC 0326 (2015), performed by Stephanie McCallum.
 CD includes *Dans l'ombre de la montagne*; *Un Prélude dominical et Six Pièces à danser pour chaque jour de la semanine*; *Choral varié*; *La Chanson de Marguerite*, Op. 5; *First Love*, Op. 6.

Guy Ropartz: Sonates vol. 2
Timpani 1C1235 (2015), performed by Jean-Marc Phillips-Varjabédian (vn), Henri Demarquette (vc), François Kerdoncuff (pf).
 CD includes Violin Sonata No. 1; Cello Sonata No. 1; Violin Sonata No. 3.

Musique classique bretonne / Sonerezh klasel breizh
Coop Breizh CBCB 2012 (CD accompanying the small book by Bodlore-Penlaez & Ripoche, see Bibliography; 2012), performed by L'Instant en Trio (Jean-Marie Lions, vn; Aldo Ripoche, vc; Laurence Allix, pf).
 CD includes Louis Aubert: *Berceuse* (vc, pf); Louis-Albert Bourgault-Ducoudray: *Ma douce Annette* (vn, vc, pf); Jean Cras: *Paysage maritime* (pf); Maurice Duhamel: extract from *Chants de la fiancée* (vc, pf); Paul Ladmirault: *La Chevauchée. Fantaisie sur des reels écossais* (vn, vc, pf); Jean Langlais: *Ar Baradoz* (vn, vc, pf); Paul Le Flem: *Chants des genêts* (pf); Jef Le Penven: *Étude sur Me 'zo ganet e kreiz ar mor* (vc); Rhené-Baton: *Divertissement sur un vieil air breton* (vn, vc, pf); Guy Ropartz: *Final de la Sonate No. 1* (vn, pf); Louis Vuillemin: *Évocation* (vc, pf).

Piano 4 mains: Musique française
Skarbo DSK 4073 (CD, 2008), performed by Laurent Boukobza and Jean-Pierre Feray
 CD includes Paul Ladmirault: *Rhapsodie gaélique*; Gabriel Fauré: *Dolly Suite*, Op. 56; Jean Cras: *Âmes des enfants*; Maurice Ravel: *Ma mère l'oye*.

en homage: Joachim Mendelson
EDA Records EDA 040 (CD, 2014), performed by Polish Radio Symphony Orchestra cond. by Jürgen Bruns, Frédéric Tardy (ob), Ulrike Petersen (vn), Ignacy Miecznikowski (va), Claudio Corbach (vc), Tatjana Blome (pf).
 CD includes Violin Sonata, Oboe Quintet, Chamber Symphony, Symphony No. 2. The Chamber Symphony by Joachim Mendelson (1892–1943), published 1938 by Eschig, is dedicated to Swan Hennessy.

Index

A., Lucienne   448
Adam, Auguste   83, 452, 500, 511
Adam, Jacqueline   460
Adam-Pineau, Ida   83, 193n, 229, 233, 471, 474, 511
Adler, Josef   441, 443
Ajalbert, Jean   285, 286, 392, 443, 446
Alavoine (monsieur)   480
Albrecht, Otto Edwin   60, 447, 522
Aleman, Madeleine d'   286, 443, 506
Alexander, Elizabeth   442
Alkan, Charles-Valentin   154, 308
Allix, Laurence   559
Altenburg, Detlev   149
Altmann, Wilhelm   12, 305, 306n, 401, 550
Alwens, Edmund   33, 429
Alwyn, William   158
Ames, John Carlowitz   428n
Andolfi, Argéo   486
Andreae, Volkmar   137, 210
Anemoyanni, Alcibiade   74n, 246, 471
Anssono (Mme)   442
Antheil, George   356
Arnitz, Hélène   480
Ashbourne (Lord)   371
Association des Compositeurs Bretons   16, 174, **197–206**, 215–7, 220, 225–9, 245, 251, 253, 280, 284, 331, 332n, 411, 432–3, 515
Astruc, Suzanne   424, 437, 444, 446, 480, 485
Aubert, Louis   196, 197n, 200, 202, 204–5, 226, 331, 338, 340, 433, 515, 556, 558
Aubert, Yvonne   444
Augener (publishing house)   31, 42, 51, 61, 82, 87n, 114, 398, 430, 448–51, 470, 495, 551
Aulich, Bruno   14, 550
Auric, Georges   251n, 347, 352

Bach, Johann Sebastian   35, 81, 84, 101, 342, 378
Bailly, Jacques (?)   477
Bairstow, John Holroyd   59

Balakirev, Mily   199
Ballets russes, Les   234–5
Banciu, Andreea   9, 556
Bankart, Ethel   474, 482
Bantock, Granville   66, 330, 431
Barber, William T. Scott   450, 500
Barbillion, Jeanne   340
Bardac, Raoul   182
Barnes, Djuna   356
Barraine, Mathieu   304, 477
Barrère, Georges   478
Barrett (Mr)   316
Bartók, Bela   196, 259, 510
Basso, Alberto   12, 550
Bast, Henri   265, 316
Bataille, Henri   198
Bath, Hubert   66
Baudelaire, Charles   91, 285–6, 439, 443, 534
Bax, Arnold   17, 66, 249, 268–9, 330, 434
Bayne, David   470
Bayreuther, Rainer   35, 551
Bazaillas, Albert   218, 219n
Bazelaire, Paul   344
Beach, Sylvia   356
Beaufort, Sonia de   557
Beaven, Edna   195, 454
Beckett, Samuel   332
Bedenne, Germaine   480
Beethoven, Ludwig van   75, 81, 134n, 378
Belassène, Mathilde   9
Belinkoff, Raymond   480
Bellaing, Véfa de   16, 199n, 200n, 504, 515, 519, 550
Bellanger, Lucien   475, 478
Bempéchat, Paul-André   10, 16, 198n, 199, 200n, 551
Bender, Gabriel   337–8, 340, 347n
Benecke, Amy M.   76–7
Benecke, Marie   76
Benecke, Victor   76
Benedict, Julius   65
Berlin (concerts)   18, 88, 96, 99, 107, 137–8, 156, 168, 172, 173, 174, 178,

208, **210–4**, 215, 218, 220, 224, 257–9, 267, 269, 272, 273, **287–93**, 294, 295, 297, 300, 302, 311, 333, 366, 429, 437, 439, 441, 447, 452–3, 457–9, 461–3, 465, 471–5, 477–9, 482, 487, 511
Berlin, Irving   259
Berlioz, Hector   329
Bernard-Krauß, Geneviève   198n, 205n, 508n, 551
Bernheim, Marcel   172, 338, 340, 381n
Bernstein, Theresa   420, 421n, 553
Bertelin, Albert   137, 210, 344, 384n
Berthier, Paul   480, 483
Bertrand, Paule   476
Besset, Lilette   441
Bevant, Yann   15n, 254n, 332n, 552
Bibliothèque Nationale de France   9, 37, 63n, 186, 201, 206n, 285, 357, 384n, 435, 462, 508n, 521
Bickhoff, Nicole   8, 29n, 31n, 551
Bishop, Lesley   9
Bispham, David   60, 428, 447, 500, 522
Bizet, Georges   118, 163, 258, 308, 378, 460, 500
Blanche (monsieur)   442
Blanchemain, Prosper   396, 446, 537
Blanchon-Mialin, V.   476, 478
Blanquart, Gaston   304n, 305n, 371, 422, 424, 482–3, 500, 503, 508, 521, 547
Blanquer, Rachel   308, 465, 501
Bleuzet (Mme)   371
Bleuzet, Louis   215
Blin, A.   458
Bliss, Arthur   14
Blois, Pierre   394n
Blome, Tatjana   558
Blottière, Cécile   442–3, 476
Blume, Friedrich   550
Bodlore-Penlaez, Mikael   551, 559
Boehland (Mr)   420
Boisvert, Mélanie   556
Bomberger, Douglas   10, 30n, 429, 551
Bonis, Mel   390, 482
Bonnal, Ermend   215, 379
Bonne, M.   482
Bonniol-Bondy, Pierrette   351n, 441
Booth, Madeleine   107, 447

Bordes, Charles   203, 508
Borodin, Alexander   112, 185, 199, 378–9, 467–8, 510, 531
Bottrel, Simone   440–1, 445
Boucher, Jacques   476, 478
Boughton, Rutland   66, 330, 431
Bouillard, Jeanne   247, 471
Boukobza, Laurent   558
Boulanger, Lili   245
Boulanger, Nadia   355, 503, 506, 512
Boulmé, Roger   484
Boulnois, Jane   351n
Boulnois, Joseph   351n
Bourbaki Ensemble   555
Bourgault-Ducoudray, Louis-Albert   202, 204, 205, 228, 371, 558
Bouserez, Ludovic   396, 439, 444, 446
Boydell, Barra   7, 17n, 66n
Boydell, Brian   317
Boyle, Ina   268, 317
Bozza, Eugène   503
Brady, Eoin   9
Brady (Miss)   314, 473
Brahms, Johannes   35, 53, 67, 203, 308, 311n, 322, 342, 378–9, 398, 400–1, 414, 429, 467–8, 486, 506, 531
Breen, Denis   13, 74, 184, 194, 293–8, 314, 317, 371, 433–4, 463, 481n, 501, 515, 520, 550–1
Breithaupt, Rudolph Maria   15
Breitkopf & Härtel (publishing house)   31, 39, 75, 210, 337n, 448, 451, 495
Breitner, Marguerite   396, 446, 501
Brennan, Marjorie   10, 551
Bresnan, C.   471
Bret, Gustave   358
Bretenaker, Henri-Eugène   477
Brett, George H.   265, 266, 273, 316, 434, 472–3, 475
Bréville, Pierre de   340, 344
Britt, Horace   478
Brittany (region and influences) (see also Association des Compositeurs Bretons)   15n, 16, 17n, 36, 192, 198–9, 201–5, 217, 219, 226–8, 251–4, 331–2, 374–5, 432–3
Britten, Benjamin   14
Brocq, Nicolas   508n, 553

Brulé (Mlle)   479
Brun, Paul   306, 336, 478, 501, 540
Bruneau, Alfred   338
Bruns, Jürgen   558
Bruns, Peter   557
Brussels (concerts)   61, 122, 370, 385–6, 388, 440, 444–5, 456, 466, 468, 476, 481, 484, 506
Buérick, Robert   479
Bunting, Edward   375, 445
Buonamici, Giuseppe   64, 514
Burkart, Sebastian   10
Burns, Michael   503n
Bussine, Romain   196
Butler, Thomas O'Brien   66n, 330
Byk, Richard   381–2, 403, 463, 467–9, 481, 484, 487, 501, 510, 531–2
Byrne Bodley, Lorraine   10

Cabarat, Philippe   10
Cahuzac, Louis   477
Caldwell, Conor   10
Campbell, Kia   9
Caméléon (concert hall)   252–3, 323, 325, 333, 335–6, 371, 441–4, 451–3, 455–6, 459, 465, 472–3, 475, 477–9, 481–2
Canteloube, Joseph   16n, 203, 338, 417, 511
Caraher, Brian   329n
Carasso, Émile   444
Carlioz, Colette   481
Carol-Bérard   352, 483, 501, 541
Carolan, Turlough   371, 481n
Casadesus, Francis   245
Casella, Alfredo   338, 340, 379
Castéra, René de   344
Cazes-Novello, Nilda   438–9, 441, 444, 447
Cellier, Alexandre   480, 483
Celticism / Celtic elements   7, 14, 15–7, 55, 65–7, 94, 163, 182, 184, 191–5, 200, 202, 206, 210, 215–9, 227–9, 233, 241, 251–4, 264–5, 267, 270, 272, 276–85, 287–92, 306–13, 316, 318, 320, 326–7, 329–32, 359, 374, 378, 403, 418, 433–4
Chabrier, Emmanuel   134n, 185, 378–9, 467, 531–2

Challet-Vicq, Gaëtane   438, 440, 455, 457, 471, 474
Chantôme, Robert   304, 306, 311, 314, 318–20334–5, 337, 354, 394, 422, 424, 432, 475–80, 483, 485, 502
Chapuis, Auguste   338, 344
Charaitecher, A.   455
Charpentier, Gustave   136–7, 182
Chausson, Ernest   249
Chester Arthurs (Mr)   316
Chevaillier, Lucien   12, 13, 29, 55n, 56n, 62n, 65, 79, 130n, 185, 253, 278, 279n, 280, 309, 310, 311n, 398, 411–2, 413, 417–8, 426, 432, 486, 502, 513, 550
Chevaillier, Suzanne   398, 422, 424, 482, 486, 502
Chicago (residence)   11, 22–8, 29, 30, 49, 50, 97, 241, 427
Chiffoleau, Yvan   557
Chopin, Frédéric   85, 110, 111, 167, 168n, 287, 308, 378, 386, 387n, 467–9, 531–2
Chrétien, Raphaël   557
Clarens, Jean   452
Clementi, Muzio   375, 378–9, 381, 386–7, 467–9, 531
Cliquet-Pleyel, Henri   379
Cocteau, Jean   251
Coeuroy, André   358
Coffer (Mlle)   228
Coggins, Valmai   9
Coghill, Rhoda   317
Coll-Anemoyanni, Mme   247
Collet, Henri   12, 13n, 174, 232, 233n, 251, 267, 272, 277, **282–4**, 294, 344, 374, 402, 405, 432, 445, 502, 511, 536, 550
Collin, Charles-Augustin   200, 228, 331
Combarieu, Jules   108n, 117–8, 119, 432, 456, 502, 533
Cools, Denise   440, 444–6, 503
Cools, Eugène   311n, 367, 374, 425, 426n, 445, 502–3, 536
Cools, Janine   172, 311n, 401, 455, 458–9, 461, 486, 503
Cooper, David   187, 552
Coppola, Piero   344

Corbach, Claudio   558
Cork (heritage, city)   7, 8, 21–2, 64, 66n, 74, 187n, 192–4, 208, 223, 255, 261, 265, 267, 269, 294–7, 309, 315, 317, 320, 332, 371, 430, 433–4, 453, 463, 471, 487, 501, 505, 506, 509, 514, 515, 520
Corkery, Daniel   193, 296
Couperin, François   118, 370
Courant, G.   460
Cowell, Henry   33, 356, 428
Cox, Gareth   10
Craig, David Millar   14, 470, 550
Cras, Jean   16, 199, 202, 331, 390, 433, 561, 557, 559
Cras-Tansman, Colette   556
Crofton, William Mervyn   316
Crofts, Gerald   265, 316
Crofts, Joseph   268, 297, 316
Croiza, Claire   308
Crome, Fritz   161n, 164n
Cui, César   112, 199
Czerny, Carl   259

Dahms, Walter   358
Dambly, Paul   228, 229n
Daniel, Laurent   15n, 254n, 332n, 552
Darb, Tina   10
Darley, Arthur   18, 265, 266, 296, 314, 316, 434, 472–3
Darzins, Andra   555
Daugareil, Roland   557
David, Marc   171
David, Romain   556
De Koven, Reginald   428
de Valera, Éamon   265, 297, 317
Debussy, Claude   35, 84, 93, 100n, 115, 117, 121, 136n, 149, 151, 157, 174, 183–5, 226, 234, 245, 251, 186, 321, 322, 333, 350, 358, 359, 360n, 378–9, 381, 383–4, 412, 431, 467–8, 500, 507, 508, 520, 531, 558
Dechert, Carl   487
Dedieu-Peters, Madeleine   344
Defrance, Yves   10, 15, 17, 199n, 331, 332n, 552
Dejean Quartett   9
Delaborde, Eraïm Miriam   308, 501
Delacour, André   326, 335–7, 422n, 443, 505, 512, 535
Delacroix, Auguste   74, 101, 111–4, 245, 453, 458, 471, 503, 515, 525
Delage, Maurice   259
Delannoy, Marcel   343
Delibes, Léo   247
Delmas, Marc   344
Delmet, Paul   378, 380, 467, 531
Delorme-Jules Simon, Jeanne-Charlotte   440, 503, 534
Delune, Louis   344
Deman Quartett   291, 479, 487
Deman, Rudolf   292, 487
Demarquette, Henri   558
Demarquez, Suzanne   370
Demets, Eugène (person)   123, 125, 128, 130, 134, 158, 238, 258, 304, 387, 389, 453, 456, 503, 525, 525
Demets, E. (publishing house)   82, 83, 85, 91, 93, 98, 99n, 101, 108, 111, 123, 148–51, 157, 174, 186, 191–2, 220, 229, 241, 258, 269, 273, 300, 304, 384, 431, 438–41, 452–6, 458–63, 465, 472–6, 496–7, 503, 527, 535
Demolière, Viviane   445–6
Déré, Jean   340, 344, 390
Derry   269, 474
Dervan, Michael   10, 66n, 317n, 552
Despiau, Gaston   476
Diaghilev, Sergei   234
Dibble, Jeremy   66, 552
Diesterweg, Adolf   288n
Donaldson, Walter   259
Donisch, Max   374n
Doreau (monsieur)   477
Doucet, Clement   341
Dowdall, Rita   316, 472
Dowling, Martin   295, 552
Doyle, J.   314–5, 471
Drouet, Georges   475, 478
Dublin (concerts, travels)   51, 59, 64, 70, 192, 195, 224, 229n, 254, 265, 269, 273, 277, 294, 295, 298, 314, 315, 316, 317, 332, 388n, 430, 433–4, 454–5, 462, 471–7, 506, 507, 513
Dublin String Quartet   316
Dubois, Théodore   137, 210

Ducasse, Roger   79
Duchesne, Louis   480
Dufrenne (monsieur)   477
Duhamel, Maurice   198, 200, 201, 204, 205, 215–6, 217n, 218, 226, 228–9, 285, 371, 514, 519, 559
Dukas, Paul   100n, 196, 333, 344, 403, 504
Dumesnil, Maurice   215–6
Dumesnil, René   13–4, 550
Dupin, Paul   134
Dupré, Madeleine   439, 474
Dupuy, Géo   401, 476, 486
Durand [et Schoenewerk] (publishing house)   38, 55, 149, 269n, 450, 495, 515
Durey, Louis   251n
Dvořák, Antonín   67, 245, 278, 378–9, 467–8, 531
Dwyer, Benjamin   10
Dyke, Charles   75

Eadie, John and Mary   50
Edinburgh (marriage, concerts)   30, 49, 50, 313, 430, 470
Efron, Julia   486
Eichberg, Richard Johannes   209n, 213n, 224
Eisner, Bruno   173, 174, 291–2, 300, 458–9, 461, 463, 465, 487
Elgar, Edward   67
Eliott, T. S.   356
Enoch & Cie. (publishing house)   63, 470, 495
Ensemble Più   9, 306
Erdsieck, Marie   468
Erlanger, Camille   182
Ernst, Moritz   9, 556
Eschig, Max (person)   304, 503
Eschig, Max (publishing house)   108, 123, 245, 269n, 285, 293, 300, 302, 304, 305, 306, 309, 311, 317, 320, 323–6, 348, 351, 364, 367, 371, 374, 378–9, 384, 388, 390, 394, 398, 402, 421, 431, 436, 441–3, 445–6, 450, 453, 455, 463–7, 470, 475, 477–84, 503, 504, 515–6, 520, 546, 548, 559
Esposito, Michele   66, 188n, 317, 330
Esrabat-Eytmin (Mme)   439, 442

Estignard (Mme)   442
Etherington (Mr)   476
Eudes, Jeanne   438, 445
Evans & Co. (publishing house)   297–8, 309, 315, 320, 463–4, 498, 506
Evins, W.   482

Fabrègue, Lili   258, 384, 422, 438, 442, 445–6
Fache, Jules   453, 455
Faisst, Immanuel   33, 35
Falla, Manuel de   163, 196, 246, 304, 403, 417
Father Mathew Feis   195, 296, 314, 317, 434, 455, 462, 471, 473
Fauré, Gabriel   89, 134n, 136, 158, 202, 226, 378–9, 467–9, 502, 504, 506, 515, 531, 559
Faure, Michel   250–1
Feis Ceoil   64, 295–6, 315, 434, 515
Félix, H.   246, 471
Ferail (Mme)   442
Feray, Jean-Pierre   558
Ferchault, Guy   12, 21, 29, 550
Ferris, Catherine   10
FitzGerald, Edward   11n
Fitzgerald, F. Scott   356
Fitzgerald, Mark   10, 315n, 552
Fleischmann, Aloys   296, 317, 375n
Fleury, Viscount de   36–8
Flood, William Henry Grattan   317
Flotow, Friedrich von   329
Fontenay-en-Vexin   387, 389, 520
Fossier-Brillot, Marcelle   480, 485
Foster, Stephen   348
Foulds, John   66, 330, 403, 409, 431
Fouquerière, M. & S.   461
Fourment, Adrien   311, 314, 478, 504
Fournier, Louis   228
Franck, César   77, 100n, 104, 202, 247, 342, 359, 360n, 378–9, 467–8, 531
François, Yvonne   480
Frank, Jonathan   9
Frank, Paul   12
Fryer, Herbert   84, 111–4, 430, 452, 458, 513, 516
Fuchs, Jean   443, 476
Fuchs-Barbazanges, M.   443

Fulcher, Jane F.   15, 181n, 196n, 244, 358, 360, 363, 552

G., Marcelle van   451
Gael, Henri van   145, 149
Gaelic League   74, 295–6, 471, 501
Gage, Lyman S.   249
Gander, Roberto   555
Gard, Lucy   442
Gaspariantz, M.   482
Gauthier, Éva   258–60, 356, 428, 442
Gaveau, Marie-Antoinette   456, 459
Gebruers, Staf   316
Geibel, Emmanuel von   173, 258, 429, 441, 535
Geiger, Max   454
Gellée, Andrée   195, 454
Gély, Roger   352, 483
Gentilhomme, Paul   479
George, Jack W.   476
Géraldy, Paul (pianist)   441
Géraldy, Paul (poet)   384
Gerar, Marcelle   286, 311n442–3, 504
Gérardy, Paul   384, 445, 536
Gershwin, George   258–9, 261, 301, 354–6, 428, 553
Gibon, Jehan de   200, 228
Gilligan family   50
Glaser, Karl   475
Gmeinder, Johannes   555
Godard, Benjamin   378, 383–4, 386, 467–9, 520, 531
Godowsky, Leopold   158
Goethe, Johann Wolfgang von   60, 392–4, 446, 447, 522
Goetschius, Gretchen   55, 450, 504
Goetschius, Percy   33–6, 39, 41, 44, 55, 83, 210, 427–9, 448, 504, 551
Gonin, Philippe   198n, 508n
Gonne, Maud   332
Goossens, Eugene   14
Gosling, Andreas   9
Gottschalk, Louis Moreau   301
Goujeon, Y.   480
Gounod, Charles   118
Gouvy, Théodore   357
Graffin, Philippe   556
Graine, Mohamed   9

Grainger, Percy   66, 223–4, 554
Green, Marika   8–9
Greene, Harry Plunket   33, 428n
Grieg, Edvard   67, 74, 320, 378–80, 386, 464, 467–9, 531
Groult, Denise   438, 441, 444
Grovlez, Gabriel   161, 340
Guellette (Mme)   442
Guiffan, Jean   245, 255n
Guillerm, (abbé) H.   371
Gurlitt, Wilibald   12, 550
Gwin, William   438–40, 547

H., Georgette   450
Haas, Monique   471
Haessler, Johann Wilhelm   70
Hahn, Reynaldo   234, 338–9
Hamelin, Gaston   483
Hamelle (publishing house)   79, 81, 90, 91–2, 93, 440, 450–1, 496, 534–5
Hamilton, (Mme) Drechsler   470
Handel, George Frederick   215, 378, 380–1, 467–8, 532
Hannigan, David   193n, 255n, 509n
Hanson, Howard   33
Hardebeck, Carl Gilbert   66, 74, 268, 295, 297, 471
Hart (monsieur)   340
Hart, Charles   442
Harty, (Herbert) Hamilton   17, 66, 188, 317, 342, 398, 552
Hasselt, Willem van   281
Haudebert, Lucien   134n, 200, 205, 259, 293, 309, 331, 433, 464, 504
Hauser, Georgette   476
Hauser, Marguerite   476
Hayet, Ch. (publishing house)   119, 456, 497, 527
Heffner, Carl   134, 220, 429, 472, 505, 543
Heffner, Elisabeth   134, 220, 429, 457, 505, 526
Heimeran, Ernst   14
Heine, Heinrich   45–6, 60n, 178, 258, 437, 441, 463, 535, 553
Heller, Stephen   118, 378, 380, 467–8, 531
Hemingway, Ernest   356

Hennessy, Aline   7, 355, 420
Hennessy, Brigitte   7–8, 301n, 355, 420, 436
Hennessy, Claire (née Przybyszewska)   7, 24, 26, 61–2, 82, 83, 107, 250, 302, 324, 355, 364, 385, 398, 414, 419–21, 422, 428, 430, 431, 435–6, 451–2, 455, 505, 511, 521, 524, 526, 548
Hennessy, David   21, 245
Hennessy, Lila   23, 27–8, 36–8, 62, 95
Hennessy, Lucie Mabel   51, 57–9, 430
Hennessy, Lucy (née Roper)   31, 45, 49–51, 55, 57, 437, 512
Hennessy, Martin Richard Furneaux   51, 57, 59
Hennessy, Mary (née Hayes)   21, 245, 433
Hennessy, Michael David   21–9, 36, 59, 60, 62, 114, 145n, 168, 193n, 214, 241–3, 245–6, 249–50, 419–21, 433, 457, 461, 505, 529
Hennessy, Monique   421
Hennessy, Sarah J. (née Swan)   23–4, 26–7, 36–8, 50, 56, 201, 245, 375, 385, 433
Hennessy, (Edward) Swan
  Critique of avant-garde   179–82, 250, 345–7, 357–66, 392, 411, 412, 554–5
  Divorce (1893)   49, 56–7, 59, 60, 61, 427, 430
  Education   11, 29–31, 33–6, 55, 73, 197, 210, 212, 261, 294, 312–3, 427, 429–30
  Family   7–8, 21, 23–8, 36–8, 49–51, 56, 59, 61, 149, 193, 241–3, 245, 249, 356, 392, 411, 421, 427, 433
  Jazz influences   98, 259, 300–1, 347–56, 370, 401, 428
  Opus number changes   60, 76, 88, 95, 119, 130, 211n, 234, 256–7, 300, 308–9, 326
  Portraits (images)   62, 162, 243, 260, 281, 305, 330, 377, 387, 389, 410, 423, 425
  'Swan Hennessy Festivals'   333–7, 422–6

Works
À la manière de …   15, 55, 185–6, 245, 320, 333, 362, **378–84**, 386–7, 401, 411, 429, 450, 463–4, **467–9**, 494, 497–8, 501, 508, 520, 527, 531–2
Adagio et allegretto du quatuor à cordes, Op. 46bis   206n, **462**, 491, 497, 549
Album-Blätter, Op. 8   **51–2**, 55, 101, **449**, 488, 495, 513
Album celtique   298, 309, 329, 398, 403, 407, 450, 463–4, **470**, 498
Allegretto du quatrième quatuor a cordes, Op. 75bis   **469**, 493, 527, 531
Au bord de la forêt, Op. 21   **82–3**, 107, 368, **452**, 489, 496, 511, 549
Au village, Op. 22   **95–9**, 100, 172, 211, 301, 347, 429, **452**, 489, 496, 512, 524, 549
Aus dem Kinderleben, Op. 19   **75–9**, 115, 337, **451**, 489, 495
Banlieues …, Op. 69   253, 320, 333, **367–70**, 386, 398, 424, **466–7**, 493, 498, 499, 513, 531, 547
Berceuse, Op. 13   49, **63–4**, 65, 71, 367, 430, **470**, 489, 495, 507
Carneval-Studien, Op. 6   31, 32, 34, 39, **42–5**, 55, **449**, 488, 495, 509
Croquis de femmes, Op. 33   **119–22**, 124n, 130, 138, 190n, 334, 386, **456**, 469, 490, 497, 502, 533, 549
Croquis parisiens, Op. 47   19, 172, **174–8**, 211, 289, 301, 347, 428, **462–3**, 491, 497, 515, 526, 549
Deux Études (en ut mineur) pour la main gauche seule, Op. 15   **79–80**, 81, **450**, 489, 496, 524
Deux Mélodies, Op. 30   87, 88, **91–2**, 107, 285, **439**, 490, 496, 512, 534, 547
Deux Mélodies, Op. 73   19, **384–5**, **445–6**, 493, 498, 536
Deux Mélodies, Op. 79   **396–7**, 423–4, **446–7**, 493, 498, 501, 537
Deux Morceaux, Op. 68   337, **348–51**, 352, 370, **482**, 492, 497, 507, 541
Deux Petites pièces bi-tonales   **346–7**, **465**, 494

Deux Pièces celtiques, Op. 77   **394**, **485**, 493, 502

Deuxième Quatuor, Op. 49   13, 14, 49, 149, 193, 255–7, **261–9**, 270, 273, 277, 280–1, 287, 296–7, 314, 316, 403, 408, 430, **473–4**, 491, 497, 509, 538, 544, 555

Deuxième Sonatine, Op. 80   **397–400**, 409, 424, 434, **485–6**, 493, 499, 502, 542

Douze Canons à deux voix à tous les intervalles, Op. 64   257, **324**, **466**, 492, 497, 511, 530

Eaux fortes, Op. 24   **83–4**, 95, 107, 337, **452**, 489, 496, 500, 511, 516, 525, 549

Ein Spinnerliedchen, Op. 2   31, 32, 39, **41**, **448**, 488, 495

En passant ... (Études d'après nature), Op. 40   138–9, 147–8, **151–7**, 168, 172–3, 176, 186, 211, 291, 334, **459–60**, 490, 497, 517, 528

Épigrammes d'un solitaire, Op. 55   257, 297, 315, **320–2**, 367–8, 378, **464**, 467, 492, 498, 506, 530

Epiphanie, Op. 26   87, 88, **90**, 91, 107, 211, **438–9**, 489, 496, 513, 534

Étude, Op. 25   13, **84–7**, 88, 95, 111n, **453**, 489, 496, 503, 525, 549

Étude de concert, Op. 60   257, **308**, 424, **465**, 492, 497, 501

Étude-Fantaisie, Op. 9   **52**, **450**, 488, 495

Fêtes, Op. 36   122–5, 127–9, **134–8**, 141, 143, 145, 154, 186, 210, 220, 234, 291, 347, 423, **457–8**, 490, 496, 505, 517, 549

Gitaneries, Op. 42   161, **163–4**, **460**, 491, 497, 500, 528

Huit Pièces celtiques, Op. 51   257, 297, **298–300**, 315, 371, 382n, 398, **463**, 467, 470, 491, 498, 501, 506, 532

Im Gebirg, Op. 7   **51–2**, **449**, 488, 495, 506, 549

Impressions humoristiques, Op. 48   **178–80**, 186, 234, 357, **463**, 491, 497, 533

Incunabula, Op. 39   138–9, 147, 148, **150–1**, **459**, 490, 497, 515, 517, 518, 549

Introduction, variations et fugue sur un thème obligé, Op. 38   88, **111–4**, 138, 234, **458**, 490, 496, 511, 516, 527

Kinder-Album, Op. 35   111n, **114–8**, 119, 138, 337, 434, **457**, 490, 496, 505, 532

Ländliche Skizzen, Op. 1   **39–41**, 209, **448**, 488, 495, 504, 549

Les Noces du soldat de bois, Op. 37   **234–40**, **458**, 490, 526–7

Lieder an den Mond, Op. 10   14, 31, 40, 51, **53–4**, 55, 289, **470**, 488, 495

Lydia, Op. 23   87, **88–90**, 91, 96, 211, 220, 326, **437–8**, 489, 496, 511, 533

Mazurka et Polonaise, Op. 17   **82**, 107, **451**, 489, 495, 511, 524

Miniatures, Op. 11   31, 38, 49, **55**, 60, 63, 378, 430, **450**, 488, 495, 500, 504, 508, 512, 515, 531

Nouvelles feuilles d'album, Op. 27   95, **101–5**, 211, **453**

Petit album, Op. 18   **80–1**, 87, 107, **451**, 489, 496, 511, 524, 549

Petit trio celtique, Op. 52   9, 13, 256, 257, **273–8**, 280–1, 287, 334, 336–7, 371, 373, 386, 423, 433, **475–6**, 491, 497, 502, 507, 508, 537–8, 555

Petite suite irlandaise, Op. 29   21, 111n, 187, 188, **191–5**, 199n, 208, 223, 226, 270, 294, 428, 433, **454–5**, 472, 490, 496–7, 525

Petite suite sur les notes Mi Do Mi Fa Si Mi, Op. 34   119, 122–4, 126–9, **130–4**, 138, 141, 143, 145, **456**, 490, 496, 503, 517, 518, 526, 547, 549

Pièce celtique, Op. 74   386, **388**, 398, **484**, 493, 498, 506, 507, 510, 542

Pièces celtiques, Op. 45   199n, 204, **206–9**, 211, 382, 433, **461–2**, 491, 497, 529, 549

Praeludium et fuga, Op. 16   **81–2**, **451**, 489, 496, 524, 549

Quatre Mélodies, Opp. 23, 26, 30   91, 438–9, 534

Quatre Morceaux, Op. 71   **351–4**, 370, 424, **483–4**, 493, 498, 501, 510, 541–2
Quatre Pièces celtiques, Op. 59   9, 19, 257, **306–7**, **478**, 492, 497, 501, 507, 540, 555
Quatrième Quatuor, Op. 75   14, 333, 389–92, 421, 424, **484–5**, 493, 498, 545–6, 556
Rapsodie celtique, Op. 50   13, 49, **229–33**, 241, 247, 257, 277, 287, 473, **474–5**, 491, 497, 539
Rapsodie gaélique, Op. 63   13, 257, **323**, 334, 386, **481**, 492, 497, 507, 510, 514, 540
Rapsodie irlandaise, Op. 67   257, 311, **328–9**, 398, **466**, 470, 492, 498, 505, 530, 540–1
Reel irlandais   434, **469**
Sentes et chemins (Nouvelles études d'après nature), Op. 44   **168–74**, 177, 186, 211, 289, **461**, 491, 497, 505, 529, 549
Sérénade, Op. 65   13, 14, **325**, 337, 371, **481**, 492, 497, 508, 546, 556
Sonate en Fa (style irlandais), Op. 14   13, 61, 65, 67, **70–5**, 84, 87n, 101, 209, 246, 287, 295, 314, 317, 397, 430, **470–1**, 489, 496, 513, 522, 547
Sonatine, Op. 43   **164–8**, 185, 211, 212, 309, 336, **460–1**, 491, 497, 510, 529, 549
Sonatine, Op. 78   333, **395–6**, 433–4, 469, **485**, 493, 540
Sonatine, Op. 81   398, **400–1**, **486**, 493, 499, 510, 542
Sonatine celtique, Op. 53   257, 297, 309–11, 317, 336, 398, **464**, 470, 491, 498, 504, 506, 529–30
Sonatine celtique, Op. 62   13, 15, 257, **317–20**, 334, 337, 397, 424, **479–80**, 492, 497–8, 502, 507, 533, 540
Suite, Op. 46   13, 14, 134, 199n, 201, 210, 211–2, 215–6, **220–5**, 261, 270, 287, 316, 334, 364, 366, 373, 433, **472–3**, 491, 497, 505, 529, 543–4, 555
Tarantelle, Op. 20   **472**, 489

The Blackbird has a Golden Bill, Op. 5   31, 32, 38, 39, 42, **46–7, 437**, 488, 495, 512
Trio, Op. 54   13, 60n, 256–7, **269–73**, 278, 280, 289, 293, 317, 371, 373, 469, **476–7**, 492, 497, 506, 536, 539, 555
Trio, Op. 70   305n, 333, **371–4**, 424, **482–3**, 493, 498, 499, 500, 503, 508, 521, 531, 538
Trois Chansons celtiques, Op. 72   92n, **374–7**, 384, 385, 386, 396, 433, **444–5**, 485, 493, 498, 502, 512, 513, 536
Trois Chansons écossaises, Op. 31   18, 87–8, **92–5**, 211n, 280, 326, 337, 386, 423, **440–1**, 490, 496–7, 503, 506, 511, 534–5
Trois Chansons espagnoles, Op. 42bis   257, **258–9**, 289, 293, 311n, 334, 366, 424, **441–3**, 491, 497, 511, 535
Trois Mélodies, Op. 56   257, **285–7**, 337, 393, **443**, 446, 492, 497–8, 504, 506, 514, 535
Trois Mélodies, Op. 66   92n, 257, **326–8**, 337, 386, 423, **443–4**, 492, 497, 505, 512, 535
Trois Petits trios pour voix de femmes, Op. 76   333, **392–4**, **446**, 493, 512, 547
Trois Pièces exotiques, Op. 57   257, 289, 291, **301–2**, 334, 347, 351, 428, **464–5**, 483, 492, 497, 530, 541
Troisième Quatuor, Op. 61   14, 257, 291, **311–4**, **478–9**, 487, 492, 497, 502, 504, 507, 508, 545, 547, 556
Two Studies, Op. 4   39, **42**, 64, **448–9**, 488, 495, 514
Valses, Op. 32   **107–11**, 119, 138, 153, 337, 368, 423, 424, **455**, 490, 496, 511, 526
Valses caprices, Op. 41   138, 147–8, **157–62**, 172–3, 185, 186, **460**, 491, 497, 517, 519, 528, 549
Variations sur un air irlandais ancien, Op. 28   67, 187, **188–91**, 317, **453**, 490, 496, 525

Variations sur un thème de six notes,
  Op. 58   9, 13, 257, **302–6**, 336,
  477–8, 492, 497, 521, 546–7
*Variations sur un thème original dans le style
  irlandais*, Op. 12   49, 61, 64, 65–
  70, 398, 407, 430, **450**, 470, 488,
  495, 498, 514
Vier Lieder, Op. 3   31, 39, **45–6**, 424,
  437, 488, 495, 512, 547
Hennessy, (Michel) Patrice   7, 193, 243,
  318, 328, 355–6, 419–21, 428, 436,
  443, 466, 505, 521, 533, 535, 541
Hennessy, Richard   21
Hennessy, Simonne   421
Henniker, Ann Margaret   59
Henniker, Robert John Aldborough   57,
  58n
Henniker, John Granville   57
Henry, Leigh   473
Henry, Paul   332
Herault-Harlé, Jane   438–9, 441, 444,
  447
Herbert, Victor   33, 195, 428, 454
Hérédia, José-Maria de   90, 438, 534
Herterich, Herbert   7
Hervé, Raymond   200, 226
Hindemith, Paul   259
Hinson, Maurice   15, 319, 479, 552
Hoerée, Arthur   298, 299n, 309
Höfer, Matthias   555
Hoffmann, E.T.A.   235
Holbrooke, Joseph   66
Holland, James A.   24
Hollenberg, Otto   173, 178n
Holmès, Augusta   329
Hone, Evie   332
Honegger, Arthur   154, 251n, 253, 308,
  319–20, 335, 336, 340–1, 394, 504
Honegger, Marc   12, 550
Hoth, Manfred   555
Housman, Rosalie   278n
Hubbard, Charles   286, 337, 428, 440,
  441, 443, 506, 535
Hughes, Herbert   188, 434, 547
Hugon, Georges   438, 440, 442, 444
Hull, Arthur Eaglefield   13, 87, 222, 551
Hunt, Úna   9, 15n, 191n, 229n, 323n,
  388n, 553

Huré, Jean   200, 215–6, 217n, 218, 226,
  228, 287, 331, 338, 504, 557
Huth (Mrs)   474

I., Élise   449
I., Gabrielle   451
Imbert, Maurice   157, 319, 328, 370,
  424–5
Imfeld, Martin   555
Indy, Vincent d'   16n, 100n, 181, 202,
  203, 333, 360n, 363–4, 378–9, 467,
  508, 511, 531, 548
Ireland (travels, relations)   21–3, 49–51,
  57–9, 64–5, 70, 74, 107, 187–8, 191–
  4, 254–6, 265–6, 268–9, 273, 293–8,
  309, 314–7, 329–32, 374–5, 411, 417,
  422, 433–4
Ishay, Roglit   557

Jacquon, Alain   556–7
Jaffe, Max   258–9, 442
Jamet-Mottet, P. M.   440
Janssens, Francine   385–6, 476
Jazz (see 'Jazz influences' under Hen-
  nessy's name)
Jellett, Mainie   332
Jemain, J.   474
Jensen, Adolf   80, 81n
Joannon, Pierre   331n, 552
Jolivet, André   503
Jonas-Stockhausen, Ella   137–8, 210–1,
  457
Jongen, Joseph   79
Joplin, Scott   98, 301
Jozé, Thomas Richard Gonsalvez   317
Jude, Marie-Josèphe   557
Julienne, Janick   8
Just, Josias   555

Kabisch, Thomas   158
Karl Friedrich Alexander, King of Würt-
  temberg   33
Kaskevitz, Simone   440, 447
Katzbichler, Bernd   10
Kavanagh, Michael   297–8, 309, 320,
  430, 434, 441, 463, 464, 474, 506, 530
Keebaugh, Aaron   10, 195n, 454
Keil, Werner   317

Kelley, Edgar Stillman   33–4
Kelly, Barbara L.   15–6, 157n, 174, 186, 196n, 203–4, 251, 347n, 552
Kennedy Cahill (Dr)   316
Keogh, Dermot   265n
Keown, Gerard   265n
Kerdoncuff, François   556, 558
Kern, Jerome   259
Kerney, Leopold H.   371
Khramouchin, Alexandr   556
Kirchner, Theodor   55, 101, 429, 449, 506
Kieran, R.   471
Klengel, August Alexander   81
Kleyle, Francis   481
Kliachko, Samuel   481
Klingler, Karl   88, 437
Klingsor, Tristan   75, 122n, 157, 354, 394
Knoertzer, Jeanne   438–9, 470
Koch, Philippe   556–7
Koechlin, Charles   118, 149, 196, 338, 346, 510, 557
Kohl, Leonhard   272–3, 293, 477
Körner, Emily   306n, 555
Kotlaroff (Mme)   438–9
Koukl, Giorgio   557
Krieger, Georges   245
Kronke, Emil   145, 149
Kufferath, Fernande   385–6, 388, 476, 481, 484, 506
Kuhn, Laura Diane   12, 550
Kulenkampff Quartett   267, 268n, 287, 472–3
Kulenkampff-Post, Georg   287, 289, 471, 474–5
Kurth, Sabine   8

La Villemarqué, Théodore Hersart de   202
Labayle, Marie-Louise   440, 444–5
Labey, Marcel   245, 344, 485
Lacombe, Alain   258
Lacour, Marcelle de   462
Ladmirault, Paul   100n, 192, 195, 198–202, 204–5, 216, 217n, 218, 225–6, 228–9, 244–5, 251, 269–70, 282, 283n, 285, 331, 332n, 342–3, 357, 371, 433, 477, 506–7, 514, 538, 551, 557–8
Ladoux, Robert   306, 311, 314, 323, 334–5, 337, 475–6, 478, 481, 484, 507
Lagardère (monsieur)   478
Laloy, Louis   174
Lancelot, Jacques   557
Landormy, Paul   174, 338
Lane, Adelaide   474
Langley, Beatrice   63, 430, 470, 507
Laparra, Raoul   163, 285, 329, 338, 343, 384n
Lapommeraye, Pierre de   349n
Laporte, Jean   198
Larchet, John F.   66
Larchet-Cuthbert, Sheila   64, 514, 553
Latapi (Mme)   480
Laugwitz, Alfons   138n
Laurent, René   317, 337, 348, 350, 351, 432, 477, 480, 482, 507, 540–1
Lavaillotte, Lucien   478
Lavello-Stiévenard (Mme)   74n, 471
Lawton, Ralph   258, 441
Lazzari, Sylvio   198, 218, 338
Le Borne, Fernand   338
Le Braz, Anatole   374–5, 384–5, 444–5, 536
Le Breton, Marthe   130n, 335, 370–1, 381, 387, 421, 422, 432, 448, 451, 454–5, 457–8, 460–1, 464–5, 467–8, 472, 474, 484, 508, 531
Le Feuve, Gaston   215–6, 219
Le Flem, Paul   8–9, 198, 200, 202, 204–5, 216, 217n, 218, 226, 229, 267, 274–5, 282, 283n, 304–5, 308, 311, 331, 335, 349, 351, 356, 358–9, 363, 371, 433, 461, 472, 475, 508, 537, 551, 557–8
Le Marc'Hadour, Yvon   445
Le Métayer, André   478
Le Nail, Jacqueline   9
Lebert, Sigmund   33
Lecointe, Suzanne   471
Leconte de Lisle, Charles   88–9, 92, 94, 326, 374, 437, 440, 443–4, 505, 512, 533–6
Leduc (publishing house)   149, 553
Leichtentritt, Hugo   86, 111, 117

Lemaire, F.   476
Lencsés, Lajos   306, 555
Lenczner, Lionel   8
Lenczner, Swan   8
Lenormand, René   285, 338, 403
Léopold II, King of Belgium   61
Lesage, Alain-René   217
Lestrade, Marguerite   484
Lévy, Lazare   344
Lévy, Michel Maurice   338
Lewis, Katie   450, 508
Leykam, Ulrich   555
L'Instant en Trio   558
Lions, Jean-Marie   558
Lipnitzky, Boris   162, 260, 330, 377, 410
Liszt, Franz   33, 308, 378, 467, 531–2
Lizotte, Jean-Marcel   340
Llano, Samuel   16, 163, 552
Lods, Nicolas   8
Lods-Lenczner, Sophie   8
Loesel, William   481
Loevensohn, Marix   107, 137, 211–3, 437, 439, 441, 447, 472
Loewenguth, Alfred   476
Loewenguth, Roger   476
Logeart, (Mme) Raoul   476
Loiseau, Émile   304, 306, 311, 314, 318, 325, 334–5, 337, 371, 395, 475–8, 481, 482, 485, 500, 503, 508–9, 540, 546, 553
Loiseau (Mme)   311n, 323, 334–6, 479, 481
Londeix, Jean-Marie   15
London   9, 22, 38, 51, 59, 60, 70, 74, 76, 84, 107, 187, 209–10, 220, 241, 298, 316, 500, 507–8, 511–3, 516
   Concerts   64, 70, 84, 107, 320, 430, 441, 447, 450, 452, 464, 468, 474, 513–4
   Publications   31, 38, 42, 49, 51, 61, 63, 65, 70, 80, 82, 114, 188, 224, 257, 297, 298, 309, 315, 320, 398, 448–51, 463–4, 470–2, 475, 488–92, 495–6, 506, 514
   Residence   27, 31, 38, 42–3, 49–51, 56 62–3, 65, 67, 97, 430
Longley, Ernest   34, 43, 449, 509
Loth, Georges   111, 113–4, 458

Lovejoy, Suzanne   9
Lover, Samuel   65
Luzel, François-Marie   198, 202
Lyadov, Anatoly   112

MacBride, Seán   332
MacCunn, Hamish   65
MacDowell, Edward   34, 301
Mackenzie, Alexander   65
Mackenzie, Colin   470
Macnie (Miss)   316
MacSwiney, Mary   265
MacSwiney, Terence   8, 18, 193–4, 255, 261, 263, 266, 296, 317, 430, 433, 509
Madin, Henry   329
Magnard, Albéric   196, 197n, 249
Maguire, Mary   316
Maizier, Christiane   445, 486
Malézieux, Odette   422, 474–6, 478, 481
Mallen, Mizzi de   438, 441, 444
Manteufel, Tina   422, 471, 474–6, 480
Mantu, Adrian   9, 555
Marchessaux (monsieur)   336
Marie Henriette, Queen of Belgium   61
Markievicz, Constance   265
Markovitch, Ivan   438–40
Marot, Robert   199n, 202–3, 553
Martineau, Paul   195, 198, 200, 204, 216, 217n, 219, 226, 228–9, 245, 251, 282, 283n, 454
Marouzeau, Jules   335–6
Marx, Wolfgang   10, 269n
Massenet, Jules   247, 333, 378, 380–1, 386, 467–9, 513, 532
Masson, Paul-Marie   98
May, Frederick   315–6, 434
May (Mrs.)   316
Mayer, Paulette   440
McCallum, Stephanie   558
McCleave, Sarah   329n
McDonald, Annabel   107, 447, 509
McGowan, James   285n
McGraw, Cameron   15
McHale, Maria   10
McKay, George Frederick   548
McKinley, William   249
McMullin, David   8
McWhinnie, H. G.   482

Mélicourt, Paulette   442
Melmeister, Julieff   486
Mendelssohn-Bartholdy, Felix   33, 35, 45, 74, 76–7, 81, 309, 342, 357, 378, 380, 400–1, 429, 467–8, 531
Mendelson, Joachim   364, 402, 405, 516, 558
Menu, Pierre   285
Mercereau, Alexandre   253
Merry, Jan   483
Messiaen, Olivier   352–3, 484
Meyer, G.   195, 454
Meyerowitz, William   420, 421n, 553
Meynieu, Suzanne   483
Michaux, Henri   478
Michelet, Victor-Émile   390
Miecznikowski, Ignacy   558
Mignan, Édouard   446
Migot, Georges   251, 283–4, 311n, 338–9, 342, 344, 401–3, 413–6, 418, 432, 521
Milet, Alice   438–9
Milhaud, Darius   251n, 253, 259, 286, 341, 346–7, 363, 504
Miry, Elisabeth   385–6, 440, 444–5
Molié, Denyse   156–7, 311, 456, 459, 463–4, 466
Molinier, G.   392, 446
Möller, Heinrich   8, 89, 94, 101, 107, 139, 167, 196–9, 206, 214–5, 218, 234, 429, 447, 460, 510, 521, 547–9
Monnier, Madeleine   401, 481, 484, 486–7, 510, 542
Monteverdi, Claudio   85
Moody, John   273, 314–5?, 475
Moore, Christopher   347n, 552
Moore, Thomas   329
Moraly, Stéphanie   556
Moreau, Léon   200, 226, 338, 340
Morgan sisters   371
Morschel, Richard   555
Moses, Karen   9
Moyse (monsieur)   478
Mozart, Wolfgang Amadeus   75, 85, 88, 220, 378
Müller, Charles   379, 551
Murphy (Miss)   314, 473
Musk, Andrea N.   16, 203

Mussat, Marie-Claire   357n, 553
Mussorgsky, Modest   118, 173, 199, 293
Mützelburg, Adolf   272, 273n, 293, 477

Neilz, Jacques   476
Nevin, Ethelbert   145, 149
Ní Uaidh, Eibhlin   471
Nic Ruaidhrí, Treasa   453
Nic Uidhir, Máire   471
Nicola, Ingrid   9, 555
Nijinsky, Vaslav   235
Nin, Joaquín   338, 344
Noël, Marcel   344, 378, 467, 531
Nolan (Miss)   314, 473
Nucelly (monsieur)   316, 228

Obey, André   338–9
O'Brady, Liam   74, 295, 296, 471
O'Brien, Dermod   316
O'Brien, Grace   13n, 551
O'Brien, Laoise   9
O'Brien, Vincent   317
O'Connor, Frank   296
O'Connor, Terry   265–6, 473
O'Conor, Roderic   332
Ó Dochartaigh, Seóirse   9
Ó Dúbhgaill, Aidán   9
O'Dwyer, Robert   66, 297, 317, 330
Oehme, Robert   145, 149
O'Flynn, John   10
Oireachtas na Gaeilge   295–6, 317, 434, 453, 471, 501
O'Kane, John   9
O'Kelly family   7, 329, 332
O'Leary, Arthur   317
O'Mara (Miss)   316
O'Reilly, Joseph   316
Orenstein, Arbie   10, 356
Ornstein, Leo   33
O'Shea, G.   471
O'Sullivan, John   332
Oxford (education)   29, 31, 59, 430

P., Alice   451
Paladilhe, Émile   247
Palmer, Geoffrey M.   66, 297, 316–7
Papin, Marguerite   440, 447, 486

Paris
   Concerts   61, 70, 74–5, 84, 122,
      134, 156, 172, 195, 206, 224–5,
      229, 233, 259, 286, 297, 300, 311,
      318, 323, 325, 326, 348, 370, 371,
      374–5, 384, 390, 392, 394, 396,
      398, 401, 431–2, 437–68, 470–87
   Montparnasse quarter   7, 8, 175,
      178, 193n, 252–3, 301, 325, 356,
      413, 415–6, 421
   Publications (see *Demets, Durand,*
      Eschig, Hamelle, Hayet)
   Residence   61, 241, 252, 356, 368,
      431–2, 503
Paris, Louise   480
Paris, Suzanne   480
Pascal, André   471
Pasler, Jann   347n
Patterson, Annie W.   297, 515
Paulich, Zoltan   306, 555
Pavlovski, Valentin   438, 445, 470
Pazmor, Radiana   258, 289, 293, 366, 411, 441–2, 511
Pearse, Patrick   254, 268
Peintre, Lionel   556
Pellion, E.   440
Pénau, Roger   200, 228, 245, 285, 331, 514
Permentier (monsieur)   228
Péronne, A.   483
Perroud, Jacques   10
Petersen, Ulrike   558
Petit, Henri   319, 320n, 374n
Petrie Collection   67, 187–8, 192, 194, 208, 223, 307, 374–5, 395, 399, 433, 445, 453–4, 462, 469, 472, 485, 552
Petrie, George   187n
Petzelt, Kurt   482
Peyrot, J.   161n
Phillips-Varjabédian, Jean-Marc   558
Pierné, Gabriel   344, 511
Pierne, Paul   338
Pijper, Willem
Pikulski, Maciej   557
Pillois, Jacques   219, 220n
Pineau, Gabrielle   83, 448–52, 500, 511
Piriou, Adolphe   200, 202, 228
Plantard, Robert   557

Plé, Simone   344
Polia, Mildah   258, 422, 442–3
Polignac, Armande de   338
Pollack, Howard   10, 258, 553
Popoff, Sonia   8
Porter, Cole   356
Poueigh, Jean   338
Poulenc, Francis   249, 251n, 347, 503
Pound, Ezra   356
Pradier, Marie-Antoinette   300, 388, 422, 439, 441, 444, 447, 463, 466, 471, 484
Prieberg, Fred K.   363n
Prokofieff, Sergey   403
Proust, Marcel   17, 333
Przybyszewska, Rose Claire E.   61
Przybyszewski, Stanisław   61
Pruckner, Dionys   33
Pühn, Ullrich   9

Quatuor Andolfi   389–90, 402, 404, 414, 424, 473, 485
Quatuor Bastide   390, 407, 473, 485
Quatuor Calvet   311, 407, 473, 479
Quatuor Krettly   311, 407, 479
Quatuor Le Feuve   216, 219, 220n, 472
Quatuor Liger   557
Quatuor Loiseau   306, 311, 318, 334–7, 371, 389–90, 402, 407, 409, 414, 432, 442, 472–3, 479, 481, 485, 502, 504, 507, 509, 545
Quatuor Louvigny   557
Quatuor Malézieux   390, 422, 442, 474, 481, 485
Quatuor Roth   364–6, 389, 402, 404–5, 407, 473
Quellien, Narcisse   192
Quijoux, P.   452
Quintin, Alice   478

R., Madeleine   452
Rabaud, Henri   329
Raby, Marcel   439, 441
Rachmanoff (Mlle)   401, 438–9, 486
Raff, Joachim   70
Rameau, Jean Philippe   118
Rao, Arun   9, 388n

Rasch, Hugo   79, 80n, 88, 95–6, 101, 105n, 111, 112–4, 117, 121, 128–9, 133, 136–7, 142–3, 161, 162n, 167, 173–4, 190n, 195–6, 259, 293, 363, 380, 429, 437–8, 440, 458, 511–2, 518–9, 533
Raucheisen, Michael   287, 289, 471, 474
Ravel, Maurice   35, 79, 87, 91, 100n, 118, 149, 157–8, 163–7, 185, 196, 204, 234, 308, 309, 329, 333, 338–9, 347, 354–6, 363, 378–80, 398, 414, 431, 467–8, 500, 502, 504, 511, 532, 558
Realtor, Andrée   394n
Reboux, Paul   379, 551
Redmond, Chamisa   9
Reed, Leonard   320, 464, 468
Reger, Max   8, 80, 81, 95, 96–7, 100–1, 157, 161, 222, 366, 378, 380, 429–30, 452, 460, 467, 512, 524, 528, 531, 548
Regionalism   15–6, 203, 227, 254, 364, 432
Reid (Miss)   314, 473
Renner, Birgit   8
Rhené-Baton   200, 226, 282, 283n, 331, 342–3, 370–1, 557–8
Rialan, Rachel   392, 446
Riegger, Wallingford   33
Righetti, Bruno   555
Rimsky-Korsakov, Nikolai   111–2, 167–8, 199, 251n, 510
Rind, Adelaide   441
Riol, Maximilien   477
Ripoche, Aldo   551, 558
Roberts, Wesley   15, 319, 479, 552
Robijns, Jozef   12, 560
Robin, Albert   413
Rockford, Illinois (place of birth)   8, 23–7, 265, 419–20, 427
Roget, Henriette   481
Roland-Manuel   174, 286, 338
Rolland, Romain   206, 243–4, 462, 510
Ronchaud, Louis de   392, 446
Roosevelt, Theodore   249
Ropartz, (Joseph-)Guy   16n, 196–8, 200, 202, 204–5, 215, 217–20, 226, 229, 333, 343–4, 371, 390, 433, 556, 558
Roper, Elizabeth (née Home)   49–51

Roper, Robert Ormsby   49–50
Ross, Alexander and Isabella   38, 512
Ross, Isabella C.   38, 437, 512
Rossini, Gioacchino   378–80, 386, 467–9, 531
Roudier, Jean-Michel   508n, 553
Roulmann, François   10
Rousseau, Samuel   340
Roussel, Albert   286, 340, 344, 504, 508, 511, 519
Roussel, Cécile   475
Roussel, Maurice   475
Royal Irish Academy of Music   70, 265, 513
Royer, Lucienne   442
RTÉ ConTempo Quartet   9, 269n, 311, 390n, 555–6
Rubinstein, Anton   158, 247
Rückward, Fritz   88, 437
Ruyssen, Pierre   442–3, 476
Ryan, Isadore   7, 553
Rywkind, Joseph   88, 437

S., Odette   450, 452
Sachs, Joel   356n
Sachs, Léo   344
Sangor, Mona   440, 444, 446
Saint-Saëns, Camille   196, 244n, 333
Saisset, Marthe   258, 286, 326, 334–7, 375, 384, 392, 396, 422, 424, 432, 437–47, 512, 535
Salomonsohn, Max   482
Samain, Albert   285–6, 443, 535
Samazeuilh, Gustave   286, 338, 344
'Santillane'   217
Sartoni, Gino   439, 512
Satie, Erik   13, 103, 149, 157, 174, 185–6, 251n, 341, 366, 378–9, 411, 431–2, 467, 520
Sauvrezis, Alice   200, 215–8, 252, 331, 371, 390
Scahill, Adrian   10, 68n
Scarlatti, Domenico   378, 467–8, 531
Schaarwächter, Jürgen   8
Schattmann, Alfred   273, 287, 288n
Scheiwein, Louis   272–3, 293, 477
Schirmer (publishing house)   448–9, 550–1
Schlegel, Friedrich von   107, 447, 537
Schmidl, Carlo   12, 560

Schmidt, Dörte   30–1n, 35n, 551–3
Schmidt, Leopold   137n
Schmidt-Hensel, Roland   9
Schmitt, Florent   237, 338, 504, 507
Schmitt, Joseph   265–6, 273, 316, 434, 455, 472–3, 475–6
Schönberg, Arnold   177, 180–1, 196, 250, 259, 303, 345–6, 357–63, 366, 378, 432, 463, 500, 518, 548, 553–4
Schönberger, Esther   8
Schott (publishing house)   8–10, 31–2, 61, 65, 70, 80, 114, 119n, 122–34, 138–51, 153, 157, 188, 190n, 195, 210, 224, 280, 337n, 401, 429–30, 451, 453, 456–7, 470, 496, 510, 517–9, 522–3, 528, 549, 550
Schubert, Franz   46, 53, 67, 110, 293, 360, 361n, 378, 381, 429, 467–8, 532, 554
Schumann, Clara   55–6, 429, 449, 506, 513
Schumann, Robert   39, 43–6, 52–3, 55, 67, 76, 81, 84, 94, 100–1, 104, 118, 156, 167, 168n, 309, 342, 364, 378, 380–7, 390, 405, 429, 450, 467–9, 506, 513, 531
Schwerke, Irving   9, 11, 33, 350–1, 364, 366, 370, 381, 393, 401–9, 413, 416–7, 428, 517, 520–1
Schwers, Paul   99, 137–8, 213, 224–5, 273, 292
Schweyer, Bruno   557
Scize, Pierre   374–5, 444–5, 513, 536
'Scotch snap'   67–8, 102, 206, 231, 263–4, 274–5, **278–80**, 299, 304, 307, 323, 329, 375, 388, 395
Segnitz, Eugen   156n, 225, 232n, 266n, 277n, 294
Seifriz, Max   33
Sénart (publishing house)   149
Serres, Jacques   401, 455, 486
Servais, Maurice   134, 300, 302, 320, 334–6, 367, 370, 422, 424, 432, 437–9, 444, 446, 448–9, 451–3, 455–6, 459, 461, 464–6, 468, 513, 531
Settembrino, Giuseppe   555
Séverac, Déodat de   16, 196, 197n, 203, 417, 553

Seymour, Joseph   317
Shakespeare, William   107, 167, 447, 509, 510, 513, 537
Shapiro Quartet   481
Shapiro, Max   481
Sheehan, Tony   10
Sherlaw-Johnson, Austin   10
Shermann, R.   471
Sibelius, Jean   67
Simonetti, Achille   70–1, 74, 76–7, 430, 471, 513
Singer, Winnaretta   356
Slonimsky, Nicolas   12, 550
Smetana, Bedřich   67
Société Artistique et Littéraire de l'Ouest   199, 251, 370, 390, 403, 414, 433
Société Musicale Indépendante   196, 432
Société Nationale de Musique de France   196, 205
Sofei, Bogdan   9, 555
Sonntag, Marguerite   107, 211–3, 437, 439, 441, 447
Soret, Marie-Gabrielle   9
Soulage, Marcelle   338, 484
Soulary, Joséphin   88, 91, 439, 534
Souvignet, Paulette   482
St Thomas Aquinas   392, 446
Stanford, Charles Villiers   65–7, 73n, 187–8, 194, 210, 307, 317, 395, 398, 433, 552
Stanley, Roy   9, 315n
Stark, Marie   107, 438, 447, 513–4
Stein, Gertrude   356
Stein, Richard H.   158n, 161n, 167n
Steinhagen, Otto   173n, 268n, 293n
Stephens, James   332
Steuermann, Eduard   358
Stivel, Sophie   474
Stone, Frederick   195, 454–5
Strauß, Johann   70, 111, 378, 380–1, 386, 467–8, 532
Strauss, Richard   35, 100, 245, 320, 363, 378–80, 429, 464, 467–8, 512, 531
Stravinsky, Igor   196, 228, 234–5, 243, 286, 346, 378, 500, 503
Strecker, Ludwig   119n, 122–31, 133, 138–51, 518–9
Stuart, Alexander   57, 512

Stuttgart, Konservatorium für Musik   8, 11–2, 27, 29–36, 39, 42–3, 45–6, 51, 55, 58–9, 197, 210, 312–3, 427, 429–30, 504, 509, 517, 551–2
Sullivan & Co. (publishing house)   297, 309, 320, 463, 487, 506
Sullivan, Arthur   210
Suscinio, Jean   285, 439, 441, 443, 514
Swan, Arthur Wellesley Peckham   56
Swan, Joseph Rockwell   23–4, 27, 427
Switzerland (travels, war time)   10, 26, 32, 49, 59–60, 95, 109, 123, 127–8, 130, 153, 229, 241–6, 249n, 256, 269, 306, 411, 428, 433, 456, 468, 483, 505, 517–8

Tailleferre, Germaine   251n
Talayrach, E.   438, 445
Tansman, Alexandre   338, 344
Tausig, Carl   70
Tchaikowsky, Pjotr Ilyich   510
Tcherepnin, Alexander   344
Teissier, André   325
Temperley, David   280n
Temperley, Nicholas   280n
Temple, Hope   332
Tenroc, Charles   344–5
Terrade (monsieur)   476
Thiessen, Karl   80, 121, 190n
Thirion, Louis-Claude   557
Thompson, Aidan   10, 17
Thomson, Virgil   249, 356
Three Piece Suite   9
Tieck, Ludwig   107, 447, 537
Tiessen, Heinz   137, 210
Tolmie, Rachel   555
Torre, Paul della   470
Tosti, Paolo   169
Touche, Francis (& *Concerts Touche*)   229, 233, 273, 304, 323, 326, 331, 336, 441, 444, 464, 474–5, 477–8, 481, 514, 540
Townshend, Carrie   64–5, 67, 70, 316, 430, 433–4, 448, 450, 514–5
Tracey (Mr)   476
Trembelland, A.   304, 477–8, 483
Trépard, Émile   344
Trimble, Joan   317, 434

Trio d'Ance di Bolzano   555
Trio Hochelega   558
Trio Pasquier   476
Trio Pleyel   555
Tupac   178, 459, 463, 515, 528
Turina, Joaquín   100n, 163, 196, 197n, 344, 378–9, 467, 531

Ua Braoin –> see Breen
Union Syndicale des Compositeurs de Musique   205, 501

Valencin, Anne   438, 440, 444
Vanderborght, Edmond   385–6, 476
Vanston (Mrs.)   316
Vaughan Williams, Ralph   14
Veluard, Antoinette   206, 215, 462
Verdi, Giuseppe   378, 386, 467–9, 531–2
Verlaine, Paul   396, 446, 537
Veytaux (CH) (residence)   241–3, 245, 249, 505, 531
Vierne, Louis   338–9
Villa-Lobos, Heitor   304
Villain, Julien   486
Viñes, Ricardo   253
Vogel, Wladimir   364, 402, 405
Vollerthun, Georg   258, 293, 441
Vrassy, Aristodème   478
Vuillemin, Louis   81, 99, 110–1, 113–4, 121–2, 130–1, 133–4, 136–7, 155–6, 160, 167–8, 174, 178, 197–8, 200, 202, 204–5, 208, 215–7, 219, 226, 229, 251, 282…3, 331, 356, 363–4, 433, 462, 515, 526, 558
Vuillemin, Lucy   215–6, 228
Vuillermoz, Édouard   311, 390
Vuillermoz, Émile   174, 216–8, 226, 228, 251, 302, 347, 358, 390, 432
Vulliaud O'Sullivan, Mme Paul   371

Wagner, Richard   35, 60, 85, 118, 123, 218, 308, 328, 342, 358–60, 378–9, 412, 429, 467, 500
Wagschal, Laurent   556
Walsh (Mr)   316
Waters, Roger F.   16, 203, 553
Watson, Laura   10, 15, 190–1, 323, 329, 332, 553

Weber, Carl Maria von   173, 378, 386–7, 467–8, 531
Weber, Édith   199n
Werfel, Franz   173
Whelan, Kevin   331n, 552
White, Harry   10, 15, 17n, 66, 73n, 553
Widor, Charles-Marie   137, 210, 502, 508
Wiéner, Jean   340–1
Williams, Arthur   88, 437
Williams, Gillian   9, 229n
Winckle, (Mrs) van   340
Wolf, Hugo   89–90, 378, 380–1, 467–8, 532
Wolff, Pierre   225

Wolska, Helia   258, 406, 442
Wood, Charles   317
Woollett, Henry   13, 338, 344, 551
Wronsky, Édouard   467

Yamakata, Yukie   9
Ygouw, Opol   357

Zegers Veeckens, Lambert   450, 515
Zighéra, Léon   422, 471, 483
Zijlstra, Miep   12, 550
Zimmermann, Martin   555
Zumsteeg, G. A. (publishing house)   31–2, 35n, 39, 42, 437, 448–9, 495, 551

www.ingramcontent.com/pod-product-compliance
Lightning Source LLC
Chambersburg PA
CBHW080802020526
44114CB00046B/2696